MICHAEL LEIFER

Selected Works on Southeast Asia

The **Institute of Southeast Asian Studies (ISEAS)** was established as an autonomous organization in 1968. It is a regional centre dedicated to the study of socio-political, security and economic trends and developments in Southeast Asia and its wider geostrategic and economic environment.

The Institute's research programmes are the Regional Economic Studies (RES, including ASEAN and APEC), Regional Strategic and Political Studies (RSPS), and Regional Social and Cultural Studies (RSCS).

ISEAS Publications, an established academic press, has issued more than 1,000 books and journals. It is the largest scholarly publisher of research about Southeast Asia from within the region. ISEAS Publications works with many other academic and trade publishers and distributors to disseminate important research and analyses from and about Southeast Asia to the rest of the world.

MICHAEL LEIFER

Selected Works on Southeast Asia

Compiled and edited by
Chin Kin Wah and Leo Suryadinata

LSEAS INSTITUTE OF SOUTHEAST ASIAN STUDIES
Singapore

First published in Singapore in 2005 by
Institute of Southeast Asian Studies
30 Heng Mui Keng Terrace
Pasir Panjang
Singapore 119614
E-mail: publish@iseas.edu.sg
Website: http://bookshop.iseas.edu.sg

The responsibility for facts and opinions in this publication rests exclusively with the editors and contributors and their interpretations do not necessarily reflect the views or the policy of the publisher or its supporters.

ISEAS Library Cataloguing-in-Publication Data

Leifer, Michael, 1933–2001
Michael Leifer : selected works on Southeast Asia / compiled and edited by Chin Kin Wah and Leo Suryadinata.
 1. Asia, Southeastern—Politics and government—1945-
 2. Asia, Southeastern—Foreign relations.
 3. ASEAN.
 4. Regionalism—Asia, Southeastern.
 5. Asia, Southeastern—Strategic aspects.
 6. National security—Asia, Southeastern.
 I. Chin, Kin Wah.
 II. Suryadinata, Leo, 1941-
 III. Title.
DS525.7 L52   2005
ISBN 981-230-270-0 (hard cover)

Every effort has been made to identify copyright-holders; in case of oversight, and on notification to the publisher, corrections will be made in the next edition.

PHOTO CREDIT
Photo of Michael Leifer on the front cover reproduced courtesy of the London School of Economics.

Typeset by International Typesetters Pte Ltd
Printed in Singapore by Seng Lee Press Pte Ltd

Contents

Director's Message

K. Kesavapany

Michael Leifer was one of the most distinguished scholars in the field of Southeast Asian Studies. He was a teacher of international repute at the London School of Economics, and in a professional lifetime spanning nearly forty years he published more that twenty single-authored and edited books and innumerable scholarly articles covering not only the international relations of Southeast Asia, which was his field of specialization, but also the domestic politics and foreign policies of key Southeast Asian countries.

The enduring quality and the encyclopaedic range of his works deserve to be commemorated in this volume of his selected writings, which ISEAS is sponsoring. It is hoped that students and later generations of scholars, researchers, and policy-makers will find resonance and relevance in his works on the region. This volume also includes a most comprehensive bibliography of Leifer's published as well as unpublished works, which will be an invaluable asset to researchers.

I wish to compliment Dr Chin Kin Wah and Dr Leo Suryadinata for completing this scholarly enterprise within a period of eight months.

Finally, this volume highlights Leifer's professional links with ISEAS, which were developed over the years and culminating in his appointment as Senior Professorial Fellow of the Institute between 1995 and 1997.

Preface

Chin Kin Wah and Leo Suryadinata

Michael Leifer, Emeritus Professor of International Relations and founding director of the Asia Research Centre at the London School of Economics and Political Science, was a highly respected scholar in the field of Southeast Asian Studies. When he died in March 2001 Michael left behind a rich legacy of works on Southeast Asia — nearly 300 published and unpublished articles and twenty single-authored and edited books ranging over some of the most momentous developments in post-colonial Southeast Asia. While his expertise in the international relations of the region was widely recognized, he also made substantial contributions to the study of the domestic politics and foreign policies of Southeast Asian states. The depth and reach of his expertise on the region and the enduring quality of his publications made it possible to contemplate this volume of selected works when we sought to commemorate his scholarship in Southeast Asian studies.

In this endeavour we were greatly helped by the existence of a comprehensive collection of his works at the Institute of Southeast Asian Studies (ISEAS) library where Michael himself had researched during his numerous visits to Singapore. Moreover the ISEAS library had just brought out an excellent bibliography, which covers his entire corpora of works on the region published between 1961 and 2002. We are fortunate to be able to include this valuable bibliography in the book.

Our familiarity with Michael's works was derived from our personal and professional associations with him. Michael had been External Examiner (1979–83) and Visiting Professor (1986) at the Department of Political Science, National University of Singapore where we had both taught courses in the international relations as well as comparative politics of Southeast Asia. One of us had also been a student of his at the LSE.

This volume of selected works is essentially the voice of Michael Leifer heard over nearly four decades. The depth of his reflections ensures that the voice will not be lost in the years ahead as Southeast Asia continues to undergo transformation and adaptation in coping with the forces of change.

In the preparation of this volume we laboured under the nagging concern that we might not be able to do sufficient justice in reflecting Michael's encyclopaedic range of interest in the region. Both constraints of space and budget meant that we had to be extra-selective in the works to be showcased. Where we encountered prohibitively high copyright fees to reproduce an item, we have had to substitute with articles that cover similar issues though perhaps not in an exactly similar analytical framework. Most of the articles have been considerably shortened but we were guided by the importance of letting Michael speak up in his original coherent way.

This book is divided into two parts: Part I focuses on the international relations of the region including the roles and impacts of the major external players. Part II deals with domestic politics and foreign policies of Southeast Asian countries. Each part begins with an introduction by the respective editors to provide a better appreciation of the sections that follow. In the case of Part I, the sections are presented thematically while Part II covers the regional states. Introductory comments on the chapters are provided at the beginning of each section. Given severe constraints of space most of the chapters are presented in abridged form. This is to avoid unnecessary overlaps but where a chapter in one part touches on issues that are linked to or have bearing on a chapter in the other part of the book, a cross-reference is provided in the relevant introductory commentary. We have not drawn too heavily from Michael's single-authored books, as these are readily accessible to those who are interested in the field.

Readers who wish to locate other items not included in this collection may turn to the bibliography for guidance. The contents of the bibliography have been arranged in a manner that complements the organization of the chapters.

Many hands have contributed to the preparation of this book. Special thanks are owed to the ISEAS Librarian Ch'ng Kim See and her dedicated library staff for their labour of love in compiling the bibliography. In this endeavour, Gandhimathy Durairaj served admirably as principal searcher and compiler.

To the ISEAS Publications Unit, in particular its Managing Editor Triena Ong and Production Editor Rahilah Yusuf, we are much indebted. They have been unstinting in their co-operation and support, which made possible the expeditious processing of an enormous manuscript. We would also like to thank Teo Kah Beng for his timely assistance in going over the proofs.

We are thankful to the London School of Economics for permission to reproduce the photograph of Michael Leifer on the cover and Part Opening pages of this book. Finally, a special word of gratitude is owed to Mrs Francis Leifer for her kind permission to republish some of her late husband's articles in this volume.

We alone are responsible for any errors of compilation and interpretation.

Foreword

Wang Gungwu

Michael and I first met on the eve of the formation of the Federation of Malaysia. I was at the University of Malaya in Kuala Lumpur engaged in producing the volume of essays, *Malaysia: A Survey*, to explain and celebrate this new and controversial political entity. He had been attracted to the growing conflict in the former French territories of Indochina and had focused his attention on the fate of Cambodia, lodged between neighbouring Vietnam and Thailand. But the common interest we had in British efforts to tidy up their messy political arrangements in Southeast Asia led us to talk about the future of the region in broader terms. Beyond our concerns for the increasingly uncomfortable relations between Singapore and the Federal Government, we discussed the probable outcomes of Sukarno's *konfrontasi* policy and the American military involvement in Vietnam. He was then at the University of Adelaide and about to return to Britain, and was deeply concerned to analyse what the British could still do. On my part, I wanted to understand the likely outcomes for newly independent states in Southeast Asia with the Cold War hotting up on their doorsteps.

Needless to say, we both encountered surprises in the years ahead. For him, the American war in Vietnam and its consequences called for a thorough re-examination of Southeast Asia's place in the security structure of the Asia-Pacific region. And he played an important role at various levels of thinking about that structure for at least three decades. For myself, I was fascinated by the drama of Mao Zedong's Great Proletarian Cultural Revolution, not only because it highlighted the unbridgeable chasm between China and the Soviet Union but also because it challenged everything I had learnt about the nature of Chinese culture and history. For these reasons, our work over the next decades barely touched. There was, however, one subject that brought us together from time to time. That was the future of the Association of Southeast Asian Nations (ASEAN). The ups and downs of ASEAN during the next three decades provided the core of our common interests, Michael from his diplomatic and security point of view and I from the past and future of China's connections in eastern Asia.

Michael was more constant in his focus, always exploring what the superpowers and their allies had in mind for Southeast Asia. It is, therefore, most appropriate that his most enduring works on the region have been collected in this volume and edited by two scholars who have followed his work closely over the decades. From the collection, we can see how deeply Michael had immersed himself in the region's fate and how much he served as the questioning and critical voice that tracked and captured the region's history since the early 1960s. It was this steady examination of the possibilities of a viable regional structure that gave us all much to admire in Michael's work.

When I returned to work in Singapore in 1996, I met him again while he was engaged in putting together the letters that David Marshall had written during his visit to China as an independence-seeking leader from Singapore. I learnt how much he felt about Marshall's Jewish background and how that background influenced what Marshall thought about an earlier phase of China's revolution. This was a side of Michael I never knew. The juxtaposition of that perspective of David Marshall and Michael's own reading about a happier China before the Great Leap Forward was eye-opening. This was the first time I had heard him speak with feeling about developments in China and it was the beginning of several conversations we had before his last visit in January 2001 about how China's transformation would force ASEAN towards a more coherent community. This became all the more important as we looked at how the region faced yet another harsh test of its capacities. How will ASEAN evolve to deal with the unexpected financial crisis of 1997–98 that had halted its promising development?

Michael was then deeply engaged in writing his last book, *Singapore's Foreign Policy.* This is indeed a subject that had engaged his attention ever since he first began to work on Southeast Asia in the early 1960s. His regular visits to Singapore over a period of almost forty years had given him an extraordinarily realistic understanding of the island state's vulnerability. When the book appeared, I was not surprised to find that, despite his usual cool analysis, it revealed a deep feeling that he rarely showed in his writings. One sentence sums it up, "Singapore's attempts to drive its region have been successful up to a point. They have not served to transform its security environment that displays a disconcerting continuity." The same comment about success up to a point might also apply to ASEAN as a whole as that organization tries to adapt to the larger East Asian community. Michael did not live to see the world after September 11. In the context of the wise words he has given us about Southeast Asia, we would dearly love to hear him tell us what we should look out for now.

With Tan Sri Dato' Dr Mohamed Noordin Sopiee, Chairman of the Institute of Strategic and International Studies, Kuala Lumpur, and Mr S. Rajaratnam, Distinguished Fellow, ISEAS and formerly Singapore Senior Minister, at ISEAS 25th Anniversary celebrations on 29 September 1993.

With Professor Chan Heng Chee, former Director of ISEAS, and Professor Somsakdi Xuto, a member of the ISEAS Regional Advisory Council, at the ISEAS 25th Anniversary celebrations on 29 September 1993.

With Dr Francois Godement, Director of Asia Centre, French Institute of International Relations, and Dr Kusuma Snitwongse, Chairperson of the Advisory Board of the Institute of Security and International Studies, Chulalongkorn University, Bangkok, at a dinner held after the Conference on Strategic Concepts and Strategic Cultures in East Asia and Europe at The Regent, Singapore on 10–11 November 1995.

Speaking at a seminar during his stint as a Senior Professorial Fellow at ISEAS in January 1997.

Front row, left to right: Mrs Jean Marshall, wife of Singapore's first Chief Minister Dr David Marshall, Mrs Frances Leifer, Mr K. Kesavapany, Director of ISEAS, Mrs K. Kesavapany, Mrs Barry Desker, and Mr Barry Desker, Director of the Institute of Defence and Strategic Studies, Singapore, at a ceremony to inaugurate the annual Michael Leifer Memorial Prize held in ISEAS on 18 May 2004.

Left to right: Ms Ch'ng Kim See, Head of ISEAS Library, Mr Jeremy Leifer, Dr Chin Kin Wah, Mrs Frances Leifer, Mrs Jean Marshall, and Dr Leo Suryadinata at the display of Professor Michael Leifer's works in ISEAS Library.

Introducing Southeast Asia

In this *tour de force* of Southeast Asia, Leifer highlights three characteristics of the region: first, its great socio-cultural, religious, ethnic, and political diversity; second, the legacy of colonial political boundaries (with enduring implications for the forces of separatism and irredentism) and parliamentary democracy (with a more chequered outcome); and third, the absence of geopolitical coherence until the establishment of ASEAN in 1967, which provided at least a conventional, if limited, coherence. Post-World War II nationalism found expression in anti-colonial struggles of varying intensities. The Cold War and its conjunction with the struggles between local Communist and anti-Communist movements added to regional fragmentation. Such conjunction of local and international conflicts was most evident in the first and second Indochina wars while the third was essentially a fall-out among the Communist powers themselves albeit with disturbing consequences for ASEAN's vision of regional order. The end of the Cold War and Vietnamese weariness in Cambodia opened the way to regionwide conciliation culminating in the identification of all existing Southeast Asian states with ASEAN by the end of the twentieth century. Ironically, just when a new regional coherence was being realized, it was diluted by strategic and economic changes that obliged ASEAN to expand its regional horizons.

Southeast Asia

South-East Asia comprises ten states: Myanmar (formerly Burma), Thailand, Vietnam, Laos, Cambodia, Malaysia, Singapore, Brunei, Indonesia, and the Philippines. They are diverse in human and physical geography, their territorial boundaries a legacy of colonial interventions and accommodations.

At the outset of the twentieth century, the term South-East Asia did not enjoy common currency; its disparate territories were objects of empire and not subjects of international relations, with Thailand, known as Siam until 1939, as the sole exception. They did not begin to enjoy international status until after the end of the Pacific War in 1945.

The term South-East Asia came into effective usage only during the Pacific War. It was employed by the Western Allies as a military-administrative arrangement for dispossessing Japan of wartime gains. A South-East Asia Command (SEAC) was created in August 1943.

Reprinted from Michael Leifer, "Southeast Asia", in *The Oxford History of the Twentieth Century*, edited by Michael Howard and Wm. Roger Louis (Oxford: Oxford University Press, 1998), pp. 227–39, by permission of the publisher.

Based in Ceylon (now Sri Lanka), its responsibilities were confined initially to Burma. Thailand, Malaya including Singapore, and the island of Sumatra. In July 1945, at the Potsdam Conference, SEAC's domain was enlarged to include British northern Borneo, the whole of the Netherlands East Indies (except western Timor), and French Indochina south of the sixteenth parallel of latitude but not the whole of South-East Asia. When SEAC was disbanded in November 1946, a common understanding of South-East Asia's bounds still did not exist.

South-East Asia began to assume a geopolitical coherence only during the last quarter of the twentieth century. That coherence came to be registered through the activities of the Association of South-East Asian Nations (ASEAN) established in August 1967 by Thailand, Malaysia, Singapore, Indonesia, and the Philippines. Brunei became a member on resuming sovereignty in January 1984. But it was only at the end of the cold war from the early 1990s that the three states of Indochina (Vietnam, Laos, and Cambodia) as well as Myanmar acknowledged ASEAN's regional credentials, attracted partly by the economic achievement of most of its member states. Vietnam became its first communist member in July 1995.

Colonialism was imposed on South-East Asia from the sixteenth century but its consolidation was not completed until the early years of the twentieth century concurrent with the first stirrings of nationalism. By 1900 the British were ensconced in Burma, in Malaya, including Singapore, and northern Borneo, as were the Dutch in their East Indies archipelago incorporating in the main Java, Sumatra, Sulawesi (Celebes), and the major part of Borneo. The French had established dominion over Indochina, while the USA had just succeeded to Spanish rule in the Philippines. The Portuguese retained a vestige of empire in the eastern half of the island of Timor. Only Thailand enjoyed an independent status as a buffer zone between British and French colonial domains.

Colonial rule disrupted and changed traditional society. For example, kingship was either removed, as in Burma and Vietnam, or remodelled to lend legitimacy to the machinery of colonial government, as in Malaya, Cambodia, and parts of the Netherlands East Indies. Colonialism also made an impact through promoting plantation agriculture and extractive industry. Metropolitan economies profited from exchanging their manufactures for tropical products. This kind of economic development was accompanied and stimulated by flows of migrant workers from southern China and to a lesser extent from southern India and Ceylon. These migrants served the colonial economic design in filling the roles of labouring and economic middlemen and in consequence stirred up local resentments which were a factor in the emergence of modern nationalism. Nationalism was stimulated also through educational provision for indigenous élites to service the needs of colonial society.

Modern nationalism developed in urban centres where Western-educated indigenous élites who had assimilated liberal ideas experienced frustration and humiliation because of the racialist structure of colonial societies. Nationalism proved to be a containable challenge until Japan overthrew the colonial orders within a matter of months from December 1941.

The first major expression of nationalism took place in the Philippines when a short-lived independence was declared in June 1898 in the political vacuum created by the Spanish–American War. The United States decided to retain possession. It crushed all resistance but then coopted the mestizo élite which had evolved during Spanish dominion. Political accommodation with this landed oligarchy was sealed with the establishment of civil government on the American democratic model in July 1901. National independence was never in contention but a matter of timing, which was agreed during the 1930s and upheld after the Pacific War, despite a brutal and destructive Japanese interregnum.

Collaboration was also a feature of colonial experience in Vietnam but in tandem with strong élite resistance to French rule inspired partly by Japan's modernization and China's republican revolution. Nationalist parties modelled on Chinese example were crushed by French repression which provided scope for the clandestine Communist Party of Indochina which the Vietnamese exile Ho Chi Minh founded in Hong Kong in 1930.

Elsewhere, nationalism arose from a religious source. In Burma, Buddhism was a vehicle for anti-colonial resistance after the First World War but was overtaken during the 1930s by a radical student-based movement influenced by Marxist ideas. Led by Aung San, this movement established a military link with the Japanese before the Pacific War and took part in their invasion of Burma. Buddhism played a corresponding role in Cambodia during the 1930s.

In the Netherlands East Indies, Islam provided an organizational frame for nationalism stimulated by resentment of alien Chinese competition in traditional textiles. The *Sarekat Islam* (Islamic Union) was set up in 1912 and attracted a mass following and also a Marxist affiliate which developed in 1920 into the Communist Party of Indonesia. Internal division and governmental repression destroyed its viability, while a Communist revolt in 1926 was put down ruthlessly. A distinctive Indonesian political identity crystallized nevertheless during the late 1920s from a secular base. Leadership was provided by a young architect named Sukarno, who was confined to internal exile by the Dutch before collaborating with the Japanese during their occupation in the nationalist interest. In Malaya, nationalism also had an Islamic source as a basis for upholding an indigenous Malay identity threatened by alien migration. Religious nationalism, however, did not gain the support of the Sultans or rulers of the Malay states, who enjoyed a privileged role under British rule.

Thailand was not subject to colonial rule but registered an anti-Western nationalism under a military regime which had come to power through overthrowing the absolute monarchy in 1932. Modernizing reforms introduced during the late nineteenth century by King Chulalongkorn had generated tensions between the court and the bureaucracy over political prerogatives which were resolved in the latter's favour. Japan provided a model for emulation which was employed by the military leader Marshal Phibun Songkhram, who pursued irredentism at French colonial expense. After the fall of France in June 1940. Thailand went to war to recover territory in western Laos and Cambodia, securing its end through Japan's mediation, which foreshadowed its subsequent aggression in December 1941. From June 1940, Japan secured military access to Indochina, from which its forces were able to strike at colonial South-East Asia.

Japan launched airborne attacks on the US naval base at Pearl Harbor on 7 December 1941. Concurrent attacks were launched within South-East Asia, beginning with an air raid on Clark airfield in the Philippines and a sea-based assault on southern Thailand, from which the invasion of Malaya, Singapore, the Netherlands East Indies, and Burma proceeded. By May 1942, with the fall of Corregidor in the Philippines, the Japanese conquest of colonial South-East Asia was complete. The superiority of Europe was exposed as a hollow myth as its surviving soldiers and colonial civil servants were herded like cattle into prison camps.

With Japan's displacement of the colonial orders, the pace of political change was strictly controlled to serve its war effort. A nominal independence only was conferred on Burma and the Philippines in

August and October 1943 respectively, and in Indochina in March 1945, when the French Vichy administration was removed in favour of local nominees. The human effect of Japan's occupation was profound, with economies devastated and subject peoples and colonial captives treated with great brutality. Japan was driven forcibly from South-East Asia by Allied forces only in Burma and in part in the Philippines, which meant that there was minimal opportunity to redeem a shattered colonial reputation. Elsewhere, Japan's dispossession followed from the atomic bombing of Hiroshima and Nagasaki.

Returning colonial powers divided into the compliant and the dogged. The United States was the most compliant, honouring a promise made in the 1930s by according independence symbolically on 4 July 1946 to the Philippines. Manuel Roxas, a nominee of General Douglas MacArthur and a collaborator of the Japanese, was elected as the first President of an independent Republic. Britain made concessions in the face of an assertive and popular Burmese nationalism organized through the Anti-Fascist People's Freedom League led by Aung San. An agreement on independence was concluded in January 1947. The assassination of Aung San by a political rival in July did not interrupt the timetable for the transfer of sovereignty, which took place on 4 January 1948, with U Nu as Burma's first Prime Minister.

In Malaya, including Singapore, Britain did not face pressing demands for independence. The indigenous Malay majority were apprehensive of the large ethnic-Chinese community which had provided most recruits for armed resistance to the Japanese through the vehicle of the Malayan Communist Party. A Malay nationalism emerged with the formation of the United Malays National Organization (UMNO) in March 1946 in reaction to a British proposal for a Malayan Union, excluding Singapore, in which non-Malays would enjoy ready access to citizenship, while the Sultans, the symbols of Malay rule, would lose their constitutional status. In the event, Singapore remained a separate British colony and naval base, while Malaya was reorganized into a Federation with the status of the Sultans restored in return for a more gradual acquisition of citizenship by non-Malays.

The eruption of Communist insurrection in Malaya in June 1948 delayed Malaya's progress to independence. The transfer of sovereignty occurred on 31 August 1957 with Tunku Abdul Rahman as Prime Minister after a Malay–Chinese political accommodation at élite level which has been the basis for political rule ever since. Singapore became self-governing in June 1959. British possessions in northern Borneo had reverted to direct colonial control for reasons of good government. Sarawak was transferred from the personal rule of the Brooke family and North Borneo (now Sabah) from that of a chartered company, while Brunei was restored as a protected state. Portugal resumed control over the eastern half of the island of Timor.

Fierce struggles for independence took place in the Netherlands East Indies and Indochina. The Republic of Indonesia was the first new state to assert independence, proclaimed by nationalist leaders Sukarno and Hatta on 17 August 1945 just two days after Japan's surrender. Indonesia's independence was achieved through a combination of armed struggle and negotiations, with the embryonic Republic being accorded quasi-international status and representation at the United Nations from August 1947. The Dutch were obliged to transfer sovereignty in December 1949, but relations with Indonesia remained strained by their unwillingness to concede the western half of the island of New Guinea. Indonesia's struggle for independence was aided by Cold War considerations. Initial US support for the Dutch was withdrawn after the Republic had put down a communist-supported revolt in Madiun in East Java in September 1948.

In the case of Indochina, however, and in particular Vietnam, US Cold War calculations served French interests. Unlike Indonesia, Vietnam had declared independence under the aegis of the Communist Party. In July 1941 Ho Chi Minh, operating from southern China, had established the League for the Independence of Vietnam or *Viet Minh* which attracted nationalist support. In August 1945 it took advantage of Japan's surrender by seizing Hanoi and forcing the abdication in its favour of the Emperor Bao Dai. The proclamation of the Democratic Republic of Vietnam took place in Hanoi on 2 September 1945, with Ho Chi Minh employing the idiom of the United States' declaration of independence in an abortive attempt to secure international recognition.

Indochina had been divided along the line of the sixteenth parallel of latitude with responsibility for taking the Japanese surrender shared between the Nationalist Chinese forces of Chiang Kai Shek to the north and those of SEAC to the south. The Chinese dispossessed the *Viet Minh* in North Vietnam, while SEAC enabled the return of French administration to South Vietnam, Laos and Cambodia. A *modus vivendi* between the French and the *Viet Minh* against a background of Chinese withdrawal broke down at the end of 1946. The political future of

Vietnam, as well as of Laos and Cambodia, was then to be decided by force of arms in two stages.

Thailand was an exception to the regional pattern. It was an independent state but had become tainted politically through association with Japan's aggressive design. The United States sought Thailand's international rehabilitation, however. Bangkok's declaration of war had not been communicated by the Thai legation in Washington nor accepted by the US government, while Britain's and France's wish for retribution was interpreted as an expression of an abiding colonialism. With a civilian government restored, Thailand was treated little differently from any other country liberated from Japan's tyranny, albeit obliged to return its wartime territorial gains. But when that government was overthrown by a military *coup* in the wake of the unexplained violent death of the young King Ananda in June 1946, cold-war priorities interposed to sustain American patronage.

The post-colonial states of South-East Asia began their independent existence with two legacies: the colonial political boundaries and the parliamentary democracy deemed a necessary symbol of international legitimacy, given the global dominance of the United States. Those state boundaries contained fissile social diversities which were not readily willing to accept the cultural and economic imperatives of alien political centres. For example, Burma was afflicted with ethno-regional dissent and challenge which has persisted for over half a century. Neighbouring Thailand also experienced a separatist pull from its mainly Muslim south stimulated by the rise of Malay nationalism. Indonesia in its archipelagic condition was most vulnerable to centrifugal political forces, encouraged by Dutch policy before the transfer of sovereignty.

Communist insurrection was another endemic feature of South-East Asia in the wake of the Pacific War. It made a major impact in Burma and the Philippines shortly after independence and in Malaya and Indonesia before the transfers of sovereignty, although ultimately failing. In the important case of Vietnam, the communist movement assumed the mantle of nationalism to attain ultimate military and political success.

Despite an endemic separatism aggravated by communist insurrection, none of South-East Asia's post-colonial states have experienced involuntary dismemberment. The Federation of Malaysia took a conscious decision to eject Singapore to independence in August 1965. Irredentism has enjoyed greater regional import, for example, in

Indonesia's recovery of the western half of the island of New Guinea (known now as Irian Jaya) in May 1963 and in the unification of Vietnam in April 1975. With minor exceptions, the territorial inheritance of colonialism has been transferred intact. But Indonesia's annexation of the eastern half of the island of Timor in December 1975 was inconsistent with the nationalist *raison d'être* based on the Dutch colonial domain.

The political inheritance of the West has been much less durable. Parliamentary systems have experienced a chequered record and were placed under great strain in Burma and Indonesia during the 1950s as tensions between polity and society were aggravated by economic difficulties. Both states opted for authoritarian solutions, as did Thailand. The Philippines maintained the form of democracy into the early 1970s, but then President Ferdinand Marcos assumed dictatorial powers for over a decade. Malaya/Malaysia and then Singapore sustained their initial parliamentary practices on independence but increasingly employed legislatures as rubber stamps for one-party government.

The post-colonial era coincided with and was affected deeply by the Cold War and the determination of the United States to contain international communism. In Indochina, France's confrontation with the *Viet Minh* was represented as a theatre of global conflict. Its failure to contain the *Viet Minh's* advance by early 1954, however, prompted the United States to contemplate direct military intervention, which caused alarm among regional states of a neutralist disposition. The governments of Burma and Indonesia combined with those of three South Asian states in Ceylon's capital Colombo to appeal for moderation. That meeting led on to a wider Asian–African Conference in the Indonesian city of Bandung in April 1955, which registered for the first time the international agenda of post-colonial states.

The historic Bandung Conference convened in the wake of the First Indochina War. France had suffered a devastating military reverse at the hands of *Viet Minh* at the battle of Dien Bien Phu in the north-west of Vietnam close to the border with Laos. The surrender of the French position took place on 7 April 1954, one day before an international conference convened in Geneva to address the Indochina conflict. Ceasefire agreements were concluded for Vietnam, Laos, and Cambodia, together with an unsigned Final Declaration endorsing their terms. Vietnam was divided along the line of the seventeenth parallel of latitude for the purpose of regrouping military units. That line solidified into a *de facto* international boundary enduring for over twenty years. A communist government led by Ho Chi Minh took power to its north; to its south an anti-communist administration headed by former exile Ngo Dinh Diem was installed. Under the terms of the Geneva agreements, nationwide elections were to be held in Vietnam within two years, but they never took place as the country became the locus of the Cold War in Asia.

Communist-supported revolutionary movements in Laos and Cambodia were not recognized at the Geneva Conference. Cambodia was restored to independence under the leadership of King Norodom Sihanouk, who abdicated in favour of his father in March 1955 to set up a Vichy-style organization through which he dominated politics for a decade and a half. Laos was also restored to a fragile independence; two of its provinces abutting China and Vietnam remained under control of *Viet Minh*-controlled Laotian forces. The United States sought to hold the line against further communist advance in Indochina through a Collective Defence Treaty for South-East Asia concluded in Manila on 8 September 1954 whose members assumed unilateral obligations to Cambodia, Laos, and South Vietnam. Within South-East Asia, only Thailand and the Philippines signed up. A South-East Asia Treaty Organization (SEATO) was set up in Bangkok in February 1955 but without a military command. From the early 1960s, the south of Vietnam reverted to armed struggle, with Laos drawn into that conflict because of the importance of its eastern uplands as an infiltration route into South Vietnam — which achieved notoriety as the Ho Chi Minh Trail.

In Indonesia, President Sukarno replaced Indonesia's parliamentary system with an authoritarian Guided Democracy in July 1959 in the wake of abortive regional uprisings. He commanded the country's political heights through remarkable oratorical skills and by playing off the armed forces and the large Communist Party. He also exploited nationalist issues — in particular, Holland's refusal to transfer the western half of the island of New Guinea. Fear of Communist advantage attracted US support for this irredentist cause, but its realization encouraged Sukarno's engagement in external diversion as a way of maintaining political control in deteriorating economic circumstances. A revolt in the British-protected Sultanate of Brunei in North Borneo in December 1962 provided a pretext for challenging the formation of the Federation of Malaysia.

In May 1961 the Prime Minister of Malaya, Tunku Abdul Rahman, proposed unifying the Malay Peninsula with self-governing Singapore and British possessions in North Borneo as a way of containing local communist and Chinese influence in Singapore seen as synonymous. Indonesia's challenge to the legitimacy of Malaysia from January 1963 was distinguished by the term *Konfrontasi* (Confrontation) — a form of coercive diplomacy which had been used against the Dutch over West New Guinea. Malaysia was established on 16 September 1963 but without Brunei's adherence. Indonesia's "Confrontation" and Sukarno's "Guided Democracy" collapsed in the wake of an abortive *coup* in October 1965 attributed to the country's Communist Party. On 11 March 1966 power was assumed by Lieutenant-General (later President) Suharto, whose military-based administration embarked on economic development and regional cooperation involving reconciliation with Malaysia and a newly independent Singapore.

Political crisis and change in Indonesia occurred concurrently with political decay and military confrontation in South Vietnam. The leadership of President Ngo Dinh Diem had failed to prise the nationalist standard from the grasp of the *Viet Minh*, who were reconstituted under the leadership of the Communist Party as the National Liberation Front of South Vietnam (NLF) in December 1960. Buddhist protest against the government in Saigon, seen as dominated by Catholics, as well as the lamentable military performance of its army against a rural insurgency, led to a withdrawal of American support for Diem who was murdered during a military *coup* in November 1963, just days before the assassination of President Kennedy. A series of juntas then exercised power but without any grasp of the requirements for political victory which led the United States to assume growing responsibility for the conduct of the widening war. By March 1965 the United States had changed its nature by embarking on the sustained aerial bombardment of North Vietnam. When this attempt to impose an unacceptable cost on the ruling party in Hanoi failed, more than half a million combat troops were introduced progressively into the south but without inflicting the desired miliary reverse on the communist army increasingly stiffened by infiltration from the north.

The turning point in the conflict came at the end of January 1968 during the Tet festival for the Vietnamese lunar new year when the NLF launched coordinated attacks against urban targets. Although a military failure, the Tet Offensive proved to be a historical turning point because of its political impact within the United States where popular protest was rising in opposition to the heavy price in lives and casualties being paid by American servicemen. A peace agreement concluded in Paris in January 1973 left the government in Saigon in place but not for long. A Vietnamese communist military offensive in March 1975 in the central highlands set off a rout among the southern army, with northern forces seizing Saigon on 30 April. Formal reunification took place on 2 July 1976 with the promulgation of the Socialist Republic of Vietnam.

A communist victory had also occurred in neighbouring Cambodia on 17 April when Phnom Penh was invested by a revolutionary movement known as the Khmer Rouge. This movement had its roots in a nationalist–communist alternative to the neighbouring Vietnamese party but had acquired military and political significance only in the wake of Prince Norodom Sihanouk's overthrow by a right-wing *coup* on 18 March 1970. The restoration of the royal government in April 1975 was short-lived, to be replaced on 5 January 1976 by an ironically termed "Democratic" Kampuchea and Prince Sihanouk's resignation and house arrest. Under the leadership of the fearsome Pol Pot, a gruesome social experiment was inaugurated. Cambodia was transformed into a primitive agricultural work camp combining the worst excesses of Stalin and Mao in which around a million people died from execution, starvation, and disease. An attempt to conceal the failings of economic dogma through xenophobic nationalism led on to military confrontation with Vietnam. Laos, subject to a fragile coalition, also succumbed to communist control during the course of 1975. In December, the constitutional monarchy was removed and the Laos People's Democratic Republic was established in a close relationship with Vietnam.

As the Vietnam War intensified, a group of non-communist states began an experiment in regional cooperation. Thailand, Malaya and the Philippines set up the Association of South-East Asia (ASA) in Bangkok in July 1961, based on the rationale that economic progress through regional cooperation would provide a foundation for national security. ASA fell victim to Indonesia's "Confrontation" and the claim by the Philippines to the part of North Borneo incorporated into the Federation of Malaysia as Sabah. ASA was superseded in August 1967 in Bangkok by ASEAN, with the additional membership of Indonesia and Singapore.

ASEAN was an attempt to provide a framework for regional reconciliation. Its declaratory goals were economic and cultural cooperation but security was uppermost in mind among governments which shared a common experience of resisting internal revolutionary challenge and which also had misgivings about the regional staying power of the United States. A progressive willingness to cooperate in avoiding and managing conflict served to engender external business confidence in regional economies which, beginning with Singapore under the dynamic leadership of Lee Kuan Yew, came to emulate Japan's example of export-led growth.

In February 1976, after the success of revolutionary communism in Indochina, ASEAN demonstrated its collective nerve by holding the first meeting of its heads of government in Indonesia. A political agenda was set and an agreement reached to establish a secretariat in Jakarta. Moreover, Japan began to take ASEAN seriously. Prime Minister Takeo Fukuda with his Australian and New Zealand counter-parts attended the next meeting of heads of governments convened in August 1977 to commemorate the tenth anniversary of ASEAN's formation. Japan had returned to South-East Asia in an economic role during the 1950s through the vehicle of reparations agreements. That role expanded over the years as access to raw materials and market opportunities was succeeded by capital investment to take advantage of cheaper labour and land, pointing the way for burgeoning multi-national enterprise.

The Third Indochina War marked the final occasion in the twentieth century when a local conflict within South-East Asia would serve as a focus for global conflict. It began in December 1978, when Vietnamese forces invaded and occupied Cambodia. The belligerent Khmer Rouge regime was driven out to find active sanctuary in Thailand, and a People's Republic of Kampuchea was established in January 1979 in a special relationship with Vietnam. China responded by launching a punitive expedition into North Vietnam in February. The United States and Japan applied economic pressure on Vietnam while the ASEAN states played an active diplomatic role, with the alignment supporting an armed resistance against the Vietnamese occupation, including the Khmer Rouge.

The burden of the Third Indochina War broke the back of Vietnam's resolve to engage concurrently in socialist development and to uphold a special relationship with neighbouring states in Indochina. In the event, Vietnam lost the countervailing support of the Soviet Union and was obliged to appease China in particular by withdrawing its forces from Cambodia from the end of September 1989. ASEAN then took a back seat diplomatically, as the permanent members of the Security Council assumed the initiative for a peace settlement through the vehicle of a United Nations Transitional Authority in Cambodia (UNTAC) provided for at an international conference in Paris in October 1991. UNTAC conducted nationwide elections in Cambodia in May 1993, despite the recalcitrance of the Khmer Rouge, leading to the restoration of the constitutional monarchy under Norodom Sihanouk in September and the formation of a fragile coalition government in October. Complete peace was not restored, however, as a diminished Khmer Rouge continued to fight for a share of power as a basis for resuming its exclusive exercise.

The end of the Cambodian conflict registered the regional impact of changes in global politics at the end of the century. It also registered an acknowledgement by the ruling party in Hanoi that it had lost its way economically and had placed its legitimacy at risk. During the Third Indochina War, the members of ASEAN, augmented by an independent Brunei from January 1984 and with the exception of the Philippines, continued to prosper as they benefited from concentrating on comparative advantage in manufactures. Vietnam faced penury as the cost of prosecuting the Cambodia war compounded the failings of the rigid application of socialist doctrine. Revision in Hanoi came in December 1986 a the Third National Congress of the Communist Party which appointed the economic reformer Nguyen Van Linh as General Secretary. A new doctrine of *Doi Moi*, meaning renovation or renewal of the economy through free-market practice, was promulgated and applied progressively, despite resistance from party diehards.

Doi Moi registered the need to encourage free-market economics and inward investment if Vietnam was to raise standards of living to match those of its regional neighbours. Such a repudiation of economic doctrine, replicated in Laos, was not matched by a revision of the political system. On the contrary, economic change was undertaken in order to protect the leading role of the Communist Party. To that extent, a convergence of a kind emerged in political systems with some other regional states which had pioneered successful economic growth through a practice of developmental authoritarianism whereby the state intervened to ensure political demobilization in the interest of social stability and economic progress. Such a practice had been demonstrated in the case of Indonesia under the leadership of President Suharto and Malaysia under Dr Mahathir Mohamad, and strikingly so in the case of Singapore, whose Senior Minister and former Prime

Minister, Lee Kuan Yew, was invited to Vietnam to offer economic advice.

In the wake of the Cold War, the astounding economic successes of a number of South-East Asian states provided a source of self-confidence in rebutting attempts by the West to impose its own democratic values. The issue of democratization within the region had arisen well before the end of the Cold War in the Philippines, where the venal rule of President Marcos had provided a political opening for the insurgent Communist Party. Against a background of political and economic decay Marcos called a snap election in February 1986. He was challenged by Mrs Corazon Aquino, the widow of his one-time principal political opponent, Benigno Aquino, who had been murdered at Manila Airport in August 1983 on his return from exile in the United States. Fraudulent conduct of that election served as the context for a military revolt in Manila led by Fidel Ramos, the deputy Chief of Staff of the Armed Forces, and Juan Ponce Enrile, the Defence Minister. Marcos loyalists were prevented from crushing that revolt in support of Mrs Aquino by the physical interposition of civilian demonstrators encouraged by the Catholic Church. That display of so-called "people power" persuaded the United States to withdraw its longstanding support for Marcos, who, with his family, went into exile in Hawaii, leaving Mrs Aquino to be inaugurated as President. She restored the democratic process, but a stable political order had to await the election in June 1992 of her successor Fidel Ramos, whose loyalty as Defence Minister had thwarted a series of military *coups*.

Democracy triumphed also in Thailand. A false start had been made in October 1973 when student revolt and intervention by King Bhumibol restored the parliamentary system, but it was soon overturned by another military *coup* three years later. During the 1980s benign military rule and respect for constitutionalism ensued under Prime Minister General Prem Tinsulanond. When the military removed his elected successor, Chatichai Choonhavan, by a *coup* in February 1991, King Bhumibol distanced himself from the junta, who chose civilian caretaker, Anand Panyarachun, as Prime Minister. Fresh elections were held in March 1992, but the appointment of an unelected former army commander, General Suchinda Krapayoon, provoked angry demonstrations in Bangkok reminiscent of Manila in February 1986 but culminating in a bloody confrontation. The King intervened to restore democratic order, with further elections in September 1992 giving rise to an elected government with a civilian base which has been sustained. In both the Philippines and Thailand, popular protest but in contrasting economic circumstances had served the democratic interest. Corresponding protest in Burma, however, resulted in the flowering of democracy being ruthlessly crushed.

Burma had been ruled by a military regime headed by General Ne Win ever since the armed forces had seized power in a *coup* which displaced the democratic regime in March 1962. A mixture of Marxist and Buddhist nostrums provided a doctrinal basis for a so-called "Burmese Road to Socialism" under the monopoly rule of the Burma Socialist Programme Party (BSPP). The outcome by the late 1980s was a condition of national penury indicated by application to the United Nations for Burma to be accorded the status of "least developed country" in order to secure grants in aid. Demonetization of larger currency notes in circulation in September 1987 provoked student unrest which rose to a crescendo during August and September 1988, to be met with ruthless military repression. Ne Win had resigned as head of government in 1981 and gave up the leadership of the BSPP in July 1987, but he retained a dominant political influence despite his ailing physical condition. In the face of popular protest which was inspired by the presence in the country of Aung San Suu Kyi, the daughter of the revered nationalist martyr Aung San, the armed forces launched an "incumbency *coup*". All state and party organs were abolished by the new junta, which styled itself the State Law and Order Restoration Council (SLORC) and which in June 1989 changed the name of the country to Myanmar.

Elections were held in May 1990 in which the National League for Democracy — led by Aung San Suu Kyi, who had been placed under house arrest in July 1989 — won an overwhelming majority over the National Unity Party, which was the political vehicle of the military junta. That electoral outcome was not honoured and the SLORC went ahead with drafting a new constitution designed to entrench the political role of the armed forces along the lines of the Indonesian model as well as to exclude Aung San Suu Kyi from power.

Through its diplomatic performance and economic accomplishments, ASEAN had become increasingly attractive to non-members, giving the region a historically unprecedented coherence. The prospect seemed good for realizing the aspiration of transforming South-East Asia into a Zone of Peace, Freedom, and Neutrality (ZOPFAN) which had been articulated at a meeting of ASEAN's foreign ministers in November 1971. In fact, with the end of the cold war, the strategic environment in East Asia, including South-East Asia, changed in a way that did not permit the members of ASEAN to shape regional order in a prerogative manner. South-East Asia did not enjoy a self-contained condition but was linked by land, water, and politics to a more extensive East Asia. This geopolitical linkage was pointed up in contention over the Spratly Islands in the South China Sea, which had not been dominated or delimited by colonial powers.

The People's Republic of China had pressed a claim to all the islands of the South China Sea from its establishment, had employed force to secure the northerly Paracel Islands at Vietnam's expense in the mid-1970s, and had seized a limited number of the southerly Spratly Islands in the late 1980s with a further armed occupation in the mid-1990s. Claims to partial jurisdiction in the Spratly Islands had been asserted also by Malaysia, the Philippines, and Brunei — all members of ASEAN — while Vietnam, which joined the Association in July 1995, sought jurisdiction over both the Paracel and Spratly Islands. China's irredentist disposition was displayed at a time when it had come to enjoy an unprecedented regional strategic latitude free from any major adversary and had begun to modernize its armed forces with an increasing ability to project naval and air power southwards. Moreover, the United States had conceded nationalist demands and had withdrawn its once formidable military presence from the Philippines by the end of 1992.

Despite a sustained commitment to a ZOPFAN, ASEAN governments have never shared a common perspective of external threat; nor has the Association been willing to engage in defence cooperation. In the circumstances, ASEAN opted to extend its approach to regional security based on multilateral dialogue to a wider East Asia in order to cope with an assertive China and a retreating United States. In July 1993 in Singapore, the annual meeting of ASEAN's foreign ministers was used to host an inaugural dinner for eighteen foreign ministers to launch the ASEAN Regional Forum (ARF) intended to promote a predictable and constructive pattern of relationships in Asia-Pacific. Apart from the six ASEAN states, and their seven dialogue partners from the United States, Japan, Australia, New Zealand, Canada, South Korea, and the EU, there were Papua New Guinea, Vietnam, and Laos as well as China and Russia. The first working meeting of the ARF convened in Bangkok in July 1994.

South-East Asian governments have also found themselves obliged to accept a wider framework for economic cooperation. ASEAN has long had a formal commitment to economic cooperation but it was only in January 1992 that a decision was taken by its governments to set up a free trade area. By this juncture, however, through Australian initiative in 1989, a wider consultative forum for Asia-Pacific Economic Cooperation (APEC) was established which has assumed a growing importance through annual meetings between its heads of government.

By the end of the twentieth century, the governments of an expanding ASEAN have given coherence to the concept of a South-East Asia. Ironically, just as this coherence has been registered, they have been obliged to expand their regional horizons in order to cope with changing strategic and economic environments in a way which casts doubt on the very viability of the concept of South-East Asia.

PART I
International Relations

Introduction to Part I

Chin Kin Wah

Michael Leifer's interest in Southeast Asia was awakened during his first academic appointment at the University of Adelaide where he spent more than three years in the 1960s. In his first book on Southeast Asia[1] published after his return to the United Kingdom, Leifer admitted to having fallen prey to the Australian "national habit" of continually looking to their "near north" — a habit that was to distinguish his own academic achievements in ensuing years. Interestingly Leifer's early research skills were honed in quite a different field — Zionism and Palestine in British Opinion and Policy — a doctorial dissertation topic, which led to his coming under the joint supervision of Elie Kedourie at the London School of Economics. In a tribute to his former teacher, Leifer acknowledged the intellectual influence of Kedourie from whom he acquired "a fuller understanding of the activity of politics and what might be expected of those who indulged in it". Such an understanding, he felt, stood him well in his subsequent endeavours to interpret a vastly different regional field of study.[2]

In an academic career spanning over three decades, Leifer witnessed and sought to make sense of the historic transition of Southeast Asian states from being objects to subjects of international relations. In his academic lifetime (when his first book was published the United States was getting increasingly embroiled in the Vietnam War), he also observed a region undergoing transformation — in a process often punctuated by turbulence — from being "a category of convenience" associated with a wartime military command and from the so-called "Balkans of the Orient", to one with a growing sense of regional oneness and geopolitical coherence. By the time of his death in March 2001, the whole of Southeast Asia had become identified with ASEAN, thus fulfilling the regional association's putative vision of "one Southeast Asia".

In this saga of regional transformation, the formal emergence into statehood often marked the beginning of a chapter in the struggle for survival and stability. Indeed the problem of how the new and often vulnerable states of the region were to maintain their independent existence in a less than benign regional environment that threatened to engulf them, posed a central puzzle and refocused his attention albeit in a different context, on "the activity of politics" and "those who indulged in it". It was not surprising that his early works on Southeast Asia sought to address the security challenges faced by some of the most vulnerable of successor governments in the region — Cambodia seeking a precarious independent foreign policy against the backdrop of an unfolding American intervention in Indochina; the new Malaysian Federation then being confronted by neighbouring Indonesia; Singapore struggling to come to terms with an unexpected independence. The interplay of external providence (or improvidence) and enlightened domestic leadership (or the lack of it) were to result in radically different outcomes for those who indulged in the activity of politics in post-colonial Southeast Asia. These "domestic" developments of regional states are taken up in greater detail in Part II of this volume. Part I looks at Leifer's analysis of the broad forces at work which shaped the patterns of international relations in Southeast Asia.

His Theoretical Underpinnings and Method

On reading Leifer one is often struck by the detachment of his analysis and avoidance of intellectual faddishness. Others have been left with an impression of his being a-theoretical. He often avoided stating upfront his theoretical approach in his numerous studies of the region, but his largely empirical works were by no means lacking in theoretical underpinnings. Nor was he unfamiliar with the contending schools of thought in international relations. Indeed he often evinced a strong underlying realism although as a former colleague of his at the LSE noted, it was a tough realism uniquely blended with humanity that made it difficult to categorize him in simple terms.[3] If he had appeared traditional and even conservative in his approach it was because his method was one which tended to draw heavily on "substantive examples which have an illustrative function"[4] — in other words the diplomatic record was usually grist to his analysis of international politics. Be that as it may, his analyses of current events were often cast in cogently developed intellectual frameworks.

Leifer's realist assumptions were quite consistently reflected in the attraction that power and balance of power analysis held for him in his interpretation of the shifts in foreign policies and patterns of regional relations; in his essentially state-centric "billiard-ball" perspective of international politics and the importance of national interests and national sovereignty as determinants of state action as well as regional co-operation. In his first book on a regional state's foreign policy, he noted Cambodia's hypersensitivity to shifts in the regional balance of power and anticipated that it would "maneuver in any direction to preserve its national independence".[5]

In subsequent works Leifer sought to explain the elusive balance of power concept in terms of a dimension he deemed pertinent to the ASEAN experience namely, of a balancing policy pursued with a view towards preventing undue dominance by one or more states. Such balancing purpose was as he saw it, reflected in the way ASEAN provided a structure for regional partnership that would place checks ("constraints" in later-day parlance) on a willingly accepting Indonesia previously known for its hegemonial aspirations. Leifer also saw a balance of power purpose reflected in the way ASEAN responded as a diplomatic community to Vietnam's invasion and occupation of Cambodia. His masterly analysis of external power intervention in the conflict similarly highlighted the balance of power considerations behind the respective policies of China, the former Soviet Union, the United States, and Japan. That said, Leifer did not elevate the balance of power to an immutable law of state behaviour in an anarchic world. On the contrary he acknowledged the existence of international society (for which he could be said to reflect a defining strand of thought in the "British School of International Relations") but without exaggerating the constraining role of the norms therein.

With the end of the Cold War, the changing balance of power and the prevailing condition of stability had made it possible for ASEAN to venture into multilateral security co-operation in the form of the ASEAN Regional Forum (ARF) that took it beyond its geostrategic ambit by the end of the last century. However, to the extent that it was very much dependent on a pre-existing stable balance of power situation (which could change over time, and where the one state capable of redressing that change would be the United States, an extra-regional power), it was seen as an imperfect diplomatic instrument, lacking in teeth and, as Leifer colourfully but also realistically put it in his seminal work on the ARF, not unlike "making bricks without straw".

A vein of realism also runs through much of Leifer's reflections on regional co-operation and association. While he saw that ASEAN held forth the possibility of widening functional ties, he did not see much promise in David Mitrany's theory of functionalism (with its assumption of deepening regional co-operation leading eventually to supra-nationalism) being fulfilled in a Southeast Asian setting given that regional leaders tended to guard jealously their nation's sovereignty. Such a view held in his early observations of ASEAN co-operation had been sustained through subsequent regional transitions and expanding regional membership and has not lost its relevance in the arena of high politics, despite the rhetoric of regional integration and community-building which has gained currency in recent times.

Although Leifer took an essentially "statist" approach in his analysis of the international relations of the region, he was nevertheless conscious of the non-state variables and the ethical (as opposed to the power) elements to a contentious international issue. This is vividly illustrated in his almost magisterial treatment of the clash of principles over Vietnam's intervention in Cambodia, cast in terms of the debate between the Rights of State versus the Rights of People. A similar non-partisan approach was reflected in an earlier discussion of Southeast Asian responses to the Vietnam War. If he appeared too much of a realist to some (indeed he never quite rejected the realist label) it could be because the objects of his analysis often seemed to hold a mirror to his own realist inclinations.

Some Recurring Themes

Conflict, co-operation, and order were some of the recurring themes in Leifer's study of the international relations of the region. His entry into

Southeast Asian studies coincided with the intensifying Cold War manifested in the most cataclysmic manner in the Vietnam conflict, which like the subsequent Cambodia conflict (pivot to another Cold War this time, among the Communist powers themselves) marked a conjunction of local, regional, and global contestations. At the local level, there was also a template of traditional conflicts, which were rooted in pre-colonial antagonisms, contested state identities and disputes over boundaries — which questioned the viability of "regional solutions to regional problems" and set parameters to attempts at regional association.

But it was the management of political order (intertwined between the domestic and regional levels) or how to achieve that condition of politics that is characterized by stability and predictability rather than conflict and violence that preoccupied him intellectually. At the level of international relations he most persistently pursued the issue of ASEAN's vision of and capacity to bring about a Southeast Asian-wide regional order — a capacity that was found wanting during the Cold War. Indeed with the emergence of an Indochina sub-system following the American departure from Vietnam, Southeast Asia was left with two contending visions of regional order. Be that as it may, Leifer was ungrudging in his acknowledgement of ASEAN's achievement in sustaining a condition of orderliness (in the sense of a relative absence of violence in the conduct of intra-mural relations) among the members of the regional association. ASEAN effectively presented a viable structure of regional confidence-building, which at the conclusion of the Cold War was embraced by its hitherto regional antagonists. He was more sceptical of ASEAN's attempts to extend its model of regional order beyond its ambit.

Leifer's interest in the problem of managing regional order was pursued into the maritime realm where China's policy has a critical bearing on how local states could bring about more "orderliness" in the South China Sea environs, seen by Leifer as the last frontier of Southeast Asia. His realist inclinations led him to see assertions of maritime claims as most likely where the regional balance of power is in flux and where countervailing power seems doubtful. The post-September 11 regional environment is however witnessing changes in the way maritime security is being redefined. New areas of functional needs to counter threats to maritime security are presenting new opportunities for co-operation between regional and extra-regional states. Complicating such co-operation are the traditional notions of sovereignty, which Leifer had so usefully explored.

And Some Lacunae

Leifer graduated in politics and economics from Reading University, but there is little hint of this background in his works on Southeast Asia. Indeed he seems not to have given fuller treatment to foreign economic policy or the economic aspects of foreign policy-making by the more developed regional states. Where he has attempted a limited politics cum economic approach it has been in connection with his later-day analysis of China's and Taiwan's economic engagement with the region. A sharper political economy angle on the region itself and considerations of emerging new economic interdependence might have provided a prism to a different pattern of regional dynamics and made better sense of the growing impacts (and consequent political implications) of China and India on the geoeconomic terrain of Southeast Asia.

If he were to look at the region today he would probably have more sharply factored in the rising profile of India, which in his time seemed to be diplomatically distant — serving almost as a contrasting footnote to the rise of China. This despite the fact that he anticipated the growing influence of India in the region. Today as India reorientates its international outlook and attitudes towards the Southeast Asian region and extends its strategic reach, it will be an increasing reminder to ASEAN of its strategic presence on its western flank. Indeed the region has never had to face the rise of both China and India at the same time as it is currently, and Leifer would have compared and contrasted their respective impacts.

Among the major external powers which had shaped the strategic environment of Southeast Asia, the United States and China consistently took much of Leifer's attention. Since the demise of the Soviet Union and the onset of economic malaise in Japan, Moscow and Tokyo seemed to have lost their appeal although Leifer had directed his attention on their interests in and diplomacy towards the region during the Cold War years. His interest in the Sino-U.S. relationship underlines its importance to the stability of East Asia of which ASEAN is a part.

Today Leifer would perhaps have linked more clearly the greater significance of an evolving East Asian mega-region to the economic and strategic environment of ASEAN especially since there is growing acceptance of the need to factor in economics in any security and foreign policy evaluations. Regional states' economic entry into China is also redefining traditional notions of space as they increasingly grow their stakes in the internal stability of China itself — a significant transformation from the early Cold War years when China was all too readily seen as a threat to their domestic security. More importantly he would have revisited the question of regional identity and what underpin that, in the light of what has been claimed as a growing East Asian consciousness and relate that back to ASEAN's place in the greater game of today in East Asia.

Leifer died before the horrendous events of September 11 and the emergence of a transnational threat posed by a non-state network of terror. Since September 11, a whole host of non-traditional security concerns (but particularly international terrorism) are crowding into the security agenda of the region — a phenomenon that would have given exciting materials for Leifer to reflect on although he might still be inclined to focus on the level of states' response and co-operation.

His Sense of the Paradoxical and the Ironic

In his years of observing Southeast Asia, Leifer was able to look out for the paradoxical and the ironic without seeming to be cynical. In his study of Singapore's foreign policy, he drew out several paradoxes including the observation that the island-state needed the region and yet sought to transcend it. The old ASEAN-5 had also seemed like a paradox to Leifer. It was best contemplated as a security organization of a kind — in the sense that its members shared a common interest in preventing radical internal political change and sought to promote mutual security by consultation and co-operation wherever practical. Yet paradoxically, it did not possess the form or the structure of an alliance and its corporate activity was devoted in the main to regional economic co-operation. This "paradox" was "a function of the perception of threat held by the individual governments of the association and of other limits to the degree of co-operation between them".[6] Leifer returned to this paradoxical element in his comments on the strains registered on Malaysia–Singapore relations as a consequence of Israeli President Chaim Herzog's visit to Singapore in 1986. He saw that the visit once again pointed to a paradoxical quality of ASEAN, present at its creation. "ASEAN was established between adversaries of different kinds in an attempt to promote a structure of reconciliation. The regional enterprise was embarked upon in the full knowledge that certain underlying facts of political life could not be changed at will, including the sense of vulnerability of some member states; some partners in reconciliation would remain potential enemies."[7]

In taking stock of ASEAN developments, Leifer often revealed a sense of the ironic. He noted for example that by the end of the last century, the governments of an expanding ASEAN had given coherence to the concept of a Southeast Asian region. "Ironically, just as this coherence has been registered, they have been obliged to expand their regional horizons (through the creation of the ARF) in order to cope with changing strategic and economic environments in a way which casts doubt on the very viability of the concept of South-East Asia."[8]

Leifer clearly recognized ASEAN's need at century's end to reinvent itself — the alternative being institutional atrophy. Yet every solution seems to have its own problems! The dilemma for ASEAN is that the diversity that came with expanding membership underlined the value of "a tightly restricted model of regional security" based on the principles of respect for national sovereignty and non-interference in the domestic affairs of neighbours. Keeping in view the debate about revisiting the terms of intra-regional engagement, Leifer warned that, "ASEAN cannot be expected to expand beyond its role which means that the Association is condemned to suffer from the defects of its qualities and the evident limitations of its collective competence ... Its prime saving grace ... has been to sustain an original role of containing and managing intra-mural tensions which is an accomplishment not to be disparaged in an imperfect world. In that respect, ASEAN lends itself to an old adage that in contemplating its future role the best should not be made the enemy of the good."[9]

Leifer's familiarity with the region and its many key policy-makers did not lead him into the realm of advocacy. It was as if he believed that vision making was best left to regional visionaries. What he did was to bring a sense of the realistic to bear on the prescriptions of the day — "regional solutions to regional problems", "going the ASEAN way", "constructive/flexible engagement in ASEAN", "towards 'one Southeast Asia'" — dissected them and spelt out their implications. He subjected to close scrutiny such concepts as diplomatic community, security community, defence community, co-operative security, and the notion of a distinctive ASEAN peace process, which have entered regional discourses. In so doing he forced many to clarify their own thoughts and review the empirical evidence even as they sought to take issue with his brand of realism. It is this role as the constructive critic that will be sorely missed in Michael Leifer.

Notes

1. Michael Leifer, *Cambodia: The Search for Security* (London: Pall Mall, 1967).
2. Michael Leifer, "A Personal Note", in *Elie Kedourie CBE, FBA, 1926–1992: History, Philosophy, Politics*, edited by Sylvia Kedourie (London; Portland OR: Frank Cass, c1998), p. 29.
3. Adam Roberts, "Obituary: Professor Michael Leifer", *The Independent*, 9 April 2001.
4. Michael Leifer, *Dilemmas of Statehood in Southeast Asia* (Singapore: Asia Pacific Press, 1972), p. xi.
5. *Cambodia: The Search for Security*, p. 19.
6. Michael Leifer, "The Paradox of ASEAN: A Security Organisation Without the Structure of an Alliance", *Round Table* No. 271 (July 1978), p. 261.
7. Michael Leifer, "ASEAN's Search for Regional Order" (Singapore: G Brash for Faculty of Arts and Social Sciences, National University of Singapore, 1987), p 18.
8. "Southeast Asia", *The Oxford History of the Twentieth Century*, edited by Michael Howard and Wm. Roger Louis (Oxford: Oxford University Press, 1988), p. 239.
9. Michael Leifer, "The Limits of ASEAN's Expanding Role", unpublished paper written in mid-1997 in connection with an ISEAS commemoration of ASEAN's 30th anniversary, p. 16.

Southeast Asia: Conflict and Co-operation

INTRODUCTION

Conflict and co-operation are traditionally "such stuffs" as international relations are made on, and to Leifer, an understanding of their nature and inter-play is an essential point of entry to making sense of the international relations of Southeast Asia — an academic endeavour which for him had begun during the Cold War. Three sources of regional conflict during that era attracted his attention. These were contests over state identity; pre-colonial historical antagonisms, such as those between Vietnam and China and Kampuchea (Cambodia) and Vietnam; and legacies of the transfers of sovereignty resulting in disputes over state boundaries. Such conflicts — whether internal, for example, Communist insurgency in Thailand, Malay(si)a, South Vietnam and Burma (Myanmar), or separatism in Southern Thailand and the Southern Philippines, or inter-state, for example, boundary disputes and territorial claims — although rooted in the region, acquired particular saliency when conjoined with the competitive interests of external powers. Such was the fate of local powers that lacked the capacity to manage regional order on their own (Ch. 2).

33

The conflicts that existed during Leifer's early academic entry into the region were a hinderance to regionwide co-operation. Revival of traditional antagonisms reflecting old fears and new anxieties between regional states and "mutual antipathy" underlay relations between Cambodia and its neighbours, namely, Vietnam and Thailand. Malaysia–Thai border problems, Confrontation, the Philippines' claim to Sabah, and post-separation Malaysia–Singapore tensions suggested a lack of trust and limited scope for regional integration. Leifer questions the notion of "Asian solutions to Asian problems" which assumed that regional commonality necessarily made for a conciliatory approach (Ch. 3).

By far the most cataclysmic regional conflict since World War II was the Vietnam War, which to Thailand especially, appeared as a fusion between historical threat and an emerging Communist menace. In a hitherto unpublished paper written in 1986, Leifer notes that the public impact of the war on regional states outside Indochina was low compared to what transpired in America. Regional responses depended largely on the political identities, experience and, above all, the security priorities of the governments. Regional dispositions ranged from neutrality to alliance. But even between regional allies of the United States (Thailand and the Philippines), interests and responses were differentiable. Despite varying strategic perspectives, Leifer saw that non-Communist Southeast Asia shared a common desire for the United States to play the role of prime manager of the regional balance of power. Such hope was not fulfilled in Indochina as the war came to an end (Ch. 4).

Besides seeking to understand regional conflict, Leifer also turned his attention to indigenous attempts to create institutional frameworks for regional association. He examines (in Ch. 5) the dynamics of regional diplomacy leading to the formation of the Association of Southeast Asia (ASA) and its subsequent grounding by the Philippine claim to Sabah and the unfolding Confrontation against Malaysia by Indonesia. The Maphilindo proposal was stillborn given its hasty conception against the backdrop of Confrontation. The Association of Southeast Asian Nations (ASEAN) that superseded ASA was more promising in view of the transformed regional environment following the end of Confrontation and the inclusion of Indonesia. At the time, Leifer already saw that although such a regional association reflected essentially limited functional ties, its scope could well be extended as the habit of co-operation developed. Indicative of his realist outlook

Leifer felt that such progress would be determined by the self-interest of participating states.

Such a realist perspective was evident in his critique of David Mitrany's seminal theory of functionalism applied to the Southeast Asian context (Ch. 6). To Leifer, Southeast Asian political leaders guarded jealously their national sovereignty over any notion that regional co-operation might either render the state-form superfluous or lead to supranationality as suggested by functionalism. Reviewing the experiences of the Baguio and Bandung conferences of the 1950s, SEATO, ECAFE, ASA, early ASEAN and the Lower Mekong Basin Committee (the last, seen as a clearer example of functionalist endeavour), Leifer concluded that functional co-operation or rather "pseudo-functionalism" in Southeast Asia was most likely where it served the particular and separate interests of participating states — a practice which worked counter to the very process that Mitrany had sought to promote.

2

Sources of Regional Conflict

It is possible to identify three general sources of either internal or inter-state conflict within Southeast Asia, although they are not necessarily mutually exclusive. In this analysis, internal conflict is not differentiated from inter-state conflict as a factor relevant to the problem of regional order because, in its various forms, it has long been of major importance in attracting not only the interests of regional states but also the competitive involvement of external powers. The three sources of regional conflict may be described as: issues of state identity; historical antagonisms; and legacies of the transfers of sovereignty.

Issues of State Identity

This subject comprises the basic values which inform the social and political character of the state. It will be discussed under three headings:

Reprinted in abridged form from Michael Leifer, *Conflict and Regional Order in Southeast Asia*, Adelphi Paper No. 162 (London: International Institute for Strategic Studies, 1980), pp. 4–13, by permission of Oxford University Press.

revolutionary social challenge; separatism and irredentism; and nation-building and alien minorities.

Revolutionary Social Challenge

Revolutionary social challenge has been a fundamental source of internal conflict, manifesting itself from the onset of decolonization. The circumstances of its expression have varied in each case of transfer of sovereignty and have depended, in part, on whether or not the colonial power in question was dogged or conciliatory in response to nationalist claims. The common feature of such conflict has been organized armed opposition to successor elites to colonialism by alternative elites who offer a radically different vision of modernity and social order. The appeals of such alternative elites are cast doctrinally in terms of the values of distributive justice and are designed to attract groups alienated by poverty, by gross disparities of private wealth and by the intolerance of a dominant culture. However, the prospect of adventure and a career is relevant to recruitment to revolutionary forces, as is resort to terror.

In every case of relatively peaceful and negotiated transfer of sovereignty within Southeast Asia, the authority of the successor government has been challenged by an insurgent Communist party which established a position of internal strength during the course of the Pacific War. The experience of Burma, Malay(si)a, Singapore and the Philippines may be cited in this respect, while Thailand, which was never subject to direct colonial domination, has shared that experience only during the past two decades. In Indonesia, where the colonial power used force in an attempt to deny nationalist claims, a Communist party enjoyed a tense co-existence within the mainstream of the nationalist movement until September 1948, when it became implicated in an abortive rebellion against the Republican government in Yogyakarta. After independence this party was rehabilitated, and it pursued its political goals within the framework of succeeding political systems. In October 1965 it was again implicated in an abortive coup whose outcome served to outlaw it.

In the special case of Indochina, where the colonial power also resisted nationalist claims, the Indochinese Communist Party — with a patrimonial political role in Laos and Kampuchea — was able to assume the leadership of Vietnamese nationalism. Indeed, it was the only Communist party in the region to attain this position, and this had a decisive effect on the course of the struggle against the French in the First Indochina War. In Vietnam, the Communist Party succeeded to power only North of the 17th Parallel, with the conclusion of the Geneva Conference on Indochina in July 1954. Internal conflict, as such, was resolved only in part. Armed opposition revived South of the 17th Parallel in the late 1950s against an American-backed government in Saigon, as it did in Laos, where the Pathet Lao revolutionary movement exercised *de facto* control of two provinces bordering North Vietnam. It was not to revive, in any substantive sense, in Kampuchea until after the deposition of Prince Norodom Sihanouk in March 1970. From this point all of non-Communist Indochina was beset by a revolutionary challenge, which was successful in 1975.

Conflicts which result from revolutionary challenges to internal social and political orders tend not to stay self-contained. Whether a particular challenge is incipient or fully fledged it gives rise to a form of civil war, and the dynamics of this bitter activity — especially where ideological issues are involved — encourage contending internal parties to seek access to external support. In terms of geographic scale, such outside involvement in support of internal revolutionary challenge within South-east Asia has not been widespread in any substantial sense. For example, internal revolutionary challenge in Burma, Malay(si)a, Singapore, Indonesia and the Philippines has not been serviced significantly by regional parties or governments, if one represents China as external to South-east Asia although marching with it. External support has been more readily forthcoming for regimes subject to revolutionary threat.

Although Vietnam's Prime Minister, Pham Van Dong, admitted his government's past support for revolutionary movements in Thailand and Malaysia during visits to those countries in 1978, decisive regional backing for such internal challenge has depended on facility of access and has obtained, primarily, in Indochina, where extra-regional interests have also been engaged heavily. The most striking example of such support was provided by the Vietnamese Communists during the course of the Second Indochina War. A client revolutionary movement in Laos was stiffened and sustained in order to ensure control of the eastern uplands of the country which provided logistical links between North and South Vietnam. A primary interest was the prosecution of the war South of the 17th

Parallel, which took priority over any fraternal party obligations. Thus, in the case of Kampuchea, the Vietnamese Communists saw more practical advantage in reaching a working accommodation with the conservative and ostensibly neutral government of Prince Sihanouk rather than in promoting the political interests of the fledging Kampuchean Communist Party. It was only when Prince Sihanouk was deposed in March 1970 by a right-wing coalition, which threatened Vietnamese Communist use of logistical and sanctuary facilities within Kampuchea, that support for this neighbouring revolutionary party was forthcoming.

External support for internal revolutionary challenge has been bestowed also, primarily and with most effect, in Indochina. The geopolitical position of China has been most important in this respect. After October 1949 it was possible for the insurgent Vietnamese Communists to be assisted materially across a common border. And after July 1954 such material assistance was more easily conveyed, with access possible by sea as well as by land. China's provision for the Communist Party of Burma has also been of significance; but it has been of a limited order which has enabled that revolutionary party only to sustain itself militarily in the North-east of the country, and not to pose a decisive challenge to the government in Rangoon. With the intensification of Sino-Soviet conflict and the onset of China's attempt to rally South-east Asian governments in a countervailing united front, its support for revolutionary challenge has become increasingly ritual in character, if sustained in principle.

Revolutionary social challenge to incumbent governments within South-east Asia has been a persistent feature of the region and a continuing source of internal instability. Nonetheless, its ability to attract significant regional and extra-regional support has been restricted in geographic scope and has depended, in great part, on facility of access. The radical Revolutionary Front for the Liberation of East Timor, which declared the establishment on an independent republic in the former Portuguese possession in November 1975, was speedily overthrown by Indonesian military intervention across a common border; it was beyond the reach of external assistance. Internal revolutionary challenge has only succeeded, so far, where such assistance has been forthcoming in a practical manner. In the main, substantive assistance has come from external forces and has been forthcoming where the outcome of internal conflict has been perceived to have importance beyond the bounds of the region. Indeed, it has been that very fact of external intervention which has been of major significance for regional conflict.

Co-operative regional responses to conflict arising from such internal challenge have assumed three primary forms: *ad hoc* military co-operation; political and economic co-operation; and formal alliances with external powers.

(1) Specific *ad hoc* bilateral military co-operation has been undertaken among ASEAN states with the object of striking at centres of insurgent activity along common borders. Such co-operation between the armed forces of Thailand and Malaysia, and also between those of Malaysia and Indonesia, has been conducted outside the formal framework of regional organization. It has taken the form also of maritime surveillance (which is equally relevant to the control of piracy and smuggling), of combined military exercises and of a measure of standardization of equipment and operational procedures, as well as exchanges of intelligence.

(2) A regional organization like ASEAN does not have a military function. Nonetheless, the five member governments share a sense of common predicament in relation to internal security: indeed it is their primary security concern.

(3) Formally structured alliance arrangements designed to provide for both external and internal security have been on the wane. The South-east Asia Treaty Organisation (SEATO) was disbanded in June 1977, though the alliance obligations remain, in principle, in force. The Anglo-Malaysian Defence Agreement which had relevance for the internal security of Malaysia and Singapore was superseded in November 1971 by a Five-Power (consultative) Defence Agreement with an external security function only. Its limited external military underpinning has eroded with the passage of time, although interest in its revival was generated following an initiative by Australia's Prime Minister, Malcolm Fraser, in September 1980. The Mutual Security Agreement between the Philippines and the United States in 1951, and the revised bases agreements of 1979, provide a nexus for military assistance, while the residual obligations of the United States to Thailand under the Manila Pact of September 1954 have been disinterred and used to justify increased arms supplies. An unpublished exchange of letters remains the basis for Britain's deployment of a battalion of Gurkhas in Brunei, at least until the end of 1983, when that state reverts to sovereignty.

Separatism and Irredentism

Political boundaries in South-east Asia have tended to follow a colonially inspired pattern of demarcation arrived at for reasons of administrative convenience. State forms have been stamped out in a part of the world distinguished by its great social diversity. As a result of a combination of colonial policy and ethnographic circumstances the successor states of the region have included within their bounds territorially-based minorities, some of whom have been unwilling to reconcile themselves to political dominance from culturally alien centres. Regional minority dissidence has been most marked in Burma, Thailand, Laos, Vietnam, Indonesia and the Philippines. In some cases such dissidence has severely tested the soundness of the successor state, and has also been a factor in generating tension between regional states. Once again, the issue of external — including regional — support has been critical to the significance of the conflict. This type of conflict can become joined to revolutionary social challenge. For example, alliances of varying quality have been struck between Communists and dissident minority groups in virtually every state in the region. At times this has affected relations between Burma and Thailand, Thailand and Malaysia, Malaysia and Indonesia, and Malaysia and the Philippines.

Separatism has been a recurrent source of conflict within South-east Asia, if not the most dominant politically. Regional states have dealt with the threat which it poses bilaterally and, to an extent, within regional organization. Once again it should be pointed out that this kind of conflict has assumed its most far-reaching consequences when support has been extended (even if informally) by a major power.

Undoubtedly, minority dissidence expressed either in demands for autonomy or independence has caused friction between regional neighbours. Thai tolerance of the cross-border activities of Burmese minorities has been responsible for a recurrent downturn in relations. The attendant friction (much reduced after the end of the Second Indochina War) has never made a political impact beyond the bilateral relationship and has not engaged the interests of third parties. The same general conclusion applies concerning difficulties in the relationship between Thailand and Malaysia over the separatist activities of Moslems in the southern provinces of Thailand which abut the northern and dominantly Moslem provinces of Malaysia. This particular source of conflict does have a wider dimension in so far as it has engaged the interests of Moslem governments within the framework of the Islamic Conference. However, the limited effectiveness of Moslem separatists operating within Thailand has restricted opportunities for external exploitation. A more significant example of external support for separatist-based conflict has obtained in the case of the southern Philippines. Open rebellion on the part of the Moslem community dates from October 1972, shortly after the declaration of martial law by President Marcos. This rebellion has been sustained by external support initially provided within the region from the neighbouring territory of Sabah, a constituent state of the Federation of Malaysia. This support came partly as an act of reprisal because of the past prosecution of a Philippine claim to Sabah. The internal rebellion has also attracted external support from Islamic states, especially and importantly in financial form from Libya. A significant regional consequence has been the strain imposed on relations between ASEAN partners.

Attempts by cultural minorities to secure separate political identity have neither been remarkably successful nor engendered major regional conflicts within South-east Asia. A primary part of the explanation for this limitation of conflict arises from the fact that separatism is not an easy enterprise to undertake. Singapore's independence from Malaysia was an involuntary act; it represented rejection, not successful separatism.

Separatism is endemic to South-east Asia as a source of conflict, but the intensity of that conflict has been limited in impact, even if it has strained the resources and tested the integrity of states such as Burma, Indonesia and the Philippines. Despite the serious domestic weaknesses which are characteristic of virtually all South-east Asian polities, dissident cultural minorities have not demonstrated sufficient capability to exploit these weaknesses to full advantage. The success of such an enterprise would seem to depend on decisive external support which has not been forthcoming.

Irredentism, of a kind, has enjoyed a better record within the area. For example, the unification of Vietnam can be placed within this category, as can Indonesia's incorporation of the western half of the island of New Guinea, if not that of East Timor. None of these episodes, however, arose from the inability of an alienated cultural minority to reconcile itself to the entrenched political dominance of a resented cultural majority. The two examples cited represent aspects of partially frustrated decolonization.

The example of West New Guinea merits limited discussion because the conflict involved assumed more than just a regional dimension. From the mid-1950s the Soviet Union had begun to engage in political competition with the United States in Asia. An obvious prize in South-east Asia was Indonesia, which was in serious dispute with her former colonial master, Holland, over the disposition of the western half of the island of New Guinea, which had been set aside in the transfer of sovereignty in 1949. The unwillingness of the United States to apply the same kind of pressure on Holland which had been a decisive factor in precipitating the transfer of sovereignty, and her initial partiality for the regional rebels in the late 1950s, encouraged a developing association between Indonesia and the Soviet Union whose nexus was the provision of arms. An enhanced Indonesian military capability lent credibility to a practice of coercive diplomacy and brought with it the prospect of armed confrontation whose outcome could have worked to both internal Communist and Soviet advantage. This prospect prompted American diplomatic intervention to contain and resolve the conflict. In these circumstances the conflict had its source in Dutch denial of the nationalist claim to the total territorial inheritance of colonialism, but it was brought to a point of crisis through external involvement.

It should be pointed out that the eastern half of the island of East Timor, which was forcibly incorporated into Indonesia, was never a part of the Netherlands East Indies: it had been colonized by Portugal. Indonesia's military intervention was in no sense an act of irredentism, although it may have been intended to deter any separatist tendencies elsewhere within its distended archipelago. It represented an attempt to deny the establishment and consolidation of a government of incompatible political philosophy within the ambit of the Indonesian state.

Nation-building and Alien Minorities

South-east Asia is distinguished by an immense cultural diversity which is made up, in part, of minorities without territorial roots within its post-colonial states. Most of these minorities are ethnic Chinese, most of whose antecedents migrated from Southern China from the nineteenth century onwards. Significant minorities from the Indian subcontinent settled in Burma, Malay(si)a and Singapore, while Vietnamese moved into Kampuchea and Laos under French dispensation and also, in smaller numbers, as refugees into the north-east of Thailand during the course of the First Indochina War. Lao and Khmer refugees from successive Indochina Wars as well as Vietnamese 'boat people', have also sought sanctuary in Thailand.

In the main, alien ethnic minorities serviced the needs of colonial economy and administration and attracted the resentment and envy of the autochthonous people as a consequence. The degree of such resentment and envy was governed, of course, by individual state experience and, in this respect, cultural differences between regional states gave rise to differing degrees of acceptance of such minorities.

Policies of discrimination against alien minorities justified in the nation-building interest have affected relationships among regional and external states. A major local source of conflict arising from intra-regional migration has been Kampuchean resentment of Vietnamese settlement facilitated by colonial rule. In Kampuchea deep-seated racial hatred exploded with the killing of Vietnamese residents in April 1970, in the wake of the deposition of Prince Sihanouk and with the onset of armed intrusion by the Vietnamese Communists. Looked at in perspective, the gory episode in April 1970 was a subordinate dimension of a wider conflict rooted in the prospect of a unification of Vietnam on Communist terms. Tensions between Thailand and Vietnam over the repatriation of Vietnamese minorities have also been encompassed by this conflict.

The treatment of alien minorities by national governments has not evoked a uniform external response. In the case of Burma, her government adopted discriminatory measures against her large Indian minority in the early 1960s, resulting in a major repatriation. Subsequently a largescale exodus of Moslem residents of Bengali origin took place during 1977–8. In both these cases the issues between the governments concerned were settled on a bilateral basis without other political interests being engaged. Indian–Burmese relations were not subject to evident deterioration as a consequence of the application of nationalization measures to the retail trade, although Indian restraint was almost certainly governed by her embittered relationship with China.

A more evident source of conflict and consternation in bilateral relations has been seen regarding overseas Chinese residents. The policy of the People's Republic of China towards these overseas communities changed in the mid-1950s with the negotiation of a treaty with Indonesia designed to resolve the contentious issue of dual nationality. Beijing's intention was to improve government-to-government relations by denying openly any legal obligation towards those residents of Chinese origin who had assumed the citizenship of their host country. Indeed, overseas Chinese were actively encouraged to assume such citizenship and to obey the laws of their adopted lands. In practice, the attitude of Chinese governments towards the overseas Chinese communities has tended to vary according to political circumstances. At times it has been found politic to overlook the most cruel treatment — for example, in the case of Kampuchea after April 1975 — while on other occasions their condition has been a matter of public controversy with the host government.

A bitter exchange over the alleged persecution of the resident Chinese community in Vietnam occurred in 1978. This issue, however, was not a source of conflict in itself.[1] It served to impair further an underlying relationship between China and Vietnam which had begun to deteriorate before the end of the Second Indochina War. In the circumstances the issue was more a symptom than a source of conflict.

In the case of the Chinese community in Vietnam, their alleged persecution became an issue which accelerated the momentum of conflict. It involved a matter of identity in so far as their ethno-cultural distinctiveness and affinity with people across the northern border made them suspect as a potential fifth column. The relationship between the overseas Chinese community and their mother-country became a weapon in the wider conflict over the pattern of power in the region as the government of Vietnam sought to represent all overseas Chinese in South-east Asia as insidious agents of Beijing. To some extent this charge was given greater credence by a revision of interest in the overseas communities by the Chinese government from early 1978. Regional states with significant resident Chinese communities were given cause for some apprehension, as indeed they were also when China exhibited a willingness to use force in her conflict with Vietnam in February 1979. The Vietnamese policy of encouraging, at a profit, the exodus of ethnic Chinese across the South China Sea was intended to reduce an undesirable alien presence and, probably, to demonstrate China's inability to protect them. In some of the countries of South-east Asia it had the effect of intensifying inter-communal friction and also introduced an element of strain into intra-ASEAN relations.

Since her revolution China has never enjoyed the luxury of dealing with states to her south to the exclusion of other concerns. It has been those other concerns — namely, threats posed successively by the United States and the Soviet Union — which have governed Chinese policies. In this respect China's response to discriminatory treatment of overseas Chinese residents — whether citizens or not — by regional governments has been determined by extra-regional factors, most recently by the spectre of an assertive Vietnam rejecting Chinese leadership for an unholy alliance with the Soviet Union.

Historical Antagonism

South-east Asia assumed its present political-territorial form as a direct result of colonial domination. That domination contained and subordinated antagonisms between pre-colonial kingdoms which comprised political rivalries and also deep-seated differences of culture and identity. Where colonialism served to sustain state identity rather than to merge it with others in a wider administrative framework which became the basis for post-colonial succession, such antagonisms have survived in most conspicuous and politically relevant forms.

It is in the mainland of South-east Asia that such a phenomenon has assumed major significance as a source of conflict. In the maritime part of the region, including Malaysia, the transfers of sovereignty have had the effect of establishing states which had never existed in that form before the advent of colonial rule. Only minuscule Brunei, which is now a fraction of her former size and which survived because of colonial "protection", has experienced conflict arising, to a limited extent, from her pre-colonial identity. And even mainland states such as Burma and Thailand, which were antagonists before the advent of colonial rule, have experienced a post-colonial relationship marked by alternating tensions and accommodation rather than by a sustained revival of historical conflict. Kampuchea's relationship with Vietnam provides the striking regional example of such a revival, which might suggest that Communist rule reinforces traditional conflicts.

The experience of Vietnamese occupation of Kampuchea in the 1830s, when an attempt was made to eradicate a traditional culture and to supplant it with an alien one, has left its legacy. Although it became conventional wisdom during the rule of Prince Sihanouk to label Vietnam and Thailand equally as political predators, it was Vietnam who was regarded with more apprehension. Fear of Vietnam — above all, a Communist Vietnam — was an abiding theme of

Prince Sihanouk's foreign policy, even when expressed in the form of political accommodation. This fear was inherited by both his right-wing and left-wing successors. Indeed, the restoration of historical antagonisms appeared as virtually an article of faith in the public rhetoric of the Kampuchean Communist government which came to power in April 1975.

Correspondingly, a similar pattern of relations has developed between Vietnam and China. At the onset of French colonial rule Vietnam was a formal vassal of China, if not subject to her direct political control. Over a number of centuries the two states had engaged in intermittent warfare, with Vietnam seeking to defend her independence from a dominating China. For China, a critical element in her conflict with Vietnam at the end of that decade was the burgeoning relationship between the governments of Hanoi and Moscow. Vietnam's invasion of Kampuchea was perceived as serving the Soviet interest. However, the openly expressed desire by the Chinese leadership to put Vietnam in her place suggested a view of her southern neighbour which had its source in pre-colonial experience.

Although Thailand and Vietnam have never shared a common border their post-colonial relationship has also been shaped by historical experience of competition — in this case between culturally distinct peoples — for influence and advantage in the interposing states of Laos and Kampuchea. This competition resulted in an acceptable balance of advantage just before the coming of French colonial rule. From the viewpoint of governments in Bangkok the recent eradication of the "buffer" function of eastern neighbours by a vigorous Vietnam has posed a major threat to security and has encouraged active, if not open support for internal opposition to its dominance within Kampuchea.

Colonialism has had a major impact on the history of South-east Asia. Yet, in historical perspective, it represents only an interlude. The accompanying revival of some pre-colonial antagonisms has had an undoubted effect on the course of conflict within the region. If traditional Kampuchean-Vietnamese and Thai-Vietnamese antagonisms, as well as those between Vietnam and China, have been a source of conflict, the competitive engagement of external interests has served to fuel its furnaces. Indeed, it has been such competitive engagement combined with the revival of historical antagonisms which has served to make mainland South-east Asia the epicentre of regional conflict.

Legacies of the Transfers of Sovereignty

The transfer of sovereignty from colonial powers to independent governments was a mixed experience for South-east Asia, and the impact and the legacy of those transfers has varied from state to state. One such legacy, which has been cited above, has been the determination of state boundaries. This inheritance has not been uniformly well received: post-colonial boundaries have been challenged in the form of irredentist claims, for example. One such claim has been made by the government of the Philippines to the Malaysian state of Sabah, and this has yet to be relinquished in acceptable legal form. Conflict over this issue has tested the cohesion of ASEAN and has persisted, ironically, because of Moslem rebellion in the southern islands of the Philippines. Boundary issues have been a factor also in relations between Brunei and Malaysia; and between Malaysia and Thailand there has existed a latent tension arising from a boundary settlement determined by British colonial power in 1909. Boundary demarcation has also been a source, if not the root, of conflict between Kampuchea and Vietnam, and between Vietnam and China.

Conflict over state boundaries has assumed an important maritime dimension. The attractions of off-shore oil deposits have generated competing claims around the littoral, and over the islands and continental shelf of the South China Sea. In this context one notable legacy of the transfers of sovereignty has been the projection of Indonesia's archipelagic claim across the South China Sea as a consequence of an Anglo-Dutch treaty of 1824 whereby off-shore islands were placed under Dutch and, ultimately, Indonesian jurisdiction.

The transfers of sovereignty have also affected intra-regional conflict when the colonial power has been reluctant to give up its position. Dogged colonial rule was demonstrated in the case of the Netherlands East Indies and in that of French Indochina where independence was attained only after violent revolutionary struggles. Where the attainment of independence involved such struggle, political attitudes of suspicion and hostility have been engendered towards neighbouring states which have not undergone the same experience and which have even been involved, in some way, in seeking to frustrate nationalist goals.

This experience of socialization on the part of Indonesia affected the outlook of the government of President Sukarno which could not comprehend the legitimacy of the Federation of Malaysia either at its conception or its subsequent establishment.

In general terms political boundaries bequeathed by colonial rule have not been an acute source of regional conflict in themselves even where less than well defined. The actual experience of the transfer of sovereignty has had a greater impact in particular circumstances. For example, the wider issue of regional order, which requires the acceptance of shared assumptions among the resident states, has undoubtedly been prejudiced by Vietnam's bitter and protracted experience of attaining independence.

These sources of conflict are in no sense mutually exclusive; they exercise influence in an inter-locking manner. What is most evident about their impact, however, is that, where acute, it conforms to a general global pattern. In other words, although they are rooted within the region, such conflicts take on special significance when the interests of major external powers become competitively engaged. Such is to be expected in the case of South-east Asia, where resident powers capable of assuming a regulating role in regional relationships are conspicuously absent.

Note

1. For a discussion of this issue see Bruce Grant, *The Boat People, an "Age" investigation* (Harmondsworth, Middx: Penguin Books, 1979), Chapter 4.

3

Regional Association
Sources of Conflict

Perhaps the most striking example of the revival of traditional antagonism, albeit in modern form, has been demonstrated in the case of Cambodia. This country, independent according to national legend in 1953, is the diminished legatee of the once great Khmer Empire. The apogee of Khmer dominance was in the twelfth and early thirteenth centuries. But from about the middle 1300s it was subject to territorial encroachment and challenge by the T'ai (Siamese), who by 1431 forced the Khmer to abandon their capital site at Angkor. Imperial decline in the west was accompanied from the seventeenth century by encroachment from the east by the Annamites (Vietnamese), who eventually annexed the Mekong delta region. By the nineteenth century Cambodia was wedged between competing antagonists and preserved only a semblance of independent existence. Only the intervention of France in 1863 and the establishment of a protectorate prevented the piecemeal territorial erosion of what remained of the Khmer state.

Reprinted in abridged form from Michael Leifer, "Regional Association: Sources of Conflict", in *Dilemmas of Statehood in Southeast Asia* (Singapore: Asia Pacific Press, 1972), pp. 115–29, by permission of the copyright-holder.

Following the fall of metropolitan France in June 1940, Thailand with Japanese encouragement and support reasserted claims to rice-growing provinces restored to Cambodia by France in 1907. This episode served not only to undermine the reputation of the "protecting" power but also to sustain the national image of the predatory Thai. This image was reinforced for Cambodia after the attainment of independence when relations with Thailand were shaped by old fears and new anxieties.

Thailand was to align itself with the Western powers in the years after the Second World War and in 1954 became a member of the Southeast Asia Treaty Organization. Cambodia, however, because of internal political circumstances and her geo-political situation was attracted to the idea and practice of non-alignment which was widely expounded in the wake of the 1954 Geneva Conference by India's first Prime Minister. Thus Thailand and Cambodia came to be divided by past history and the cold war. Thailand and Cambodia's easterly neighbour South Vietnam both came to look on Cambodia's international position with resentment based on traditional attitudes and concern at what they regarded as a certain point of entry for communist activity. As Cambodia improved and harmonized its relationships with communist countries, in part a consequence of political difficulties with her aligned neighbours, the state of conflict intensified. The ousted Cambodian Head of State, Prince Sihanouk, frequently publicized his version of Thai encouragement and support for anti-government forces and has made no secret of his sensitivity to the personal slights and insults which he has received at the hands of Bangkok. Symptomatic of the mutual antipathy between the two countries was the extended dispute over the possession of the ruins of an ancient Khmer temple situated along their common northern border. This dispute, which was responsible in part for a total rupture in diplomatic relations in October 1961, was decided in favour of Cambodia by the International Court of Justice in June 1962. The degree of personal feeling involved in the hostile relationship was demonstrated fully in December 1963 when Prince Sihanouk proclaimed a national holiday to celebrate the death of the Thai Prime Minister, Marshal Sarit.

Thai-Cambodian relations have for the most part been sustained on the basis of mutual invective fed by border incidents and territorial transgressions. It should be pointed out, however, that this state of hostility has been shaped also by foreign policy needs. More recent experience of both countries has led to a significant modification in the hostility pattern. Cambodia, having experienced a measure of fall-out from China's Cultural Revolution and subject to increasing territorial intrusions by communist Vietnamese, showed signs of willingness to coexist more readily with a Thailand equally flexible in the face of a need to adjust to an unpredictable measure of American disengagement from the mainland of Asia. With the Vietnamese communist challenge to Cambodia in 1970, the government of General Lon Nol repaired relations with Bangkok. It also countenanced the prospect of Thai military assistance.

Cambodia's relations with South Vietnam had, until recently, been no better than those with Thailand and, because of the regular spill-over of the conflict in Vietnam onto Cambodian territory, had tended to be appreciably worse. Historical experience, cultural differences and the role of the Vietnamese minority introduced during French hegemony laid a foundation for bad feeling. Although Cambodia does not now proclaim irredentist designs on territory under the formal jurisdiction of the regime in Saigon, there remains a legacy of resentment which centres on the significant Khmer minority which is domiciled across the border. Territorial disputes have occurred over the possession of certain off-shore islands in the Gulf of Siam. However, the most constant irritant in past relations was the violation of the border by South Vietnamese and American military formations engaged in hot pursuit of Vietcong. For its part, the Saigon regime had charged for nearly a decade that Cambodian territory served as an active sanctuary for the Vietcong. This charge came to have increasing substance from the end of 1967, and by 1969, the former Cambodian Head of State was himself complaining publicly of Vietnamese communist intrusions.

It was the furore over this issue which provided the pretext for the deposition of Prince Sihanouk. With the apparent threat to the successor regime and the military intervention of South Vietnam, relations were restored between Phnom Penh and Saigon, and the Cambodians found themselves obliged to tolerate the military presence of former antagonists in common cause against the communists.

One consequence of the political fall of Prince Sihanouk (regarded by the Vietnamese communists as an affront) was to revive the prospect of Thailand and a Vietnamese regime restoring the dual suzerainty over Cambodia which existed before the French Protectorate. In the face of communist challenge by an ethnic foe, historical antagonisms have been subsumed. If this challenge is successfully met, one could expect a reversion to an earlier pattern of relations with Cambodia seeking to sustain a tenuous independence between two more powerful neighbours.

This brief account of the outline of Cambodia's relations with Thailand and the adjoining part of Vietnam is but one example of a tendency for history and geographic propinquity in Southeast Asia to work against regional co-operation. The UN-sponsored scheme for the development of the Mekong River basin affecting the riparian countries may be seen as an exception to this evaluation. However, the degree of co-operation that has taken place should be seen in the special context of the compartmentalized tangible advantages for the riparian states.

Cambodia and her neighbours present, perhaps, an obvious case of regional discord. There are, however, other intra-regional frictions which have a source that antedates independence. The relations between Thailand and Malaysia have, on the surface, been harmonious and fruitful. Yet, there is a basis of discord between the two countries which might one day disrupt the present state of good relations.

[T]he four northern states of mainland Malaya were transferred from formal Thai control at the beginning of the present century. When Malaya became independent in 1957, the four northern states, which had been returned temporarily during the Japanese hegemony, were included automatically within the new federation and have remained within Malaya and its successor, Malaysia. The population of the four states of Kedah, Perils, Kelantan, and Trengganu is predominantly ethnic Malay with a very small Thai minority. The population of the southern provinces of Thailand is also populated in the main by ethnic Malays who share the same religion, language, and culture as the people on the Malaysian side of the international border. The Malays of southern Thailand are thus set apart from the politically dominant Buddhist Thai and feel both a sense of physical and cultural difference from the regime in Bangkok. Following the Second World War and with the restoration of the northern states of Malaya to British administration, there emerged a significant if short-lived Malay irredentist movement which gave the Thai Government serious cause for concern.[1] Such concern has been sustained up to the present and is an important factor in explaining any measure of reluctance on the part of the Thai Government to co-operate with any enthusiasm with their Malaysian counterparts in rooting out the increasingly active remnant of the Malayan People's Liberation Army which was obliged to seek refuge along the border region by the mid-1950s.

The Thai-Malaysian conflict is latent rather than active in terms of the overall relations between the two countries but it is certainly not overlooked by their respective foreign ministries. An even more striking example of the repercussions of ethnic straddling across international lines of demarcation is the case of Laos. Laos's problems and the consequent conflict arise from the lack of congruency between its French-created form and the mixed sense of identity of its population. Apart from traditionally rooted internal competition between scions of rival families, there is the ethnological and cultural divide between the valley Lao and the more numerous hill tribes who have a much greater sense of identification with counterparts on the North Vietnamese side of the border. And it is this divide based on altitudinal frontier which has provided an effective point of entry for communist direction.[2] The related regional and international significance arising from the Laotian situation is the correspondence of the present struggle for dominance to the historical struggle between the Thai and the Vietnamese interrupted by French imperial design.

For examples of international conflict arising out of the process of decolonization, there are no better cases in Southeast Asia than the "confrontation" of Malaysia by Indonesia between 1963 and 1966 and the continuing claim by the Philippines to the Malaysian state of Sabah (North Borneo). These two conflicts are of special significance because of their bearing on the progress of regional association.

Indonesia's confrontation of Malaysia is associated with the Sukarno era in which romantic nationalism came to be blended with deep-seated anti-colonial feeling. Indonesia had not objected to the independence of Malaya which occurred in August 1957. At the time Sukarno was engaged, with the assistance of the army, in overturning constitutional democracy. Malaya, however, was not regarded with undue benevolence, in part because its experience of obtaining independence was completely alien to that of Indonesia. The question of the Emergency and the need to crush a communist insurgency meant little in the Indonesian order of things. Independence against the Dutch had been achieved only after violent and bloody struggle. As a consequence of totally different political cultures, independent Malaya was regarded with patronizing tolerance. Such regard was to turn to irritation when it came to be believed in Djakarta that assistance and sanctuary was being provided for some of those engaged in the

1958 regional risings against the Republic Government. Personal annoyance crept into the relationship when the Prime Minister of Malaya Tunku Abdul Rahman attempted to mediate in the Indonesian dispute with Holland over the disposition of the western half of the island of New Guinea.

When confrontation came it was directed against Singapore also. The Indonesians had long felt resentment at the economic role of the entrepot, whose predominantly Chinese population in association with overseas Chinese in Indonesia controlled the major portion of the legal and illegal trade of the Republic.

The above factors were some of those that served as a backdrop to the announcement of confrontation in January 1963, nearly two years after the Malayan Prime Minister had first made public the prospect of a wider federation to include Singapore and the British Borneo territories. It was an incident in North Borneo which provided the pretext for forthright and active opposition to the Malaysia scheme.

An internal uprising in the British-protected state of Brunei in December 1962 sparked off official Indonesian support for the "people" of North Borneo, who, it was claimed, were resolutely opposed to the formation of Malaysia. The actual story of confrontation as it affected Malaysia together with accompanying diplomatic encounters has had its chroniclers and does not need repetition here.[3] More relevant in this context are the roots of the conflict. Of special significance was Sukarno's resentment that a colonial power could decide the territorial configuration of a part of Southeast Asia vital to the security of Indonesia without its participation or approval. Related to this attitude was the Indonesian experience in attaining independence. There was a belief that genuine independence could not be granted by a colonial power but had to be taken forcibly. Malaysia seen in terms of these values appeared as a puppet; a neo-colonial construct designed to preserve and perpetuate the interests of the British. In the event, confrontation led to a temporary augmentation of the British military presence.

Resentment of the augmentation of territory by Malaya is believed also to have derived from personal ambitions to enlarge Indonesia beyond the territorial bounds of the former Netherlands East Indies. Evidence to support this view has been taken from the record of a conference held in June 1945 to discuss the form of the as yet unborn Indonesia. At this conference, Sukarno made public his dream of a greater Indonesia to include not only the Dutch colony but also

British North Borneo, Malaya, and even the Philippines.[4] Symptomatic in this episode in relation to the period of confrontation was a long-standing Indonesian desire to the considered the dominant power in, at least, the maritime part of Southeast Asia by virtue of its historical myths, size, and population. The formation of Malaysia coincided also with political conditions within Indonesia which had gestated a style of rule in which national chauvinism was given full expression.

Confrontation moved into lower gear following the abortive coup of 1 October 1965 and was eventually brought to a halt following a dramatic change in internal political circumstances which had promoted its prosecution.[5] The initial reconciliation between Djakarta and Kuala Lumpur involved a certain euphoria expressed in emphasis on ties of blood and culture across the Strait of Malacca. The rhetoric of reconciliation was soon to give way to a more guarded and cautious mutual relationship.

Co-operation to counter communist insurgency along a common border in Borneo has, however, taken place between Malaysia and Indonesia; they have also participated in wider regional association. At this juncture, it is sufficient to point to the hesitancy with which Malaysia views Indonesia not merely in terms of the recent experience of confrontation but also because of the enormous disparity in almost every respect between the two countries. Even more circumspect is the behaviour of Singapore, now also in limited institutional association with Indonesia. Singapore, which is predominantly Chinese in population, was for nearly two years a part of the Malaysian Federation and experienced the impact of confrontation in the rupture of all trading ties and in the form of terrorist bomb attacks. After confrontation, Indonesia established diplomatic ties with the independent island-republic and trade was resumed beyond 1963 levels. There is, however, more than a measure of apprehension among the members of the Singapore Government about the propensities of Indonesia. It is primarily for this reason that the Singapore Government sought, in advance of the completion of British military withdrawal, to establish a ground-to-air missile defence system. An indication of the underlying state of relations with Indonesia occurred in October 1968 following the execution in Singapore of two Indonesian marines convicted of the murder of civilians in a bomb attack on a bank building. The hangings provoked widespread demonstrations within Indonesia not only against the Singapore diplomatic mission but also against local Chinese. For a brief period trade was suspended between the two countries.

If Singapore's principal source of apprehension lies to the south, it experiences concern also in the other direction. Singapore separated from Malaysia in August 1965 while confrontation was still in progress and the fact that such a rupture could have occurred at a time of external threat is a clear indication of the full measure of animosity between the communities within Malaysia; an animosity that was to find more violent expression in May 1969. The reason for the separation resided in the differing and incompatible conceptions of Malaysia held on the one hand by the former Prime Minister of Malaya Tunku Abdul Rahman and on the other by the Prime Minister of Singapore Lee Kuan Yew. Lee's attempt to promote the ideal of a "Malaysian Malaysia", while highly praiseworthy in democratic theory, was regarded by the Malay ruling group as a direct challenge to the governing system of which they were the beneficiaries.

In the aftermath of separation, mutual suspicion based on sad experience continued to mar relations between two entities whose representatives have agreed publicly that their defence interests are inseparable.[6] At the time of the formal termination of confrontation in 1966, with such an expression of blood-brother talk in Kuala Lumpur, genuine alarm spread within Singapore on the prospect of becoming the nut between Malaysian and Indonesian arms of the nutcracker. This spectre soon lost its immediacy but the prospect of joint Indonesian-Malaysian action against Singapore continues to be a factor in Singapore's attitude towards her neighbours. Militarily and economically Malaysia and Singapore are interdependent but the racial issue obstructs genuine *rapprochement*. Coexistence and mutual irritation is the present sum of their relations. Malaysia tends to look with jealous eyes at the social and welfare achievements of the island-state and Singapore views with trepidation the Malaysian political scene lest the type of communal conflict which erupted in 1969 has repercussions which affect her national security. There is, however, underlying the fierce emotionalism of this testy relationship a measure of realism and even a modicum of trust between some cabinet counterparts on either side of the Johore Strait.

The Philippine claim to Sabah (North Borneo) has served not only to disrupt normal diplomatic relations with Malaysia but also the most extensive attempt at regional association from within. The actual progress of the dispute can be considered in more detail elsewhere.[7]

For our purposes, it is sufficient to note that the claim was first pressed in June 1962 while North Borneo was still a possession of the British Crown and while the Malaysia scheme was in the process of realization. The political purpose of the claim urged on legal grounds was to effect the obstruction of Malaysia's formation, which was objected to by President Macapagal on the grounds that it was of colonial inspiration — a ploy, in part, to solicit Indonesian support — and also that it would encourage communist penetration of a part of Borneo that represented a vital security interest of the Philippines. Such arguments may be dismissed as implausible but they had a mythological credence within the Philippines where lack of knowledge of other parts of Southeast Asia is quite striking.

More basic reasons for the urging of the Philippine claim may be sought in the personality of the Philippine President who initiated it and also in the international position of the country. The Philippines was the first Southeast Asian country to become independent but because of the peaceful transfer of power and her subordinate relationship with the United States, she was not regarded as in the mainstream of Asian nationalism. The pejorative "little brown brother", which was often used by the more ardent of Filipino's nationalists, had a bitter ring of truth. With the Presidency of Carlos Garcia, there emerged an attempt to institute a more autonomous Asian policy.[8] Initially this took the form of anti-(local)Chinese legislation in domestic policy; externally, there evolved the promotion of regional association with Thailand and Malaya. But it was only with the claim to Sabah, which became entangled with the diplomacy of confrontation that the Philippines emerged as a participating member of the Southeast Asian world. Manila became, if only for a short spell, the focus of diplomatic action and the birthplace of a new concept in regional association. In incongruent partnership with a forceful Indonesia, the Philippines sought to erase the image of a willing subordinate of the United States. It is perhaps more than a coincidence that the period of the Philippine claim coincided with a more strident expression of anti-American feeling within the country and the renegotiation, to Philippine advantage, of agreements affecting American rights in the country.

The presentation of the claim was a way of giving notice that the Philippines sought a new role within Southeast Asia. The manner of the urging of the claim has been less than conventional particularly under the presidency of Ferdinand Marcos. And in a country where personal relationships play such a large part in everyday life, there would seem to have been a transfer of domestic values to the international scene. The stand taken on the claim by the Philippine Government has involved the question of force. Malaysia, for its part, because of domestic considerations in Sabah and because of a conviction of rightful title, has not been inclined to adopt the kind of flexible response which might possibly promote an accord with a country with which it would appear to have many interests in common.

One point that might be adduced to explain any continuing friction between the Philippines and Malaysia is that mutual and tangible co-operation has not always been valued in Manila. Indeed the Philippine Government was willing to risk the break-down of a practical anti-smuggling agreement with Malaysia so as to satisfy its feelings over the claim. It went so far as to sponsor the training of Muslim Filipino guerrillas for infiltration into Sabah. A willingness to go to such lengths, which became public knowledge soon after a state visit to Malaysia by President Marcos and his wife in January 1968, indicated the value which the Filipinos placed on amicable relations with the Government of Malaysia.

From this unduly brief survey of more recent intra-regional conflicts within Southeast Asia it is possible to see that there are many points of friction and that a factor in this condition is the common regional situation. In the cases of Cambodia, Thailand and Vietnam, Indonesia, Malaysia, and Singapore, and even the Philippines and Malaysia, geographic proximity has been an undoubted factor in making for the conflict situation. One conclusion that we may draw at this stage is that the states of Southeast Asia are nor necessarily any different, in conducting their mutual relationships by dint of their being Asian or of having suffered the experience of colonial domination. Thus the same element of anarchy is present in Southeast Asia as anywhere else within the international system of states. In the case of Southeast Asia, the states themselves suffer also from a varying measure of internal anarchy and their domestic orders do not augur well for their ability to establish a viable regional one between them.

On the evidence we have considered above it would seem that the prospects of regional integration within Southeast Asia are limited. Co-operative ventures between states have to be related to tangible advantage and a factor in promoting perception of such advantage is trust. Trust is sadly lacking in a Southeast Asia where the individual states, as elsewhere, evaluate schemes for co-operation on the basis of what specifically is in it for them. To be sceptical, as this writer may seem to be about the notion of Asian solutions for Asian problems is not to suggest that they are not in themselves desirable and praiseworthy. One of the diplomatic achievements of Thailand has been its willingness to provide neutral ground and congenial surroundings for Southeast Asian antagonists to try and resolve their common problems. The point of the argument, however, is not that the notion of Asian solutions for Asian problems should be disparaged, but rather that to assume in any glib manner that because common antagonists are Southeast Asian they are invested automatically with extraordinary qualities for conciliation is to engage in highly erroneous and misleading conceptualization. Conciliation like more positive association can take place only if there is a congruence of interests of the parties concerned, irrespective of regional situation.

Notes

1. See Pierre Fistié, *L'Evolution de la Thailande Contemporaine*, Paris, 1967.
2. See Hugh Toye, *Laos, Buffer State or Battleground*, London, 1968.
3. Good examples are Arnold C. Brackman, *Southeast Asia's Second Front*, London, 1966; Bernard K. Gordon, *The Dimensions of Conflict in Southeast Asia*, New Jersey, 1966; and Peter Boyce, *Malaysia and Singapore in International Diplomacy*, Sydney, 1968.
4. See Gordon, *op. cit.*, pp. 80–87.
5. Franklin B. Weinstein, *Indonesia Abandons Confrontation*, Ithaca, 1969.
6. Michael Leifer, "Astride the Straits of Johore: Commonwealth Rivalries in South-East Asia", *Modern Asian Studies*, July 1967.
7. Michael Leifer, *The Philippine Claim to Sabah*, Zug, Switzerland, 1968, and "The Philippines ad Sabah Irredenta", *The World Today*, October 1968.
8. See J. L. Vellut, *The Asian Policy of the Philippines 1954–61*, Canberra, 1965.

4

The Vietnam War and the Response of Southeast Asian Countries

The Vietnam War was the most cataclysmic episode to afflict the region of Southeast Asia since the Pacific War. In its physical effect on the countries of Indochina, it was a far more destructive experience. Some 7 million tons of bombs were dropped on Vietnam alone during the war waged by the United States to sustain the separate political identity of the southern half of that country. That figure may be doubled to take account of naval artillery and other ordnance employed. The catalogue of destruction may be expanded to include the employment of toxic defoliants which have had a continuing effect on survivors on both sides.

When one considers the intensity of the conflict, especially from the mid-1960s as well as the scale of casualties,[1] it is noteworthy that outside of Indochina the Vietnam War made far more of a public impact within the United States than within the other countries of

Reprinted in abridged form from Michael Leifer, "The Vietnam War and the Response of Southeast Asian Countries", unpublished paper presented at the 30th Anniversary International Conference of the Japan Association of International Relations on 4–8 September 1986, pp. 346–66.

Southeast Asia. Combat troops from Thailand and engineering units with infantry support from the Philippines were despatched to Vietnam for limited periods. Their restricted military roles meant that the emotive issue of battlefield losses never entered into the domestic political processes of either of America's two regional allies in any way comparable to their penetration and disruptive impact in the United States, where conscription also bulked large.

Outside of Indochina, only the government of Indonesia assumed a vocal anti-American position, openly endorsing the National Liberation Front of South Vietnam. President Sukarno condemned American air raids on Vietnamese installations in 1964 in the wake of the Gulf of Tonkin incident. He went on to denounce "outside imperialist forces" for disturbing the security of Vietnam, Laos and Cambodia at the Conference of Non-Aligned States held in Cairo in October 1964. Within a year, however, Sukarno's political position had been irreparably compromised by the circumstances and outcome of an abortive coup attributed to Indonesia's Communist Party. The period of most intensive American military intervention coincided with a substantive reappraisal of Indonesia's foreign policy. If popular sympathy still obtained for the cause of national liberation in Vietnam, its expression was controlled by an anti-Communist government in Jakarta which maintained a studied ambivalence towards America's military role. Despite misgivings about that role, the government of Burma adopted a correspondingly passive position.

The general contrast between the visible impact of the Vietnam War in Southeast Asia beyond the bounds of Indochina and in the United States is not a sufficient indication of its regional significance. That war which came to encompass the whole of Indochina was a factor of the utmost importance in the calculations of regional governments. Those governments took positions on the war according to their own political identities and experience and, above all, with reference to their own security priorities. These considerations governed their mixed responses.

In the course of the transfers of sovereignty after the Pacific War, all post-colonial successor states experienced challenge of one kind or another from revolutionary Communist movements. Their object was to replace conservative nationalist elites with an alternative social and economic order. That experience, in the context of a bi-polar world, led some governments to the view that national security would be served best by avoiding Cold War entanglements. For others, that experience confirmed the requirement for assured access to external countervailing power. Such a position was reinforced by an acceptance of prevailing conventional political wisdom in Washington; namely, that Southeast Asia had become the object of threat from a monolithic international Communism whose chosen prime vehicle for expansion in the region was the People's Republic of China. These two alternatives of non-alignment and alliance, in terms of underlying rationale for each, gave expression to alternative responses within Southeast Asia to the Vietnam War. Over time, however, the non-aligned complement of states in the region was reduced while the alternative disposition, at least in terms of alignment if not formal alliance, increased. By the end of the Vietnam War, only Burma had maintained a true consistency in its non-aligned position which it sought to demonstrate in 1979 by leaving the Non-Aligned Movement because it had compromised its principles at the Havana Summit. Cambodia had effectively repudiated non-alignment with the overthrow of Prince Sihanouk in March 1970, while the government of Laos had become a party to American military policy with the breakdown of the 1962 Geneva Accords. As for the ASEAN states, Ngo Dien, assistant to Vietnam's Foreign Minister Nguyen Duy Trinh, remarked at the Conference of Non-Aligned States held in Colombo in August 1976 that they had been "directly serving or indirectly serving the US aggressive war in Vietnam, Laos and Cambodia in complete contravention of the principles of the non-aligned movement."[2]

In April 1954, during the final stages of the siege of Dien Bien Phu, five Asian states (including Burma and Indonesia) met in Colombo to warn publicly against American military intervention seen as likely to lead to another direct confrontation with the People's Republic of China. Their stand against bringing the Cold War to Asia proved not to be fully representative of regional governments. One notable achievement of the meeting of the Colombo powers was the convening, though Indonesian initiative, in April 1955 of the historic Asian-African Conference in Bandung. This conference was significant as the first occasion on which post-colonial states gave notice that their collective views should be taken into account by the major powers. It was not a fully harmonious occasion, however. By that juncture, the United States had inspired the Collective Defence Treaty for Southeast Asia which was signed in Manila in September 1954. Its institutional form, the Southeast Asia Treaty Organisation (SEATO) had been established at a meeting of treaty partners in Bangkok in February 1955, provocatively close to the Bandung meeting.

The object of the Manila Pact had been to signal a drawing of the line of containment along the 17th parallel of latitude in Vietnam as well as placing Cambodia and Laos under a mantle of protection. The Philippines and Thailand had become enthusiastic parties to that alliance because their governments shared the strategic perspective of the United States. Their governments had welcomed the commitment to uphold the separate political identity of South Vietnam. They did so because of apprehension that domino theory, as enunciated by President Eisenhower in April 1954, might have operational validity and also because after Dien Bien Phu and the Geneva Conference on Indochina, the regional guarantor role of the United States was on trial.

The position taken by the governments of the Philippines and Thailand at Manila and Bandung led on to direct participation in the American war effort in Vietnam. They became parties to the Vietnam War "with the intention of establishing an obligation for the United States to help them in time of need."[3] That sense of need was most acute in the case of Thailand. Sustaining sovereignty during and beyond the colonial era, it had not experienced internal revolutionary challenge but the revival of historical threat and the emergence of Communist menace fused in a single source. That threat had manifested itself in Viet Minh penetration of both Laos and Cambodia in the early 1950s with the prospect of a trans-Mekong buffer zone becoming incorporated within an Indochinese Communist centre of regional power. Accordingly assured access to credible external countervailing power became a strategic imperative. It has been pointed out that after July 1954 "the Thai government was less concerned with supporting South Vietnam for its own sake than with the fact that the continuation of the struggle with the South diverted North Vietnamese attentions from lowland Laos."[4] The failure of SEATO to respond with resolution to the crisis in Laos in the early 1960s generated a lack of confidence in Bangkok in the American commitment as did the willingness to become a party to a superficial neutralization. But when the internal conflict within South Vietnam was construed in Washington as a test of American credibility, the Thais took heart. Accordingly in 1966, the ruling military establishment responded positively to American entreaties to despatch combat units as part of President Johnson's "Many Flags Programme" of third country support.

As part of an exercise designed to lend international legitimacy to American military intervention, some 11,000 combat troops were despatched in all with the first contingent arriving in Saigon in July 1967. Some three years earlier the Thai government had granted the United States the right to establish a network of bases for bombing North Vietnam. As a result, "from 1965 to 1968 at least 75 per cent of all bombing of North Vietnam emanated from Thai bases".[5] Concurrently, the prospect of retaliation moved the Thai government to enter into a secret agreement with the United States to secure protection in the event of a direct external threat.[6] Also in secret, some 25 battalions were deployed in Laos subject to CIA control in confrontation with units of the Pathet Lao.

There was a financial nexus to Thai participation in the American war effort but the underlying motivation was national security. The Thai government sought to pursue that security through identification with America's display of military resolution in Vietnam. When that resolution weakened and the United States Government agreed to engage in negotiations to which Thailand would not be a party, acute political embarrassment followed. Political options, however, were exceedingly limited. The most that could be undertaken was a measure of damage limitation. Accordingly, soon after the enunciation of the Guam Doctrine by President Nixon in July 1969, Foreign Minister Thanat Khoman announced the withdrawal of Thai forces from South Vietnam on the grounds that they were required to fight insurgency at home, in part an opportunity cost of alliance with the United States. Correspondingly, the Thai Government acted with a measure of caution after the overthrow of Prince Sihanouk in March 1970 refraining from direct military intervention in the ensuing civil war. America's right to continue using Thai bases for aerial bombardment was not denied, however. Thai bases were employed in American attempts to blunt the Vietnamese Communist Spring offensive in 1972 and at the end of the year in renewed bombing of North Vietnam designed to lend credence to cosmetic changes to the terms of the Paris Peace Agreements concluded finally in January 1973. The bombing of Cambodia was conducted from Thai bases until the action of Congress led to its halt in August 1973.

For the government of Thailand, the Vietnam War was both a source of regional threat and an opportunity to overcome it through alliance association with the United States. In the event, alliance policy proved to be a provocative and wasting asset. It placed Thailand on the losing side, leaving it not only used and abused but also vulnerable and exposed because the United States had proved unable to guarantee the separate existence of South Vietnam. Although the American option was never formally repudiated after the end of the Vietnam War, Thailand was not obliged to pay the price of American failure. For it became the security beneficiary of a changing structure of related global and regional alignments. Ironically, its government now enjoys access to an external source of countervailing power which as recently as the first signs of a faltering American resolve over Vietnam war was still regarded in Bangkok as the principal source of regional threat.

The Philippines, although conditioned to rely on American protection, did not share quite the same acute sense of security threat over Vietnam which had been experienced by Thailand. Despite internal Communist challenge after the transfer of sovereignty, the geo-political circumstances of the two allies were not the same. Moreover, a separate mutual security agreement with the United States in 1951, together with extensive American military bases on its territory under an accord in 1947, served to compensate for an intrinsic vulnerability. If a willing signatory of the Manila Pact, the Philippine government insisted with a measure of success on the inclusion of an appendix incorporating a statement of democratic principles.[7] One reason for the measure of ambivalence in the alliance relationship was the open political process in the Philippines which gave full opportunity to opposition Congressmen to voice their misgivings about the degree of dominance exercised by the United States.

The Filipino involvement in the Vietnam War was much more of an opportunistic exercise than that of the Thais. Nonetheless, underlying the different participation of both countries was a concern to ensure the engagement of the United States in regional security. Their mixed participation may be construed as an insurance premium on an alliance insurance policy which failed to pay out. It is worthy of note, however, that when SEATO was finally abolished in June 1977, the governments of Thailand and the Philippines were content to leave intact the Collective Defence Treaty for Southeast Asia.

The measure of security provided through the Anglo-Malayan Defence Agreement — with which Australia and New Zealand became associated — made it possible for the Malayan government to repudiate the idea of adhering to the Manila Pact. It had established a tangible link to that Pact through its security relationship with Britain, Australia and New Zealand but without unduly alienating neutralist neighbours as well as its sizeable Chinese community given the evident anti-Chinese purpose of that alliance.[8]

Under the political leadership of Tunku Abdul Rahman, however, Malaya adopted an unequivocal anti-communist line in foreign policy. Moreover, the first foreign visit by the Tunku was to South Vietnam.[9] Malaya also identified itself conspicuously with the Indian cause with the onset of the Sino-Indian border war in October 1962. Moreover, in 1964, Malaysia was the only Southeast Asian country to respond to the American appeal for non-military assistance to South Vietnam. American support had been solicited to counter Indonesia's campaign of confrontation.

In material terms, Malaysia provided only token support for the American war effort in the form of training for South Vietnamese in police administration as well as providing motor-cycles. Open vocal support for the American military role was quite explicit, however, especially when President Johnson paid a visit to Malaysia in October 1966, during which he announced concessions over control of releases from tin and rubber stockpiles.[10] By the time that Tun Abdul Razak had succeeded Tunku Abdul Rahman as Prime Minister, the United States had embarked on the agonizing reappraisal of its Vietnam policy. Under Tun Razak, Malaysia sought to pioneer neutralization as a formula for Southeast Asia's international political ills. Non-alignment for Malaysia, although an attempt to dissociate the country from a conspicuous identification with American policy, did not mean an endorsement of the cause of the Vietnamese Communists.

On independence in August 1965, Singapore identified itself as a non-aligned state. This declaratory attempt to avoid unnecessary provocation of Indonesia while confrontation was still in train did not reflect its government's attitude to the outcome of the Vietnam War. Misgivings about America's involvement were matched by concern at the consequences of a hasty withdrawal. Moreover, Prime Minister Lee Kuan Yew shared the American conviction about the operational validity of domino theory.

For Singapore, the experience of having independence thrust upon it had generated an acute sense of vulnerability. Apart from a deep-seated anti-Communism which was a product of overcoming the united front strategy in domestic politics, the leadership of the island-state was deeply apprehensive at the prospect of any resident Southeast Asian state establishing a position of regional dominance. Accordingly, it upheld as a fundamental priority of foreign policy, the promotion of a regional balance of power in which the United States would be a necessary makeweight. During the Vietnam War, public statements were tailored to this requirement. A measure of defence cooperation was undertaken also. In 1966, Singapore was used as a centre for rest and recreation for American serviceman from Vietnam, while camp construction materials had been furnished even earlier by private contractors.

The four countries discussed above came together with Indonesia in August 1967 at the height of the Vietnam War to form the Association of Southeast Asian Nations (ASEAN). Indonesia was distinguished from its new regional partners by having renounced with consistency any alliance association with an external power.

Under President Suharto's New Order, Indonesia repudiated the bellicose stance of Sukarno restoring in principle an independent and active foreign policy expressed in returning to the United Nations and in endorsing the conventional virtues of non-alignment. If the ruling miliary establishment shared a virulent anti-communism with the government in Washington, non-alignment and support for America's policy in Vietnam were not compatible. American support for the economic rehabilitation of Indonesia was essential. Accordingly, Indonesia's policy makers sought to square the circle. A gentleman's agreement appeared to obtain between the governments in Jakarta and Washington, whereby mild token of criticism of military intervention in Vietnam was readily tolerated because of Indonesia's new political orientation.

In November 1972, shortly after a tentative accord had been reached on a peace agreement for Vietnam, the Indonesian Government agreed at America's request to participate in the International Commission of Control and Supervision which would monitor its implementation. Indonesia's participation proved to be a mixed blessing. It became a member of an important body serving as an American nominee. Pride at being the only Asian participant in the ICCS, an opportunity to monitor the resolution of a conflict of regional significance had to be set against a disposition on the part of Hanoi to regard the government in Jakarta in a similar light to those of its ASEAN partners which had actually sent troops to fight in Vietnam.

The remaining Southeast Asian country outside of Indochina is Burma which did not adopt a distinctive position of commitment towards the Vietnam War. During its most intensive phase, Burma's non-alignment and equidistant posture was strained because of political fall-out from China's Cultural Revolution. Burma's government was naturally keen to see an end to the war because of concern at its escalation and entangling character. At one juncture, Burma did express a willingness to lend its good offices to help resolve the conflict. During 1965 when U Thant was Secretary-General of the United Nations, he sought to promote private talks and explored the possibility of Rangoon as a venue for that purpose. General Ne Win gave permission for this meeting but it never materialised because the United States set preconditions which the Vietnamese Communists were not prepared to meet.[11]

Of the Indochinese states other than the divided country of Vietnam, Laos, which became engulfed by the war, became identified with the American war effort. After the breakdown of the accord on neutralization worked out in Geneva in 1962, Prime Minister, Prince Souvanna Phouma openly endorsed American policy in Vietnam, including bombing of the North. Although Souvanna Phouma had assumed office because of his neutral credentials, the survival of his government came to rest almost entirely on the support of the United States with whom he became increasingly identified.

In Cambodia, Prince Sihanouk tried to keep the Vietnam War at arms length through his policy of neutrality which became in practice one of accommodation to the perceived winning side.[12] That practice of accommodation included denunciation of the United States with which diplomatic relations were severed in 1965. It also took the form of accepting a diplomatic mission from the National Liberation Front of South Vietnam in 1967. Accommodation was expressed also in tolerance of the use of Cambodian territory adjacent to the border with South Vietnam as a sanctuary zone for the Vietnamese Communist insurgent army. In the event, that tolerance was abused and served as the formal justification for Sihanouk's overthrow. His deposition was followed by a radical reversal of policy and a provocative and self-destructive challenge to the Vietnamese Communists who responded by nurturing and unleashing the Khmer Rouge.

It is not possible to dwell much in generality on the responses of the Southeast Asian countries to the Vietnam War. At its active outset only the government of Indonesia demonstrated any tangible sympathy for the Communist side. That sympathy was replaced by mixed feelings when Sukarno's political system of guided democracy was superceded by Suharto's New Order. Of the Southeast Asian states, Thailand was the most committed from a geo-political strategic perspective which has been sustained with perfect continuity in current challenge to Vietnam's occupation of Cambodia from January 1979. That commitment to the American cause was governed by the requirement for assured access to external countervailing power because of a sense of acute vulnerability to historical threat in Communist guise. Lesser commitment on the part of most other regional states was governed also by a corresponding consideration. If regional strategic perspectives were not exactly the same, they shared in the main a desire for the United States to fulfil a role as prime manager of the regional balance of power. For that reason, its policy in Vietnam was generally approved if with mixed feelings. It failed in its undertaking in Vietnam, but outside of Communist Indochina that same regional expectation has been sustained but without the same sense of confidence in American resolve and capability.

Notes

1. See Guenter Lewy, *America in Vietnam,* Oxford University Press, Oxford, 1978. Appendix I, Civiliam Casualties: A Quantitative Analysis, pp. 442–453.
2. B.B.C. *Summary of World Broadcasts,* FE/5298/A3/3.
3. Leszek Buszynski, *SEATO: The Failure of an Alliance Strategy,* Singapore University Press, Singapore, 1983, p. 96.
4. Charles E Morrison and Astri Suhrke, *Strategies of Survival. The Foreign Policy Dilemmas of Smaller Asian States,* University of Queensland Press, St. Lucia, 1978, p. 119.
5. George McT. Kahin, *Intervention: How America Became Involved in Vietnam,* Alfred A. Knopt, New York, 1986, p. 325.
6. A. Casella, "U.S.–Thai Relations", *The World Today,* March 1970.
7. J. L. Vellut, *The Asian Policy of the Philippines 1954–61,* Australian National University, Canberra, 1965, pp. 13–16.
8. See the discussion in Chin Kin Wah, *The Defence of Malaysia and Singapore,* Cambridge University Press, Cambridge, 1983 and also Dato' Abdullah Ahmad, *Tengku Abdul Rahman and Malaysia's Foreign Policy 1963–1970,* Berita Publishing Sdn. Bhd., Kuala Lumpur, 1985, pp. 26–27.
9. See T. H. Silcock, "The Evolution of Malayan Foreign Policy", *Australian Outlook,* April 1963.
10. The Tunku reiterated his endorsement of American policy in Vietnam made in September 1966. He pointed out that, "I have never failed to give solid backing to what America is doing in South Vietnam and to help explain to the rest of the world the great sacrifices made by America in

assisting freedom-loving people defend their rights and sovereignty" quoted in Peter Boyce, *Malaysia and Singapore in International Diplomacy,* Sydney University Press, Sydney, 1968, p. 169.

11. Kahin, op. cit., pp. 243–5.
12. See Michael Leifer, *Cambodia: The Search for Security,* Praeger, New York, 1967.

5

Regional Association
From ASA to ASEAN

In Southeast Asia there was not to be any positive move towards an institutional framework for association until July 1961. Then, Malaya, the Philippines, and Thailand — after a false start in attempting to promote a Southeast Asia Friendship and Economic Treaty (SEAFET) — set up the Association of Southeast Asia (ASA). The idea for SEAFET was first mooted in August 1959 by the Malayan Prime Minister Tunku Abdul Rahman during a visit to Manila. The response to this initiative varied in the main between the lukewarm and the blatantly hostile. The non-aligned countries made it apparent that they regarded the proposed association as not much more than an adjunct of SEATO.

The measure of negative response to the Tunku's initiative led to further revision of the scheme and its emergence in institutional form as ASA composed only of Malaya, the Philippines, and Thailand. The association was inaugurated formally on 31 July 1961 and described as a non-political enterprise, independent in every way from any power

Reprinted in abridged form from Michael Leifer, "Regional Association: Convergence of Interests", in *Dilemmas of Statehood in Southeast Asia* (Singapore: Asia Pacific Press, 1972), pp. 130–50, by permission of the copyright-holder.

bloc or military alliance and founded on an authentic Southeast Asian initiative. ASA's declared aims were limited to economic and cultural association.

But if ASA provoked little fury outside of its limited ranks, this negative accomplishment was not accompanied by any activity of significance that could not have been as easily promoted outside of its framework. ASA as such was never to demonstrate a potential for growth; it was to spend the greater part of its short-lived existence as a divided house. The conflict over the formation and the legitimacy of Malaysia and in particular the presentation of the Philippine claim to Sabah served to undermine the basis for continuing association. During confrontation, ASA was relegated to a state of limbo and following its formal termination in August was revived but not reactivated. In August 1967 it was superseded by a wider regional body which has since found itself subject to similar strains.

If ASA was founded ostensibly as a non-political body, the movement to Malaysia was to gestate the most far-reaching proposal for political integration ever mooted in Southeast Asia. This was the notion of Maphilindo coined by the former Indonesian Foreign Minister Dr Subandrio but conceived by the Philippine President Diasdado Macapagal as a confederation between his country, Indonesia, and Malaya.

Within the maritime part of Southeast Asia, the concept of a Malaysia, that is, a union of Malay peoples, had enjoyed occasional currency in the twentieth century. The Malaysia scheme proposed publicly in May 1961 by Tunku Abdul Rahman was not, however, a genuine exercise in regional integration. In one sense, it was part of the *ad hoc* process of decolonization; in another it marked the extension of the authority of the Government in Kuala Lumpur across the Johore Strait and the South China Sea.

To return to the notion of Maphilindo, this conception crystallized during the course of negotiations held during the early part of 1963. Their ostensible purpose was to resolve the conflict between Malaya, on the one hand, and Indonesia and the Philippines on the other over the formation of the new federation. The original initiative, however, for what was to be described as a Greater Malayan Confederation came during a press conference held on 27 July 1962 by President Macapagal.

There is reason to believe that the initiative was an attempt to forestall a political *fait accompli* by associating the future of North

Borneo with a proposal separate from both the Malaysian Federation and the Philippine claim. It is of interest also to consider that in its initial form the proposed confederation excluded Indonesia — the natural core of any wider association of Malay people.

It was only following the Brunei uprising of December 1962 that Indonesia proclaimed open opposition to the formation of Malaysia. The next month discussions were held in London between representatives of the British and Philippine Governments to consider among other subjects the claim to North Borneo. These discussions were to result in deadlock but during their course, the Philippine Foreign Minister Emmanuel Pelaez demanded a solution to the problem of North Borneo which would be satisfactory not only to the Philippines but also to Indonesia. He, then, called for a permanent accommodation among the three "Malay" countries and echoed President Macapagal in advocating their rediscovery of a sense of common destiny and brotherhood. It was at this juncture that the Malayan Confederation idea was to be extended in scope to provide for the participation of Indonesia: a highly significant extension in view of its recent open opposition to the formation of Malaysia.

The Philippines moved to propose a tripartite diplomatic exchange to which both Indonesia and Malaya agreed. So was gestated the notion of Maphilindo, in nomenclature an acronym composed of the first syllables of the names of the countries involved.

A meeting of the three heads of government, President Sukarno, President Macapagal, and Prime Minister Tunku Abdul Rahman, took place also in Manila from 30 July to 5 August 1963. An ostensible purpose was to establish a procedure whereby the conflict over the formation of Malaysia might be resolved. Of course, resolution was not readily subject to any common perception. The procedure agreed on was that of a determination of opinion towards the formation of Malaysia in British North Borneo to be conducted through a representative of the United Nations Secretary-General. But in advance of this provision, on 31 July a document described as the Manila Accord which had been drafted at the preceding ministerial meeting was signed. What emerged in the Manila Accord was provision for an exceedingly loose system of consultation.

Maphilindo foundered and sank over the formation of Malaysia. Less than two months after the tripartite agreements, duly signed in Manila, diplomatic relations were broken off between Djakarta and Manila on the one hand and Kuala Lumpur on the other. From that time on Maphilindo has never been a subject for any serious discussion.

In one sense, however, confrontation did not change the need for regional co-operation but demonstrated that it had a function for the amelioration of conflict.

The event which was catalytic in creating a fresh climate for a new initiative in regional association was the abortive coup in Indonesia of 1 October 1965. Following this episode, the Indonesian Communist Party was subject to liquidation, the Sukarno regime was replaced by pragmatic military government and Indonesia's relations with the Chinese People's Republic changed radically. In August 1966 confrontation was formally terminated. Relations between the Philippines and Malaysia had improved much earlier; in August 1964 consular relations were established and formal diplomatic recognition came in June 1966. The previous month, in Kuala Lumpur, there had been a meeting of ASA working parties; the first such gathering for three years.

The change in international orientation of the regime in Djakarta, the more moderate posture of the Philippines, and an increasing general concern at the outcome of the conflict in Vietnam appeared to make for greater common interest between the countries involved previously in the ASA and Maphilindo enterprises. Malaysia was keen to encourage Indonesian participation in regional association to prevent the revival of past animosities. It was concerned also to widen the limited Maphilindo association to deny charges of an anti-Chinese juncture of interests. The Government in Singapore was also disposed to see the formation of an institutional framework which might mitigate local conflicts and in particular to ward off any alignment of Malay states against predominantly Chinese Singapore. In the case of Singapore, there were also trading interests to consider; both Singapore and Malaysia looked to a revival of trade with Indonesia particularly after April 1967 when the initial British decision to withdraw its military presence from east of Suez was communicated privately. Thailand had been consistently an advocate of regional association in the hope of securing a local counter to outside threats to the region. Indonesia, for its part, saw such an exercise as a way to establish credentials of international respectability and thus qualify for desperately needed economic assistance.

In August 1967 the Foreign Ministers of Indonesia, Malaysia, the Philippines, Thailand, and Singapore met together in Bangkok to set up the Association of Southeast Asian Nations (ASEAN). This organization was to supersede the more limited ASA whose members came together only once more under its auspices. ASEAN substituted for ASA but also assumed more ambitious terms of reference relating to peace and security. The most significant practical difference between the two groupings is the extended membership of the more recent organization to include Indonesia, a country which, since the end of confrontation, has made a firm commitment to the progress of regional association.

Strains of the kind that had served to impair the working of ASA upset also the early functioning of ASEAN. Internal discord was a direct consequence of the active revival by the Philippines of its claim to Sabah.

The potential for conflict within ASEAN is not restricted to the relationship between Malaysia and the Philippines. ASEAN, however, has served as a modest vehicle for the reduction of tension among its members. The dispute between Malaysia and the Philippines has not had the same debilitating effect on ASEAN as it had on ASA. The wider membership would seem to be important in this respect.

An essential element in the popular movement for union which arose in Western Europe in the aftermath of the Second World War was a strongly held belief by some that the conventional nation-state has ceased to fulfil its primary function and has therefore lost its *raison d'etre*. It was thus advocated that the nation-state in Western Europe ought to be superseded by a different kind of polity. No such ethic moves hearts or minds in Southeast Asia; if anything, it is the reverse.

At the level of regional association there has yet to be demonstrated any prevailing conviction that mutual benefit is likely to arise from more than limited functional ties. As the habit of co-operation develops and mutual confidence grows such limited ties may be extended to present an aspect different from that which characterizes contemporary Southeast Asia. Also, changing perceptions of common security problems may stimulate much greater collaboration to mutual advantage. Progress in regional association will be determined by the states' perceptions of self-interest.

6

The Limits of
Functionalist Endeavour
The Experiences of Southeast Asia

In his seminal approach to the problems of world order,[1] Professor
Mitrany indicated his approval of "the functional alternative" applied
on a less than universal scale. The utility of such "administrative
devolution" was admitted if promoted outside the context of a
"sectional union" which in close form was alleged to be merely a
rationalised nationalism. In the case of South-east Asia, a region which
possesses greater conventional than actual coherence, functionalist
endeavour has been attempted both within the framework and under
the aegis of universal organisation and also to some extent on a more
exclusive basis. The experience and achievement of such endeavour
has been limited, however, and understandably so given the factors
sustaining the fragmentation of a region characterised by some as the
Balkans of the Orient.

Reprinted from Michael Leifer, "The Limits of Functionalist Endeavour: The
Experiences of South-East Asia", in *Functionalism: Theory and Practice in
International Relations,* edited by A. J. R. Groom and Paul Taylor (New York:
Crane, Russak & Company, 1975), pp. 278–83, by permission of the copyright-
holder.

With the exception of Thailand, all of the states of South-east Asia — from Burma to the Philippines — have been subject to direct colonial domination. Their acquisition of international status dates only from after the termination of the Second World War. In partial consequence, their political leaderships cherish jealously individual national sovereignty and have not demonstrated, in any sense, a propensity to render the state-form superfluous or to facilitate any slicing off of sovereignty to any supranational seat of authority. In addition, the states of South-east Asia have been beset by a variety of mutual differences and antagonisms whose sources lie in both pre-colonial and modern experience. Intensely aware of conflicts of state interest and of the reality that geographic propinquity does not necessarily make for international harmony, the political leaders of South-east Asian countries have shown themselves to be extremely cautious in the extent to which they have been willing to commit themselves to regional cooperative enterprise.

Apart from the predilections and apprehensions of the political beneficiaries and successors of colonialism, a common feature of the states of South-east Asia is for popular horizons and cognitive patterns to be circumscribed by primordial or sub-national considerations. While such a common condition might appear appropriate for some as a context in which to attempt to channel loyalties beyond the idea of nation-state, the overriding emphasis of governmental action is directed to the goal of political integration and the consolidation of the territorial entity which succeeded to colonial rule. In consequence the prospects for functionalism, which in principle gravitates against such a goal, is somewhat bleak. Indeed, that small measure of success in functionalist endeavour which has been attained has been possible only where it has operated well within the conventional context of the state system and where it has appeared to assist that particularistic practice which Professor Mitrany had hoped would be overcome through the application of the functional alternative.

In so far as functionalism may be understood to mean international cooperation in piecemeal or special purpose enterprise of an ostensibly non-political kind, this chapter will not seek to evaluate that aspect of regional association which has been expressed in unequivocal political form.[2] Rather, it is hoped to assess those more specific forms of cooperative endeavour which, although falling within the scope of regional association, fit more closely the criteria of Professor Mitrany's conception.

Functionalism is not an activity which emerges simply in response to some objective notion of common need. If such were the case, South-east Asia might well be a suitable *milieu* for its active promotion. Functionalist activity tends rather to be the product of a convergence of perceived interests underpinned by suitable political and economic circumstances. In the case of South-east Asia, convergence of perceived interests has been minimal and the majority of enterprises which possess a functionalist component have represented in practice a deliberate attempt to secure an exclusive form of political advantage. In this respect, it is possible to write of pseudo-functionalism, that is, where the functionalist argument serves as the ostensible reason for promoting the enterprise in question.

During 1950, the President of the Philippines, Elpidio Quirino, sought to sponsor an anti-communist alliance among Asian states. Motivated by the success of communist revolution in China and distressed by a failure to interest the United States in the idea of a Pacific Pact, he managed to secure the attendance of a number of Asian and Australian political leaders at the hill resort of Baguio, near Manila, in May 1950. But in order to attract the participation of important Asian states, such as India and Indonesia, whose attitude to Cold War enterprise was well defined, the Philippine President found himself obliged to exclude South Korea and Taiwan who had been involved in the original sponsorship of a conference. Thus, the underlying purpose of the gathering was compromised at the outset. In addition, it became necessary to represent the meeting as a forum for the promotion of economic and cultural cooperation. In the event, the functionalist facade was not sufficient to engender any sense of genuine rapport among the participants at Baguio. The occasion was marked instead by the passage of pious and vacuous resolutions and by a failure to agree on any practical proposal for economic cooperation. Functionalism, in so far as it possessed any relevance to the conference, served solely as an implausible cover to facilitate its convening.

At Bandung in Indonesia in April 1955, there occurred a somewhat different type of gathering with a constituency also beyond that of South-east Asia. This was the Asian-African Conference which was intended to promote the international standing of the host country, assist the China policy of India and also demonstrate Afro-Asian solidarity. A more honest occasion than Baguio, the Bandung Conference also did little more than produce fine sounding declarations. There was no response from among the delegates to suggestions for a technical cooperation council for mutual assistance, while no progress was made in promoting intra-regional trade.

One of the issues which divided delegates to the Bandung Conference was membership of the South-east Asia Treaty Organisation (SEATO), established in Manila in September 1954. For a country like the Philippines which had sponsored the ill-fated Baguio Conference, the advent of SEATO was a welcome addition to its provision for national security. But by the end of the decade there arose increasing doubts about the efficacy of the organisation and especially the degree of commitment to its purposes by the extra-regional powers. Such doubts were strengthened with the onset of crisis in Laos at the beginning of the 1960s. Concurrently, two members of SEATO, Thailand and the Philippines, together with Malaya which was in close defence association with a SEATO member, sought to sponsor a regional association in part to satisfy personal ambitions of national leaders but also to promote common political interests. It was perhaps unfortunate that their preliminary initiative took the proposed form of a South-east Asia Friendship and Economic Treaty, represented in acronym as SEAFET. This expression, together with the alliance associations of the sponsors of the treaty, suggested to the non-aligned countries of South-east Asia, including Indonesia and Cambodia, that an indigenous alternative to SEATO was in the making. In addition, the Soviet Union, the Chinese People's Republic and North Vietnam all denounced the undertaking.

Both Malaya and the Philippines persisted in the joint enterprise but changed the name of the proposed association. In July 1961 they sponsored, with Thai support, the Association of South-east Asia (ASA). This body was represented as a vehicle for economic, social and cultural cooperation. However, in spite of the declared non-political objectives of the association, it failed to attract members in addition to its three founders. The non-aligned states of the region had no desire to compromise their status and also had little inclination to incur the antagonism of Peking and Hanoi over a suspect venture. Even the exclusion by its sponsors of South Vietnam did not make the association an attractive prospect.

ASA represents another example of pseudo-functionalism in that the prospect of non-political forms of inter-state cooperation was held out as a bait to promote a regional association of undoubted political significance. In the event, the actual functional enterprise of ASA between its three members was little more than nominal. Apart from the inauguration of an express train service between Kuala Lumpur and Bangkok, already in rail communication, the various joint projects announced never went beyond the stage of consultation. Various governmental, official and expert committees were established to assist in consultation but no progress was made towards the establishment of a common secretariat for the association. ASA did not promote any real measure of economic integration between states whose economies, as with others in South-east Asia, did not stand in any complementary relationship.

However, before ASA had any real opportunity to demonstrate either success or failure over time, it was disrupted by the onset of Indonesian Confrontation against Malaysia and the claim by the Philippines to Sabah (North Borneo). During the three and a half year period of confrontation in which the Philippines was aligned diplomatically with Indonesia in order to advance its territorial claim, ASA rested in a state of suspended animation. With its termination, the foreign ministers of ASA met once more in formal session only to adjourn *sine die*. In effect, ASA was to be subsumed within a new regional grouping called the Association of South-east Asian Nations (ASEAN) which was established in August 1967. Indonesia and Singapore joined the new association in addition to the three founder members of ASA.

ASEAN, although undoubtedly limited in its achievements, has emerged as much less of a pseudo-functionalist body than its regional predecessors. Its initial purpose was political. Indeed, its founding document made reference to the temporary nature of foreign military bases in South-east Asia. ASEAN represented an institutional means whereby a politically transformed Indonesia might find scope for a measure of regional leadership without displaying the urge for dominance suggested by the rhetoric and bellicose conduct of the Sukarno era. In essence, however, ASEAN has operated in a manner somewhat similar to ASA before that body was seized with internal discord. Although the members of ASEAN jointly pay attention to matters of regional security and have committed themselves in principle to the goal of neutralisation for South-east Asia, the energies of its membership have been directed in the main to limited functional enterprise.

The members of ASEAN, however, have not sought to force the pace of regional cooperation. They have come to recognise that their divergent conceptions of security interest plus competitive economic policies do not permit any rapid move in this direction. To this end, ASEAN, which is regarded as a useful if modest vehicle for diplomatic consultation and possible harmonisation of goals has a pragmatic cast about its activities. In its degree of institutionalisation it does not represent a dramatic advance over the limited achievement of ASA. For example, it does not possess a common secretariat. On the other hand there is an awareness of the value of functional cooperation if only because this is the only kind of cooperation that is really practical. To this end permanent sub-committees do exist in national capitals to oversee functional projects in food production and supply, civilian transport, communications and civil air traffic, shipping, commerce and industry.

Bureaucratic arrangements do not of themselves make for meaningful cooperation and ASEAN has yet to achieve the condition of embryonic form of regional functionalism. In essence, it is a diplomatic forum within which common interests can be identified and cooperation planned on that basis. At this point in time, the visible achievement is minimal. Nonetheless, the members of the association do not show any signs of wishing to dismember or replace it. On the contrary, it has come to represent a symbolic assertion of local autonomy in a region which has been long subject to the influence of external powers.

A more authentic example of regional functionalism, albeit with a wider geographic compass, from Iran to the West Pacific, is demonstrated in the workings of the United Nations Economic Commission for Asia and the Far East (ECAFE) established in March 1947 which has its permanent headquarters in Bangkok. At its initial formation ECAFE did not assume a functionalist role. It began activities as an instrument for post-war economic reconstruction. As such it received a mandate from the Economic and Social Council to make or sponsor studies of economic and technical problems and also to collect, evaluate and disseminate economic information. It has been pointed out that there was an early realisation that ECAFE was not likely to assume an important role in the channelling of external economic assistance because prospective donors preferred bilateral arrangements.[3] Also, because of great power and UN Secretariat obstruction, it had considerable difficulty in assuming an administrative role in the UN technical assistance programme. It was not until the 1960s with the designation of the ECAFE secretariat as executive agency for the UN special fund for the Lower Mekong

Project that the Commission began to take an operational responsibility of any kind.

ECAFE serves as an all embracing organisation which sponsors activities of a functional kind. But in the main because of limited access to funds and the greater willingness of governments to promote economic development through bilateral associations with external powers, it has been restricted in its activities to the investigation and collection of data, the provision of advisory services and assisting states in the promotion of regional cooperation.

In the realm of functional endeavour, it has two well-established undertakings in hand. First, it oversees the Asian Highway Project. The Commission assists in providing surveys and specifications for routes, bridges and road signs. Its main role, however, is advisory, including the organisation of motor rallies. The project itself does not point up the special merits of functionalism. It has been explained: "The Asian Highway did not raise serious political difficulties as much of the project is part of the national road development plans to be executed by the governments concerned".[4] Indeed, the example and the experience of the Asian Highway Project, which has been seriously interrupted by war in Indochina, underpins an earlier argument that interstate cooperation of a functionalist kind is most likely to occur when it serves the particular and separate interests of the participating states.

Such an axiom has been borne out in the experience of what has been the most notable achievement of ECAFE and the most significant example of functionalist endeavour in South-east Asia. As far back as 1952 a preliminary report had been prepared on the prospects of controlling and utilising the waters of the lower reaches of the river Mekong and its tributaries which run through Thailand, Laos, Cambodia and South Vietnam. But it was not until 1957 that a project under ECAFE auspices assumed tangible form. In effect, the Committee for the Coordination of Investigations of the Lower Mekong Basin was established by the governments of the riparian states. It works, however, in close conjunction with the secretariat of ECAFE. The actual financing of the project had been on a multilateral basis with over $200 million in funds being received from twenty-six external donors as well as from UN agencies and private foundations. A notable feature of the progress of the project, which has experienced numerous difficulties because of the political condition of Indochina, is the extent to which the riparian states have demonstrated a continuing willingness to cooperate despite recurrent strains in their mutual relations. Indeed, the Committee proceeded with its task with full membership even when diplomatic relations were ruptured between some of the participant states. However, there has been no evidence that the degree of interstate cooperation inspired by the project has been able to prevent a deterioration in inter-state relations arising out of political differences.

A special feature of the Mekong Project has been that the prospect of advantage for participating states has been approximately equal. This is reflected in the distribution of the specific programmes within the overall project which takes the form of ten for the main stream and sixteen in the tributaries divided equally between the four riparian states. This somewhat fortuitous circumstance has been unique within South-east Asia and the extent of functionalist endeavour, although significant and meritorious, does not show any sign of servicing as a means of transforming the nature of inter-state relationships which in Indochina in particular are beset by great strains.

The habit of cooperation of a functionalist kind has been demonstrated in other ways in South-east Asia, in great part through ECAFE,[5] and since the mid-1960s a number of standing ministerial conferences have been established to discuss matters of common regional interest. For example, there is the South-east Asian Agricultural Development Conference and also the South-east Asian Ministerial Conferences on Development and on Education. However, in the main, such gatherings do little more than exchange informed views, while the annual meeting of finance ministers serves more than anything else as a means of channelling economic assistance from Japan.

The needs of the state in South-east Asia as perceived by the various governments do not suggest much prospect of the extensive adoption of functional techniques of cooperation. Besides a plenitude of political differences, the nature of the economies of the region are such that, with the exception of Singapore, they have a minimal complementary relationship. They are concerned in the main to provide for import substitution in industrial development and, where it does not yet already exist, self-sufficiency in rice production. That measure of specificity from which complementary interest might facilitate substantive functional activity has yet to be attained within South-east Asia.

Professor Mitrany conceived of the functional approach as a way of limiting authority to specific activity and hopefully in the process to break away from the traditional link between authority and defined territory. Only in the example of the Mekong Project has there been any resemblance to such a process within South-east Asia. The states of the region in common with others elsewhere whose political and economic situation is similar are not prepared to contemplate the functional approach in any genuine sense unless there is a clear prospect of tangible advantage of a kind which in practice will work against the very process which Professor Mitrany has sought to encourage and promote.

Notes and References

1. David Mitrany, *A Working Peace System,* Chicago, Illinois: Quadrangle Books 1966.
2. For such an evaluation, see Michael Leifer, *Dilemmas of Statehood in South-east Asia,* Singapore, 1971. Chapter 9.
3. L. P. Singh, *The Politics of Economic Cooperation in Asia: A Study of Asian International Organisations,* Columbia, University of Missouri, 1966. p. 57.
4. *Ibid,* p. 126.
5. Regional projects related to ECAFE include:
   (a) Committee for the Coordination of Investigations of the Lower Mekong Basin.
   (b) Asian Institute for Economic Development and Planning.
   (c) Asian Highway Coordinating Committee.
   (d) Asian Industrial Development Council.
   (e) Committee for Coordination of Joint Prospecting for Mineral Resources in Asian Offshore Areas.
   (f) Typhoon Committee (in Manila — in association with World Meteorological Organisation)
   (g) ECAFE Trade Promotion Centre.
   (h) Asian Coconut Community (Djakarta)
   (i) Asian Statistical Institute (in Tokyo)
   (j) Trans-Asian Railway Project.
   (k) Asian Centre for Development Administration.

ASEAN and Regional Order

INTRODUCTION

Leifer applied much intellectual effort to understanding the problem of managing regional order in Southeast Asia. He saw the linkage between regionalism and international order as being governed by the perceptions of key players of the international system that have the capability and will to intervene in a regional context to protect or advance their vital interests. Southeast Asia, unlike Eastern Europe during the Cold War, was characterized by the absence of a resident global power. As such, regional states could conceivably shape regional order and indirectly temper international order if they could stabilize their domestic political orders and achieve intra-mural accord, thereby reducing the opportunities for external competitive interventions. The advantage for members of ASEAN was that their subregion at least was not subject to imminent external threat. That said, a measure of regional autonomy reflecting a shared view to guide collective action was deemed necessary for the promotion of regional order (Ch. 7).

ASEAN's search for a Southeast Asian regional order is addressed at much greater depth in Chapter 8. Such an attempt during the Cold War proved elusive because of differences in strategic perspectives and limitations in aggregate capability despite an ambition to manage regional order as reflected in ASEAN's founding declaration. ASEAN's 1971 ZOPFAN (Zone of Peace, Freedom and Neutrality) declaration was not operationalized, and with the fall of Indochina to Communism, ASEAN soon faced a competing regional order. Vietnam's invasion of Kampuchea (Cambodia) further polarized the region and showed that regional order in a grand sense was beyond ASEAN's capacity although on a limited scale the successful management of intra-mural relations suggested regional order of a kind. But even this was not to be taken for granted as the diplomatic fall-out of the Herzog visit to Singapore demonstrated.

The end of the Cold War fundamentally changed the relationship between ASEAN and Indochina (increasingly a category of convenience) and presented opportunities for expanding the basis of regional co-operation. But the central problem of managing regional order did not go away. While the accommodation of the Indochinese states within ASEAN was on the cards and a larger ASEAN presented an important structure for regionwide confidence-building, Leifer was less sanguine about regional capability to overcome the problem of power as China's new assertiveness in the South China Sea demonstrated. Despite a growing regional coherence, the problems of Southeast Asia could not be addressed in isolation of the wider East Asian strategic context, which seemed to be generating new uncertainties and apprehensions (Ch. 9).

Indeed, Leifer challenged the notion of a distinctive ASEAN peace process that could be directed at solving specific intra-mural problems or addressing core regional issues such as the competing claims over the South China Sea (Ch. 10). This is not to understate ASEAN's achievements as a diplomatic community (which reached an apogee during the Cambodia conflict) or its engagement in a "diluted form" of co-operative security — the latter conceivably, an alternative to balance of power practice. Nevertheless, it was questionable whether the culture of regional relations associated with ASEAN's success in containing intra-mural tensions merited the label of a distinctive "peace process" that could be brought to bear on the looming new generation of post-Cold War security problems.

Nevertheless ASEAN's success in coping with intra-mural problems merited the label of a "security community". In Chapter 11, Leifer compares ASEAN as a security community with the alternative models of "political community" and "defence community", which are deemed irrelevant. In two senses ASEAN fits the model of a security community namely, as a vehicle for intra-mural conflict avoidance and management and as a diplomatic community being able to articulate effectively common diplomatic positions. However, these aspects of the security community suffer two flaws: ASEAN has never invoked its own dispute settlement mechanism to resolve intra-mural disputes; and its autonomy to manage regional order is limited.

At the beginning of the new century Leifer returns to the notion of "regional solutions to regional problems" (Ch. 12) in the ASEAN context and sees it as inherently flawed, given the intra-regional differences over issues of regional identity and strategic perspectives. Nor has the ASEAN Regional Forum (ARF), which reflected an extension of the ASEAN model of extra-regional engagement, a remit for regional problem solving on, say, South China Sea problems. Essentially, resident states of the wider region did not necessarily share the same view of the nature of regional problems or how to address them.

Leifer views the ARF as a venture into multilateralism at a time of critical post-Cold War transition aimed at promoting stable relationships among the major powers in the Asia-Pacific. For Leifer, it remains an imperfect diplomatic instrument given its dependence on a pre-existing stable balance of power situation rather than being able to create such a situation. In Chapter 13, Leifer has sought to explain the elusive balance of power concept as reflected in the ASEAN approach of attempting to "contain" a potential hegemon within a structure of multilateral engagement. Within the Asia-Pacific where the rising power of China is being felt, Leifer still sees the United States as underpinning the balance of power situation. Nevertheless he recognizes the neofunctionalist assumption of the ARF whereby stable political relationships could follow an incremental dialogue process. But this replication of the ASEAN model of external engagement is essentially a limited contribution to a stable balance of power by other than traditional means (Ch. 14).

ASEAN's evolution as a security model and its expanding role is reviewed by Leifer in an unpublished paper, written to commemorate ASEAN's thirtieth year (Ch. 15). Although ASEAN's vision of regional order was tested by the regional Cold War, the Cambodia conflict was a mixed blessing — ASEAN's collective diplomatic voice was enhanced but with the dissipation of the Cold War and resolution of that conflict, the international alignments that had supported ASEAN's diplomatic achievements began to change. Seeking to overcome marginality, ASEAN extended geographically its model of regional security. Concurrently its corporate membership was expanded to encompass the whole of Southeast Asia. The former process reflected ASEAN's lack of competence on its own to manage security problems in its regional locale, while the latter brought with it the seeds of discordant diversity.

7

Regionalism, the Global Balance, and Southeast Asia

I should like to discuss the links between regionalism and international order. By international order, I mean that condition of international political life which is the product of shared assumptions about interests and conduct on the part of those states which play the major role in determining the central or global balance of power. Such a condition, if realized, expresses itself in arrangements of a regulating kind which make possible the stable management of critical relationships. Whether such an order is, in fact, possible depends, of course, on the nature of the prevailing international system. However, it does become possible to speak in a meaningful manner of international order when those states which possess the capability and the will to maintain it or disrupt it, accept the legitimacy of the prevailing *status quo* and agree on ways to maintain or change it. I am not seeking to imply that the present condition of international political life represents

Reprinted in abridged form from Michael Leifer, "Regionalism, the Global Balance and Southeast Asia", in *Regionalism in South-East Asia* (Jakarta: Center for Strategic and International Studies, 1975), pp. 55–70, by permission of the publisher.

international order in the somewhat ideal terms in which I have defined it. However, the advent of détente has brought about a greater approximation to such a state of affairs than has been the case for many decades.

The actual link between regionalism and the promotion, maintenance or disruption of international order is governed by the perceptions of those key states which possess the capability and will to intervene in a regional situation to protect or advance what are envisaged as vital interests. Such intervention may be expected where the region in question occupies a place of high priority in the strategic awareness of a major power which is coupled to the balance of competitive advantage between that power and its principal global adversaries. The prospect for such competitive intervention will depend on the degree of antagonistic polarity within the international system and on the consequent extent to which regional domestic disorders and conflicts are drawn into the tension which characterizes the global balance. In a context of competitive quest for regional access the link between regional condition and international order is demonstrated where, for example, domestic upheaval contains within it the prospect of either sharp discontinuity in political succession or the emergence of a separatist new state with sharp discontinuity in its international alignment. In the light of this analysis, it is understandable why competitive intervention in Southeast Asia had been intense in the years since the end of the Second World War. These years have coincided with both antagonistic polarity within the international system and a historically rapid process of decolonization giving rise to new states and new leaderships, often in a less than stable political context.

Before taking this analysis any further, it is necessary to draw a crude distinction between two kinds of region. On the one hand, it is possible to identify a region in which is situated a major power constituting an integral part of the global balance. On the other hand, one can point to a region where no such power is domiciled. In the first case, the region in question is likely to be an exclusive zone within which the major power may act, if not with total freedom and success, with the expectation that its global adversaries will not engage in any substantive attempts at competitive access. An obvious example of a major power acting in such a manner would be the Soviet Union in Eastern Europe; action which it has sought to dignify and legitimate through the promulgation of the Brezhnev Doctrine of limited sovereignty applicable to the states of the Socialist Commonwealth. In so far as major power adversaries respect one another's zones of exclusive intervention then regional disorder need not enter into the global balance.

(T)he second kind of region is marked by the absence of a resident global power. In a region of this kind — exemplified by Southeast Asia — great power intervention has been facilitated by the subordinate character of the regional system and impelled by the degree of strategic awareness of the major powers concerned, that is the extent to which the regional balance has been perceived as an integral component of the global balance. Such a sense of strategic awareness has been experienced, above all, by the United States. Thus, following the end of the Pacific War (with the onset of the Cold War and the attendant policy of the containment of Communism on a global scale) the American Government perceived a direct link between the regional balance in East and Southeast Asia and the global balance of power. Governed by a conviction that there existed an expansionist monolithic Communism with China as its vehicle in Asia and swayed by a belief in the theory that any Communist territorial success would work to the political advantage of both China and international Communism, the American Government coupled Southeast Asia to its global strategic view. The American determination to hold the line in Southeast Asia was exemplified by President Nixon's description of Vietnam as "the cork in the bottle of Chinese expansionism in Asia".

Such a view preceded the promulgation of the Nixon Doctrine. Indeed, it is evident that Mr. Nixon's visit to Peking together with the Paris "settlement" of the Vietnam issue — designed primarily to permit a tolerable American disengagement — as expressions of that Doctrine have indicated a fundamental change in the premises of American policy. And such a change has been shaped not only by the American experience of military intervention but also by the prospect of managing a central adversary relationship with the Soviet Union through limited rapprochement with China. To this end, the United States has decoupled Southeast Asia from its strategic perspective and its mode of intervention has been modified. In consequence, the scale of competitive intervention has been reduced and an era of international politics in Southeast Asia has come to an end. I would qualify this assertion only to the extent that the United States during the tenure of office of President Nixon and after, has been concerned to influence the mode of political change in Indochina, that is to sustain the "peace with honour" formula which translated means that America's allies should not be violently overthrown because such a process of change would reflect on the global credibility of the United States.

I am not suggesting, however, that extra-regional powers no longer possess identifiable interests in Southeast Asia. Both the Soviet Union and China have intervened in the past and at present are engaged in a competitive quest for influence and advantage at the level of governments and dissident movements. Indeed, it is possible to point to a whole range of external interests. For example, the United States and the Soviet Union have taken a common stand on the question of naval passage through the Straits of Malacca and Singapore. China has a territorial claim to the Spratly Islands, while it gives open encouragement to revolutionary movements, within Southeast Asian states and in the case of Burma has intervened more concretely during the past year. China's interests do not only conflict with non-Communist states in the region. It is fairly self-evident that the Chinese Government would be displeased to see the hegemony of the Vietnamese Communists established throughout Indochina. And its support for Prince Sihanouk's government in exile represents an attempt to shape the sectoral balance. The Soviet Union, for its part, has given notice in the form of the Brezhnev collective security proposal of its own desire to counter any extension of Chinese influence. Its enunciation in June 1969 shortly after the clashes along the Amur and Ussuri rivers was almost certainly more than coincidental. In addition, it has engaged in naval display in the Indian Ocean. Japan is another state with great power potential which has undoubted political interests. In its case, above all, a concern to sustain ready access to the region, arising out of a ubiquitous if not fully comfortable economic position. And finally, the application of the Nixon Doctrine does not mean a withdrawal to Hawaii but rather a policy of encouraging friendly states in the region to become militarily and otherwise more self-sufficient and so to ensure an acceptable stability in those states which make up the bounds of the opposite extremity of a shared ocean.

Although the American experience of the costliness of intervention has probably been salutary in capitals other than Washington, there still remains a link between regional and international order in so far as the interests of external powers are concerned. What appears to have changed, however, in great part as a consequence of the application of the Nixon Doctrine is that Southeast Asia has become for the time being somewhat less of a cockpit for the interventionist practice of external powers. In this respect, it is possible to suggest that as between regional and global dimensions peace may come to be increasingly divisible — and not indivisible — and that any regional disorder could well foster unconstrained or without undue stimulation in that it ceases to have a major impact beyond conventionally acknowledged bounds. However, changes in the strategic awareness of any of the global powers or in the political condition of regional states could reverse such a situation in the future.

I should like to direct my attention now to the question of how countries of the region of Southeast Asia — or rather those of them willing to engage in regional association — might make a contribution to both regional and international order. At one level they can do very little in that the strategic awareness of the three principal global powers is governed by the nature of their triangular relationship. One can suggest, nonetheless, that in so far as regional states are able to act collectively to shape regional order then they will influence, if indirectly, the temper of international order. By this I mean that in so far as they are willing and able to invest political systems and international relations within Southeast Asia with a strong measure of stability and regularity, then both the opportunity and the propensity for external intervention will be reduced, and equally the prospect of engaging regional issues into global competitiveness.

Regional association within Southeast Asia operates, however, within a context of constraints. For example, ASEAN is not an alliance in the traditional sense and to my knowledge it has never been the intention of any of its members that it should become one. Besides, with the possible exception of Thailand, situated on the sidelines of the Indochina War, the states of ASEAN do not face the imminent prospect of conventional external threat. In consequence, it would seem that an appropriate approach to regional order in Southeast Asia is for those who possess the interest and the will to cooperate and consult to concentrate on critical aspects of their domestic orders which if neglected could serve to attract outside interest. By promoting settled and acceptable conditions of public life in part through attention to social and economic injustice then the opportunity for external intervention on the side of competing internal political forces will be reduced. In addition, by giving adequate attention to such matters intra-regional differences will be more readily moderated and resolved through pacific settlement and once again the opportunity for the external exploitation of internal political turbulence will be limited.

Of course, to be able to act collectively in this way there has to be a developing sense of regional partnership based not only on the recognition of sovereign equality but also of the differing interests among the members of the association. This means that regional action will tend to be determined by the lowest common denominator of interests. The self-evident task is to raise such a common denominator to the highest possible point.

In the light of these remarks, I should like to conclude with a comment on the likely efficacy of any proposal for the collective promotion of regional order, whatever label one might attach to it. I would suggest that any scheme for regional order to have a reasonable chance of success must have some kind of autonomous regional basis which reflects — in a word which has become well-known in Southeast Asia — the resilience of the participating states. The weakness of any scheme for regional order which places undue reliance on understandings between external and regional states and between such external states is not just that the regional system remains subordinate and not coordinate within the international system, but that where such understandings are based on a particular status quo, any change in that status quo which violates such understandings could precipitate a reversion to competitive intervention; an experience which Southeast Asia has known for too long at too much cost. Some measure of regional autonomy would seem to be necessary to define jurisdiction where possible and to invest regional association with adequate authority for dealing with security issues. This is not to say that understandings with external powers are intrinsically not of value. They may well be. However, undue dependence on them may merely build the prospect of a reversion to intervention into a system of regional order.

Such prescription, of course, like all advice from those who don't have to follow it is much easier to offer than to apply practically. And one obvious reason for this gap between suggested policy and application is that within all regional associations, states possess differing perceptions of their interests and vulnerability and in consequence may be unwilling to give up any available options of access to external countervailing support, whether bilateral or multilateral. Nonetheless, what I have tried to indicate is valid if the goal is a viable regional order which can contribute at the same time to international order. To this end, some basis of regional autonomy would seem to be necessary and for this to materialize the prerequisites of interest, will and capability expressed in stable domestic order and intra-regional accord have to be demonstrated. In other words, there must pre-exist some kind of shared central or integral view to guide the collective action of regional partners.

It is a fact, nonetheless, that regionalism is not a ready made panacea for security and prosperity but merely an approach to such ends with possibilities for success. It is in no sense a form of supranational expression but rather a variant of inter-sovereign state association which is fraught with all kinds of perils and which can so easily be founded on the rocks of conflicting interests. This said, I would hope that, although Southeast Asia is experiencing a process of uncertain change, that this is not a time for pessimism.

8

ASEAN's Search for Regional Order

Regional order is a high-sounding aspiration which is difficult to define with any precision. In general terms, it means the existence of a stable structure of regional inter-governmental relationships informed by common assumptions about the bases of inter-state conduct. It other words, regional order refers to a condition of security obtaining between regional states which is upheld by their deferring to a formal or informal set of rules.

If regional order is difficult to define with any precision, it is even more difficult to promote because, like beauty, that ideal condition tends to reside in the eye of the beholder. Obstacles to its realisation may arise, for example, from differences in the strategic perspectives — or threat perceptions — of regional states, even though in aggregate capability those states may well be in a position to impose an order on their locale. Where differences in strategic perspective arise between states without such appropriate aggregate

Reprinted in abridged form from Michael Leifer, "ASEAN's Search for Regional Order", Faculty of Arts and Social Sciences Lecture 12, National University of Singapore, 1987, by permission of the copyright-holder.

capability, then any quest for regional order becomes an even more elusive undertaking.

The Association of Southeast Asian Nations fits within the second category of regional states. Its members exhibit differences in strategic perspective and also serious limitations in aggregate capability. Those differences and limitations have never prevented the ASEAN states from pursuing the goal of regional order. Its realisation, of course, has been another matter.

At the outset, the member governments of ASEAN did not articulate an operational doctrine of regional order to which they were all committed. The process of negotiations, which culminated in the founding declaration of 8 August 1967, was marked by strong divergences of view and interest which reflected the prior contentious experience of *Konfrontasi* as well as the attendant sense of vulnerability of some of the prospective regional partners. Moreover, although it was hoped that ASEAN would include all the countries of Southeast Asia, the basis of initial membership was sub-regional, without any early prospect of wider association because of the Vietnam War. The new-found partners did have an eye to its termination. But, August 1967 marked the peak of American military involvement without any end to it in sight.

To fend off external condemnation, priority of stated purpose was given to unexceptional economic coooperation. But inherent in the founding declaration was an evident ambition to manage regional order. This ambition derived directly from longstanding Indonesian ideas which had been carried over from President Sukarno's discredited political system of Guided Democracy. Indeed, it is significant just to what extent the premises for such management were drawn intact from agreements concluded at a series of regional conferences which convened in Manila during 1963 which were intended ostensibly to resolve differences over the advent of the Federation of Malaysia.[1] At those conferences, the viewpoint of Indonesia's delegation prevailed up to a point. It expressed a vision of order predicated upon a proprietary management of regional relationships by the resident states of Southeast Asia.

In Bangkok in August 1967, elements of this unrealised vision were incorporated in the preamble to the founding declaration but as a statement of ideals rather than as a binding commitment. For example, longstanding security arrangements with extra-regional states which obtained for every member government, with the exception of

Indonesia, were not repudiated. Those arrangements constituted a practical operational reality deemed relevant to national security as opposed to the aspirational character of the preamble to the founding declaration. The incorporation of some of its passages — including, for example, the affirmation that all foreign bases were temporary — constituted an expression of deference to Indonesia's political sensibilities because of the welcome change in its prevailing political orientation under General Suharto and the significance of its new-found commitment to regional cooperation.

Despite the evident gap between declaratory intent and operational reality, ASEAN was conceived by its founding members as an embryonic security community. At the outset, however, security was approached in a piecemeal manner which was necessary in order to overcome the legacy of suspicion engendered in part by *Konfrontasi*. Reconciliation among new-found regional partners was the first priority.

ASEAN began its institutional life in a way that demonstrated continuity with the premises and cooperative practice of the defunct Association of Southeast Asia (ASA) which it had superseded. All member governments attached great importance to domestic political stability which served as the basic common denominator of their security concerns.[2] Regional cooperation was intended to promote such stability through containing and reducing intra-mural tensions. To the extent that within the bounds of the Association, threats might be contained, managed and even eliminated, national governments would be able to devote their limited resources more fully and with more confidence to the goal of economic development deemed to be the appropriate antidote to problems of domestic political stability. This process of linkage was intended to give rise to that idealised condition which the Indonesians came to dignify with the term "national resilience". Moreover, to the extent that security, as an expression of domestic political stability, was conceived as an indivisible condition among regional partners, this fruitful linkage might find aggregate regional expression. Such expression matched in aspiration the collateral Indonesian term; regional resilience.

Security and regional order were approached tentatively on a limited geographical scale on the basis of what may be described as a theory of collective internal security. The climate of reconciliation, and a corresponding commitment to regional cooperation, was expected to counter any revival of threats between member governments. In addition, an attendant ability to address problems of domestic political stability through the mechanisms of economic development would, it was hoped, prevent the contagion of internal disorder from spreading to infect the body politic of regional partners. If such an exercise in political prophylaxis could work, it would deny the opportunity for extra-regional political predators to fish in troubled waters; a disposition deemed a longstanding affliction of post-colonial Southeast Asia. If conditions for such denial could be created, then a zone of regional stability would be established, albeit on a limited geographical scale.

The operational reality of intra-ASEAN co-operation, certainly in its formative years, did not meet the expectations of this inferred limited model for regional order. The habit of cooperation took time to cultivate impeded by the revival of bilateral tensions, while its economic dimension hardly proved inspiring. Moreover, although *ad hoc* political cooperation (i.e. common foreign policy) did proceed, albeit at a limited pace, it did not make any tangible impact beyond the geographic bounds of the Association. For example, ASEAN as a corporate entity was not of direct relevance to the central regional conflict in Vietnam, although most of its governments in one way or another became parties to the controversial process of American military intervention. In effect, the ASEAN states constituted a group of political spectators to the resolution of the Second Indochina War.

In addition, the vision of regional order implicit in the founding Bangkok Declaration was not shared fully among ASEAN's members, especially the goal of an autonomous system which might portend the emergence of a dominant regional power. It was to avoid such a political spectre in the wake of *Konfrontasi* that ASEAN had been established. Moreover, the early 1970s heralded a series of unilateral initiatives by member governments which had discordant intra-mural effects. For example, Indonesia's convening of an international conference on Cambodia (now Kampuchea) was not well received in Singapore for reasons intimated just now. A collective view was not established on whether or not the People's Republic should represent China in the United Nations. The matter of legal regime in the Straits of Malacca and Singapore gave rise to a measure of contention among coastal states and also incurred ironically the joint displeasure of the superpowers. Most importantly, the government of Malaysia took it upon itself to prescribe for regional order by advocating unilaterally an ambitious scheme of neutralisation for the whole of Southeast Asia.

It was in the context of this unilateral initiative and the admission of the People's Republic of China to the United Nations that the Foreign Ministers of the ASEAN states met in Kuala Lumpur in November 1971, although not in a corporate capacity. Although the Kuala Lumpur Declaration did contain an endorsement, in principle, of neutralisation, a central feature of that international practice — namely, a prescribed role for external guarantors — was discarded. In place of a well-established term with standing in international law, a diluted alternative was substituted which lacked the former's precision. The alternative formula of a Zone of Peace, Freedom and Neutrality (Zopfan) did not contain classical provision for neutralisation but corresponded closely to Indonesia's conception of proprietorial management of regional order by resident states. Underlying that conception was a conviction that close cooperation among regional states would have an insulating political effect, thereby overcoming the need for any demeaning policing function being accorded to external powers.

The implications of the Zopfan formula were disturbing to some ASEAN states because it foreshadowed an unpalatable regional dominance. But the practical prospects of its operational application were deemed to be so unlikely that it could be readily accepted by all member governments as a symbolic common denominator of ASEAN's regional role and intent.

Before the end of the Second Indochina War, however, this collective commitment to Zopfan, although subject to mixed response from external powers, did not possess any direct practical relevance to wider debate about regional order. With the end of that war in 1975 and the success of revolutionary Communism throughout Indochina, the ASEAN states were obliged to confront a new pattern of regional power. And it was in this context that their ideal formula came to be regarded with intense suspicion and repudiated as a prescription for regional order. For the government in Hanoi, in particular, the credentials of ASEAN were suspect, together with Zopfan. It was construed as an insidious design intended to prosecute the interests of Vietnam's defeated but still menacing adversary.

At the next conference of non-aligned states, convened in Sri Lanka in August 1976, the Zopfan formula was attacked by the Laotian and Vietnamese delegations as an unacceptable basis for regional order. In consequence, it was denied a place in the final communiqué.[3] One effect of this successful assault on the symbol of ASEAN's aspiration was to encourage member governments to close ranks and to reinforce their sense of corporate identity which had been displayed at the first ever meeting of heads of government, convened in February that year in Bali. Another effect was to demonstrate beyond doubt that a system of regional order on a Southeast Asian scale was not an early practical possibility. The appropriate regional preconditions for Zopfan were not present and were also beyond the capability of the ASEAN states to manufacture.

The Zopfan formula had been reiterated earlier at the Bali Summit in February 1976 when intra-ASEAN political cooperation, as opposed to excluded defence cooperation, was placed on a formal footing. Zopfan, however, was incorporated as only one indication, among others, of common purpose within a general declaration of ASEAN concord. The conclusion of a Treaty of Amity and Cooperation was intended to encourage the institutionalisation of intra-mural dispute management and settlement. Significantly, the treaty contained an extra-ASEAN dimension in its provision for "accession" by other regional states, with Vietnam uppermost in mind. Through the provision for "accession", it was hoped to encourage Vietnam to participate in a general commitment of respect for the national sovereignty of states as a way of establishing a regional *modus vivendi*.

Vietnam did not indicate any interest in becoming a party to the Treaty of Cooperation and Friendship, but a change in the tone of its relationships with the ASEAN states became manifest during the late 1970s. That change was inspired primarily by the need to cope with the disturbing deterioration in Vietnam's relations with China. The change in the tone of relationships reached a high point of a kind during September-October 1978 with a series of visits to ASEAN capitals by Vietnam's Prime Minister, Pham Van Dong, who provided assurances of non-interference in the internal affairs of regional states. During those visits a measure of political accommodation was expressed in mutual tolerance for alternative formulae for regional order. Vietnam differed from the ASEAN states over Zopfan by insisting only on the word "independence" being interposed after "peace" and before "freedom and neutrality". In retrospect, it would seem that the point of the diplomatic exercise was to mollify the ASEAN states in advance of Vietnam's treaty with the Soviet Union and invasion of Kampuchea.[4] Following that invasion, a collective sense of betrayal was experienced by every ASEAN government.

Vietnam's invasion of Kampuchea tested the credibility of ASEAN as a corporate entity because of the importance which the Association had placed on the sanctity of national sovereignty. Consideration of the balance of power was also paramount because of the security concerns of the Thai government, imposing a requirement on regional partners to demonstrate solidarity. Nonetheless, the public justification for their collective diplomatic challenge in response to Vietnam's invasion was the need to uphold respect for the cardinal rule of the society of states.

With the diplomatic engagement of ASEAN in that conflict, the issue of regional order in a grand sense was joined in an intractable manner. That state of affairs has continued for a number of reasons:

First, the issue of the appropriate political identity of Kampuchea engaged the adverse and incompatible security interests of both Thailand and Vietnam which became entrenched through competing external power support. Conflict over that issue has served to confirm a condition of political polarisation within Southeast Asia between ASEAN and a constellation of Indochinese states.

Secondly, the question of an appropriate format for regional order, in the full sense, was relegated to a subordinate position to the more immediate issue of who is to rule in Kampuchea and on what terms. Contending formulae for regional order have been symptomatic of fundamental differences over the terms of settlement.

Thirdly, the underlying issue of the conflict, namely whether or not Vietnam will be confirmed as the dominant state in Indochina, has been from the outset more than a matter of regional significance. It has attracted the competing interests of major external powers in a manner characteristic of the prevailing pattern of conflict in Southeast Asia since the onset of the transfers of sovereignty. In the circumstances, regional order cannot be simply a matter for the ministrations of regional states.

Fourthly, in challenging Vietnam's assertion of dominance, the ASEAN states engaged in the classical practice of the balance of power, but without employing its traditional prerequisite of military capability. It should be understood that ASEAN has never incurred the obligations, or established the structure, of an alliance. It did become a party, however, to a wider coalition for coercing Vietnam, with the active intervention of external powers, above all China. As a consequence, ASEAN has been obliged to forego any practical pretensions either to a managerial regional role or to forging regional order through exclusive negotiations among resident states.

Finally, to the extent that ASEAN's common strategy has been made dependent on the role of external powers, and indeed has made the Association indirectly a party to Sino-Soviet conflict, it has also run counter to its declaratory aspiration for Zopfan which envisaged regional insulation from external quarrels. This contradiction between a declared aspiration and an operational foreign policy has had the effect of setting up tensions within the body of the Association because of the perceived adverse effects of ASEAN's stand and alignment on the security interests of some member governments.

In particular, the demerits of such a policy have been articulated by an influential component of Indonesia's military establishment. Such tensions over the principal source of external threat have been accommodated up to a point, but they have been a cause of corporate weakness in diplomatic confrontation with Vietnam, designed to encourage deference to ASEAN's regional priorities.

If regional order in the grand sense has been beyond the capacity of ASEAN, order of a kind has been realised on an intra-mural scale. The management of inter-state tensions within ASEAN, underpinned by an established habit of cooperation, has given rise to a sense of security community. The corporate attachment to principle over Kampuchea has increased the confidence of the more vulnerable member governments in ASEAN as a mechanism for ensuring respect for the sanctity of national sovereignty by self-denying ordinance. One minor fruit of this sense of confidence has been the evident utility of membership of ASEAN to Brunei after it resumed sovereignty in January 1984. For the government of Brunei, membership of ASEAN has been perceived as a way of ensuring a more secure local environment which is obviously attractive to the government of the vulnerable micro-state.[5] That said, the continuing limitation of ASEAN as an instrument for promoting regional order on even a modest scale and basis has been exposed by the external security relationships retained by all member governments, except Indonesia. Those security arrangements, with the exception of the tacit alliance between Thailand and China, were established before the advent of ASEAN and for Brunei, before it became the sixth member of the Association.

The Association has developed over the years into a working diplomatic community and has concurrently grown in international stature becoming in the process a factor of some significance in the calculations of both regional and extra-regional states. To that extent, despite intra-mural differences, it has been able to assume a prerogative role of a kind in an intermittent process of negotiations about establishing regional rules of the game. For the time being, however, the prospect for such establishment is very limited. First, the balance or distribution of power within Southeast Asia is such that ASEAN is not in any position to act corporately to revise it to promote its declaratory conception of regional order. Secondly, the interests of the two corporate poles of regional conflict, and their external patrons, are so adversely entrenched that early compromise over Kampuchea seems unlikely. Finally, and as a consequence, the rules of the game have been approached from different perspectives.

ASEAN as a corporate entity remains committed to securing endorsement of the cardinal rule of the society of states as it applied within Southeast Asia before 25 December 1978, which is when Vietnam invaded Kampuchea. The Indochinese constellation has wished to apply that rule in a more discriminate manner, since 10 January 1979 when the People's Republic of Kampuchea was established. Until it is finally decided on what basis the line is to be drawn across the page of Southeast Asian history, regional order in a full sense will remain an elusive ideal. In terms of scope and operational application, order within Southeast Asia can only be a partial accomplishment among like-minded entities who are party to regional polarisation. In consequence, for ASEAN, order is, *faute de mieux*, essentially an intra-mural undertaking.

That intra-mural undertaking and achievement is not to be treated lightly, however. Consultation and cooperation within ASEAN have created a zone of peace of a limited but valuable kind in comparison with the circumstances of the early 1960s. Moreover, the attendant cohesion displayed in crises has given ASEAN a unique hearing internationally. Its institutionalised dialogues with industrialised states are a reflection of its international standing. No other corresponding corporate entity has been able to count on the regular attendance each year, at a meeting with its foreign ministers, of counterparts from the United States, Japan, Australia, New Zealand and Canada, as well as a matching representative from the European Community.

[O]ne of the signal accomplishments of the Association has been to demonstrate that it is possible to accommodate intra-mural differences while sustaining working relationships. In practising intra-mural accommodation, ASEAN has proceeded by consensus; exemplified in the agreement to differ when Malaysia unilaterally established diplomatic relations with the People's Republic of China in May 1974. The practice of consensus has limited corporate initiative but it has also sustained corporate commitment through respect for national sovereignty.

That practice of consensus has never entailed full uniformity in foreign policy among ASEAN states. Political cooperation has been confined in the main to regional issues, without any suggestion that a veto should be applied to the foreign policy of any member government. For example, the presence of Israeli embassies in Bangkok, Manila and Singapore has never been made a test of ASEAN's solidarity; nor has Malaysia's exclusive decision to accord full diplomatic status to a mission of the Palestine Liberation Organisation.

The issue of a veto on a member state's foreign policy arose in concrete form in November 1986. Protests were lodged by the governments of Brunei, Indonesia and Malaysia at the visit to Singapore by President Chaim Herzog of Israel. The protests by Brunei and Indonesia had a perfunctory quality but in the case of Malaysia vehement objections were raised by senior cabinet ministers and both living former prime ministers as well as by an *ad hoc* action committee primarily comprising opposition parties.

In the case of Malaysia, it is necessary to consider the furore aroused by President Herzog's visit to Singapore in the context of domestic political circumstances, including growing competition for political leadership within UMNO. The visit occurred at a time of communal tension between Malays and Chinese over prerogative position, from which Singapore has never been completely insulated because of its proximity and prevailing ethnic-Chinese identity, as well as the persisting legacy of its stormy interlude as a constituent state of the Federation. In addition, it is important to take into account the extent to which Islamic credentials have come to assume a dominant place in Malay identity as well as a focal point in intra-Malay politics. Correspondingly, the cause of Palestinian nationalism has come to be viewed as a co-religionist issue. Furthermore, one must single out the firm support of Prime Minister Dr Mahathir Mohamad for that cause and also his publicly expressed conviction that Zionism is a pernicious influence threatening the well-being of Malaysia.[6] One of a number of such statements by Dr Mahathir was made less than two weeks before it was announced that Israel's President would be visiting Singapore.

In addition to formal protests, Indonesia and Malaysia, but not Brunei, registered disapproval by temporarily withdrawing the heads of their diplomatic missions in Singapore. In Malaysia, however, matters were taken further at governmental level in the articulation of indignation. Singapore's reception of Israel's President was deemed insensitive to Malaysian feelings and hence gratuitously provocative. Of relevance to the issue of regional order was the official and unofficial Malaysian argument that where such strong national feelings could be aroused, then special consideration and second-thoughts were required in the interests of ASEAN solidarity.

Although, after the event, governments in Singapore and Malaysia have attempted to limit the political damage there can be little doubt that President Herzog's visit to Singapore has placed a major strain on an important bilateral relationship within ASEAN. That strain has been reinforced by contention over the loyalty of Singapore's Malay community. In the case of Brunei and Indonesia, no apparent lasting effects have been indicated in relations with Singapore. Relations between Malaysia and Singapore, however, have been so engulfed by primordial sentiments that it would be facile to represent the episode as a mere storm in a teacup. Indeed, the Herzog visit has pointed to a paradoxical quality of ASEAN, present at its creation.

ASEAN was established between adversaries of different kinds in an attempt to promote a structure of reconciliation. The regional enterprise was embarked upon in the full knowledge that certain underlying facts of political life could not be changed at will, including the sense of vulnerability of some member states. In other words, foreign policy would always be a problem among member states; some partners in reconciliation would remain potential enemies.

The question arises as to which is the best way of sustaining a structure of reconciled relationships as a basis for a viable regional order, if only of a limited kind. Taking the rather exceptional example of President Herzog's visit to Singapore, one might ask whether it is served best by one state insisting on deferential conduct by a regional partner of a kind which might well strain the notion of national sovereignty?

The issue may be posed in a less extreme alternative form, taking into account that membership of any corporate grouping of necessity requires some limitation on freedom of action. In other words, without compromising sovereignty, it may be argued that ASEAN governments ought to be sufficiently sensitive to the interests of their regional partners not to engage in foreign policy initiatives certain to be regarded as gratuitously provocative. It was on this ground that Anwar Ibrahim, Malaysia's Minister of Education and UMNO youth leader, sought to question the wisdom, but not the right, of Singapore's government to invite the President of Israel; a view endorsed by Indonesia's Foreign Minister, Mochtar Kusumaatmadja.[7]

The difficulty involved is compounded by the prospect that a member government may feel disposed to display sovereignty from time to time in order to overcome an abiding sense of vulnerability. And that display may violate sensitivities among regional partners in circumstances where foreign policy issues readily enter into the domestic political process. If the furore aroused in Malaysia by President Herzog's visit to Singapore was an exceptional as well as a symptomatic episode, it has pointed to the persistent problem of how to sustain the bases of a regional order achieved by ASEAN on a limited scale.

In the case of ASEAN, special relationships cannot be taken for granted, as the Herzog episode and its aftermath have demonstrated. The overriding task for regional partners, as the Association moves into its third decade, is to invest the commonplace but crucial habit of consultation and consideration with critical significance.

Notes

This lecture is based on a paper presented to a workshop on "ASEAN and the Search for Order in a Changing World", Institute of Security and International Studies, Chulalongkorn University, August 1986.

1. See Michael Leifer, *Indonesia's Foreign Policy*, Allen and Unwin, London 1983, pp. 88–9 and 121–2.
2. See Franklin B Weinstein, "The Meaning of National Security in Southeast Asia", *The Bulletin of Atomic Scientists*, November 1978.
3. The Vietnamese position was made explicit by Ngo Dien, an assistant to Foreign Minister Nguyen Duy Trinh. He pointed out: "It should be made clear that the Socialist Republic of Vietnam has many times declared its support for the efforts of Southeast Asian countries for genuine independence, peace and neutrality. But we did not agree to insert this question in the resolution of the summit conference in the name of the Kuala Lumpur Declaration of ASEAN, a declaration issued at the very moment when the ASEAN countries were directly or indirectly serving the US aggressive war in Vietnam, Laos and Cambodia in complete contravention of the principles of the non-aligned movement — we decidely do not tolerate any scheme to revive a none-too-bright past of ASEAN and

to sell an outmoded and bankrupted policy of this organisation." B.B.C. *Summary of World Broadcasts,* FE/5298/A3/3.

4. See Nayan Chanda, *Brother Enemy,* Harcourt Brace, San Diego, 1986, pp. 318–20.

5. See the argument in Michael Leifer, 'Brunei: Domestic Politics and Foreign Policy', Karl Jackson et al (eds.), *ASEAN in Regional and Global Perspective,* Institute of East Asian Studies, University of California, Berkeley 1986.

6. Dr Mahathir pointed out, "Malaysia views with grave concern Zionist attempts to manipulate individuals and groups in the country to run down the government and undermine the economy through playing up certain issues", *The Straits Times,* 11 October 1986.

7. *The Straits Times,* 13 December 1986.

9

Indochina and ASEAN
Seeking a New Balance

A new balance of a kind is already in place between Indochina and
ASEAN. That much has been conspicuously evident ever since the
Cambodian peace agreement was concluded in Paris in October
1991, despite continuing problems of implementation. In the case of
Vietnam, the pace and extent of ministerial and bureaucratic exchanges
with the ASEAN states have been striking. Accelerated economic
dealings have been underpinned by an expanding network of regional
air communications.

This article addresses the changing nature of the relationship
between Indochina and ASEAN and also the measure of opportunity
which the political watershed of the Cambodian settlement provides
for expanding regional co-operation on the basis of mutual confidence and shared understandings. At issue is an obvious underlying question: how to manage regional order in fundamentally
changed strategic circumstances and more importantly, to what

Reprinted in abridged form from Michael Leifer, "Indochina and ASEAN:
Seeking a New Balance", *Contemporary Southeast Asia* 15, no. 3 (1993): 269–79,
by permission of the Institute of Southeast Asian Studies.

extent can such management be approached on a regionally autonomous basis.

By the fourth meeting of ASEAN's heads of government in Singapore in January 1992, the balance of advantage between Indochina and the Association had been transformed. ASEAN's intra-mural structure of conciliation and its role as a diplomatic community were no longer subject to derisive comment. On the contrary, Vietnam and Laos sought to accede to the Treaty of Amity and Cooperation as a step towards full membership on ASEAN's terms in much the same way that a new state might apply to join the United Nations. Vietnam and Laos have been driven by economic imperatives and also by those of national security shaped by the greater strategic latitude enjoyed by China as a consequence of the end of the Cold War. It is Vietnam and Laos which have assumed a supplicant role towards ASEAN, now viewed as a countervailing factor of advantage in regional relations. Cambodia, of course, cannot begin to address the question of regional association until its internal order is made stable.

What then is the essence of the new balance between Indochina and ASEAN in transformed regional circumstances and what is its potential?

First, it should be well understood that Indochina is now only a category of convenience rather than a set of special relationships subject to Vietnamese dominance. Vietnam's relationship with Laos has begun to change from that between virtual metropolitan power and provincial centre, with Vientiane displaying greater autonomy. Indeed, with the disintegration of the Soviet Union, Vietnam cannot afford to be its patron in a material sense. Cambodia has, of course, been prised from Vietnam's grasp and an underlying tension based on cultural differences and historical experience is expected to shape an uncertain future relationship. In consequence, the very notion of a balance between Indochina and ASEAN is already outmoded because the concept of Indochina as some kind of unitary actor needs to be radically revised.

Secondly, although ASEAN has a well defined corporate identity, it is also very much the mixed sum of its constituent parts which are not in accord on all regional issues. Its members have never shared the kind of declaratory aspirations to be found in the Treaty of Rome which still inspires the goals of the European Community. Moreover, its governments have mixed as well as common views about security and cannot be expected, for example, to seek to integrate Vietnam within a conventional collective defence structure designed to contain any creeping assertiveness in the region by China. Apart from the absence of a lobby within ASEAN with an interest in so confronting China, there is also a lack of a necessary common strategic perspective.

That said, the concept and practice of balance in the relationships between states is well understood in Singapore and among its regional partners within ASEAN even if they have not necessarily shared a common view about its particular purpose. The concept and practice of balance is traditionally associated with military power; and above all, the prospect of its collective projection in response to the advent of a menacing dominance or hegemony. But in the case of ASEAN, balance of power in the conventional sense was excluded deliberately from its corporate philosophy and declaratory vocabulary from the outset. Despite some urging, the ASEAN states have never moved in the direction of alliance formation and have excluded conventional defence co-operation from their common agenda. For example, they did not take up the challenge presented by United Nations peacekeeping in Cambodia to engage in that quasi-military undertaking on a collective basis. Instead, each member state which participated despatched a separate contingent of soldiers or police. In retrospect, ASEAN may have missed an important opportunity to lend substance to its declaratory position on regional order.

Member governments have sought to deal with problems of imbalances in the regional distribution of power in part through a structure of consultation and conciliation which has made it possible to mitigate and manage conflict within the walls of the Association. And, although they have endorsed a code of conduct for regional order in the Treaty of Amity, its dispute settlement provisions have never been invoked since promulgation in 1976. To do so could, of course, expose intra-mural tensions and conflicts of interest at the expense of corporate cohesion whereas the culture of ASEAN is disposed to concealing or minimizing such conflicts. To that extent, in limiting its security role, ASEAN has to suffer the defects of its evident qualities.

Beyond its walls, ASEAN has sought to function as a diplomatic community employing regional credentials to register a collective view on issues of common interest. But the role of the diplomatic community has changed significantly since the end of the 1980s when the Cambodian conflict was still concentrating the minds of member governments.

The strengths and limitations of ASEAN's challenge to Vietnam's occupation of Cambodia should be well understood. That challenge was a product of the Association being a party to a tacit alliance in which China assumed military obligations, and the United States and Japan in particular applied economic sanctions. Against the direction of its guiding declaratory philosophy and the political inclination of some member governments, ASEAN with a diplomatic responsibility was drawn into a classical practice of the balance of power to deny the dominance of Vietnam in Indochina. The collective strategy of attrition worked over time, especially when a vulnerable Vietnam could no longer cope with economic distress because of diminishing access to Soviet benefaction, which then ceased with the disintegration of its longstanding patron.

It should be noted that there is a conspicuous contrast in context and significance, for example, between ASEAN's stand on Cambodia from January 1979 and that on the South China Sea in July 1992. In promulgating a declaration on the latter issue at a meeting of foreign ministers in Manila, ASEAN gave notice that it had recovered its collective diplomatic voice after having been marginalized by the permanent members of the United Nations Security Council in promoting conflict resolution over Cambodia. That declaration met with Vietnam's approval, which was understandable in the light of its government's signature of the Treaty of Amity and Cooperation which gave it observer status in Manila. China, however, indicated a studied reserve at the time, if subsequently indicating a more accommodating attitude. The United States, for its part, did not at the time display any serious interest in the declaration despite the presence of its Secretary of State at the annual post-ministerial meeting. Such evident indifference came shortly before America's final withdrawal from military bases in the Philippines, with implications for the regional balance of power.

The point at issue is that the tacit alliance which had been formed at the height of the so-called Second Cold War to challenge Vietnam's occupation of Cambodia has been dissolved. The convergence of strategic interests which had made possible an international division of labour to deny Vietnam's dominance in Indochina no longer obtains. The corporate diplomacy of ASEAN is no longer underpinned by the joint countervailing power of China, the United States and Japan, among others. On the contrary, its utility is now based on the more mixed interests of both regional and extra-regional states in cultivating and accommodating the Association, whose members have in the main demonstrated both economic accomplishment and a collegial culture of relations.

The reason for this discussion is to make clear that whatever the merits of a new relationship between the Indochinese states and those of ASEAN, any attendant constellation between them will not comprise an enhanced makeweight in the regional balance of power in the conventional sense. A structure of intra-mural conciliation may be widened, and a collective diplomatic voice may be strengthened. These are desirable outcomes in themselves but they do not necessarily provide the building blocks for a new regional order in the post-Cold War era. Indeed, it is partly for this reason that the ASEAN states have begun to explore, with their observer and dialogue partners and also China and Russia, a wider East Asian structure of multilateral security dialogue which has borne embryonic fruit as the ASEAN Regional Forum.

In discussing a new balance between Indochina and ASEAN, we have to be clear on what is required as well as what is possible. From the perspective of the ASEAN states, the essence of a desirable new balance of advantage is already in place. Vietnam and Laos have committed themselves to market-based economic reform through close engagement with the regional and international economy and the momentum of that policy has been sustained. Vietnam, in particular, has overcome a one-time pariah status and is no longer perceived as the proxy of any other state; nor is it viewed as harbouring the kind of geopolitically-driven ambitions in Indochina which were articulated openly with national unification in the mid-1970s. Close proximity must sustain an abiding interest in Laos and Cambodia but Vietnam's spokesman have openly reiterated a determination not to be drawn again into the trap of Cambodia.

The ASEAN governments no longer regard Vietnam as the core of a communist menace in Indochina. They see the creed of communism as having withered away, remaining only in the form of a ruling party whose preservation of a monopoly of power is the prime consideration of its beneficiaries. To the extent that the ruling party in Hanoi is willing and able to convert itself from one kind of authoritarian structure into another devoid of doctrinal rectitude, it would have little difficulty in being accommodated into a regional order based on a mixture of market economics and conservative politics. Vietnam and Laos have come to ASEAN as supplicants, without seeking to negotiate special terms of entry and have been received on that basis.

The problem for ASEAN is that the opportunities for new forms of post-Cold War relationships in Southeast Asia, incorporating Indochina, do not in themselves necessarily make for a tolerable balance or distribution of power in which full responsibility can be assumed by regional states. Vietnam's pragmatically-driven changes of policy have been warmly welcomed, together with its desire for membership of ASEAN, which would seem to be a matter of timing. However, Vietnam's change of political heart in the 1990s in a new strategic context is of much lesser significance than a positive response to ASEAN's bridge-building initiative would have been in the mid-1970s. Progressive membership of the Indochinese states in ASEAN will certainly expand an important network of bureaucratic and ministerial consultation which can be used to address a multiplicity of disputes, especially over territory. But an expanded membership will not in itself be able to confront a wider problem of regional order arising from post-Cold War changes in the East Asian balance or distribution of power of which China has been the major beneficiary. To that extent, the problem of seeking a new balance has to an important extent become irrelevant if addressed on an exclusive Southeast Asian basis.

In 1976, a change in the form of regional relationships through, for example, Vietnam acceding to the Treaty of Amity would have signalled a critical intent to be a good regional citizen, with Vietnam at the height of its revolutionary power. Such a change of form would have been the instrument of a change of substance in relations between Indochina and ASEAN. In 1991, that accession served to confirm such intent, which had been registered progressively as Vietnam sought to overcome a predicament which threatened its domestic political order. But in 1992, Vietnam's accession represented not much more than a change in form which followed on from an earlier change in the substance of policy. As such, it has represented a far less significant act than it might have done some decade and a half earlier in a very different strategic context.

Clearly, a process of regional confidence building has been in train which membership in ASEAN should accelerate to advantage. But that process has arisen from a fundamental prior change of circumstances for Vietnam and Laos which has driven them in a political direction which pleases ASEAN. The so-called new balance arises from those circumstances and not from expanding the formal bounds of regional co-operation. Indeed, the problem of managing the regional balance of power in the wake of the Cold War will not be readily solved through the simple means of Vietnam and Laos joining ASEAN, with Cambodia to follow hopefully in time. The issue of a common strategic perspective which has been absent among the members of ASEAN and which has made defence co-operation problematic will not be resolved simply by an expansion of ASEAN.

A greater ASEAN can provide an important structure within which confidence building may proceed but without any guarantee, for example, of resolving substantive problems of jurisdiction in the South China Sea. Nor will it necessarily provide a forum for overcoming geopolitically driven differences between Thailand and Vietnam, for example, which in turn make it difficult for a common countervailing stand to be taken against a territorially revisionist China. China's new-found strategic latitude, underpinned by an extensive programme of rearmament, means that however beneficial the new balance between Indochina and ASEAN, its main significance has been to register the solution of yesterday's problem; not necessarily today's.

In politics as in life, most solutions give rise to new problems which the new balance in the making between Indochina and ASEAN cannot necessarily address with any great effect. An expanded ASEAN can only provide for common security up to a point. If it were expected to do better, then those ASEAN governments which can afford it would not be spending significant sums on arms procurement for external defence. Moreover, the very emergence of a new balance — in practice a new distribution of power — has the potential to set up new tensions arising, for example, from the extent to which China still continues to view its relationship with Vietnam in patrimonial terms.

The new balance between Indochina and ASEAN merits careful cultivation and, indeed, time and effort have been well expended in prescribing and providing for mutual trust and understanding. Its importance in the light of past turbulent experience should not be under-estimated. But it should be well understood that the new balance is not in itself a formula for regional order. The problems of Southeast Asia, despite a growing regional coherence, cannot be fully addressed if extracted from a wider East Asian regional domain whose strategic context has changed, generating in the process uncertainty and apprehension. At their last summit in January 1992, the heads of government of ASEAN pledged that the Association would move towards a higher plane of political and economic co-operation to secure regional peace and prosperity. The change in strategic context attendant on the end of the Cold War requires a wider perspective and political imagination extending beyond Southeast Asia which has been duly acknowledged by the expanded membership and terms of reference of the most recent Post-Ministerial Meeting held in Singapore in July. The ASEAN Regional Forum has been an encouraging development but it is well understood that, beyond Indochina and ASEAN, a much greater range and mixture of interests have to be accommodated.

At issue as the twenty-first century approaches is how regional states might reconcile their cultivation of the new balance between so-called Indochina and ASEAN with managing wider problems of East Asian regional security attendant on the new post-Cold War pattern of power. The new balance within Southeast Asia cannot stand on its own. It requires a wider approach which has been addressed recently in embryonic form. That wider approach offers promise in terms of opportunities for regional confidence building. But it also cannot necessarily overcome the problem of power which, despite and because of the end of the Cold War, will remain a perpetual factor in regional relations. It should be understood that the ASEAN model of security based on conflict management and avoidance has never confronted that problem. Extending that model geographically will not in itself provide a robust basis for security provision after the end of the Cold War.

10

The ASEAN Peace Process
A Category Mistake

An ASEAN Peace Process?

The notion of a distinctive ASEAN peace process may fairly be described as a category mistake in the light of the institutional experience of the Association of Southeast Asian Nations since its establishment in August 1967 (Leifer 1990; Sandhu *et al.* 1992; Acharya 1993; special issue, *The Pacific Review* 1995; Buszynski 1997/98). This assertion is not intended to deny any connection whatsoever between ASEAN's characteristic mode of activity and regional peace. Over the past three decades, the Association has played a positive role in providing a framework for avoiding and managing contention among member states. The point at issue, however, is that ASEAN's mode of activity, which has been expressed primarily in an informal process of confidence-building and trust creation, has never been directed to solving specific intra-mural problems. Preventive diplomacy, for example, which is best defined in dispute-specific terms, has been the

Reprinted from Michael Leifer, "The ASEAN Peace Process: A Category Mistake", *The Pacific Review* 12, no. 1 (1999): 25–38, by permission of Taylor and Francis Limited <http://www.tandf.co.uk/journals>.

notable exception and not the rule in the intra-mural experience of ASEAN, unless one indulges in intellectual licence and represents the multilateral structure of the Association as itself a grand exercise in preventive diplomacy.

The fact of the matter is that beyond ad hoc initiatives during 1968/69, which served to defuse tension between Malaysia and the Philippines over the latter's claim to Sabah, preventive diplomacy has been conspicuous by its absence in ASEAN's institutional experience, while formal dispute settlement has been beyond it. More to the point, the very notion of a peace process misrepresents the remit of ASEAN as a multilateral security dialogue. ASEAN relates to peace through a general influence exercised on member governments to observe standard international norms and not through applying any distinctive process to a particular conflict which may be transformed as a consequence. Authoritative confirmation of that assessment may be found in the 'Concept Paper' prepared ostensibly by Brunei's Foreign Ministry for the second working session of the ASEAN Regional Forum in Bandar Seri Begawan in August 1995. That paper explained, *inter alia*, that "ASEAN has succeeded in reducing tensions among its member states, promoting regional cooperation and creating a regional climate conducive to peace and prosperity without the implementation of explicit confidence-building measures ..." (cited in Ball and Kerr 1996: 111–15).

In addition, it should be noted that although ASEAN has acted also as a diplomatic community with a collective voice beyond its walls both within and without Southeast Asia, the Association has never been effectively responsible for regional peace-making as opposed to helping to keep the peace through exercising a benign influence on the overall climate of regional relations. ASEAN has certainly been concerned with security and peace in that general sense from its formation but it has functioned intra-murally through a process of intergovernmental dialogue whose continual flow has been regarded as a prophylactic in itself against any incidence of conflict. The Association has never been instrumental, however, in helping to devise and manage a peace process in the substantive sense that the term has been employed with reference to the Middle East, for example. ASEAN sought to do so beyond its membership in the case of Cambodia after Vietnam's invasion of that country in December 1978 but its initiatives were ultimately abortive and were superseded by the decisive role of the permanent members of the

United Nations Security Council in the context of the end of the Cold War.

The key to understanding the nature and regional role of ASEAN and its relationship to peace lies first of all in appreciating that the Association was established as the institutional fruit of conflict resolution rather than as a vehicle for promoting such resolution in any direct sense. ASEAN was a prime product of the termination of Indonesia's campaign of "Confrontation" of the Federation of Malaysia during the mid-1960s which was a direct challenge to the legitimacy of a new state through the vehicle of coercive diplomacy. "Confrontation" was brought to an end because of regime change within Indonesia in 1966. The judgement of a succeeding military leadership in Jakarta was that the international rehabilitation and economic regeneration of the Republic required a revised regional outlook and, above all, a cooperative relationship with regional neighbours, preferably in institutionalized form.

Without discounting a common anti-communism and a related concern with the military staying power of the United States among founding members, ASEAN was established in order to locate post-conflict intra-regional reconciliation within an institutionalized structure of relations. That structure was to be based, above all, on respect for national sovereignty which would sustain the momentum of that reconciliation to mutual advantage. A shared belief in the positive relationship between economic development and security served to reinforce the commitment to regional reconciliation as a way of avoiding any diversion of scarce resources away from such linked priorities. To that end, ASEAN was conceived as an aspirant security community but without clear initial expectations of how it might evolve, especially in the light of an early incidence of intra-mural tensions.

Nonetheless, it is noteworthy just how reconciliation has marked every stage in the subsequent enlargement of ASEAN beginning with Brunei's adherence on independence in January 1984 through to the historic act manifested with Vietnam's entry in July 1995. Reconciliation was also much in mind in the abortive attempt to include all three remaining states of geographic Southeast Asia in late July 1997 when Laos and Myanmar joined, but not Cambodia whose membership was postponed because of a violent coup in Phnom Penh earlier in the month. The phased stages of reconciliation point up also the fact that, for nearly three decades, ASEAN enjoyed only a subregional ambit which limited the geographic scope of its prime confidence-building role.

ASEAN as "Cooperative Security"

ASEAN is best understood as an institutionalized, albeit relatively informal, expression of "cooperative security" which may serve as both a complement and as an alternative to balance-of-power practice. Its distinctive modality may be illuminated partly by comparison and by contrast with the classical notion of collective security which is also an intra-mural arrangement. A characteristic feature of cooperative security, by contrast with collective security, is that it foregoes the vehicle of sanctions, either economic or military. It seeks to work on the basis of suasion (through peer-group pressure underpinned by the assumption of self-interest) to adhere and to be accountable to standard international norms applied without exception to national standing and circumstances.

In ASEAN's case, "cooperative security" has assumed a somewhat diluted form because of an aversion to concrete confidence-building measures. Indeed, there has been a strong claim in the rhetoric of its protagonists and practitioners that the secret of its success has been "the system of consultations that has marked much of its work" described as "the ASEAN way of dealing with a variety of problems confronting its member nations" (Moertopo 1975: 15). That somewhat elliptical view by the late Lieutenant-General Ali Moertopo, one of the key Indonesian plenipotentiaries in resolving "Confrontation" and then in negotiating the advent of ASEAN, has been more explicitly articulated by one of his Malaysian interlocutors. Former Foreign Minister Tan Sri Ghazali Shafie has revealed that in conceiving of reconciliation within the framework of wider regional cooperation, they recommended "that inter-state problems should not be aired openly no matter how small" (Ghazali 1992: 30). They had in mind "a special kind of relationship" based on a common cultural heritage and style which avoided formal legalistic agreements concluded after an adversarial process.

At issue here is the primacy of a continuing process of dialogue which is capable of forging resilient relationships able to withstand any shift to adversity in interstate ties. Such a rationale is part of the mythology of ASEAN whose governments have not shied away from entering into legal undertakings where required in the common interest as in the case of the norm-setting Treaty of Amity and Cooperation in 1976 and in that establishing a regional nuclear weapons-free zone in 1995. Such a rationale is also legitimately part of the reality of its working practice. Security, and hence peace, has been addressed by ASEAN primarily through developing a culture of intra-mural dialogue and consultation based on close working relationships between ministers and officials and an adherence to common norms; not through invoking formal legal mechanisms for dispute settlement. The so-called "ASEAN Way" as a process distinguished by an informal diplomatic style was facilitated at the outset by the limited scale of the initial regional enterprise, the intensity of personal contacts during the formative post-Confrontation period reinforced by a relative homogeneity of political outlooks. ASEAN was certainly not conceived as a political community along the lines of the European model. A prime object of the collective enterprise was to consolidate national sovereignty and not to supersede it. To that end, the norms of the Westphalian system were readily shared among member governments.

Norm-setting and peer-group pressure to adhere to them became an inherent part of the ASEAN dialogue process and has been the basis on which its later enlargement has been contemplated. ASEAN's norms of state conduct are, however, part and parcel of the standard working practice of international society writ large and not in any way particular and exclusive to the Association or its regional locale. Indeed, the attempt to codify appropriate norms as the first summit in Bali in February 1976 within the Treaty of Amity and Cooperation for Southeast Asia was based conspicuously on the United Nations Charter and not on any so-called cultural regional model. The fundamental guiding principles for intra-regional relations set out in Article 2 of that treaty are unexceptional. The rationale of a distinctive cultural style aside, in 1976 precepts such as mutual respect for national sovereignty, non-interference in other states' internal affairs, an injunction against the use of force and engagement in the peaceful settlement of disputes were hardly peculiar to Southeast Asia.

In addition, provision was made within the Treaty of Amity for formal dispute settlement through intra-mural mediation and adjudication methods of Western provenance. Moreover, although that treaty with its strong registration of the sanctity of national sovereignty has been extolled as a model code of conduct for regional relations, its provision for dispute settlement, involving the establishment of a high council, has never once been invoked but has remained totally dormant. The strong reluctance to invoke that provision has been indicative of the recognition that engaging in formal intra-mural dispute settlement could well be highly contentious and divisive and therefore self-defeating to the limited security purpose of the Association which is, above all, about conflict avoidance and management.

ASEAN was obliged to cope with a number of serious intra-mural tensions in its early years but there was sufficient of a sense of shared understanding and priorities among a relatively like-minded small number of governments to help contain and manage them. Moreover, an intra-mural threat to peace was never seriously at issue in the wake of "Confrontation", despite the degree of sabre-rattling between Malaysia and the Philippines over Sabah. With the benefit of hindsight, it is possible to argue that post-Confrontation among the founding membership there was never a credible *casus bellum* and therefore peace-making was never at issue because hostilities were most unlikely to have broken out. Over the years, a number of acute bilateral tensions have been exposed in which domestic political emotions have been involved so demonstrating the extent to which the ASEAN process is primarily an intra-elite undertaking. Nonetheless, those tensions have always been kept under control by respective governments and have never foreshadowed a mobilization of forces and the serious prospect of a clash of arms which has been a recurrent experience in South Asia, for example.

The fundamental issues of regional conflict and peace within Southeast Asia have always existed beyond the walls of the Association and, in its formative years, were located in Indo-China. In the collective attempt to come to terms with the failure of America's military intervention within that peninsula and then the success of revolutionary communism there, a renewed sense of corporate solidarity and aspirant security community were registered. Indeed, in the need to consult closely in order to cope with the challenge posed by an assertive and triumphalist Vietnam, the member governments were drawn more closely into an exclusive structure of dialogue. Aided by the relatively small scale of the enterprise and the relative homogeneity of political outlooks, the five, and then six, governments reinforced the culture of consultation and cooperation which served to buttress the original peace concluded with the termination of "Confrontation". In addition, the need to act as a diplomatic community, especially after Vietnam's invasion of Cambodia in December 1978, further reinforced the emerging quality of intra-mural security community. The entry of Brunei as the sixth member in 1984 did not mark any divergence from that pattern of relations but served to extend an existing homogeneity of political outlook.

ASEAN as a Diplomatic Community

ASEAN did seek to reach out beyond its bounds in the interests of regional security and peace but it had its initial overtures rejected. Provision had been made in the Treaty of Amity for adherence to it by non-member states which would in so doing accept an obligation to conform to those norms of conduct inherent in the idea of international society. The prime object at the time was to build political bridges to the revolutionary states of Indo-China and, in particular, a reunited Vietnam so as to come to a working accommodation in the interest of regional order. The initiative failed at the time because Vietnam was supremely confident that ASEAN would be short-lived and could be replaced by an alternative enterprise in regional cooperation more to its political liking. It is a matter of some irony that some sixteen years later a politically contrite Vietnam (together with Laos, its close political partner) was only too pleased to be allowed to sign the Treaty of Amity and to become a candidate member of ASEAN on the Association's terms.

Regional peace-making was more directly the concern of the Association in response to Vietnam's invasion of Cambodia. Ostensibly at issue was the cardinal principle of the international society of states enshrined in the Treaty of Amity which had been violated by Vietnam's invasion. Of more practical concern was the issue of the balance or distribution of power attendant on Vietnam's invasion. Vietnam's likely hegemony in Indo-China did not generate consensus within ASEAN, however, because of the more immediate perceived apprehension by some members of the security threat posed by China. That absence of a common strategic perspective within the Association was a source of intra-mural tension during the course of the conflict but a working accommodation was reached around the principle of the non-violation of national sovereignty in the particular interest of Thailand, the self-styled frontline state. In the main, ASEAN was able to display a common diplomatic front in challenging Vietnam's invasion and occupation but its efforts to resolve the Cambodian conflict must not be viewed in isolation.

ASEAN played a prominent diplomatic role during the Cambodian conflict, especially in keeping the issue in the political limelight at the United Nations. In attempting to bring pressure to bear on Vietnam to withdraw, however, it did not act alone but was part of an international division of labour, including China and the United States, which employed complementary military and economic instruments of coercion. There was a period during the late 1980s when ASEAN, under the leadership of Indonesia, which had been accorded an interlocutor role in dealing with Vietnam, held a series of informal meetings in Jakarta in an attempt to find a comprehensive solution to the conflict on a regional basis but without evident success.

In the event, the Cambodian conflict as an international problem was resolved as a consequence of the nature of the end of the Cold War whereby the Soviet Union withdrew material and diplomatic support from Vietnam which was in turn obliged to come to terms with China, its prime adversary. The process of regional peace-making was then taken out of ASEAN's hands and addressed directly and with ultimate success by the Permanent Members of the United Nations Security Council who were responsible for the terms of an accord reached at an international conference in Paris in October 1991. Although ASEAN governments were represented at that conference, and Indonesia's Foreign Minister was a co-chair with that of France, the Association had been confined, in effect, to the diplomatic margins. Moreover, when the United Nations Transitional Authority in Cambodia (UNTAC) assumed responsibility for peace-keeping in that stricken country between 1992 and 1993, ASEAN contingents participated on an individual and not a collective basis.

It is possible to argue that ASEAN took part in the peace process which resolved the Cambodian conflict as an international problem. The conflict was not resolved through an ASEAN peace process, however. As indicated above, such a process has never obtained with reference to a specific issue of regional contention. Process in the ASEAN sense refers only to a mode of dialogue bearing on the climate of regional relations. The Cambodian conflict did facilitate a unique diplomatic prominence for ASEAN, however. The pattern of international alignments during the so-called Second Cold War permitted ASEAN a unique latitude for collective diplomacy over a regional conflict. That latitude has not been sustained since its end and the disintegration of the Soviet Union.

Indeed, with the transformation of that pattern of alignments concurrent with fundamental changes in the regional strategic environment, ASEAN's collective diplomatic voice has no longer counted in quite the same way. That much became evident, for example, from the late 1980s in contention over maritime jurisdiction in the South China Sea. China, for example, a tacit alliance partner of the Association over Cambodia, displayed a studied ambivalence in response to ASEAN's attempt in July 1992 to set out a code of conduct for maritime conflict resolution within a Declaration on the South China Sea which drew heavily on the Treaty of Amity.

China's subsequent lack of regard for the political sensibilities of ASEAN in seizing Mischief Reef in the Spratly Islands close to the Philippines, as revealed in January 1995, demonstrated the limitations of dialogue as an instrument of regional security. It would be stretching a point beyond political reality to suggest that the contentious and complex issues of the South China Sea have been encapsulated by an ASEAN peace process registered, for example, in biennial dialogues between the Association and China. The truth of the matter is that the problem has been put on hold to a degree because China in particular has found it politic to arrest its maritime irredentism because of an interest in conciliating ASEAN within a wider regional context in which critical tensions have obtained with the United States and Japan (Leifer 1997). Moreover, those ASEAN governments in contention among themselves over jurisdiction in the Spratly Islands have yet to attempt any intra-mural negotiation as a way of establishing a common position against external claimants.

Problems of Regional Competence

It has been argued that it would be a category mistake to posit an ASEAN peace process other than in a loose sense whereby a characteristic modality of informal dialogue is employed which may be accommodated within the model of "cooperative security". That said, a peace dividend of a kind may be deemed to follow to the extent that member governments have developed a stake in the sustained viability of the Association as a vehicle for conflict avoidance and management and also as an instrument for collective diplomacy. Since "Confrontation", however, whose termination preceded the advent of ASEAN, and the ad hoc preventive diplomacy over Sabah, there has been an absence of any distinctive Association peace process in respect of any intra-mural dispute. The ASEAN framework has served, however, to permit bilateral dialogue over contentious issues. A concern to avoid such issues from having an adverse effect on corporate cohesion and standing has led to limited examples of a willingness to use the facility of the International Court of Justice whose modalities stand in some contrast to the so-called "ASEAN Way".

In addition to questioning the idea of an ASEAN peace process, it is intended to question an attendant implied notion that ASEAN has been able to exercise a prerogative managerial regional role. Such a role was asserted in the preamble to the founding Declaration in August 1967. It registered the strong influence of Indonesia which favoured so-called regional solutions for regional problems. The balance-of-power implications of that view were tolerated by prospective regional partners suspicious of Indonesia's hegemonic potential because of the importance of establishing the multilateral structure with the Republic's participation. In the event, Indonesia assumed a relatively self-abnegating political role within the Association which has been an important factor in promoting intra-mural harmony and the degree of success of ASEAN. Indeed, Indonesia's unassertive demeanour within ASEAN in the context of prior conflict resolution points up an extremely important difference between regional cooperation in Southeast Asia and, for example, South Asia. In the case of South Asia, the relative regional dominance of India and the absence of central conflict resolution retarded the advent of regional cooperation and also the institutional evolution of SAARC.

A prerogative managerial role for ASEAN was reasserted in November 1971 in a joint declaration whereby the five founding governments committed themselves to secure recognition and respect for Southeast Asia "a Zone of Peace, Freedom and Neutrality". The declared object was to make the region "free from any form or manner of interference by outside Powers". That formulation had been the outcome of an internal debate precipitated by a Malaysian initiative to secure the neutralization of Southeast Asia through the guarantees of the major powers. Indonesia, in particular, had objected to an initiative interpreted as likely to accord virtual policing rights within Southeast Asia to external states which would have denied the prerogative role asserted in ASEAN's founding Declaration. The so-called ZOPFAN formulation registered a consistency of declaratory purpose in approaching the subject of regional order, however. It was reiterated in a Declaration of ASEAN Concord promulgated at the Bali summit, while the Treaty of Amity with its disposition to enlargement indicated an attempt to locate that prerogative role within the wider ambit of geographic Southeast Asia.

In the event, the experience of the Cambodian conflict served to demonstrate the limitations of ASEAN's regional security role. As indicated above, ASEAN's involvement as a diplomatic community was buttressed by a distinctive pattern of international alignments. Its participation in a tacit alliance relationship was in contradiction to the ideal goal of regional order being managed on an autonomous basis as registered both in the founding Declaration and in the ZOPFAN formula. Ultimately, the Cambodian peace process was ordained and managed by the permanent members of the United Nations Security Council with ASEAN confined to the diplomatic margins.

That process was driven by the circumstances of the end of the Cold War pointed up most dramatically by the disintegration of the Soviet Union at the end of 1991. The net effect was to decouple global from regional conflict in Southeast Asia, so terminating a condition of competitive linkage and intervention which had afflicted its locale since the end of the Pacific War in 1945. Indeed, global conflict ceased to exist in the same way as a competitive point of reference for regional conflict. The nature of the end of the Cold War in the Asia-Pacific served also to effect a transformation in strategic environment with which ASEAN was not equipped to cope unaided. A new balance or distribution of power was in train, while ASEAN was essentially an instrument for cooperative security. It was in these changing and uncertain circumstances that ASEAN began to come to terms with its limitations as a security organization of a kind.

At its fourth summit in Singapore in January 1992, a willingness was signalled to address security issues beyond the walls of the Association which led on to the establishment of the ASEAN Regional Forum (ARF) in July 1993. The ARF is also a multilateral security dialogue modelled very much along ASEAN lines, although encompassing greater formality in provision for confidence-building. Its membership of twenty-one states, including all of ASEAN as well as Cambodia, extends through Asia and the Pacific from India to North America (Leifer 1996; Khong 1997).

One of the significant features of the advent of the ARF on an Asia-Pacific-wide basis is that it registered a recognition by ASEAN that it was not competent on its own to provide for regional security in a context in which Southeast and Northeast Asia were subject to a strategic fusion. ASEAN was able to demonstrate a managerial role of a kind in taking the initiative in promoting the geographically more extensive multilateral structure. Moreover, it was able to secure a novel diplomatic centrality within the new enterprise which carried its name as opposed to that of the Asia-Pacific Regional Forum which would have more faithfully reflected the scope of its membership. That membership, however, included all the major regional powers which stood in some contradiction to the more exclusive ZOPFAN formula for regional order. Because of a need to cope with a changing distribution of power pivoting, in particular, on the perceived strategic retreat of the United States and the strategic ascendancy of China, ASEAN took the initiative to extend its model of "cooperative security" beyond its limited regional bounds.

In taking such a step, ASEAN not only acknowledged its limitations in any prerogative role confined to Southeast Asia but also assumed the risk that its corporate identity might be diminished and even subsumed within the wider enterprise. In the event, that risk has not arisen, at least not so far, because it has been in the interest of China, in particular, with Russian and Indian support, to support the sustained diplomatic centrality of ASEAN within the ARF as a way of promoting a greater multi-polarity defined with reference to the post-Cold War global standing of the United States. Nonetheless, ASEAN governments have been conscious of the potential risk entailed in engaging the Association with a geographically wider enterprise subject to the influence of all the major regional powers.

For Every Solution a Problem?

It was that potential risk which encouraged an enlargement of membership to coincide with geographic Southeast Asia as a way of buttressing diplomatic centrality within the ARF. Regional reconciliation played a part also to the extent that enlargement was intended to encapsulate new-found regional partners within a working structure of good citizenship. Vietnam's entry in July 1995 paved the way to realizing the so-called vision of an ASEAN 10 through admitting Cambodia, Laos and Myanmar (Burma). The membership of the latter was a controversial matter, however, because of its military government's gross abuse of human rights. In the event, internal dissension was overcome and the incumbent members closed ranks against Western pressure relying on an established norm of non-interference in domestic affairs as a rationale for Myanmar's entry. To that extent, ASEAN behaved with a certain consistency in placing the priority of regional order before that of internal political order. If Myanmar's membership was addressed with expectation of international controversy, the same was not the case with Cambodia and Laos. In the event, the entry of Laos (with Myanmar) in July 1997 was uneventful. The case of Cambodia was highly controversial within ASEAN and its entry had to be postponed.

A violent coup in Cambodia in early July 1997, whereby Second Prime Minister Hun Sen deposed his main political rival, First Prime Minister, Prince Norodom Ranariddh, came as a matter of acute political embarrassment to ASEAN which had looked forward to completing its membership on the occasion of the thirtieth annual meeting of its foreign ministers. The fragile power-sharing arrangement which had distinguished the government of Cambodia from October 1993 had been endorsed by ASEAN as the legitimate outcome of the UN-supervised peace process in which the Association had a strong stake. Its regional credentials and international standing had been established as a result of its prominent diplomatic role during the Cambodian conflict even though its mythology does not bear close scrutiny. The Cambodian coup, involving impetuous action by Hun Sen, was construed as a political affront by ASEAN members, although not all governments were opposed initially to postponing entry. Entry, however, was linked to a restoration of some form of the political status quo which marked a radical departure from one of the Association's cherished norms; namely, non-interference in others' domestic affairs. Indeed, that very norm had been the basis, in principle, for ASEAN's collective stand against Vietnam's invasion of Cambodia nearly two decades earlier.

ASEAN had upheld the norm of non-interference in the interest of regional peace and stability and to that extent it may be seen as an integral component of its aspiration to a security community. A minor lapse only had occurred in February 1986 during the period of political upheaval in the Philippines which culminated in the flight into exile of the late President Marcos and the inauguration of President Corazon Aquino. It took the form of a tepid collective call to all parties to restore national unity and solidarity. In the case of Cambodia, the very act of postponement indicated a judgement about political change within Cambodia as a candidate member, while a concurrent decision to engage in mediation through a team of three foreign ministers took the Association into unchartered political waters.

Regional peace was not at issue, however. Tensions along common borders did not accompany or follow the coup. ASEAN's declared concern was the matter of constitutional propriety, not a breach of the peace in the conventional sense. As Singapore's Foreign Minister, Professor Jayakumar, pointed out at the time, "Any unconstitutional change of government is cause for concern. Where force is used for an unconstitutional purpose, it is behaviour that ASEAN cannot ignore or condone" (Pereira 1997). In the event, ASEAN failed to shift an obdurate Hun Sen and was obliged to give up an exclusive prerogative role in favour of its mediators cooperating with a major power grouping of so-called "Friends of Cambodia" with Japan assuming the diplomatic lead in an attempt to facilitate "free and fair" elections in which Prince Ranariddh's party could participate. The contrast between the cases of Myanmar and Cambodia was striking in terms of the norms invoked. And one cannot help but suggest that had the coup in Cambodia occurred after its entry into ASEAN, the Myanmar precedent would almost certainly have been invoked to justify non-interference in domestic affairs. In a speech in Sydney in July 1998, Thailand's Foreign Minister, Surin Pitsuwan, advanced the notion of "flexible engagement" intended to permit constructive criticism and advice where the internal practices of one ASEAN country affected another or offended its principles (Alford 1998). Such a proposal, however, stands in direct contradiction to the culture of regional relations which ASEAN has pioneered and which depends on an unqualified respect for the sanctity of national sovereignty.

The latest sorry episode over Cambodia has not done much for the international standing of ASEAN; nor has it indicated that the notion of a peace process is at all relevant to an understanding of what has transpired. Moreover, the intra-ASEAN consensus forged over the coup in Cambodia was very much of a political veneer with Vietnam and Malaysia standing out for some time for its entry together with Laos and Myanmar as agreed in the previous May. Moreover, with internal division and limited competence demonstrated in July 1997, ASEAN's round of troubles had only just begun as a period of regional economic turmoil ensued concurrently which has been well beyond the competence of the Association to address on any exclusive basis. It should be understood that it is not intended to judge the Association by its collective record over the continuing economic adversity because

ASEAN has never been more than a highly embryonic economic community with a commitment to a free-trade area entered into only in January 1992. To do so would be to invoke a false criterion in a misleading way. Ironically, regional economic adversity has not found expression, so far, in any notable rise in intra-regional tensions.

Concurrent with both political crisis in Cambodia and regional economic crisis was a regional ecological crisis whose source may be located in a failure of governance in Indonesia. The fires in the forests of Kalimantan and Sumatra have been symptomatic of the corrupt political economy of the Republic pointed up in the composition of the cabinet formed after President Suharto had been re-elected unopposed to a seventh consecutive term of office in March 1998. Moreover, there has been a clear failure of regional cooperation in addressing the problem of "the haze" caused by the fires which have afflicted a number of ASEAN states, besides Indonesia. In addition, of all the countries in the region which have required the ministrations of the International Monetary Fund, Indonesia has proved to be the most problematic in coming to terms with the structural shortcomings which have made its economic adversity most acute.

At the formation of ASEAN in 1967, the new government of an economically prostrate Indonesia showed itself not only to be contrite for the political and economic delinquencies of its ill-fated predecessor but also willing to take effective measures in regional cooperation in the interest of its international rehabilitation. ASEAN had not been the first initiative in regional cooperation within Southeast Asia. A limited undertaking called the Association of Southeast Asia (ASA) involving Malaya, the Philippines and Thailand had enjoyed a short-lived experience from 1961 but had never attracted international respect because of the absence, in part, of the largest and most populous country in the region. Indonesia's participation and political commitment as a founder member of ASEAN was critical to the Association's viability and degree of success. Indeed, Indonesia served as the political centre of gravity of the Association from the outset. Its economic debilitation and caretaker leadership following the dramatic resignation of President Suharto in May 1998 has left an enlarged and less cohesive ASEAN in a diminished condition.

Despite its tribulations from the middle of 1997, the Association has soldiered on without succumbing to any incidence of intra-mural strife arising from conflicts of economic interest. Moreover, in some circumstances, economic adversity has concentrated political minds and has led to tangible bilateral cooperation, for example, in support of Indonesia's economic recovery, and has also restored a working accommodation between Malaysia and Singapore. What this means is that ASEAN has reverted *faute de mieux* to its original role of containing intra-regional tensions which was its prime purpose in the wake of "Confrontation". It is a moot point, however, whether such a role, however worthy and worthwhile, may be dignified by the term "peace process". Certainly, the ASEAN of the late 1990s is not the ASEAN of the late 1960s. Even without Cambodia, it is a much more diverse and cumbersome entity; while the changes in its scale means that an earlier intimacy in political communication and consultation is no longer possible.

ASEAN continues to have practical utility as a vehicle for confidence-building and trust creation within a region which still encompasses a range of inter-state rivalries and tensions. It has developed a process of multilateral dialogue which is valued for its own sake as a political prophylactic factor against conflict. A distinctive peace process capable of addressing core regional issues, such as the complex overlapping claims to jurisdiction in the South China Sea, for example, is another matter entirely and another category of political activity which brings the discussion back full circle to the point of entry to this subject.

Acknowledgement

This paper was presented at a conference on "Regional Peacemaking in Comparative Perspective" held at the Leonard Davis Institute for International Relations of the Hebrew University of Jerusalem in June 1998.

References

Acharya, Amitav (1993) *A New Regional Order in South-East Asia: ASEAN in the Post-Cold War Era*, London: International Institute for Strategic Studies.
Alford, Peter (1998) 'Thais push radical shift in ASEAN', *The Australian*, 6 July.
Ball, Desmond and Kerr, Pauline (eds) (1996) *Presumptive Engagement: Australia's Asia-Pacific Security Policy in the 1990s*, St Leonards: Allen & Unwin.
Buszynski, Leszek (1997/98) "ASEAN's new challenges", *Pacific Affairs* 70(4).
Ghazali Shafie (1992) "Politics in command", *Far Eastern Economic Review*, 22 October.

Khong Yuen Foong (1997) "Making bricks without straw in the Asia Pacific?" *The Pacific Review* 10(2): 289–300.

Leifer, Michael (1990) *ASEAN and the Security of South-East Asia*, London: Routledge.

—— (1996) *The ASEAN Regional Forum: Extending ASEAN's Model of Regional Security*, London: International Institute of Strategic Studies.

—— (1997) "China in Southeast Asia: interdependence and accommodation", in David S. G. Goodman and Gerald Segal (eds) *China Rising: Nationalism and Interdependence*, London: Routledge.

Moertopo, Ali (1975) "Opening address", in *Regionalism in Southeast Asia*, Jakarta: Centre for Strategic and International Studies.

Pacific Review, The (1995) "Special issue on ASEAN", 8.

Pereira, Brenda (1997) "Asean can't condone use of force: Jaya", *The Straits Times*, 25 July.

Sandu, K. S., Siddique, Sharon, Jeshurun, Chandran, Rajah, Ananda, Tan, Joseph and Thambipillai, Pushpa (1992) *The ASEAN Reader*, Singapore: Institute of Southeast Asian Studies.

11

ASEAN as a Model of
a Security Community?

The question mark at the end of the title of this lecture is not intended to dispute that ASEAN is a "security community". At issue are: what kind of security community is ASEAN?, what are its strengths?, what are its limitations? and what are its prospects?

To give some sense of credentials, this paper is commenced with a story that goes back to the virtual beginnings of ASEAN when there was no such institution as an ASEAN Secretariat; only national secretariats. I had occasion to visit Indonesia's national secretariat and there I had discussions with senior officials who gave me a so-called confidential document containing the minutes of the previous annual meeting of foreign ministers. The most interesting portion of this document dealt with the agenda. It explained that the foreign ministers had decided that their discussions would be restricted to only one day in order that the second day could be given over to a golf competition.

Reprinted in abridged form from Michael Leifer, "ASEAN as a Model of a Security Community?", in *ASEAN in a Changed Regional and International Political Economy*, edited by Hadi Soesastro (Jakarta: Centre for Strategic and International Studies, 1995), pp. 129–42, by permission of the publisher.

Of course, one can easily make fun of that dispensation, and say: "What a characteristic example of distorted priorities". But, in fact, this anecdote is a pointer to what is at the base of the security relationship among ASEAN governments. There exists among them a very close network. They enjoy what I would describe as a "culture of consultation" that arises through a serious and sustained attempt on the part of ministers and officials to get to know each other. And there is no better way than through various kinds of social engagement, especially golf in Southeast Asia. The ASEAN network is now well institutionalized, and provides an important dimension of the regional security relationship.

I should now like to pose some basic questions about the nature of ASEAN. First, I will identify what I think ASEAN is not. Some of you may be familiar with these arguments, but I suggest that they need rehearing in the interest of identifying the strengths and weaknesses of the Association.

The first negative feature that is quite evident, if not well understood outside of Southeast Asia, is that ASEAN is not a "political community". What is meant by political community is a grouping of states which are committed ultimately to overcoming the sovereign divisions between them. Accordingly, the European Community (EC) is not a role model for ASEAN. In the Treaty of Rome of 1957 there is a commitment to merge sovereignties. ASEAN was not established on a treaty basis, although there are treaties among member governments. It was founded through a common declaration with the converse intention of reinforcing sovereignty — that is, strengthening the national entities that made up the membership of the Association. The only, albeit important, point of comparison between ASEAN and the EC is that, from the outset, they were both conceived as means for institutionalizing reconciliation. Those of you who have any familiarity with the history of the evolution of the EC know well that the founders of the European movement believed that if they could lock together the economies of France and Germany, then those two traditional enemies would not be able ever again to go to war against one another.

Correspondingly, a similar view was held around the time of the establishment of ASEAN in 1967. It was believed that if the process of reconciliation which had been taking place after the end of confrontation between Indonesia and Malaysia, Indonesia and Singapore, and to an extent between the Philippines and Malaysia could be put within a framework of constraint, it would serve to deny the opportunity for the resumption of conflictual relationships.

The second negative feature is that ASEAN is not a defence community. It does not replicate NATO which might have been, at one time, an alliance role model. When ASEAN was established, it was not on the basis of any common strategic perspective. There was no shared definition of external threat which could provide a basis for common defence planning and for the collective projection of military power at a distance. It was made quite clear, indeed, quite explicit, at the time of the first summit in Bali, in February 1976, that defence cooperation among ASEAN governments, while perfectly legitimate, should not be brought within the walls of the Association.

Having put to one side two models within which some might try and fit ASEAN — namely, ASEAN as a political community and ASEAN as a defence community — how is it possible to look at the Association in security terms?

I would suggest that ASEAN does provide two alternative models of a security community nonetheless. Indeed, I have more than hinted at one such model in my opening remarks. I think that one can claim quite categorically that ASEAN has become an institutionalized vehicle for intramural conflict avoidance and management.

Without trying to justify avoiding the solution of problems, the record of ASEAN in managing them has been quite an instructive achievement. That practice provides the first model of a security community. We may call it the intramural model.

The second model that one can identify in the practice of ASEAN is that the Association has become a vehicle for the management of regional order through its success in its intra-mural role and also through its corporate action as a diplomatic community. ASEAN through its practice of international relations among member governments has established its own informal zone of peace. That informal zone of peace fulfils the function which its formal counterpart of 1971 was intended to achieve: namely, to deny opportunity for outside powers to fish in troubled waters by actually making those waters less troubled.

Linked to that function, in terms of regional order, has been ASEAN's corporate role as a diplomatic community, that is, being able to come to a common position and to articulate it with great fluency and vigour. And we have observed ASEAN's capability in that regard during the 1980s over the Cambodian conflict, where it employed its regional credentials and helped keep the issue alive. That issue was, in part, about national sovereignty. And national sovereignty is at the very heart of the origins and institutional life of ASEAN.

What I have done so far is to look at the strengths and merits of ASEAN. I have indicated two models which are not relevant and I have then gone on to indicate two alternative models which I do think are appropriate to ASEAN and which quite accurately express what the Association has been up to during the past quarter of a century. Having said that, I want now to indicate why and to what extent these two alternative models are flawed as examples of a security community.

You may have noticed that in the Manila Declaration on the South China Sea, which is a very interesting document, the member governments drew public attention to the existence of the Treaty of Amity and Cooperation (TAC) which was concluded among the five founding governments of ASEAN at the first summit in Bali in February 1976. This treaty was represented as a model for a code of conduct for regional international relations, fitting the intramural model. When the TAC was concluded, it was certainly intended as a code of conduct. If you examine it carefully, you'll see a certain correspondence with parts of the UN Charter. The prime point of the exercise in 1976 — because in addition the Treaty was made open for the accession of non-member states — was to see whether a unified and revolutionary Vietnam might be persuaded to accede to the Treaty. To the exent that Vietnam would attach its signature to a Treaty which embodied a code of conduct for regional international relations based fundamentally on respect of national sovereignty, it would be seen as an act of good faith, and of reassurance. It would be a regional confidence-building measure.

In 1976, however, Vietnam was beset by a sense of triumphalism. Certainly at the Non-Aligned Conference in Colombo in August that year, there was a certain strutting quality about Vietnamese diplomacy. The Treaty was treated with derision and contempt and rejected. It is, of course, a matter of some irony that, having rejected that Treaty in August 1976, Vietnam went to Manila in July 1992 with its diplomatic begging-bowl seeking adherence to it.

So much for the code of conduct in the Treaty but, of course, there is another dimension to it. The TAC also provides for machinery to be established for dispute settlement. There is provision made in it for a so-called high council and there is opportunity to employ in international relations all the established techniques of industrial relations such as good offices, mediation, and conciliation. [D]espite the conclusion of this Treaty and the importance attached to it in February 1976, which was a watershed in terms of the political awakening of the Association, no member government has ever thought fit to invoke any of its terms as a way of trying to settle disputes between member governments.

To the extent, therefore, that ASEAN governments have not had the self-confidence to use their own dispute settlement machinery, which they set up in 1976, then one must conclude that it reflects badly on the credibility of the Association. If they were able to do so, it would certainly strengthen the international standing of the Association and add greater substance to its collective diplomatic voice.

Below is the description on why the second model of a security community is also flawed. The second model is that of ASEAN as a manager of regional order in part through functioning as a diplomatic community. ASEAN's role as a diplomatic community has not only strengths but also limitations. It has been limited by differences of strategic perspective held by different member governments denying the option of projecting collective power. Those differences have been registered in operational attitudes to the symbolic slogan of ASEAN's security priorities, namely the ZOPFAN.

It is important to understand the background of ZOPFAN which was both a negative as well as a positive initiative. It was a negative initiative because it was an attempt to block an earlier one by Malaysia which had put forward a proposal for the neutralization of Southeast Asia. Neutralization is a very precise term which enjoys standing in international law. The Malaysian proposal was that Southeast Asia, not just one country within the region, should be neutralized with guarantees provided by the major powers.

This proposal was not received with any warmth in Jakarta. The reason is quite simple. The Indonesian government, whose Foreign Minister at the time was the late Adam Malik, was very much opposed to outside powers, long regarded as a source of friction in the region, being allocated what amounted to legitimate policing right in this part of the world. Such policing rights would have been accorded if neutralization had gone ahead.

When the meeting of ASEAN foreign ministers took place in November 1971, the Kuala Lumpur Declaration was not issued in the name of the Association but in the name of the five governments. There was a measure of lip-service paid to the principle of neutralization, but the commitment made in the Declaration was to establish Southeast Asia as a Zone of Peace, Freedom, and Neutrality. At the time, no one seemed to know exactly what it meant. Its purpose was to provide an alternative to neutralization.

ZOPFAN is not without significance, however. It represents continuity with the founding ASEAN Declaration of August 1967 — in which security priorities were addressed. That founding Declaration made clear that the governments of Southeast Asia enjoyed the right to assume exclusive responsibility for their own security. That really is the essence of ZOPFAN. It is an ideal, however, and the governments at the time went along with that ideal because they regarded Indonesia, which advocated it, as a moderating influence. Moreover, they did not have great expectations that ZOPFAN would have operational application.

This brings me back to the issue of strategic perspective. Within ASEAN there are clearly at least two alternative approaches to managing regional security. Indonesia, for example, with its distinctive historical experience clearly believes that regional problems have certain peculiar characteristics of their own which are best addressed by regional states. That view has been put in a very sober way. There are, of course, other governments within ASEAN who recall that this view was put in a rather different way under the previous administration. Adam Malik's predecessor as foreign minister, used to call for Asian solutions to Asian problems which some governments translated as meaning that "if there were only Asian solutions for Asian problems, those problems would be solved by the strongest Asians". Accordingly, by implication, we have an alternative approach to managing regional security. That alternative is through access to external sources of countervailing power.

Whatever the imprecisions of the concept of balance of power in academic literature, that concept and practice is as old as the oldest profession. What it means is that if a state faces the prospect of an unacceptable dominance, then it will try to deal with it in one of two ways. One way is through developing its own capability. If that enhanced capability is insufficient, then the alternative is to join it to the capability of others.

These mixed attitudes to regional security are still held within ASEAN and they colour the view of ZOPFAN which has been accepted as the lowest common denominator of priorities because it has failed to demonstrate operational application. But state practice is rather different and, of course, it is conspicuous where the practice differs. For example, the Five Power Defence Arrangements (FPDA) still operate in this part of the world. They were introduced in 1971 as a diluted substitute for the Anglo-Malaysian Defence Agreement. The main point of the exercise was to bring about a greater measure of political accommodation between Singapore and Malaysia through engaging them in military cooperation.

One takes note also of the facilities that are being offered to the American Navy by Singapore, of the so-called commercial facilities which Malaysia seems willing to make available in Lumut and which Indonesia is considering in Surabaya. All these are examples of the fact that the balance of power is alive and seems to be naturally as much a part of Southeast Asia as of Europe. These examples also indicate that the model of ASEAN as a prerogative manager of regional order is flawed because it cannot address balance of power problems on a corporate basis.

On the second aspect of how the security role of ASEAN as a diplomatic community is flawed, there has been much talk after the formal settlement of the Cambodian conflict about ASEAN having lost its way. That talk is somewhat misplaced to the extent that those who know ASEAN also know that Cambodia was very much a source of dissension. One of the great achievements of ASEAN was in maintaining its corporate cohesion despite the dissension caused by trying to cope with the Cambodian conflict.

In the case of Cambodia, ASEAN played a very significant role in the management of regional security with Indonesia taking an important leadership role which culminated in the Paris Conference in October 1991. It is interesting, however, to contrast ASEAN's role as a diplomatic community over the Cambodian conflict with its attempt to act as a diplomatic community over the South China Sea. In Manila in July 1992, its foreign ministers issued a statement on the South China Sea which is regarded as an indication that ASEAN has recovered its collective diplomatic voice. But, the strategic context is now different from that when the Cambodian conflict raged.

In the case of Cambodia, ASEAN employed its regional credentials and made a major international impact. It did so despite reservations about engagement in balance of power politics within a wider coalition, even if that coalition was a tacit alliance and not formally registered.

ASEAN was linked, for example, with the US which employed an economic embargo against Vietnam. It was linked, with some displeasure in Jakarta, also with China which engaged in military action, both direct and indirect, against Vietnam. ASEAN assumed the key diplomatic role within the tacit alliance. All these countries and others joined forces to engage in "a strategy of attrition" that ultimately imposed a breaking strain on Vietnam's society. The irony is that ultimately Vietnam left Cambodia for the same reason that the US left Vietnam.

In the case of the South China Sea, the strategic context is very different. ASEAN is not part of a wider structure of alignments directed against the creeping maritime assertiveness of China. It does not enjoy the kind of linkage which enabled it to play such a prominent role as it did over Cambodia. For example, the US does not seem exercised by the Spratly Islands, which are hardly likely to become an issue in the American presidential elections. The point at issue is that in the case of Cambodia, ASEAN could indirectly play a balance of power role because of its engagement in a tacit alliance. Over the South China Sea, it has no power to deploy because it is neither a defence community nor a party to a countervailing structure of alignments. To that extent, the management of regional order eludes it.

The role of ASEAN and the autonomy of ASEAN as a manager of regional order is limited because of the very nature of the Association. This limitation is pointed up in the new strategic context since the end of the Cold War by the issue of the South China Sea which is very much one of the balance of power which ASEAN is not competent to address in its present form. What has been happening is that countries have been employing military force, partly in display and partly in confrontation, to create facts with which to shape their position in international law. Some would argue that China is not doing anything more than others in trying to create such facts. What has caused such a tremendous disturbance in this part of the world is that China is doing this at a distance of some 800 miles from its mainland. And, if it is successful, it would be in a position to interpose itself in the very mediterranean of Southeast Asia. ASEAN has only limited resources with which to cope with such a menacing forward movement.

As far as ASEAN and its security role is concerned, the Association faces a dilemma. Unless it changes its regional role, that role can only be limited. It cannot be more than an intramural mechanism for avoiding and managing conflict, and a regional mechanism for expressing a collective diplomatic voice. The very nature of the Association, especially the way in which it is conceived in Jakarta, means that change is not only difficult but, also, that the kind of change which might make ASEAN capable of addressing new threats to regional security would in all probability serve as a challenge to its very viability and identity as a security community.

12

Regional Solutions to Regional Problems?

The notion of "regional solutions to regional problems" has a beguiling simplicity and attraction within and beyond Pacific Asia. It implies an authentic "neighbourhood-watch" approach to regional security based on the underlying assumption that resident states are willing and able to act as "their brothers' keepers", and will engage collectively in constructive dispute-settlement.

Of all regional institutions of its kind, ASEAN has come closest to approximating to its declaratory intent. Its ability to impose regional solutions to regional problems is, however, another matter (Leifer 1999). In practice, "regional solutions to regional problems" is more likely to be a slogan serving a particular interest than an operational policy accepted and applied on a regional basis in any common interest.

Reprinted in abridged form from Michael Leifer, "Regional Solutions to Regional Problems?", in *Towards Recovery in Pacific Asia*, edited by Gerald Segal and David S. G. Goodman (London: Routledge, 2000), pp. 108–18, by permission of the publisher and David S. G. Goodman.

Preliminary Misgivings

The notion of regional solutions is inherently flawed because it begs a number of questions, notably those concerning the bases of regional identity and coherence. Even if shaped by geography, such an identity is governed by political considerations. Second, the idea neglects the likely prospect of regional differences over strategic perspective, or in the definition of the prime external threat. A "regional solution" may thus be both a formula for regional order, and a euphemism for regional hegemony. Finally, the notion of regional solutions assumes that a regional association can solve problems, whereas any degree of institutional success in Pacific Asia since the Second World War has depended on conspicuously avoiding a problem-solving role. ASEAN's provision for dispute-settlement, incorporated in its Treaty of Amity and Co-operation (TAC) of 1976, has never been invoked.

In the post-colonial era, "co-operative security" has been the prime vehicle for comprehensive regional approaches to regional problems. However, by its very nature co-operative security avoids solving problems because its working premise is that the ideal conditions for finding regional solutions should be sought with others, as opposed to against them (Lawler 1995; Dewitt 1994). It is thus an alternative to a balance-of-power approach, which involves collective defence co-operation against an extra-mural adversary. Co-operative security seeks to manage relations between states which are neither allies nor adversaries, although both categories could find their way into a co-operative security structure. Co-operative security contrasts with the classical notion of collective security, contained in the Covenant of the League of Nations, which has been represented as the institutionalisation of the balance of power. Both are intra-mural arrangements, but co-operative security is distinct because it forgoes the hallmarks of a collective approach — military or economic sanctions. Instead, its main vehicle is dialogue and suasion. In Pacific Asia, this practice of confidence-building has fallen short of either preventive diplomacy or dispute-settlement. The major institutional examples of co-operative security have so far addressed only the general climate of international relations, rather than specific disputes.

The ASEAN Regional Forum

The ARF does not have a remit for regional problem-solving. It has not in any practical sense addressed any of the three prime sources of conflict within Pacific Asia: Taiwan, the Korean Peninsula and the South China Sea islands. Taiwan is, of course, beyond its remit because China regards the island as a renegade province and would leave the Forum if the ARF took steps to accord Taiwan a status comparable to that which it enjoys in the Asia-Pacific Economic Co-operation (APEC) forum. Bejing does not regard Taiwan's position in APEC as a matter of national sovereignty. Taiwan is addressed at the level of intra-Chinese informal relations, and in the context of Sino-American ties. The issue of the Korean Peninsula has been the subject of pronouncements by the ARF, but the Forum has not been engaged as an institution in any practical attempts to manage the relationship between North and South. While South Korea has been an ARF participant from the outset, the North has yet to be admitted. The Korean Peninsula's problems have been addressed through bilateral dealings between the two Koreas, between Washington and Pyongyang, and in four-party talks involving Beijing and Seoul.

The ARF has been more directly concerned with the issue of the islands of the South China Sea, but has not addressed the core problem of sovereign jurisdiction. It has followed ASEAN's example in seeking to promote a code of conduct for contending states, whereby the threat or use of force would be eschewed in prosecuting claims to islands and maritime space. It has also invoked the UN Convention on the Law of the Sea as an additional source of constraint. The problem of the South China Sea islands has not been addressed directly in the ARF's prime vehicle, the separate Inter-Sessional Support Group on Confidence-Building. The sole attempt to deal directly with the matter has been made through a series of confidence-building workshops initiated by Indonesia. These initiatives have not achieved anything substantive and, given its post-Suharto problems, Indonesia has almost certainly lost enthusiasm for them.

The Myth of Regional Solutions

Implicit in the idea of regional solutions to regional problems is an assumption that not only are there "natural" regions, but also that their resident states will share the same view of the nature of regional problems and how to address them. Attempts at regional solutions in post-colonial Pacific Asia have taken a collective-security approach, but without its economic and military sanctions. Dialogue has been the prime vehicle. This medium has obvious limitations in an ungoverned world, especially where co-operative security has been undertaken in advance of dispute-settlement. This highlights a notable difference between ASEAN, at least at its formation, and the ARF. Although the ARF followed the Cambodian conflict's resolution, it was not intended to promote reconciliation between former antagonists in quite the way that ASEAN's prime purpose was to provide an institutional structure for reconciliation between Indonesia and Malaysia after Confrontation.

Since the mid-1990s, ASEAN has moved away from being the quasi-familial sub-regional grouping which had begun to make its mark from the mid-1970s. Changes in scale and increased diversity can be an impediment to building a culture of co-operation. In ASEAN, an enlarging membership encompassing a variety of strategic perspectives and, in particular, different relationships with China, has had a mixed impact on the prospects of reaching consensus on the South China Sea islands, for example. The scale of the ARF's multilateral undertaking is even larger and more diverse. Consensus-building is consequently more difficult, bearing in mind that the guiding operating principle as set out in the Concept Paper is that the Forum "should progress at a pace comfortable to all participants".

In Pacific Asia, co-operative security cannot address regional problems. The differences in strategic perspective stemming from the scale and diversity of the region's institutional undertakings make co-operative security better suited to confidence-building than to problem-solving. At issue here, most importantly in the ARF, which includes all the major Pacific Asia powers, are adverse interpretations which have arisen over the function of co-operative security.

Adverse Interpretations

At the outset, the ARF was primarily the product of a post-Cold War concern within a Western alignment of states — the ASEAN Post-Ministerial Meeting — about how to cope institutionally with America's apparent strategic retreat from East Asia. The Soviet Union had collapsed, and a rising China would seek to exploit its new-found strategic latitude, with the US withdrawing from its military bases in the Philippines. As a result, the key object was to promote a multilateral structure for security dialogue to complement and support the main bilateral alliances in Pacific Asia established by the US during the Cold War. At the same time, there was an important additional interest in coping with a rising China by engaging it in multilateral dialogue as a way of inducing Beijing to show greater respect for international norms. As the US became more enthusiastic about multilateral dialogue, and also showed its determination to retain a military presence in East Asia, the ARF's founding states became increasingly interested in constructively engaging China in a bid to encourage its "good citizenship".

Both the US and China participated in the ARF from its first working session in 1994. Each, however, had rather different expectations. For the US, Japan and others, the ARF had been envisaged as complementary to bilateral defence co-operation. These bilateral links were reaffirmed in the renewed guidelines for America's Mutual Security Treaty with Japan, and in its new understandings with the Philippines and Singapore over the use of their military facilities (Department of Defense (US) 1998). For China, as well as for countries such as India and Russia, the ARF has been seen as a way of promoting multipolarity, as opposed to multilateralism. This is, of course, code for curbing the unipolar pretensions of the US. In September 1998, for example, Chinese Defence Minister Chi Haotian reportedly indicated that his government was unhappy with the security order in East Asia, in which the US and its allies, especially Japan, played a central role (Richardson 28–29 September 1998). This view can only have been reinforced by America's military action against Iraq in December 1998, which was undertaken without reference to the UN Security Council. This structural tension in the ARF means that the inhibitions on it assuming a problem-solving role are greater than they are for ASEAN. ASEAN has differences of strategic perspective of its own, but within a group of lesser powers without evident competence in a managerial role.

Another, albeit less important, structural tension in the ARF stems from ASEAN's diplomatic centrality within it. The Forum's name derives partly from the acronym for the Association of South-East Asian Nations. Lacking a secretariat, the ARF has been tied inextricably to ASEAN from the outset. ASEAN provides the rotating chair for the ARF's annual working sessions and for meetings of senior officials. It also provides secretarial support and the co-chairs for all inter-sessional activity. As such, it has agenda-setting responsibilities. ASEAN's diplomatic centrality within the ARF is reflected in the Association's self-assumed obligation to be its "prime driving force", which was supported by participating ministers in the Chairman's Statement at the working session in Manila in July 1998.

ASEAN's diplomatic centrality in the ARF had been tolerated by other members of the Western alignment because of a realisation that China would have been reluctant to participate if the formal initiative establishing the Forum had been taken by either Japan or the US, for example. ASEAN's role has, however, prompted resistance, especially among some North-east Asian and Pacific governments, which have judged it incongruous that the Forum's diplomatic centre of gravity should be in South-east Asia, while the main regional problems are in the North-east. The view has been expressed that ASEAN's position should be transitional and that, in time, the ASEAN Regional Forum should give way to an Asian or Asia-Pacific Forum, thereby reflecting the true balance or distribution of regional power. For China, however, the current arrangement is preferable as an expression of post-Cold War multipolarity. In this, it is supported by Russia and, after its entry into the ARF in 1996, by India. Despite ASEAN's evident institutional failings — or indeed perhaps because of them — there has been no attempt to revise either the ARF's title or its format. Neither is, however, conducive to problem-solving.

Prospects

Neither ASEAN nor the ARF is a vehicle for solving regional problems. Among its participants, the ARF is viewed as a useful and relatively cost-free way of providing additional points of diplomatic contact and cushioning, and even as a way of securing a possibly progressive conformity to international norms. Judgement on ASEAN, however, has become more reserved — even sceptical — as the Association's spirit of co-operation seems to have drained away with enlargement, economic adversity and an upsurge of bilateral tensions. The issue of Cambodia's membership exposed ASEAN's disarray, in ironic contrast to the solidarity displayed by a smaller membership over the Cambodian conflict in the 1980s.

Given the region's economic crisis, ASEAN has been unable to improve the climate of regional relations. The ARF would seem to have been more successful, but not necessarily because of the development of a collegial culture of co-operation. A more likely explanation is that the ARF has reflected the condition of the more important regional relationships and, in particular, that between the US and China. However chequered, Sino-American relations have achieved some working accommodation. This cannot, however, be taken for granted, as shown by China's principled objection to NATO action in the Balkans in 1999, and by its vociferous opposition to the prospect of theatre missile defence in Pacific Asia.

Both ASEAN and the ARF are still a long way from achieving regional solutions for regional problems — which is, in any case, more a myth than a valid aspiration. According to the Chairman's Statement after the annual working session of the ARF in July 1997: "The Ministers agreed that the evolutionary approach to the development of the ARF process and the practice of taking decisions by consensus shall be maintained, taking into consideration the interests of all ARF participants and, at the same time, demonstrating the continued consolidation of the process through increased activities in relevant areas." Such a statement has little, if anything, to do with finding "regional solutions to regional problems". This remains as elusive a notion as ever, not least in Pacific Asia.

References

Dewitt, D. (1994). "Common, Comprehensive and Cooperative Security", *Pacific Review* 7(1).

Lawler, P. (1995) "The Core Assumptions and Presumptions of 'Cooperative Security'", in S. Lawson (ed.) *The New Agenda for Global Security: Cooperating for Peace and Beyond*, St Leonards: Allen & Unwin.

Leifer, M. (1999) "The ASEAN Peace Process: A Category Mistake", *Pacific Review* 11(1).

Richardson, M. (28–29 September 1998) "Gently, China Flexes Strategic Muscles in Asia", *International Herald Tribune*.

13

Truth about the Balance of Power

In academic and political debate on regional security with Southeast Asia, a dismissive attitude has arisen towards the concept and practice of balance of power. The conventional wisdom is that balance of power is a mechanical contrivance of European provenance which is not suitable for regional circumstances, especially in the wake of the Cold War. Indeed, the criticism goes further in suggesting that indulgence in the balance of power would be a self-affliction best confined to the dust-bin of history along with colonialism because it would provoke confrontation and not facilitate reconciliation.

Part of the difficulty in coming to terms with the concept of balance of power is its intrinsic ambiguity. Many tomes have been written exploring and explaining the different meanings of the concept as applied in a variety of historical circumstances. A short-cut to understanding the concept is to simplify its meanings into only two kinds.

Reprinted from Michael Leifer, "Truth about the Balance of Power", in *The Evolving Pacific Power Structure*, edited by Derek de Cunha (Singapore: Institute of Southeast Asian Studies, 1996), pp. 47–51, by permission of the publisher.

One meaning of balance of power is a description of a relationship between two or more states defined in terms of their respective capabilities. Balance of power in this sense is best understood as distribution of power and, of course, marked changes in such a distribution can have disturbing consequences as states which feel disadvantaged and vulnerable may take steps to redress any adverse change in capabilities between themselves and potential adversaries. This meaning of balance of power, which is akin to the notion of a bank balance, provides a direct link to the second, which is best explained as a policy rather than a situation. Such a policy is best understood as being directed at preventing the establishment of undue dominance by one or more states. Balance of power in this sense is undertaken with the objective of denying the emergence of a hegemonial state able to dictate the terms of regional order through forming a countervailing coalition of states. The normal name for such a coalition is an alliance defined in terms of military purpose and, traditionally, the instrument of the balance has been war.

The experience of alliance in Southeast Asia has been mixed but, where it has existed, a critical precondition has been necessary; namely, a common definition of external threat on the part of prospective alliance partners. Such a common definition has never been obtained among the members of ASEAN who have approached the management of security issues through alternative political means with some success. A reluctance to contemplate alliance has been based also on an aversion to the very concept and practice which is believed to be alien to and incompatible with non-aligned aspirations.

In point of fact, however, ASEAN's practice has contained an evident dimension of balance of power from the outset. ASEAN was established in an attempt to promote regional reconciliation within an institutional framework of multilateral constraint. "Confrontation" had revealed Indonesia's hegemonial propensities under President Sukarno. His successor, President Suharto, well understood that one practical way of restoring both regional confidence and stability would be to lock Indonesia into a structure of regional partnership which would be seen to disavow hegemonial pretensions. It was not an exercise in the balance of power in the classical sense through alliance formation but ASEAN had an evident balance of power purpose.

In the wake of the Cold War, ASEAN has taken the formal initiative to apply its own model for regional security on a wider Asia-Pacific basis. The modalities of the embryonic ASEAN Regional Forum (ARF) have been drawn in important part from ASEAN's experience at avoiding and managing conflict. In this undertaking, however, balance of power has not been discarded.

When the senior officials of ASEAN and its dialogue partners convened at a seminal meeting in Singapore in May 1993 which led on to the ARF, balance of power as well as the ASEAN model were very much in mind with China identified as a potential regional hegemon. In that context, it was pointed out that "the continuing presence of the United States together with stable relationships among the United States, Japan, and China and other states of the region would contribute to regional stability."

The object of the exercise was not necessarily to contain China. Indeed, it was hoped that the nexus of economic incentive would serve to bring about the constructive engagement which has become part of regional rhetoric. Nonetheless, the very attempt to lock China into a network of constraining multilateral arrangements underpinned hopefully by a sustained and viable American military presence would seem to serve the purpose of the balance of power by means other than alliance.

That commitment and presence is not to be taken on trust, as pointed out by American academic Donald Weatherbee. For that reason, in part, regional states which can afford it have begun unilaterally to engage in defence force modernization, which would seem to be yet another version of balance of power practice.

The balance of power may have become identified historically with a particular phase of European experience. Its underlying tenets have a universal application, however, irrespective of the manner in which they are expressed and applied. For that reason, it is possible to conclude that the balance of power is alive and well in Southeast Asia, albeit confined to the closet.

14

The Merits of Multilateralism

The ASEAN Regional Forum is an embryonic venture in multilateralism within a region that exists more as a category of convenience than as a coherent framework for inter-governmental cooperation. The ARF was established at a critical historical juncture as one global pattern of power gave way to another, which has yet to be clearly defined. The ARF is unique in that the formal initiative and organisational responsibility for its creation were assumed by a grouping of lesser states — ASEAN — rather than by the major regional powers. These major powers, for the time being, appear tolerant of the present arrangement which has not yet come into serious conflict with their individual interests.

Indeed, the prime object of the ARF, which ASEAN has sought to base on its own distinctive practice and experience, has been to promote stable relationships between those major powers in the general

Reprinted in abridged form from Michael Leifer, *The ASEAN Regional Forum*, Adelphi Paper No. 302 (Oxford: Oxford University Press for the International Institute for Strategic Studies, 1996), pp. 53–60, by permission of the publisher.

regional interest. A remarkable economic dynamism, from which all states wish to benefit further and which has been perceived positively as a hostage to the political fortunes of security dialogue and interdependence, has underpinned the new multilateralism.

The ARF, however, can be seen as an imperfect diplomatic instrument for achieving regional security goals in that it seeks to address the problem of power which arises from the anarchical nature of international society without provision for either collective defence or conventional collective security. Moreover, the degree of cooperative association the ARF has attained so far has not reduced military competition in the form of regional arms procurements. Arms procurements by a number of regional states, made possible by their astounding rates of economic growth, demonstrate the extent to which governments are unwilling to rely solely on diplomatic instruments to protect their vital interests.[1] That said, however, there is a conspicuous absence of a regional constituency for moving beyond individual force modernisation towards multilateral defence cooperation. This absence stems from a number of factors, but above all from the judgement that the traditional instrument of balance of power, if expressed in a new multilateral form, is more likely to provoke than to protect, particularly regarding China.

The problem for which the ARF is an ambitious and unproven solution is hardly new in international relations. It is that of a changing balance or distribution of power and, in particular, of the emergence of a rising power with a revisionist agenda. In the past, the emergence of such powers has invariably been associated with periods of great international turbulence, such as Asia-Pacific during the 1930s and early 1940s when Japan sought its place in the sun through militarism. The rising power in Asia-Pacific as the twenty-first century approaches is China, whose leaders harbour a historical resentment of national humiliations inflicted on their weakened state by a rapacious West. China's successful post-Cold War economic reforms have provided it with a historic opportunity to realise a sense of national destiny, which many regional states view with apprehension. The analogy with Japan does not apply in quite the same way, however, because China has not been excluded from the international economy. On the contrary, it has modernised its economy by opening up to the capitalist world, including that of the Asia-Pacific, which has reciprocated by opening up to China. In addition, there are no longer any similar revisionist states of global significance with which China could ally in challenging world order, as Japan did with Nazi Germany.

The United States has been at serious odds with China, particularly after the 1989 Tiananmen Square massacre, over human rights, arms and arms-technology transfers, trade and intellectual property issues and, most recently, over the highly contentious issue of Taiwan. The US has opted, however, for a policy of comprehensive yet conditional engagement, even if to Beijing that phrase is a euphemism for a new containment.[2] Despite heated differences over Taiwan, China is not being excluded from access to natural resources, capital, technology and markets, as was Japan in the 1930s. This was a critical factor in precipitating the Pacific War in 1941. Moreover, the United States no longer has the hegemonic power to interpose itself between China and interested and eager trading and investment partners in East Asia.

East Asia's governments have no interest in seeing the increasingly integrated pattern of trade and investment in the region disrupted as a consequence of their involvement in a military coalition to contain China. Such a policy is widely regarded not only as impractical on military grounds, but also as potentially highly provocative and destabilising. That judgement has not, however, been made by taking China's assurances of peaceful and good regional intent at face value. It is based instead on highly pragmatic reasoning about what is possible in the current uncertain circumstances in which the regional distribution of power continues to change and in which the region's states have less than full confidence in the ability of the US to sustain a countervailing role to prevent territorial change by force.[3]

Although the ARF is a highly imperfect diplomatic instrument for coping with the new and uncertain security context, there is no practical multilateral alternative available, at least for the time being. ASEAN's limited experience has produced only mild optimism that it may be able to transpose its model for managing regional security onto a wider regional plane with some stabilising effect. ASEAN has never sought to resolve a regional conflict. Doing so would have tested its very viability because member governments would have been obliged to take sides in the competing cases and causes of their regional partners. Similarly, the ARF has not been set up to address specific conflicts. If it had been, it is most unlikely that China would have participated. Indeed, engaging China through the ARF has been

ASEAN's strongest card in sustaining its central diplomatic role. The undeclared aim of the ARF is to defuse and control regional tensions by generating and sustaining a network of dialogues within the overarching framework of its annual meetings, while the nexus of economic incentive works on governments irrevocably committed to market-based economic development.

The issue of the South China Sea disputes is a test case for the ARF's viability and efficacy to the extent that the Beijing government understands that any further Chinese assertiveness there would damage its relationship with ASEAN in particular, which it has come to regard as helpful over its other more pressing problems, especially Taiwan. This does not mean that China has given up its claims to sovereignty in the Sea, which it reiterates as indisputable and irrefutable, but it does now appear willing to tolerate the status quo, however unpalatable this is in nationalist terms.

What has been the extent up to now of the ARF's contribution in promoting "a predictable and constructive pattern of relationships in the Asia-Pacific"? The answer at this juncture can only be a marginal one. Annual meetings of 21 and possibly more foreign ministers, and a limited number of inter-sessional activities on safe subjects, hardly constitute a new architecture for Asia-Pacific security. Such a multilateral structure is precluded from addressing the Taiwan issue as any attempt to do so in current circumstances would oblige China to withdraw from the ARF. The Forum has sought to address the Korean conflict, but has done little more than engage in well-meaning but bland comment. It has assumed no responsibility whatsoever for managing nuclear proliferation on the peninsula. The ARF has also only touched the surface of arms control, without any substantive progress on the issue of arms registers, either universal or regional, or on the issue of defence white paper.[4] The ARF, as an annual occasion, appears to have had some moderating influence on China's assertiveness in the South China Sea, but not necessarily through any intrinsic institutional qualities, so far. China has been willing to put its assertiveness on hold to engage in a united front strategy with ASEAN as a tacit diplomatic partner to resist pressures from the US and Japan.

Such tactical constraint by China is recognised for what it is worth within the rest of the Asia-Pacific, as is Beijing's unwillingness to compromise on matters of sovereignty during a transition in political leadership. This is also linked to the emotive nationalist issue of reunification with Taiwan. Although China has trumpeted the underlying economic advantages of a stable regional order, Singapore's Senior Minister, Lee Kuan Yew, received a frosty response in March 1996 when he attempted to point out to Beijing the possible costs of China's military intimidation in the Taiwan Strait. In the meantime, Chinese diplomats have shown themselves to be adept at controlling the pace of the ARF's progress as a vehicle for cooperative security. This may explain China's willingness to co-chair the next ISG on confidence-building measures.

China, as the rising regional power, has attracted the most attention in exploring the merits of the new-found multilateralism in Asia-Pacific, and in the degree to which that multilateralism may be capable of inducting members into the canons of good regional citizenship. Tensions generated by China's assertiveness are not the only ones in the region, however. For example, the diplomatic row between South Korea and Japan in February 1996 over sovereignty of the Dakto or Takeshima islets in waters halfway between the two states exposed an underlying embittered relationship that was not mitigated by the ARF which, coincidentally, had held a meeting on confidence-building in Tokyo only the month before.

The ARF as an expression of cooperative security is based on a model that has succeeded within South-east Asia — up to a point — because it has avoided addressing acute problems of regional security directly. To the extent that the ARF has been created in ASEAN's image, little more may be expected of it, certainly in its formative phase. On the positive side, the embryonic multilateral structure is unique to the Asia-Pacific and is also remarkable in how much it has accomplished institutionally in such a short space of time. Moreover, it is a convenient point of diplomatic contact for the major Asia-Pacific powers.

Yet how suitable is the ARF to undertake such a regional diplomatic role? In a world without common government, multilateral diplomacy, even when underpinned by economic advantage, suffers inevitably from intrinsic defects. In some circumstances, it may be a valuable adjunct to the workings of the balance of power in helping to deny dominance to a rising regional power with hegemonic potential. In the presence of a powerful revisionist state and in the absence of such a viable balance, expressed as a stable distribution of power, diplomacy, especially of the multilateral variety, can be very weak. Multilateral mechanisms like the ARF may work well in the presence of such a balance, but are not inherently capable of creating one.

Indeed, the prerequisite for a successful ARF may well be the prior existence of a stable balance of power. The central issue in the case of the ARF is whether, in addition to diplomatic encouragement for a culture of cooperation driven partly by economic interdependence, the region shows the makings of a stable, supporting balance or distribution of power that would allow the multilateral venture to proceed in circumstances of some predictability. The ARF's structural problem is that its viability seems to depend on the prior existence of a stable balance, but it is not really in a position to create it.[5]

The balance of power in the Asia-Pacific has been left primarily to the United States to uphold. This is still regarded in the region as somewhat problematic, despite assurances from the Pentagon and the resolve demonstrated by President Clinton and his advisers in responding to China's act of military intimidation against Taiwan in March 1996.[6] That military intimidation highlighted the utility of the US–Japanese security relationship, reaffirmed when Clinton visited Tokyo in April 1996, as well as the commitment to retain 100,000 US troops in East Asia. However, the collateral decision to return ten military installations on Okinawa to Japanese jurisdiction in response to popular opposition to the US military presence there has also raised regional concerns about whether "America has the stamina to maintain the balance of power in the region."[7] This concern was also reinforced by the agreement between President Clinton and Prime Minister Ryutaro Hashimoto that Japan's regional role under the security treaty should be expanded, as well as apprehension over what form that role might take.[8] Underlying uncertainty about the longer-term position of the US has encouraged regional states to make individual security provision in the form of arms procurements which threaten to start a competitive interactive trend. Uncertainty over US intentions is also linked to the ARF's ability to make practical progress in promoting concrete confidence-building measures which could help to sustain Washington's interest in the region. A proposal for a new forum for Asia-Pacific defence ministers made by US Secretary of Defense William Perry in late May 1996 suggests some frustration on Washington's part with the ARF process.

The ARF is an instrument of regional security policy, but no state would be willing to rely for its security on the Forum's ministrations alone. The ARF should be seen as serving a one-dimensional purpose only for regional states facing an uncertain security environment, but not necessarily an immediate external threat. To that extent, the ARF is a complementary diplomatic activity of the same nature as ASEAN and subject to the very same intrinsic limitations. Its initial record would not seem to support the tentative conclusion that "what is evolving might be a distinct [sic] form of multilateralism linked to alternative understandings of the roots of conflict and ways to manage them".[9] The ARF is certainly distinctive in its novelty and scope within the Asia-Pacific. But its promising performance has not so far demonstrated any alternative modes of conflict management, based on so-called alternative understandings of the roots of conflict, that reveal a distinctive way of accomplishing a stable regional order as pioneered by ASEAN.

To question whether the ARF is actually capable of solving problems and conflicts would be to make a category mistake. The ARF's limited objective is to improve the climate in which regional relations take place in the hope that bilateral and multilateral problems may be easier to manage. This, up to a point, has been ASEAN's experience and achievement.[10] The ARF's workings are informed knowingly or not by neo-functionalist assumptions that an incremental linear process of dialogue can produce a qualitative improvement in political relationships along the lines of the ASEAN experience. More consciously, it has been suggested that cultural tradition in the Asia-Pacific can facilitate greater regional security cooperation.[11] The fact of the matter, however, is that the ARF is an embryonic, one-dimensional approach to regional security among states of considerable cultural and political diversity and thus suffers from the natural shortcomings of such an undertaking. To interpret its role in terms of a new paradigm in international relations would be the height of intellectual naivety. It is more realistic to regard the Forum as a modest contribution to a viable balance or distribution of power within the Asia-Pacific by other than traditional means. Those means are limited, however, and the multilateral undertaking faces the same order of difficulty as the biblical Hebrew slaves in Egypt who were obliged to make bricks without straw. A constituency for any alternative form of security cooperation does not exist in the Asia-Pacific. But that does not change the nature of the ASEAN Regional Forum or its degree of relevance for coping with post-Cold War problems of regional security. The issue of relevance is reinforced by ASEAN's insistence on retaining the central diplomatic role in the ARF which confuses power and responsibility and generates frustration among North-east Asian and Pacific participants.

For the time being, it may be said on behalf of the ARF that bricks made without straw are better than no bricks at all. In the absence of any alternative set of multilateral security arrangements for the Asia-Pacific, the ARF provides a helpful point of diplomatic contact and dialogue for the region's major powers on which the prospects for stability and order depend. The continuing interest and participation of the United States, Japan and China, albeit for mixed reasons, sustain the momentum and constructive course of multilateralism. The challenge facing the ASEAN Regional Forum is how to develop and deepen the dialogue process among its expanding membership so that ASEAN's model and experience as a vehicle for conflict avoidance and management may be replicated with some tangible effect in the interest of a wider regional order.

Notes

1. See Desmond Ball, "Arms and Affluence: Military Acquisitions in the Asia-Pacific Region", *International Security,* vol. 18, no. 3, Winter 1993–94, and Panitan Wattanayagorn and Desmond Ball, "A Regional Arms Race?", *The Journal of Strategic Studies,* vol. 18, no. 3, September 1995.

2. For a representative account of US policy, see Winston Lord, "US Policy Toward East Asia and the Pacific, Statement before the Subcommittee on Asia and the Pacific Affairs of the House International Relations Committee, Washington DC, 9 February 1995", *US Department of State Dispatch,* vol. 5, no. 8, 27 February 1995, and *A National Security Strategy of Engagement and Enlargement* (Washington DC: The White House, February 1966), pp. 39–41. See also, James Shinn (ed.), *Weaving the Net: Conditional Engagement with China* (New York: Council on Foreign Relations Press, 1996).

3. For a discussion of US policy in Asia-Pacific based on that judgement, see Douglas T. Stuart and William T. Tow, *A US Strategy for the Asia-Pacific,* Adelphi Paper 299 (Oxford: Oxford University Press for the IISS, 1995), and also Donald Weatherbee, "US Strategic Distancing", *Trends,* no. 64, Institute of Southeast Asian Studies, Singapore, 30–31 December 1995.

4. *China: Arms Control and Disarmament,* Information Office of the State Council of the People's Republic of China, Beijing, November 1995, is primarily a propaganda exercise and not a model of what the ARF considered a defence white paper.

5. See the interesting discussion in Paul Dibb, *Towards a New Balance of Power in Asia*, Adelphi Paper 295 (Oxford: Oxford University Press for the IISS, 1995).
6. See, for example, *United States Security Strategy for the East Asia-Pacific Region*, Department of Defense, Office of International Security Affairs, Washington DC, February 1995.
7. Michael Richardson, "Asians Query US Staying Power", *International Herald Tribune*, 13–14 April 1996 and Nigel Holloway and Sebastian Moffett, "Cracks in the Armour", *Far Eastern Economic Review*, 2 May 1996.
8. *International Herald Tribune*, 14 May 1996.
9. See Paul Evans, "The Prospects for Multilateral Security Cooperation in the Asia-Pacific Region", *The Journal of Strategic Studies*, vol. 18, no. 3, September 1995, p. 214.
10. See the arguments by Peter Ho in "The ASEAN Regional Forum: The Way Forward", in Veraphol and Phenning (eds.), *ASEAN–UN Cooperation in Preventive Diplomacy*.
11. Desmond Ball, "Strategic Culture in the Asia-Pacific Region", *Security Studies*, vol. 3, no. 1, Autumn 1993.

15

The Limits to
ASEAN's Expanding Role

Over the past three decades, the Association of Southeast Asian Nations (ASEAN) has assumed a constructive security role in promoting regional order which was not anticipated at its formation in Bangkok in August 1967. Its greatest achievements have been in the realm of intra-mural confidence-building and conflict management and also in acting as a diplomatic community able up to a point to assert a prerogative position on regional security issues. Its model of regional security fits best within the theoretical paradigm known as "common or cooperative security", which may be regarded as both an alternative and as a complement to balance of power practice.[1]

That construct was not consciously in the minds of ASEAN's founding fathers when they contemplated a fresh start in regional co-operation. Moreover, that model has evident limitations in its practical application which have been exposed during the institutional experience of the Association. It also poses serious problems by way of managing consensus for an expanding and more diverse membership

This hitherto unpublished paper was originally written in mid-1997 in connection with an ISEAS commemoration of ASEAN's 30th anniversary.

in the revised strategic context in Asia-Pacific attendant on the end of the Cold War. Those problems have been compounded further since the onset of regional economic adversity from mid-1997. Nonetheless, that model, based on attaining security through co-operation with others as opposed to against others, continues to inform the workings of ASEAN in the absence of a constituency for any alternative collective way of addressing problems of regional order. Indeed, it has been extended geographically within a wider Asia-Pacific regional ambit in order to enable ASEAN to cope with security problems which it is incapable of addressing unaided.

ASEAN has now reached a turning point in the expansion of its collective role as a result of shortcomings exposed in the face of challenges to its institutional competence. An inability to cope with regional economic adversity, with regional environmental pollution with its source in Indonesia and also with the aftermath of a coup in Cambodia in July 1997, which provoked a postpone-ment of its membership, have damaged the standing and credibility of the Association. ASEAN's predicament has been compounded by the way in which economic crisis has overtaken Indonesia, in particular, which has been the pivotal state of the Association from the outset.

Indonesia's prostrate condition points to the most serious failure of ASEAN and to which criteria are most appropriate in passing judgement on the performance of the Association. To be fair, ASEAN was never in a position to address a regional economic crisis of major proportions, while the coup in Cambodia took it into the unchartered waters of intervening in the domestic affairs of a regional state. The issue of environmental pollution, however, was more directly an intra-ASEAN matter because it occurred within the territorial domain of its most important member. Indonesia's failure of governance has been compounded by a failure to show one iota of so-called ASEAN spirit in regional co-operation to resolve the matter. In the light of such failure, at issue for the Association is how to sustain a coherent institutional identity and security role while engaged now within a wider Asia-Pacific structure of multilateral dialogue which has the potential both to diminish and even to absorb ASEAN as a distinct and distinctive regional entity. Indeed, that prospect is likely to increase with an evident diminution of the international standing of the Association.

The Genesis and Evolution of a Security Model

The formation of ASEAN in August 1967 was driven by multiple factors, including a concern about the military staying power of the United States then embroiled in Vietnam.[2] The prime consideration, however, was to locate intra-regional reconciliation, after Indonesia had abandoned Confrontation, within an institutionalized structure of relations which would serve to sustain its momentum to mutual advantage. Although the prior and ill-fated Association of Southeast Asia (ASA), set up by Malaya, the Philippines, and Thailand, provided a model of a kind, it had never enjoyed regional standing because of the absence from its ranks of Indonesia, the largest and most populous regional state. After Confrontation, a fresh start was required by the new government in Jakarta. Indeed, it was the enthusiastic participation of Indonesia in ASEAN from the outset, which made the critical difference to the Association's viability and evolution.

Indonesia's need to demonstrate its pacific bona fides in the interest of its international rehabilitation and economic reconstruction led the potential regional hegemon to assume a self-abnegating political role which served over time to generate confidence and trust among its regional partners. Indonesia's willingness, in the main, not to deviate from that role has been critical to ASEAN's degree of success, so far. Moreover, the related imperative of regional reconciliation as a basis for Indonesia's regional role has underpinned the strong measure of intra-mural cohesion exhibited by ASEAN, despite a range of continuing differences and tensions among the member states. Reconciliation has marked every stage in the subsequent enlargement of ASEAN beginning with Brunei's adherence on independence in January 1984 through to the historic act manifested with Vietnam's entry in July 1995. It was also in mind in the abortive attempt to include the remaining three states of geographic Southeast Asia in July 1997. In the event, only Myanmar (Burma) and Laos joined on that occasion; the membership of Cambodia was postponed because of a violent coup in Phnom Penh earlier in the month which overturned a coalition government which had been endorsed by ASEAN on its formation in October 1993. ASEAN's response to that coup marked a departure of a kind from corporate convention which will be addressed below.

ASEAN was established with regional security uppermost in mind, albeit not openly declared because of a common interest in not provoking hostility to its inauguration. If read on its own, however, the founding Declaration which stresses economic and cultural co-operation gives a misleading impression of primary purpose. In practice, the five founding governments were drawn together by a recognition of the self-defeating nature of their past contentions. Their new regional partnership was intended to provide a vehicle for consolidating reconciliation and avoiding and containing future conflict. In its absence, fragile political systems would be more readily managed through economic development, so mitigating a shared vulnerability. The underlying practical purpose of ASEAN was well expressed by Thailand's Foreign Minister, Thanat Khoman, who had begun to employ the term "collective political defence" in searching for an alternative policy to that of doubtful reliance on the United States.[3] ASEAN represented an attempt to seek security through an undeclared political co-operation and, in that respect, served as an embryonic institutional model of common or co-operative security long before those concepts had entered into the discourse of the discipline of International Relations.

The initial purpose of ASEAN is also likely to be misunderstood if the founding Declaration is read together with its preamble. The preamble asserted a shared "primary responsibility for strengthening the economic and social stability of the region" and a determination "to ensure their (countries) stability and security from external interference in any form and manifestation". Such a grand vision of regional order, which primarily reflected Indonesian thinking, was not shared within the founding membership because of a concern by some governments about its likely use to establish a local hegemony. That vision was accepted nominally and only grudgingly at the time in the interest of institutionalized reconciliation and also because it did not seem a practical proposition involving any derogation of national interests.

Nonetheless, that contested vision did provide a basis for asserting an expanding role on the part of ASEAN. It was more openly articulated in Kuala Lumpur in November 1971 with the promulgation by the Association's foreign ministers of a collective commitment "to secure the recognition of, and respect for, South East Asia as a Zone of Peace, Freedom and Neutrality, free from any form or manner of interference by outside Powers".[4] At the time, that initiative constituted the joint undertaking of the five member governments only and not ASEAN per se. Moreover, it did not proscribe any existing security arrangements with extra-regional powers with which the Philippines, Malaysia, Singapore, and Thailand were associated. Indeed, only Indonesia was then outside of any such arrangements.

The ZOPFAN initiative had, in fact, been a collective reaction to an earlier Malaysian proposal for the neutralization of Southeast Asia to be guaranteed by the major powers which had been put forward at the summit of non-aligned states in Lusaka in September 1970. The proposal had been inspired by a felt need in Kuala Lumpur to reach an accommodation with China in the wake of serious inter-communal violence in Malaysia in the previous year. That proposal had attracted Indonesia's ire, in particular, because it appeared to accord virtual policing rights in the region to external powers, including the People's Republic of China whose assumption of a seat at the United Nations in the previous October had precipitated the Kuala Lumpur meeting. Significantly, the ASEAN governments had not adopted a common position on the issue of China's representation.

Although the ZOPFAN Declaration endorsed, in principle, the desirability of neutralization for Southeast Asia, it allocated the primary responsibility for managing regional order to regional states and excluded the guarantor role of the major powers which had been a central feature of Malaysia's proposal.[5] Irrespective of the misgivings of some member-governments about the implications of the ZOPFAN concept for the nature of the regional balance or distribution of power, it did represent a declaratory assertion of a prerogative regional role which was subsequently reiterated in the Declaration of ASEAN Concord which was one of two key documents arising from the first meeting of the Association's heads of government held in Bali in February 1976. That document enunciated objectives and principles which the Association would take into account "in the pursuit of political stability". As such, it served to register a stage in the expansion of ASEAN's role beyond the anodyne aims of its founding document. It was significant also for the Association's institutional development. Meetings of senior officials (SOM) were introduced on a regular basis to address the implementation of ZOPFAN.

The assertion of a regional role was easier to articulate than to undertake, however. The early chequered history of ASEAN before the Bali summit does not require rehearsing, except to note that the viability of the Association was severely tested by an acute revival of tensions between Malaysia and the Philippines in the late 1960s over the latter's claim to Sabah. Moreover, relations between Singapore and

Malaysia and between Singapore and Indonesia were also beset by a recurrent rancour. ASEAN survived its early tribulations through the progressive realization of the utility of membership in generating mutual respect for national sovereignty. An attendant fuller allocation of national resources for internal development served in turn to reinforce mutual confidence in managing intra-mural relations. It was that synergy which Indonesia's President Suharto had in mind when he recommended the concept of "national resilience" with its attendant counterpart of "regional resilience" to his regional partners. The underlying premise was an assumed indivisible and positive relationship between economic development and security on both an individual state and collective inter-state basis. That premise was reiterated in the Declaration of ASEAN Concord which maintained that "the stability of each member state and of the ASEAN region is an essential contribution to international peace and security. Each member state resolves to eliminate threats posed by subversion to its stability, thus strengthening national and regional resilience".

In the event, the synergy generated served to create a regional zone of peace of a kind which has proved attractive to foreign investors whose engagement has been critical to some astounding regional economic achievements up to the middle of 1997 and also to underpinning regional co-operation. ASEAN was assisted in its institutional evolution also by the small scale of the enterprise among governments of corresponding political outlooks. The development of close personal relations among both officials and ministers generated a corporate culture of close consultation and co-operation. The emergence of that quasi-familial culture was instrumental to the process of intra-mural confidence-building and served, in turn, to facilitate the role of diplomatic community which ASEAN assumed with some effect from the end of its first decade.

Overcoming Embattlement

ASEAN began to assume a growing institutional coherence from the mid-1970s in response to the dramatic successes of revolutionary communism in Indochina. In a display of collective nerve intended to demonstrate that the member states were not candidate "dominos", a first meeting of heads of government was convened in Bali in February 1976 at which it was decided to establish a permanent secretariat based in Jakarta. That meeting was notable for the assertion of a corporate political identity registered through the Declaration of ASEAN Concord considered above but which stopped short formally of declaring an explicit security role. Defence co-operation was sanctioned among members on a bilateral and even a trilateral basis but it was repudiated as a multilateral activity under ASEAN's aegis. Alliance formation was unequivocally ruled out with President Suharto asserting, for example, that "Our concept of security is inward looking".

For the first time, however, the ASEAN states concluded a treaty among themselves which was designed to promote regional order and which reflected the spirit of the Zone of Peace formulation. The Treaty of Amity and Co-operation (TAC) in Southeast Asia comprised a code of conduct for regional relations and included also provision for establishing machinery for dispute settlement.[6] These two dominant features have stood in some contradiction to one another and have had the effect of exposing some of the limitations of ASEAN's model of regional security.

The terms of the code of conduct within the Treaty were innocuous in themselves and were drawn from appropriate parts of the Charter of the United Nations. That Treaty was based, above all, on respect for national sovereignty and was intended to uphold the cardinal rule of the international society of states. It went to the very political heart of ASEAN which has been about reinforcing sovereignty among post-colonial states and not transcending that status by contrast, for example, with the declaratory objectives of the European Union. To that extent, the Treaty served a confidence-building function based on states being willing to honour quite basic undertakings in their common interest. The Treaty was designed to reinforce the intra-mural role of ASEAN but also to extend its confidence-building function within the region beyond the bounds of the Association's existing membership. This dual purpose was demonstrated in a provision made for adherence to the Treaty by regional non-members. The evident goal then was to reach out to the revolutionary states of Indochina in the hope that their governments would see utility in such an indirect affiliation based on a mutual respect for national sovereignty. To that extent, the Treaty represented an attempt to establish a *modus vivendi* with governments in Indochina which registered very different political identities to those of ASEAN's members.

That hope proved to be unfounded in the circumstances. For example, the Communist government of a united Vietnam initially exhibited an arrogant triumphalism towards ASEAN. It did not deign to take up the offer of adherence to the TAC. Instead, it called for ASEAN's dissolution and for its replacement by an alternative regional body. Vietnam also opposed successfully the inclusion of ASEAN's Zone of Peace formulation in the final document of the Conference of Non-Aligned States which convened in Colombo in August 1976. That successful objection was a pointed way of denying the legitimacy of the Association in prescribing for regional order. It is a matter of some irony that some sixteen years later a politically contrite Vietnam was only too pleased to be allowed to sign the TAC and to become a candidate member of ASEAN on the Association's terms.

The TAC began in practice with an intra-mural remit only. Such a restricted remit obtained also for the dispute settlement provisions of the Treaty. Its terms, including the establishment of a High Council with a quasi-judicial role, contained the seeds of corporate disorder, however, because of a potential obligation for members to take sides in adjudicating a bilateral dispute among regional partners. Such provision ran counter to the informal working premise on which ASEAN had been founded; namely, not to bring any bilateral differences between members openly within the walls of the Association.[7] In the event, the dispute settlement provisions of the Treaty were left dormant and have never once been invoked for good practical reason. Instead, some members have shown themselves willing in some cases to go to international arbitration over territorial disputes rather than risk damage to the fabric of ASEAN or their standing within the Association by bringing bilateral contention openly within its walls.

ASEAN's balance sheet was mixed in the immediate wake of its first summit in Bali in February 1976. Its members had shown themselves determined to stand firm in the face of disturbing events in Indochina which had exposed the limitations of the United States as a protecting external power. The attempt to build political bridges to Indochina on the basis of common norms had been rejected, however, and Southeast Asia was seen to be divided into two antagonistic blocs before an even more bitter antagonism between Cambodia and Vietnam came to be fully revealed. Moreover, ASEAN's new-found political declarations were not matched by an ability to demonstrate substantive progress in economic co-operation. That was certainly the conclusion to be drawn from the outcome of ASEAN's second summit in August 1977 held to commemorate the tenth anniversary of its formation. The failure to make good initial commitments to economic co-operation were compensated for in an important institutional development of the Association, however.

Present at Kuala Lumpur for a meeting with ASEAN's heads of government were the Prime Ministers of Japan, Australia, and New Zealand. Their participation, and in particular the subsequent articulation of a doctrine of regional engagement by Prime Minister Takeo Fukuda, registered the growing credentials of the Association which bore full fruit with the onset of the Cambodian conflict. Within a short space of time, the so-called Post Ministerial Conference (PMC), which convened immediately after the annual meeting of ASEAN's foreign ministers, would become a regular diary commitment for ministerial counterparts from Western industrialised states which had acquired the status of dialogue partners of the Association. Its international standing was enhanced accordingly. Moreover, the need to cope with the radical change in regional circumstances as well as growing intra-communist tensions and competing communist attentions made close intra-mural consultation and co-operation on the part of the diplomatic community increasingly necessary and also advantageous. ASEAN's collective and coherent diplomatic voice began to count in a way unanticipated at its formation as a consequence of these developments.

The Mixed Blessing of Cambodia

The advent of the Cambodian conflict from December 1978 gave ASEAN a prominent regional and international role as a diplomatic community. Despite removing a murderous regime, Vietnam's invasion and occupation had violated the cardinal rule of the international society of states as registered in the TAC. However, ASEAN's collective response in defence of that rule barely concealed fundamental differences of strategic perspective held by Thailand and Indonesia defined respectively with reference to Vietnam and China. These differences came to a head in March 1980 when the Indonesian President and the Malaysian Prime Minister issued a joint statement indicating their common concern over ASEAN's policy of confronting Vietnam working to China's advantage, in particular. That statement proved to be stillborn because of the objection of Thailand, as the Association's "front-line state" to the implicit acceptance of Vietnam's hegemonic role in Indochina. It was allowed to lapse in the interest of intra-ASEAN solidarity which Thailand's regional partners did not want to jeopardize.

Despite such differences, which were accommodated rather than resolved, the Association was able to uphold a common position during the course of the conflict. It refused to accord recognition to the government in Phnom Penh which had been virtually carried into the Cambodian capital in the saddle bags of the Vietnamese army. ASEAN distinguished itself in the diplomatic role which it assumed in challenging the *fait accompli* which the Vietnamese had sought to impose through *force majeure*. Although ASEAN achieved much in that expanded diplomatic role, its achievement was facilitated in important part by the Association becoming a party to an informal alliance devoted to subjecting Vietnam's society and government to breaking strain. Within that alliance, a division of labour obtained with China assuming a military role and the United States and Japan an economic one. ASEAN's diplomatic enterprise would not have carried the same weight without the support of the international alignment to which it was an active party. Indeed, it was that participation which generated resistance, in particular, on the part of the government in Jakarta which resented the informal coalition with China in the latter's strategic interest.

Employing its regional credentials, ASEAN took the lead within the United Nations with evident success in mobilizing voting support for annual resolutions adverse to Vietnam's interest. During the 1980s, the size of that majority was raised progressively from year to year in a remarkable diplomatic accomplishment. It was responsible also in June 1982 for promoting a so-called Coalition Government of Democratic Kampuchea out of disparate Khmer resistance factions as a way of overcoming the bestial identity of the legitimate alternative at the United Nations to the Vietnamese-imposed government in Phnom Penh. There can be no doubt that ASEAN's solidarity contributed to Vietnam's inability to impose its notion of a special relationship on Indochina by force of arms. In the event, its ultimate failure was more directly a consequence of political change within the former Soviet Union which was the key also to the end of the Cold War.[8]

The prime root of the Cambodian conflict lay in Sino-Vietnamese antagonism to which ASEAN was not a party; nor was it an effective mediator. The conflict was brought to an end as an international problem through Sino-Vietnamese accommodation in the context of the end of the Cold War. ASEAN's prior attempt to settle that conflict through Indonesia's assumption of an interlocutor role had not borne fruit. In the event, terms of settlement were worked out through the ministrations of the Permanent Members of the United Nations Security Council with ASEAN relegated, in effect, to the diplomatic margins. It is of interest also to note that ASEAN governments took part only individually in the subsequent peacekeeping operation in Cambodia conducted under UN auspices and did not address the possibility of despatching a collective ASEAN force in support of the mission of the United Nations Transitional Authority in Cambodia (UNTAC) during 1992–93.

A Changing Security Environment

The Cambodian conflict had been a diplomatic triumph of a kind for ASEAN in upholding the principle of international legitimacy. The Association had registered a remarkable solidarity and international standing during its course and had overcome intra-mural tensions arising from a natural diversity of strategic perspectives. Its membership demonstrated collective nerve again also in going ahead with a third summit in Manila in December 1987 when the government of President Corazon Aquino was subject to recurrent internal challenge by a disaffected and coup-disposed military. However, with the end of the Cold War and of the Cambodian conflict, the pattern of international alignments which had supported ASEAN's diplomatic achievements had begun to change in critical respects. Above all, the convergence of interests which had distinguished that pattern during the 1980s no longer obtained in the wake of the Cold War so that when the heads of government of the Association convened for their fourth summit in Singapore in January 1992, ASEAN's role was in some doubt.

A transformation of the regional security environment had been pointed up by the notice of withdrawal from its military bases in the Philippines by the United States in November 1991, the disintegration of the Soviet Union in the following month and the novel strategic latitude visited in consequence on China. China had displayed a disturbing maritime assertiveness from the late 1980s when it had occupied several islands in the Spratly group in the South China Sea following an armed clash with Vietnam. Within ASEAN then, Brunei, Malaysia, and the Philippines held competing claims with China over the territory and waters of the Spratly Islands, while the irredentist agenda of the People's Republic extended ominously to the maritime heart of Southeast Asia. At issue was the degree of uncertainty about the nature of the regional balance or distribution of power on the part of states which were not organized collectively to address problems of power, including challenges to the territorial status quo, in any robust manner.

In Singapore, the heads of government paid some acknowledgement to the changes in strategic environment by taking an unprecedented decision to address security co-operation openly through "external dialogue". They also belatedly set up an ASEAN Free Trade Area (AFTA) in an additional attempt to bolster its regional role against the background of the advent of the Asia-Pacific Economic Co-operation (APEC). More significantly, the summit meeting recommended that "ASEAN should intensify its external dialogues in political and security matters by using the ASEAN Post-Ministerial Conferences". At the time, non-ASEAN participation in those conferences was restricted to governments which were a party to a Western alignment dominated by the United States. The matter of devising an institutional structure which would give content to the collective commitment to "external dialogue" was left to senior officials who came to grips with the matter only in mid-1993. In the meantime, ASEAN would have concrete experience of the impact of the change in the pattern of international alignments of which it had been a beneficiary during the Cambodian conflict.

In February 1992, China promulgated a law on territorial waters and contiguous areas in which its extensive claims to all the islands in the South China Sea and their interjacent waters were reaffirmed. It followed up this initiative in May that year by granting an oil exploration concession in a contested part of the South China Sea to the Crestone Corporation, a little known American company based in Denver. Arising from a Philippine initiative at the annual meeting of its foreign ministers held in Manila in July 1992, ASEAN sought to reassert its prerogative regional role through issuing a Declaration on the South China Sea. That Declaration called on claimant states "to resolve all sovereignty and jurisdictional issues by peaceful means, without resort to force". Moreover, within the Declaration, the principles contained in the TAC were commended to all parties concerned as "the basis for establishing a code of conduct over the South China Sea". China, whose foreign minister had been invited as a guest to the formal part of the ASEAN meeting, was most equivocal in its response, while the United States appeared to distance itself from the issues of jurisdiction in the South China Sea.

The fact of the matter was that ASEAN, unlike its experience during the Cambodian conflict, appeared to be on its own over the South China Sea. Its Declaration did not command the international attention and respect of its earlier diplomatic interventions over Cambodia. It is possible to interpret that Declaration as a reassertion of ASEAN's collective diplomatic voice after it had been marginalized over Cambodia. More realistically, the episode served to demonstrate a diplomatic impotence based on an inability to counter China's seeming glacial drift southwards. That impotence was confirmed in February 1995 when it was revealed that Chinese naval forces had seized the unoccupied Mischief Reef in the Spratly Islands some 130 miles off the coast of the Philippines island of Palawan and had also erected living-quarters there on top of steel scaffolding.

Overcoming Marginality

ASEAN found itself at a turning point over its regional role with the end of the Cold War and its impact on the strategic environment. The Association's exclusivist approach to the management of regional order had not only concealed fundamental differences of strategic perspective among its members but also lacked operational utility. Apart from limitations in collective capability, ASEAN could not be a true manager of regional order because its model and practice of regional security was based on a process of dialogue only in its intra-mural role and, indeed also more to the point, beyond it, unless attached to a wider alignment. At issue was how to proceed in the absence of a constituency for an alternative and more robust approach to regional security which would be willing to confront the perpetual problem of power in international relations. A solution of a kind was found in extending geographically ASEAN's model of regional security through a new and enlarged Asia-Pacific structure of multilateral dialogue to include the major regional powers but within which the Association would occupy a diplomatic centrality. The outcome was the ASEAN Regional Forum (ARF) which began its working life at a meeting of foreign ministers in Bangkok in July 1994.[9]

The initial terms of reference for the ARF had been set at a unprecedented and seminal meeting of ASEAN senior officials and counterparts from its PMC dialogue partners in Singapore in May 1993. After some resistance, it was agreed to widen the multilateral structure to include China and Russia as well as candidate members of the Association, including Vietnam and Laos. The practical point of the diplomatic exercise was revealed in that part of the Chairman's statement which noted: "The continuing presence of the United States as well as stable relationships among the United States, Japan, and China and other states of the region would contribute to regional stability."[10] Through that comment, it was evident just to what extent ASEAN's approach to regional order was based on perpetuating a favourable distribution of power within which it was anticipated that the United States would play the critical role. To that extent, the establishment of the ARF represented an attempt to engage in the practice of the balance of power through non-military means along the lines of ASEAN's model of regional security. The ARF was designed in important part to reinforce America's countervailing role in the region through encouraging its engagement in political dialogue as well as to persuade China to accept and observe those international norms which had been reaffirmed in the TAC. Japan had been an encouraging voice in promoting the ARF. Its government shared a common interest with its ASEAN counterparts in not wishing to have to extend its conventional security role beyond its home islands.

A supporting premise underpinning the prospect of a greater constructive engagement by the major Asia-Pacific powers was the common incentive of economic advantage arising from the astounding economic growth of much of Asia. That development had been registered institutionally with the establishment and evolution of the APEC in 1989 which assumed an important political dimension from late 1993 as a result of an initiative by America's President Bill Clinton for convening informal annual summits. The ASEAN states joined in, some with mixed feelings partly because of the Association's lack of achievement in economic co-operation and also a reluctance to become locked into an institutional structure dominated by the United States and Japan. Nonetheless, APEC expressed an underpinning economic inter-dependence for the ARF which was seen as helpful in upholding those norms of international conduct enshrined in the TAC as the basis for regional order.

In taking the step to extend its model of security well beyond its limited conventional regional bounds, ASEAN's governments were, of course, acknowledging that they were not competent collectively to deal effectively with post-Cold War security problems in Asia-Pacific which had intruded into Southeast Asia. The Association was not organized to deal with the perpetual problems of power in an ungoverned world. Moreover, the impact of the end of the Cold War had revealed the shortcomings of Southeast Asia as a strategic concept and also the awesome geopolitical reality and indivisibility of a fused Northeast and Southeast Asia within which China had begun to register a hegemonic potential.

From the outset, the ARF was extended beyond East Asia to the Pacific in part to call in countervailing power against China. With its self-declared economic interests in mind, the ARF was intended also to give China a stake in regional order as a way of inducing self-restraint against any disposition to act unilaterally to change the territorial status quo. In taking the initiative to promote the ARF, ASEAN was going against the grain of its declared exclusivist approach to managing regional order as expressed by the Zone of Peace formula. Participation in a wider structure of dialogue with the major Asia-Pacific powers, the United States, China, and Japan (also incorporating India from 1996), raised the logical prospect of ASEAN being diminished in its identity and security role within its own region through their intervening greater political weight.

ASEAN had been able to impose its name on the Forum as a symbol of its diplomatic centrality in the collective enterprise. It was also able subsequently to determine the operational terms of reference of the ARF to its corporate advantage by securing acquiescence that the main annual working meeting be held in close conjunction with ASEAN's annual meeting of foreign ministers in the appropriate ASEAN capital. Moreover, the ASEAN host foreign minister would chair that working meeting, while his ministry would provide the secretariat support. Finally, ASEAN participants would co-chair all inter-sessional meetings of the ARF. The point was well made by Singapore's Foreign Minister, Professor S. Jayakumar, after the annual meeting of ASEAN's foreign ministers in Brunei in July 1995, that the Association had to stay in the driver's seat and take control of its own destiny or risk being overtaken by rapidly changing events.[11]

ASEAN was able to overcome initial resistance to the assertion of its diplomatic centrality within the ARF because of the extent to which the *raison d'être* of the enterprise came to turn increasingly on incorporating China within its multilateral structure. Participation in such a multilateral structure would never have been acceptable to China had it been proposed by the United States or Japan, for example. Moreover, China had come to regard ASEAN as independently-minded and as an important factor for encouraging multipolarity in an Asia-

Pacific where the People's Republic was in contention with both the United States and Japan. Its government was prepared to overcome a natural reluctance for multilateralism to join the ARF on ASEAN's procedural terms. China has continued to support its diplomatic centrality but has also been able to restrict the role of the ARF to basic confidence-building measures which has caused some ASEAN states to have misgivings about the utility of the collective enterprise. Despite these misgiving and the dangers for ASEAN of being overwhelmed within the multilateral structure, the promotion of the ARF has been a creative adaptation to changing strategic circumstances and has marked an important stage in institutional evolution. In addition, ASEAN has been able concurrently to develop a separate security dialogue with China at senior officials level beginning in Hangzhou in April 1995. At a corresponding meeting two years later in Huangshan, China's representatives agreed to discuss ASEAN members' claims in the South China Sea and also revived an earlier proposal for a code of conduct with the Association, albeit separate from the Manila Declaration and the TAC.

The Utility and Problems of Enlargement

The advent of the ARF enabled ASEAN to assume a new lease of diplomatic life but with the collateral risk that the form of its diplomatic centrality would be overtaken by the substance of the greater influence of the major powers. It was partly in the light of this prospect that ASEAN began to embark on a new and ultimate phase of enlargement. A major step in that direction had been taken with Vietnam's entry in July 1995. It was followed up with another at the fifth ASEAN summit in Bangkok in December 1995 which was notable for the invited presence of Prime Ministers from Laos, Cambodia, and Myanmar; none of which were then member states. The initial drive for completing the ASEAN circle had come from Thailand whose government saw opportunity in such expansion to register its greater centrality within the Association. All remaining new members would come from the region's mainland within which Thailand has regarded itself as the economic hub. Early resistance to Thailand's proposal was overcome partly because of the growing attraction of achieving the visionary goal of "One Southeast Asia" by the millennium. Equally important, at least, was a shared interest in underpinning the Association's diplomatic centrality within the ARF. That prerogative position had been contested by some participating governments, including Japan and South Korea, which resented having the agenda for addressing Northeast Asia in the control of counterparts from Southeast Asia without appropriate experience of the adjoining regional sector. Their grudging tolerance of ASEAN's position has indicated that its diplomatic centrality within the ARF could not necessarily be taken for granted.

The anticipated purpose and practical advantage of enlargement is that an ASEAN of ten members, able to speak with a single voice and so displaying a renewed cohesion, would enjoy greater diplomatic influence within the wider Asia-Pacific enterprise and so protect the pivotal position and the corporate interests of the Association.[12] Such a prospect was indicated at the third annual working session of the ARF in Jakarta in July 1996 when existing and prospective members of ASEAN closed ranks in the face of Western attempts to influence the timing of Myanmar's entry into the Association which had just been admitted into the ARF together with India.

At ASEAN's first informal summit which convened also in Jakarta in the following November, it was agreed to admit Myanmar to membership with the matter of timing left in abeyance through the formula that it would be admitted "simultaneously" with Laos and Cambodia. In the event, the decision to admit the three states in July 1997 was taken by the Association's foreign ministers at a meeting in Kuala Lumpur at the end of the preceding May but that timetable was interrupted by the Cambodian coup. Over Myanmar, however, ASEAN demonstrated a determination to stand firm on the terms of enlarging its membership. An ability to write the rules for regional order on a unilateral basis would seem to be another and an entirely different matter. In that respect, the efficacy of ASEAN as a diplomatic community has remained limited.

The continuing limited efficacy of ASEAN as a diplomatic community had been pointed up after the Bangkok summit in December 1995. None of the permanent members of the UN Security Council had been prepared to endorse a Southeast Asia Nuclear Weapons-Free Zone Treaty which had been concluded by ASEAN's heads of government as a step towards realizing the Association's goal of a Zone of Peace, Freedom and Neutrality. Both the United States and China raised specific objections to some of the terms of the Treaty which left it in a state of diplomatic limbo, although it came formally into force in March 1997. That experience served to point up the salutary fact of life that by taking the initiative to bring the ARF into being, ASEAN had acknowledged that it was not the ultimate master of its regional destiny. There was also the related and complicating matter of the likely impact of enlargement on the quasi-familial corporate culture and coherence of the Association. To employ the idiom of the European Union, at issue is an ability to combine "widening" with "deepening"; namely, to reconcile a new-found diversity in membership with a regional role based previously on a small working scale of membership and a relative homogeneity of political outlooks. In addition, ASEAN will have to cope with the political opportunity costs of Myanmar's membership. Indeed, one of ASEAN's most vocal protagonists has drawn attention to the likely damage to its stature and credibility so "reducing its influence".[13]

ASEAN has persisted in its commitment to enlargement with its role within the ARF partly in mind and has not set aside its interest in including Cambodia, however problematic. A corresponding diplomatic centrality was asserted and displayed also in ASEAN's successful initiative in promoting the Asia-Europe Meeting (ASEM) which was inaugurated at heads of government level in Bangkok in March 1996 and which convened for a second time in London in April 1998. An underlying objective was to promote a better balance in Europe's economic and political engagement as a counter to the regional roles and influence of the United States, Japan, and China.

Europe was represented in Bangkok and London by the members of the European Community (EU), while participating from Asia, in addition to members of ASEAN, were heads of government from China, Japan, and South Korea. ASEAN has exercised a diplomatic centrality in this novel structure of inter-regional dialogue in support of a regional role which has been called into question by the nature of its security model, the changes in its strategic environment attendant on the end of the Cold War as well as by the impact of economic adversity. Corresponding to a degree to their role within the ARF, ASEAN governments have been able to assume a co-chair responsibility in co-ordinating efforts on the Asian side in preparation for dialogue with European partners who have the advantage of institutional co-ordination within the European Union. Moreover, to the extent that ASEAN has begun to operate increasingly as a grouping of heads of governments as opposed to one of foreign ministers — signalled by the decision at their meeting in Bangkok in December 1995 to convene annual informal summits — the Association more effectively expresses the political will of national power centres. That development was extended in December 1997 to a meeting between ASEAN's heads of government and those from China, Japan, and South Korea matching the Asian side in the ASEM process. By that juncture, however, the impact of regional economic crisis had exposed the limitations of regional initiative to ASEAN's disadvantage.

Moreover, ASEAN had encountered a novel difficulty in expanding its role because of the coup in Cambodia which interrupted the timetable for enlargement. Its governments had been parties to the Paris accords of October 1991 which had settled the Cambodian conflict as an international problem. All, except that of Brunei, had participated in the peacekeeping operation under United Nations auspices which culminated in elections in May 1993. Although less than content at the way in which the Cambodian People's Party, led by Hun Sen, had forced its way into coalition government after losing the elections to the royalist Funcinpec led by Prince Norodom Ranariddh, they had endorsed the power-sharing arrangement which took effect in October 1993. In consequence, ASEAN's credibility as a diplomatic community became tied to the viability of that arrangement, at least until after a subsequent election.

ASEAN's degree of involvement in Cambodia's domestic affairs had been deemed legitimate in the exceptional circumstances of an internationalized civil war. However, the Association continued to adhere to the convention that it did not interfere in the domestic affairs of any of its members or indeed into those of other regional states, although collective concern had been communicated to the government in Manila by five of its members after fraudulently conducted elections in the Philippines in February 1986. Such a declared respect for national sovereignty provided the basis for ASEAN's policy of "constructive engagement" towards Myanmar and the repudiation of Western attempts to persuade the Association to join in treating it as a pariah on account of its government's human rights record.

The violent coup in Cambodia placed ASEAN in a political quandary, in important part because it occurred less than a month before the country was to be admitted as a full member. Previously, ASEAN had challenged the use of external force to change the government in Phnom Penh. It was now faced with the problem of how to react to such a change through the use of internal force which, by convention, was beyond the Association's remit. In the event, ASEAN broke with convention up to a point by postponing Cambodia's entry and by despatching three of its foreign ministers to mediate in Phnom Penh with the object of restoring an acceptable form of coalition government. That attempt at mediation was rebuffed rudely by Hun Sen to be replaced by an ostensibly more accommodating attitude tied to the principle of non-intervention.

Intervention of a kind had taken place, however, which marked a qualitative change in the Association's role. Moreover, its foreign ministers upheld their decision to defer Cambodia's membership and to admit only Laos and Myanmar at their annual meeting in Kuala Lumpur at the end of July, albeit without challenging Cambodia's observer status. At issue is whether or not ASEAN's experience in the wake of the Cambodian coup marks an exception to its declared conventional practice exemplified in the comment of Singapore's Foreign Minister, Professor S. Jayakumar that "Where force is used for an unconstitutional purpose, it is behaviour that ASEAN cannot ignore or condone."[14] That point taken, it would also seem to be in ASEAN's interest to include Cambodia within its fold in order to avoid the prospect of a civil war from spilling across the borders of member states and also to prevent the country becoming the object of competing external attentions.

In their joint communique, the nine foreign ministers confirmed that expectation by registering the hope that a "return to normalcy ... in the spirit of the Paris Peace Accords" would enable Cambodia to join ASEAN.[15] ASEAN's governments drew comfort from the welcome given by the succeeding ARF meeting to the Association's assumption of responsibility for helping to restore political stability. That assumption of responsibility for securing respect for the Paris Accords, including the commitment from the Phnom Penh regime to uphold the 1993 constitution and to conduct free and fair elections, marked an expansion of role. In the event, however, ASEAN's diplomacy proved to be ineffectual and the Association was obliged to defer to a Japanese initiative in the face of capital charges brought by Hun Sen's government against Prince Norodom Ranariddh in absentia intended to prevent his return to the country to lead his party in elections. A farcical formula for a royal pardon after two trials and sentences paved the way for Prince Ranariddh's return to Cambodia but in circumstances where his Funcinpec Party had been effectively destroyed and where his feeble political presence would serve only to legitimize Hun Sen's hold on power consolidated through a coup to which ASEAN had objected in vain.

Prospect

During the three decades which have passed since its formation, both ASEAN and its regional context have changed; the latter most dramatically in economic terms from the middle of 1997. In that period, the Association has demonstrated a facility for adaptation, especially from the end of the Cold War. A decisive point of adaptation occurred with the entry of Vietnam which marked a qualitative change in composition. Further enlargement has sustained that trend but, with membership beset by a much greater diversity in political identities, a working consensus will become more difficult to attain as well as making convergence in targets for economic co-operation problematic. The Cambodian coup has pointed up the difficulty of completely separating the domestic from the regional agenda which has been the case also with the environmental catastrophe caused by the forest fires in Indonesia. The display of collective impotence in the face of the pollution of the regional atmosphere as well as the more foreboding regional economic crisis has served to diminish the international standing of the Association. Moreover, it foreshadows intra-mural tensions, for example over the forced repatriation of migrant labour, which could undermine the collective diplomatic role of the Association, including its participation within the ARF.

It is with that prospect in mind that ASEAN will have to come to terms with the problem of addressing the challenge to regional order arising from China's rising power and extensive irredentist agenda.[16] There remain also a host of outstanding bilateral tensions among ASEAN states which have the potential to disturb working relationships. But they would not seem to be of the order of *casus belli*, including contending claims in the Spratly Islands. Moreover, any limited changes in the territorial and maritime status quo in the South China Sea among individual ASEAN states would not necessarily have a radical effect on the regional environment. China's claims fall into a different category, however, because of their far more extensive nature and also because their full realization would be truly revolutionary in geopolitical terms. China has maintained a steely rectitude in asserting its claims to sovereign jurisdiction which the ASEAN states have not been able to persuade Beijing to address with a view to any compromise, so far. Moreover, within an enlarging ASEAN, a mixture of interests exist in addressing the problem of a rising China. The government in Bangkok, for example, appears comfortable in its current relationship with that in Beijing which it has no interest in prejudicing over the South China Sea. The same may be said for Myanmar and Laos as newest members of the Association as well as for Cambodia whose post-coup government has looked to China to endorse its legitimacy through conciliating it over the Taiwanese commercial presence.

Although the defence of limited island holdings is within the military competence of some individual member states, ASEAN is not organized to defend the regional territorial and maritime status quo in the South China Sea; nor can it expect much support from the ARF despite a diplomatic centrality within it. The ARF is based on ASEAN's security model, while China exercises an effective veto on its security agenda. Moreover, it was left to individual governments to protest to Beijing when in May 1996, following its ratification of the UN Law of the Sea Convention, China employed the archipelago principle in drawing base-lines around the Paracel Islands which are claimed also by Vietnam. China reserved its right to declare base-lines for the more contested Spratly Islands with the implication that it would also employ the archipelago principle for that group which, under International Law, is valid only for mid-ocean archipelagic states.

In the case of the South China Sea, ASEAN has been able to adopt a collective position only on the question of modalities as expressed in its Declaration of July 1992. Its inability to move effectively beyond that position is indicative of its corporate limitations. That said, ASEAN has shown itself to be a factor in China's calculations in the context of its differences with the United States and Japan and in the light of its interest in promoting multipolarity within Asia-Pacific in its own interest. For example, in March/April 1997, a dispute between Vietnam and China over the right of one of the latter's oil exploration rigs to operate at the margins of coastal waters in the South China Sea was defused after Vietnam's Foreign Ministry called in heads of resident ASEAN missions in Hanoi for a briefing. All in all, however, ASEAN has not been able to do more than secure a measure of accommodation on China's part in its persistent pursuit of territorial and maritime claims in the South China Sea.

The role of ASEAN has evolved and expanded in a substantive sense over the decades because of the ability of member governments to contain and manage tensions among themselves. That signal achievement has contributed also to an ability to project a collective diplomatic voice in the special circumstances of the Cambodian conflict during the 1980s. ASEAN's standing was enhanced also by its members' success in economic accomplishment which served to strengthen the "cooperative security" structure. Indeed, it was that accomplishment and incentive represented as "the economic underpinnings of security" which was much in mind when the ARF was conceived. The reversal of regional economic fortunes has served to impair institutional standing accordingly.

At issue in a transformed context of regional economic adversity is whether or not ASEAN has reached the limits of an expanding role. In one important respect, however, the Association has not evolved since its formation; namely, in its reliance on dialogue as the sole instrument for containing and managing intra-mural tensions. The ARF has been established on the same premise, while its formation was also an acknowledgement that ASEAN was not competent on its own to manage the security problems of its region locale which has been called into question as discrete strategic category as a consequence. Indeed, enlargement has been embarked upon, in part, to protect ASEAN's separate political identity and prerogative regional position within a wider structure of "cooperative security". But enlargement also contains seeds of discordant diversity within it which could have adverse consequences for the Association's role as a diplomatic community.

The point has been well made that "There is nothing preordained about the future survivability of ASEAN".[17] In its most recent phase, ASEAN has been obliged to come to terms with its evident limitations exemplified before the onset of economic adversity in the promotion of the ARF. That initiative indicated a pragmatic abdication of an exclusivist doctrine for regional order and a willingness to join in security co-operation beyond Southeast Asian bounds. It may be argued, therefore, that ASEAN has reached the limits of its role and that it needs to reinvent itself or experience institutional decay. The dilemma for ASEAN in contemplating such a prospect is that the diversity attendant on enlargement obliges members to adhere to a tightly restricted model of regional security. In an ungoverned world, however, the vehicle of dialogue can only be effective up to a point which, for example, has been ASEAN's salutary experience in seeking to cope with the coup in Cambodia. ASEAN cannot be expected to expand its role beyond dialogue which means that the Association is condemned to suffer from the defects of its qualities and the evident limitations of its collective competence. Its prime saving grace, in a context of change in strategic environment and an unanticipated economic adversity, has been to sustain an original role of containing and managing intra-mural tensions which is an accomplishment not to be disparaged in an imperfect world. In that respect, ASEAN lends itself to the old adage that in contemplating its future role the best should not be made the enemy of the good.

Notes

1. For an explanation of those terms, see David Dewitt, "Common, Comprehensive and Cooperative Security", *Pacific Review* 7, no. 1 (1994).
2. For analyses of ASEAN's origins and evolution, see K. S. Sandhu et al., eds., *The ASEAN Reader* (Singapore: Institute of Southeast Asian Studies, 1992); Amitav Acharya, *A New Regional Order in South-East Asia: ASEAN in the Post-Cold War Era*, Adelphi Paper No. 279, (London: Brassey's for the International Institute for Strategic Studies, 1993); *Pacific Review*, Special issue on "ASEAN in the post-cold war era", vol. 8 , no. 3 (1995); and Manuel F. Montes, Kevin F. F. Quigley, and Donald E. Weatherbee, *Growing Pains: ASEAN's Economic and Political Challenges* (New York: Asia Society, December 1997).
3. In *Foreign Affairs Bulletin*, Ministry of Foreign Affairs, Bangkok, August–September 1968 and in an interview in *Far Eastern Economic Review*, 12 June 1969.
4. For a background analysis, see Heiner Hanggi, *ASEAN and the ZOPFAN Concept* (Singapore: Institute of Southeast Asian Studies, 1991) and also Muthiah Alagappa, "Regional Arrangements and International Security in Southeast Asia", *Contemporary Southeast Asia* 12, no. 4 (March 1991).
5. See the discussion in Michael Leifer, *ASEAN and the Security of South-East Asia* (London and New York: Routledge, 1990), pp. 55–59.
6. For a reflective analysis, see C.P.F. Luhulima, "ASEAN's Security Instrument: The Treaty of Amity and Cooperation in Southeast Asia", in *Cambodia in ASEAN*, edited by Kao Kim Hourn (Phnom Penh: Cambodian Institute for Cooperation and Peace, 1995).
7. Note the revelation of how this premise was placed at the heart of the working practice of ASEAN from the outset by Tan Sri Ghazali Shafi in "Politics in Command", *Far Eastern Economic Review*, 22 October 1992.
8. See Leszek Buszynski, *Gorbachev and Southeast Asia* (London and New York: Routledge, 1992).
9. See Michael Leifer, *The ASEAN Regional Forum. Extending ASEAN's Model of Regional Security*, Adelphi Paper 302 (Oxford: Oxford University Press for International Institute for Strategic Studies, 1966).
10. "Chairman's Statement", ASEAN Post-Ministerial Conferences, Senior Officials Meeting, Singapore, 20–21 May 1993.

11. *Straits Times*, 4 August 1995.
12. Such an expectation has been indicated by Noordin Sopiee in "Fulfilling dream of regional unity", *New Straits Times*, 6 June 1997.
13. See Jusuf Wanandi, "Partners Should Nudge Burma", *International Herald Tribune*, 5 June 1997, and also Michael Leifer, "The European Union, ASEAN and the politics of exclusion", *Trends*, Institute of Southeast Asian Studies, Singapore, 31 January–1 February 1998.
14. *Straits Times*, 25 July 1997.
15. Joint Communique of the Thirtieth ASEAN Ministerial Meeting, Kuala Lumpur, 26 July 1997.
16. See Michael Leifer, "China in Southeast Asia: Interdependence and Accommodation", in *China Rising*, edited by David S. G. Goodman and Gerald Segal (London and New York: Routledge, 1997).
17. Chin Kin Wah, "ASEAN in the New Millennium", in *ASEAN in the New Asia: Issues and Trends*, edited by Chia Siow Yue and Marcello Pacini (Singapore: Institute of Southeast Asian Studies, 1997), p. 161.

The Cambodia Conflict

INTRODUCTION

Leifer's writings on the Cambodia conflict spanned the entire saga beginning with the Vietnamese invasion in 1978 until the resolution phase, marked by the Paris agreement of October 1992 and subsequently the holding of elections under supervision of the UN Transitional Authority in Cambodia (UNTAC). The impact of the conflict on Cambodia's domestic politics and foreign policy is covered in Part II of this volume. This section contains only four of his articles focusing on the international dimensions. Constraints of space does not allow for the inclusion of more items here. ASEAN's interests and involvement in the conflict and the impact of the conflict on ASEAN's attempts to manage regional order have already been covered in the section on ASEAN and Regional Order above. The four selected pieces help to define the nature of the conflict; lay out the justifications for and against intervention in Cambodia; explicate the interests and roles of the key external players whose involvements were deemed central in sustaining the conflict; and finally provide some account of the closure of a thirteen-year contestation.

In the first selected piece (Ch. 16) published at the end of the conflict, Leifer tries to capture the saga in a nutshell. He sees the conflict essentially as a product of the Cold War whereby the competitive dynamics among the major players (the United States, USSR, and China) were linked to conflict within Cambodia itself. The end of the Vietnam War redrew the battle-lines in Indochina, with Cambodia reflecting that "fused global and regional pattern of rivalry". Here, Leifer viewed the historically rooted Sino-Vietnamese tension as most critical in sustaining the conflict. Its termination would have to await the end of the Cold War and transformation of China's relations with Vietnam. The latter had begun a major reassessment of its interests in Cambodia given the economic strains of occupation. At the local level political impasse was broken by Sihanouk's accommodation with Hun Sen. The article hardly touches on ASEAN which found itself sidelined by the major powers at the final stage of the peace process.

The international debate over the legitimacy of Vietnam's intervention in Cambodia was pursued rigorously by ASEAN and supported by the United States and China. While Vietnam sought public justification of its action on ethical grounds (that is, its removal of the genocidal Khmer Rouge regime), ASEAN questioned the legitimacy of the successor regime that had been installed by and sustained through force of Vietnamese arms. Such an act of military intervention, if tolerated, was deemed to undermine a cardinal rule of international society namely the right to independence of the state. In his review of the relative merits of the opposing arguments, Leifer noted that ethics had been subordinate to state interests even when employed in justifying intervention (Ch. 17).

The critical roles of the intervening external powers in sustaining conflict dynamics had been addressed at the very onset of the Cambodia imbroglio. In a 1980 *Adelphi Paper* (Ch. 18), Leifer argued, *inter alia*, that external power involvement in the region had continued with the end of the Vietnam War although the pattern of such involvement did change radically. Each of the external powers was guided by balance of power considerations (that is, denying advantage to its principal adversary) in their regional policies. This brought China increasingly into conflict with Hanoi notwithstanding past fraternal support. The Cambodia problem also showed how America's policy towards Southeast Asia, post-Nixon doctrine, was influenced by a wider design in ensuring strategic balance between itself, China, and

Japan on the one hand, and the then Soviet Union on the other. Japan's political outlook was one of ambivalence but its position was influenced by concerns over Soviet military access to the region although Japanese interests were not directly threatened there. It was the Soviet Union that benefited most from the deterioration of Sino–Vietnamese relations over Cambodia, gaining a strategic toehold in Indochina as a consequence — this despite that fact the region was of marginal direct interest to Moscow.

A subsequent transformation of great power relations following the end of the Cold War opened the final chapter to conflict resolution in Cambodia. UNTAC's role in this phase was to ensure a neutral political environment in which "free and fair" elections could take place. Leifer noted the relatively peaceful atmosphere in which the elections were conducted despite the Khmer Rouge's boycott and threat of disruption. However the election results proved inconclusive for the royalist FUNCINPEC led by Norodom Ranariddh and Hun Sen's Cambodian People's Party (Ch. 19). This sowed the seeds for future political contestation despite a power-sharing arrangement. It culminated in a coup by Hun Sen against Ranariddh in July 1997, the consequences of which for the expansion of ASEAN's membership are discussed in Chapter 28.

16

The Indochina Problem

The Indochina problem was a product of the Cold War. It arose initially when conflict over colonial restoration in Vietnam became linked among competing external interests to both the regional and global balances of power. With the radical change in strategic context which has marked the end of the Cold War, that competitive linkage has been disconnected making the outcome of domestic conflict within Indochina of diminished international significance. The Indochina problem has, therefore, ceased to exist; at least, in characteristic form. Its latest phase was brought to the point of settlement on 23 October 1991 when an international conference in Paris reached an accord on Cambodia.

1. What was the characteristic feature of the Indochina problem and how was it manifested, especially in its most recent expression over Cambodia?

Reprinted in abridged form from Michael Leifer, "The Indochina Problem", in *Asian-Pacific Security after the Cold War*, edited by T. B. Millar and James Walter (Canberra: Allen and Unwin, 1992), pp. 56–68, by permission of the publisher.

2. How and why has the problem changed so that a political settlement became possible in Cambodia?
3. What are the implications for regional security of the end of the Indochina problem?

The Nature of the Indochina Problem

With the end of the Pacific War and the onset of nationalist struggle against colonial restoration, Southeast Asia in general and Indochina in particular seemed to fit the circumstances of Southeast Europe before 1914. The region not only came to serve as a locus for conflict which linked competitively regional and global balances but also as a possible setting for the outbreak of World War III between rival ideological alliances. The Indochina problem, at least in the West, was regarded in terms of denying geopolitical advantage to the regional proxy of a global adversary for fear of the domino consequences of extra-regional import. That problem was central to three successive Indochina Wars all of which, while reflecting a changing pattern of international alignments, registered a common feature: an explosive junction of regional and global politics.

It has been well argued that the initial American interest in Indochina was a direct consequence of European priorities. George Kahin, for example, enjoins his readers to note the French connection as the explanation for Washington's early engagement in a problem seemingly remote from national interest.[1] The importance of the perceived link between regional and global balances was reinforced with the establishment of the People's Republic of China. This revolutionary state was deemed to be the prime vehicle in Asia for the expansionist goals of a monolithic international communism, especially after its intervention in the Korean War. China's prior alliance with the Soviet centre of that monolith, its common border with Vietnam, across which came military support for the Viet Minh insurgency, gave rise to the belief that interlocking proxies were engaged in an attempt to revise the regional balance of power to global effect.[2] The American policy of containment translated from Europe to Asia was directed against that threat. Failure to prevent the division of Vietnam to Communist advantage in 1954 served to reinforce the commitment to containment culminating in an ill-fated military intervention undertaken from the early 1960s.

The Indochina problem was modified in its strategic context when a fundamental revision of the global pattern of alignments occurred during the early 1970s. That revision, arising from Sino–American *rapprochement*, paved the way for the end of the Vietnam War because containing China in Vietnam had lost its *raison d'être*. It also served to establish the battle lines for the next Indochina conflict over Cambodia in which the United States and China were ranged together against the Soviet Union in what began as a preliminary round of the so-called Second Cold War. The Indochina problem remained the same in general terms, however, to the extent that the United States still wished to contain the regional pretensions of its Soviet adversary now seemingly exercised more directly through the vehicle of a united Communist Vietnam. Thailand, in particular, was perceived to be at serious risk from Vietnam's regional ambitions so attracting diplomatic support from regional partners. The prospect of an adverse regional dominance was still perceived in terms of global consequences. That perception was shared by the government in Beijing which had switched Cold War alignments to engage in collaborative containment of the Soviet Union. In the process, a previously obscured but historically-rooted tension between China and Vietnam was revealed. That autonomous tension was the most critical factor in the ensuing Cambodian conflict.[3]

The Indochina problem has now changed virtually beyond recognition because the end of the Cold War has given rise to a novel disjunction between global and regional politics. The nature of the change has been registered by the way in which the Cambodian conflict has been detached in turn from both global and regional relationships and relegated primarily to a domestic issue; at least, for the time being. Nonetheless, a final political settlement in October 1991 had to wait on Sino–Vietnamese *rapprochement* which took longer to effect than improvements in Soviet–American and Sino–Soviet relations.

The Cambodian Conflict

The Cambodian conflict had its origins in a nationalist-driven clash of wills between the Vietnamese and Cambodian Communist Parties over the terms of their relationship.[4] After closely consecutive revolutionary successes in April 1975, fundamental differences arose between a Vietnamese strategic perspective requiring a so-called special and unequal relationship and a Cambodian national–salvationist vision defined with reference to independence from Vietnam. Closely joined was a corresponding critical tension between Vietnam and China also over the terms of their relationship in which alignment with the Soviet Union was a key issue.[5] Cambodia came to be the central object of contention between the ruling parties in Hanoi and Beijing, both of which regarded the country's political identity and attendant external affiliation as directly relevant to their competing geopolitical interests in Indochina. Their indirect confrontation both reflected and reinforced a fused global and regional pattern of rivalry, incorporating Thailand in particular because of its historical rivalry with Vietnam in the trans-Mekong. As indicated above, both China and the United States looked on the Cambodian conflict as a dimension of their fraught relationship with the Soviet Union. Correspondingly, the Soviet Union was drawn into that conflict in response to an adverse global balance and in support of a fraternal state.

At the outset, the Cambodian conflict was primarily an international problem. The Vietnamese, in treaty relationship with the Soviet Union, drove out the incumbent Khmer Rouge regime and substituted an administration of their own political manufacture. The principal response to this intervention was international with the object of removing the Vietnamese military presence and eliminating its political legacy. A Chinese military riposte across its southern border against Vietnam was complemented by promoting, in collaboration with Thailand, insurgent challenge to Vietnam's presence in Cambodia. Economic sanctions were imposed primarily by the United States and Japan, while diplomatic pressure was exerted by the states of the Association of Southeast Asian Nations (ASEAN). The object of the collective enterprise was to apply a strategy of attrition at Vietnam's expense which over time would subject its government and society to breaking strain so obliging it to abdicate its geopolitical advantage.

Although international in its origins, the Cambodian phase of the Indochina problem assumed an increasingly important domestic dimension as the competing external parties promoted warring internal clients. That internal application of force failed to resolve the conflict which seemed set in a stalemate for much of the 1980s. Among the external parties, military stalemate proved least satisfactory and most costly to Vietnam which was unable to pacify the country and also to create a viable party organisation with which to incorporate Cambodia into an ideal close structure of Indochinese relations. Moreover, concurrent with its occupation of Cambodia, it had been afflicted with grievous economic problems which could be overcome only through the assured benefaction of the Soviet Union which served also as its sole source of external countervailing power.

The Road to Political Settlement

The Indochina problem, which was locked in stalemate, began to unravel from the mid-1980s after Mikhail Gorbachev became General Secretary of the Communist Party of the Soviet Union. Driven by internal economic imperatives, the new Soviet Government set out to address its domestic priorities by improving global relationships. Both the United States and China made such an improvement conditional on progress in resolving regional conflicts. Cambodia was made the prime issue in the bilateral relationship by China after Mr Gorbachev failed to grasp the nettle of the problem in his important speech in Vladivostok in July 1986. That issue was progressively detached with Vietnam's phased removal of its troops from Cambodia and the withdrawal of Soviet countervailing power from Vietnam, which was demonstrated in March 1988 by the absence of any supportive response to a Sino–Vietnamese naval clash in the Spratly Archipelago. Despite serious misgivings about the political direction of the Soviet Union, China acted to repair the bilateral relationship. Cambodia was effectively detached from it in May 1989 when Mr Gorbachev paid his historic albeit uncomfortable visit to Beijing. Soviet–American relations much improved after the accord on Afghanistan the year before were further reinforced by the shift in the Soviet position on Cambodia. But an end to the Indochina problem had to wait on a change in Sino–Vietnamese relations which only came about after the government in Hanoi felt obliged to make a choice between two competing security priorities.

The revision in global relationships attendant on the rise of Mikhail Gorbachev located the Indochina problem squarely in regional context pivoting primarily on Sino–Vietnamese ties. Reconciliation seemed a forbidding task initially as neither side appeared willing to compromise on strategic priorities defined with reference to the political identity and external affiliation of Cambodia. China's objection to the political legacy in Phnom Penh of Vietnam's invasion did not seem to be mitigated by the change in the tone and substance of Sino–Soviet relations. Within a relatively short time, however, both sides found good reasons to come to terms and indeed to begin to detach Cambodia from their bilateral relationship.

Vietnam had began to adjust its economic priorities in advance of adverse changes in Soviet policy, at first without revising its strategic priorities.[6] At the Sixth National Congress of the Communist Party in December 1986, the conventional Socialist economic model was replaced by a commitment to *Doi Moi* or Renovation. Such market driven reform had become a matter of political necessity bearing on regime security. The legitimacy of the ruling party was being called into question by its failure to fulfil the economic promise of the revolution. A special alliance relationship with Laos as well as Cambodia was reiterated, nonetheless.

At the next Congress in June 1991, the term special alliance relationship had given way to that of special friendship and solidarity but the underlying policy towards Indochina appeared to be the same.[7] By that juncture, however, negotiations on a Cambodian settlement had been taken out of a purely regional forum and placed within the competence of the five permanent members of the United Nations Security Council while Vietnam's international position had become even more isolated and vulnerable. The officials of the permanent five explored an Australian plan to overcome the problem of power sharing among Cambodian factions which had caused the failure of an international conference on the conflict which had convened in Paris in July 1989. Vietnam had been less than enthusiastic about the United Nations initiative which took shape as a framework agreement in August 1990, especially the provision for the Khmer Rouge to be a party to a political settlement. Nonetheless, it faced pressing economic problems as a consequence of the fundamental change in the relationship with the Soviet Union and the refusal of the United States to remove its long-standing embargo on trade and investment.

Vietnam was faced with a critical conflict of priorities reflected in the content of documents endorsed by the Seventh Party Congress in June 1991. Economic reform had become a matter of political necessity. Success in that reform, made more pressing because of the end of Soviet benefaction, required access to the international economy as well as improved bilateral relations with China. Cambodia, which had once been represented as the key to national security, now stood in the way of economic progress which was itself a matter of regime security. A false start in *rapprochement* with China during 1990 was remedied by political changes at the Seventh Party Congress, especially the removal from the Politburo and Central Committee as well as the cabinet of Foreign Minister Nguyen Co Thach who enjoyed the reputation of a Sinophobe. It may be deduced that China required his political head as the price for an improved relationship and as a symbol of deference which was essentially at issue in the border war of 1979 in which China claimed to have taught Vietnam a lesson. China was also encouraged by Vietnam's attempt to reconcile market economics with a reaffirmation of faith in the Socialist ideal which indicated a convergence in the political economies of the two states against the trend in Eastern Europe.

By that juncture, the United States triumphant, in the Gulf War, had reiterated rigid terms for normalising relations with Vietnam tied to a complete settlement of the Cambodian conflict. Moreover, the outcome of the abortive coup in the Soviet Union in August 1991 had a traumatic political impact challenging the very basis on which the Vietnamese state was constituted. There was little alternative in the circumstances but to come to terms with the traditional adversary, China, which had upheld the sacred model of socialism. Such considerations told also with China, conscious of its diminished significance in American calculations in the light of the new pattern of international hierarchy. The following month, Vietnam's new Foreign Minister, Nguyen Manh Cam, travelled to Beijing to meet his Chinese counterpart, the first such visit since the onset of the Cambodian conflict. A visit to Beijing by Party leader Do Muoi and Prime Minister Vo Van Kiet in early November completed the process of normalisation.[8] The pace of Sino–Vietnamese *rapprochement*, however opportunistic, had a direct impact on the condition of the Indochina problem. It was reflected in a series of political agreements among Cambodian factions beginning with that in the Thai resort of Pattaya at the end of June 1991 in marked contrast to the evident impasse displayed only weeks before at their meeting in Jakarta.

The key to the political breakthrough among the Cambodian factions was the initiative taken in June by Prince Norodom Sihanouk with China's sanction to seek an accommodation with Prime Minister Hun Sen of the Phnom Penh Government. Previous such attempts by Prince Sihanouk had all proven abortive as a consequence of China exercising a veto power, usually through the vehicle of the Khmer Rouge. Among the motives governing Prince Sihanouk's deferential conduct has been the conviction that China, unlike neighbouring

Vietnam and Thailand, possessed a clear interest in preserving the integrity of the Cambodian state. The measure of progress in brokering a settlement was indicated in July when the Supreme National Council held an informal meeting in Beijing. That Council had been conceived in the United Nations plan as a symbol and repository of Cambodian sovereignty which would overcome the obstacle of power sharing by delegating powers to a transitional authority charged by the world body with holding general elections. The meeting marked the first visit to the Chinese capital by Prime Minister Hun Sen, previously depicted as a Vietnamese puppet.

China's position has been critical to the progress attained in the dialogue over Cambodia, especially since the end of June 1991. The balance of advantage in the adversarial relationship with Vietnam has shifted progressively in China's favour. By the end of the 1980s, China was no longer confronted militarily by either the United States or the Soviet Union. It had also become a legitimate party to an international community initiative over Cambodia which, if implemented, would limit Vietnamese influence in Cambodia. To the extent that global and regional politics were separated with the end of the Cold War, China was permitted an unprecedented latitude in regional affairs, especially in relation to Vietnam and Cambodia. It did not seem likely that a Cambodian settlement which failed to attract China's endorsement would be viable. Prince Sihanouk's political conduct reflected such a calculation.

It would be facile to draw the conclusion that time was so much on China's side that its government could afford to tolerate the Cambodian conflict continuing indefinitely. The Chinese Government had good reasons to want to see its end, especially given the revised relationship with the Soviet Union and also that between the Soviet Union and Vietnam. The persistence of tensions with the United States over the Tiananmen Square massacre at a time when China has lost its former strategic significance served to concentrate minds in Beijing. Moreover, an imperative concern to sustain the legitimacy of Socialist political systems undoubtedly encouraged a new relationship with Vietnam provided that the government in Hanoi was prepared to accept that it could no longer enjoy an exclusive association with its counterpart in Phnom Penh.

China had also begun to acknowledge the disutility of conspicuous patronage of the Khmer Rouge, a party at its insistence to the political settlement of the Cambodian conflict, despite their gruesome record in power. The Beijing Government had never been committed to the Khmer Rouge as a revolutionary ally. They had always been treated as a dispensable instrument of anti-Vietnamese purpose and since the withdrawal of Vietnamese main force units in September 1989 doubts had arisen about their military performance. But support for a deal between Prince Sihanouk and Prime Minister Hun Sen which appeared to distance China from the Khmer Rouge did not foreclose on the option of reactivating them should the outcome of a political settlement appear to serve Vietnam's interest. In the meantime, there was a good prospect that China's object of denying Vietnam's dominance in Cambodia would be protected through the person of Prince Sihanouk in accommodation with the incumbent government in Phnom Penh, no longer a client of Hanoi.

The Phnom Penh Administration cobbled together by Vietnam has always been a political *mélange* kept together in part by hatred and dread of the Khmer Rouge. A strong indication that Hun Sen and his close supporters regarded their career interests better protected in association with Prince Sihanouk than through weakened Vietnamese patronage was provided in mid-October 1991. An extraordinary congress of the ruling People's Revolutionary Party repudiated its ideological identity in favour of political pluralism and expressed a willingness to accept the overall leadership of Prince Sihanouk. Moreover, Prince Sihanouk's triumphal return to Phnom Penh in November 1991 was marked by an immediate tactical collaboration with the incumbent administration in a coalition government.

Conflict Resolution and Regional Security

The most recent phase of the Indochina problem has been brought to the point of resolution because of a fundamental change in its strategic context making possible an uncoupling from both global and regional considerations. An international dimension of the problem remains in the form of a peacekeeping exercise of daunting order because the domestic dimension of conflict has assumed an importance which was not present at the outset. Moreover, some of the internal Cambodian parties represent alternative versions of national identity which are not readily reconciled.

The political settlement endorsed in Paris in October 1991 makes provision for general elections within a multi-party political system.

Prince Sihanouk is virtually guaranteed the dominant role in such a system at the outset but any settlement which pivots unduly on his person will almost certainly be a fragile one, enduring only for as long as his remaining years. Much will depend on Prince Sihanouk's ability to sustain a working relationship with the incumbent administration in Phnom Penh, especially at the expense of the Khmer Rouge, which would survive his incapacity or demise. He turned 70 in November 1992 and has enjoyed mixed health. His son, Prince Ranariddh, who has been his principal representative, is not an automatic political successor. He does not enjoy his father's national and international standing and has been the object of family intrigue. Prince Sihanouk's demise in the absence of institutionalised politics of a kind could invite the employment of *force majeure* to resolve differences among Cambodian adversaries representing incompatible political traditions.

The Khmer Rouge constitute one such tradition. They may well secure sufficient votes under a provincially-based scheme of proportional representation to claim a legitimate place in public life and so poise themselves to take advantage of any future power vacuum.[9] Despite provision for demobilising factional fighting units in the Cambodian settlement, there is a general expectation that all sides will cheat so as to insure against its breakdown. The Khmer Rouge would seem to be in a better position to cheat than any other faction and have resisted compliance with the disarmament provisions of the UN peace plan. Their resumption of power would certainly be of international significance. Indeed, political change of any kind in Cambodia will continue to be of interest to Thailand and Vietnam both of which has a long record of trans-Mekong intervention. Renewed intervention in response to political change will obviously depend on its geopolitical implications for Cambodia's immediate neighbours and, above all, on the state of Sino–Vietnamese relations. Intervention from a Western source would not seem very likely, however, once United Nations peacekeeping forces depart, despite humanitarian concern over the likely return of the Khmer Rouge.

Irrespective of the outcome of domestic political conflict, the Indochina problem has ceased to engage competing regional and global interests in a once characteristic way. Political change within all of its states has been detached for the time being from those considerations of balance of power which gave the problem its dynamic quality from the end of the Pacific War. The problem has been resolved, above all, in China's geopolitical interest and against that of Vietnam which has been obliged to acknowledge, by abdicating its guardian role in Cambodia, that it has been taught a lesson by its historical enemy. To the extent that the government in Beijing now believes that it enjoys a greater entitlement to manage regional order, then the Indochina problem could be succeeded by other regional problems. Such an eventuality would be in the nature of all politics whereby solutions tend to give rise to new problems.

Centrally at issue in the many phases of the Indochina problem has been the question of the regional balance of power. At the outset of the Cambodian conflict, it was commonplace to represent Vietnam as some kind of Asian Prussia within an Indochinese federation as its goal. Indeed, its formula of exclusive special relationships applying among the states of Indochina seemed to presage the emergence of a historically unprecedented centre of power to which other regional states would be obliged to defer. Loss of political will and fear of loss of political identity in adverse economic circumstances have obliged Vietnam's Communist Party to give up its geopolitical ambitions and submit to Chinese primacy. The regional implications of the Cambodian settlement are mixed, however. China has displayed a steely consistency of purpose over Cambodia and also its claim to the islands of the Spratly Archipelago. It has been unwilling to make any concessions over maritime jurisdiction. Yet at the same time, its government is conscious of its diminished international position attendant on the end of the Cold War and the collapse of Soviet power. It faces a more recalcitrant United States buoyed by its Gulf War success and annoyed by China's contribution to nuclear proliferation. China also faces a suspicious set of states within ASEAN with which it wishes to engage in closer economic cooperation. Moreover, whatever its ambitions in Southeast Asia, it may find its energies distracted by an increasingly self-confident Taiwan capable of exercising a growing attraction for China's coastal provinces as well as Hong Kong.

Vietnam has been obliged to defer to China but correspondingly has begun to rehabilitate itself politically in Southeast Asia. A visit by Prime Minister Vò Van Kiet to Indonesia, Singapore and Thailand from late October 1991 was especially significant in marking the removal of a pariah status. Indonesia has long adopted an accommodating attitude towards Vietnam and President Suharto visited Hanoi in November 1990 well in advance of the Cambodian settlement. Thailand and Singapore, however, had been the most hardline of ASEAN states in insisting that Vietnam liquidate its occupation of

Cambodia and play a constructive part in removing the political legacy of its invasion. The willingness of their governments to permit the first visit by a Vietnamese Prime Minister since the invasion of Cambodia represented a political breakthrough giving Vietnam an opportunity to establish countervailing relationships to that accepted on sufferance with China.

In July 1992, Vietnam and Laos acceded to the Treaty of Amity and Cooperation concluded by the ASEAN states at their first summit in February 1976. The terms of this treaty constituted a code of international conduct based on the United Nations Charter. It had been made open for signature by non-ASEAN states in the hope that it might serve as a political bridge to the revolutionary governments which had recently come to power in Indochina. At the time the Vietnamese Politburo was in a triumphalist frame of mind and treated ASEAN with derision. Sixteen years later, the revised composition of that Politburo reflects a chastened experience, with Vietnam committed to a course of economic reform requiring a peaceful and cooperative regional environment of which the ASEAN states form an important part.

Post Cambodia, the condition of security in Southeast Asia no longer reflects a problem which lent definition to linked regional and international alignments. Despite its polarising effect, the problem of Indochina did place a number of regional tensions on hold, including land and maritime boundary disputes among member governments of ASEAN and also between some of them and those of China and Vietnam, themselves in competition over land and sea.[10] The significance of the end of the Indochina problem is that paradoxically it removes both a focus for conflict and an important factor of constraint from the conduct of those regional states which have been ranged in loose coalition against Vietnam. The measure of common interest present in that coalition has now been replaced by different considerations, including the countervailing one of a Vietnam keen to secure regional rehabilitation.

The problem of Indochina was a particular expression of the classical problem of the balance of power. That problem still obtains in Southeast Asia as the pattern of external influences has been subject to marked change, including the withdrawal of America's military presence from the Philippines. There is no equivalent problem which now joins domestic political change to external affiliation. There are evident matters of political succession to be resolved within the region but they do not appear likely to involve the kind of shift of ideological identity which made Indochina such a political cockpit for so many decades. There is, of course, much speculation about rising aspirants likely to succeed to America's waning regional role.[11] But with the disappearance of the measure of constraint engendered by the Cambodian conflict, at issue is the difficulty of forging a structure of cooperative relationships through which to address security issues. Such a structure is not easy to contemplate in the wake of the Indochina problem. Common threat has become even more difficult to define and there has been an attendant reluctance on the part of regional states to assume new obligations.

That reluctance was indicated in Singapore in January when ASEAN heads of government held their fourth summit. In addressing problems of common security, all that could be agreed was that annual post ministerial conferences with external dialogue partners should be utilised to discuss such matters but without going beyond consultation. The subsequent post-ministerial conference held in Manila in July following the annual meeting of ASEAN's foreign ministers considered regional security but did no more than talk about it. Although Vietnam and Laos acceded to ASEAN's Treaty of Amity and Cooperation in Manila and were accorded observer status, there was no indication that they were joining a security regime capable of addressing those regional tensions which had previously been kept on hold because of the problem of Indochina. ASEAN did rediscover its collective diplomatic voice to the extent that the Association issued a declaration on the South China Sea calling for the peaceful resolution of competing claims to its islands. But as it does not uphold the strategic perspective and dispose of the capability of an alliance, ASEAN was not in any position to confront the new problem of the regional balance of power which had succeeded that of Indochina.

Notes

1. George McT. Kahin, *Intervention. How America Became Involved in Vietnam*, Alfred A. Knopf, New York, 1986.
2. Paul M. Kattenburg, *The Vietnam Trauma in American Foreign Policy, 1945–75*, Transaction Books, New Brunswick and London, 1980.
3. An instructive account of these tensions from a Vietnamese perspective may be found in *The Truth About Vietnam–China Relations Over the Last Thirty Years*, Ministry of Foreign Affairs, Hanoi, 1979.

4. For accounts of the origins of the Cambodian conflict, see David W. P. Elliott (ed.), *The Third Indochina Conflict*, Westview Press, Boulder, Colorado, 1981; Grant Evans and Kelvin Rowley, *Red Brotherhood at War*, Verso Books, London, 1984, and Nayan Chanda, *Brother Enemy: The War After the War*, Harcourt Brace Jovanovich, San Diego, California, 1986.

5. See Charles McGregor, *The Sino–Vietnamese Relationship and the Soviet Union*, Adelphi Papers no. 232, IISS, London, Autumn 1988.

6. See Michael Leifer and John Phipps, *Vietnam and Doi Moi: Domestic and International Dimensions of Reform*, RIIA Discussion Papers no. 35, London, June 1991.

7. Note the terms of the Political Report reprinted in *BBC, Summary of World Broadcasts*, FE/1109 C1/11.

8. Normalisation of relations was registered in the joint communique, see *BBC, SWB* FE/1227 A3/1–2.

9. See Nayan Chanda, "Pol Pot's Plans for Peacetime Cambodia", *The Asian Wall Street Journal Weekly*, 9 September 1991.

10. For a comprehensive account of the important maritime dimension of regional conflict, see Douglas M. Johnson and Mark J. Valencia, *Pacific Ocean Boundary Problems*, Martinus Nijhoff, Dordrecht, 1991.

11. See, for example, William T. Tow, *Encountering the Dominant Player: US Extended Deterrence Strategy in the Asia Pacific*, Columbia University Press, New York, 1991.

17

Vietnam's Intervention in Kampuchea
The Rights of State v. the Rights of People

It is notoriously difficult to formulate a precise definition of intervention which can fit all cases. Intervention is best understood as an act that can be placed along a continuum of state practice which may include such diverse undertakings as economic sanctions and radio broadcasts. The particular example of Vietnam's intervention in Kampuchea[1] is straightforward, however. On 25 December 1978, the Vietnamese Army carried a new government into Kampuchea almost literally in their saddlebags. They displaced an established government which enjoyed international recognition, including a seat at the United Nations, and installed a new government of their own choosing.

The formal agency for intervention was a so-called National Salvation Front for National Liberation,[2] made up in the main of dissident Khmer Rouge; that is, dissidents from the ruling revolutionary

Reprinted in abridged form from Michael Leifer, "Vietnam's Intervention in Kampuchea: The Rights of State v. the Rights of People", in *Political Theory, International Relations, and the Ethics of Intervention*, edited by Ian Forbes and Mark Hoffman (Basingstoke, Hampshire and New York: Macmillan Press and St. Martin's Press, 1993), pp. 145–56, by permission of Palgrave Macmillan.

party in the so-called Democratic Kampuchea. Vietnam acted in support of this National Salvation Front through the deployment of "volunteers", in the same way as China had conducted its intervention in Korea at the end of 1950.

Vietnam's public justification was the need to remove a genocidal regime. Clearly, in light of what we now know went on inside Kampuchea between April 1975 and December 1978, that justification carries a high degree of validity. On 18 February 1979, Vietnam entered into a Treaty of Friendship with the government of the new People's Republic of Kampuchea, which had been set up in early January. That Treaty of Friendship served as the legal basis for the acknowledged presence of Vietnamese troops inside the country until their declared withdrawal in September 1989.

Public v. Private Justifications

There is a fundamental difference between the public justification for intervention and the private and informal positions which the Vietnamese have been willing to reveal. In discussions in Hanoi and outside the country, it has been quite clear that human rights violations in Kampuchea were not the pressing priority. Indeed, the whole process of human rights violations of the most gruesome kind, beginning with the invasion of Phnom Penh by the Khmer Rouge in April 1975 and the forcible despatch of its population to the countryside, failed to attract Vietnamese condemnation — until it was politically convenient. For the Vietnamese, the requirement in December 1978 to remove the government in Phnom Penh and replace it with one of their own choosing was a matter of strategic imperative rooted in geopolitical doctrine.[3] That doctrine contemplated Indochina as a natural entity in strategic terms which had to be maintained. Otherwise the integrity and political identity of the Vietnamese state might be placed at risk. This was a view which had been adopted partly from a long-standing proprietary attitude of pre-colonial vintage, and also importantly from Vietnamese Communist experience of fighting both the French and the Americans during the First and Second Indochina Wars. The lesser countries of Laos and Kampuchea were regarded as platforms from which Vietnam could be threatened (partly because of its vulnerable geographic shape). Such platforms had been used to military purpose by both the French and the Americans. It was deemed necessary therefore to establish a close structure of special political relationships in the interests of Vietnamese security.

Public Condemnation and Private Interests

International recognition and acceptability of the new Kampuchean regime was crucial to validate Vietnam's action. The public explanation offered, that it was justifiable to remove a genocidal regime, related to that purpose. In the declaratory position of the Vietnamese government, the ethical dimension was integral to the legitimacy of Vietnamese support through "volunteers" for the agency of intervention. When Phan Van Dong went to Phnom Penh to sign a Treaty of Friendship on 18 February 1979, he stated:

> In the atmosphere of this friendly meeting our delegation warmly welcomes the fraternal Kampuchean peoples' historic victory. A victory which has smashed the tyranny of the Pol Pot clique, eliminated for good the genocide and slavery imposed by this clique.... The victory of the Kampuchean revolution is a victory of the indomitable struggle of the people, who for independence and national sovereignty and for the right to live, oppose the treacherous scheme of expansion and hegemony of the Peking rulers and the fascists' regime of the Pol Pot clique, unprecedented in human history.

The Vietnamese represented themselves as supporting an act of liberation and self-determination. The declaratory position adopted indicated the way in which public justification was sought for action in support of the agency of intervention. In other words, the National Salvation Front which they had promoted had been engaged in legitimate acts. Moreover, the Vietnamese never admitted direct intervention at the outset. What they did admit was a measure of retaliation against the Pol Pot regime to defend their frontiers and preserve their national integrity.[4] The actual troop presence was only admitted and justified in retrospect under Article 2 of the Treaty of Friendship. That article states that "[o]n the principle that national defence and construction are the cause of each people, the two parties undertake to whole-heartedly support and assist each other in all domains and in all necessary forms in order to strengthen the capacity to defend their independent sovereignty and unity". This was cited as an act of consent by the People's Republic of Kampuchea (PRK) to the presence of "fraternal" Vietnamese troops in Kampuchea.

These pronouncements were seen by the Vietnamese, at least in principle, as functional in international debate, and as a way of trying to rally diplomatic support for their position (though with limited success). They also had relevance to domestic control. To the extent that the spectre of the return of a genocidal regime was the only alternative, then clearly a temporary alien presence in Kampuchea would be less objectionable than the terrorism of Pol Pot. However, informal communication made it explicit that the intervention had been a matter of strategic necessity. It was put in terms of *realpolitik* rather than of ideology. The different justifications might be explained with reference to the practice of price discrimination in different markets. Where the market is the formal arena of the General Assembly of the United Nations and the aim is to secure legitimisation, then arguments with reference to the publicly accepted norms of that organisation have been advanced. In the corridors, other appeals to governments with differing interests have been made, albeit in conflict with public positions.

There were a number of other related issues at stake in the public discourse about the Kampuchean conflict. First, there was the question of the nature of the ousted government of Democratic Kampuchea, changing in form to become the Coalition Government of Democratic Kampuchea from the middle of 1982. Clearly ethical considerations were relevant to this change. The demonic side of the ousted government had been played up by Vietnam and its supporters. Correspondingly, that aspect had been played down and diluted by the Association of South-East Asian Nations (ASEAN), primarily concerned about the sanctity of national sovereignty. It went out of its way to promote that dilution by encouraging a coalition through the addition of the two non-communist factions. Second, there was the question of representation in the United Nations. If, for example, the PRK could displace the Coalition of Democratic Kampuchea from its United Nations seat, then other important consequences could follow. It would reinforce the legitimacy of the government in Phnom Penh and make it more difficult to continue diplomatic and other support to the Khmer resistance. It would also give the PRK government access to avenues of economic support previously denied it, while Vietnam would be released from a pariah diplomatic position.

To sum up, then, the Vietnamese employed a public justification for intervention based on appeal to the humanitarian norms of the international community. Private or informal justification was couched, however, in terms of perception of the strategic requirements in Indochina, made up of three separate states. On both counts they were unable to overcome a critical objection: namely, the violation of the cardinal rule of the society of states to respect the sanctity of national sovereignty.

Intervention and the Consequences for Legitimacy

The main argument against the Vietnamese relates to their propping up the PRK government which was established through a military initiative. This role distinguished the situation from some other interventions such as India in Pakistan and Tanzania in Uganda, which were limited operations, not a prelude to externally contrived political reconstruction. That argument animated public debate in the United Nations. When the Vietnamese complained that they had done no more than other governments who had not been put in the dock, the reply was that the government of the PRK existed only because Vietnamese armed forces were in the country and that the removal of those forces would mean the disappearance of that government. The ability of the government in Phnom Penh to sustain itself independently without Vietnamese military support had regularly been an issue in UN debates. For example, Singapore's one-time Ambassador to the UN, Tommy Koh, speaking on behalf of the ASEAN group, said that, "That government of the PRK is nothing more than a puppet regime installed by Vietnam and kept in office by more than 200 000 troops in Kampuchea". A fundamental question had been the legitimacy of that regime. ASEAN regarded it as illegitimate because, it was claimed, the PRK could only sustain itself with the support of an external agency.

This raises the question of whether it is possible to determine the legitimacy or illegitimacy of a particular regime with reference to ethical considerations. The debate over Kampuchea suggests a presumption that regimes are illegitimate if they are put in place by another country by force of arms, even if they continue in power. Indeed, the solution to the conflict over Cambodia worked out by the permanent members of the UN Security Council turns on "free and fair elections" to determine the political future of the country. If there could be clearly specified criteria for the legitimate existence of a regime, then ethical considerations might inform judgement about intervention. However, the fundamental problem for international society is that an act of military intervention is deemed, in principle, to threaten the independence of the state, which if tolerated threatens the independence of all states. Therefore, all governments have, in principle at least, a general and equal interest in opposing all interventions, even if justified on ethical grounds.

Ethics and Sovereignty

The ethical factor in the Kampuchean conflict had been a utilitarian one, employed by one side. The terms of public debate about the merits and demerits of intervention were set by international norms. These norms are enshrined in the United Nations Charter and have informed the vocabulary of international discourse. To the extent that states see themselves as beneficiaries of these norms, then they are willing to support them in principle. But the issue of ethics has entered this conflict primarily by way of trying to secure justification or international legitimacy for adverse positions adopted. The Vietnamese used the argument of necessity with reference to the removal of a genocidal regime. That was not effective and was blocked by the far more well-established cardinal rule of the society of states.

The arguments that have been made against the Vietnamese and which have prevailed as arguments are best regarded as prudential rather than ethical. They hold that the nature of the state and its government cannot really be regarded as a criterion for membership or exclusion from membership of international society. Notwithstanding the way that members of international society share ideas and norms, a state which appears to have transgressed certain ethical values is not deemed to be void of legitimacy. Traditionally, therefore, a state's record in human rights is not one of the criteria by which to approve or reject the credentials of a delegation to the UN. Were it introduced into the necessary qualifications for membership of the UN, then at least half the governments would be excluded.

Two other arguments were put forward within the General Assembly. First, accepting the validity of Vietnam's action would set an extremely dangerous precedent. Second, the key issue was the sanctity of national sovereignty and its violation. All member governments have a general interest in upholding that sanctity. A convergence of separate realist interests occurred which served to sustain that general interest. To that extent, the issue of the sanctity of sovereignty has been upheld against arguments based upon ethical considerations of human rights. The rights of state took priority over the rights of people. This prevailing reasoning may be set against the Vietnamese private justification for their presence in and hold on Kampuchea until their declared unilateral withdrawal in September 1989. That position is that the Kampuchean state, in light of its experience of civil war, has been so debilitated in its physical and personal infrastructure that it cannot be an independent entity. It cannot sustain itself as a buffer state, which would serve the security interests of Vietnam, without external protection. To the extent that it is believed that Kampuchea can only be a satellite of another country, the Vietnamese have been determined on geopolitical grounds, as far as their resources have allowed, that it should be their satellite.

Before Vietnam's intervention there was no full public debate on the merits of intervention in Kampuchea on ethical grounds. In part this was because of an absence of full information until well after the event. The internationally condemned intervention by Vietnam suggests a terrible irony. Its direct effect was to halt the process of slaughter in Kampuchea. That was not its prime purpose. Vietnam was unable to use the effect of its intervention to justify its purpose.

Conclusion

Vietnam's intervention was the culmination of a process of conflict involving China in particular. The Politburo in Hanoi came to the view during 1978 that there was no other way of dealing with a hostile and ferocious government in Phnom Penh, whose unhygienic political relationship with China seemed designed to place Vietnam in a strategic trap. That government had conducted deep penetration raids into southern Vietnam employing Chinese artillery to shell population centres. Nevertheless, the cardinal rule of the society of states, namely respect for the sanctity of national sovereignty, prevailed as a basis for judging Vietnam because most states share a vested interest in upholding that sanctity. ASEAN resolutions in the General Assembly of the UN calling for the withdrawal of Vietnamese forces from Kampuchea drew progressively increasing majorities during the course of the 1980s, with only lip service paid at the end of the decade to a concern over human rights violations.

In response to international pressure and its own economic distress, Vietnam repeatedly expressed its willingness to withdraw troops from Kampuchea. Nominal withdrawals began in 1982, while a finite date of 1990 was set in the mid-1980s. The transformation in major power relations and an international conference on Cambodia, albeit abortive, prompted a declared accelerated withdrawal in September 1989. However, an attendant upsurge in Khmer Rouge military pressure made it necessary to return "advisers" to stiffen the resistance of the Phnom Penh government. At issue as far as international response was concerned was the absence of any authoritative monitoring of withdrawal. Provision for the United Nations to undertake this role in the context of a comprehensive political settlement was accepted by Vietnam. National security has been Vietnam's abiding priority in the diplomacy over a settlement; its object has been to uphold the tenure of the incumbent government in Phnom Penh and correspondingly to deny political success to the Khmer Rouge. Condemnation of the Khmer Rouge's bestial record has not been sufficient to overcome international pressure for a settlement designed to deny the legitimacy of Vietnam's intervention and its political outcome through an electoral process. United Nations' management of that process cannot provide a guarantee that Cambodia will be freed of the scourge of the Khmer Rouge, whose military strength has made them, of necessity, a party to a political settlement.

In considering the experience of Kampuchea between 1975 and 1978, the motivation for intervention should ideally have been humanitarian. In the event, intervention was governed by strategic priorities and the international responses to that intervention by the corresponding priorities of interested parties. The ostensible basis for counter-intervention challenging Vietnam's action has been the cardinal rule of the society of states. On both sides of the argument, for and against intervention, ethics have been subordinate even when employed in its justification.

Notes

1. Democratic Kampuchea was the official name of the state (now the State of Cambodia) at the time of the initial act of intervention.
2. This is a rather interesting representation. Usually one thinks of national *liberation* fronts. This terminology led Singapore's Prime Minister Lee Kuan

Yew to quip: "When Communists want to take over capitalist countries or overthrow capitalist governments, they set up national liberation fronts. When they want to take over or overthrow communist governments, they set up national salvation fronts".

3. It is worth bearing in mind that the Vietnamese support for a Kampuchean attempt to remove the Pol Pot regime represented a change of public position from April 1975. That change occurred in the context of a corresponding threatening change in their strategic environment: namely, a concurrent and serious deterioration in the relationships between Vietnam and Kampuchea — both governments and the Communist Parties — and also between Vietnam and China — again between the governments and the Communist Parties. Previously, the Vietnamese had defended the record of the Democratic Kampuchean regime during an attempt in 1978 by the British government, through Evan Luard, then junior minister in the Foreign and Commonwealth Office, to raise the issues of human rights violations in Kampuchea before the United Nations Human Rights Commission in Geneva.

4. When discussing the justifications offered privately in terms of national security, the Vietnamese might subsequently have had recourse to a self-defence claim in relation to Kampuchean deep-raids and shelling. Vietnam was very careful to assess the weak points in the possible case against them and to defend them, but they did have a *prima facie* right of self-defence under the UN Charter if they were being attacked. They could have intervened in a legitimate way, with due observance of the principle of proportionality. There had been a previous intervention into Kampuchea in December 1977, with the object of imposing a sanction in the hope that it would deter the Khmer Rouge. Instead, it had just the opposite effect.

18

Cambodia Conflict
Interests and Roles of
External Powers

Although the pattern of external power involvement in South-east Asia has changed radically since the end of the Second Indochina War, the practice has persisted, for the same reason that it arose during the course of the First Indochina War. Competitive external-power involvement in South-east Asia has been the consequence of a coupling of either internal or intra-regional conflict to strategic perspective and priorities. In this respect Kampuchea has assumed the kind of international significance attributed earlier to Vietnam, in that the outcome of internal conflict was perceived both within and outside the region as likely to transform not only the political identity of the Khmer state but also its external affiliations. The implications for the regional balance of power were not confined to South-east Asia. With this wider inter-relationship arising from the conflict over Kampuchea in mind, we must examine the interests

Reprinted in abridged form from Michael Leifer, *Conflict and Regional Order in Southeast Asia*, Adelphi Paper No. 162 (London: International Institute for Strategic Studies, 1980), pp. 13–23, by permission of Oxford University Press.

and roles of the People's Republic of China, the United States, Japan and the Soviet Union.

The People's Republic of China

Of all the major states outside South-east Asia, China has the most direct interest in the pattern of power within the region. Indeed, in terms of location and historical associations, China is hardly external. She shares common borders with Burma, Laos and Vietnam, and is a coastal state in the South China Sea, over which she maintains extensive claims. Within the states of South-east Asia there reside large communities of ethnic Chinese, approximately seventeen million in number, who play a central role in their economies out of all proportion to their numerical strength. China's policy towards these communities has never been completely free from ambivalence, which has engendered an abiding concern on the part of regional governments that Peking might seek to influence their behaviour to political ends.

China's policy has never been free from ambivalence in another sense. In her role as a revolutionary state she has never relinquished a moral commitment to support fraternal revolutionary movements on her southern periphery. However, the dominant theme in her policy towards South-east Asia has been the denial of advantage to her principal international adversaries. The balance of power has been the prevailing consideration in this endeavour. Thus the re-unification of Vietnam on the terms of the Vietnamese Communist Party was a lesser priority than the elimination of an American strategic threat. The management of a revised relationship with the United States when the Soviet Union was perceived as the supreme external menace to the security of the Chinese state also took priority over Vietnamese interests. It was in this context that the apparent close political association between Peking and Hanoi did not survive the end of the Second Indochina War. Its marked deterioration and junction with Sino-Soviet relations became the central factor in China's policy towards the countries of South-east Asia.

From the end of the Second Indochina War Vietnam was viewed increasingly as an ingrate and an upstart: an ingrate because her government had refused to acknowledge the extent to which revolutionary success had been facilitated by Chinese assistance; an upstart because she had expressed her independence in an obdurate and uncompromising manner, especially in her refusal to acknowledge

China's international doctrine and in her willingness to endorse Soviet diplomatic positions. The issue of Kampuchea served as the catalyst in moving relations with Vietnam past a point of no return, and the alleged persecution of resident Chinese community from the early months of 1978 was a major aggravating factor. Central to Chinese calculations was her perception of Vietnam as the political surrogate of the Soviet Union for the fulfilment of her regional ambitions. The consolidation of Vietnamese–Soviet economic ties through the former's membership of the Council for Mutual Economic Assistance (CMEA) in June 1978, and then the conclusion of a Treaty of Friendship and Co-operation with the Soviet Union in the following November confirmed the client role of the Vietnamese government. Indeed, it was regarded as more than a coincidence that the Treaty was signed just one month before the proclamation of a so-called Kampuchean National United Front for National Salvation, in opposition to the incumbent government in Phnom Penh and with open Vietnamese support and evident inspiration as well as Soviet endorsement.

As a matter of political self-respect, and in response to its view of Vietnam as an externally inspired regional poacher, the Chinese government set out to act as regional gamekeeper to restrain her smaller neighbour. Her credibility and reputation as a regional power was at stake. China's limited military intervention was not intended to challenge the existence of the government in Hanoi; it was intended to underline the geopolitical context of Sino–Vietnamese relations and to demonstrate that Vietnam could readily be chastised despite a Treaty of Friendship with the Soviet Union which contained a security clause.

China set out to register a political gain by military means. In the event, she demonstrated that her army possessed the firepower (as well as the dispensable manpower) to break through Vietnam's defence perimeter and to lay waste her northern border region. China's military intervention undoubtedly increased the price which Vietnam has been obliged to pay for the sake of asserting a special relationship with Kampuchea. But there has not been any indication since that act of punishment was concluded in March 1979 that the Politburo in Hanoi has entertained any willingness to compromise over the internal transfer of power within Kampuchea.

It may be argued that China's punitive policy has been self-defeating and has served to demonstrate the shortcomings of her general military capability. She could not prevent Vietnam from discharging her ethnic

Chinese community into the South China Sea. To the extent that China has succeeded in driving Vietnam deeper into the political embrace of the Soviet Union, the outcome of that policy may be regarded as a distortion of strategic priorities. The object of the exercise was to counter the extension of Soviet influence, not to promote it. Nonetheless, it may be argued also that her government was obliged to react strongly to Vietnam's invasion of Kampuchea as a matter of political self-respect; otherwise her standing as a regional power would have been diminished.

China's policy is best contemplated as a long-term undertaking. She has been adamant in her refusal to be reconciled to Vietnamese hegemony within Indochina and conducts her policy not on the basis of success or failure being realised in the course of just one dry season. China's geographical position enables her to apply persistent pressure on Vietnam throughout Indochina at acceptable cost. She has maintained a high level of tension along her borders with Vietnam and Laos, holding out the prospect of a second "lesson", and has been able to provide material support to the Pol Pot resistance inside Kampuchea. More to the point, her intention would seem to be to make Vietnam over-reach herself and drain her resources in the process — to the point of virtual collapse. In addition, China seeks to demonstrate to the Soviet Union that she is throwing good aid after bad and to Vietnam that no ultimate profit can accrue from an unhygienic political relationship.

China's refusal to be reconciled to the prospect of Vietnamese hegemony in Indochina has been a function of traditional interest and of a bitter adversary relationship with the Soviet Union reinforced by events in Afghanistan. She has been encouraged in opposition to Vietnam by the diplomatic solidarity expressed by the ASEAN states, which she has sought to sustain.

An earlier endorsement of ASEAN's Zone of Peace proposal and support for the regional role of the Association in the cause of denying Soviet advantage has been complemented by an attempt to forge a united front in the wake of Vietnam's invasion of Kampuchea. Coincidence of interest has been most evident in the case of Thailand, whose leadership has valued China's public commitment to that kingdom's external defence, and who exercises a veto power over any joint ASEAN initiative designed to promote a political settlement with Vietnam over Kampuchea. As long as China can assure a government in Bangkok of the utility of seeking to deny Vietnamese dominance in

Kampuchea, other ASEAN states will be obliged to sustain a common diplomatic position with Thailand or risk threatening the cohesion of the Association.

For China the conventional imperative of the balance of power is the guiding principle of her policy in South-east Asia. And yet such a policy is not without ambivalent aspects. For example, as long as the Communist Party of China sustains its support, if only in principle, for revolutionary movements in the region — as part of its strategy of denying the penetration of Soviet influence — non-Communist governments in the region are depicted as illegitimate. In addition, the claim by China that the overseas Chinese communities resident in South-east Asia represent a patriotic united front and that there exists a "flesh and blood relationship between the overseas Chinese and the people of the motherland"[1] appears to make a demand on the loyalties of nationals of regional states. From the point of view of these regional states, China's strategy of denial in relation to Vietnam and the Soviet Union is well understood. There is considerable uncertainty and apprehension in assessing her intentions beyond that, particularly as China has demonstrated a willingness to resort to force in a conflict which involved the ill-treatment of an overseas Chinese community.

The United States of America

In the wake of her related *débâcles* in Vietnam and Kampuchea in 1975 the United States government visibly lost interest in mainland South-east Asia. Military withdrawal from Thailand by the middle of 1976 was countered, however, by a desire to retain air and naval bases in the Philippines, although negotiations over the revised terms of their operational use were not concluded when Jimmy Carter became President. His campaign promise, incorporated into policy, (although subsequently much modified), to withdraw American ground-combat forces from South Korea served to confirm apprehensions among South-east Asian governments that the United States was in strategic retreat in Asia, although she had taken a firm position over rights of naval passage through the Straits of Malacca and Singapore.

A re-orientation of American policy was indicated following the Vietnamese invasion of Kampuchea, although earlier expressions of interest in South-east Asia were exemplified by the visits of Vice-President Mondale to the Philippines, Indonesia and Thailand in April 1978 and by the ministerial dialogue conducted with ASEAN governments in Washington in August that year. Coincidentally, January 1979 marked the successful renegotiation of the military bases agreements with the government of the Philippines, as well as the fall of Phnom Penh to Vietnamese forces. The conclusion of these agreements, which had involved protracted discussions, represented concrete evidence of an American strategic interest which extended through South-east Asia to the Indian Ocean and on to the Persian Gulf.

The United States Administration expressed its strong opposition to the Vietnamese overthrow of the Pol Pot regime and its replacement by an evident Hanoi puppet. It was a matter of some irony that the Carter Administration, which had denounced the Pol Pot regime for its gross violation of human rights, should be so aroused by its removal. The concern displayed reflected balance-of-power considerations arising from Vietnam's relationship with the Soviet Union as indicated, for example, in the measure of tolerance accorded to China's military intervention in Vietnam. The immediate response of the United States to the invasion of Kampuchea was to suspend negotiations over the establishment of diplomatic relations with Vietnam, in marked contrast to the formal resumption of such ties with China celebrated by the visit to Washington in January 1979 of Vice-Premier Deng Xiaoping. For the non-Communist states of South-east Asia a limited revival of confidence in American interest in the region was derived from the visit to Washington in February 1979 of Thailand's Prime Minister, General Kriangsak Chamanand. President Carter expressed his commitment "to the integrity, freedom and security of Thailand" and reaffirmed the validity of the American commitment under the Manila Pact (or SEATO Treaty) of September 1954. He promised also to step up arms deliveries although the Thai government was less than satisfied with the scale of material assistance until an acceleration in arms transfers after a Vietnamese military incursion in June 1980.

American support for the integrity of Thailand was extended, if less explicitly, to the whole of ASEAN. In July 1979 the American Secretary of State Cyrus Vance met the Foreign Minister of the ASEAN states on the island of Bali at the termination of their annual meeting. His presence there was due, in part, to the acute problem for some ASEAN governments which had arisen from the flow of refugees from Vietnam. It reflected also a greater sense of commitment to ASEAN as an institution and to the denial of Vietnamese political goals. The

United States made other gestures which confirmed the direction of her policy including increased naval deployment in the Indian Ocean. Most significant was the decision announced in July that President Carter had halted indefinitely the withdrawal of American combat troops from South Korea.

The issue of Kampuchea turned on the consolidation of a pattern of power which had seemed likely to assume a definite form in April 1975. The invasion of that country brought about not only an immediate revival of that prospect but also Soviet backing of Vietnamese dominance. In consequence, the United States became associated with the governments of ASEAN and China in seeking to restore the independence of Kampuchea. But, apart from pursuing the issue within the United Nations, the United States Administration has played a secondary role if supporting an international relief aid operation to Kampuchea across the Thai border which has served to sustain the Pol Pot resistance. Its policy has followed the direction set out by President Nixon on the island of Guam in July 1969 — above all in encouraging military self-reliance on the part of regional allies. In response to the crisis which followed the events of January 1979, the US Administration took this course while urging a peaceful resolution of outstanding issues. There was no consideration of troop deployments. Cyrus Vance sought to promote the idea of an international conference on Kampuchea following his meeting with ASEAN's Foreign Ministers in July; to no avail. In October 1979, in Bangkok, Richard Holbrooke, the United States Assistant Secretary of State for East Asian and Pacific Affairs, offered an improvement in his government's relations with Vietnam in return for a withdrawal of its forces from Kampuchea in order to pave the way for a political settlement. But Nguyen Co Thach, then *de facto* Foreign Minister of Vietnam, refused to link the two issues and the attendant diplomatic impasse has been sustained.

American policy towards South-east Asia is an integral, if subordinate, aspect of a wider design in Asia in which the prime object is to ensure that the strategic balance between the United States, China and Japan on the one hand, and the Soviet Union on the other, is not disturbed dramatically, either in a general sense or in respect of a particular sector of the region. Interestingly, the general priorities of policy in Asia, namely, a strong flexible military presence to help maintain the balance of power, the cornerstone quality of the relationship with Japan, the commitment to normalizing relations with China and the promotion of United States trade and investment

— did not have direct relevance to South-east Asia. It was the crisis over Kampuchea which brought South-east Asia within the compass of a revised American policy in Asia. In so far as the governing factor in United States global policy is her relationship with the Soviet Union, then she has been concerned to limit the influence in Asia of any states directly identified with the Soviet interest, a view which has been reinforced by events in Afghanistan. Those events may well have indicated the merits of encouraging the disengagement of Vietnam from her close association with the Soviet Union, but such a policy could be promoted only by conceding Vietnamese interests in Indochina, which would bring the United States into conflict with some ASEAN states and China.

Historically, the United States has never shown a major direct interest in South-east Asia but has intervened in the region as a consequence of her governments' perceptions of the place of the region in a global framework. Although the focus of her involvement has altered ever since *rapprochement* with China, containment of a kind has been her objective. From the onset of the Third Indochina War in December 1978, containment has been expressed in an attempt to limit the direct influence of Moscow's regional beneficiary and to ensure the integrity of an allied state most directly affected by that war. This practice of containment has been conducted with restraint and without direct involvement in the prosecution of conflict. The priorities of the United States include upholding the independence of the non-Communist states of the region and maintaining the freedom of sea-lanes essential to the deployment of naval power from the Pacific to the Indian Ocean, as well as to the passage of oil supplies.

Japan

Japan's interest and involvement in South-east Asia was barely interrupted by her failure to enforce her co-prosperity policy during the course of the Pacific War. In the context of the United States' post-war practice of containment of Communism in Asia, the medium of reparations served the process of economic recovery and promoted a relationship of mutual economic dependence with states of the region. Japan's priorities in South-east Asia have been that of access to raw materials, markets and investment opportunities and to safe commercial maritime passage for oil supplies from the Middle East. With the passage of time the balance of economic dependence has shifted to favour Japan, while the region has never occupied the same importance as North-east Asia as a zone of security. Nonetheless, South-east Asia has remained of considerable attraction as an area of economic opportunity which requires stability to be sustained in that role. Although Japanese governments have not been conspicuous in assuming political responsibilities, they have undertaken some diplomatic initiatives in an attempt to reduce regional tensions.

The evolution of ASEAN has been in some ways a mixed blessing for Japan in that some of the collective initiatives of the Association have been directed towards redressing the balance of economic advantage. Japan prefers to deal in economic matters on a bilateral basis. However, the measure of intra-regional reconciliation and co-operation achieved as a result of that process of evolution has been regarded as an asset to Japanese policy. Commitment to ASEAN and to economic co-operation with its members on a collective, as well as a bilateral, basis was indicated in the attendance of Prime Minister Takeo Fukuda at the meeting of the Association's Heads of Government held in Kuala Lumpur in August 1977 to commemorate the tenth anniversary of its formation. The terms of that co-operation were articulated by the Japanese Prime Minister in a speech which he made in Manila in the same month, before returning to Tokyo. Yet Japan's relationship with the ASEAN states was not regarded as an obstacle to engaging in economic dealings with Communist countries within the region after the end of the Second Indochina War. The prospect of additional access to energy resources was an incentive to explore economic co-operation with Vietnam. Indeed, the underlying philosophy of Japan's foreign policy has been to open up options and to avoid having to make invidious choices.

Japan's response to the Vietnamese invasion of Kampuchea has corresponded, in form to that of the ASEAN states, China and the United States. She has continued to recognize the ousted Democratic Kampuchean government. Indeed, she has continued to receive its emissaries, including Foreign Minister Ieng Sary. Japan voted in the United Nations for a withdrawal of Vietnamese forces from Kampuchea but also recorded disapproval of China's "punishment" of Vietnam. Before the invasion of Kampuchea Japan had provided economic assistance to Vietnam. For the financial year 1979 a total of US$58.5 million had been committed. A concrete measure taken by Japan in response to that invasion was her suspension in April of that aid, even though it entailed prejudicing the undertaking assumed by the government in Hanoi to repay a large debt incurred in the past by the Thieu government in Saigon. Although the suspension of aid has been regarded as provisional in Tokyo, it was renewed for the financial year 1980. Although Japan has well understood the sense of alarm engendered within ASEAN as a result of Vietnam's invasion of Kampuchea, her government, under the late Mr Ohira, was keen to promote a political settlement. A major factor in her calculations has been the belief that any military solution satisfactory to ASEAN could be effected only through Chinese pressure, which would have the consequence of further consolidating the relationship between Vietnam and the Soviet Union.

Vietnam's invasion of Kampuchea and the probable establishment of Vietnamese political dominance throughout Indochina was not regarded in Tokyo as a direct threat to Japanese interests. Indeed, recent experience had demonstrated that Japan need not be obliged to choose between Communist and non-Communist South-east Asia in economic relations. However, she has been very concerned about the potential threat posed by the build-up of Soviet military forces in the close vicinity of her home islands. That concern was articulated in the Defence White Paper issued in July 1979 which provided for an expenditure of over US$10 billion — an increase of more than ten per cent over the 1978 military budget. In assessing the strategic environment the White Paper drew attention to the enhancement of the military capabilities of the Soviet Union in the Pacific, including the deployment to Vladivostock of the aircraft carrier *Minsk* and supporting craft. It noted also that, for the first time in eighteen years, Soviet ground forces had been deployed on Kunashiri and Etorofu, two of the four northern islands which have been a constant source of contention since the end of the Pacific War, affecting the basis of relations between the two countries. In addition, after mentioning that the ability of the United States to control sea areas might be further reduced in the future, it stated that, should the Soviet Union gain improved access to port facilities in Indochina, this would affect the military balance in the area and the safety of Japan's sea lines of communication. Although the content and tone of this White Paper and its successor do not indicate any fundamental material revision in Japan's long-term defence planning in response to changes in strategic environment, there is no evidence of complacency.[2] A prime consideration is the prospect of a continuing expansion of Soviet naval capability. And in this respect the position of Vietnam is believed to be of major importance borne out by the sighting of the *Minsk* in Cam Ranh Bay in September 1980.

In the light of the above analysis it is evident that the interests of the ASEAN states and Japan over the issue of Kampuchea have been less than fully congruent, although when Japan raises the prospect of Soviet advantage accruing from the continuation of conflict in Kampuchea, a chord is struck in ASEAN capitals. It was for this reason, among others, that Japan's former Foreign Minister Sunao Sonoda, put forward the idea of an international conference on Kampuchea when he met the Foreign Ministers of ASEAN in July 1979 after their annual meeting in Bali. This initiative encountered hostile response from the Vietnamese government which maintained that the situation in Kampuchea was irreversible, while the Chinese government was equally unenthusiastic. Although Japan was unable to induce any movement into the diplomacy of political settlement, she did not relinquish an interest in promoting a weakening of Vietnam's dependence on the Soviet Union.

Although sustaining its suspension of economic aid to Vietnam, the Japanese government persisted with an attempt to promote a political settlement in Kampuchea in the face of the perceived reality that the Heng Samrin government would not be removed by military means. However, when Mr Ohira visited China in December, he found an adamant refusal to consider such an approach. In the event Japan was obliged to give up her political initiative and also to sustain her suspension of economic aid to Vietnam. With the assumption of office by Zenko Suzuki in July 1980, Japan pledged full and active support for ASEAN initiatives to find a political solution to the Kampuchean conflict.

For Japan the issue of Kampuchea, which has served as a catalyst in regional conflict, is not clear-cut; certainly not in the manner it has been to China or to Thailand and Singapore. Like some other members of ASEAN, Japan's political outlook betrays a sense of ambivalence. This ambivalence arises from the fact that the interests of Japan's trilateral associates (China and the United States) as well as those of ASEAN as a diplomatic community, have disposed them to seek the international isolation of Vietnam, which has, accordingly, been obliged to rely on the Soviet Union as her major external source of economic benefaction and military assistance. Japan's concern arises from the prospect that in order to ensure the continuation of that benefaction and assistance Vietnam may have to make naval base facilities available to the Soviet Union on full operational terms and that such an enhancement of Soviet naval power and reach will not necessarily be matched or countered by the United States.

Such a consequence is regarded with greater apprehension in Tokyo than any consolidation of Vietnamese dominance in Indochina. At the same time there is no doubt that Japan wishes to preserve the various rights of access which she enjoys within non-Communist South-east Asia, whose governments share her economic philosophy and her principal external affiliations. To this end she is willing to act in a bountiful manner where necessary to help regional governments fend off internal challenges to political stability. However, the effects of regional conflict on the pattern of power in Indochina — to which external contentions have become attached — are beyond the capacity of Japan to regulate, to serve her complex economic and security interests.

The Soviet Union

The interests and the policies of the Soviet Union within South-east Asia have been governed by relationships with her principal adversaries, which have had their focus in other regions. Nonetheless, these relationships have prompted increased competitive involvement, particularly since the incorporation of China within their ambit and the transformation of Sino-American relations. The most important co-operative relationship which Soviet governments have maintained within South-east Asia has been with their counterparts in Hanoi — a relationship consummated by treaty in November 1978 and consolidated as a consequence of China's military intervention in Vietnam in February 1979.

Although Soviet involvement in South-east Asia was prompted initially by competition with the United States, exemplified in Indonesia as well as in Vietnam, growing rivalry with China was more important. Over Vietnam the Soviet Union sought, with some success, to reconcile the conflicting objectives of promoting the cause of the government in Hanoi and of advancing the attainment of detente with the United States. It also demonstrated the meaning of the term "adverse partnership" in the joint stand taken with the United States over the issue of unimpeded naval passage through the Straits of Malacca and Singapore.

Towards China, the Soviet Union has long sought to practice a strategy of containment, and this was indicated formally in June 1969 when Leonid Brezhnev put forward a less-than-precise proposal for a system of collective security in Asia. Although this proposal has never received serious consideration from the governments of South-east Asia, the Soviet Union did extend her diplomatic ties in the region. However, a striking example of her abiding concern to secure the political disadvantage of China was her reluctance to break diplomatic contact with the Lon Nol administration in Phnom Penh when the ousted Prince Sihanouk set up a government-in-exile in Peking in May 1970.

In the wake of the Second Indochina War, the Soviet Union has been a political beneficiary of the progressive transformation in relations between Vietnam and China. The Soviet Union conducted her relations with Vietnam from a position of considerable advantage, both because of the kind of economic assistance she was able to offer for post-war reconstruction and development, and also because history and geography had combined to render her much less of a threat to Vietnamese interests than her rival China. Indeed, Vietnam appeared to express her independence of undue Chinese influence through her relationship with the Soviet Union. That alignment developed into an intimate political relationship after the open armed confrontation between Vietnam and Kampuchea drew China to the support of Kampuchea. The Soviet Union profited from this development: from the serious economic difficulties facing Vietnam which were aggravated by the termination of Chinese economic assistance; from the limited ability of the government in Hanoi to attract aid from the Western world; and from a failure to reach a political accommodation with the United States. In the circumstances the Soviet Union would appear to have made an offer which the politburo in Hanoi could not refuse. In June 1978 Vietnam became a full member of the CMEA.

From this moment Soviet and Vietnamese policies in South-east Asia proceeded in evident harmony in competition with China. For example, the two governments embarked concurrently on an apparent change of public heart towards ASEAN by expressing a willingness to look more favourably on the Association's formula for regional order — the establishment of a Zone of Peace, Freedom and Neutrality. However, the course of events in the latter months of 1978 dictated that the Soviet Union should make a choice with consequential costs to her relations with the governments of ASEAN. On 3 November the

Soviet Union and Vietnam entered into a Treaty of Friendship and Co-operation which the politburo in Hanoi had not found necessary during the entire course of the Second Indochina War.

The signature of the Treaty between the Soviet Union and Vietnam indicated the willingness and the ability of the government in Moscow to make a decisive political choice. [I]ts outcome appeared to serve the principal purposes of the Soviet Union in the context of her rivalry with China. First, the Treaty sanctified the ideological standing of the Soviet Union through an act of identification with a renowned Third-world Communist state. Second, the evident connection between the Treaty, which contained a security clause, and the unhindered invasion of Kampuchea demonstrated the virtues of the Soviet Union as an ally. However, in undertaking a security obligation to Vietnam in advance of the invasion of Kampuchea, the Soviet Union took the calculated risk that her credibility as an ally might be called into question. She may have assumed also that a Vietnamese army would be able to pacify Kampuchea within the course of one dry season, and that the cost involved in supporting its expedition would be limited. On the other hand, the Soviet government may have calculated that Vietnam's undertaking in Kampuchea would entail such a measure of dependence on the Soviet Union that her government would be able in time to secure operational naval and air-base facilities of major strategic advantage for military deployment in East as well as in South-east Asia.

In response to China's military intervention in Vietnam on 17 February 1979, the Soviet Union behaved with caution. Although her obligations under the Treaty of Friendship with Vietnam were reaffirmed, Soviet reaction was confined to a vigorous denunciation of China's "shameless aggression", limited naval deployment and aerial reconnaissance in the Gulf of Tonkin, and an airlift of arms to an ally stretched militarily in containing the intervention across its northern border while engaged also in protracted pacification in Kampuchea. Soviet prudence would seem to have been governed, in part, by the preference of Vietnam to cope herself, independent of any direct military support. Her conduct would seem also to have been governed as much by the realization that it is easier to initiate a limited punitive strike than it is to bring it to a satisfactory military conclusion as by a reluctance at the time to embark on a course which might prejudice the Strategic Arms Limitation (SALT) negotiations. In addition, the Soviet Union's presumed forebearance gave some credence to her vilification of China as an international deviant, especially among those non-Communist states of South-east Asia disconcerted by the sight of Beijing action as regional gamekeeper.

The military obligations of the Soviet Union were never put to a full test because Sino–Vietnamese confrontation was not played out à *outrance* on the field of battle. Nonetheless, her credibility as an ally was tarnished somewhat, for China's military intervention in Vietnam represented a demonstration of resolution in the face of Moscow's support for Hanoi. It was also the first occasion on which the territory of a formal ally of the Soviet Union had been invaded, except, of course, by the Soviet Union herself. In consequence, in the absence of direct military support for Vietnam, it became incumbent on the Soviet Union to assist her ally to consolidate its dominance in Indochina. The burden of that obligation has become more onerous with the failure of the Vietnamese army to crush the Pol Pot resistance inside Kampuchea within the course of two dry seasons. Indeed, the cost of sustaining the economy and the defence of Vietnam, as well as her expeditionary forces in Laos and Kampuchea, has been put by Richard Holbrooke at US$3 million a day. The Soviet government may have some mixed feelings about such costly benefaction, particularly as it serves to reinforce the sense of political alienation promoted among the ASEAN states by her connivance in Vietnam's invasion of Kampuchea. Vietnam's Prime Minister has been emphatic that the Soviet Union has not been, and would not be, given military bases, if conceding that she had been accorded normal facilities offered to friendly countries.[3] The Soviet government has confirmed that its warship have been using the facilities of Cam Ranh Bay under the terms of its Treaty of Friendship with Vietnam.[4] This usage has given rise to growing Japanese and American concern. In April 1980 the Philippine government protested to the Soviet Union at the intrusions into its air space of TU-95D reconnaissance planes based at Danang. And in November 1980, the Thai government protested at the deployment of the *Minsk* and three support vessels in the Gulf of Siam.

The recent burgeoning of Soviet–Vietnamese relations has been encouraged by force of circumstances which have engaged the complementary interests of Moscow and Hanoi. That relationship has not always been easy or necessarily natural when not forged by the imperatives of the balance of power. In the case of the Soviet Union, the principal incentive in the relationship has been the opportunity to deny political advantage to China.

The treaty relationship between the Soviet Union and Vietnam marks the most successful Soviet diplomatic engagement in the political affairs of South-east Asia. Indeed, the Soviet Union has never before enjoyed such an exclusive association with any state in the region. However, one cost of cementing that association has been the evident increase in suspicion and mistrust on the part of the ASEAN states, and articulated most vigorously by the government of Singapore.

The Soviet Union views South-east Asia, from the standpoint of a global power, as a region of marginal direct interest but one where competitive involvement is demanded because of her own rivalry with principal adversaries. Her ideas about regional order, *vis-à-vis* the pattern of power in Indochina and the issue of naval passage in the maritime part of the region, are a product of this global outlook.

Notes

1. *Beijing Review*, 26 May 1978.
2. See Ian Nish, "Japan's Security Preoccupations", *The World Today*, November 1980.
3. In May 1979. See BBC Summary of World Broadcasts (SWB), FE/6127/A3/5 and again in September 1980, SWB FE/6532/A3/2.
4. *International Herald Tribune*, 15 May 1979.

19

UNTAC Fulfils Its Mission

The end of the Cold War had been a decisive factor in making possible a comprehensive political settlement of the Cambodian conflict. By the end of 1992, however, the agreement reached in Paris in October 1991 appeared to be in serious jeopardy despite the transformation in international and regional environments, including a *rapprochement* of a kind between China and Vietnam. The Khmer Rouge, which had been a signatory in Paris, had refused to honour the military provisions of the accord due to be implemented from June 1992 and had also refused access to zones under its control to UNTAC personnel engaged in registering voters. By the end of the year, a campaign of violent intimidation against contingents of the U.N. peace-keeping force as well as Vietnamese residents was well under way. The growing violence prompted a Japanese warning in April that its peace-keeping contingent might have to be withdrawn. UNTAC's task of holding the ring politically in order that it might conduct elections to determine the

Excerpted from Michael Leifer, "Expanding Horizons in Southeast", in *Southeast Asian Affairs 1994* (S'pore: Institute of Southeast Asian Studies, 1994), pp. 4–21, by permission of the publisher.

future governance of the country seemed then to be well beyond its collective grasp.

In the event, with the sanction of the U.N. Security Council, UNTAC assumed a calculated risk by embarking on elections according to schedule during 23–28 May. Polling was conducted without serious disruption, despite the call for a boycott by the Khmer Rouge. Political violence by the incumbent government of the State of Cambodia (SOC) against candidates of the rival royalist FUNCINPEC, led by Prince Norodom Ranariddh, the eldest son of Prince Sihanouk, also failed to subvert the electoral process. The political outcome matched the plan and timetable formulated in Paris, whereby an elected constituent assembly would convene to draft and approve a liberal democratic constitution after which that assembly would transform itself into a legislative body from which a new government would be drawn. The actual course of events did not go exactly to plan, even though Yasushi Akashi, the head of UNTAC, was able to claim that its mission had been a success despite the death of twenty-one of its personnel.[1]

In its mandate, UNTAC had been entrusted with responsibility for ensuring "a neutral political environment" conducive to free and fair elections. To that end, it was charged also with exercising "direct control" in spheres of foreign affairs, national defence, finance, public security, and information over the administration left in place by the Paris accords. Both of these tasks proved to be beyond UNTAC's capability, partly because of a strict adherence to its conventional peace-keeping mandate in addressing the problem of the Khmer Rouge and also because of a failure to attempt seriously to control the way in which the SOC employed its security apparatus against political opponents. The shortcomings of the U.N. presence, which gave rise to rampant inflation and social ills, prompted a public attack on its performance by Prince Sihanouk in February. In the run-up to the elections, the security situation deteriorated dramatically with some 200 deaths, 338 injuries, and 114 abductions occurring.

In April, Khieu Samphan, the nominal leader of the Khmer Rouge, who had been based in the capital since the multi-factional Supreme National Council (SNC) had been located there at the end of 1991, left Phnom Penh. His departure seemed to suggest that any attempt to conduct elections would be both dangerous and foolhardy. His departure had been prompted by a speech to the SNC by UNTAC's head, Yasushi Akashi, guaranteeing that elections would be held in

May. That speech had followed a statement by Khieu Samphan that the Khmer Rouge's National Unity Party would not participate in the forthcoming elections, which were depicted as a theatrical farce designed to hand over Cambodia to Vietnam. The withdrawal of Khieu Samphan and all of his officials except a residual staff was succeeded by military offensives by the Khmer Rouge in the north and northwest of the country.

Despite its shortcomings and the great difficulty of its task, the U.N. presence had a decisive impact on popular Cambodian attitudes and on the electoral outcome. Its information and education division pioneered the effective use of radio in providing advice and instructions about the nature of free and fair elections. Its broadcasts reached and influenced an extensive audience who were assured that the vote would be secret. In addition, its electoral division, employing courageous volunteers in the rural areas, proved able to register some 4.6 million voters. Fear of Khmer Rouge intimidation was overcome as nearly 90 per cent of registered voters cast their ballots in a poll that was subsequently endorsed by the U.N. Security Council as having been free and fair. A striking feature of the elections, which took place in a relatively peaceful atmosphere, was the absence of a concerted attempt by the Khmer Rouge to disrupt them, in some provinces even encouraging voting for FUNCINPEC. One hypothesis advanced for their conduct is that a deal had been struck with Prince Sihanouk in Beijing that in return for the Khmer Rouge not disrupting the elections, he would include them in some capacity in a future government.

The electoral outcome was inconclusive with no one party securing an overall majority in the Constituent Assembly of 120 seats. FUNCINPEC won a narrow majority with fifty-eight seats with over 45 per cent of the vote. The Cambodian People's Party (CPP), which had dominated the SOC, won fifty-one seats with just over 38 per cent. The Buddhist Liberal Democratic Party which emanated from the Khmer People's National Liberation Front led by former Prime Minister Son Sann, won ten seats with just under 4 per cent, while Moulinaka, one of the original resistance groups against the Vietnamese occupation, obtained only one seat with just over 1 per cent. The elections had been organized through a system of proportional representation within each province.

The immediate outcome of the elections in late May gave rise to a short period of political turbulence. The CPP challenged both their conduct and results on the grounds of malpractice and called for fresh polls in a number of provinces. An abortive assumption of executive powers by Prince Sihanouk, possibly justified from a fear of SOC military intervention, was followed by an abortive attempt to establish an autonomous zone in seven eastern provinces by Prince Norodom Chakrapong, the estranged half-brother of Prince Ranariddh and a deputy prime minister in the SOC. UNTAC refused to endorse either of these political stratagems and by mid-June, the CPP had reached an internal accord and grudgingly accepted the results of elections, which it had confidently expected to win. A Provisional National Government of Cambodia was established in which power was shared primarily between FUNCINPEC and the CPP with Prince Ranariddh and Hun Sen, head of government in the SOC, registering political parity as co-prime ministers. Such compromise was sustained throughout the deliberations of the Constituent Assembly, which convened on 16 June to vest full and special powers in Prince Sihanouk as head of state and also to declare null and void the right-wing coup that had deposed him on 18 March 1970. The Assembly took until 21 September to draft and ratify a new liberal constitution, which reinstated the monarchy.

Norodom Sihanouk promulgated the constitution and was enthroned as constitutional monarch in Phnom Penh on 24 September, nearly four decades after he had abdicated the throne in order to free himself of its constraints so as to play a full political role. His resumption of the throne was ironically an indication of a continuing ability to play such a role irrespective of his formal status. He had proved to be an essential ingredient in any political settlement because of his remarkable standing among the Cambodian populace and because of the international support which he has enjoyed, especially from China whose antagonism with Vietnam had been at the root of the Cambodian conflict. Nonetheless, an innate political wilfulness and a determination to be treated as indispensable made him also an unpredictable political factor ready to wreak havoc should his pride or dignity appear to have been affronted.

The Constituent Assembly transformed itself into a National Assembly on 28 September but failed to elect its President. It only did so on 25 October with the appointment of CPP leader and hardliner, Chea Sim. A new government was announced four days later with Prince Ranariddh and Hun Sen in the offices of first and second prime ministers with parity of political position giving way to a clear order of precedence. The delay was a consequence of internal debate within the CPP, which had difficulty in coming to terms with the practice of power-sharing. In the event, the distribution of portfolios reflected the control which the CPP had long exercised over the armed forces and police, which would be critical should the post-electoral political accommodation break down. Indeed, the elections did not challenge the CPP's control of political organization in the provinces.[2] The coalition government barely concealed considerable tensions beneath the surface of politics, which were contained by a shared understanding by the principal parties that a failure to cooperate would prejudice the flow of essential foreign aid.

The last of the UNTAC military presence left the country by mid-November and by the end of the year Cambodia continued to enjoy a political stability beyond the expectations of most observers. Moreover, a unique measure of military co-operation had begun from July between members of the new coalition against Khmer Rouge strongholds in the north and west of the country in an attempt to remove their control from centres of population. The military capability of the Khmer Rouge had appeared to diminish after the elections as fears of its powers of retribution drained away, while defections from its ranks reached more than 2,000. Nonetheless, it proved able to launch a small military offensive in northerly Kompong Thom province at the end of the year.

The Khmer Rouge formally recognized the new constitution and Norodom Sihanouk as king but delayed acknowledging the new government, which was depicted as a political surrogate for Vietnamese interests. Despite their repudiation of the elections and their failure to disrupt them, they sought a role in public life through advisory positions in government. It has been suggested that

> The PDK aim would be to be well positioned should the new government stall due to politics, incompetence, inactivity, or failure of the foreign donor community to address its genuine needs in a timely manner.[3]

King Sihanouk encouraged the Khmer Rouge ostensibly in the interest of national reconciliation. In late November, he offered the Khmer Rouge, with the exception of its notorious leadership, a role in government, including ministerial positions, if they agreed to a cease-fire, to dissolve their army, and to hand over territory under their control. That offer was then withdrawn after Prince Ranariddh had challenged its constitutional propriety.

Notes

1. See the assessment before the elections in Yasushi Akashi, "The Challenges Faced by UNTAC", *Japan Review of International Affairs* 7, no. 3 (Summer 1993), and after the event in Timothy Carney and Tan Lian Choo, *Whither Cambodia?* (Singapore: Institute of Southeast Asian Studies, 1993).
2. Nate Thayer, *Far Eastern Economic Review,* 9 December 1993.
3. Carney and Tan, op. cit., p. 14.

External Actors and Southeast Asia

INTRODUCTION

Leifer was ever mindful of the impact of external actors and influences on Southeast Asia, likened at one time to the "Balkans of the East". The emergence of regional states from being objects to subjects of international relations and their struggles for nationhood were, among other things, processes that attracted him. The formation of Malaysia, Confrontation, the Sabah claim, the merger and then separation of Singapore (a new and vulnerable state emerging) from Malaysia held his attention during his early research into the region. These were *problematiques* in the security of maritime Southeast Asia that also engaged the interests of extra-regional powers.

Among them, Britain (a declining power on the verge of colonial divestment but still having "parental concern" for the security of the new Malaysian state) and the United States (a global power fixated on the wider competition with the Soviet Union and China respectively) offered interesting contrasts. Their different approaches were reflected in their responses towards Confrontation. Britain was more concerned with the immediate situation of Malaysia while the United States sought albeit without much success, a more flexible response towards

239

Sukarno, cast within a wider regional framework (Ch. 20). Britain however was caught in an invidious position between Singapore and Kuala Lumpur with the latter increasingly resentful of Lee Kuan Yew's special access to London as the local players drifted towards separation. Given the continuing post-separation tensions between the local clients and the financial strains of the East of Suez policy, Leifer stressed the unrewarding aspects of Britain's continuing defence obligations even as he saw its only clear-cut role as one of maintaining stability between Malaysia and Singapore. Significantly, he questioned Britain's capacity to influence the power balance in Asia (Ch. 21).

Among the external powers, the United States and China were most consistently observed in Leifer's treatment of the Cold War and post-Cold War regional security environments. However, he also analysed the interplay of Soviet and Japanese interests during the Cambodia conflict (see Ch. 18 in the Cambodia Conflict section) and with reference to sea-lane security (Ch. 30 in the Security and Order: The Maritime Dimension section); as well as U.S., Chinese, and Japanese participation in multilateral co-operative security within the ARF (Ch. 14 in the ASEAN and Regional Order section) With the demise of the Soviet Union, Moscow's relations with Southeast Asia have been marginalized, and Leifer paid little attention to the subject thereafter. An excessively high copyrights fee has precluded the inclusion of a separate chapter on the Soviet Union and the region. The item is recorded, however, in the bibliography. Nevertheless, Moscow's Cold War interests in Southeast Asia have been covered in other selected chapters.

Leifer's principal focus on the United States and China reflected above all the importance of the Sino-U.S. relationship to stability in the wider Asia-Pacific environment. Here, his main frame of reference was the balance of power/influence considerations. This aspect of foreign policy calculation was, as he saw it, at work from the very outset of China's relationship with the Southeast Asian states. The relationship evinced a linkage between China's regional interests and the wider global dimension of great power competition. China's main concern was to avoid any united front ranged against it. Consequently it has related to the region with pragmatism despite earlier problems, which centred on the overseas Chinese issue and support for fraternal communist movements in the region. Growing economic interdependence with the region led to accommodation albeit within limits, with regional states on the South China Sea problem (Ch. 22).

The leeway that ASEAN states obtained vis-à-vis China was also reflected, though in a limited extent, in their continuing ties with Taiwan. The One China policy adopted by all ASEAN states did not preclude the continuation of their economic linkages with Taiwan. But the latter failed to overcome the impediments to attaining a separate international status no matter how it sought to pursue its brand of "pragmatic diplomacy" towards the region (Ch. 23). For Southeast Asia, the engagement of China, which Leifer clearly recognized as a "rising power" with increasing strategic latitude, dominated over any consideration of furthering linkages with Taiwan. However, the importance of Taiwan to the management of the Sino–American relationship and the critical countervailing role of the United States in constraining any Chinese use of force over Taiwan (that would in turn have serious consequences on the whole Asia-Pacific environment) is well recognized by Southeast Asian states. In a post-Cold War environment in which they cannot take for granted that the United States would be a guardian of their interests or act multilaterally, Leifer poses the intriguing question of who it is (China or the United States), that really needs to be engaged (Ch. 24).

ASEAN's engagement with the outside world involved not just state actors but also regions. Of the latter, the EU (previously the EC) was among the earliest of ASEAN's dialogue partners. But the dialogue between the two regions in the post-Cold War period has been complicated by differences over human rights and Myanmar's membership in ASEAN. As Leifer notes, democracy is part of the EU's "organic identity" which is not the same for ASEAN, which is essentially a diplomatic rather than political community (Ch. 25). The contrasting organizing principles between the two regions are further compared in the section that follows.

The end of the Cold War also had its positive impact on the Israel–PLO peace process and enabled Israel to expand its contacts with Asia. The final selected article in this section (Ch. 26) focuses on developments in Israel's relations with three regional states following the conclusion of the 1993 Oslo Accord. It reflects Leifer's personal interest in Israel given his strong Jewish background, as well as his academic interest in Malaysia and Indonesia with their substantial Muslim populations (in Indonesia's case, the largest Muslim population in the world), which find resonance in the fate of the Palestinians; and Singapore with its close relationship with Israel. Leifer compares the varying impacts of the peace dividend on Israel's relations with these regional states, which culminated in the visit to Jakarta and Singapore by then Israeli Prime Minister Yitzhak Rabin. With prescience, Leifer concludes that Israel's problems with the world at large would have to be resolved through attending to its immediate political environment and not the other way around.

20

Anglo-American Differences over Malaysia

Britain and the United States are in close accord over long-term priorities in South East Asia. Their Governments recognize the threat posed by the Chinese People's Republic and see the need to sustain the independence of non-communist States. But there is not always the same harmony over matters of more immediate concern within the area. One by-product of the present dispute surrounding the establishment of the Federation of Malaysia has been the evident conflict of interest between the two countries.

U.S. policy in South East Asia has been increasingly dominated by the anti-communist struggle in South Vietnam. It has therefore been disinclined to alienate the present regime in Indonesia — a country which, though notable for a large Communist Party, it regards as the one potential Great Power in South East Asia, and as the natural leader of any neutral and anti-Chinese grouping there. Britain's policy, on the other hand, has been primarily to defend the integrity of her former

Reprinted in abridged form from Michael Leifer, "Anglo-American Differences over Malaysia", *World Today,* vol. 20, no. 4 (1964): 156–67, permission of the Royal Institute of International Affairs.

colonial possessions in South East Asia, now regrouped as Malaysia, in the face of Indonesia's "confrontation" campaign in North Borneo.

Britain's parental concern for Malaysia has been respected and approved in Washington. At the same time, however, the U.S. Government has been anxious to prevent conflict in North Borneo from being carried to the stage where the strain on British resources could lead either, as in the case of Cyprus, to a call for American assistance, or, more alarming still, to an upgrading of the order of conflict. In January, therefore, President Johnson, through his Attorney-General, Mr Robert Kennedy, took the initiative in bringing the war "out of the jungle", to be considered, if somewhat inconclusively, at the conference table in Bangkok. Subsequent discussions in February in Washington, between the President and the British Prime Minister reaffirmed U.S. support for "the peaceful national independence of Malaysia" and indicated lessening American tolerance of the Indonesian position. This accord, however, has not removed altogether the likelihood of renewed Anglo-American differences.

Britain's Stand

The British support for Malaysia has been unequivocal and sustained. From the time of the public announcement by Tunku Abdul Rahman in May 1961 of the possibility of a federation to incorporate Malaya, Singapore, and the British Borneo territories, the British Government provided diplomatic encouragement and material assistance to bring it about.[1] Malaysia was seen in a multiple role. First, she would provide a solution to the anomalous position of Singapore, already cast by many as a potential "South East Asian Cuba". Secondly, she would facilitate decolonization in North Borneo within a far more stable framework than separate independence could hope to provide. Finally, she was seen as an instrument of stability in the region; her Prime Minister has had no inhibitions in describing the new Federation as "a bastion against communism in South East Asia".

At an early stage it was agreed between the British and Malayan Governments that "... in the event of the formation of the proposed Federation of Malaysia, the existing Defence Agreement between Britain and Malaya should be extended to embrace the other territories".[2] The military implications for Britain of the extension of the Anglo-Malayan Defence Agreement of 1957 became clear before the establishment of Malaysia — namely, at the time of the uprising in Brunei in December 1962.[3] With the subsequent announcement by the Indonesian Foreign Minister, Dr Subandrio, of a policy of "confrontation" against Malaysia and the almost simultaneous incursions by Indonesian-based marauders into Sarawak,[4] it became necessary to commit large numbers of British troops, of which there are, at the time of writing, approximately 9,000 in North Borneo, including four Gurkha infantry battalions. In spite of military obligations elsewhere, the British Government has given no sign of willingness to withdraw these troops, while the basic attitude of Indonesia towards Malaysia remains, apparently, unchanged.

This position does not reveal a failure, on Britain's part, to appreciate Indonesia's potentialities as an obstacle to communist ambitions in South East Asia. In her maritime insulation she is better placed than the mainland States of the region to withstand Chinese pressure. Also, her highly developed sense of national identity, together with a deep resentment of the overseas Chinese, is a factor militating against the influence of the Chinese People's Republic. Nevertheless, the present leadership in Indonesia is regarded in Britain with intense suspicion; British officials find no evidence to suggest that it is capable either of trust or of responsibility. Personalities have played an important role in this assessment, and the flamboyance of President Soekarno arouses little sympathy, particularly since the burning of the British Embassy and other British property in Jakarta last September. There is little inclination to see the Indonesian President as the only alternative to the 2-million-strong Indonesian Communist Party. Indeed, it is probably felt that continued U.S. assistance for Soekarno's regime cannot but be of advantage also to the Communists, since their support is necessary to him to counteract the influence of the army.

America's Reserve

The U.S. Government, on the other hand, has tended to temper its support for Malaysia with some reserve. Although President Kennedy gave his blessing to the proposed Federation on 14 February 1963, the U.S. Government's posture was seen as one of "non-involved cordiality"; this was recommended by Majority Leader Senator Mansfield later the same month in a report to the Senate Foreign Relations Committee following a world tour made at the request of the President. Meanwhile, the reception accorded to Malaya's Deputy Prime Minister, Tun Abdul Razak, when he visited Washington in April last year, suggested that Malaysia could not expect more than "moral support" from the United States.

This is not to suggest that the United States had little sympathy for Malaysia. On the contrary, she was regarded highly in the press,[5] while the State Department sought privately to dissuade Soekarno from reckless behaviour. The official American attitude was that Malaysia made a contribution to the stability of the area, but that it was Britain's prime responsibility to sponsor the new Federation and to provide it with economic assistance. The U.S. Government had little desire to become actively involved to the extent that it might incur the hostility of Indonesia or Malaysia's lesser antagonist, the Philippines. Such a likelihood, it was considered, could work only to the advantage of the Indonesian Communist Party which had played a prominent role in the anti-neo-colonialist campaign directed against Malaysia. Moreover, in the first half of 1963, there was an expectation that the United States would come to exercise greater influence within Indonesia and that the Indonesian Government would turn its attention from foreign adventures to the rehabilitation of a rundown economy. The visit to Jakarta in April of Soviet Defence Minister Malinovsky, who came, it is believed, to demand prompt repayment of outstanding debts, served to confirm this. Less comfort was derived, however, from the visit the same month of Chairman Liu Shao-Ch'i, who, it was reported, offered the Indonesian Government credits to buy Chinese rice and textiles.

Indonesia and the Philippines withheld recognition of the new Federation after its establishment on 16 September and withdrew their Ambassadors from Kuala Lumpur. The Malaysian Government immediately severed all diplomatic ties with both countries. In Jakarta, one dramatic reaction was the burning and sacking of the British Embassy. This event produced a strong U.S. protest both in Washington and in Jakarta. The U.S. Government also made it known that it would withhold, at least for the time being, all new aid programmes for Indonesia.

U.S. and British Assessments of the Situation

It seemed that the U.S. Government, though angered by the happenings in Jakarta, felt that a complete break with Soekarno might produce undesirable internal repercussions detrimental to American interests. The State Department's preoccupation with the Indonesian Communist Party was influential in this respect. There was no desire to take any action which might work to the advantage of this party, which would certainly profit from a further deterioration of living standards in Indonesia. On the other hand, it was considered impossible, in the circumstances, to proceed with plans for stabilizing the Indonesian economy, if only because of the heated response expected from the House of Representatives Foreign Affairs Committee which, the previous August, had written into the Foreign Aid Authorization Bill a ban on further economic or military aid to Indonesia without a public finding by the President that such aid was vital to U.S. security interests.

Apart from the above measures, there was little to indicate that the U.S. Government was considering any radical change of policy towards Indonesia. There was still some expectation that, in spite of the furore over the establishment of Malaysia, the United States might, by continuing economic assistance, exercise some restraining influence over President Soekarno.

The British Government, however, further galled by the take-over of British economic interests in Indonesia, no longer placed any confidence in, or cherished hopes of, Soekarno's regime. In its view, economic aid would not only help Indonesia in continuing her opposition to Malaysia but would also mean throwing good money after bad; any Indonesian retreat in response to U.S. pressure was likely to be no more than tactical.

An American Initiative

The American decision to intervene diplomatically followed a visit by President Soekarno to President Macapagal in Manila from 7 to 11 January. On 13 January it was announced in Washington that the Attorney-General, Mr Robert Kennedy, would go to Tokyo to meet President Soekarno, who was to holiday there after a short stay in Cambodia which he visited on his way from the Philippines.

This announcement reflected growing American concern at the military situation in North Borneo and a fear of the conflict spreading.[6] A letter sent by President Johnson to the Indonesian President on 2 January, expressing concern at the state of affairs in North Borneo, had had no visible impact at the time. A direct personal approach was therefore to be made through a man who, two years previously, had visited Jakarta when the United States was seeking to mediate in the West Irian dispute between Indonesia and the Dutch. American anxieties over the likely escalation of the conflict in North Borneo were probably aggravated by the resolute statements made by the British Minister of Defence, Mr Peter Thorneycroft, whilst on a tour of Malaysia early in January; in one speech, he was reported as saying that full-scale war could result from Indonesian attacks on Sarawak and North Borneo.[7] Very little perception was needed to appreciate that, if the conflict in Borneo got out of bounds, Malaysia would probably make a request for military assistance from Australia and New Zealand, both of whom were participants in the Commonwealth Strategic Reserve in Malaya. The United States was bound to both Australia and New Zealand by the ANZUS Agreement of 1951 and could, therefore, find herself involved more directly in the dispute.

Mr Kennedy's Mission

In Tokyo, Mr Kennedy was at pains to emphasize his limited role in the dispute and to insist that any solution had to be resolved and determined by the Asian countries acting alone. President Soekarno was evidently most amiable with the American Attorney-General and appeared happy with this formula. The British Government, which would have liked recognition of Malaysia made a precondition of renewed negotiations, drew little comfort from what was construed as consistent American softness towards Soekarno. This was particularly the case when the Indonesians began to advance demands for the withdrawal of British troops not only from Borneo but also from Singapore, as an integral part of any settlement — demands which seemed to find some measure of American support. British suspicions that Robert Kennedy was recreating the role of Ellsworth Bunker, the American diplomat whose intervention led to the Dutch withdrawal from West Irian,[8] were not allayed by the outcome of the talks. President Soekarno did not announce the end of confrontation or the withdrawal of armed infiltrators from North Borneo. Kennedy, apparently, did not ask for this but implored the Indonesian President to seek a solution at the conference table, whilst making it clear that the fighting in Borneo would have to stop before any meeting with Malaysian representatives could be arranged.

The impression gained in London was that Kennedy, like others before him, had become captivated by Soekarno's charm and that the meeting signalled no hardening in American policy towards Indonesia.

From Tokyo, Mr Kennedy went on to Manila where he conferred briefly with President Macapagal, and then to Kuala Lumpur where he met Tunku Abdul Rahman and also Prince Norodom Sihanouk of Cambodia, who was in process of arranging a separate meeting between the Philippines President and the Malaysian Prime Minister. When Kennedy left for Jakarta, Tunku Abdul Rahman had not withdrawn his demand that respect for Malaysia's integrity and a recognition of her sovereignty were essential preconditions of renewed talks with President Soekarno.

On 23 January, the Indonesian President issued a cease-fire order to his troops on the Borneo border. At the same time, it was announced that the three Heads of Government had agreed to meet in an effort to improve relations, the meeting to be preceded by one at Foreign Minister level. Indonesia, meanwhile, made it clear that she was not prepared to accept recognition of Malaysia as a precondition of any peace negotiations and wished the question of recognition to be discussed at the forthcoming tripartite talks. On the day the cease-fire was announced, Dr Subandrio told a mass rally in Jakarta that Indonesia would continue her policy of confrontation against Malaysia in order to give real independence to the peoples of Singapore, Malaya, and North Borneo, while President Soekarno pointed out that Indonesia did not stand alone in her struggle to "crush Malaysia".

British Reactions

Mr Kennedy, during his visit to London, made no attempt to exaggerate the diplomatic success of his mission, though he was hopeful of its results. In fact, his mission, which had been arranged without the consultation of the British Government, served to bring to the surface points of difference with the American Government on the whole issue of Malaysia. President Soekarno had not been seen to shift his position and there was no doubt, in the eyes of the British, that military confrontation could be turned on like a tap, as easily as it had been turned off.

The general distaste at Kennedy's mediation was intensified by the continued process of expropriation of British investments in Indonesia concurrent with his visit to London. But the most disturbing feature for Anglo-American relations was the report that "in an obviously inspired whispering campaign he [Kennedy] is being accused of all manner of devious intent."[9]

Notes

1. See "Proposals for Malaysia" by T. E. Smith, in *The World Today*, May 1962.
2. Cmnd. 1563, p. 3.
3. See "Progress towards Malaysia and the Brunei revolt" and "The Brunei Revolt, background and consequences" by T. E. Smith, in *The World Today*, January and April 1963.
4. See "Communism and the guerrilla war in Sarawak" by Justus van der Kroef, in *The World Today*, February 1964.
5. See, for example, *New York Times*, 6 February 1963: "The best hope of stability for the area lies in the British–Malayan plan to terminate British colonial rule in Borneo by creating a new independent Malaysian state. Both the Philippines and Indonesia would do well to abjure their tendency to imitate the very nineteenth-century imperialism they profess to despise."
6. This particular question was reported as having been discussed at an unannounced meeting of the National Security Council. (*New York Times*, 14 January 1964.)
7. *Daily Telegraph*, 13 January 1964.
8. See 'The West New Guinea problem' by Justus van der Kroef, in *The World Today*, November 1961.
9. *The Times*, 1 February 1964.

21

Astride the Straits of Johore
The British Presence and Commonwealth Rivalry in Southeast Asia*

In September 1963, with the formation of Malaysia, British military establishments situated on either side of the Johore Straits were brought within the compass of a single polity. Within less than two years the Malaysian union was put asunder and those military establishments were divided by national frontiers. Such a situation was viewed with displeasure by the British Government which had supported the establishment of Malaysia in part to avoid such a prospect. To add to the problem of dealing with two governments, there was the complicating factor of the unhappy relationship between them and with it the danger of Britain being caught up in the interplay of differences to the extent of prejudicing the value of her military presence.

There is no guarantee that the present muted hostility across the Johore Straits will not flare up in such a way as to involve Britain and

Reprinted in abridged form from Michael Leifer, "Astride the Straits of Johore: The British Presence and Commonwealth Rivalry in South-East Asia", *Modern Asian Studies* 1, no. 3 (1967): 283–96, by permission of the Cambridge University Press.

possibly impair the value of its principal military establishment east of Suez. The problem is made more acute as a result of the impression created and confirmed by Britain that it is less than impartial as between Singapore and Malaysia. There is strong feeling in Kuala Lumpur that the British Government is more favourably disposed towards Singapore than Malaysia.

Britain had sought to encourage a merger between Malaya and Singapore. It was a major British objective to relinquish residual authority in Singapore within a context of political stability and so ensure the continuing use of military base facilities centred on that island. When the Malayan Prime Minister made public his initiative for a wider union, this received enthusiastic British support.

The onset of the active stage of Indonesian confrontation made a British military presence more welcome, but it also had the effect of involving Britain more deeply in the affairs of its former possessions; involvement that was only tolerated because of the special circumstances. Britain had, of course, been a principal party to the negotiations that had preceded the formation of Malaysia. And as such it was involved in the political squabbling that was to bedevil the Federation, even before its establishment. During the course of the negotiations it became apparent that there existed more than a measure of ill-will between political principals in Malaya and Singapore, irrespective of communal factors. The actual signing of the Malaysia Agreement was almost postponed at the eleventh hour because of a failure to come to terms between the Malayan and Singapore Governments. The British Government played a major part in helping to resolve these differences which centred in the main over the proposal to establish a common market for manufactured goods for the new Federation. Singapore was the protaganist of such an arrangement and in supporting this proposal Britain may have suggested itself as a lever with which the government of Lee Kuan-yew could seek its ends within Malaysia. Thus, before the inception of Malaysia, Britain was to find itself in the invidious position of appearing unduly sympathetic towards a prospective constituent of the Federation which the government in Kuala Lumpur was coming increasingly to regard as troublesome and as a potential challenge to its authority.

Such an alignment was also suggested following the brief postponement of the inauguration of Malaysia which was undertaken as part of an attempt to persuade Indonesia and the Philippines to welcome the formation of the new Federation. At the time the Prime Minister of Singapore played a leading role in organizing pressure from the Borneo states to try to influence the Malayan Government to adhere to the timetable agreed in London. As part of this exercise, which was related to domestic imperatives, the Singapore Government was to declare a *de facto* independence and presumed to hold the defence and external affairs powers in the hands of the Singapore head of state until Malaysia came into being. The significance of this episode lies not only in the animosity aroused in Kuala Lumpur at Singapore's act of arrogation but also in its concurrence with the stand taken against the postponement of Malaysia by the British Secretary of State for Commonwealth Relations, Duncan Sandys.

Following the formation of Malaysia there developed a genuine concern at Lee's ability to convey his point of view to leading members of the major political parties in Britain and to the British press.

Britain's prime function in Malaysia was to assist in safeguarding the territorial integrity of the Federation. But as animosity increased between Kuala Lumpur and Singapore, especially after the P.A.P. intervention in the mainland Malayan elections of April 1964, Britain assumed an additional role of marriage counsellor.

Britain's concern was to sustain as a going concern the Federation which it had helped to create and to whose defence it was committed. Its special position in providing the principal underpinning for the defence of Malaysia offered an opportunity to play a more positive internal role than would otherwise have been tolerated. The leverage which lay in this position was not only recognized by Lee Kuan-yew, but was also evident to the Alliance leadership when they deliberated with their Singapore counterparts on separation without informing these governments that were providing for Malaysia's defence.

Following the separation, Britain took the lead in assuring both Malaysia and Singapore that it would continue to assist both countries in their external defence. It was announced that assurances given by the Governments of Malaysia and Singapore, that the facilities accorded to British forces would be unchanged, had made this possible. The instruments of separation had made provision for safeguarding British facilities in Singapore; those in Malaysia were still covered by the Malaysia Agreement of 1963.

The terms of separation had appeared to provide for the continued use of military facilities in Singapore as if nothing had changed. The alternative uses of the bases were still such that Britain could employ its forces other than for the defence of Malaysia, Singapore and Commonwealth territories.

The British Government must have drawn reassurance from Article V of the Separation Agreement whereby Malaysia and Singapore were to establish a joint defence council for purposes of external defence and mutual assistance. There was also provision for the Government of Malaysia to continue to maintain bases and other facilities used by its military forces within Singapore.

Whatever satisfaction may have been derived by the British Government from the Separation Agreement was to be short-lived as relations between Malaysia and Singapore rapidly deteriorated.

The obstacles to a defence treaty between Singapore and Malaysia, as provided for by the Separation Agreement, and a general arrangement to formalize the British position were to loom especially large after February 1966. In that month a situation of crisis developed between Singapore and Malaysia over the determination of the latter to retain an infantry battalion on the island. At that time of separation it was agreed that a battalion of the Singapore Infantry Regiment should serve in Borneo and that a Malaysian battalion should be stationed in its place in Singapore. The dispute arose when the Singapore battalion, on its return from Borneo, sought to re-occupy its former barracks which had served in the meantime as quarters for the Malaysian battalion. The Singapore Government wished to see the Malaysian battalion return to its camp on the mainland and it would seem that advance units had already begun to move when the Malaysian Government was to insist that it was obligatory under Article V (3) of the Separation Agreement for the Singapore Government to allow the Malaysian troops to remain in their current quarters or to provide suitable alternative accommodation. The issue was resolved after much acrimony in public by the decision of the Singapore Government to find alternative accommodation. The episode did much to heighten fears in Singapore that Malaysia sought a permanent military presence on the island to ensure the obedience of its government.

April saw a further episode indicative of the inability of Malaysia and Singapore to come to terms on defence matters. Singapore was to withdraw its representation from the Joint Defence Council established at the time of separation. Reports that a new council would be set up failed to materialize and discussions between officials of the two governments begun in May 1966 yielded no fruit.

The Separation Agreement had rescinded those annexes of the Agreement relating to Malaysia providing for a common market and had substituted a provision to co-operate in economic affairs. Nothing had come of this. Indeed, just the opposite to co-operation had taken place.

Singapore's future was seen to depend on progressive industrialization and finding markets for the products of such industrialization. In South-east Asia Malaysia offered the best prospect in terms of *per capita* income and ease of physical access. It was thus to become the policy of the Singapore Government to dangle a package of agreements on both defence and economic co-operation in the hope that Malaysia would agree to economic arrangements to Singapore's advantage in return for a satisfactory defence treaty.

It was not to be long before Britain was drawn into the vortex of unresolved differences between Singapore and Malaysia. It seems likely that when the Singapore Prime Minister visited London in April 1966 he not only had discussions with appropriate ministers on defence matters but also succeeded in putting across his view in the necessity for closer economic association between his country and Malaysia. The following month, the Malaysian Minister of Finance, Tan Siew-sin came to London with the object of seeking economic assistance, in particular to provide for his country's continuing defence build-up. The visit proved to be most unhappy. Tan left London empty-handed after having been informed that the British Government was not in a financial position to help Malaysia. On his return to Kuala Lumpur, he announced that the reason for the British decision was more political than financial. Undoubtedly, the British Government was reluctant to make further financial commitments to the defence of Malaysia while outstanding defence issues had yet to be resolved with Singapore.

In addition to this, public expression was given to resentment over alleged British interference in the Borneo territories and charges were levelled that attempts had been made to subvert local loyalty. But most important, the British Government had once again given the impression that it desired to sponsor the interests of Singapore against those of Kuala Lumpur.

The Malaysian Government, for the time being, shows no desire to alter formal defence arrangements with Britain. Nevertheless, its Prime Minister has foreshadowed foreign policy changes. He said in August 1966 "If Malaysia is to become a permanent and cohesive national unit, she must be regarded by neighbours as a specifically

Asian country and not as a creation or protégé of Britain which some still suspect her to be". The British presence would thus appear to be more directly related to the interests of Singapore rather than to those of Malaysia. Singapore desperately needs the economic infusion which the bases provide as well as a protective shield against intimidation by Malaysia or a liaison between Malaysia and Indonesia. For the British Government, the military arrangements with both governments are such that at present no difficulties ensue and therefore the *status quo* is both tolerable and tolerated even though reciprocal obligations to Singapore have still to be defined.

A continuing role in relation to Malaysia and Singapore was suggested in *The Defence Review* in that the "visible presence of British forces by itself is a deterrent to local conflict". However, in the circumstances of bad feeling between Malaysia and Singapore the visible presence of British forces could be interpreted as a means of keeping Lee Kuan-yew's chestnuts out of the fire. The more this would appear to be the case, the more difficult relations could be expected to become with the government of the Malayan hinterland, whose hostility could undermine the British position.

The British presence is seen to relate also to the security of Australia and New Zealand. In reality this has been an American responsibility for some time.[1] The British contribution is regarded as of marginal import and one might suggest that it provides mild comfort rather than security. At the present time Britain and Australia and New Zealand have a different order of priorities about regional security. This is reflected in their differing attitudes to the war in Vietnam. Britain has avoided physical involvement and as a result doubts must be entertained in Canberra and Wellington as to the prospect of Britain using its military facilities in South-east Asia for intervention in the region.

Britain's membership in S.E.A.T.O. has formal relevance for the defence of Australia and New Zealand. But it is difficult on the basis of past performance to conceive of the military facilities in Singapore and Malaysia being used by Britain for a S.E.A.T.O. purpose, within South-east Asia.

Harold Wilson has argued that the British cannot leave the East of Suez area to the other principal powers. However, one has to question whether Britain, in her present parlous state, has the capacity to exercise a determining influence on the power balance in Asia. In terms of purpose, it would appear that the only clear-cut role for

Britain is to maintain stability as between Malaysia and Singapore. But, once again, it must be stressed that there are unrewarding aspects involved in continuing this obligation.

Notes

* This article was presented in slightly different form as a paper at a seminar on Commonwealth Relations held in January 1967 at the Institute of Commonealth Studies, University of London.

1. See Coral Bell "Asian Crises and Australian Security", *The World Today*, February 1967.

22

China in Southeast Asia
Interdependence and
Accommodation

China's Shadow

The relationship between China and the states of Southeast Asia has displayed features of interdependence from the outset. From China's perspective, its regional interests have been invariably linked to a wider global dimension. An illuminating example of such linkage very early in the relationship was the contentious issue of the national status of ethnic-Chinese resident in the countries of Southeast Asia.[1] Its resolution served to demonstrate the extent to which an autonomous Chinese policy entailed opportunity costs in the case of the emerging post-colonial governments of the region. The prospect of their alienation in a Cold War context became a matter of some concern in Beijing leading to an attendant clarification of policy.

Despite this important example of political sensitivity, the relationship between the People's Republic of China and the states of Southeast Asia has long been problematic.[2] With the end of the Cold

Reprinted in abridged form from *China in Southeast Asia: Interdependence and Accommodation*, by Michael Leifer, CAPS Paper No. 14 (Taipei: Chinese Council of Advanced Policy Studies, 1997), pp. 1–19, by permission of the publisher.

War, that relationship has changed for the better in many important respects, in part at China's initiative, but has remained replete with difficulties nonetheless. At the centre of those difficulties is the fact of geopolitical life that China, which shares and disputes common land and maritime borders with Southeast Asian states, is a rising and potentially dominant regional power.[3] A successful policy of economic reform has given it the resources with which to begin to take advantage of the transformation in strategic environment within Asia-Pacific after the end of the Cold War. Indeed, the People's Republic of China has come to enjoy a unique regional latitude because for the first time in its troubled history of international relations, it is free of the persistently hostile attentions of a global power.

Despite a conscious attempt to cultivate the ASEAN states which dates from the mid-1970s, China continues to cast a shadow over the states of Southeast Asia because of its huge size, enormous population, close geographic proximity and considerable economic potential. It does so, in addition, because it asserts an irredentist agenda in the South China Sea with a steely and self-righteous nationalist determination underpinned by a programme of military modernization. That modernization holds out a worst case prospect that in the early Twenty First Century, China may be in a position to pursue that irredentist agenda by superior force of arms.

Interdependence and a United Front Policy

China is not a totally free agent in its dealings with Southeast Asia. Its government has embarked on a process of economic reform from which there would not seem to be any turning back because of the likely domestic political consequences for the ruling Communist Party. That process depends for its success on an important measure of external confidence. China has a continuing need to attract direct foreign investment, including capital from enterprises controlled by members of ethnic-Chinese communities in Southeast Asia. In addition, although the end of the Cold War has permitted China an unprecedented regional latitude, its relationships with major Asia-Pacific powers are sometimes tense and those tensions have a bearing on policy towards Southeast Asia. The Chinese relationship with the United States has lost the degree of shared interest and strategic convergence that were present when confronting the Soviet Union and its regional allies during the second phase of the Cold War.

Especially since the bloody events in Beijing in June 1989, the relationship has come to be distinguished by mutual mistrust. Issues of trade and intellectual property, transfers of arms and military technology as well as human rights violations have continued to cause trouble. Major security disputes include the unresolved issue of Taiwan and the matter of freedom of navigation in the South China Sea. Moreover, Beijing's perception that the United States has begun to renege on its commitment to recognize only one China, implicit in the terms of the Shanghai Communiqué of 1972 and two others and in the agreement to establish diplomatic relations in 1979, has generated nationalist fury.

Relations with Japan have also not been trouble-free. An underlying tension, in part a legacy of Japan's militarist past, has been aggravated by a progressive diplomatic assertiveness on the part of the government in Tokyo.

The problem of managing relationships with the United States and Japan, both of whom possess capabilities to affect Chinese interests, means that China's latitude in pursuing its interests within Southeast Asia would seem to be subject to a measure of constraint. China has been consistent, in the main, in seeking to avoid provoking a united front against itself within Asia-Pacific and to that end has taken some care to differentiate between its various regional relationships. Up to a point, this degree of care on China's part has been to the advantage of Southeast Asian states. It should, of course, be pointed out that China is not an embattled state either globally or regionally. As a rising power in Asia-Pacific, it has not found itself in the predicament of Japan before the onset of the Pacific War. China has been committed to economic modernization for nearly two decades but has not been impeded in that aspiration by other global or regional powers. China has not been denied access to the international economy. On the contrary, the world has opened up to China concurrently with China opening up to the world. China has been able to develop in tune with the prevailing economic temper of the times and has been a party to the so-called East Asian Miracle. That said, Southeast Asia is an integral part of the economic constituency towards which China has looked from the late 1970s to help expedite its economic reform process. To that extent, China's policy of economic reform would seem a hostage to its fortunes as a rising regional power.

For its part, Southeast Asia in the form of an expanding Association of Southeast Asian Nations (ASEAN) has not shown any intention of mobilising countervailing military power against an assertive China. But ASEAN is a diplomatic community of some international standing which China would not wish to alienate unnecessarily in the light of its economic interests and its recurrent problems with the United States and Japan. Moreover, there is a legacy of political interference by Beijing in Southeast Asia which lingers on in the region and which ensures that whatever the public rhetoric there about China being an opportunity and not a threat, the People's Republic's declarations of good intent are not taken totally at face value.

China's agenda in Southeast Asia has changed radically over the years making possible, for example, a restoration of diplomatic relations with Indonesia in August 1990. Singapore and Brunei then followed suit in October 1990 and October 1991 respectively, but it meant that it had been over forty years from the establishment of the People's Republic before China had been able to enjoy diplomatic relations with all ten states of the region. Communism as an ideology is no longer at issue; nor is support for revolutionary movements. The problem of the relationship with resident ethnic-Chinese communities has not disappeared completely, however, despite the long-resolved issue of dual nationality. As China exhibits a growing sense of nationalist feeling in place of a moribund ideology, there is always the possibility of a resented diplomatic intervention should an ethnic-Chinese community in the region appear to have been ill-treated, as was the case in Medan in Indonesia in April 1994.

For China, however, policy towards Southeast Asia after the initial wave of revolutionary enthusiasm, which followed the establishment of the People's Republic, has been mostly pragmatic and selective (discounting the turbulent fall-out from the Cultural Revolution). For example, in the case of Myanmar (Burma), border concessions were made in order to curry political favour as China contended with India over territorial issues. China's policy may be said to have followed a standard united front practice whereby potential alignment partners, irrespective of political identity, were cultivated to the extent that they were considered useful in helping to cope with hostility from major powers.[4]

Such united front practice was an implicit admission of the vulnerabilities of interdependence and an attempt to come to manage them. The relationship with Cambodia during the rule of Prince Norodom Sihanouk was a notable example of such practice during the 1950s and 1960s, while the tacit alliance with ASEAN during the Cambodian conflict in the 1980s was even more striking. The Cambodian conflict provides a useful point of reference for assessing such practice in a post-Cold War context. During the Cambodian conflict, China's priority was to deny Vietnam (viewed as an agent of the Soviet Union) the prospect of achieving an undue dominance in Indochina and so revising the distribution of power in the peninsula to Beijing's disadvantage. To that end, its government engaged in a united front policy with the states of ASEAN among others in a successful attempt to reverse the outcome of Vietnam's invasion of Cambodia in December 1978. Although that alignment was problematic and a source of some discord within ASEAN because of differences of strategic perspective over the identification of primary external threat, it held together during the course of the conflict because of a particular correspondence of interests. With the end of the Cambodian conflict, that correspondence of interests no longer obtained. ASEAN no longer served the function of diplomatic agent of China, while China was no longer required to help contain Vietnam. The degree of divergence of interests was signalled towards the end of the 1980s when China clashed with Vietnam in the South China Sea so registering a new phase of maritime assertiveness. Such divergence was confirmed in February 1992, when China promulgated a law on territorial waters and their contiguous area which reiterated extensive territorial and maritime claims in the South China Sea.

The Problem of the Spratlys

ASEAN's attempt to secure a commitment to moderation on China's part through a Declaration on the South China Sea at a meeting of its foreign ministers in Manila in July 1992 produced only an equivocal response from Beijing. Concern at such equivocation turned to alarm in February 1995 when it became known that Chinese forces had seized control of a reef in the Spratly Islands claimed by the Philippines, as well as by Vietnam, and had erected naval-support structures on them. Moreover, China's participation in a series of unofficial regional workshops on managing potential conflict in the South China Sea, which have been convened by Indonesia with Canadian financial support, has not provided any indication of compromise beyond an ambiguously expressed willingness to engage in joint development.[5]

The issue of the Spratly Islands has served to divide ASEAN from China, despite a growing economic engagement. Apart from shared geopolitical concerns, two of its founding members are also claimant states to some of those islands. Accordingly, the long-standing irredentist objective of China began to harm the relationship with members of the Association which was put on a formal basis in July 1992 when China's Foreign Minister, Qian Qichen, attended the annual meeting of his ASEAN counterparts as a guest. It was that meeting in Manila which issued the Declaration on the South China Sea. China had been consistent in its territorial claims in the South China Sea ever since Japan had renounced its sovereign jurisdiction there in the San Francisco Peace Treaty of September 1951 after having surrendered Taiping (Itu Aba), the largest of the Spratly Islands, to forces of the Nationalist government of Chiang Kai-shek after the end of the Pacific War. Direct confrontation over competing maritime claims had arisen before the end of the Cold War only with Vietnam; first with the former Republic of Vietnam in 1974 over the Paracel Islands and then with a united Socialist Republic of Vietnam over the Spratly Islands soon after unification in 1975. The issue had been set aside in China-ASEAN relations during the greater course of the Cambodian conflict only reviving towards its end.

The issue of the Spratly Islands has highlighted the problem of interdependence for China in its dealings with the states of Southeast Asia. It turns on how Beijing seeks to reconcile conflicting priorities of irredentist goals and good regional relations. In the case of the Spratly islands, an untrammelled pursuit of irredentist ambition could run counter to the promotion of economic interests and the management of relations with the United States and Japan. The Chinese political and military establishment is in no self-doubt about the legitimacy of the People's Republic's claim to island territories in the South China Sea. Underlying the strident manner in which entitlement to sovereignty has been represented as both indisputable and irrefutable has been the conviction that the territories in question have been Chinese from time immemorial and that other regional claimants which have seized a good number of the Spratly Islands have engaged in unacceptable acts of trespass which are said to date only from the 1970s.[6] Their ability to encroach on China's rightful domain has been regarded as just one more example of how China's past weakness has been exploited in the face of constraints on its action imposed by the nefarious policies of major powers. China in its rising nationalist mood is determined in time to rectify the historical record. A full rectification would, of course, move China's jurisdiction and potential reach southward some 1,000 nautical miles from its mainland in a historic and revolutionary act of geopolitical fusion between Northeast and Southeast Asia. Such a prospect was indicated by an article in China's Army newspaper in March 1995 which pointed out that "After years of active probes, a South Sea Fleet naval base has successfully integrated into a systematic whole the procurement, transport and supply of materials to islands and reefs in the *Nanshas* (Spratlys) ... treating it as a strategic problem under conditions of high-tech war."[7]

At issue is to what extent will China's relations with the countries of Southeast Asia be allowed to stand in the way of the People's Republic asserting its historical title in the South China Sea. It is here that considerations of interdependence interpose. Such an irredentist objective would seem to be in direct conflict with China's more immediate economic priorities and also its united front interest of generating good relations with the ASEAN states.

Another conflict of priorities has been pointed up by the problem posed for China of separating its policies towards Southeast Asia from those in Northeast Asia, especially in the case of Taiwan over which national feeling is very much stronger than over the Spratly Islands. The protracted problem of Taiwan has proven continuously frustrating for Beijing, despite recurrent acts of intimidation designed to influence the political process within the so-called renegade province, as well as serving a domestic political function within a People's Republic beset by a rising nationalism. Those acts of intimidation, especially the displays of armed force in the run-up to Taiwan's presidential elections in March 1996, in addition to the way in which China has conducted itself at times over the terms of recovery of Hong Kong, have not served the cause of confidence-building and united front practice with Southeast Asian states. For example, in March 1996, Singapore's Senior Minister, Lee Kuan Yew, who occupies a special position as an interlocutor between the mainland and Taiwan, was so disturbed by the escalation in military display by China that he interceded publicly in the cause of moderation without directly criticizing China's conduct. In reflecting regional concerns, Singapore's elder statesman was making the obvious point that Chinese policy in Southeast Asia cannot be separated from its conduct in Northeast Asia and indeed that the two were then at odds with one another.

Despite the emotive nationalist priority of Taiwan, China's leaders have been obliged to take into account the important interest of sustaining the momentum of economic and diplomatic cooperation with Southeast Asia. They would not willingly wish to manoeuvre the People's Republic into a position of diplomatic isolation whereby an alienation of regional states compounds difficulties experienced with the United States and Japan over Taiwan and other matters.

An additional and related problem has arisen as the ASEAN's heads of government concluded a treaty in Bangkok in December 1995 with the declared object of making Southeast Asia a nuclear weapons-free zone. The geographic terms of reference of that treaty include the exclusive economic zones and continental shelves of the signatory states. China has refused to sign a protocol to the treaty endorsing its terms for fear of prejudicing its territorial claims in the South China Sea.

China, ASEAN and the ASEAN Regional Forum

It would be an oversimplification to see China's relations with the states of Southeast Asia solely in terms of its dealings with ASEAN as a unit. Individually, China enjoys mixed relationships within Southeast Asia. It much prefers to deal with ASEAN's members on a bilateral rather than on a multilateral basis so as to limit the constraints arising from interdependence. For example, relations with Vietnam have remained chequered despite the restoration of party to party ties expressed in reciprocal visits by respective party secretaries general. Sino-Vietnamese contention over disputed territories has continued to disturb the association. China has not recorded any public displeasure at Vietnam's entry into ASEAN but its unilateral action in seizing Mischief Reef could have been inspired by its timing which had been announced a year in advance in July 1994. A practical demonstration of Sino-Vietnamese accommodation was the reopening of cross-border rail links in February 1996 after an interruption of seventeen years. Bilateral tensions revived visibly in April 1996, however, when Petro-Vietnam granted exploration leases for two blocs some 400 kilometres southeast of Ho Chi Minh City to Conoco, the American oil major. China entered a formal protest in response to the grant which covered half of the zone which Beijing had leased to America's Crestone Corporation in May 1992.[8] Those tensions had moderated sufficiently by the following June 1996 for Prime Minister Li Peng to attend the Eighth National Congress of Vietnam's Communist Party.

The relationship with the Philippines has become correspondingly testy because of the direct conflict of interests over competing claim in the Spratly Islands. Matters came to a head when, in response to the revelation in February 1995 that Chinese naval forces had seized Mischief Reef, Philippines naval units began to blow up Chinese markers on nearby unoccupied reefs and also conveyed journalists to the vicinity of Mischief Reef. China's Foreign Ministry responded with an explicit warning before tensions moderated.[9] Tensions have arisen also with Indonesia over the ambiguity of China's clarification of maritime claims within that part of the Republic's exclusive economic zone extending from the Natuna Islands at the western periphery of the South China Sea. Indeed, such tensions are believed to have had a bearing on Indonesia's willingness to enter into an unprecedented security agreement with Australia in December 1995. By contrast, for example, the relationship with Singapore has been exceedingly good with the island-state acting as a key economic partner in a joint venture to create a satellite city in Suzhou, near Shanghai, modelled on its own successful experience of urban development. Equally, Malaysia has also opened up to China with great enthusiasm. Moreover, China's relationship with Myanmar has burgeoned because of extensive economic cooperation and military assistance which has been a critical factor in maintaining the ruling State Law and Order Restoration Council (SLORC) in power.

China's relationship with ASEAN as a corporate entity has been of paramount importance, however, because of the leading role that the Association has played in transposing its model of regional security dialogue onto a wider Asia-Pacific canvass.[10]

It was well understood in Beijing that a prime purpose of the initiative was to address the uncertainty in regional strategic environment concerning rising Chinese power. It was not in a position, however, to avoid participation because of the Asia-Pacific wide scope of participation and remit of the new Forum. The pragmatic judgement was made that such a Forum would be better influenced from the inside than from an isolated outside. Moreover, a very important consideration was that the formal initiative for the security dialogue had come from ASEAN rather than from any major regional power such as Japan or the United States which would have aroused even greater Chinese suspicions. In addition, it became quite clear early on that ASEAN was set on assuming a diplomatic centrality within the embryonic venture.

Misgivings about participation in the ARF may well have been sustained as a result of the first working session in Bangkok in July 1994 at which the issue of the South China Sea was raised briefly. However, after the second working session in Brunei in August 1995, it would appear that China's view had softened somewhat. In the interim, China had been confronted with the diplomatic ire of ASEAN at an initial security dialogue between senior officials of respective foreign ministries which was held in April 1995 in Hangzhou. At an informal dinner, the evening before the meeting, ASEAN's permanent secretaries registered their common position in reproaching China for its unilateralist action in seizing Mischief Reef. In addition to that collective admonition, the ASEAN side took great pains to explain the consensual culture and modalities of the Association. To the extent that ASEAN was determined to transpose its own model of security dialogue to the wider framework of the ASEAN Regional Forum, the Chinese officials had their initial apprehensions of multilateralism reduced.

Interdependence and Accommodation

The point at issue is the diplomatic context of interdependence. China showed itself to be comfortable to a degree with its participation in the ARF as part of a general strategy towards Southeast Asia. During the last ARF, Foreign Minister, Qian Qichen, indicated the strong degree of convergence between his government and those of ASEAN over how the ARF ought to proceed.[11] Moreover, at a meeting between Qian Qichen and his ASEAN counterparts in Brunei shortly before the ARF convened, a number of concessions in form were made which indicated the priority placed by China on its relationship with the Association. Without offering any compromise on the issue of sovereignty, he registered his government's recognition of international law, including the basic principles and rules of the United Nations Convention on the Law of the Sea, as a basis for negotiating a settlement of the Spratlys issue. This was a modification of position from a rigid insistence on the historical foundations of China's claim.[12] He also revived the prospect of shelving the dispute in favour of joint development as well as reiterating the great importance which China attached to safe and free passage in international sea lanes in the

South China Sea. Qian Qichen departed from a previous insistence on addressing the matter of the Spratly Islands on solely a bilateral basis between contending parties by indicating a willingness to having it discussed on a multilateral basis between Chinese and ASEAN officials. Close to that time, Qian Qichen also held a bilateral meeting with Domingo Siazon, the Secretary of Foreign Affairs of the Philippines, at which he promised that China will not take any action towards the complication of the situation in the region as both China and the Philippines are concentrating on economic construction which needs a peaceful and stable peripheral and international environment.[13]

Such concessions were of form only, particularly as China had then yet to ratify the Law of the Sea Convention and had also failed to clarify publicly the precise extent and nature of its maritime claims in the South China Sea, including the relevance of a dotted median line drawn in 1947 by the Chiang Kai-shek regime which overlapped with Indonesia's exclusive economic zone from the baselines of the Natuna Islands. Such concessions, however, indicated an undoubted willingness to accommodate the concerns of ASEAN governments about the perceived creeping assertiveness of China aggravated by the Mischief Reef episode.

China has continued in its cooperative mode albeit in its own interest. In May 1996 the Standing Committee of China's National People's Congress announced the ratification of the United Nations Convention on the Law of the Sea. Baselines for the territorial sea were defined for China's mainland and for the Paracel Islands (disputed with Vietnam) but no mention was made of the Spratly Islands towards which four ASEAN states have differing claims.[14] Strong individual protest followed from Vietnam and the Philippines but not from ASEAN as a whole. Moreover, a second security dialogue between senior officials of China and ASEAN states convened in Indonesia in early June 1996 at which the Spratly Islands and the nuclear weapons-free zone treaty were addressed without undue contention and with a tentative agreement on an exchange of views between respective legal advisers. Correspondingly, the third working session of the ASEAN Regional Forum in Jakarta in July 1996 did not provoke Chinese open annoyance, despite addressing the issue of the Spratly Islands.

The Mischief Reef episode would seem to have been a defining diplomatic moment for China in ordering its priorities with the states of Southeast Asia. China demonstrated a vulnerability to the workings of interdependence. It is too early to say that a line has been drawn under further acts of unilateral territorial revisionism in the South China Sea. That said, the more rational strategy, and the considered view of China's Foreign Ministry, would seem to be that it is in the People's Republic's continuing interest to cultivate good relations within Southeast Asia.[15] The Association is no longer regarded as a compliant client of the West but is seen as an increasingly autonomous entity with international standing and with its own agenda. On the issue of the sanctity of national sovereignty and a resentment of foreign interference in domestic affairs on the grounds of human rights violations, China has found common cause with ASEAN in resisting the imposition of Western values.

China's policy within Southeast Asia has become largely governed by a rational ordering of national priorities in the interdependent context of economic interests and continuing tensions with the United States and Japan. Such a policy, which requires self-restraint in asserting perceived legitimate territorial objectives in the South China Sea is based in part on a recognition of the lack, so far, of a decisive military capability for projecting power to the south of Hainan Island.[16] Correspondingly, China has been obliged to take into account the air and maritime force modernization on the part of some ASEAN states, which are also claimants to islands in the Spratly group, and which could make the irredentist task of even a strong China in the future exceptionally difficult. A cautious calculation would seem to have been made, for the time being.

The states of ASEAN would seem in the main to have based their overall relationship with China on a corresponding rational basis, in part because they lack the collective resources and resolve to do otherwise. The vehicle of the ASEAN Regional Forum enjoys their strong support in the interest of inducting China into habits of good regional citizenship underpinned by the nexus of economic incentive. ASEAN states retain the fail-safe expectation of engaging the United States in a balance of power role. In encouraging such a policy of constructive engagement, the states of Southeast Asia have become a party to helping China's government to realize an historical ambition of creating a strong state of truly global significance. They may also therefore be a party to China escaping the constraints of interdependence. The more optimistic calculation in Southeast Asia, based on the premise of interdependence, is that if China is given enough economic rope it will tie itself down and behave differently from the way in which rising powers have conducted their international relationships in the past. It is this kind of calculation which caused ASEAN's governments in July 1996 to respond positively to China's request to become a formal dialogue partner of the Association and to participate in the ASEAN-Post-Ministerial Conferences.

As the Chinese like to say, only history will decide. For the time being, China's policy would seem to be to avoid engaging in policies likely to generate political alienation within Southeast Asia, so as to be able to focus on the more critical priorities of economic development and on managing relationships with the United States and Japan.

Notes

1. See, Stephen Fitzgerald *China and the Overseas Chinese: A study of Peking's changing policy, 1949–1970,* Cambridge University Press, Cambridge, 1972.
2. See Michael Yahuda *The China Threat,* Institute of Strategic and International Studies, Kuala Lumpur, 1986 and also his general discussion in David Goodman and Gerald Segal (eds.), *China Rising,* Routledge, London, (forhcoming) "How much has China learned about Interdependence? The problems of Engagement".
3. A survey of the relationship with the ASEAN states which highlights their attitudes towards China may be found in Leszek Buszynski, "China and the ASEAN Region" in Stuart Harris and Gary Klintworth (eds.) *China as a Great Power: Myths. Realities and Challenges in the Asia-Pacific Region,* Longman, Melbourne and St. Martin's Press, New York, 1995.
4. See Peter Van Ness *Revolution and Chinese Foreign Policy: Peking's Support for Wars of National Liberation,* University of California Press, Berkeley, 1970 and J. D. Armstrong *Revolutionary Diplomacy: Chinese Foreign Policy and the United Front Doctrine,* University of California Press, Berkeley, 1977.
5. See Mark J. Valencia *China and the South China Sea Disputes,* Adelphi Paper 298, Oxford University Press, for International Institute for Strategic Studies, London. October 1995, pp. 20–22 and also *The Straits Times.* 12 October 1995 for an account of the inconclusive outcome of the sixth workshop in October 1995.
6. For a representative view see, Pan Shiying "The Nansha Islands: A Chinese point of View" *Window Magazine,* Hong Kong. 3 September 1993. See also, Chen Jie "China's Spratly Policy" *Asia Survey,* Vol. xxxiv, No. 10, October 1994 and Sheng Lijun "Beijing and the Spratlys" *Issues and Studies,* Vol. 31, No. 7, 1995.
7. Cao Baojian and Ding Feng "Years of Effort by a South Sea Fleet naval base results in integrating the procurement, supply and transport of materials to *Nanshas* into a system." *Jiefangjun Bao,* 17 March 1995 in BBC *Summary of World Broadcasts,* FE/2260/G 1-2.

8. Adam Schwarz and Matt Forney, "Oil on Troubled Waters", *Far Eastern Economic Review*, 25 April 1996.

9. Its spokesman advised "the Philippine side not to misinterpret the Chinese side's restraint. The Philippine side had better return to the correct course of settling the relevant dispute through peaceful talks. If the Philippine side continues to act wilfully and recklessly, it should be responsible for all consequences arising therefrom." *Xinhua New Agency*, 16 May 1995.

10. For a representative benign Chinese view of ASEAN, see Lu Jianren, "Characteristics of the Present Security Situation in the Asia-Pacific Region" *Foreign Affairs Bulletin*, Beijing, September 1995.

11. He pointed out that "The Chinese side advocates the development of regional cooperation in security matters in stages in the spirit of dealing with issues in ascending order of difficulty, and of seeking common ground while reserving differences. For some time to come, the countries concerned may hold preliminary informal discussions and consultations on the principles, content, scope and method of cooperation in security matters. Meanwhile, they should carry out specific activities of cooperation on which the parties have reached a consensus or which are not highly contentious, and institute some practical and feasible confidence-building measures in a practical manner". *Xinhua News Agency*, 1 August 1995.

12. *Op cit*, 30 July 1995.

13. *Ibid*.

14. The press announcement stated that 'The Government of the People's Republic of China will announce the remaining baselines of the territorial sea of the People's Republic of China at another time.' *Xinhua News Agency* 15 May 1996.

15. See, Shi Min "Background and Impact of a 'Greater ASEAN'" *Foreign Affairs Bulletin*, Beijing, December 1995.

16. It has been widely noted that China has entered into a US$2 billion licence-production agreement with Russia to produce SU-27 long-range fighter aircraft (of which it has already taken separate delivery of 26 with another 24 on order). Deployed from a base being developed on Woody island in the Paracels, the SU-27 could patrol over the Spratly Islands for at least an hour on each mission. See, *International Herald Tribune*, 8 February 1996.

23

Taiwan and Southeast Asia
The Limits to Pragmatic Diplomacy

The relationship between the island of Taiwan and the states of South-East Asia during the 20th century has enjoyed only a limited temporal autonomy. Autonomy was denied during much of the first half of the century because of Japan's colonial rule over the island and because the countries of South-East Asia, with the exception of Thailand, were subject to Western colonialism. It was only with Japan's defeat in the Pacific War and the onset of decolonization, and also with the end of the civil war on the mainland of China that relations between Taiwan as a discrete expression in political geography and independent South-East Asian states began to assume a kind of autonomy. The pattern of relations was never uniform, however, because the states of the region adopted differing Cold War positions towards the governments in Taipei and Beijing; at least until after the issue of the China seat in the United Nations had been resolved in October 1971,

Reprinted in abridged form from Michael Leifer, "Taiwan and South-East Asia: The Limits to Pragmatic Diplomacy", *The China Quarterly*, no. 165 (March 2001), pp. 173–85, by permission of the publisher, Cambridge University Press and the copyright-holder, the School of Oriental and African Studies.

and the end of the Vietnam War. By the end of the century, all ten states of the region had adopted a "one-China policy" in favour of Beijing, while enjoying economic advantages from non-diplomatic relationships with Taipei. In consequence, Taiwan's relations with those states have been confined to a diplomatic limbo, which its government has sought to transcend without success. Indeed, Taiwan's relations with the states of South-East Asia may be understood as an example of the attempt by the government in Taipei to engage with international society from which it has been denied normal membership.

Taiwan's Predicament

The island of Taiwan has long faced a problem of international legitimacy that shows no sign of being resolved. The problem existed even when the government resident in Taipei occupied China's seat in the United Nations because of the recurrent challenges to its status posed within the world body. When that challenge was ultimately successful in October 1971, the problem became acute. It was compounded in 1979 when the United States revoked its diplomatic relations with Taiwan in favour of those with the government in Beijing, and also revoked a critical mutual security treaty. The subsequent passage by America's Congress of the Taiwan Relations Act has served as a practical consolation for upholding a separate existence, but it has not had direct relevance to the problem of international legitimacy whereby Taiwan has been denied normal membership of international society. That problem was not brought any closer to resolution with the remarkable democratic election of Chen Shui-bian as President of Taiwan in March 2000 in succession to Lee Teng-hui. The assumption of political power by the Democratic Progressive Party in place of the long-ruling Kuomintang has served to reiterate a *de facto* independence. It has not brought about any significant change in the basis on which Taiwan is permitted to participate on sufferance within international society.

Such participation as permitted to Taiwan in multilateral forums in the company of the People's Republic of China, from sporting occasions to regional economic gatherings, has required the employment of a politically demeaning nomenclature. This has been insisted on by the government in Beijing as a way of registering its island counterpart's lack of conventional international status and legitimacy. It could be argued that, although nomenclature such as

"Taipei China" is politically demeaning, it nevertheless serves to register a separate identity for Taiwan as in the case of membership of the Asian Development Bank and Asia Pacific Economic Co-operation (APEC). However, such registration has not paved the way for Taiwan to participate correspondingly in the sole comprehensive regional institution devoted to multilateral security dialogue in the Asia Pacific. China has exercised a veto on Taiwan's participation in the ASEAN Regional Forum (ARF) on the ground that membership, as with the United Nations, is a prerogative of sovereign states. And even in the "track-two" Council for Security Co-operation in the Asia Pacific (CSCAP), where participation is on a non-official basis, representatives of Taiwan have been denied a place at plenary sessions and have to be content with a role in subordinate working groups. It is the denial of sovereign status that has been continually frustrating for the government in Taipei, more especially since a constitutional amendment in 1991 recorded a separate jurisdiction from that of the People's Republic over the mainland of China.[1]

        In its countervailing attempts to register and defend an incomplete international status, the government in Taiwan has pursued diplomatic and other ties with the states of South-East Asia, partly on grounds of regional propinquity. By April 1999, with Cambodia's entry, making ASEAN and geographic South-East Asia fully coincident, all its resident states had established diplomatic relations with the People's Republic of China; the last to do so was Brunei in September 1991.[2] However, well before that complete correspondence of membership of regional association and diplomatic relationships with Beijing, Taiwan had not enjoyed extensive diplomatic ties within South-East Asia.

        They had existed for a time with the Philippines and Thailand, both signatories of the American-inspired Manila Pact and members of the South-East Asia Treaty Organization (SEATO) based in Bangkok, as well as with the now defunct Republic of (south) Vietnam. In those three cases, the correspondence of special relations with the United States was a critical factor. Consular relations were established with Malaysia in 1964 but ten years later the government in Kuala Lumpur broke these off on entering into diplomatic relations with Beijing. The next year, with the reunification of Vietnam under communist rule and the end of Taipei's diplomatic relations with the government in Saigon, the Philippines and Thailand followed suit.

        The absence of diplomatic ties did not mean the end of substantive links with states of the region, especially economic ones that involved engagement with the influential local Chinese communities. Moreover, many regional governments established non-official offices in Taipei through which *de facto* inter-state business was conducted. After the success of the Chinese communist revolution, Taiwan's relations with South-East Asia developed primarily as a consequence of the island's astounding economic success and attendant interest beyond trade in exporting investment capital along the lines of the Japanese model. Apart from the special cases of Singapore and Indonesia, with which it has been engaged also in defence co-operation, Taiwan's basis of association with South-East Asia has been primarily economic, with the region becoming the second largest recipient of overseas investments. Economic inducements have been the currency of a so-called pragmatic diplomacy which has been conducted in an attempt to mitigate diplomatic isolation and to generate support for some form of international status which would acknowledge Taiwan's separateness from the Chinese mainland and its government.

The problem with pragmatic diplomacy, which requires dealing with governments in diplomatic relations with Beijing, is that it is likely to be of some utility only for as long as the government in Taipei does not take vigorous steps to register and secure recognition of an unambiguous international status. That limited utility has taken the form of practical unofficial links, which do not require Southeast Asian governments, all in formal diplomatic relationships with Beijing and committed to the one China formula, to make a choice about diplomatic ties. Indeed, it may be argued that once the government in Taipei, irrespective of the merits of its case, seeks actively to secure clarification of its international status then its diplomacy ceases to be pragmatic. The most recent example of the difficulty of combining pragmatic diplomacy with a clarification of international status occurred in early July 1999. In an interview with the German radio station *Deutsche Welle*, President Lee Teng-hui explained that, under constitutional amendments in 1991, the mainland and Taiwan enjoyed "a state-to-state relationship or at least a special state-to-state relationship" as opposed to "an internal relationship between a legitimate government and a renegade group or between a central government and a local government."[3]

The furious reaction from Beijing may have obscured for some the political reality that no SouthEast Asian state indicated any support for that clarification and yet these are among the states that have been courted in the interest of a pragmatic diplomacy. That lack of support had been signalled much earlier by a refusal of observer status to Taiwan by ASEAN. Moreover, at its annual ministerial meeting in late July 1999 in Singapore, its foreign ministers, representing every state in the region, felt the need to reaffirm a corporate commitment to their one China policy. It was significant also that in Singapore, which has long enjoyed the use of Taiwanese facilities for military training and which refused to give them up as the price of diplomatic relations with Beijing, the English language vehicle of government advised that, in dealing with China, Taiwan might find that "it pays to leave well alone."[4]

The Evolution of Pragmatic Diplomacy

From Taiwan's point of view, engagement with South-East Asia was initially driven by a genuine interest in reaping economic benefit from trade ties and from the investment advantages of the lower costs of labour and land.

In the five founder members of ASEAN (Indonesia, Malaysia, the Philippines, Thailand and Singapore), burgeoning trade and investment ties with Taiwan were supported by quasi-diplomatic establishments in each other's capitals. Diplomatic privileges and immunities were accorded to Taiwanese staff whether or not diplomatic relations had been established with Beijing. The extent of those privileges varied according to the economic dependence and political nerve of the government concerned.

China has not been in a position to challenge seriously these growing economic arrangements with diplomatic overtones between Taiwan and South-East Asia, even though trade offices established in Taiwan have had more than an economic purpose. As long as the government in Taipei and its regional trading partners have adhered to a one China policy, especially from the mid-1970s, their counterpart in Beijing was willing to tolerate attempts to mitigate a diplomatic isolation that were most unlikely to bear any tangible diplomatic fruit. Moreover, because the Chinese government in Beijing has had every interest in cultivating good relations with South-East Asia, especially among the members of ASEAN with which it joined in tacit alliance against Vietnam and the Soviet Union over Cambodia from the end of the 1970s, it would have been impolitic to have brought undue pressure to bear on most regional states. Recurrent objection was taken, however, to visits to South-East Asian states by senior political figures from Taiwan, especially when they were received by local political counterparts. From the point of view of South-East Asian governments, such visits signalled to Beijing that the interests of regional states should not be taken for granted, as well as indicating to local Chinese communities that the links with Taiwan were valued.

These visits, with their implied recognition of international status, have, of course, been an anathema to China. Its government was particularly annoyed by the willingness of some regional governments to receive President Lee Teng-hui in the course of his so-called vacation diplomacy in early 1994, especially his reception by Thailand's King Phumibol which implied a state visit. Beijing has been willing, however, to make an exception and turn a blind eye in the case of Singapore, certainly after Prime Minister Lee Kuan Yew's first visit to Beijing in 1976. Singapore has in the past welcomed President Lee Teng-hui. In March 1989, he was acknowledged as the President from Taiwan, while in the previous November, Hau Pao-chuan, Taiwan's Chief of General Staff, was awarded a military honour by President Wee Kim-wee. Moreover, in April 1989, in an extraordinary example of Singapore's role in its dealings with both Taipei and Beijing, a man accused of murder in Taiwan was extradited from China to Taiwan via Singapore's Changi Airport. In April 1993, Singapore was the trusted venue for the historic meeting between China's Association for Relations across the Taiwan Straits and the Taiwan Strait Exchange Foundation. Singapore, as an exceptional ethnic-Chinese majority state, has undoubtedly been given special treatment by Beijing, although objections have been raised to some visits, such as that by Vice-President Lien Chan in January 1998.[5] For Taiwan, however, the advantages of its pragmatic dealings with Singapore have been mixed because Singapore has never wavered from a one China policy even before it established diplomatic relations with Beijing, which only took place in October 1990. Indeed, in October 1971, its United Nations representative had voted for Beijing's assumption of the China seat in place of Taipei.

Taiwan's links with Southeast Asia have also had an overseas Chinese dimension for both economic and political reasons. Their networks have been viewed in Taipei as giving rise to political advantage to the extent that they have facilitated economic links that have, in turn, permitted quasi-diplomatic relations. Beyond that, they have had to be treated with caution because of the political sensitivities of local governments, which Taiwan has sought to court. It merits noting, however, that despite the nature of the constitutional amendments of 1991, there is still provision for overseas Chinese representation in Taiwan's legislature.

Pragmatic diplomacy on Taiwan's part with reference to South-East Asia was given a new impetus by historic political change within Taiwan during the 1980s. The end of martial law and the onset of democratization had an international impact in revealing the fallibility of Taipei's claim to be the government of all of China. The injunction that all surviving mainland-elected politicians from 1947 had to retire by December 1991 underlined matters. The death of President Chiang Ching-kuo in January 1988 and his succession by Vice-President Lee Teng-hui was significant for a number of reasons but particularly because the new President was a native Taiwanese, which implied a separate identity from the mainland.

At the national party congress of the ruling Kuomintang in July 1988, Lee Teng-hui announced that his government would adopt a more pragmatic, more flexible and more forward-looking approach to upgrade Taiwan's external relations.

That offensive began unsurprisingly in Singapore where the foreign minister, Lien Chan, paid an unpublicized visit in December 1988, which paved the way for a state visit by President Lee in March 1989. It was unsurprising in so far as Lee Kuan Yew, while prime minister, had made countless visits to Taiwan, some to discuss defence co-operation. Pragmatic diplomacy was, in effect, a *de facto* two China policy without articulating that political reality.

Vietnam's great need for foreign investment provided an opportunity for Taiwan whose first trade mission was welcomed in Hanoi in 1988. That dimension of the relationship was readily tolerated in Beijing, including a visit by a vice-minister of economic affairs in September 1993. Indeed, by the end of 1991, Taiwan had already become the leading foreign investor in the Socialist Republic. The limits of the relationship were pointed up, however, in 1993 when China's intervention in objecting to China Airlines, Taiwan's official carrier, flying directly to Ho Chi Minh City with the Republic of China flag on the tail of its aircraft, led to the suspension of the service. It was resumed the following year by Eva Air, a private Taiwanese carrier without the national flag.

In the interim, opportunities for developing new relations within South-East Asia, such as with Vietnam, and building on established ones were taken by Taipei with special attention given to publicized exchanges of visits of political leaders in the face of objections from Beijing. From the South-East Asian point of view, however, such visits have tended to be driven by economic considerations with the exception of Singapore which, in its own interest, has sought to contain tensions across the Taiwan Strait. Its defence co-operation links with the government in Taipei are well known and have been tolerated grudgingly in Beijing. It is notable that in March 1996, during the crisis precipitated by China's attempt through live-firing missile exercises to intimidate Taiwanese voters in advance of the first popular elections for the office of president, Singapore's was the only regional voice willing to urge caution on the government in Beijing through a public statement by Lee Kuan Yew. Ironically, two Singaporean naval vessels had dropped anchor in the port of Kaohsiung in early March 1996 after exercises with the Taiwanese navy concurrently with China's acts of intimidation.

Irrespective of the material interests of many regional governments in their relations with Taiwan, they all formally acknowledge the government in Beijing as the government of China. Within the socially diverse states of South-East Asia, separatist sentiment is endemic, albeit frustrated. Support for an independent Taiwan could have domestic consequences for governments that have still to overcome fully the lack of congruence between state and society within inherited colonial political boundaries. Ambiguity is favoured also because any clarification of Taiwan's international status could pose problems that South-East Asian governments would prefer not to face.

In the special case of Singapore, without expressing sympathy for President Lee Teng-hui's policies, former prime minister and now senior minister, Lee Kuan Yew, as indicated above, has spoken out publicly to Beijing against its display of force in approaching unification though not in favour of a separate international status for Taiwan. Such an intervention has been the exception and not the rule within South-East Asia despite a general concern over China's willingness to use force in settling conflicts.

The South China Sea

Irrespective of the degree of success of Taiwan's pragmatic diplomacy, it may be argued that its assertion of sovereign jurisdiction over islands and other features in the South China Sea, initially on behalf of the government of China, works in direct contradiction to the aims of that policy. It has been pointed out that Beijing and Taipei "assert Chinese sovereignty identically as based on history."[6] Indeed, it was the government of the Republic of China which in 1947 produced the controversial dotted-line map of historic waters in the South China Sea, which has been taken up as its own by the government of the People's Republic to register national claims. Although the government in Taipei has deployed troops on its sole occupied Taiping (Itu Aba) Island, it has never engaged in any physical competition with its counterpart in Beijing over sovereign jurisdiction. Moreover, when in December 1988, Cheng Wei-yuan, the Republic of China's defence minister, was asked by journalists what his government would do in the event of an armed clash between Beijing and Hanoi in the Spratly Islands, he answered that Taipei would stand side by side against Vietnam as the people on both sides of the Taiwan Strait were Chinese.[7]

Taiwan has only a toehold in the Spratly Islands that fall beyond its immediate strategic environment. Taiping Island, on which Taipei has maintained a small garrison, lies some 860 nautical miles southwest of Taiwan and poses a problem of power projection. Taiwan has avoided engaging in the kind of creeping assertiveness that has distinguished the policy of Beijing, Hanoi and Kuala Lumpur. Indeed, in November 1999, Taiwan's defence minister, Tang Wei, confirmed that marine units stationed on Taiping Island would be replaced by coastguards to avoid possible conflict.

Taiwan's representatives, ostensibly in a personal capacity, and subject to politically demeaning titles, have been engaged since the early 1990s in "track two" preventive diplomacy workshops on the South China Sea sponsored by Indonesia and Canada, but without any notable success. Pressure from Beijing, which also sends participants to the workshops, has prevented Taiwan from sponsoring a technical working group on the safety of navigation, which shows its diminished status. Beyond these less than satisfactory workshops, Taiwan cannot engage in substantive negotiations over its island claims because the lack of full diplomatic status denies it any interlocutors or, for example, the right to approach the International Court of Justice.

It may be argued additionally that such a policy serves Taiwan well, *faute de mieux*, in that it prevents its claims coming into practical conflict with its policy of pragmatic diplomacy directed at the states of South-East Asia. The matter interposes primarily in some of the relationships in principle only.

How Pragmatic is Pragmatic Diplomacy?

Pragmatic diplomacy in Taiwan's case is a euphemism for trying to overcome a fundamental impediment to separate international status, which is inherent in the concept of sovereignty that is the organizing principle of international society. In pursuing such a diplomacy in and beyond South-East Asia, the government in Taipei has sought to use economic engagement as a way of securing degrees of recognition which would give it greater freedom of international manoeuvre and thus deny the claim of the government in Beijing that it is no more than a renegade province. The problem for Taiwan is that while it has made considerable advances in securing a quasi-diplomatic association with the more important regional states on a bilateral basis, none of them, with regional security in mind, has been willing to offend the government in Beijing over the indivisible matter of sovereignty.[8]

Such lack of support has not been reflected in an unwillingness to sustain a fruitful economic association with Taiwan which, ironically, may be said to be in Beijing's interest because of its dependence on investment capital from both Taiwan and overseas Chinese business networks within South-East Asia. That economic association, while of considerable importance in Taipei, does not go far enough to satisfy its underlying objective of pragmatic diplomacy.

Taiwan enjoys a fruitful relationship with most of the states of SouthEast Asia, which is expressed, in part, in quasi-diplomatic links which have served to give the government in Taiwan a greater international profile. From the perspective of the South-East Asian states, however, these links are mainly intended to facilitate a fruitful economic association without prejudicing conventional diplomatic ties with the government in Beijing.

Notes

1. For general analyses of Taiwan's predicament, see Christopher Hughes, *Taiwan and Chinese Nationalism, National Identity and Status in International Society* (London: Routledge, 1997), and Bernice Lee, *The Security Implications of the New Taiwan*, Adelphi Papers No. 331 (Oxford: Oxford University Press for the IISS, 1999).

2. An exception within geographic Southeast Asia is the eastern half of the island of Timor. East Timor, formerly a Portuguese colony, was invaded by Indonesia in December 1975 and integrated into the Republic in July 1976 but was relinguished in October 1999 against a background of political violence. The territory has reverted to non-self governing status under United Nations tutelage with independence in prospect within two to three years.

3. The full text of the interview may be found in *Taipei-London*, Newsletter No. 13, August 1999, Taipei Representative Office in the UK. See also Lee Teng-hui, "Understanding Taiwan: Bridging the perception gap," *Foreign Affairs*, Vol. 78, No. 6 (November/December 1999).

4. *The Straits Times*, 5 August 1999.

5. For an assessment of why the government in Beijing might make an exception in tolerating Singapore's links with Taiwan, see Chen Jie, "The Taiwan problem in Peking's ASEAN policy," *Issues and Studies*, April 1993, pp. 116–122.

6. See Chen Hurng-yu, "A comparison between Taipei and Peking in their policies and concepts regarding the South China Sea," *Issues and Studies*, September 1993; Kuan-ming Sun, "The Republic of China's policy toward the South China Sea: a review," *Issues and Studies*, March 1996; and Cheng-yi Lin, "Taiwan's South China Sea policy," *Asian Survey*, April 1997.

7. Chen Hurng-yu, "A comparison between Taipei and Peking," p. 50.

8. See Michael Yahuda, "The international standing of the Republic of China on Taiwan," in David Shambaugh (ed.), *Contemporary Taiwan* (Oxford: Oxford University Press, 1992), pp. 292–93.

24

Who's It that Really Needs to be Engaged?

It has become a conventional wisdom in the West that China, as a rising power, should be "engaged" so as to ensure that it learns and observes the rules of international society. Within China, however, the English language concept of engagement gives rise to confusion.

Engagement as employed in the West is certainly not intended as a prelude to marriage so that the Chinese are inclined to regard the term as a euphemism for containment by other than military means.

China's rising power is a matter of genuine concern within East Asia where the People's Republic has come to enjoy a unique measure of strategic latitude in the wake of the Cold War.

Anxiety over its hegemonic potential is widespread, even if most governments are reluctant to voice that apprehension for fear of compounding matters.

Reprinted in abridged form from Michael Leifer, "Who's It That Really Needs to be Engaged?", *Bangkok Post,* 9 February 1997, by permission of the Post Publishing Public Company Limited.

And yet despite its demonstrable economic progress and its degree of aggrandisement in the South China Sea, China remains a weak power militarily.

Last March, it shrank from confrontation over Taiwan in the face of a display of American resolve.

But even without American deterrence, China is still far away from a position from which it could mount a successful invasion at acceptable cost.

The fact of the matter is that, despite a persisting reluctance to risk ground forces in battle, the United States is a military giant compared with China.

Its advanced technology, its unmatched international standing and a deep-seated sense of ideological rectitude have encouraged a persistent drive to promote a world order in the American image.

The absence of any counter-balancing international peers in the wake of the disintegration of the Soviet Union and the international enthronement of market economics have reinforced the underlying view that what is good for the US is almost certainly good for the rest of the world.

In addition, although President Clinton's policy of "enlarging market democracies" has been modified out of considerations of prudence, the underlying determination to remake the world in the image of American democracy has been sustained, albeit directed against soft targets and not at the cost of material interests as relations with China have demonstrated.

In the case of the UN, the American government has given the impression of believing in unequal representation with minimal taxation.

In the light of this kind of conduct, the question might be posed: should the US, as well as China, also attract a measure of engagement for the benefit of international society? In East Asia, however, the shortcomings of America's outlook and assertiveness are tolerated by most governments because it is regarded by them as the least objectionable major power, even if a number do not repose great confidence in its longer-term political will and staying-power.

The spectre of a rising China, concern about a rearmed Japan and the likely fall-out from Sino-Japanese tensions have given the US, at the very least, a grudging countervailing role in the interest of a good number of regional states.

Moreover, the US has demonstrated responsibility as well as prudence in its East Asian security policy.

Its military deployment off the coast of Taiwan last March was well below the horizon, except on CNN.

Patience and persistence in dealing with North Korea over its nuclear policy, despite the adverse effect on relations with its southern ally, would appear to have produced due political reward.

And while Washington cannot be expected to take sides in the complex disputes over jurisdiction in the South China Sea, it has registered an unequivocal position on freedom of navigation through its waters.

As a security partner, the US has been, on balance, a responsible superpower in East Asia, despite Beijing's view that Washington's current policy of engagement is a euphemism for containment.

The US has also been forbearing towards ASEAN, which as a grouping of lesser states, has assumed, for some presumptuously so, the central diplomatic role within the embryonic ASEAN Regional Forum (ARF).

Moreover, ASEAN's promotion of multilateral dialogue through the ARF serves the dual purpose of incorporating the US as well as China within a context where powerful states have to take some account of the views of lesser ones.

The US has been a relatively benign superpower but as the sole survivor of this rare species it exists on a different plane to those lesser states which seek to benefit from its countervailing role in East Asia.

For that reason, they cannot afford to assume that the US will act either as a political equal or as a disinterested guardian of their interests.

It is certainly not desirable for any one state to dispose of an overweening power which might enable it to rule the roost.

And for that reason, engaging the US, in a corresponding way to that advocated for China, has much to commend it, at least in principle.

The fact of the matter, however, is that despite any perceived shortcomings in its ideological outlook and diplomatic practice, the US is not seen to pose a security threat regionally through, for example, articulating territorial claims or modernising its armed forces.

For that reason, regional states in the main tolerate and cope as best they can with Washington's intrusive agenda for world order, however appealing may be the logic of upholding common standards of engagement.

25

The European Union, ASEAN, and the Politics of Exclusion

Ever since the end of the Cold War, the relationship between the EU and ASEAN has been troubled by a tension over human rights. That tension has been registered most explicitly over how to deal with the unelected military regime in Yangon. Indeed, an EU-ASEAN Joint Cooperation Committee meeting due to have been held in Bangkok in November last year was cancelled because the EU side had refused to accept Myanmar's participation with the status of an official observer, despite its full membership in the association from the previous July.

That cancellation prompted speculation that the issue of Myanmar's representation might well prejudice the second Asia-Europe heads of government meeting scheduled to convene in London in April 1998. The leaders of the Yangon government have been banned from visiting EU capitals under visa restrictions imposed as part of a package of sanctions in 1996. The prospect of an ASEAN boycott as a demonstration

Reprinted from Michael Leifer, "The European Union, ASEAN and the Politics of Exclusion", *ISEAS Trends, Business Times*, Weekend Edition, 31 January–1 February 1998, p. 7, by permission of the copyright-holder, the Institute of Southeast Asian Studies.

of a refusal to be subject to a European diktat over representation arose when a source close to the Philippine chair of its Standing Committee threatened the EU with exclusion from security dialogues under the ASEAN Regional Forum and the ASEAN Post-ministerial Conference.

In the event, the issue of Myanmar's representation has not been allowed to threaten the second ASEM which exists on a different plane to the relationship between EU and ASEAN. It was made clear at the historic first meeting between the heads of government of ASEAN and their counterparts from China, Japan and South Korea in Kuala Lumpur in mid-December last year that there would not be automatic membership in ASEM for ASEAN governments which had joined the association since the first meeting in Bangkok in March 1996. Indeed, no new members would participate in London.

Disentangling ASEM from the relationship between the EU and ASEAN, at least for the time being, has not solved the problem which arose over Myanmar. That problem exemplifies fundamental differences of policy which may be defined with reference to the concept of exclusion. The EU has taken a high moral tone towards the military regime in Yangon in keeping with its resolution on Human Rights, Democracy and Development in November 1991. In protest at the deplorable human rights record of that regime and its refusal to embark on a dialogue with Aung San Suu Kyi, the EU has sought to punish Myanmar through a policy of exclusion from political dialogue, albeit not to the extent of breaking off diplomatic relations either on an individual or an EU basis.

That policy of exclusion was pursued in the EU's abortive attempt to persuade ASEAN not to admit Myanmar to membership until its human rights record had improved. Since its entry in July 1997, the EU has refused to accord Myanmar ASEAN-member status at meetings with the association which led to the cancellation in Bangkok last November. ASEAN has long taken a diametrically opposite view towards Myanmar expressed in the notion of "constructive engagement". That policy of inclusion is justified on the grounds that sanctions will only reinforce the doggedness of the Yangon government and also encourage it to develop an even closer relationship with Beijing.

On ASEAN's side, there is an evident resentment of the European presumption to dictate the terms of the association's enlargement. Moreover, the perceived spurious legalism of the EU's rationale for excluding Myanmar on the grounds that it was not a signatory of the original Cooperation Agreement of 1980 is also deemed offensive.

Added to those factors is the evident sensitivity within ASEAN of the way in which its new-found economic adversity has been greeted in Europe and the failure of the EU, which seemed to rediscover Asia in 1994 from a sense of economic opportunism, to demonstrate a greater willingness to help in mitigating that adversity.

It has been suggested that part of the problem between the EU and ASEAN last November was the measure of diplomatic rigidity displayed by the Luxembourg Presidency. A greater diplomatic imaginativeness and flexibility is not going to be sufficient in itself as a basis for rebuilding the troubled relationship with Britain replacing Luxembourg in the EU presidential role. Indeed, Britain's Foreign Secretary, Robin Cook, has registered the ethical dimension of his government's foreign policy which is driven, in part, by the close link between a number of UK-based NGOs and the ruling Labour Party.

From ASEAN's point of view, in seeking to make an issue of Myanmar, the EU is attacking a soft target with which economic engagement is limited by contrast, for example, with China where confrontation has been deliberately avoided. European inconsistency over human rights and ASEAN's sensitivity to the EU's presumption to interfere in the management of its own affairs drives a disposition to diplomatic solidarity, even on the part of those members strongly committed to democratic values and uncomfortable about Myanmar's membership.

If the EU may be accused of inconsistency, so may ASEAN in its exclusion, albeit temporarily, of Cambodia from membership as a result of Hun Sen's successful violent coup in July last year. Moreover, the EU may be reluctant to compromise over human rights and Myanmar as the sense of economic opportunity which prompted its Asian initiative in 1994 gives way to a more pessimistic regional outlook.

The fact of the matter is that for domestic reasons in EU countries the issue of exclusion in the case of Myanmar is not likely to go away, certainly as long as the government in Yangon refuses to attend to its lack of political legitimacy which has not been achieved by a recent change of nomenclature. For the EU, democracy is part of its organic identity which is not the same for ASEAN which has always been a diplomatic and not a political community. For ASEAN, however, the EU's policy of exclusion is no more than a posture without practical merits and to be resisted for that reason as well as for its presumptuous nature.

26

The Peace Dividend
Israel's Changing Relationship with Southeast Asia

One of the more unanticipated and intriguing consequences of the Declaration of Principles on Interim Self-Government Arrangements, reached on 13 September 1993 between Israel and the Palestine Liberation Organization (PLO), has been the first open and publicized contact between the Jewish state and Indonesia. On 15 October, Yitzhak Rabin, who had just completed the first visit to China by an Israeli prime minister, changed his itinerary at very short notice and flew to Indonesia instead of Uzbekistan where he was expected. His three-hour visit was only announced to the Indonesian press after he had left the country for neighbouring Singapore.

Prime Minister Rabin was received by President Soeharto at his private residence in a meeting described by the state secretary, Moerdiono, as one "between mature, wise and insightful statesmen". It was made clear that President Soeharto had acted in his capacity as chairman of the Non-Aligned Movement and that the meeting was

Reprinted in abridged form from *The Peace Dividend: Israel's Changing Relationship with South-East Asia,* by Michael Leifer, IJA Research Reports, no. 1 (February 1994), pp. 2–13, by permission of the Institute for Jewish Policy Research.

not intended to signal a prelude to diplomatic relations. Nonetheless, the brief encounter at head-of-government level between two former military commanders was an event of some political significance both for Israel and for Indonesia.

The end of the cold war has enabled Israel to extend the range of its diplomatic relationships in Asia, with normal ties now established with such major regional states as India and China which had long resisted them. That post-cold war transformation has meant that the first open contact between Israel and Indonesia has been less dramatic than it would have been in different circumstances. However, Rabin's visit remains of considerable importance. Not only does the republic of Indonesia currently head the Non-Aligned Movement but it is also home to the largest Muslim population in the world. In Indonesia, as well as in neighbouring Muslim Malaysia and Brunei, the conflict between Israel and the Palestinians has been interpreted at the popular level as a co-religionist issue. A willingness on the part of the government in Jakarta to treat with Israel as a normal country has relevance for the climate of opinion within the Islamic world as a whole towards the peace accord. It also affects the international legitimacy of the Jewish state.

There is a related factor bearing on Israel's international relationships arising from Yitzhak Rabin's presence in South-East Asia. From Jakarta, Rabin travelled on to Singapore for two days during which he visited the prime minister, Goh Chok Tong, and received senior minister and former prime minister, Lee Kuan Yew. Israel and Singapore have enjoyed diplomatic relations since May 1969 and have long engaged in military co-operation. Rabin's visit to Singapore was reported while he was in the island state but was not announced in advance. Such caution was almost certainly intended to avoid the kind of political difficulty with neighbouring Malaysia which had arisen from the visit to Singapore by former President Chaim Herzog in November 1986. Prime Minister Rabin's reception at the highest level removed any suspicion of reserve on Singapore's part about the relationship and served also as a reminder to Malaysia, which had objected strongly to Chaim Herzog's presence, that the sovereign prerogatives of the island state should be respected.

The initiative for this first open contact came from the Israeli side which has long sought to expand its diplomatic relationships within South-East Asia, especially with countries with distinct Muslim identities. Islam is the official religion in both Malaysia and Brunei but

Israel has not yet been able to establish working contacts in either of those countries. Islamic communities are also to be found in Thailand and the Philippines but, in those countries, Muslims are clear minorities, albeit concentrated geographically. Israel entered into diplomatic relations with Thailand and the Philippines respectively in 1954 and in 1957. Indonesia has not taken an active role as a vociferous opponent of Israel but its government has been an extremely hesitant diplomatic partner. Nonetheless, it should be placed in a different category from Malaysia and Brunei because of the greater degree of working contacts.

There has long been [an] active covert relationship between the two states which has been expressed in transfers of arms and agricultural technology. Indonesia's resistance to Israel's interest in open contact has been a function of its domestic political context and also of its longstanding desire to assume recognized leadership within the Non-Aligned Movement.

The Opening to Israel

President Soeharto is a master of the art of political balance. He had seen the unreality of an absence of diplomatic relations with China as the cold war was coming to an end. Correspondingly, as chairman of the Non-Aligned Movement, he saw advantage in burnishing that role in responding to an Israeli initiative which would also signal to Indonesia's Muslims that his more recent political indulgence towards them should not be misconstrued. His new-found activism as spokesman for the Non-Aligned Movement has struck a chord among Indonesia's political public who have long felt that membership of the Association of Southeast Asian Nations (ASEAN), the regional organization established in August 1967, has constrained the republic from playing the full international role to which it is entitled on account of its physical and human geography.

Prime Minister Rabin flew from Shanghai to Halim Perdanakusumah military airbase outside Jakarta, where he was met by state secretary Moerdiono and taken without ceremony in an unmarked car to President Soeharto's private residence. The two heads of government held discussions for over an hour in the presence of only one personal adviser each before Rabin was taken back to Halim airbase to travel on to Singapore. The nature and place of the meeting without any state protocol was quite deliberate so as to avoid generating expectations of impending diplomatic relations. Foreign Minister Ali Alatas was excluded from the discussions on the ground that Israel's foreign minister was not accompanying his prime minister.

In a radio interview in Singapore, Yitzhak Rabin gave his account of the brief unannounced visit, explaining that Yassir Arafat had visited Indonesia in the previous month and that he had thought it fitting to present the Israeli position to the man who heads the 108-state Non-Aligned Movement.

Although Rabin's visit to Indonesia was only announced some four hours after he had left the country, it was widely reported the next morning on the front pages of the national press together with photographs taken by staff of the State Secretariat of the two heads of government together. The meeting was also shown on state television. Indonesia's press was informed that after performing his Friday prayers, the president had received "a courtesy call" from Israel's prime minister that had been based on his role as chairman of the Non-Aligned Movement. Indeed, the timing of the visit between Friday prayers for Muslims and the Jewish sabbath, so enabling Rabin to arrive in Singapore before its onset, served the interests of both leaders in coping with their domestic constituencies.

It was explained to the Indonesian media that the meeting had been requested some time before, presumably in the knowledge of Prime Minister Rabin's impending visit to China. They were told also that the reason why President Soeharto had decided to meet Rabin was because the Non-Aligned Movement aimed to promote global peace. In addition, it was made known that the president had instructed the foreign minister, Ali Alatas, to convene a meeting of the Non-Aligned Committee on Palestine with a view to recommending steps to its Co-ordinating Bureau in New York that the Movement might take following mutual recognition between the PLO and Israel. Finally, it was emphasized that Indonesia was not in a hurry to establish diplomatic relations.[1]

For both Israel and Indonesia, formal diplomatic relations were not at issue. Both states had derived benefit from the meeting between the two heads of government. President Soeharto had raised his profile as a statesman to domestic applause as well as enhancing the international role and standing of the republic. Prime Minister Rabin had broken through an Islamic wall of containment with the expectation that President Soeharto would employ his good offices as chairman of the Non-Aligned Movement on Israel's behalf. Indeed, after attending the informal summit of Asian leaders convened by

President Clinton in Seattle in November, President Soeharto returned via Tunisia and Iran and met again with Yassir Arafat. In addition, in Israel, Yitzhak Rabin revealed that President Soeharto had expressed a willingness to open channels for bilateral co-operation.[2] In return, Indonesia found in Israel an unlikely spokesman for its interests. For example, when Rabin was in Washington in November, he urged Americans not to push for human rights at the expense of undermining governments that could be helpful in combatting the spread of Islamic fundamentalism.[3]

The Singapore Connection

Israel's close relationship with Singapore was forged after the island state had independence thrust upon it on expulsion from the Federation of Malaysia in August 1965.

The relationship has always enjoyed a low profile because of regional sensitivities and Singapore's concern not to offend Arab-Islamic states more than necessary. A reassessment of the relationship by the government of Singapore occurred after the controversial visit by President Chaim Herzog in November 1986 which was announced a month in advance. That visit caused particular offence in Malaysia, which led the way in regional protests, because of the political embarrassment caused to the prime minister, Dr Mahathir Mohamad, whose strictures against Zionists and Jews, employed interchangeably, had become prominent in his public pronouncements in the preceding months.

For Singapore, the visit by Yitzhak Rabin enabled its government to demonstrate that Malaysia could not exercise a veto over which guests it chose to receive. The occasion was highly opportune for such a purpose, coming after his visit to Indonesia, the largest and most important member of ASEAN. Indonesia's government had only gone through the motions of protest when Chaim Herzog had visited Singapore in November 1986. Shortly afterwards, in February 1987, President Soeharto had paid a cordial visit to the island state approaching it by road across the causeway from Malaysia, which had been his first call. Singapore has long taken care to cultivate President Soeharto's Indonesia. A good working relationship had developed between him and Prime Minister Lee Kuan Yew, sustained by his successor Goh Chok Tong, by contrast to the personal tensions between Indonesia's president and Malaysia's prime minister, Dr Mahathir

Mohamad. Yitzhak Rabin's brief visit to Jakarta provided Singapore with an ideal opportunity to raise the profile of its relationship with Israel in the interest of reasserting its sovereign independence. In his meeting with Prime Minister Rabin, Senior Minister Lee Kuan Yew responded positively to a renewed longstanding invitation to visit Israel.

For Israel, the visit by Yitzhak Rabin to Singapore was of lesser importance than the brief encounter in Jakarta. Its government deferred to Israeli political sensibilities when Senior Minister Lee Kuan Yew called on Yitzhak Rabin at his hotel during the Jewish sabbath, while Prime Minister Goh Chok Tong waited until its termination before receiving him at his office. Apart from discussing the accord reached with the PLO, Rabin also raised the question of Israeli servicemen missing in action. The Singapore connection does not have the same significance for Israel in promoting the accord with the PLO as that established with Indonesia. Nonetheless, it continues to be useful, especially in growing economic co-operation. That connecton has now been freed of the inhibition which had been the legacy of the earlier visit by Chaim Herzog. Singapore's ministry of foreign affairs had no qualms about welcoming the meeting between the Indonesian president and the Israeli prime minister.

Conclusion

The Israel-PLO accord has been one of the positive consequences of the end of the cold war. It attempts to address a fundamental political problem arising from the very establishment of the state of Israel. To that end, its successful implementation in the face of considerable difficulties will depend greatly on the ability of the principal parties to arrive at necessary compromises consistent with their interests. Successful implementation will depend also on an ability to engage other Middle Eastern governments constructively in the peace process. The wider international context is not unimportant, however. And it was for this reason that Yitzhak Rabin sought an opening to Indonesia.

It had been the end of the cold war which gave credence to Indonesia's aspiration to head the Non-Aligned Movement, which was only realized in September 1992. The republic presented its qualifications for that office in terms of concrete achievement in economic development and not in rhetorical confrontation with the West which had once been a requisite for leadership. The changing priorities and agenda of the Non-Aligned Movement based upon international co-operation have made Indonesia an ideal interlocutor for Rabin's purpose in securing the widest possible international support for the accord with the PLO and also greater international acceptability for Israel itself. President Soeharto's willingness to take on that role constitutes a diplomatic success for Israel in its search for greater dialogue with the Islamic world. It has to be said, however, that the progress of that dialogue and the ability of President Soeharto to act as interlocutor will depend on progress in more central dialogue between Israel and the PLO. Elsewhere in Southeast Asia, the prime minister of Malaysia welcomed the Israel-PLO accord as a positive development but Dr Mahathir has also been conspicuously cautious in his response, possibly influenced by his known personal animosity to Israel. For example, although an Israeli doctor visited Malaysia in August 1993 as part of an invited delegation of international specialists, its government has yet to reverse its official prohibition on visits by Israelis.[4]

Without discounting necessary caution, Rabin's visit to Indonesia and, to a lesser extent, to Singapore has served to help change the perception of Israel among those for whom it has long been regarded as a pariah. For example, it is significant that another leader of Indonesia's Muslim *Ulemas* Council, Ali Yafie, felt able to say that the peace accord between Israel and the PLO meant that the republic no longer had to shun the Jewish state.[5] Such a remark may be only of small comfort in Jerusalem, but it represents a major advance in Jakarta. It also serves to demonstrate that Israel's problems with the wider world have to be addressed and overcome through attending to the country's immediate political environment and not the other way around.

Notes

1. See the account of the press briefing, *Radio Republic Indonesia*, 15 October 1993, in BBC *Summary of World Broadcasts (SWB)*, FE/1823 B/7-8.
2. BBC *SWB*, ME/1824 MED/3. Also Neal Sandler, "Indonesia: Israel's new trade hot spot", *Jerusalem Report*, 18 November 1993.
3. *International Herald Tribune*, 18 November 1993.
4. Lindsey Shanson, *Jewish Chronicle*, 1 October 1993.
5. *Asian Wall Street Journal*, 18 October 1993.

Between Regions:
ASEAN and the EC/EU

INTRODUCTION

The word "between" in the heading of this section refers to the relations between regions and to the comparison being drawn between the respective models of regionalism. The three selected articles relate to three phases in the development of European and Southeast Asian regionalism. ASEAN's early phase of intra-regional co-operation characterized by a loose institutional structure whereby major decision-making and co-ordination were largely decentralized despite the existence since 1976 of a central secretariat, forms the backdrop to the first article which was published in 1986 (Ch. 27). Its European counterpart (or dialogue partner) at the time was the European Community with which ASEAN is being compared. A key contrasting feature is that while the European model contained from the very outset a treaty-bound commitment to political and economic integration, ASEAN was essentially a diplomatic community acting in concert. In short, ASEAN had never aspired to supra-nationalism. Such a comparison would have been a bland exercise were it not for Leifer's observation of the ironic. The underlying strains of political decision-making and mixed record of foreign policy co-ordination in the EC belied its professed tight regionalism whereas despite its looser regionalism ASEAN achieved a remarkable cohesiveness as a diplomatic community conducting an effective foreign policy over the Cambodia issue that epitomized for ASEAN a classic case of national sovereignty under threat. Leifer noted the irony that it was ASEAN, which upheld the states system of European derivation, while it was the EC which sought to transcend it.

By the time of the second selected article (Ch. 28) published in 1998, the EC had deepened into the European Union and changing circumstances in both regions were affecting the ASEAN–EU relationship. Adding to a more complex relationship and a less consistent approach on the European side was its peculiar six-monthly rotating presidency of the Council of Ministers and the "troika" partners of past, current, and next presidents. At a time when the revision of the ASEAN-EC/EU Co-operation Agreement, which had provided the legal framework for inter-regional co-operation since 1980, was stalemated by the position taken on East Timor by new EU member, Portugal, and when the much wider Asia-Europe Meeting (ASEM) process was taking off, Leifer wondered whether ASEAN could maintain its centrality in Europe's expanding relations with Asia.

The final article in this section (Ch. 29) is Leifer's last published article on ASEAN. Completed at the end of the last century when ASEAN finally realized its aspiration for "One Southeast Asia" but against the backdrop of the still reverberating Asian financial crisis and controversies over Cambodia's and Myanmar's entries into ASEAN, this article shows Leifer in his more sombre moments. Comparing ASEAN's regionalism with that of the EU, Leifer draws out the perils over the benefits of regional expansion faced by ASEAN. Regional expansion conceivably could lead to bigger international clout if the expanded region could speak with a single voice. The peril is that the collective political culture could be diluted by a greater diversity of political interests and identities, thus making it more difficult to achieve consensus. ASEAN's intra-mural differences over the issue of "intervention" with regards to the domestic political situation in Myanmar and in Cambodia following the July 1997 coup and the less than coherent response to the regional haze as well as to China's creeping expansion into the South China Sea area and failure to play a collective role in the "second decolonization" of East Timor added to a sense of frustration as Leifer surveyed ASEAN at century's end.

27

Regional Decision-Making and Corporate Foreign Policies

As corporate entities, ASEAN and the European Community are very different. Differences express themselves not only in the comparative quality of economic cooperation but also in the formal commitment to political integration. Both ASEAN and the European Community operate within the international legal order which underpins the states' system but the former is committed in principle to uphold it regionally, while the latter is committed in principle to transcend and revise it. The object of this paper is to assess the manner of collective decision-making within the two international institutions in the light of their fundamental differences and to consider what effect, if any, it may have on corporate foreign policies and on their bilateral relationship. The analysis is governed by the maxim "never mind the principle, look at the practice".

Reprinted in abridged form from Michael Leifer, "Regional Decision-Making and Corporate Foreign Policies", in *ASEAN-EC Economic and Political Relations,* edited by R. H. Taylor and P. C. I. Ayre (London: External Services Division, School of Oriental and African Studies, 1986), pp. 63–71, by permission of the publisher and the copyright-holders.

It is only possible to assess the nature of ASEAN, and therefore the manner in which it differs from the European Community, by taking full account of the regional environment at the time of its formation. The key to its advent and to its measure of success was the common commitment to regional reconciliation evident in the aftermath of Indonesia's Confrontation. Regional order of a kind required an affirmation of respect for the national sovereignty and territorial integrity of neighbouring states. Any hint of the kind of political aspiration which had inspired the European movement would have prevented the Association from getting off the ground. It should be noted that the founding document of ASEAN is a multilateral declaration and not a treaty. Sovereignty was not at issue, except that the object of the corporate exercise was to reaffirm it. The emphasis of the founding declaration was as much on equality as on partnership. Any element of supranational intent was conspicuous by its absence by contrast with the institutional antecedents of the European Community. The initial service functions for the Association were assumed by National Secretariats which were integral parts of members' foreign ministries.

ASEAN has never looked beyond an inter-governmental structure. The ASEAN states may be joined in a parliamentary union of a kind but they are not in any way committed to a common assembly on the European model, let alone to direct elections. The European Community may be compared with ASEAN in terms of formative incentive with reconciliation in the wake of conflict a regional imperative. But in the case of the European Community, from the outset there has existed a commitment in treaty form to political integration. However qualified over the years and diluted through the impact of an expanding membership, that commitment has shaped the aspirational identity of the corporate institution. For example, the adoption in February 1984 by the European Parliament of a Draft Treaty on a European Union was an indication of the underlying strain of political aspiration which has no place within ASEAN.

In the case of ASEAN, when its heads of government reached the stage of expressing common interest and aspiration in treaty form in February 1976, political union was certainly not on their minds, not even in principle. The Treaty of Amity and Co-operation concluded on the occasion of their first joint meeting constituted an attempt to institutionalise the peaceful settlement of disputes within a wider structure of rules for states behaviour. In other words, at its most ambitious the Treaty was intended to provide a code of conduct for regional order to which it was hoped, at the time, the states of Indochina might adhere. Central to the terms of the Treaty was the sanctity of national sovereignty which its signatories were enjoined to respect and protect.

No hint of superseding national sovereignty has ever been a feature of any ASEAN document. If there had been the government of Brunei would not have been willing to overcome its misgivings in becoming the sixth member of the Association in January 1984. Although membership of ASEAN does not provide any assured guarantee of Brunei's independent existence, any conspicuous challenge to it by a regional partner would certainly damage the cohesion and standing and possibly the viability of ASEAN. Moreover, to the extent that ASEAN has adopted a principled stand since 1979 over Kampuchea which highlights the violation of national sovereignty by Vietnam, then the Association has reinforced its commitment to a public philosophy which provides a measure of reassurance to a vulnerable Brunei.

Given the different perspectives, if only in principle, towards the legal order which governs Community and Association relations *inter se*, it might appear to follow that the European Community would enjoy a better record than ASEAN in conducting political cooperation, that is a corporate foreign policy, beyond declaratory diplomacy. In effect, the reverse has been the case if only over one issue. ASEAN has distinguished itself in a corporate diplomatic role in response to Vietnam's invasion and occupation of Kampuchea. Their achievement has been to a large extent a function of special regional circumstances which have been beyond the direct experience of the European Community and of a different order, for example, to Argentina's invasion of the Falkland Islands. It has been assisted by a longstanding cultivated practice of ministerial and bureaucratic consultation between a limited number of states. Indeed, the limited scale of the Association, hardly disturbed by Brunei's admission to membership, has facilitated the practice of political cooperation which was only put on a formal basis with the Bali Summit in February 1976.

It has been the overriding significance of the Kampuchean issue which has served to embellish the record of ASEAN in political cooperation. That significance has two dimensions. First, given its public philosophy expressed in treaty form, it was imperative — in order to deny the establishment of an alarming precedent — to prevent a blatant infringement of national sovereignty in South-East Asia from being endorsed or profiting by default. Secondly, the strategic environment of a member state had been violated which required at the very least a public demonstration of solidarity if the cohesion and future of the Association was not to be put at serious risk.

Given the issue on which ASEAN has been able to conduct an effective common foreign policy, the Association presents a paradox in a way that the European Community does not. ASEAN is an inter-governmental body which indicated a corporate interest in regional order from the outset and went on to prescribe for it if in less than precise declaratory form. During the past decade, it has become preoccupied increasingly with problems of external security. But aside from primarily bilateral cooperation in defence outside the walls of the Association, its member governments have never been willing to contemplate any formal set of multilateral obligations to defence cooperation or to develop even the semblance of an alliance structure. It is as a diplomatic community acting in concert on a matter of security that ASEAN has made its greatest impact and has received international recognition accordingly.

The European Community, if inspired by a longstanding grand political design, has made its international mark through institution-alising a structure of economic cooperation and integration. ASEAN's record has been exceedingly modest in this regard. In political cooperation, the European Community has developed a measure of institutionalisation also but it has proceeded very much on an *ad hoc* basis. The practice of political cooperation has reflected the balance of sovereign states interests. It has relied upon the convergence of those interests without a specific body of officials involved on a full time basis with European foreign policy making until the decision of the Luxembourg Summit in December 1985 to set up a small permanent Secretariat. Indeed, it has been concluded that "the socialisation process, as it had developed by the early 1980s, probably depended, however, too strongly on the chance juxtaposition of particular politicians and administrators who found each other, sometimes to their mutual surprise, congenial. A changing political scene and the retirement of key officials, could rapidly undermine what measure of socialisation had been achieved".[1] It is not difficult to apply such a sober evaluation to the condition of ASEAN if one assumed some form of resolution of the Kampuchean conflict and took into account the close prospect of the concurrent departure from the political scene of a number of national figures whose long tenure of office has served to lend continuity to intra-ASEAN relationships. In the case of the European Community it has been further concluded that "in the early 1980s, the achievement of harmonised positions depended on a convergence of perceptions of national interests; it was circumstantial and conditional rather than a product of any sense of the overriding importance of unified action".[2] However, in the case of ASEAN, the circumstantial and the conditional in its regional environment would seem more constant and compelling in generating an overriding sense of the importance of unified action, if only diplomatic. The question of regional security possesses a greater immediacy even if divisions of interest obtain in strategic perspectives. To that extent, there would seem to be a greater compulsion to close ranks.

The European Community clearly differs from ASEAN in its lesser degree of preoccupation with matters of regional security. It is in no sense an alternative to the North Atlantic Treaty Organisation (NATO) which has the continuing prime function of providing for Western European defence. Moreover, the correspondence in membership between the European Community and NATO, with the notable exception of the Republic of Ireland, is not matched in the case of ASEAN. Although every member of ASEAN, with the exception of Indonesia, has a security relationship of a kind with a state or states external to South-East Asia, these links do not comprise a unified structure; nor does the countervailing power to which they provide access offer the same measure of credibility as in the case of NATO. The states of ASEAN reside in a regional environment which has long experienced the competitive intervention of external powers but without any sense of assurance that the United States, for example, possesses the political will to act decisively to contain threats to their security. If ASEAN does not seek to assume any formal collective responsibility in military terms for the security of South-East Asia, its member governments do employ their collective diplomatic means primarily to serve that end.

Despite important differences in political cooperation with respect to regional security, the European Community and ASEAN arrive at corporate foreign policy decisions on a corresponding basis. In the years since the report of the Davignon Committee was accepted by the Council of Ministers in 1970, the responsibility for the administration of political cooperation has been in the overall charge of the foreign minister of the member state which holds the presidency. The net result has been a succession of rotating secretariats each acting in a coordinating role for a six month period. The correspondence with the practice of ASEAN with an annually rotating Standing Committee serviced by an appropriate National Secretariat is only too evident. In effect, in both institutions, decision-making in political cooperation has been a logical function of the requirement for consensus which means some kind of common denominator.

The experience of the European Community and ASEAN in decision-making would not seem to have been affected by any differences in principle over the desirability or not of political integration. The manner in which common positions are worked out through meetings of senior officials and ministers would appear to be standard practice in inter-governmental association. Indeed, the ideal of political integration which is one of the features which distinguishes the European Community from ASEAN does not make any fundamental difference to the practice of collective decision-making. Both institutions work within the framework of the conventional international legal order and proceed where possible on the basis of corporate consensus. If, to some extent paradoxically, ASEAN has suggested a greater measure of corporate coherence in foreign-policy decision-making, it has been because the security of one member-state has been at particular risk in the context of a common sense of apprehension at the condition of a regional environment for which there is no overarching security structure. In the case of the Falklands, Argentina's invasion did not represent quite the same threat to national interests. Nonetheless, Britain's European partners not only condemned the invasion and imposed an embargo on arms sales but also suspended the importation of Argentinian goods into the Community with notable exceptions until after the reoccupation of the islands. Where there is a difference, if in style, between ASEAN and the European Community, it is in the sustained commitment of the former to the centrality of consensus. Open intra-mural confrontation is avoided which has not been the experience of the European Community. Cultural factors as well as apparent greater concern at the political dangers of compromising the cohesion of ASEAN would seem relevant to this commitment.

When it comes to relations between ASEAN and the European Community, the same structure of decision-making applies to a more complicated extent because of the scale of the undertaking. It is complicated additionally on the European side because of the division of competences between the Commission and the Council. Nonetheless the requirement for consensus was made manifest during the meeting in Kuala Lumpur in March 1980 which convened to conclude a Cooperation Agreement, the first between the European Community and any regional grouping. Europe's foreign ministers travelled to the Malaysian capital after having worked out a common position on Afghanistan in Rome during February which they expected to have endorsed by their ASEAN counterparts. Somewhat to their surprise, they confronted an insistence by ASEAN counterparts on a corresponding endorsement of the Association's position over Kampuchea. Such an endorsement together with specific identification of the Soviet Union and Vietnam was forthcoming only after a strong and protracted measure of debate both within and between corporate delegations. That joint statement on political matters was kept separate from the agreement on economic cooperation. It was suggested, at the time, that the political statement constituted an important benchmark "in the Community's future ties with ASEAN".[3]

Since the joint ministerial meeting in Kuala Lumpur, there has been a continuing linkage of Afghanistan and Kampuchea if with certain reservations on the European side as well as a widening of expressions of common interest in international issues. For example, at the joint ministerial meeting held in Bangkok in October 1983, reference was made also to "the present dangerous situation in the Middle East". In Dublin in November 1984, the scope of such declaratory diplomacy was extended to cover East-West relations, while the Iran-Iraq war was mentioned in the expression of common concern over the Middle East. An ability to engage in such declaratory diplomacy by consensus has given the relationship between ASEAN and the European Community the quality of a mutual-admiration society.[4] Such a quality of relationship arising from dialogue partnership and post-ministerial meetings is not to be derided. In international relations as in life it is easier to make enemies than to make friends.

If one looks back on the manner of regional decision-making within ASEAN and the European Community, it is evident that neither entity has been free of intra-mural tensions. ASEAN has been the more successful in managing the practice of consensus and indeed in avoiding open contention more so than the European Community. One reason for this measure of success has been discussed above; namely, the greater immediacy of security problems. ASEAN, however, is also a much more limited undertaking than the European Community and is not obliged to confront the complexity of economic issues arising from its rules of the game and the expansion of its membership. It is also more limited in its propensity to pontificate on international issues. When it comes down to the inter-corporate relationship, differences in identity and form and, of course, political aspiration do not seem to count for much. In economic terms, the structure of dialogue turns on a bargaining relationship between mainly industrialised and industrialising states with the latter concerned to secure better access to the markets of the former for both traditional and new products. That bargaining relationship has been influenced up to a point by a correspondence in political outlooks between governments in each regional grouping. Their political interests, however, like their economic ones are not in perfect harmony but they are sufficiently so to make possible a process of inter-corporate decision-making based on a realistic common denominator, if expressed in declaratory terms. There is no practical expression to the irony that it is ASEAN which upholds the states system of European derivation, while it is the European Community which purports to wish to transcend it.

Conclusion

The striking differences between ASEAN and the European Community in terms of quality of economic cooperation and ideal political goals are self-evident. These differences might suggest that the European Community should enjoy a far better prospect of conducting a common foreign policy. But it is ASEAN which has been more successful in this respect for reasons which arise from regional environment and not from its structure of corporate decision-making. It is the immediacy of the issue of regional security and the close link between that issue and the cohesion and viability of the Association which have been decisive. In effect, there is a close correspondence between the structure and practice of decision-making in both ASEAN and the European Community based on a conventional requirement for consensus. That requirement governs the practice both within the two regional groupings and also in their inter-corporate relationship, if expressed in the latter in declaratory diplomacy outside of their economic dealings.

Notes

I should like to express my appreciation to my colleagues Dr Christopher Hill and Dr Paul Taylor for their helpful comments on a draft version of this paper.

1. Paul Taylor, *The Limits of European Integration*, New York: 1983. Columbia University Press, P. 148.
2. Taylor, *op. cit.,* p. 149.
3. See *The Times,* 12 March 1980.
4. *The Joint Declaration 5th EC/ASEAN Ministerial Meeting,* Dublin, 15 & 16 November 1984, concluded "the EC Ministers recognised ASEAN as a cohesive regional grouping playing an independent and positive role in the search for peace and stability in South East Asia. The ASEAN Ministers expressed their appreciation of the important role of the European Community as a stabilising influence in a world facing many problems." For a general account and assessment of the relationship between the two institutions, see Stuart Harris and Brian Bridges, *European Interests in ASEAN* (London: Routledge and Kegan Paul for the Royal Institute of International Affairs, 1983.)

28

Europe and Southeast Asia

The European Union and ASEAN are two very different expressions of regionalism, despite enjoying a common element of provenance in their attempts to promote regional reconciliation through institutional cooperation. Above all, by their very different natures, identities and political aspirations, they partake of very different forms of collective decision-making, which reflect their differing corporate goals. In addition, the greater part of the economic policies pursued by the member states of the European Union towards ASEAN and vice versa, above all in trade and investment, are conducted on an individual and not a collective basis. Moreover, the European experiences of and degrees of interest in Southeast Asia vary considerably among member states without an evident congruence.[1] This lack of congruence has been reflected in the mixed degrees of commitment to the relationship displayed by succeeding Presidents of the Council of Ministers and

Reprinted in abridged form from Michael Leifer, "Europe and Southeast Asia", in *Europe and the Asia Pacific*, edited by Hanns Maull, Gerald Segal, and Jusuf Wanandi (London: Routledge, 1998), pp. 198–205, by permission of the publisher and the copyright-holders.

their "troika" partners.[2] Indeed, this six-monthly rotating pattern of European leadership has proved to be a critical and a disconcerting factor in the relationship, making for a less than consistent approach, despite the continuity of the bureaucratic structure of the Commission. Although a procedural feature of the European Community/Union, it has also been a symptom of the balance between form and substance in the relationship with ASEAN.

European Community/Union policies towards ASEAN have evolved and changed concurrently with changes in the regional circumstances and priorities of both entities over more than a quarter of a century and especially with the end of the Cold War and have combined economic and political interests. Europe has engaged with ASEAN at ministerial and officials level to mixed effect. However, an initiative by the European Commission in July 1994 expressed in the document "Towards a New Asia Strategy"[3] was endorsed by the Council later in the year. An imaginative response by Singapore's Prime Minister, Goh Chok Tong, initially in September that year which was endorsed by ASEAN in the following July and then agreed with its European Union dialogue partner in August in Brunei, paved the way for an Asia–Europe Meeting (ASEM) which convened in Bangkok in March 1996. That meeting, at heads of government level, would seem to have opened up the prospect of a qualitative change in the relationship between the EU and ASEAN even though existing forms of institutionalised contact will certainly be maintained. At issue is the degree to which European policy towards ASEAN in the broad sense will come to be subsumed within a wider structure of East Asian relationships and how that might affect the longstanding relationship in its post-Cold-War form.

ASEM represented an ASEAN-driven initiative to which the EU responded through strong French encouragement. The wider geographic partnership in prospect, involving China, Japan and South Korea initially, may give rise to a measure of intra-Asian tension should ASEAN seek to retain the diplomatic initiative as in the case of the ASEAN Regional Forum (ARF).[4] The EU collectively will want to avoid being drawn into such a tension, while benefiting from the wider framework of co-operation. The EU-ASEAN dialogue may well be sustained as the core of the wider Europe–Asia dialogue process which has yet to be institutionalised. However, the management of overlapping processes of dialogue opened up by the first ASEM in Bangkok could pose a diplomatic test for the EU. ASEAN has registered a determination to sustain its separate identity. The degree of resistance by some East Asian and Pacific states to that determination being expressed in a prerogative role within a wider Asian context has generated differences within the ARF, of which the EU is a member.

The European Union, with its treaty base, is committed, at least in principle, to transcending the Westphalian model of the states system in its European locale, while ASEAN is committed in more than principle to upholding that system of separate sovereignties in its Southeast Asian context. Those differences in political model have been reflected in the somewhat different bases of political representation, with Europe enjoying the advantage, in principle, of a single locus of institutionalised decision-making. In practice, however, ASEAN has been able to proceed in less ambitious joint enterprises through the vehicle of annual meetings of foreign ministers complemented by less frequent but regular meetings of heads of government, which have set specific mandates for officials to implement.

The fundamental differences in underlying political purpose and conception of regionalism have not stood in the way of a co-operative relationship based on common and complementary interests. But to the extent that global and regional circumstances have changed significantly with the end of the Cold War, there have been evident changes in priorities on the part of both entities without any underlying desire to impair fruitful aspects of inter-regional co-operation.

Europe and ASEAN made initial institutional contact in the early 1970s at formative stages in their respective developments. The initiative for an institutional link came from the ASEAN side in 1972 driven by an evident concern by its two Commonwealth members, Malaysia and Singapore, about market access over loss of preferences occasioned by Britain's impending membership of the European Community as well as an underlying interest in the transfer of technology. This collective concern found initial expression in contacts between officials in Brussels. These contacts developed into formal consultations which did not bear full fruit at the political level until November 1978 which then marked the beginning of a full dialogue relationship leading to regular attendance at the ASEAN Post-Ministerial Meetings (ASEAN-PMC) with other industrialised states from Asia Pacific. In March 1980, an unprecedented Co-operation Agreement of a framework kind was concluded which has stood unrevised ever since as a testament to changing political priorities on the European side but without impairing the practical relationship. It is worth noting that it was only in October 1985 that a meeting between economics ministers was convened and that the inter-institutional relationship on the ASEAN side has been conducted by foreign ministries, despite the greatest practical interchange between states being expressed in economic terms. Indeed, the great paradox of the relationship between the European Community/Union and ASEAN is that it has been managed to a great extent as an exercise in political co-operation as understood in Brussels, while the terms of the surviving Co-operation Agreement are about trade and economic co-operation. To be fair, that agreement has provided a basis for practical co-operation with limited European Union funds allocated for encouraging trade, joint venture investments through the European Investment Bank, industrial training, human resource development, scientific and technical co-operation as well as modest development aid among other forms of provision.

That Co-operation Agreement is a good starting point for assessing the nature of the relationship. Although the European Union ranks third among ASEAN's trading partners, the Agreement has not served as an instrument for negotiating trade policies, except to the extent that the application of the Generalised System of Preferences (GSP) has been of varying benefit to members of the Association. It is best seen as a framework for inter-regional co-operation within which various facilitating devices exist for promoting a number of functional activities of mutual benefit. Total trade between European Union and ASEAN members has risen dramatically since 1980 when it amounted to just over 12 billion Ecu. In 1994, trade between members of the two entities had risen to nearly 58 million Ecu (US$71 billion) with a continuing but fluctuating balance in favour of the ASEAN states. That trade has been primarily a function of endeavours by individual states on both sides; the same can be said for direct investment in ASEAN economies aided by investment promotion facilities on the European side. Investment flows of late have not matched trade ones, however.

The Co-operation Agreement has remained unrevised since its conclusion, despite a commitment to revision in Luxembourg in May 1991, because of the interposing issue of East Timor after Portugal's entry into the Community and in particular an abhorrence at the killing of young demonstrators at Santa Cruz Cemetery in Dili in November 1991. In October 1992, ministers from both sides meeting in Manila agreed to sustain the relationship without the benefit of a new framework. Indeed, by that juncture, the pressing need for a formal revised structure with which to underpin the relationship had passed. ASEAN had moved into the tiger business, which was reflected in changing bases of economic interchange. Again members of the European Union, while taking an increasing proportion of ASEAN exports, have not been decisively responsible in any collective sense for changing the terms of the economic relationship. ASEAN's growing impact on European markets has been a product of governments' policies within Southeast Asia to the extent that it became a matter of economic imperative to overcome the recession of the mid 1980s when the total volume of EU-ASEAN trade was only just over 20 billion Ecu. A commitment by individual governments to policies of economic liberalisation encouraging greater direct foreign investment for exports would seem to have been a critical factor in accelerating the momentum of trade relations from the turn of the decade.

The ability to deal with the then [European] Community on an inter-institutional basis registered the corporate identity and international standing of the Association. An interest in encouraging a more extensive European economic presence was motivated in part by a desire to offset the degree of economic dependence on Japan and the United States as sources of foreign investment and as trading partners; an interest which has been sustained as a factor in encouraging a wider Europe–Asia dialogue.

An evident attraction of ASEAN for Europe was the ambition to play a role through inter-regional links in upholding regional and global order in the Western interest and to a degree in competition with the United States. ASEAN was perceived as part of the Western global alignment whose governments were determined to defeat the challenge of revolutionary communism. Moreover, the conclusion of the framework Co-operation Agreement in March 1980 had coincided with the outbreak of the so-called Second Cold War defined by the Soviet invasion of Afghanistan in the previous December. In the following year, the European Community achieved the status of dialogue partner of the Association with right of access to the annual Post-Ministerial Conferences. Indeed, it was this status of dialogue partner which enabled the European Union to become a founder member of the ASEAN Regional Forum (ARF). That membership stands in sharp contrast to Europe's absence from APEC.

It may well be that in seeking ASEAN's support for the European position on the issue of Afghanistan, opportunity was thrust upon its members. At the meeting in Kuala Lumpur in March 1980 at which the Co-operation Agreement was concluded, the Europeans were confronted by an insistence on ASEAN's part of a corresponding endorsement of their corporate position on Cambodia, then subject to Vietnamese occupation. To that extent, it would seem to have been ASEAN which made the wider link between regional and global security which, from then on, was better assimilated on the European side. [T]he European Community supported the Association's lead and collective purpose by suspending economic aid to Vietnam and in contributing financially to the resettlement of Vietnamese refugees as well as giving due recognition to ASEAN's declaratory commitment to make Southeast Asia a zone of peace, freedom and neutrality.

The Cambodian issue served as a basis for co-operation with ASEAN playing a leading diplomatic role. But the way in which that conflict was brought to a conclusion as an international and regional problem pointed up the extent to which ASEAN's leading diplomatic role had been as an agent of Sino-American alignment to which the European Union had been joined. The evident marginality of ASEAN in the ultimate process of conflict resolution, managed in the main by the permanent members of the United Nations Security Council, was reflected in a slackening in the momentum of European–ASEAN co-operation. Moreover, with the end of the Cold War and the reunification of Germany, Europe's attention was drawn towards the problems of Central and Eastern Europe. In addition, from the European side, with the end of the Cold War and the downfall of communism as an ideology, there was a tendency to emulate the United States in articulating human rights priorities which had always been part of the European political agenda, especially within the Parliament. The impasse over differing conceptions of sovereignty and respect for domestic jurisdiction was pointed up over the issue of East Timor, which proved to be the obstacle to a formal revision of the Co-operation Agreement through Portugal's obduracy.

In retrospect, however, the Co-operation Agreement, forged in the heat of the Second Cold War, did not demonstrate anything like a special relationship. Indeed, the relationship comprised more of form than of substance. It has been well noted that after the high point of the Co-operation Agreement and convergence over Afghanistan and Cambodia the substantive content of the political consultation stagnated somewhat.[5] The momentum of accord over Cambodia was sustained with some difficulty as some European states indicated their distaste for the inclusion of the Khmer Rouge in the so-called Coalition

Government of Democratic Kampuchea set up in June 1982 as a diplomatic device to confront Vietnam. In addition, there was a corresponding European reluctance to engage in a policy of isolating Vietnam completely. Moreover, when, in an attempt to find a wider basis for political dialogue, contentious issues such as the Middle East and Southern Africa were discussed, the degree of divergence in international outlooks became even more pronounced. To that extent, given the stalement over revising the Co-operation Agreement, the relations between the European Union and ASEAN had come to be distinguished by a strong sense of political inertia compounded by irritation at the interposition of a human rights agenda.

In the years since the end of the Second Cold War, however, there has been a reassessment of the utility of the relationship with ASEAN in the light of the economic achievements of many of its member states. This reassessment was reflected in the document submitted by the Commission of the European Union to the Council of Ministers in July 1994 entitled "Towards a new Asia strategy" which urged that Asia be accorded a higher priority. It was recommended that the European Union should seek to develop its political dialogue with Asia and should look for ways to associate Asia more and more in the management of international affairs, working towards a partnership of equals capable of playing a constructive and stabilising role in the world.

The Commission's strategy document set out policy priorities across Asia, including a list of functional interests such as arms control, human rights and drugs as well as ways of strengthening the European economic presence in Asia. In setting out these priorities, the Commission identified its existing policy instruments in its relations with Asia and it was only here that ASEAN received particular mention in terms of regular meetings at ministerial and at senior officials level within the context of the longstanding and unrevised Co-operation Agreement, participation in the annual Post-Ministerial Conferences and in the wider context of the ASEAN Regional Forum. At the time there were only four European representations in ASEAN capitals, namely: in Bangkok, Manila, Hanoi and in Jakarta, out of ten in Asian countries overall. It would seem of some significance that the European Union's main representation is a delegation in Bangkok, with another in Manila and in Hanoi but with only an office in Jakarta which is the site of ASEAN's Secretariat. With the exception of a general exhortation to strengthen the Union's relations with regional groups such as ASEAN, the Association was not singled out for particular attention in the strategy document. Rather, it was subsumed within the overall concluding policy recommendations from the Commission to the Council of Ministers and not mentioned specifically in them. Neglect on the European side was made up for with an inaugural meeting of EU–ASEAN senior officials in Singapore in May 1995. That inaugural event was a product of a ministerial meeting in Karlsruhe in September 1994 which recognised the need to reinvigorate the relationship on the basis of a partnership of equals. In the event, the senior officials meeting served to pave the way for the ASEM in Bangkok in March 1996.

Given that so much effort and energy has been invested in the wider relationship between Europe and East Asia, with the object of institutionalising the enterprise in regular bi-annual meetings, what is the future of the association between Europe and ASEAN, which works on an annual roll-over basis without the benefit of a revised co-operation agreement? The Commission's strategy document does not offer much comfort here given its much wider horizons. The declared aim of the ASEM has been to reinforce the weak link in the triangle of relations between Asia, North America and Europe. A general East Asian interest has been expressed in having Europe pay much greater attention to, and have a greater presence in, Asia so as to balance their relations with other partners. These are high-sounding aspirations as well as somewhat mechanical ones. Europe may wish to assert a new political relationship but geography and the absence of a common military presence to ensure balance in the conventional sense stand in the way of such a grandiose objective.

For all the talk of a new partnership, at issue has been the prospect of gaining a larger share of the region's exponential growth in terms of trade and investment as well as to counter American trade unilateralism.[6] For their part, Asian officials indicated caution against expecting any immediate increase in trade and investment coming from the Bangkok summit. Any new partnership between Asia and Europe was identified as an evolutionary process driven by the ability of heads of government meeting together to focus on the so-called big picture and not be bogged down by the detail of the complex set of relationships.

The ASEM process offers the prospect that a possible Asia–Europe Co-operation Framework might take the place of the EU–ASEAN Co-operation Agreement which has still to be revised from its initial 1980 form. Moreover, the commitment to process on the part of the heads of government at the ASEM foreshadows also a greater demand on diplomatic resources on the part of states which are heavily engaged in multilateralism in Asia and in Europe. Given such demands, which will place some foreign ministries close to breaking point in terms of the availability of skilled human resources, it is almost inevitable that critical choices will have to be made in national and collective priorities. It is in this context that the relationship between the EU and ASEAN will have to be reconsidered. That relationship has been reinvigorated up to a point, in the context of much wider horizons on the part of both entities, but very much more so as far as Europe is concerned. At issue will be how Europe copes with balancing the priorities of regenerating the relationship with ASEAN while developing a new relationship with a wider Asia of which ASEAN is only a part. A pointer in the direction of Europe's objective has been a policy paper on relations with ASEAN, issued by the European Commission in July 1996, which announced the intention of keeping the Association as the centrepiece of Europe's expanding relations with Asia. For the time being, that declaration of intent has removed any acute fears on both sides that the dynamics of ASEM might interpose in a longstanding relationship. Moreover, ASEM has barely begun to take on institutional form.

Notes

1. See, Stuart Harris and Brian Bridges, *European Interests in ASEAN* (Routledge and Kegan Paul for RIIA, London, 1983).
2. It is notable that the Danish, Greek, Spanish and Swedish Prime Ministers were unable to find the time to attend the first Asia–Europe Meeting (ASEM) which convened in Bangkok in March 1996.
3. "Towards a new Asia strategy", Commission of the European Communities, Brussels, 13 July 1994.
4. See, Michael Leifer, *The ASEAN Regional Forum Extending ASEAN's Model of Regional Forum*, Adelphi Paper No. 302 (Oxford University Press for IISS, London, July 1996).
5. Elfriede Regelsberger "The relations with ASEAN as a 'Model' of a European Foreign Policy", in Giuseppe Schiavone (ed.) *Western Europe and Southeast Asia* (London: Macmillan, 1989), p. 84.
6. Note the comment in *International Herald Tribune* (17 January 1996).

29

Regionalism Compared
The Perils and Benefits of Expansion

"Widening" and "Deepening"?

In any regional grouping, scale is likely to be a mixed blessing. Ideally, an expansion in membership will bring with it a greater international standing, particularly if such an expansion makes the membership of the grouping fully coincident with its geographic locale. An increase in the number of governments speaking with a single voice on the same issue with full regional credentials may reinforce the quality of diplomatic community associated with a regional organisation. It is in this respect, among others, that the European Union has sought to link the notion of "widening" to that of "deepening" the quality of integration. Scale, however, can also have an adverse effect on regional association should an increase in membership add to the diversity of political identities and interests within the grouping as well as to its levels of economic development. Such an increase may dilute its

Reprinted from Michael Leifer, "Regionalism Compared: The Perils and Benefits of Expansion", in *The Asia Pacific in the New Millennium: Political and Security Challenges*, edited by Mely C. Anthony and Mohamed Jawhar Hassan (Kuala Lumpur: ISIS Malaysia, 2001), pp. 499–504, by permission of the publisher.

collective political culture and make more difficult the task of managing consensus, which is the *modus operandus* of regionalism, irrespective of regional locale. That difficulty may extend beyond intra-mural relations to those with external counterparts.

The issue of expansion has been most significant in the case of the Association of Southeast Asian Nations (ASEAN) where membership became coincident with regional geographic bounds at the end of the last century. The completion of the so-called "One Southeast Asia" took place with Cambodia's entry in April 1999 before Indonesia was obliged to abdicate sovereignty over East Timor, which is now under a form of UN trusteeship pending independence. Expansion has relevance also in the case of the ASEAN Regional Forum (ARF) but such expansion that has occurred since its first plenary session in 1994 has not made any substantive difference to the workings of the multilateral security dialogue. The same may be said for Asia-Pacific Economic Co-operation (APEC), which has expanded to incorporate a Latin-American dimension.

In the case of ASEAN, the goal of "One Southeast Asia" was registered in the founding document of the Association and was driven by the criterion of reconciliation. Indeed, reconciliation post-Confrontation was the key to ASEAN's conception and formation. At issue was to locate that reconciliation within an institutionalised structure of relations. Every single stage of expansion has been driven, to a degree, by the same priority, especially the historic reconciliation marked by Vietnam's membership in July 1995. When it came to completing the ASEAN-10, considerations of international standing were more directly at play. The strategic circumstances that had permitted ASEAN to play such a prominent diplomatic role over Cambodia had changed. Indeed, it was the change in those circumstances that enabled a resolution of the Cambodian conflict as an international problem through the role of the permanent members of the Unted Nations Security Council and not the collective diplomacy of ASEAN.

It was also that change in strategic circumstances that inspired the advent of the ASEAN Regional Forum (ARF). Although that initiative registered a diplomatic centrality on ASEAN's part, which was subsequently institutionalised within the ARF, it also required a compromise over strategic priorities. ASEAN had long held to a declaratory doctrine of a Zone of Peace, Freedom and Neutrality (ZOPFAN) for Southeast Asia, which assumed the exercise of a prerogative role in managing regional order to the exclusion of the major powers. However, the functional remit and geographic ambit of the ARF is subversive of and supersedes the exclusive terms of reference of ZOPFAN. In that context, an ASEAN-10 was conceived as likely to register a stronger diplomatic voice in the weighty company of the major Asia-Pacific powers and to uphold diplomatic centrality. That diplomatic centrality has been contingent ironically on China's reluctance to participate in a multilateral security dialogue at the explicit initiative of either the United States or Japan. It has been challenged within Northeast Asia and beyond but China has attracted Russian and Indian support for continuing ASEAN's diplomatic role.

In the event, the final stage of ASEAN's expansion also coincided with the onset of a contagious and devastating regional economic crisis that had the effect of undermining the Association's international standing. Indeed, the impact of that crisis on Indonesia, in particular, gave rise to an acute problem of leadership and direction, which was aggravated because of the way in which expansion had become informed by controversy over the entry of Myanmar and then Cambodia. Indeed, in the latter case, consensus visibly broke down, to be patched up in a superficial way as ASEAN was obliged to tolerate the use of violence to effect constitutional change within a candidate-member state, poorly camouflaged by an election of a kind. Moreover, despite, the fine-sounding words in the ASEAN Vision 2020 and in the Hanoi Plan of Action, the Association has yet to re-establish itself as a vibrant, diplomatic community.

Is Expansion the Problem?

There is no doubt that expansion has brought more perils than benefits to ASEAN. Expansion has not only added to the diversity of membership but has been linked to political controversy with the effect of exposing intra-mural divisions. These divisions have been exposed by a sterile debate over whether or not the Association ought to qualify its cardinal rule of non-intervention in members' domestic affairs in special circumstances, particularly if events in any member state spill over its borders to affect adversely any of its regional partners. That debate has been conducted by way of weasel-word euphemism, with terms such as "flexible engagement" and "enhanced interaction" deployed by governments whose degree of political development makes them comfortable with the principle of non-intervention, and also sufficiently self-assured that a breach of a basic injunction in the United Nations Charter would be unlikely to apply to them. In that respect, expansion is a problem to the extent that ASEAN's enlargement has diversified the pattern of political identities concurrent with a measure of democratisation among some founder-states, which has been reinforced by the impact of the economic crisis from the end of the 1990s. Democratisation has given some governments the confidence to try to stretch ASEAN's parameters without necessarily taking full account of why the Association was formed in the first place.

The initial priority of regional reconciliation was tied closely to reinforcing national sovereignty on the part of post-colonial states and was far removed from the model of the European integration as indicated in the founding Treaty of Rome. All post-founder members, from Brunei onwards have looked on ASEAN as a vehicle for collective political defence, which is a function identified initially by Thanat Khoman, Thailand's elder statesman. That priority has been sustained consistently by subsequent members, especially Myanmar and the states of Indochina, which have not engaged in multilateralism in order not to lose control of their sovereign prerogatives. Indeed, it may well be that a concern about creeping democratisation within ASEAN has contributed to political division in addition to an economic division, which is acknowledged in the different targets set for tariff reductions under the terms of the ASEAN Free Trade Area (AFTA).

An indication of a reversionary fragmentation within ASEAN was the little-reported meeting in October 1999 in Vientiane of the heads of government of Cambodia, Laos and Vietnam. It will be recalled that during the 1980s, during the height of the Cambodian conflict, those three states constituted a separate bloc in an adversary relationship with ASEAN. That bloc appeared to have been dissolved with the resolution of the Cambodian conflict as an international problem in 1991 and then Vietnam's membership of ASEAN in 1995. The revival of a pattern of meetings separate from the other members of ASEAN would seem an ominous development. It is worth noting that the meeting in Vientiane stressed the need of these three to further strengthen their traditional solidarity, recalling the rhetoric of political polarisation within Southeast Asia during the Cambodian conflict. Since October 1999, there have been subsequent functional subject meetings dealing with electricity generation and malaria control, which on the surface would seem to fall within ASEAN's remit rather than any subordinate alignment.

Is it the Same ASEAN?

This example of political differentiation with ASEAN would seem to suggest that in its case, "widening" has not been accompanied by "deepening." Indeed, it may be suggested that ASEAN is not and cannot be the same entity that was established in August 1967, primarily to cement institutionally the settlement of Confrontation. The nomenclature and institutional form is the same but the substance of the undertaking has changed. Up to the end of the Cold War, especially given an unusual continuity in political leadership, ASEAN had registered a quasi-familial quality based on shared political outlooks, albeit without coincident political identities. Moreover, the minimal expansion in January 1984 with the entry of Brunei did not bring with it any special problems that spilled over beyond its bounds to affect intra-mural or extra-mural relationships. Matters changed considerably over the controversial entry of both Myanmar and Cambodia, while the issue of the "haze" emanating from Indonesia pointed to how failings of governance in one member state could afflict the environment of others. The debate over qualifying the cardinal rule of non-intervention demonstrated not only how the political agenda of ASEAN had changed but also how the expansion in membership had changed the very nature of the Association, despite a declaratory commitment to an elusive "ASEAN Way." ASEAN had been established on a limited scale to cement the solution to Confrontation aided importantly by an important degree of political self-abnegation on the part of Indonesia, which gave the Association so much of its working idiom. The process of institutional cementing was facilitated by the intra-mural diplomacy required by exigencies of the Cambodian conflict. With the end of that conflict, precipitated by the end of the Cold War, ASEAN was confronted by a new strategic environment, which facilitated the advent of the ARF.

For ASEAN, however, beyond its minimalist function of conflict avoidance and mitigation, there was an absence of a ready consensus about purpose and direction, which has been compounded by enlargement. ASEAN has never been an alliance defined by a common strategic perspective, while enlargement has diluted any sense of political community. Intra-mural diversity and the change in strategic circumstances have also undermined its standing as a diplomatic community built up over Cambodia. Indeed, that standing received a signal blow by the churlish way in which its mediating mission of foreign ministers was received in Phnom Penh in the wake of the violent coup in July 1997. With a sense of economic recovery, an attempt has been made to advance in co-operation over AFTA but the pace of substantive tariff reduction remains in the balance, exemplified by concessions made to Malaysia, in particular, at the meetings of economics ministers in Yangon in May this year. Moreover, the attempt to address destructive currency speculation has required extending the economic ambit of the Association to include China, Japan and South Korea. It may be argued that just as ASEAN was obliged to concede the primary regional security role to the ARF, it has now conceded its regional economic primacy to a version of Dr Mahathir's East Asian Economic Caucus (EAEC).

These attempts at progress in economic co-operation have not mitigated the degree of difficulty ASEAN faces in dealing both within and beyond its regional bounds. It has failed to co-ordinate members' positions on contending jurisdictions within the South China Sea, while it allows China to toy with it over a maritime code of conduct. It has also been acutely embarrassed over its inability to play a collective role in the second de-colonisation of East Timor, in which Australia assumed an effective professional military leadership. That failing to assume any responsibility for regional peace-keeping may have had its source in ASEAN's failure to even consider that prospect in the case of Cambodia, which was addressed on an individual basis only. The case of East Timor also demonstrated the extent to which the debate over non-intervention has been somewhat spurious.

ASEAN may have changed in scale and political complexity but its working model of inter-governmental association has not. It is for that reason that the membership of Myanmar continues to cause difficulty with the European Union, for example. Myanmar's Foreign Minister has felt sufficiently confident of his government's place within ASEAN to assert that the Association would not discriminate against one of its own members by sidelining it as a condition on engaging in multilateral dialogue with the EU. In other words, the cardinal rule of the Association still obtains.

It may be argued that ASEAN is not the same institutional entity that was formed in August 1967. At issue, however, is not scale as such but the differential nature of new membership that can reinforce a diversity of political identities and interests. Whatever the benefits of institutional enlargement so as to enhance diplomatic weight, the key to the efficacy of any regional institution is its ability to display consensus with credibility. ASEAN has yet to find its way in that respect in circumstances of political heterogeneity that seem unlikely to change in the near future. Moreover, it is likely to have to face another challenge of expansion when East Timor is deemed ready for sovereign statehood by the United Nations.

The perils of expansion experienced by ASEAN are a price that has had to be paid for ensuring a coincidence between regional association and political geography. Apart from the difficulties arising from greater economic and political diversity, there is another dimension that needs to be addressed. That is the problem of what "deepening" means in an ASEAN context. It cannot mean the same as "deepening" in an EU context based on the principle of transcending national sovereignty.

For ASEAN, the problem of "deepening" has to be located in the context of separate and jealously-guarded sovereignties. For that reason, the issue at hand is the developing of a common culture of consultation and like-minded conduct. This clearly had dissipated, otherwise Singapore would not have felt the need to host a retreat to address basic matters of institutional process during the foreign ministers meeting in July 1999. How that may be realised is easier said than done. It requires giving new content to the idea of an "ASEAN Way," which has degenerated into little more than a rhetorical device. It will not be realised by pious declarations or unearthly visions but will require hard diplomatic ground-work on the part of governmental representatives so that confidence and trust become an intrinsic part of the regional political climate. In other words, ASEAN needs to define itself far more in terms of the practical requirements of confidence-building, which was at the centre of the founding model of the Association more than three decades ago.

Security and Order: The Maritime Dimension

INTRODUCTION

The three articles in this final section of Part I address the maritime security and order. In the first article (Ch. 30), which was published before the 1982 UN Convention on the Law of the Sea entered into force, Leifer notes that an embryonic global framework for the maritime dimension of regional order already existed. However, he emphasizes that a stable maritime regime for East Asia, including the South China Sea environs, require firstly agreement on how to apply the terms of the Convention and secondly, an agreement with respect to the determination of the extent of the territorial sea, archipelagic waters, the exclusive economic zone and continental shelf — the resolution of which are as much dependent on inter-state relations. The political context is clearly established wherein coastal and maritime states' interests, including the prospect of an assertive China making its territorial claims felt in the South China Sea could be assessed. Consonant with his realist outlook, Leifer concludes, noting the record of the use of force to assert maritime claims in East Asia, that such recourse is most likely where the regional balance of power is in flux. To Leifer the only extra-regional state that could provide such countervailing power is the United States.

In the above article published in 1991, Leifer also points to three threats to the freedom of navigation and considers the prospect of their occurrence/recurrence. These are firstly, armed clashes arising out of coastal states seeking to prosecute territorial claims by acts of force; secondly, attempts by coastal states to unilaterally regulate maritime passage against the letter and spirit of the UN Convention; and thirdly, attempts at interdiction of sea lanes by coastal states or external maritime powers. All these relate essentially to the actions of state actors. However, Leifer also notes other elements prejudicial to the freedom of navigation, namely, accidents and bad seamanship as well as acts of piracy and terrorism. In the post-September 11 world the last two elements in combination are increasingly being articulated as constituting a new threat to Southeast Asian sea-lanes including the crucial Straits of Malacca. Such concerns have generated fresh controversies over sovereign rights of littoral states in the realm of security co-operation with extra-regional powers such as the United States. In the early 1990s Leifer's concern over the safety of navigation through the Straits of Malacca, regarded as an international waterway, was focused on the risk of accidental collisions. As such he called for new measures on the part of littoral states to regulate passage and ensure safer traffic management despite the principle of unimpeded right of transit passage introduced by the 1982 UN Convention (Ch. 31).

In the final item in this section (Ch. 32) Leifer returns to the South China Sea, the islands and waters of which he calls "the last frontier of Southeast Asia", which has been as fully explored and invested as possible. In the absence of settlement, the existing competing claims to sovereign jurisdiction could most aptly be described as "stalemate". Reflecting prudence, China has not since 1995 (when it occupied Mischief Reef) engaged in further acts of maritime assertiveness. However though tolerable, stalemate does not bode well for regional order in a "strategically-fused East and Southeast Asia that lacks a strategic architecture reflecting consensus over the existing status quo." Also such a stalemate is not to be taken for granted. With pointed reference to the very extensive Chinese claims over the South China Sea, Leifer remarks that the realization of such claims would place China in a position to command "the equivalent of the Mediterranean of Southeast Asia" — a revolutionary transformation that no other coastal state could possibly effect.

30

The Maritime Regime and Regional Security in East Asia

The Maritime Regime

All regions of the world have been encompassed by the non-sea-bed terms of the United Nations Convention of the Law of the Sea which provide a comprehensive set of rules for ordering international relations in their maritime dimension.[1] Security and welfare cannot be separated in practice and the Convention provides for national jurisdiction in both respects. It extends the breadth of the territorial sea (including corresponding air-space) to twelve nautical miles and sets a limit of twenty-four nautical miles to the contiguous zone. It permits the designation of mid-ocean archipelagic (i.e. internal) waters, defined by joining the outermost points of outermost islands and drying reefs. It prescribes for exclusive economic (i.e. resource) zones extending up to two hundred miles from baselines from which the breadth of the territorial sea is measured and also authorizes continental shelves to extend, in special circumstances, up to a limit of three-hundred-and-

Reprinted in abridged form from Michael Leifer, "The Maritime Regime and Regional Security in East Asia", *Pacific Review* 4, no. 1 (1991): 126–36, by permission of Taylor and Francis Limited <http://www.tandf.co.uk/journals>.

fifty nautical miles from the same baselines. Under the Convention, territorial sea and archipelagic waters lend themselves in general respects to the same quality of sovereign jurisdiction as over land. That justification is qualified for the territorial sea by the limited right of innocent passage (i.e. not prejudicial to the peace, good order or security of the coastal state) and, where it encapsulates straits used for international navigation, by the liberal right of transit passage (i.e. freedom of navigation and overflight solely for the purpose of continuous and expeditious transit). Jurisdiction is qualified for archipelagic waters by the right of innocent passage and by the right of archipelagic sea lanes passage (i.e. continuous, expeditious and unobstructed) through designated sea (and air) routes provided through normal passage routes, including those through straits used for international navigation. Jurisdiction over exclusive economic zones is limited to exploring and exploiting, conserving and managing both living and non-living resources, while that over the continental shelf beyond an exclusive economic zone is limited to the non-living resources of the sea-bed and harvestable organisms either immobile or which move only in constant physical contact with the sea-bed or the sub-soil.

In principle, the Convention tries to establish a balance between the interests of coastal and mid-ocean states, concerned with enclosure of sea-space and those of maritime powers concerned to ensure as much freedom of navigation as possible. In East Asia, resident states display both interests and are obliged to reconcile conflicting national priorities. In a strictly legal sense, the Convention on the Law of the Sea is not yet in force because there have not been sufficient acts of governmental ratification. As of writing, only forty-four of the required sixty states have done so. In general, however, those provisions cited above would appear to have become part of the body of international legal practice and may be deemed to enjoy customary status. Some regional states signed the Convention with reservations; others have resented the refusal of the United States and other maritime powers to endorse it as a whole, while insisting that the non-sea-bed provisions for freedom of navigation are part of customary international law.[2]

Since the Convention has been open for signature, there has been only one significant contentious incident precipitated by a regional coastal state affecting freedom of navigation. In September 1988, Indonesia provoked controversy by temporarily suspending passage through the Straits of Sunda and Lombok ostensibly to conduct naval firing exercises.[3] That unilateral act may have been an attempt to test the interpretation of the maritime authority of archipelagic states by seeking to invoke article 25 of the Convention which permits suspension of innocent passage specifically for weapons exercises. However, it would have known that the regime of innocent passage which applies in archipelagic waters is subject to article 54 of the Convention which makes explicit that there shall be no suspension of archipelagic sea lanes passage in the same way that suspension of transit passage is also prohibited. In the event, there has not been any repetition of the controversial episode by Indonesia or by any other regional coastal state commanding straits used for international navigation either within or beyond archipelagic waters. That said, neither Indonesia nor the Philippines have designated archipelagic sea lanes so far; nor have they recognized the International Maritime Organisation as a legitimate party to their adoption.

A stable maritime regime for East Asia as elsewhere, requires agreement on how to apply the terms of the Convention on the Law of the Sea. There are two decisive factors to be determined in such an exercise. The first is the extent of national sovereignty over territory, including islands, which provides justification for asserting maritime jurisdiction. The second factor, which is related, is agreement on exactly where baselines should be drawn from in order to establish the precise breadth of the territorial sea, the scope of archipelagic waters, that of exclusive economic zones and the extent of the continental shelf. Guidance on this matter has been provided by the Office for Ocean Affairs and the Law of the Sea of the United Nations.[4] But resolution of differences over the location of baselines depends as much on the condition of political relations between states, exemplified by the agreement concluded between Indonesia and Australia in December 1989 which provided for joint exploitation of oil and gas reserves in the continental shelf between East Timor and northern Australia. That agreement stands in contrast to the failure, so far, of Indonesia and Vietnam to reach an accord on delimitation of their continental shelf in the South China Sea. One qualification needs to be added to this general statement about the bases for a maritime regime. It concerns the status of islands which have a critical relevance to jurisdiction over sea-space and access to marine and sea-bed resources. According to the Convention on the Law of the Sea, "Rocks which cannot sustain human habitation or economic life of their own shall have no exclusive economic zone or continental shelf".[5] Many of the islands in the South China Sea would seem to be affected by this injunction.

Maritime Jurisdiction

The problems of maritime jurisdiction in East Asia have been addressed extensively in the abundant literature on the regional politics of the Law of the Sea.[6] The respective legal merits of the various contending maritime claims are not the direct concern of this article, although they are of obvious relevance to the subject under discussion. Nor is it intended to mention each and every contentious maritime issue in East Asia. This article will deal in general terms with two related matters which bear on the security concerns of regional states: namely, jurisdiction over sea-space and its relevance to freedom of navigation which is of more than regional interest.

The movement for sea-space enclosure in East Asia, as elsewhere, has been encouraged by mixed motives of access to marine and sea-bed resources and security considerations. In the specific cases of Indonesia and the Philippines, archipelagic status has been confirmed by the Law of the Sea Convention. Generally at issue for adjacent and opposite coastal states is the demarcation of offshore regimes. This task has been approached in East Asia in an *ad hoc* manner with mixed success and remains unresolved in the complex case of contested mid-sea islands some of which are close to heavily used sea lanes. The most striking example of such complexity obtains in the Spratly Archipelago in the South China Sea where physical control is shared and disputed between China, Taiwan, Vietnam, the Philippines and Malaysia. Contention over the more northerly Paracel and Pratas Islands is significant but currently less acute. Control by China and Taiwan respectively is not shared and armed clashes are less likely to occur by miscalculation. In North-east Asian waters, contention between China, Taiwan and Japan over the Senkaku (or Diaoyutai) Islands was muted for some time. It revived towards the end of 1990 when the Japanese turned back a number of Taiwanese fishing vessels carrying athletes seeking to plant an Olympic torch as a symbol of a claimed sovereignty. The dispute between Japan and South Korea over Liancourt Rock in the Sea of Japan is over access to resources. The island is occupied by South Korea and attracts recurrent Japanese notes over jurisdiction but without serious contention. The longstanding conflict between Japan and the Soviet Union over the

Northern Territories has an obvious relevance for maritime jurisdiction. But these islands are not generally regarded as the likely *casus belli* over which Japan would make good its declared intention to deny passage to Soviet naval vessels through its inter-island straits. Correspondingly, China's claim to Taiwan has maritime implications but primarily in terms of the side-effects on freedom of navigation of armed confrontation to settle possession.

Threats to Regional Security

Threats to regional security over adverse views of the maritime regime would seem possible from three general sources. First, coastal states may prosecute claims to sea-space and resources by acts of force. Apart from the likely effect on regional relationships, freedom of navigation could be disrupted in the process, depending, of course, on where an armed clash occurred and for how long. Arms control is not the subject of this paper but it is relevant to mention in passing that a number of coastal states have begun to enhance their external defence capabilities with maritime interests in mind.[7] Secondly, even where jurisdiction is internationally recognized, a coastal state might deem it in its interest to seek to regulate maritime passage unilaterally against the spirit and letter of the Convention on the Law of the Sea. Some regional states have established coastal security zones within (as well as beyond) territorial waters in which limitations on movement of vessels are more stringent than under the regime of innocent passage. Obviously, unilateral regulation by a coastal state is likely to have the greatest repercussions if applied to established sea lanes, especially where they pass through straits used for international navigation.

At issue so far is the prospect of a coastal state engaging in a display or use of force either in pursuit of a maritime claim or to demonstrate the scope of its jurisdiction. Both cases have implications for regional relationships and for freedom of navigation which extend beyond East Asia. So far, however, freedom of navigation has not been disrupted by either of the two sets of wilful state action suggested above. Challenges to freedom of navigation by display or threat of force have not been part of the general experience of East Asia. Professor Lewis Alexander has concluded in an exhaustive study of global scope that "There have been in fact few instances in the past several decades where direct challenges to foreign navigation have been made by coastal states".[8] Since his study was published, in East Asia there has been only the exceptional example of Indonesia cited above which has not been repeated, despite an earlier Malaysian concern expressed over implications for maritime passage and overflight between its Peninsula and Borneo wings arising from a treaty concluded between Jakarta and Kuala Lumpur in July 1982 which recognized Indonesia's archipelagic status.[9]

Given the experience of conflict in East Asia since the end of the Pacific War, it is necessary also to take account of a possible third source of threat; specifically to freedom of navigation from beyond regional bounds. Such threats could take the form of attempts at interdiction of Sea lanes. Such worst-case speculation became rife when the customary legal status of the Straits of Malacca and Singapore was first subject to challenge in the early 1970s and before the right of transit passage had been embodied in the Convention on the Law of the Sea. Such speculation, turning on the prospect of superpower rivalry at sea leading to armed confrontation was encouraged by opportunistic anti-Soviet rhetoric from China during the 1970s and beyond. Such speculation also corresponded with conventional wisdom in the American navy indicated by the not uncommon assertion that "The Soviet presence is a significant threat to the security of the sea lanes..."[10] In the event, superpower rivalry failed to materialize over straits used for international navigation and for sea lanes in East Asia in any worst-case sense. The significance of such straits and sea lanes in East Asia is that they provide means of access to non-adjacent areas in which all maritime powers have a corresponding if not uniform interest. That corresponding interest was displayed in the common position adopted on a liberal regime of passage during the course of the Third United Nations Conference on the Law of the Sea.[11] Japan's interest in that regime is of long standing, partly because of the geographical location of its major source of energy supply. The ocean-based strategic perspective of the United States is also well known. In the case of the Soviet Union, at stake is access from the Black Sea ports to Vladivostok and Nakhodka, while China has a growing trading interest through East Asian waters with its commitment to modernization. Worst-case interdiction by an external power is a possibility that can never be ruled out but would not seem to be a likely probability. Moreover, to the extent that global tensions have been much reduced, then their regional expression over maritime passage would be very much unexpected.

The Coastal State Factor

On the basis of limited historical experience, there would seem to be a greater possibility of freedom of navigation being interrupted by regional coastal states than by maritime powers. Coastal states have on balance been more willing to take risks than maritime powers all too conscious of the nuclear factor. Certainly, attempts at blockage of passage by coastal states would seem more likely than by external states in the case of straits, if the experience of the Suez Canal and the Gulf is any guide. In principle, however, sea lanes through high or disputed seas lend themselves as readily to interdiction as blockage of straits because it would not take many acts of force to deter commercial shippers and their insurers. Such an undertaking would still be a risky venture because of the interests likely to be challenged in the process.

Coastal state interdiction of naval passage would be even more risky. In East Asia since the end of the Pacific War, interdiction has been a matter for war games manuals and academic speculation, notwithstanding the controversial case of the Gulf of Tonkin in 1964. Not uncommon, for example, with reference to contested claims to jurisdiction in the Spratly Archipelago is the assertion that control of its islands could mean control of the major sea-lines of communication.[12] Such control, however, would require more than taking advantage of recognized jurisdiction. It would require, at the very least, appropriate capability to be able to stand off likely retaliation. In the case of the Spratly Islands, such speculation is grounded in the fact that Japan used one of them as a naval base and as a staging area for invading colonial South-east Asia at the outset of the Pacific War. Indeed, the Imperial Navy engaged successfully in interdicting Allied shipping in the South China Sea. But, to argue in extrapolation on the basis of Japan's salutary experience of war is misleading. Any calculated act of interdiction could only follow from possession of the kind of capability appropriate for imposing regional naval dominance and not from mere occupation of islands which, in most cases, barely warrant the name and which provide a questionable basis under the terms of the Law of the Sea Convention for pressing claims to maritime jurisdiction. Moreover, any attempt to control sea-space and shipping routes from barely sustainable garrisons difficult to reinforce from a distance would invite retaliation. It has been well argued that "To claim, however, that control over those islands would give the controlling nation a stranglehold on Japan or a veto on the strategic movements of the great powers seems to exaggerate the strategic importance of what in fact are specks of land".[13] The measure of control exercised by contending states, so far, does not represent much more than a toehold, even though displays and use of force have been used to secure them.

The Spratly Islands

The more realistic prospect of interruption of freedom of navigation would arise as a side-effect of armed clashes between coastal states engaged in pressing claims to maritime jurisdiction including those to mid-sea islands. Serious military confrontation has taken place between China and Vietnam, but without evident effect on freedom of navigation. In January and February 1974, China employed force against the Republic of Vietnam so consolidating control over the Paracel Islands. From January 1988, China began to establish a foothold on a limited number of islets in the Spratly Archipelago not occupied by any other coastal state. In March, an armed clash was precipitated with the inferior naval forces of the Socialist Republic of Vietnam which resulted in their defeat. China went on to entrench its limited position which has not been challenged physically by any coastal state or external power.

China's claim to islands in the South China Sea as well as some in the East China Sea has been pressed consistently and without any qualification ever since China raised objections to the terms of the Japanese Peace Treaty of 1951. Force has been employed in pursuit of some claims but with a measure of discrimination in geopolitical context. The Paracels expedition in 1974 may be interpreted as a pre-emptive exercise undertaken in the expectation of a communist victory in Vietnam which would have delivered around half of the islands to the jurisdiction of the government in Hanoi. That successful expedition occurred against a background of rising Sino-Soviet antagonism and suspicion in Beijing of a Moscow–Hanoi axis and importantly with the benefit of Sino-American *rapprochement*.[14] China attacked South Vietnamese shipping to lay physical hold on all the islands of the Paracel group; not with an immediate intention of dictating the local maritime regime. China has not yet made explicit its full terms for such a regime. The net effect, however, was to indicate a willingness to employ force to serve political ends if the circumstances were such that the cost of doing so was deemed acceptable. China's subsequent act of punishment against Vietnam in February 1979 in an unchanged geopolitical context demonstrated the extent of that willingness.

The more recent Spratly's expedition by China in 1988 was also a pre-emptive exercise up to a point. It was set against the background of Sino-Soviet *rapprochement* and had the effect of testing the credibility of Soviet countervailing power in Vietnam's interest. It was probably also undertaken in some expectation of a conclusion to the protracted Cambodian conflict. It is instructive to note that although objecting strongly to both Philippine and Malaysian claims to some of the Spratly Islands and their physical presence on them, China has, so far, avoided any military confrontation. Indeed, the same has been true in its dispute with Japan over the Senkaku (or Diaoyutai) Islands, although a somewhat bizarre form of military display was undertaken during the early 1970s. In the case of the Spratly Archipelago, the requirement of a united front strategy over Cambodia against Vietnam involving the ASEAN states has almost certainly been a factor responsible for China desisting from such a course. None the less, the military action taken by China in March 1988 which exposed the limits of Soviet–Vietnamese security co-operation made a major impact on ASEAN governments which China almost certainly calculated in advance as an acceptable political cost.

China and the Use of Force

China's military action in the Paracel Islands in 1974 occurred in the context of intense Sino-Soviet antagonism and a fear of Soviet–Vietnamese alliance. Its military action in 1988 took place in a different strategic context. Indeed that action served to confirm the measure of change that had ensued in the intervening period. China's maritime military initiatives have been undertaken within the framework of consistently held and pressed claims which are extensive within the South China Sea, albeit somewhat ambiguously defined as far as actual jurisdiction over sea space is concerned. China's maritime behaviour indicates a calculated opportunism determined in part by naval capability. That capability has expanded over the years from a coastal defence role to an ability to project power further offshore and has assumed greater significance in the case of South-east Asia in the light of Soviet military disengagement from Vietnam.[15] However, despite an evident blue water potential, it has been pointed out that "the reality is that it (China's navy) is still a coastal water force" without aircraft carriers to provide long-range air-cover.[16] Not discounting the vulnerability of aircraft carriers to anti-ship missiles, China has still to acquire the kind of military reach which would be required for sustained operations distant from its mainland. In the case of the Spratly Islands, which are the most contentious multilateral maritime issue in East Asia, China has considerable logistical difficulties to overcome in asserting the kind of military control which might be turned to strategic advantage. The Spratly Islands are well dispersed within the South China Sea and the nearest of them are about six hundred miles from China's regional naval base on Hainan Island. The ability to display naval supremacy over a debilitated Vietnam in contention over islets in the Spratly Archipelago does not yet constitute an ability to enforce a maritime regime to the disadvantage of the welfare and security of other regional states.

That said, China has been the only regional power to engage in a clash of arms to assert a claim to islands and thus to jurisdiction over sea space and related resources. It also reserves the right to use force to recover Taiwan. Occupation of South China Sea islands by Taiwan, Vietnam, the Philippines and Malaysia have involved displays of force rather than its use. Vietnamese firing on a yacht close to Amboyna Quay and Malaysia's arrest of Filipino fishing vessels, although related to maritime jurisdiction, have not been of the same order and significance as China's actions. In that respect, the prospect of an assertive China filling a regional power vacuum caused by Soviet and possibly American military disengagement has become a matter of some concern to local states. To aspire to such a task would, of course, require a scale of augmentation of capability which China cannot yet afford and also a willingness to risk confrontation likely to provoke the deployment of countervailing power. However, the Chinese government has upheld maritime claims with great tenacity.

The projection of military power in order to advance maritime claims has been limited in the case of East Asia in terms of its extent. That measure of limitation has not been an indication of any general disposition on the part of the coastal states to seek a practical accommodation of differences. Domestic politics, of course, have always been an obstacle in this respect, as the experience of the longstanding

Philippine claim to Sabah would seem to indicate. Moreover, the maze of overlapping claims in the case of the South China Sea are so extensive that the kinds of bilateral agreements which have been worked out in some cases over territorial sea and continental shelf would not be adequate in themselves to establish a stable maritime regime within the context of the Convention on the Law of the Sea. The threat of claims being pressed by military means cannot be ruled out with freedom of navigation at risk as a consequence. That threat comes most directly from the unresolved antagonism between China and Vietnam which lies at the root of the Cambodian conflict. Their respective claims to coastal waters and mid-sea islands are both comprehensive and mutually exclusive compared to those of the Philippines and Malaysia.

Jurisdiction Over Sea-Space

The central and related issues of the maritime dimension of regional security are those of jurisdiction over sea-space and freedom of navigation. In the case of the former, limited display of force has been employed to prevent oil exploration in contended jurisdiction but such acts of denial have not settled matters of jurisdiction to the advantage of any one party. In the absence of full agreement on bounds of maritime jurisdiction bearing on resources, the only rational interim alternative is to negotiate terms for joint exploitation of the sea-bed exemplified by agreements between Thailand and Malaysia, Australia and Indonesia, and Japan and South Korea. Such a measure has also been hinted at by China in discussions with Japan in the past over the Senkaku (or Diaoyutai) Islands but has not been raised since the revival of contention over sovereignty. During a visit to Singapore in August 1990, China's prime minister, Li Peng, returned to the prospect of joint exploitation this time for the disputed Spratly Islands but without attracting a constructive response from interested parties.[17] That kind of provisional solution, however, turns on the quality of political relations. It would not seem to be an early option, for example, in the Gulf of Tonkin between China and Vietnam where the question of maritime jurisdiction is not separate from contention over island groups in the South China Sea. In the absence of comprehensive working accommodation required for joint exploitation, a stable maritime regime with reference to resource allocation would seem doubtful.

Freedom of Navigation

The issue of freedom of navigation has been catered for up to a point by the Convention on the Law of the Sea. Only in the case of the Straits of Malacca and Singapore, however, has there been provision for a traffic separation scheme in the interest of safety of navigation which was a consideration relevant to the deal over a regime of passage worked out between maritime powers and coastal states in the Convention. Provision for transit and archipelagic passage makes a major contribution, in principle, to freedom of navigation which can always be prejudiced by accidents and bad seamanship as well as by acts of piracy and terrorism. The liberal nature of those regimes might be affected for naval vessels should a nuclear weapons-free zone be introduced into any sector of East Asia. ASEAN has made a declaratory commitment to such a zone but that formal commitment does not conceal evident differences among regional partners and the problems of implementation.[18] However, the issue of unimpeded navigation which corresponds to the security of sea lanes does not lend itself to truly rigorous analysis. None the less, signs of change in the balance of regional naval power have given rise to genuine concern about its consequences for the security of sea lanes. That said, up to now freedom of navigation has not been at serious risk through established sea lanes between the Indian and Pacific Oceans. For example, the seizure of the *Mayaguez* off the Cambodian coast by Khmer Rouge forces in May 1975 was very much the exception and not the rule, although indicating the possible dangers to navigation arising from a radical change of regime in a coastal state. Such a change in an archipelagic state, such as the Philippines could have far-reaching consequences. It is possible to argue that the issue of interdiction of sea lanes by coastal states and maritime powers has been something of a red-herring which the sceptical might attribute to special pleading by naval interests engaged in budgetary competition. In the past, interdiction of sea lanes has been contemplated in Armageddon-like circumstances which have become more doubtful between major powers ever since Mikhail Gorbachev began to expound his "New Political Thinking". The changing climate of global politics has also served to reinforce the significance of international economic relations, particularly given the astounding economic achievement of much of East Asia, which is a hostage to the fortunes of the regional maritime regime. Ideally, such interdependence governed by rational considerations should be sufficient to maintain its embryonic integrity. Regrettably, we do not live in an ideal world and political intemperance by coastal states may arise. It is for this reason that countries that live by trade and which feel especially vulnerable to interdiction of sea lanes may take it upon themselves to develop the capability to project naval power for their protection generating regional tensions in the process. Japan has, of course, been encouraged to move in this direction by the United States in the interest of burden-sharing. Japan has the capability in technology and financial resources to go beyond provision for its agreed task of mounting protection of waters within a perimeter of 1,000 nautical miles from the island of Honshu. A long-range sea lane defence strategy is in prospect, indicated by the procurement policy of its Self-Defence Agency.[19]

The American Factor

Despite Japan's evident interest in denying threats to sea lanes arising from changes in the regional naval balance, its government would almost certainly prefer not to assume such a role, especially if conflict arose as a consequence with states which have long given it ready access to raw materials, markets, investment opportunities as well as maritime passage. Indeed, its navy rejected a controversial invitation in May 1990 by the Thai government to take part in joint exercises in the South China Sea.[20] The critical consideration in Japanese calculations is the policy of the United States which is in some doubt partly because of the uncertain outcome of the negotiations over the renewal of the leases on military bases in the Philippines. The Pentagon however has declared an intention to sustain the place of the United States as a Pacific power based on forward-deployed forces. It has put forward *A Strategic Framework For The Asian Pacific Rim* which is intended to shape policy into the twenty-first century.[21] A measure of regional apprehension has been aroused because this policy entails an initial limited scaling-down of American force levels by around 11 per cent over three years. Concern arises from the possibility that this limited scaling-down might be merely the first stage in a more extensive programme of regional military disengagement encouraged by changes in the tone of global international relations, financial stringency and any reappraisal attendant on the Gulf War.

That concern has been expressed most vocally in Singapore whose government has offered to provide support facilities for the American navy and air force to help sustain forward deployment of its military presence in Asia. The deputy-prime minister, Lee Hsien Loong, has argued strongly that a persuasive United States presence in South-east Asia is needed to avoid a power vacuum that others will scramble to fill. In pointing out that a smaller American commitment to the region may force others to take on its role, India with its growing blue water capability has been identified together with Japan as a candidate for the role of regional policeman.[22] The regional balance of power, including its naval dimension, is in some flux with the greatest uncertainty arising over the intentions of the United States allayed in the short run by its resolute military response to Iraq's invasion of Kuwait. Although threats to freedom of navigation and security of sea lanes have probably been grossly exaggerated, regional anxieties will undoubtedly increase should the insistence of the American Congress on a peace dividend after the Gulf War lead to a larger scale of force reductions than intended by the Pentagon. That trend is likely to be resisted by the American administration which appreciates that, despite a transformed security environment in Europe, there are still potential trouble spots in East Asia. Moreover, American economic interests have become so substantial in the Pacific basin in the years since the retreat from Indo-China, that it would not make good sense to abdicate the role of prime makeweight in the regional balance which, according to the under secretary of defence, Paul Wolfowitz, costs only 6 per cent of the country's total military establishment.[23] As long as the United States maintains a credible maritime forward deployment in East Asia, then it would seem most unlikely that any maverick external power or coastal state would undertake any inconsequential initiative challenging freedom of navigation. But in the event of uncertainty over America's role, renewed assertion of maritime claims could have disruptive consequences.

Conclusion

The problem of discussing the relationship between maritime regime and regional security in East Asia is that the subject lends itself readily to speculative generalization but without the benefits of adequate empirical data upon which to base firm conclusions. A global framework does not exist for the maritime dimension of regional order, but it is embryonic partly because of the unratified condition of the Convention on the Law of the Sea. Moreover, matters of contention between coastal states and maritime powers over rights of passage still obtain. In addition, there are a host of disputes between coastal states over adjacent and opposite maritime boundaries and over mid-sea islands. This pattern of contention has been sustained concurrently with a significant improvement in the global climate of international relations which has had a mixed regional effect.

At issue is the extent to which changes in the regional balance of power may make it opportune for a coastal state with the requisite capability to attempt to extend maritime jurisdiction by force, disrupting freedom of navigation in the process. On the basis of the limited record, the prime candidate for such miscreant activity is the People's Republic of China which has been ready to employ force as an instrument of maritime policy in the South China Sea. Those acts of force at sea have been directed exclusively against Vietnam for whom the current leadership of China feels a special animus. Moreover, those acts would seem to have been carefully calculated to take advantage of circumstances which would limit the political costs involved in the undertaking. Any coastal state, including China, would be more likely to be deterred from engaging in any naval action disruptive of maritime order if the regional balance of power were so constituted that the opportunity costs of such action would be conspicuously evident. It is for this reason that the role of the United States remains critical, however much regional states might prefer to manage their security environment themselves. For that role to be effective it would require more than preemptive flag-showing to avoid having to cope with the proverbial worst-case. Required also is an evident preparedness to act without discrimination, even if it means confronting China. The record of the use of force in East Asia to assert maritime claims indicates that it is most likely to occur when the regional balance is in flux and countervailing power can be discounted. Regional security would seem to require that such countervailing power, if it cannot be generated locally on a cooperative basis, should be available from an acceptable external source for which there is only one candidate.

Notes

I am pleased to acknowledge the helpful comments of my colleague Ron Barston on a draft of this article which was initially presented in August 1990 at a conference in Hong Kong held under the auspices of the Centre for Asian Pacific Studies of Lingnan College.

1. *Official Text of the United Nations Convention on the Law of the Sea with Annexes and Index.* (New York: United Nations, 1983). All references to the provisions of the Convention are taken from this text.
2. See, Mark J. Valencia and James Barney Marsh, "Access to Straits and Sea lanes in South East Asian Seas: Legal, Economic and Strategic Considerations", *Journal of Maritime Law and Commerce,* Vol. 16, No. 4, October 1985, pp. 523–6.
3. See, Michael Leifer, "Indonesia Waives the Rules", *Far Eastern Economic Review,* 5 January 1989.
4. See, *Baselines: An Examination of the Relevant Provisions of the United Nations Convention on the Law of the Sea.* Office for Ocean Affairs and the Law of the Sea. (New York: United Nations, 1989).
5. *Official Text,* p. 39.
6. See, J. V. R. Prescott, *The Maritime Political Boundaries of the World* (London and New York: Methuen, 1985), Chaps. 8 & 9; George Kent and Mark J. Valencia (eds.), *Marine Policy in South East Asia* (Berkeley: University of California Press, 1985); Marwyn S. Samuels, *Contest for the South China Sea* (New York and London: Methuen, 1982); Chang Pao-min, *The Sino-Vietnamese Territorial Dispute* (Washington DC: Praeger, 1986); Lo Chi-kin, *China's Policy Towards Territorial Disputes: The Case of the South China Sea Islands* (London and New York: Routledge, 1989); Ma Ying-jeou, *Legal Problems of Seabed Boundary Delimitation in the East China Sea* (Baltimore: University of Maryland, 1984); Lawrence E. Grintner and Young Whan Kihl (eds.), *East Asian Conflict Zones* (New York: St Martin's Press, 1987), Chapters 3 & 6. Choon Ho Park, "The South China Sea Disputes: Who owns the Islands and the Natural Resources?" *Ocean Development and International Law* 37 (1973); Diane C. Drigot, "Oil Interests and the Law of the Sea: the Case of the Philippines", *Ocean Development and International Law,* Vol. 12, No. 1/2, 1982; Mark J. Valencia, "The Spratly Islands: Dangerous Ground in the South China Sea", *The Pacific Review,* Vol. 1, No. 4, 1988. Phiphat Tangsubkul, "East Asia and the Regime of Islands", *South-East Asian: Spectrum,* April–June 1976, and Mark J. Valencia, "North-East Asia: Petroleum Potential, Jurisdictional Claims and International Relations", *Ocean Development and International Law,* Vol. 20, No. 1, 1989; "Special issue on South China Sea", *Foreign Relations Journal,* Manila, March 1990; Gordon Jacobs, "Islands in Dispute", *Jane's Defence Weekly,* 9 June 1990, and R. Haller-Trost, *The Spratly Islands. A Study on the Limitations of International Law* (Centre of South East Asia Studies, University of Kent at Canterbury. Occasional Paper No. 14, October 1990).
7. Note the article by Steven Erlanger, *International Herald Tribune,* 7 May 1990.

8. Lewis M. Alexander, *Navigational Restrictions Within the New LOS Context. Geographical Implications for the United States* (Rhode Island: Offshore Consultants Inc., 1986), p. 325.

9. See, B. A. Hamzah, "Indonesia's Archipelagic Regime: Implications for Malaysia", *Marine Policy,* January 1984.

10. Admiral Noel Gayler, "Security Implications of the Soviet Military Presence in Asia" in Richard H. Solomon (ed.), *Asian Security in the 1980s* (Cambridge, Mass.: Oelgeschlager, Gunn and Hain, 1980), p. 67. See also, for corresponding speculation, Yaacov I. Vertzberger, *Coastal States, Regional Powers, Superpowers and the Malacca–Singapore Straits* (Berkeley: Institute of East Asian Studies, University of California, 1984).

11. Note the discussion in Michael Leifer, "The Security of Sea-Lanes in South East Asia", *Survival,* January–February 1983.

12. See, Valencia, "Spratly Islands", p. 439; Djalal, "Conflicting Territorial", p. 42, and Joseph R. Morgan and Donald W. Fryer, "Defence" in Kent and Valencia, *Marine Policy,* p. 238.

13. Donald Weatherbee, "The South China Sea: From Zone of Conflict to Zone of Peace?" in Grintner and Kihl (eds.), *East Asian Conflict Zones,* p. 127.

14. See, Lo, *China's Policy* and Gerald Segal, *Defending China* (Oxford: Oxford University Press, 1985). For a recent statement of China's maritime interests, see Xu Shiming, "Perspectives of Maritime Security in the Asian-Pacific Region", *International Strategic Studies* (Beijing) March 1990.

15. *International Herald Tribune,* 16 and 19 January 1990.

16. Tai Ming Cheung, "Force Projection", *Far Eastern Economic Review,* 27 July 1989. Note also, the authoritative comment that "The Chinese Navy continues to be slimmed down. The only new completion we can confirm are the commissioning of a fourth *Han*-class SSN and a new mine countermeasures vessel", *The Military Balance 1989–1990* (London: Brassey's for the International Institute for International Studies, 1989), p. 145. Discussion of China's current logistical limitations can be found in Marko Milivojevic, "The Spratly and Paracel Islands Conflict", *Survival,* January–February 1989.

17. *The Straits Times,* 14 August 1990.

18. See, Muthiah Algappa, *Towards A Nuclear-Weapons-Free Zone in South East Asia* (Kuala Lumpur: Institute of Strategic and International Studies, 1987).

19. Tai Ming Cheung, "Sea Lanes Strategy" and Gordon Jacobs, "Japan; Guarding Vital Sea Lanes", *Jane's Defence Weekly,* 13 January 1990. Note also the reports of regional concern in *International Herald Tribune,* 20 February 1990, as well as Dov Zakheim on the need for the United States to maintain its military role on East Asia, *ibid,* 26 June 1990.

20. *International Herald Tribune,* 10 May 1990.

21. *A Strategic Framework for the Asian Pacific Rim: Looking Toward the 21st Century,* (Washington DC: Department of Defense, April 1990). See also, *Jane's Defence Weekly,* 28 April 1990.
22. *Singapore Bulletin,* Vol. 18, No. 4, 1990.
23. Quoted in *Far Eastern Economic Review,* 3 May 1990.

31

The Straits Are Not Protected

Prime Minister Mahathir bin Mohamad of Malaysia has acquired notoriety as an abrasive advocate of Third World causes. There is a tendency in the West to discount his prescriptions as political self-indulgence. However, his recent call for ships using the Straits of Malacca and Singapore, one of the busiest international waterways in the world, to pay a toll to finance improved navigation and safety measures should be very seriously considered.

The oil spillage and fire following Thursday's collision between two supertankers near the northern entrance to the straits only underline the need for urgent action.

In the last 12 months, a series of collisions in the straits that run between Indonesia, Malaysia and Singapore have caused loss of life and pollution. They call into question the viability of the general maritime regime for straits as well as the system worked out specifically for the Straits of Malacca and Singapore in 1977.

Reprinted from Michael Leifer, "The Straits Are Not Protected", *International Herald Tribune*, 23 January 1993, by permission of the New York Times Syndicate.

The latter, which extend some 600 nautical miles, provide the shortest sea route between the Indian and Pacific oceans. They are a vital maritime supply line for countries such as Japan, South Korea and Taiwan that depend heavily on imports of crude oil from the Gulf. But the straits constrict to a point only 3.4 miles wide in one section opposite Singapore. They are also relatively shallow and increasingly congested.

Concern about safety of navigation in the straits became an issue in the early 1970s with the increase in size and number of oil tankers plying between the Gulf and Japan. In the context of international negotiations for a new law of the sea, Indonesia, Malaysia and Singapore took it upon themselves to work out a traffic separation regime that would reduce the risk of collision. An agreement was concluded in 1977 incorporating two major provisions: first, that vessels in passage should maintain a minimum under-keel clearance of at least 3.5 meters; second, that a traffic separation plan should be instituted for shipping on a voluntary basis.

That regime provided a nexus for a general regime for straits used for international navigation. It was incorporated in the UN Convention on the Law of the Sea enacted in 1982. A new principle of transit passage was introduced providing an unimpeded right, with no financial charge, to all ships proceeding through such straits on certain conditions, one of which was prevention of collision and pollution.

But the number and size of vessels using international straits, and the often hazardous nature of the cargoes they carry, have increased dramatically. An average of some 200 large merchant ships ply the Straits of Malacca and Singapore each day, together with an armada of about 1,800 smaller craft, including fishing trawlers. (In addition, piracy in some sections of the straits and surrounding waters has revived to an alarming degree in the past few years.)

The latest collision underscores the need to work out ways for safer traffic management. Clearly, a self-policing system is no longer adequate to cope with the growing volume of shipping. The recent spate of accidents are evidence of abuse by users. Such license is not tolerated in the air; it should no longer be tolerated at sea.

The time has come for the Straits of Malacca and Singapore, at least, to be treated much like a canal, with dues charged to cover the cost of navigation aids, and introduction of trained pilots to ensure that traffic separation is strictly observed.

Objections to a compulsory, fee-based regime of passage will almost certainly arise on grounds of expense and delay. There will also be concern that a precedent is being established that will pose a general threat to freedom of navigation. Singapore, for example, is almost certain to be reluctant to approve any change that might constrain access to and from its free port.

Such objections should be strongly resisted because of the overriding imperative of maritime safety, which has been neglected at obvious human and environmental cost in Southeast Asia.

The so-called new world order promised with the end of the Cold War is predicated on international community values. They should be applied and upheld rationally in the case of the Straits of Malacca and Singapore, with the lead being taken by the major maritime powers.

32

Stalemate in the South China Sea

The Last Frontier?

[T]he islands and waters of the South China Sea constitute the last frontier in South-East Asia to the extent that the maritime zone was not effectively incorporated within the delimited and demarcated domains of the respective colonial powers, bearing in mind the classical distinction between boundaries and frontiers.[1] Moreover, where applicable in the case of the South China Sea, their islands were not necessarily incorporated within post-colonial transfers of sovereignty; nor were they provided for by way of specific transfer of sovereignty in the political settlement of the Japanese Peace Treaty in 1951. This neglect, benign or otherwise, is of considerable significance because the South China Sea may be represented as the maritime heart of South-East Asia. Its domination by a single power could over time have far reaching strategic consequences

Reprinted in abridged form from Michael Leifer, "Stalemate in the South China Sea", in *Perspectives on the Conflict in the South China Sea,* edited by Knut Snildal (Oslo: Centre for Development and the Environment, 1999), pp. 1–9, by permission of the publisher.

affecting the geo-political and economic interests of both regional and extra-regional states.

Since the end of the Pacific War in 1945, irredentism, as well as more conventional expansionism, has actively been at play in respect of the islands, reefs, atolls and cays of the South China Sea and their attendant maritime space but not in respect of settled peoples in search of political redemption. In the case of the South China Sea, that irredentism, and more conventional expansionism, has become most contentious since the end of the Cold War which has seen the emergence of a new pattern of international relations in a strategically fused East and South-East Asia. That new pattern has emerged with the decoupling of China from the tacit alliance ranged against Vietnam arising from its occupation of Cambodia. Contention arising from irredentism and more conventional expansionism has become most acute in the case of the southerly Spratly Islands.

Driving coastal state conduct has been a common territorial imperative reinforced by historical grievance. It has also been motivated by the prospect of economic benefit from access to sources of energy supply through expanded rights under an evolving International Law as well as by perceived security advantages.

It is important to note in the case of the South China Sea that virtually every island and reef capable of supporting some kind of military presence has already been occupied. And that there has not been any attempt by a claimant state to assert its sovereign jurisdiction by force at the expense of another claimant for over a decade. [T]he so-called last frontier in the South China Sea has been explored and as fully invested as possible. For that reason, it is possible to employ the term stalemate for the South China Sea conflict in the absence of attempted solutions either by force or by some negotiated form of multi-national condominium or by judicial arbitration.

The Post-Cold War Balance

The contest for the South China Sea has been affected, nonetheless, by changes in the regional security environment attendant on the end of the Cold War. The prime beneficiary of those changes up to a point has been the People's Republic of China which has extensive claims to islands and maritime space within South-East Asia, albeit not without some ambiguity.

Although very much a worse-case scenario in current circumstances, the realisation of China's extensive claims would have the effect of moving its sovereign jurisdiction some one thousand nautical miles southwards and would place it in a position to command the equivalent of the Mediterranean of South-East Asia. No other coastal state has the potential to effect such a revolutionary transformation of the regional distribution of power.

China was able to consolidate its hold over the Paracel islands at the expense of the former Republic of Vietnam in January 1974 attendant on its historic rapprochement with the United States but the second phase of the Cold War had been a constraint on more southerly maritime assertiveness. It was only with a revision of strategic perspective towards the Soviet Union during the late 1980s that China felt enabled to disregard the impact of its seizure of some of the islands of the Spratly group, primarily at the expense of the Socialist Republic of Vietnam, on its alignment partners within the Association of South-East Asian Nations (ASEAN). The point at issue in the case of China's long-standing claims is the sense of grievance that its coastal-state competitors, whose own claims are deemed to be dubious, were able to engage in a seizure of islands backed by force because China had been constrained by Cold War circumstances.[2] After the end of the Cold War and the withdrawal of the United States from its military bases in the Philippines, and even after China had judged it advantageous to engage in regional multilateral dialogue within the ASEAN Regional Forum (ARF), it was deemed politic to seize the virtually underwater Mischief Reef some 130 miles off the coast of the Philippines in a calculated act of national defiance and in a demonstration of an unprecedented new-found strategic latitude and licence.

Since January 1995, however, despite a persistent reiteration that its sovereign jurisdiction in the South China Sea is indisputable, China has not engaged in any further substantive acts of maritime assertiveness.[3] The only exception, on paper, would be the delimitation in May 1996 of its maritime base-lines around the Paracel Islands employing the archipelagic principle which is valid under International Law only for mid-ocean archipelagos, while reserving its position for the Spratly Islands. Moreover, the prior occupation of Mischief Reef was an act of stealth and not one of open acquisition in the face of armed resistance. That act of stealth was symptomatic of limitations in China's military capability.

The seizure of Mischief Reef was far more symbolic of China staking a proprietary claim beyond the geographic limits of its structural tension with Vietnam so giving notice to ASEAN claimants in advance of Vietnam's membership that it had no intention of sacrificing sovereignty for the sake of good regional relations. An ability to do more than consolidate its position on the highly vulnerable platform that is Mischief Reef is very unlikely, however.

Irrespective of the motivation for the seizure of Mischief Reef, it was in a sense a reef too far. As former Foreign Minister, Qian Qichen, pointed out in July 1995, while the impact of Mischief Reef was still reverberating within South-East Asia, "The top priority of China's foreign policy is to maintain a stable peripheral environment so as to safeguard normal economic circumstances at home. China regards the establishment of long-standing and stable good relations with ASEAN as an important factor in attaining this goal." There would seem to be an obvious contradiction between Qian Qichen's declaratory goal and China's claims within the South China Sea, especially in the case of the Spratly Islands where they come into conflict over territory with Malaysia, the Philippines and Vietnam and over maritime space, additionally, with Brunei.

China has not budged one iota in its insistence of the rectitude of its sovereign jurisdiction but has been accommodating up to a point in its diplomatic dealings with ASEAN as a corporate entity.[4] Indeed, it has sought to wrap its claim to sovereign jurisdiction within the Convention on the Law of the Sea, which it ratified in May 1996. Moreover, it has made recurrent gestures in the form of offers of joint development but without ever presenting a concrete proposal for a scheme, which is not believed to be workable on a bilateral basis because of the overlapping nature of national claims.

Among the claimants to the Spratly Islands, China is the most dissatisfied. Vietnam, whose claims are almost as extensive as China's also harbours a strong sense of grievance, especially over the Paracels which are totally subject to Chinese dominion, but in the case of the Spratlys, where it occupies 35 features, it appears relatively content for the time being and has certainly not sought to pursue claims against any of its ASEAN partners on which it looks for a measure of diplomatic support against China. Militarily, it is not in any position to engage in maritime assertiveness, although it has been resolute in defence of its energy-rich continental shelf, which China disputes on the basis of its claim to the Spratly Islands.

An inability to engage in maritime assertiveness is also conspicuously the case with the Philippines, which found itself vulnerable to Chinese initiative with the withdrawal of American naval power from Subic Bay. Its government has been obliged to confine itself to military display for public relations effect in an attempt to keep the issue in the international limelight and also to ensure the passage through the Senate of the visiting forces agreement with the United States. The claims of the Philippines are limited as are those of Malaysia, albeit overlapping with one another and with Vietnam, while Brunei seeks control only over a portion of maritime space. Malaysia is also relatively content with its holdings, which it is probably capable of defending against the most resolute and well equipped attacker. It should be noted that all of these claims, with the possible exception of that to maritime space by Brunei, have shortcomings under International Law, albeit of a different order to those which may be identified in China's case and also that of Vietnam.

International legal niceties aside, the point at issue is that ever since the late 1980s, when a limited naval battle occurred somewhat inadvertently between China and Vietnam, there has not been any attempt to seize any occupied territory in the South China Sea. However obvious, it should be pointed out that Mischief Reef was unoccupied at the time of China's seizure for the likely reason that neither the Philippines nor Vietnam saw any point in investing a feature which was mainly under water for most of the time. Indeed, in order to establish its naval/fishing station on the reef, the Chinese were obliged to drill down into the rock below the water-level.

Stalemate

For the time being, none of the competing claims to sovereign jurisdiction in the South China Sea have been set aside; nor have they been subject to any measure of compromise. Because the maritime last frontier does not offer any further scope for national aggrandisement other than through acts of force, a condition of stalemate would appear to have set in. Claimant states are either satisfied up to a point with their incomplete holdings or do not deem it politic to pursue their claims by even diplomatic means. The exception to this mode is the Philippines whose government has expressed itself most aggrieved at China's recent consolidation of its position on Mischief Reef but has experienced nothing but frustration and humiliation in fruitless dialogue with Chinese officials without tangible support from ASEAN partners. Indeed, that bilateral dialogue in March 1999 was one of the deaf with China adamant that "Meiji Reef is Chinese territory" and that it would not dismantle expanded structures on it.[5]

Overcoming Contention

An evident feature of the contention over islands and maritime space in the South China Sea is that there has been a lack of political will to employ any regional or international machinery to try to resolve them. There have been a limited number of agreements over joint exploration and exploitation of contested maritime space in South-East Asia, the most notable in the case of the Timor Sea between Australia and Indonesia, albeit controversial and subject to challenge before the International Court of Justice. Limited resort to the International Court of Justice has been agreed between Malaysia and Singapore and Malaysia and Indonesia, but the issues in contention have yet to be joined in legal argument. The Philippines has also indicated a willingness to go to the Maritime Court in Hamburg over Mischief Reef but without prompting a Chinese response. The government of Indonesia with Canadian support has sponsored a series of workshops on the South China Sea over the past decade but these workshops at the "track two" level have not had the effect of generating any semblance of substantive accommodation whatsoever. They have been obliged to confine themselves to technical subjects in the interest of confidence-building and to avoid political contention.

The issue of the South China Sea has been addressed in biennial dialogues between ASEAN and China with some strong talking at the initial occasion in April 1995 in the wake of the revelation of the seizure of Mischief Reef but without any practical outcome for conflict resolution. Correspondingly, the issue of the South China Sea has been raised in general terms within the working sessions of the ASEAN Regional Forum (ARF) which includes, *inter alia,* all the claimants to sovereign jurisdiction in the South China Sea. The ARF, like ASEAN, is not a problem-solving vehicle but is concerned primarily with general confidence-building and has not taken any significant initiative to try to resolve the competing claims to sovereign jurisdiction.

[T]here is an absence of any regional machinery for addressing the complex contention which is not in itself a failure of institutions but one of political will on the part of the adverse claimants.

Stalemate and Regional Order

The main contention over islands and maritime space in the South China Sea has arisen in respect of minuscule territories which colonial powers were either unwilling or unable to incorporate within their respective domains. Accordingly, the near-to golden rule of respecting post-colonial political boundaries for fear of stirring up a multitude of competing territorial claims has not obtained, while, of course, for China the very notion of a colonial boundary is an anathema. In the case of contention over islands and attendant maritime space, possession whether through colonial transfer or through unilateral assertion has been treated as more than nine tenths of the law. Moreover, claims to sovereignty over islands and attendant maritime space have been upheld with a steely rectitude by all parties without any sign of compromise which does not bode well for regional order which has to be based on some shared view of the political-territorial status quo.

In a sense, therefore, the unresolved contention over the South China Sea is symptomatic of the problem of regional order in a strategically-fused East and South East Asia, which lacks a security architecture, based on a consensus over the status quo.

The stalemate that marks the condition of the contention over islands and maritime space in the South China Sea cannot be assumed to be a permanent feature of the region, however. Changes in strategic circumstances may offer new opportunities for assertiveness. Indeed, the timing of China's acts of acquisition in the case of the Paracel Islands in the mid-1970s and then that in the case of the Spratly Islands in the late 1980s corresponded with changes in regional strategic circumstances which made such unilateral armed action opportune. The current stalemate is tolerable for the contending claimants for the time being, however. It does not seem likely to be disturbed in the near future which is every reason for seeking a resolution sooner rather than later. Should that stalemate be disturbed for one reason or another, then the consequences for regional order could well be revolutionary. But, for the time being, a stalemate persists which has not been affected substantively by the economic adversity, which has afflicted East and South-East Asia from the middle of 1997.

Notes

1. For a helpful synthesis of seminal studies, which lead to the conclusion that a boundary refers to a line, while a frontier refers to a zone, see J. R. V. Prescott *Boundaries and Frontiers*, Croom Helm, London. 1978.
2. For a comprehensive and scholarly assessment of China's position, see Greg Austin *China's Ocean Frontier*, Allen and Unwin, St. Leonards, New South Wales, 1998. See also, Mark J. Valencia *China and the South China Sea Disputes*, Adelphi Paper 298, Oxford University Press for IISS, London, 1995 and Michael Leifer "Chinese Economic Reform and Security Policy: The South China Sea Connection" *Survival*, Vol. 37, No. 2, Summer 1995.
3. See, Pan Shiying *The Petropolitics of the Nansha Islands-China's Indisputable Legal Case*, Economic Information and Agency, Hong Kong. 1996.
4. See Michael Leifer "China in Southeast Asia: interdependence and accommodation" in David S. G. Goodman and Gerald Segal (eds.) *China Rising: Nationalism and interdependence*, Routledge, London. 1997.
5. Nirmal Ghosh "China's Spratlys structures will stay" *The Straits Times*, 23 March 1999.

PART II
Domestic Politics and
Foreign Policies

Introduction to Part II

Leo Suryadinata

Michael Leifer was better known as a scholar of international relations of Southeast Asia rather than of comparative politics. However, an examination of his publications shows that he was outstanding in both fields. In fact, good regional studies should be based on an adequate understanding of the countries in the region. It was, therefore, not surprising to discover that Leifer had conducted research on Southeast Asia's countries. The number of such studies is comparable to his international relations of the region. Nevertheless, due to his strong interest in international relations, his country studies are also often connected with foreign policy studies of the individual country.

Despite the fact that Leifer wrote a doctoral thesis on Zionism and Palestine in the British policy, he was able to make himself a Southeast Asianist. This was related to his first teaching appointment at Adelaide University in Australia where he was persuaded to focus on Southeast Asia.[1] Perhaps as a Jew he was interested in the survival of Israel, which was a new state. In Southeast Asia there were plenty of such states whose survival were then in question: Cambodia, Singapore, and Malaysia can be considered as new and fragile states. Another additional factor for his selection of Malaysia and Singapore was probably due to his British background as both countries are ex-colonies of the United Kingdom. Since Malaysia and Singapore are in close proximity with Indonesia and there have been intensive interaction, Leifer was also drawn into this nation of thousand islands.

Focusing on Southeast Asia

Leifer's first country study on Southeast Asia was on Cambodia, which was published in the *Pacific Affairs* in 1961. Cambodia was not only the earliest country that Leifer wrote about but was also the subject of the largest number of papers that he produced. He even published a book entitled *Cambodia: The Search for Security* in 1967. Many of his works on regional order and international politics were focused on this country.

Leifer also worked on Malaya/Malaysia and Singapore in the early 1960s. His earliest published works on Malaysian politics was in 1964, and he first wrote on Singapore politics in the same year. He kept up his interest in these two countries, especially Singapore, on which he published his last foreign policy book in 2000, a year before he passed away.

Not long after his research on Malaysia and Singapore, he was also drawn into the studies of Indonesian politics and foreign policy. He published his first article in 1965 on the Confrontation between Indonesia and Malaysia. In 1978, he produced a book on the Straits of Malacca, dealing with the positions of Indonesia, Malaysia, and Singapore. He became very interested in Indonesia and eventually published a book on Indonesia's foreign policy (1981).

Leifer also studied other Southeast Asian countries such as Vietnam, Brunei, the Philippines, and Thailand, but on these four countries, his publications were fewer and not as in-depth compared to those on Cambodia, Malaysia, Singapore, and Indonesia.

General Studies

In fact, his in-depth and systematic treatment of Southeast Asian domestic politics and foreign policies was reflected in his *Dictionary of Southeast Asian Politics* (1995, 1st ed.). It is comprehensive and very useful for students of Southeast Asian politics and foreign policy. By the time he passed away, the book had gone into third edition.

In his early life as an academic Leifer published two general books. The first was *The Dilemmas of Statehood in Southeast Asia* (Singapore: Asia Pacific Press, 1972), which reflected his concern with new states and their problems. The survival of these new states was his major concern. This was his first book on Southeast Asian politics and a useful introduction to the subject. Unfortunately, this book was not widely circulated. In 1974, he produced another general book entitled *Foreign Relations of New States* (Victoria: Longman Australia, 1974). The general impression was that it was a continuation of his first book, but in it he examined their foreign relations rather than domestic politics. Unlike his first book, this book was well distributed and received tremendous attention. Many were impressed by his analysis of the problems in this region and adopted the book for courses on international politics of Southeast Asia.

Themes and Concepts

In examining Leifer's publications, both books and journal articles, one can easily notice a number of common themes running across his studies. In the field of comparative politics and foreign relations, his major concern was with political stability, institutionalization, succession, civil society, and democracy. He also paid attention to ethnicity and religion, which played an important role in both domestic politics and foreign policy. When dealing with foreign policy, he was particularly interested in the relationships between domestic politics and foreign policy, characteristics of foreign policy, and foreign relations with neighbouring states and major powers.

As Southeast Asian states were mainly new, and many were weak, Leifer focused on the vulnerabilities and limitations of their foreign policy. In fact, he developed the concepts of vulnerability when dealing with Singapore and Vietnam, and the concept of engagement, with Indonesia. His article on Indonesia–China relations details the special nature and limit of the engagement concept, highlighting both unilateral and multilateral engagements. However, he did not come upfront and develop them into theories of foreign policy.

When Leifer dealt with domestic politics, he used concepts in comparative politics. For instance, when examining Indonesia, he discussed the democratic system and civil society even though his theoretical underpinning was not clearly spelt out in many of his articles as he was not particularly interested in the development of theories. Nevertheless, he addressed conceptual issues in some of his articles. For instance, he wrote a piece on the civil society with special reference to Indonesia, explaining the difficulty in applying this Western concept; another piece was on the "linkage politics" between Islam and Indonesian foreign policy without explicitly using that term.

It may be argued that Leifer was not a "theory-builder" in the American political science/international relations tradition. He was more interested in political and diplomatic analysis rather than abstract conceptualization. No doubt, he had his theoretical underpinnings but he seldom made them explicit in his articles. Some of his writings read like international history or diplomatic history. Because of this tendency, Leifer's works have much less appeal to American scholars steeped in international relations and foreign policy theory. Nevertheless, those who are interested in diplomatic history would appreciate his works.

There is no doubt Leifer had a deep appreciation of both domestic politics and foreign policies of many Southeast Asian countries. He was also very perceptive in his analysis. However, his seemingly elliptical writing style coupled with the absence of useful sub-headings in his long articles do make reading him a heavy-going experience at times.[2]

Individual Country Analysis

In analysing the politics of Cambodia, Malaysia, Singapore, and Indonesia, he addressed the issue of institutionalization and argued that this was the root of political stability. Succession became a problem because of weak institutionalization. There were no clear rules on political succession and on the transfer of political power in many Southeast Asian countries. This was particularly problematic in Cambodia and Indonesia, resulting in political instability, if not chaos. However, Malaysia and Singapore appeared to have stronger institutionalization than Cambodia and Indonesia, and hence were more stable than Cambodia and Indonesia.

However, these four countries had problems with civil society and democracy. Leifer noted that the concepts of Western liberal democracy and civil society could not be literally applied to Southeast Asian countries as these states had different histories and political cultures. Leifer advocated that to understand the politics of Southeast Asian countries, an in-depth understanding of the countries' history and society was crucial. Multi-ethnicity and ethno-nationalism were often sources of conflict. Ethnicity and religion, together with ideology, were also reflected in the foreign policy of Southeast Asian countries.

Indonesia, for instance, has a large Muslim population but, due to the plurality of the Muslim population and the dominance of liberal Muslims in the leadership, Islam was not clearly reflected in the conduct of Indonesia's foreign policy, at least up to the period of Soeharto. However, Leifer was aware of the importance of Islam and noted that it gradually showed in the leaders' decision-making process in Indonesia's foreign policy.

Leifer noted that Indonesia, being the largest country in Southeast Asia, had always harboured the desire of regional entitlement to the leadership role. However, due to its internal weaknesses, this dream could not be entirely realized. Before the 1997–98 economic crisis, it appeared to have been leading ASEAN. But it was problematic for Indonesia. The concept of "regional entitlement", as Leifer called it, became more problematic after the fall of Soeharto. Examining Leifer's writings on Indonesia's foreign relations, this concept and political culture (Islam) were always present.

On the other hand, he focused on different aspects when writing about Singapore. He often focused on the problems posed by vulnerability and the nature of exceptionalism. Leifer argued that pragmatism had become the basis of Singapore's foreign policy. Conscious of its vulnerability, Singapore was eager to build its own defence and to have the presence of major external powers. He was particularly interested in Lee Kuan Yew's role in, and his impact on, Singapore's domestic politics and foreign policy. He gave credit when it was due and offered criticism when it was needed.

On Malaysia, Leifer noted that the role of Islam was often reflected in the conduct of its foreign policy, and it became more obvious during the latter period of Mahathir's tenure as prime minister. Sectarian conflict in the Middle-East had often became part of Malaysian domestic politics. This was different from Soeharto's Indonesia which suppressed political Islam. Anti-Semitism had become a characteristic of Malaysia's foreign policy and Leifer called it "anti-Semitism without Jews", referring to Malaysia's "anti-Semitism" without the presence of a Jewish community in the country. This anti-Semitism policy was meant to serve Mahathir's domestic politics.

When analyzing Cambodia, Leifer focused on its problems of vulnerability and the hostile external environment for the survival of an independent Cambodia. He noted that Cambodia's foreign policy tried to maintain neutrality in the conflict between neighbouring states. Sihanouk succeeded temporarily but he lost eventually. The sovereignty of Cambodia was later lost to Vietnam as it became the victim of international politics before it became "independent" again.

Leifer paid special attention to the role of strong leaders. Much were written about Lee Kuan Yew, Mahathir, Soeharto, and Sihanouk. When analysing Singapore, Malaysia, Indonesia, and Cambodia, Leifer often focused on these leaders who had heavily influenced, if not determined, the politics and policy of their countries.

A New Type of "Area Specialist"?

Leifer was different from the traditional area specialist who works on one country and extensively uses the local language source. Leifer had a reading knowledge of Malay/Indonesian, but he did not extensively use the Malay/Indonesian sources in his writings. Nevertheless, he understood the local situation well and conducted fieldwork regularly. He had many graduate students who worked on or in these countries. His intensive interactions with them contributed to his deeper understanding of Southeast Asia.

Also, traditional area specialists focus on mainly one country. Unlike them, Leifer expanded his specialties to at least four Southeast Asian countries: Cambodia, Malaysia, Singapore, and Indonesia. This was perhaps one of the reasons why he never claimed any Southeast Asian country in his studies as "his country of specialty". He treated many Southeast Asian countries as an object of his studies and attempted to give a more balanced picture. He was detached and not emotionally involved in any Southeast Asian country; this was reflected in his sober writings.

His in-depth understanding of these individual countries provided the basis for his studies in international relations and comparative politics of the region. He became aware of the similarities and differences of many Southeast Asian countries and discussed the issues in the regional rather than the country's perspective.

Leifer was not accepted by area specialists as one of them. A leading Indonesian historian noted to me that Leifer was not a historian on Indonesia because he did not use Indonesian sources. Leifer never claimed that he was a historian of any country. In fact, he studied political science at the London School of Economy (LSE) and was never trained as a traditional "area specialist" which requires a mastery of vernacular languages. But it is difficult to deny that he was a specialist on the region of Southeast Asia. He read Western literature widely and conducted interviews locally. He attempted to understand the general patterns of the country and the region. He was not concerned with unique facts or detailed description of a particular country but was able to highlight major characteristics of a political system or an international system without losing sight in history.

His writings on Indonesian nationalism and foreign policy can be used as an illustration. In his chapter on Indonesian nationalism in the book *Asian Nationalism* (Routledge, 2000), he examined the "temper" of nationalism, the changing characters of this movement and its changing functions. He did not present many new historical facts but presented Indonesian nationalism in a new light. It throws light on the studies of Asian nationalism in general and Indonesian nationalism in particular, including the meaning and function of nationalism.

Leifer's book, *Indonesia's Foreign Policy* (Allen & Unwin, 1983), presented no theory, but a concise diplomatic history of Indonesia. Unlike American-trained scholars who wrote on foreign policy of Indonesia, who often applied the framework of foreign policy analysis, Leifer painstakingly looked at the long process of diplomacy from independence to the beginning of the Soeharto period. He identified Indonesian foreign policy behaviour, which was concerned with "regional entitlement" to the leadership role, a major characteristic of Indonesian foreign policy across various periods. Nevertheless, when Leifer discussed the interactions between Islam and foreign policy, he abandoned the diplomatic history approach. He focused on the conflict between secular nationalism and Islam, highlighting their unique manifestation in Indonesia's foreign policy during various periods.

Leifer tried to put himself in the shoes of Southeast Asians with his careful and sharp observations and analyses of the Southeast Asian scene. He was critical of certain policies and practices by Southeast Asian governments, but did not go out of his way to deplore and condemn them. Leifer was a realist; he tended to see things in its reality and was concerned with power relationships. He was also interested in political order and stability. He could see a merit in the status quo, while others would have been more inclined to challenge.

When Leifer passed away, the world and Southeast Asia were undergoing rapid changes. Terrorism was on the rise, and then the

September 11 incident occurred. Leifer's publications do not foresee this development and hence do not address the issue, especially its impact on Southeast Asian politics and foreign policy. Nevertheless, Leifer did discuss Islam in some of his writings and noted the increasing importance of this religion as a significant political force. He had noticed this when dealing with Indonesia and warned his readers not to overlook this issue. Regardless of the gap in his writings on the new development, Leifer's works are still useful in providing insights on Southeast Asia prior to and beyond September 2001. His contribution to the Southeast Asian studies should be recognized. Future generations of scholars who would like to study Southeast Asia's international relations and domestic politics will need to refer to his work to better understand Southeast Asia.

Notes

1. Michael Yahuda, "Obituary", *The London School of Economics and Political Science News and Views* 25, no. 1 (23 April 2001).
2. For instance, the following long articles do not have sub-headings: "Cambodia and Her Neighbouurs" (1962, 14 pages); "Politics in Singapore: The First Term of People's Action Party" (1964, 17 pages); "Singapore in Malaysia: The Politics of Federation" (1965, 17 pages); "The Islamic Factor in Indonesia's Foreign Policy: A Case of Funtional Ambiguity" (1983, 19 pages); "Brunei: Domestic Politics and Foreign Policy" (1986, 11 pages); "Uncertainty in Indonesia" (1992, 20 pages).

Cambodia

INTRODUCTION

Leifer wrote one book and more than twenty articles on Cambodia's politics and foreign policy. The earliest article was published in 1961 while the latest was in 1995. This section on Cambodia reproduces eight of those articles, mostly in abridged form, to present the important issues discussed by Leifer.

From the start, Leifer noted that Cambodia was precarious. Its independence was not natural but came about through the careful playing of the balance of power game. Of course, this was based on one condition that Cambodia itself should also be politically stable. Without domestic political stability, it would not be able to stop external intervention. Nevertheless, Leifer pointed out that Cambodia continued to adhere to tradition, and the god-king concept prevailed. There was no political institutionalization in Cambodia, and the role of a traditional authority — in this case the king — was crucial (Ch. 33). This crucial issue of political succession was never resolved (Ch. 34). Sihanouk, due to various reasons, was not interested in institutionalizing the political process, resulting in an uncertainty. The rebellion in 1967 and 1968 was said to be a result of the domestic politics and external intervention, but Leifer argued that the domestic situation should not be overlooked. Leifer noted that Sihanouk might "fail to appreciate the relationship between social change and popular expectations and demands and the sense of frustration of those educated young men who oppose his personal style of government" (Ch. 35).

Leifer stressed that Cambodia had a precarious status, and its survival was a result of playing the balance of power game. Thailand, North and South Vietnam, and China were the regional actors, and the United States, a super power that might determine the survival of this small kingdom (Ch. 36). Prince Sihanouk was able to allow the communists from South Vietnam to use it as a sanctuary so that North Vietnam would not subvert the country. Cambodia also attached importance to its relations with the People's Republic of China, hoping that the PRC would eventually protect its independence. In Leifer's words, "So far this policy of balance — on the one hand, using China as a counter to Thailand and South Vietnam, and on the other the United States with its aid donations to retain a certain freedom of manoeuvre in dealing with communists — has paid dividends. This equilibrium, however, hardly appears stable." Indeed, soon after that, Cambodia experienced crisis. To understand the Cambodian issue in perspective, four articles in Part I (Chs. 16–19) dealing with external power's involvement should also be consulted.

The "pro-communist" policy resulted in the right wing coup in Cambodia and Sihanouk was ousted. The pro-American General Lon Nol ruled the country, but was soon replaced. Cambodia became the "playground" of regional and major powers. The communist Khmer Rouge led by Pol Pot took over and introduced a murderous policy aimed at "cleansing" Cambodia. When there was a split in the Khmer Rouge, Vietnam invaded Cambodia and installed Heng Samrin and, later, Hun Sen to rule the country. The Khmer Rouge started a guerilla war. Vietnamese occupation of Cambodia, which was supported by the Soviet Union, was unacceptable to the regional powers during the Cold War. The United Nations intervened, and the new Cambodian regime was unable to gain rognition; Hanoi-backed Hun Sen refused to budge. The politics of attrition in Cambodia started (Ch. 37).

Lacking in other alternatives, China and ASEAN supported Pol Pot to force Vietnam to release its grip. Nevertheless, the Vietnamese troops only departed from Cambodia after the end of the Cold War, and an election was eventually conducted under the supervision of the UN (Ch. 38). The power-sharing formula was introduced. Hun Sen's People's Party gained the majority of seats and controlled both the government and the army. King Sihanouk was restored. Nevertheless, the vulnerability of Cambodia's politics remains (Ch. 39). The Cold War was over and the regional and international communities, feeling tired of the Cambodia issue, were reluctant to get involved again, risking the return of crisis and the authoritarian regime to Cambodia (Ch. 40).

33

The Failure of Political Institutionalization in Cambodia

The political system of Cambodia is often — and not inaccurately — described as one of the most stable in Asia. Such description is apt to be justified by reference to the relative absence of upheaval and disturbance which have been the fate of several new Asian states. Surface indications of stability, however, can give rise to exaggerated assumptions about the institutionalized nature of a political system, in the sense that an induced pattern of political activity has jelled to make the system a going concern. The object of this article is to examine the distinguishing features of the Cambodian political system with a view to establishing whether surface appearance reflects an inner resilience or fundamental structural weakness.

In trying to establish the characteristic features of a policy it is useful to identify those turning points in time which serve to mould the pattern of political activity. A much cited example of the utility of such historical explanation is the French political system, the

Reprinted from Michael Leifer, "The Failure of Political Institutionalization in Cambodia", *Modern Asian Studies* 2, part 2 (1968): 125–40, by permission of Cambridge University Press.

main features of which have been shaped by events whose legacy remains embedded in the body politic. In modern Cambodia it is possible also to identify landmarks on the political landscape which in retrospect can be classified as major watersheds. The most significant of these was established in March 1955 when the sovereign, Norodom Sihanouk, abdicated his throne in order to play a more positive political role, albeit without divesting himself of royal attributes.

The Shaping of the System

The major part of Sihanouk's reign, which began in 1941, occurred under French colonial rule. In consequence, whatever authority he possessed could be exercised only within the limits of externally imposed constraints. And while colonial rule endured, the monarch enjoyed a diminished national appeal by appearing to countenance, at least for seven years, a subject relationship for his kingdom. The Cambodian political elite, many of whom had been educated in France before participating in electoral activity and National Assembly politics following the Second World War, were not only personally ambitious and factious in association but also sufficiently secularized not to be in awe of the myth of semi-divinity which served to legitimate the form of royal authority in the countryside. The traditional reverence for the Cambodian monarchy, which the French had sought to sustain for their own political purpose, had limited relevance for the small educated class, many of whose members tended to view the throne as a compliant tool of colonial authority, an impediment to constitutional advance, and an obstacle to personal preferment. Indeed, some displayed an attitude to the throne which bore a close resemblance to the sentiments expressed by the promoters of the 1932 coup in Thailand, which abolished the absolute monarchy and replaced it by a formal constitutionalism.

In Cambodia in 1946 there began a process of constitutional reform under the supervision of the colonial power. The initial effect of this reform was to produce an atmosphere of political liberality in the capital and the appearance of Western-type political organization. Royal absolutism was abolished, although the royal prerogative did not completely disappear. Nevertheless, in constitutional terms, the monarchy was a drastically weakened force, and thenceforth the path to the exercise of limited power lay in securing support from a newly created electorate which was in no way restricted by special qualifications.

Norodom Sihanouk was to remark years later, with some bitterness, on the French suggestion that he hand over his royalty to a handful of politicians.[1] The French-tolerated post-war constitutional structure indicated that, in principle, the King would reign more and rule less. The King, no doubt looking to a restoration of monarchical authority rather than to a further diminution of powers, resisted the logic of constitutionalism. Thus there ensued continuous conflict between the throne and the elected politicians which endured beyond the acquisition of independence. In this conflict, and because of special circumstances, the King achieved success but without the assurance of an entrenched political dominance. Despite his personal achievement in diplomatic endeavour which hastened the departure of the French, his constitutional position remained an obstacle to political control. The Cambodian constitution was so framed as to ensure the assumption to power in an independent country of those political groupings whose factious wranglings Sihanouk regarded as inimical to national unity and personal authority.

Irrespective of the predisposition of the King, the Cambodian representatives to the 1954 Geneva Conference on Indo-China (which gave international sanction to an independent Cambodia) pledged their country to an open and unrestricted political process, to be demonstrated through free elections conducted under international supervision. In effect, this accord signified that the constitutional monarch would be obliged to acquiesce in the outcome of a new electoral contest, which seemed certain to be won by that political grouping — the Democratic Party — which was disenamoured of royal prerogative. From his elevated position, the King was powerless to intervene effectively to impair this process. He made one attempt to have the electoral system amended with a restricted suffrage and increased royal authority, but was baulked by members of the International Commission for Supervision and Control who were charged with the function of overseeing the elections to be held in March 1955.[2] He therefore adopted a more drastic measure to escape from the constricting cloak of constitutionalism. He decided to divest himself of the monarchy, to which he had been appointed by the French to succeed his maternal grandfather, in favour of his father, Norodom Suramarit.[3] Free from the bonds of the throne, he would be able to compete for the political affections of the kingdom.

Now as Prince Norodom Sihanouk he was to relinquish all prospect of a figurehead role, and with the backing of the public relations machinery of state he set out to create his own political following, *Sangkum Reastre Niyum* (Popular Socialist Community). This took the form of a *rassemblement* — a mass organization cutting across party lines and founded on coincident loyalty to the nation and to the ex-King. This organization, under the leadership of Sihanouk, enjoyed overwhelming success in the national elections held eventually in September 1955. The personal magnetism of the former King and his ability to employ the resources of state proved more than sufficient to counter the attraction of the more conventional political parties. The International Control Commission was to comment: "The entrance of Prince Sihanouk into public life transformed the national scene and served as a major factor in the overwhelming victory of the Popular Socialist Community".[4]

The electoral road to power had decided advantages for a man who enjoyed not only the reverential appeal of a Cambodian King but also a legendary reputation as the father of independence. Intervention in the electoral process enabled Sihanouk to enjoy the reaffirmation of that popular support which had been demonstrated in a referendum of February 1955, when the people had been asked to pass judgement on the King's endeavours to secure national independence. His ability to by-pass the political elite in direct communication with the people, and to establish the dependence of the former on his benefactions, marked a fundamental change in the character of the Cambodian political system. The pre-independence constitutional framework remained intact but now Sihanouk was its beneficiary and not its victim. Political alignments were to alter with Sihanouk's change of formal status. The principal pre-independence party — the Democratic — was able to sustain the elements of organization needed to contest the elections but failed to obtain a single seat in the National Assembly. The remaining groupings, with one exception, folded and their membership joined in the move to *Sangkum* which also attracted many Democratic adherents. Thus was established a framework for political activity which has endured through the subsequent three national elections in which *Sangkum* has run unopposed.

The Constituencies of Politics

The effect of Prince Sihanouk's intervention in the elections was to establish that he enjoyed a base of personal power independent of and divorced from the political elite. Furthermore, that section of the political elite unwilling to be associated with Sihanouk's following was shown to have only a vestigeal appeal, while the much larger section which was willing to be associated with Sihanouk was entirely dependent on his bounty, since it had sparse political resources of its own.

The principal constituency from which Sihanouk drew — and still draws — his political strength was the electorate which is composed in the main of rural dwellers. One must include with the rural people the Buddhist monks who live both physically and spiritually close to the peasant villagers, and whose influence has political import. The Cambodian peasantry are a conservative people bound largely by the coincident cycles of religious and agricultural life. Their devotion to the man who was once King stems in part from a traditional cosmology but also from his neo-traditionalist activity as a patron of the widely diffused Buddhist faith. Sihanouk is no distant potentate of Angkor vintage; he involves his person in the daily life of his constituents. The relative absence of grievance resulting from land hunger or excessive rural indebtedness, together with the legendary and perceived qualities of national leadership, has cemented a bond which is an invaluable source of political strength for Sihanouk.

At a different level, there is the constituency of *Sangkum* which is also, though to a lesser extent, the preserve of Sihanouk. This organization was formed as a loose coalition out of a combination of cliques, and factions based on royal connexions, family extension, redundant political groupings, special interests and ideological leanings. Accordingly, *Sangkum* is not a naturally cohesive grouping but reflects the disparate affinities of those involved in Cambodian political life. Such division within *Sangkum* was demonstrated in the vote in the National Legislature in October 1966 to choose a new Prime Minister. The outcome was a four-way split, with the victor emerging with a plurality of only eight votes. The degree of political unity — or rather the degree of absence of political dissension — within *Sangkum* is a function of the dominant position of Sihanouk. However, this unity is of a tenuous kind and *Sangkum* without Sihanouk would not be able to contain its strong centrifugal tendencies. Sihanouk himself has felt obliged to remark: "I note with sadness that although the Cambodians may be united around me, I have not succeeded in uniting them amongst themselves".[5]

Sihanouk's support within *Sangkum*, and more especially among members of the National Assembly, is not so readily forthcoming as among the electorate at large. He has, however, at his disposal the sanction of popular appeal — a monopoly resource. He is also well aware that internal divisions within *Sangkum* make his leadership the only feasible possibility, and that there is no grouping within *Sangkum* which could command a majority in the National Assembly without princely mandate. Indeed, *Sangkum's* standing in the country derives from the umbilical political union between Sihanouk and the people.

The two constituencies, that of the electorate and of *Sangkum*, merge in the institution of the National Congress. This Congress is a forum of *Sangkum* members, urban dwellers and selected provincials which meets every six months in Phnom Penh on the site of an ancient royal cremation ground. It began as a limited gathering restricted to *Sangkum* members but from April 1956 it became a less exclusive association. The National Congress is intended to represent a microcosm of the national political scene but its prime function is to demonstrate the political strength of Sihanouk. It serves as a populist tool whereby Sihanouk, who has been head of state since his father's death in 1960, seeks to stand above other people's politics in direct relationship to the people who sanction the prevailing political system. It serves also to remind the political elite, including Administration members, to keep their place which they enjoy as a princely dispensation. The National Congress functions as a means to remind *Sangkum* members of the broad base of political support enjoyed by their chairman, to which they are permitted access only through his good grace. It is both a symbol of Sihanouk's political dominance and also a means to ensure that such dominance is not unduly disturbed. Such is Sihanouk's skill and political success on Congress occasions that he sometimes calls special or extraordinary Congresses to serve his ends. Thus, following a minor left-wing demonstration in the capital in March 1967, Sihanouk announced his intention to call a special Congress; the demonstrators were requested to attend "to discuss the problem with the people".

The Style of Political Leadership and the Modes of Political Activity

Prince Sihanouk has divested himself of his throne but not of his royal attributes. His political strength derives from his skill in building upon the foundation of the appeal of kingship in Cambodia. The modern Khmer state has the quality of a monarchical political system. Yet Sihanouk is no longer King and his role is not totally that of rulers of the illustrious age of Kambuja — of a latter-day Jayavarman VII. It is more accurate to describe Cambodia as a quasi-monarchical political system in which the erstwhile absolute ruler has tempered his traditional role to meet a changed situation.

Prince Sihanouk is not the sole initiator of political activity within Cambodia but he is certainly the dominant political actor. It is possible to differentiate the political style that he employs in terms of the constituency divisions enumerated above. Split level politics is perhaps a convenient, if somewhat crude, way to describe Sihanouk's political style in terms of areas of activity. The levels are of a Court and plebiscitary kind.

At the Court level Sihanouk has to deal with a French-educated elite composed of ministers, Assembly members and bureaucrats. Those among them who are his confidants, and they include foreign advisers, pay him extraordinary regard and deference which he accepts as his rightful due. But he reacts in a volatile manner to what he construes as acts of *lèse-majesté*. In this situation, he rests at the apex of the political hierarchy but that does not mean that his courtiers are without influence, particularly if they know how to exploit the known sensibilities and predilections of their patron. Sihanouk does accept advice from his courtiers but their role is somewhat Byzantine. They respond to princely mood with sensitivity based on experience and intuition; in this way they retain their political heads. Sihanouk, for his part, sustains a political balance among those who surround him through a skilful process of accommodation, manipulation and neutralization. Thus an extreme leftist is removed from the Cabinet Secretariat out of harm's way to a public relations function but later elevated to cabinet office from which in turn he is removed as a public political sinner. The Commander-in-Chief of the Army is eased out of that office by being elected Prime Minister by an inspired plurality of the National Assembly, while a trusted uncle is placed in charge of military administration. At this level of activity one is faced with an interesting paradox. The political mode among the French-educated and secularized elite is that which one associates with the closed political system of royal absolutist variety. In dealing with the public at large, Sihanouk consciously exploits tradition but employs modern techniques of political communication.

With the electorate at large, Sihanouk consciously seeks to operate an agitational plebiscitarian style of politics. This style does not follow automatically from the dire political necessity of providing diversion from the hardships of life. Cambodia, although not a rich country, in no way approximates to India's pitiful poverty. The tendency to flamboyant rhetoric on Sihanouk's part derives in part from personal experience of the time when effective public relations promoted diplomatic success against France, and also from a belief that he has to deal with a people whose concentration tends to lag and who need to be constantly enthused to stay politically awake. His public platform to the nation tends in the main to be Radio Phnom Penh. But he takes care also to establish a more direct contact, and at the village level he employs an earthy manner which seems to yield dividends. The agitational style is related to problems of mobilization but also to the personality of Sihanouk, whose more volatile moods lend themselves to an emotional form of self-expression. In this activity he has a natural feeling for theatre and public drama, and this is reflected also in his leisure occupation of producing films for the Cambodian cinema.

Political activity of a kind takes place also within the chamber of the National Assembly. Here the fractious representatives debate the formal matters of state. They can, on occasions, be obstructive and may press for the withdrawal of members of the cabinet. Their decisions, however, are rarely of major consequence although their squabbling may affect political stability. But this political activity is somewhat domesticated because in the background there exists the controlling organ of the National Congress, through which Sihanouk exercises his authority. By means of this extra-parliamentary base, Sihanouk is able to demonstrate to politicians and ministers that he enjoys a special relationship from which they are excluded, and as a consequence their freedom for political manoeuvre is limited. In November 1966 Sihanouk challenged his politicians in the following manner:

> I want you to understand that I am not yet 60, like old Sukarno; I am only 40 years old. I have not yet accepted defeat in my life. You can do as you wish but you must not think you can defeat me, for I am the kind of man who never accepts defeat. I will only accept punishment from the people, for you are not the people. *You belong to a special category, another class, for you are neither Prince nor people.*[6]

These few phrases provide a deep insight into the functioning of the Cambodian political system. They demonstrate the pattern of relationships between Sihanouk, the people and the politicians and how, because of Sihanouk's exclusive relationship with the people, the politicians appear to be at a serious disadvantage in seeking to promote their ambitions.

There is a further consideration in the patron-client relationship between Sihanouk and the politicians. The disparate political groupings — which contend among themselves and annoy Sihanouk — are not able to mobilize physical resources to by-pass his special relationship with the people in order to displace him. For the time being, the Army leadership is loyal to the Head of State and appears to be directly opposed to those more active politicians who seem inclined to effect changes in the structure of the political system. The Army, thus, fulfils a functional role in relation to the system.

The Nature of Political Opposition

So long as opposition groups present a fragmented aspect and can also be denied effective access to popular support and physical means for the exercise of power, one would expect the system, which rests upon princely mandate, to be sustained. Nevertheless, opposition is not to be dismissed as of no consequence.

Opposition in Cambodia can be divided into two categories, inner and outer opposition. By outer opposition is meant those groups, prescribed or otherwise, which exist outside the ranks of *Sangkum*. There are two outer opposition elements which occupy extreme ends of the political spectrum in Cambodia. First, there are the *Khmer Serai* (Free Cambodians) who originate from that section of the anti-French resistance associated with former Prime Minister, Son Ngoc Thanh. Thanh remained alienated from the King following the acquisition of independence, and subsequently was instrumental in sponsoring sporadic insurgent activity in the forested Western provinces which border Thailand. There is good reason to believe that such activity, which has increased of late, has been encouraged and promoted also by the governments in Thailand and South Vietnam and at one time by the Central Intelligence Agency. The *Khmer Serai* is an illegal organization in Cambodia. The threat that it presents is of doubtful substance but the facts that it is associated with the traditional enemies of Cambodia and indulges also in personal villification of Sihanouk through a clandestine radio transmitter cause great annoyance to the Cambodian leader. He gives no quarter to any members of the illegal organization apprehended by the Army; they end their days before a firing squad.

Left-wing outer opposition takes concrete form in the *Pracheachon* (People's) Party which was formed by members of the Viet-Minh active in Cambodia. It sought, without success, to contest the 1955 elections but in more recent years has avoided electoral contests. The *Pracheachon* is believed to have a limited membership composed of part-Vietnamese or Cochin-China Khmer. Sihanouk has announced publicly that the political mentors of the *Pracheachon* reside in Hanoi. The party is also accused of association with Left-wing members of *Sangkum*. *Pracheachon* has a tenuous existence. It is not proscribed officially but is subject to a variety of sanctions, including the threat of capital punishment for its members. Sihanouk is in no way disposed towards the objectives of *Pracheachon* but appears disinclined to apply a formal ban on the organization. He seems to feel that it is less of a threat than a totally covert body with perhaps some form of recognized status in Hanoi. *Pracheachon* also provides Sihanouk with a convenient target for nationalist abuse which he exploits at appropriate times.

Both outer opposition groupings have a minimal following within Cambodia and their political significance follows from their external associations.

The category of inner opposition refers to the disparate elements with *Sangkum*. Sihanouk has loosely identified the divisions:

> The *Sangkum* is not a party but a vast assemblage of all the old parties and all the new tendencies. One finds on the right, the old conservatives, the youth of bourgeois origin and men who even regret the renunciation of American aid. Among others, a handful of communists is to be found in the body of the *Sangkum*.[7]

Those whom Sihanouk describes as "a handful of communists" are perhaps more clearly identified as leftist intellectuals. Known colloquially as the *Khmer Rose*, they tend to be drawn in part from the ranks of French-educated university and school teachers and their youthful following. The leftist or progressive intellectuals would appear to be ideologically motivated and attracted to an anti-imperialist ethic as expressed in Sukarno's conception of New Emerging Forces. Over the years, Sihanouk has sought to accommodate the personal ambitions of leftist intellectual leadership even up to cabinet level. This tactic, however, has not been demonstrably successful. Indeed, following the last Cambodian elections, in September 1966, the leading leftists within *Sangkum* refused cabinet office allegedly because of their ideological distaste for the former Army Commander-in-Chief, Lon Nol, as Prime Minister.

The strength of youthful left-wing dissent has been steadily growing, though not necessarily to alarming proportions. This growth has come partly as a result of governmental education policy. Secondary and post-secondary education has boomed in Cambodia as a direct consequence of governmental benefaction. One outcome has been an overabundance of young diploma-holders who feel themselves fitted for the prestige accorded by employment in the bureaucracy. Unfortunately, the necessity of late for financial stringency in Cambodia has reduced the number of openings in the bureaucracy and these openings are not always filled on the basis of achievement. Youthful frustration on the part of those who are temperamentally unsuited to leave urban life may well build up to produce a threatening reservoir of political discontent. For the time being, however, Sihanouk, who can be more anti-imperialist than his intellectual left, has not lost his ability to control his young men. In terms of popular appeal the leftists have yet to make an impact on the National Assembly. In the Legislature election of October 1966 for the position of Prime Minister, their nominee received only 19 votes out of the 163 cast.

The remaining elements within *Sangkum* are less easy to identify in terms of crystallized groupings with perhaps the exception of a moderate leftist wing. The National Assembly which reflects alignments within *Sangkum* is dominated, to use Sihanouk's terminology, by "centre-rightists". They are divided by factional conflict rather than ideological persuasion, and may be described as royalists, right-wingers, some with republican tendencies, and plain self-seekers. A good number may be said to resent the political omnipotence of Sihanouk but, as they are denied access to any extra-elite basis of support, they are obliged to vent their wrath in private. And in this respect the centre-rightists have more recently developed a heightened sense of grievance as a consequence of economic stagnation and a governmental austerity campaign. Financial stringency has its source in the rejection by Cambodia of all forms of American economic assistance at the end of 1963. This assistance was allocated in part as budgetary support, and the benefactions from America enabled the pleasure-loving urban elite of Phnom Penh to enjoy a standard of living beyond the country's real capacity.

An interesting variant of opposition was formally created by Sihanouk in October 1966. The Cambodian leader, for obvious reasons, much prefers a quiescent internal political existence for his country, that is, as far as other people's political activity is concerned. In September 1966 he permitted a degree of innovation from which followed somewhat disturbing consequences. In previous general elections Sihanouk had supervised personally the nomination of *Sangkum* candidates for the various constituencies. And only one *Sangkum* member was permitted to contest, unopposed, each vacant seat in the National Assembly. Sihanouk withdrew this restriction to permit *Sangkum* members to compete among themselves for the vacant seats. The net result was to see the election of a more conservative, testy and independent-minded Assembly, although known opponents of Sihanouk were also returned, to his displeasure. More significantly, Sihanouk forwent also his prerogative to select the cabinet. By a slim majority, the Assembly elected Army Commander-in-Chief, Lon Nol, to the office of Prime Minister and the cabinet which he formed eventually had a strong rightist composition. Sihanouk, apparently, took alarm at this indication of political imbalance beyond desirable limits, and to satisfy his own priorities and to appease a protesting left he announced the formation of a largely extra-Assembly "opposition government" composed of moderate leftists with some radical stiffening. Sihanouk claimed to be seeking the creation of an opposition party within *Sangkum*, from which he would draw a shadow cabinet which would serve to ensure governmental accountability. It would seem that Sihanouk sought not only to provide a check to right-wing government but also to try to institutionalize the checking forces so that left-wing reaction could be given expression within a framework of constraint. Sihanouk sought to create a controlled and organized opposition group to serve his own ends and to act as a political safety valve. Unfortunately for the Cambodian leader, the consequence of this initiative was considerable inter-elite dissension which forced Sihanouk to employ the whole range of his manipulative skills and communicative techniques to try to establish a more tolerable political order. Indeed he was obliged eventually, in May 1967, to take the reins of government into his own hands, and to find a new cabinet outside the National Assembly, in order to quell the unrest among elite circles and also to isolate a more active and allegedly violent leftist group.

This latter initiative serves to demonstrate both the strength and the weakness of Sihanouk's position. He has the ability to resolve intra-elite conflict through personal intervention, but he has been obliged to demonstrate his indispensable role as arbiter on perhaps too many occasions. While this may be flattering to his person, it does not augur well for the stability of the political system.

The Temper of Legitimacy

Legitimacy tends in practice to be a somewhat elusive quality whose constituents are difficult to identify with any precision in terms of a general rule. The regime in Cambodia rests its authority on all three of the ideal grounds advanced by Max Weber. Leadership is respected because of its traditional position: it draws authority from "the eternal yesterday" as personified by "the patrimonial prince of yore". Exceptional personal qualities are displayed by "the plebiscitarian ruler", while the legality of electoral procedure rests "upon a rationally enacted and interpreted constitution".

In practice, legitimacy arises out of the unquantifiable sum of relationships between ruler and ruled. In Cambodia it is demonstrated periodically in ritual manner through a process of referenda and elections.[8] There is, undoubtedly, a clear bond between Prince Sihanouk and the rural people who compose the vast majority of Cambodia's population of six million. They revere him as some sort of latter-day God-King. But their reverence is not only based on the acceptance of immemorial practice but is also a response to a carefully conceived neo-traditionalist role. Sihanouk has gone out of his way to identify himself closely with the life of the rural people, and an aspect of this identification is his patron-like but respectful relationship with the Buddhist orders. These orders are influential in the countryside and possess the potential to interpose themselves between Sihanouk and the rural people. Such an interposition has indeed occurred under the military regime in Burma where it accounts in part for the degree of rural resistance displayed in the face of attempts at innovation. Sihanouk has sought to prevent the development of a comparable situation in Cambodia and consequently associates his person with religious ceremonies connected with the rural agricultural cycle. In this context he has more recently revived the ancient ceremony of ploughing the sacred furrow which is held to coincide with the time of the first rains.

Particularly in relation to the rural population, the leadership qualities of Sihanouk are akin to those identified by Max Weber in his conception of charisma. He is the nation personified, the voice which articulates its hopes and fears and gives expression to national fulfilment. His legendary heroic role in the "Royal Crusade for Independence" and his continuing ability — so far — to ward off the threats of traditional enemies to national territorial integrity add to his political lustre. Sihanouk is also the man associated with the manifold material *realisations of Sangkum* which represent the physical symbols of personal and national achievement. He is the plebiscitarian ruler who exploits such a position to underpin a legal constitutional process of electoral activity to serve personal and national purpose. The legitimacy of the regime in Cambodia derives from princely achievement. It is not just a euphemism for apathetic acquiescence, based on relative absence of grievance like land shortage or peasant indebtedness. It is of a positive character and is demonstrated in terms of popular response and personal rapport as a visible rather than an invisible guardian of the community.

This legitimacy, however, would appear to rest on somewhat shallow foundations. The traditional and legal bases for the exercise of governmental authority derive from the person of Sihanouk rather than from ancient office and constitutional propriety. It is Norodom Sihanouk who, through his personal qualities, is able to invest office and constitution with vitality and significance. He is now in his mid-forties and may well serve as his country's principal political resource for many years to come. Nevertheless his expectation of political life cannot disguise the impermanence of the legitimacy which he has engendered to underpin the exercise of authority. There is no automatic successor with the qualities or appeal of Sihanouk who can be expected to inherit with ease his political kingdom. Sihanouk has a number of sons, some of doubtful character, who in traditional Southeast Asian fashion are candidates for internecine activity. One of these, Naradipo, educated in Peking, has been nominated by his father to succeed him, though in what constitutional capacity, it is none too clear. But there is no guarantee that he will step into his father's shoes nor that he will have the ability to employ his techniques and enjoy the popular appeal of Sihanouk. Political succession is uncertain, and as a consequence the continued stability of the Cambodian political system is far from assured. For the time being, stability and legitimacy derive from the man who enjoys the mandate of most of the people, but who has yet to demonstrate that his indispensability is not a source of future weakness as well as of current strength.

Political Institutionalization

The periodic and public expressions of personal despair by Sihanouk at the degree of intra-elite dissension within Cambodia are indicative of the lack of integration of the Cambodian political system. Prince Sihanouk has been able to promote a surface stability, though not without interruptions, by exploiting his personal resources, but he has failed effectively to institutionalize the political system so that it would be able to sustain his departure without clear prospect of disintegration. His political hold derives from an ability to establish a plebiscitarian relationship with a personal constituency and to deny the disparate and disunited political elite the means and the opportunity to make inroads into this power base. Indeed the lack of unity among the elite, their failure to associate with and to aggregate interests reflects Sihanouk's political strength. Yet even reserves of charismatic strength have their limits. Of late, it would seem that Sihanouk has been obliged to employ all his skill and resources to restore and sustain political equilibrium. There would appear to be a number of explanations. There is the fact of continuing economic crisis, and allied to this evidence of princely failure there has arisen a more vocal sense of youthful frustration directed against those members of the regime who could be more safely criticized in public. Following the assumption of prime ministerial office by Lon Nol, the youthful left became more active, and in April 1967 Sihanouk alleged that some of their number had indulged in violence against provincial guards in a number of places in Battambang Province. Whether this was an expression of what Sihanouk has seen fit to decry as action by "Khmers Viet-Minh" is subject to possible questioning.[9] It was admitted by Sihanouk that there had been criminal administrative neglect in Battambang, which may account for the incidence of violence there. The net outcome, however, was the personal intervention by Sihanouk to arrest what he may have regarded as an impolitic drift to the right and an equally serious reactive response from the left. His more genuine concern was probably expressed when he announced, "what I fear at the end is not so much communism but civil disputes and national disunion". There is clearly dysfunctional activity within the Cambodian body politic which takes the form of what Sihanouk has described as "the endless disputes among the high personages", some of whom he claims "have no time to serve the nation, since they are only busy exchanging slanders and accusations". Through personal intervention Sihanouk has prevented factional rivalry from getting out of hand. However, he shows no sign of being able to eradicate that factiousness which poses a long-term threat to political stability.

Those factious elements within the Cambodian political system seem incapable of genuine co-existence. And Sihanouk is not a bridge between them but rather a father figure who has it in his power only to rebuke, chastise and bring to heel extremely troublesome children. In the case of Cambodia, there is always the prospect that the political system could be transformed as a result of external intervention, but the passing of its father figure, by means natural or otherwise, would seem bound also to lead to fundamental political change. The psychic cement which he has, so far, provided does not appear sufficiently durable to sustain in self-continuing and institutionalized form the political system which was shaped in 1955.

Notes

1. *Neak Cheat Niyum* (The Nationalist), Phnom Penh, 25 August 1963.
2. The Commission reported that "Any informal suggestions that were made by the Commissioners in their individual capacities were meant to persuade the government before it took any final decisions to examine quietly and carefully the problem whether or not the royal reforms were compatible with the international obligations undertaken by Cambodia at the Geneva Conference". *Second Progress Report of the International Commission for Supervision and Control in Cambodia for the period January 1st to March 31st, 1955*, London, H.M.S.O., 1955, Cmd. 9534, p. 15.
3. Prince Sihanouk told Malcolm MacDonald (then British Commissioner General in South-east Asia) in April 1955 that he had considered the possibility of abdication for some time "but that he only decided that the moment for the step had arrived when he was opposed in his wish to alter the constitution". Malcolm MacDonald, *Angkor*, London, 1958, p. 147.
4. Cmd. 9761, p. 17.
5. Quoted in *Kambuja*, Phnom Penh, December 1966, p. 80.
6. *B.B.C. Summary of World Broadcasts*, Part III, The Far East, 7 November 1966, FE/2310/13/12. (Author's italics.)
7. *B.B.C. Summary of World Broadcasts*, 10 November 1966, FE/2313/13/16.
8. See Michael Leifer, "The Cambodian Elections", *Asian Survey*, September 1962.
9. In October 1967 Prince Sihanouk warned Cambodia's so-called number one friend, China, against seeking to inspire communist rebellions and subversion in Cambodia. See *The Times*, London, 6 October 1967.

34

Problems of Authority and Political Succession in Cambodia

The manner of political succession is related intimately to the nature of political authority. Where such authority derives from the qualities of person rather than from those of institutionalised office then the matter of political succession is more likely to present special problems. Indeed, in such circumstances the process of succession may well disrupt the stable functioning of a political system. For this process is less bound by a set of agreed procedures and the changing of the political guard need not necessarily be orderly or peaceful.

This is not to argue that stability is a value to be cherished for its own sake in every political circumstance; nor is there any desire to indicate the most or more desirable process of political change. Nevertheless, where the process of political succession is free from institutionalised procedure the seeds of future disorder are embedded

Reprinted in abridged form from Michael Leifer, "Problems of Authority and Political Succession in Cambodia?", *Nationalism Revolution and Evolution in South-East Asia*, edited by Michael Leifer (Zug: Inter Documentation Company, 1970), pp. 148–74, by permission of the copyright-holder, Centre for South East Asian Studies, University of Hull.

in fertile political soil. The absence of agreed procedures may encourage political competition of an unlimited kind. Political discontinuity and sudden structural change are built in consequences of such situations which tend to be transformed through upheaval rather than orderly ritual. The modern Cambodian political system exhibits the potential for such a process of political change.

A Continuing Problem of Succession

By assuming the office of Head of State of Cambodia, Prince Sihanouk had resolved a crisis of dynastic succession. But the process of solution had avoided rather than dealt firmly with the problem of political succession. A piece of constitutional juggling and resort to plebiscitarian methods had demonstrated the political primacy of Norodom Sihanouk. The events of April to June 1960 had appeared to highlight the indispensable position of the new Head of State. Nevertheless what had been achieved related to the personal qualities of one mortal being and there had not been an attempt at an institutionalisation which would more permanently prop the political system in Cambodia.

Shortly before being sworn in as Head of State, Prince Sihanouk gave an interview to the Cambodian press. He announced "An important aspect of my assignment will be to prepare the 'melting-pot' in which the future sovereign will, if I may be permitted to use the expression, be 'moulded'". He continued:

> In effect if our Monarchy wishes to survive, it must of necessity evolve. The young Prince who will one day ascend the Throne of Cambodia must be a Sovereign who is perfectly aware of the desires and needs of the people. He must for this reason live as often as possible among the people and not be enclosed in a palace, to be exposed to the flattery of courtiers who are skilled in the fashioning of intrigues.[1]

This expression of opinion by Sihanouk was an indication that he understood well enough the temporary nature of the solution to the question of monarchical and political succession. One can sympathise with the course which he adopted. It was undeniable that no member of the royal family would have been able to unite around his person popular support in the manner of a Sihanouk. This fact stands irrespective of whether Sihanouk would have been displeased at such a prospect of unity around one other than himself. Prince Sihanouk is a relatively young man. At the time of the death of his father he was under forty. Given his age and political standing it would have been impolitic and foolhardy to have upset totally an arrangement that worked not only to personal but also the national advantage. The consequence was the Head of State solution. However, he was also not entirely unmindful of the need eventually for orderly succession. And he was soon to appear to make tentative moves to establish a political if not a royal successor.

At the end of 1963, following a tumultuous episode in which Cambodia unilaterally revoked her economic and military assistance agreements with the United States, Prince Sihanouk announced that he wished to be succeeded by a son called Naradipo. This announcement was prompted possibly by the circumstances of the death of President Ngo Dinh Diem of South Vietnam. Sihanouk who is given to melancholia and periodic depression may have felt that his own end was near; hence the necessity to nominate a successor. It seems, however, that this announcement caused some consternation in palace circles especially among mothers of the royal princes. Sihanouk, who though subject to depression has amazing powers of recovery, decided then to moderate his enthusiasm for Naradipo for reasons of personal peace and the lessening need to think about succession. Nevertheless three years later in 1966 he was again to make public reference to Naradipo as his political heir.

The more recent direction of Cambodia's foreign policy has indicated a strong desire to establish a harmonious relationship with the Chinese People's Republic. This desire was based on the expectation that China would become the dominant force throughout Asia and as such she might find it in her interest to interpose her power between Cambodia and her predatory neighbours, particularly the Vietnamese. As part of a process of showing good faith towards communist countries Prince Sihanouk has had various of his sons educated in their schools. But to Peking the capital of the power seen as suzerain in South-East Asia was despatched Prince Naradipo who was to live in the house of Chen-yi, China's foreign minister. It would seem more than coincidence that a personal symbol of continuing legitimacy was to reside in Peking.

Whether or not Naradipo will eventually succeed Sihanouk who is still in his mid-forties is a matter of sheer conjecture at the present time.[2] As a young man in his early twenties Naradipo lacks political experience. Indeed the process of grooming does not seem to have begun with any real seriousness. He does not receive undue prominence in the Cambodian press or in the literature of the Cambodian Ministry of Information and has not begun to be involved in any public acts substituting for his father. He has, therefore, not had so far, the opportunity to try and establish any personal tie among the rural population and to demonstrate special personal qualities which are the basis of Sihanouk's authority. Much will depend upon the inclination of Sihanouk to take initiatives to establish a public image for his son, which in turn depends on his continuing desire or need to promote a son as successor during his lifetime. Sihanouk, who probably finds it difficult, given the aura of deference with which he is continually surrounded, to differentiate at times between his person and the body politic of Cambodia, may well be temperamentally incapable of tolerating what may appear to be a situation of latent competition in his own lifetime. While he may in a thoughtful or intemperate moment initiate the machinery of succession he is as likely to reverse the process almost overnight. If he does decide to go ahead more formally with preparing a son for succession there is no guarantee that such a son will perform in the role expected of him by his father.

If Sihanouk for one reason or another neglects the matter of succession or is unable to control the process of preparation then the issue moves further along the plane of speculation. If, for example, for one reason or another, Prince Sihanouk was to depart the political scene earlier than expected and in precipitate manner, then the prospects for someone like Naradipo would not be promising; nor would the prospects for continuing political stability within Cambodia. One could expect a contest for power and position among factional groupings who might possibly resort to the use of force in the absence of any well-founded claim to legitimacy.

It is possible, although it cannot be assumed, to speak of the Army as a unified element that could seize control in such circumstances. It should be pointed out that Sihanouk has always tried to prevent the crystalization of too unified an army and has sought to neutralize its more striking leaders. Whether the group of up and coming younger colonels would be able to act decisively and in unison cannot be established in advance of events. By and large, the Army is a force for order rather than revolution and its political complexion is not left-wing. The Army has tended to suffer from the break with the United States and some of its leading figures are thought to be unhappy at

Cambodia's close ties with communist countries. Some of its members look back with nostalgia to the days when its budget was provided by the United States and their standard of living and the quality of equipment was much higher. There would appear to be similar sentiments within the civil service whose salaries have been pegged for several years and who have become, in some cases of necessity, embroiled in the activity of corruption.

In any struggle for succession in which Sihanouk does not play a leading role much will depend also on external factors. Although both the Government of North Vietnam and the National Liberation Front of South Vietnam recognized the existing frontiers of Cambodia in the middle of 1967, there is no guarantee that the ambition of a completely communist Indo-China has been foresworn forever. The Chinese for their part have more recently demonstrated greater interest in the internal affairs of Cambodia. Whereas once their attitude towards internal affairs could be described as impeccable, they appeared to modify their position during 1967. Some sources claim that they were actively engaged in promoting subversion through Cambodian proxies.[3] One rationale for more recent Chinese behaviour may be related to the question of political succession in so far as political trends within Cambodia may have indicated to Peking that Sihanouk is losing his grip on the country. Such an assessment is said to have led the Chinese to try and establish a political foothold among restless students and intellectuals in the towns as insurance in the event that Sihanouk is removed by or connives at a right-wing coup, possibly from within the Army.

The more recent upsurge of left-wing activity in Cambodia, following the general elections of September 1966, which has been demonstrated with increasing student involvement and growing factional squabbles within the political elite together with unrest in the provinces[4] is evidence enough, irrespective of any alleged Chinese or Vietnamese involvement, that if Sihanouk departs the political scene in a hurry then the process of political succession could be disorderly.

The problem which is faced in Cambodia derives not only from a failure to institutionalise the process of political succession. The problem derives also from a closely related factor, namely the nature of political authority. Whether the form of this authority is categorised by expressions like plain charismatic or routinized charismatic it is, in terms of the activity of politics, of a kind that inhibits the promotion of orderly succession. Also given the nature of existing authority then a candidate for succession is very likely to be denied the political resources which can enable the creation of genuine legitimacy.

The Cambodian Head of State has moulded the political system which he controls in a way that the political life of the kingdom pivots on him. Although setting off from a traditional base which provides special political assets, his path to success has been created in the main through personal skills.[5] It is Sihanouk who has invested office and constitution with vitality and greater significance. To contain centrifugal forces or to restore what he would regard as political equilibrium Prince Sihanouk draws from time to time, and more frequently of late, on his personal resources. These resources which are demonstrated, for example, in plebiscitarian techniques tend to have a diminishing marginal utility. However, Sihanouk has few other means at his disposal and tends not to think of employing other means to achieve his domestic political ends. Resort to such techniques has a shoring-up effect. In other words the system holds together through the personal skills of Sihanouk. However, although these skills made possible a remoulding of the political system from 1955, their nature and the fact that they are peculiar to Sihanouk gives no guarantee that he has created a going concern which will endure. Instrumental factors are important also in helping to underpin authority and Sihanouk has been only moderately successful in efforts to stimulate the development of the Cambodian economy and in improving the quality of administration especially in the rural areas. One consequence is that Sihanouk is obliged to draw continually on a diminishing political banking account. In such circumstances where he is obliged to over-indulge in well-tried methods which relate to personal as opposed to institutionalised authority the matter of providing for orderly political succession obtains a much lower priority than attempts to stabilise the Cambodian ship of state. Equally important, and irrespective of the degree of difficulty experienced in sustaining the system, the political style of Sihanouk and the world that he has built for himself since 1955 is so Sihanouk-centric that he must find it almost impossible to think beyond. He rules in the tradition of the God-Kings of Angkor past and his style is for the present and not future generations. The prospect of succession itself may well be an unbearable thought and as such the role of living-God tends to inhibit serious consideration of how to pass on the title to rule and to avoid the political upheaval which is likely to be associated with competition for such a mandate.

Notes

1. *Cambodian News,* Canberra, Vol. 1, No. 4, July 1960, p. 3.
2. In reply to a correspondent's question what will happen to the monarchy after you, Prince Sihanouk replied: "It depends on the people's will. They will have to choose between a monarchy with a king and one without. Our monarchy is elective not hereditary. It all depends on the vote of the Council of the Crown. It could be a *de facto* Republic as is the case now."

   To a further question enquiring as to which son he would like to become his successor, he responded: "I have thirteen children, with six daughters. I have no right to choose. I cannot propose either. I must leave the matter for the Council of the Crown to decide freely". *Kambuja,* 15th December, 1968, p. 18.
3. In October 1967, Prince Sihanouk publicly warned Peking, "that any campaign to inspire communist rebellions and create subversion in Cambodia would mean the fall of his own regime and a power takeover by the Army which would turn towards the Americans" *The Times,* London, 6th October 1967.
4. Michael Leifer "Rebellion or Insurgency in Cambodia?" *Current History,* February 1969.
5. Note the comments on the combination of the legacies of monarchical authority and the personalization of power in C G Cour, *Institutions Constitutionelles et Politiques du Cambodge,* Paris, 1865, pp. 124–6.

35

Rebellion or Subversion in Cambodia?

The phenomenon of peasant unrest and rebel activity has not been associated with independent Cambodia. In 1967 and 1968, however, the Cambodian government drew attention to armed challenges to authority in the rural areas which it claimed were "radio controlled" from outside its borders.

The question is whether the process of insurgency which Cambodia has recently experienced is a product of internal circumstances or whether it can be justly attributed to outside intervention. The position of the Cambodian government is categorical. It insists that the uprisings are the direct result of a political decision taken outside Cambodia. "The Khmers Viet Minh are not North Vietnamese but Cambodians converted by the Viet Minh before 1954 when they occupied certain zones of Khmer territory."[1] In other words, the insurgents are Khmer (or part Khmer), but their overall direction is external.[2]

Reprinted in abridged form from Michael Leifer, "Rebellion or Subversion in Cambodia?", *Current History* 56 (February 1969): 89–91; 112–13, by permission of Current History Inc.

There is much to indicate that Cambodia did not experience a peasant uprising *per se* but something else. There would seem to be a connection between radical intellectual leftist opposition in the capital and dissidence in the rural areas. Teachers reportedly left their homes for the *maquis* and certain radical deputies and a significant number of their youthful followers came from a peasant background. There is also evidence of a sophisticated level of urban political organization. Prince Sihanouk has always claimed that organizations directing subversion are the Thailand Patriotic Front and the Pathet Lao, acting as proxies for Peking and Hanoi. As yet there is little by way of hard evidence to substantiate this claim. Sihanouk has said that in the Pailin region of Battambang literature printed in Thai but published in Peking was discovered together with military uniforms. He has revealed also that in Preah Vihear province, Vietnamese agents from Laos have been apprehended. Meanwhile in March, 1968, authorities announced the capture of a junk off the south coast with three Vietnamese on board carrying a large quantity of arms and ammunitions for rebels in Kampot province. However, nothing more by way of such evidence has been produced.

While one would not subscribe to the theory of a general peasant uprising within Cambodia one should not neglect the possibility that there may be circumstances favorable to unrest in some part of the rural areas which are capable of exploitation by organized opposition forces. That said, it is important to point out that Cambodia is distinguished in Southeast Asia by an absence of major social grievances in the rural areas. There is limited peasant indebtedness, while the bulk of agricultural land is held by small-scale independent proprietors.

Since the end of 1963, the state has sought to exercise a complete monopoly in the buying of rice. It is possible that dissatisfaction at the price the government agency is willing to pay for rice compared to the financial gain to be made from smuggling across the South Vietnamese borders is of significance. It may also be true that in some regions peasants and townsfolk have been increasingly resentful of the government-sponsored voluntary manual labour programs, which smack too much of *corvée,* and the constant appeals for financial contributions for *Sangkum* projects, even though these are for public benefit. Finally, there may well be a growing reaction against the well-publicized practice of corruption in government and public service circles; this has been especially emphasized in leftist literature.

Prince Sihanouk has sought to counter the arguments of those who do not see any foreign hand in the Cambodian uprisings.[3] The Prince has gone to great lengths to explain the absence of peasant grievance, and the role of Viet Minh zones along the Cordamome ranges, noting that the alleged peasant rebellion occurred just where the Viet Minh had placed its cells and arms caches.[4]

It would be profitable, at this juncture, to look at another and more concrete case of dissidence. In Ratanakiri province in the northeast, the Cambodian government has claimed that the various hill tribes,[5] equipped with excellent weapons, are in fact secessionists in foreign pay.[6] In the general region of the northeast there is the likelihood of outside and irredentist intervention; for example, in the Lao-peopled Siampang region of Stung Treng province. However, Prince Sihanouk himself offered a convincing explanation for the roots of dissidence in Ratanakiri, noting that the Montagnard population seemed to be less interested in ideological struggles than in isolation. He admitted that they had opposed enforced regroupment which would permit them "to enjoy the social achievements which *Sangkum* offers."[7] A key factor in understanding political behaviour in this region would seem to be Montagnard resistance to threats to their traditional way of life. There might also be resentment of government attempts to settle retired soldiers in this region. It is, of course, possible that tribal dissidence in the northeast is being encouraged by external forces.

While one can raise doubts about the question of foreign intervention in the Cambodian uprisings, the widespread acts of rebellion do not seem to be related entirely to rural issues. The uprisings appear to have urban associations, and political initiative appears to be centered in the capital. Why should this be so, apart from the financing presence of the Chinese Embassy? There can be little doubt that, in spite of the manifold modernizing achievements of the *Sangkum*, a malaise has affected a small but significant proportion of young Cambodians. While educational development, promoted in part by popular demand, has proceeded at a great pace, with the government giving it 20 per cent of its annual budget, it has run ahead of the absorptive capacity of the country. Thus young diploma-holders and contenders for such awards have a deep sense of frustration at the lack of status-job opportunity; they resent most of all that qualifications do not necessarily ensure promotion to positions of responsibility. In the context of other Southeast Asian countries it has been pointed out that

> where there exists an underemployed, educated, politically conscious and highly nationalist youth disappointed in the progress of their own country and finding life frustrating and unrewarding, a great deal of anger can accumulate.[8]

These words were written with special reference to Indonesia and the Philippines, but they are relevant to Cambodia. It has been possible to make a strong ideological appeal to a section of the youth of Cambodia who resent a style of national leadership which denies them political expression.

In the case of Cambodia, there is evidence of interference through the Chinese embassy, probably to consolidate a hold among students and a base in the countryside in case Sihanouk tumbles from the tightrope of external and internal neutrality and the pieces are picked up by the rightist Army leadership. The advent of the Lon Nol government in October, 1966, appeared to herald such a prospect and so precipitated a directed rebellion in well-chosen areas. On the other hand, in urban areas and the countryside there is a situation capable of exploitation by those with the requisite skills and organization. There is certainly an intellectual sophistication among the radical left in the capital and there is most probably a complementary factor in parts of the countryside.

At this point in time, Cambodia is by no means aflame. The government gives the appearance of being in control, while the basis of effective rebel support would appear to be restricted. The rebels have an ability to create conditions of insecurity, but their prospect of success will depend (discounting external factors) not only on the exploitation of genuine grievance but also on an ability to identify with the nationalist cause for which Prince Sihanouk has been the most ardent and passionate advocate. This would seem unlikely.

The political practice of Sihanouk, in any case, is not beyond question,[9] and he may fail to appreciate the relationship between social change and popular expectations and demands and the sense of frustration of those educated young men who oppose his personal style of government.

Notes

1. *Réalités Cambodgiennes,* August 4, 1967.
2. *"Pekin et Hanoi n'ont pas voulu se compromettre directement, mais leur empreinte dans cette affaire est, hélas, trop visible,"* ibid., February 2, 1968.
3. See, for example, M. Jacques Decorney in *Le Monde* (Paris), February 2, 1968.
4. See *Le Sangkum,* August and September, 1968.
5. For a breakdown of the ethnic variety in Ratanakiri see *Kambuja,* March 15, 1968, pp. 44–5.
6. *B.B.C. Summary of World Broadcasts,* F.E./2860/A3/4. It is perhaps significant to note that the scale of insurgency would seem to be larger than in the northeast of Thailand. See J. L. S. Girling, "North-East Thailand: Tomorrow's Viet Nam?" *Foreign Affairs,* January, 1968, p. 396.
7. *Réalités Cambodgiennes,* February 16, 1968.
8. See editorial in *The Times* (London), October 26, 1968.
9. See Michael Leifer, "The Failure of Political Institutionalization in Cambodia," *Modern Asian Studies,* April, 1968.

36

Cambodia and Her Neighbours

Among the successor states of Indo-China, Cambodia stands out in its attitude towards the former colonial power. The French are regarded with less bitterness than might be expected. One explanation for this attitude is that the establishment of the protectorate over Cambodia by France in 1863 is believed to have preserved the independent identity of the country from the territorial aggrandisement of hostile neighbours to the east and west. Located at the southern end of the Indo-Chinese peninsula and opening out on the Gulf of Siam, Cambodia has common boundaries with Laos, Thailand and South Vietnam. The two latter countries, Thailand to the West and South Vietnam[1] to the east, have sustained over the years a variety of belligerent relationships with their mutual neighbour. These unhappy relationships, which more recently have been aggravated because of Cold War alignments, periodically erupt into open conflict. One such episode, involving both Thailand and South Vietnam, occurred in

---

Reprinted in abridged form from Michael Leifer, "Cambodia and Her Neighbours", *Pacific Affairs* 34, no. 3 (1961–62): 361–74, by permission of the University of British Columbia.

October 1961 when Cambodia suspended diplomatic relations with the former country and was involved in troop clashes on the borders of the latter.

Cambodia's immediate fears are directed to its neighbours, Thailand and South Vietnam, which are seen as joined in common endeavour to undermine Cambodian independence now that the protective arm of France is gone. In fact the Cambodian government is firmly convinced, with good reason, that much more than tacit assistance is being given to Cambodian dissidents seeking to overthrow the ruling Popular Socialist Community movement led by Prince Sihanouk and to change the direction of Cambodia's foreign policy. Allegations of plots against the regime emanating from Thailand and South Vietnam with United States backing (as well as from North Vietnam) have been frequent in Cambodia. In these allegations the name of Son Ngoc Thanh always figures prominently, serving in Cambodia the role of a Trotsky or better still an Emmanuel Goldstein.

Early in 1959 two leading Cambodian personalities, Sam Sary, who led the Cambodian delegation to Geneva and had been one time ambassador to London, and General Chhuon Mchulpich, Royal delegate for the province of Siem Reap, were both implicated in a foreign-sponsored plot against the government. It appears that this plot (in which the Cambodian government asserted that not only Thailand and South Vietnam but also the United States were involved) was in some way related to the Cambodian recognition of the Chinese People's Republic in July 1958 — a decision that brought an official expression of displeasure from Washington. On the occasion of this recognition "China regretted the unfriendly acts of some of Cambodia's neighbours in blockading and invading her territory."[2] The Cambodian government is firmly convinced of the involvement of the United States[3] whom she sees as arming Cambodia's neighbours so that they can destroy her. It is partly for this reason that she gives the impression of leaning so heavily toward the Communist camp.

There is no doubt that there are active enemies of the regime, for in August 1959 a bomb, concealed in a parcel sent to the Queen, exploded in an ante-chamber in the Royal Palace, killing the chief of protocol and two other palace staff. Allegations of plots, however, have not been all one-sided. Cambodia is also concerned about the intentions of North Vietnam. During the Indo-China war Viet Minh forces invaded Cambodia in substantial numbers and managed to seize control of a significant section of the Issarak movement. In these activities they were assisted by the Vietnamese minority in Cambodia. The Geneva agreement provided for the complete evacuation of the Viet Minh and did not permit it to retain a foothold (as in the case of Laos). In spite of this, it seems that the North Vietnam regime has been actively connected with the Pracheochon party in Cambodia which follows the Communist line.[4] In spite of his close relations with the Communist powers, Prince Sihanouk has had no hesitation about publicly denouncing the intervention of the North Vietnamese in his country's affairs. In February 1960, while visiting a dam site in the province of Svay Rieng, accompanied by both the Soviet and Chinese ambassadors, Sihanouk claimed publicly that he had abundant proof (including Viet Minh documents) that the Pracheochon party was "working indefatigably for the Communist world and specifically to bring Cambodia under the heel of North Vietnam."[5]

Cambodia's relations with the Chinese People's Republic must be seen as a counter to North Vietnam as well as to Thailand and South Vietnam. There is no doubt that Prince Sihanouk feels that survival for Cambodia depends upon a policy of non-provocation toward Peking. At the same time such a policy brings its benefits, not only in economic aid with which China has been the most generous of Communist-bloc countries, but in support against Thailand and South Vietnam and in restraints placed on the Chinese minority within Cambodia and (it is hoped) on North Vietnam. According to Herz,[6] on Prince Sihanouk's first visit to Peking in 1956 he was informed that if he had any trouble with the Viet Minh he had only to appeal to Peking to have it stopped. On May 6, 1960, at a Royal Khmer Socialist Youth rally Chou En-lai declared publicly, "I can assure you that in the struggle to safeguard national independence you and the whole Cambodian people can count on the unfailing support of 650 million Chinese." At a press conference later in the day when pressed on this point by Reuter's correspondent, he replied, "If there is a threat, no matter where it comes the 650 million people of China are on the side of Cambodia."[7] Cambodia turns to China not merely because it is convinced of the hollowness of SEATO and feels an accommodation in time may preserve national identity[8] but because of the proximity of two enemies, whose patron, the United States, gives no indication of guaranteeing Cambodia's future from them. And in this respect Prince Sihanouk is reported to have declared in October 1961 that he had completely lost confidence in the Americans and was personally ready to break off diplomatic relations.[9]

Cambodia also shares a common border with Laos. However, despite geographic proximity, relations have been generally limited, though friendly. Recent Cambodian interest in Laos has been dictated by reasons of security following the success of the Pathet Lao forces in consolidating their position in the country. Cambodian fears are natural, for if Laos should completely fall to the Communists, Cambodia would have a common frontier with a third antagonist (North Vietnam) easily able to infiltrate the country taking advantage, as before, of Cambodia's Vietnamese minority. For this reason Prince Sihanouk proposed to the U.N. General Assembly in September 1960 the establishment of a neutral zone including Laos and Cambodia which would be guaranteed by the great powers and their allies.[10] It was also the reason why he sought to initiate the Geneva conference on Laos which has so far progressed very slowly. There can, of course, be no doubt that the plan for a neutral guaranteed zone is as much related to Cambodia's differences with South Vietnam and Thailand. However, Cambodia would certainly not wish to see a complete circle of hostility around her, although little optimism is expressed on this score.[11]

Hemmed in and pressed by traditional enemies, Cambodia seeks to preserve its independence using countervailing powers. So far this policy of balance — on the one hand, using China as a counter to Thailand and South Vietnam, and on the other the United States with its aid donations[12] to retain a certain freedom of manoeuvre in dealing with Communists — has paid dividends. This equilibrium, however, hardly appears stable. In the situation of flux that exists today in Indo-China, Cambodia's neighbours to the east and west, who express a pathological dread of Communist expansion, may feel a desperate need to shift the balance in their own favour, at the expense of Cambodia.

Notes

1. South Vietnam (the Republic of Vietnam) only assumed a separate identity from the rest of Vietnam in July 1954 following the Geneva Conference on the future of Indo-China.
2. See Department of External Affairs, *Current Notes on International Affairs,* Canberra, April 1959, p. 181.

3. At a rally on March 2, 1959 Prince Sihanouk gave full details of the plot. Besides referring to Thailand and South Vietnam, he left no doubt that he believed the United States was involved. "Enfin nous devons mentionner les déclarations du second frère de Dap Chhuon, l'exdéputé Slat Peou, révélant qu'il était chargé de prendre des contacts réguliers avec une ambassade d'une "grande nation seatiste"... J'ai érit au President Eisenhower pour demander l'intervention des Etats-Unis pour stopper ce patronage illégal de nos voisins." Ministère de l'Information, *Principaux Discours et Allocations de S.A.R. Le Prince Norodom Sihanouk en 1959*, Phnom Penh (no date), pp. 24–25. See also speech to Asia Society, New York, on September 26, 1961 (reprinted in *Réalités Cambodgiennes*, October 20, 1960).

4. A. Doak Barnett, *Communist China and Asia*, New York, 1960, p. 482.

5. See *Cambodian Commentary*, March 1960, p. 7. Prince Sihanouk has also announced publicly details of a secret Communist conference held in Cambodia at the end of 1959 linked with North Vietnam. For details of alleged Communist plot to assassinate Prince Sihanouk, see *Cambodge d'Aujourd'hui*, February 1960.

6. M. F. Herz, *A Short History of Cambodia*, London, 1958, p. 127.

7. *Cambodian Commentary*, April–May 1960, pp. 22 and 34.

8. See editorial "Avoiding the Inevitable," *Manchester Guardian Weekly*, August 3, 1961.

9. *The Times* (London), November 7, 1961.

10. *Cambodian Commentary*, August 1961, p. 12.

11. On anxieties over the Laotian crisis, see R. M. Smith, "Cambodia's Neutrality and the Laotian Crisis," *Asian Survey*, July 1961.

12. Cambodia with her neutral posture accepts aid from both the Communist bloc and the West, on the understanding that no strings are attached. The largest Communist donor, China, began the process of giving aid in 1956 with an initial grant equivalent to $22.4 million in the form of factories, commodities and technical assistance. This association worsened Cambodia's relations with her neighbouring antagonists. The Soviet Union plays a lesser role and has not been so generous; apart from occasional gifts presented on Prince Sihanouk's visits to Russia, it has concentrated its aid on one hospital project (the Khmer-Soviet Hospital of Friendship). The United States is the largest donor to Cambodia and has provided military assistance almost from independence, as has France. America's outstanding contribution has been the construction of a highway linking Phnom Penh, the capital, with Sihanoukville, the new seaport built with French aid to remove undue dependence on Saigon and Bangkok. Foreign aid has been mentioned in the above article only where it throws light on the relations between Cambodia and her neighbours. In this connection, it should be noted that Cambodia's receiving aid from both sides in the cold war serves to intensify differences. Both Thailand and South Vietnam

find it difficult to accept the fact Cambodia should receive aid from their ally, the United States, while at the same time encouraging, so they believe, the advance of Communist influence in Southeast Asia.

37

Kampuchea in 1980
The Politics of Attrition

The nature of the protracted conflict within and over Kampuchea has made it most unlikely that any form of political settlement can precede a decisive change in the military fortunes of the belligerent parties. In practical terms, such a change would mean either the elimination of the Khmer Rouge resistance or the inability of the Vietnamese to sustain their expeditionary force in the field, whether as the direct result of a loss of political will or from their Soviet patron's unwillingness to continue in the role of quartermaster. Neither of these two prospects materialized during the course of the year. The Vietnamese expeditionary force has remained entrenched within Kampuchea, sustained and reinforced by Soviet benefaction but without being able to destroy the military arm of the Khmer Rouge. For their part, the Khmer Rouge have demonstrated a resilient capacity for survival as a viable insurgency but have not posed a major immediate threat to the security of the government in Phnom Penh. Nonetheless that capacity

Reprinted in abridged form from Michael Leifer, "Kampuchea in 1980: The Politics of Attrition", *Asian Survey* XXI, no. 1 (1981), pp. 93–101, by permission of the University of California Press.

for survival has been significant in servicing a process of attrition designed to inflect a breaking strain on Vietnamese society.

An anticipated dry season offensive by the Vietnamese did not occur in any conventional sense. Counterinsurgency operations were stepped up from the beginning of 1980 in western Kampuchea with the object of exercising more effective control of the border area with Thailand. Limited sweeps were undertaken but actual engagements were not decisive. For example, in January an attack was launched on a Khmer Rouge position at Phnom Chat north of Poipet which could not be pressed home because the defending force was able to retreat through mined and booby-trapped jungle: Less accessible Khmer Rouge redoubts to the south in the Phnom Malai and the Cardamom Mountains were not the object of direct attack.

The scale, mobility, and disposition of Khmer Rouge deployment did not make for conventional search and destroy operations. Above all, the continued porous quality of the extensive border with Thailand enabled the Khmer Rouge to avoid unnecessary confrontation and to have ready access to sanctuary and material supply. This facility served to restore their vitality as a fighting force during the course of the 1979–1980 dry season. Their forces were estimated at over 30,000 at the outset of the 1980 wet season, well provided with Chinese equipment including field radios which sustained an intact command structure.

In an attendant diplomatic initiative, Kampuchea was firmly incorporated within an Indochinese international front inaugurated in January when the foreign ministers of Vietnam, Laos, and Kampuchea convened a meeting in Phnom Penh during celebrations marking the establishment of the People's Republic. On that occasion, they offered to engage jointly in an exchange of views and to sign nonagression treaties with the governments of the Association of Southeast Asian Nations (ASEAN) and Burma. A reluctance to intrude into a special relationship dominated by Vietnam may account for the failure of Kampuchea and the Soviet Union to enter into a standard treaty of friendship when Heng Samrin paid an official visit to Moscow in February. Foreign Minister Hun Sen explained that Kampuchea was not yet ready to sign such a treaty, although it was evidently in a position to conclude one with the East German government in March.

The ruling People's Revolutionary Council established in January 1979 had been cobbled together from disparate political elements at short notice. It became evident that Heng Samrin's formal position as its president did not correspond to the actual exercise of power or with the standing of its members in the eyes of the Vietnamese guardians of the state. In February, when Heng Samrin undertook an official visit to the Soviet Union, he appeared to be accorded lesser political regard than his accompanying Vice President and Minister for Defense, Pen Sovan, who was believed to enjoy closer ties with Hanoi and its greatest trust. Rumors of Heng Samrin's political demise were reinforced in April when there was no reference to his participation in the national day celebrations. In the event, this proved to be only a temporary absence from public life. Indeed, it has been suggested that the reason for the continued maintenance of the formal hierarchy of the People's Revolutionary Council with Heng Samrin at its apex has been the close identification of Pen Sovan with the Vietnamese masters of Kampuchea.

In January, Heng Samrin rejected the possibility of broadening his government's base to give it a more neutral aspect. In a speech marking the first anniversary of Pol Pot's overthrow, he dismissed suggestions that the administration be widened to include non-Communist Khmer groups. In June, seventeen captured members of the anti-Communist *Khmer Sereika* movement were tried in Phnom Penh and received jail sentences of three to twenty years for antigovernment activities. These trials appeared to indicate the end of any prospect for accommodation with the most credible of these groups — namely, the Khmers People's National Liberation Front led by Son Sann — on the basis of a common repudiation of Pol Pot. During the course of the year, recurrent armed clashes in refugee camps along the Thai border between followers of rival warlord leaders over control of smuggling rights and international relief aid served to discredit every non-Communist resistance group except that led by Son Sann. At its first national congress held somewhere in Battambang Province in April, the Khmers People's National Liberation Front rejected participation in a united front with the Khmer Rouge, if not refusing a de facto nonaggression agreement. The general political acceptability of Son Sann's organization in Western chancelleries, embarrassed by the need to proffer diplomatic support to so-called Democratic Kampuchea, has not been matched by any demonstration of military capability within Kampuchea. In addition, its political standing has suffered because of a failure to attract the adherence of Prince Norodom Sihanouk. Prince Sihanouk engaged in an abortive attempt to promote a political settlement in the early months of the year but admitted on his return to Beijing in April that he did not have the means to act. Once again in Beijing in October after interrupting a stay in Pyongyang, he maintained that "in no case and in no circumstances" would he consent to play any political role in his country's future.[1] The government in Phnom Penh sustained a hostile attitude to Prince Sihanouk whom Pen Sovan denounced as a traitor in a speech in Battambang Province in October.

The Khmer Rouge persisted without any success in an attempt to redeem their reputation and to promote a united front in opposition to Vietnam's occupation of Kampuchea. In December 1979, Pol Pot relinquished the office of Prime Minister in the ousted Democratic Kampuchean Government in favour of Khieu Samphan, its head of state. This transfer of power proved to be no more than a cosmetic political exercise. It was announced concurrently that Pol Pot would remain Supreme Military Commander, while in August it was revealed that Pol Pot had continued in office as Secretary General of the Kampuchean Communist Party. In a press conference for Western journalists, Khieu Samphan acknowledged that the Khmer Rouge experience was "a murderous utopia." He explained that Communism was dead and that "to reject Communism once and for all is undoubtedly the best way of uniting all Kampucheans in the anti-Vietnamese crusade as part of a national front."[2] By the end of the year, no such national front had materialized. The military resilience of the Khmer Rouge was not matched by its political standing. Indeed, within Kampuchea the legacy of its bestial rule has served as the decisive negative source of tolerance for a Vietnamese imposed government. As one observer commented, "It is difficult to stop at any hamlet along Kampuchea's highways without being led by people — some silent in their anger, others weeping — to the graves. Each village seems to have its local Auschwitz. ..."[3]

The Vietnamese military incursion into Thailand in June and the Vientiane resolution in July indicated that the principal priority of the Heng Samrin government and its Vietnamese patron was international recognition which conflicted with the priorities of the international relief agencies. An objective of the military action and the subsequent political initiative was to ensure that all international relief operations be conducted exclusively through dealings with the government in Phnom Penh. They reflected concern not only about a portion of relief aid reaching the Khmer Rouge but also at the attraction of the "land bridge" in undermining the authority of the Kampuchean government. Initially, the international relief agencies gave in to demands that they should cease their operations along the border with Thailand and that they should concentrate their efforts within Kampuchea in liaison with the government in Phnom Penh. However, the Thai government's refusal to allow its territory to be used as a base for relief operations directly aiding the Heng Samrin government as well as U.S. pressure led to the reversal of this decision. After a compromise formula had been arrived at whereby aid deliveries along the Thai border would not take place at points of Khmer Rouge control, relief operations were resumed at the end of July.

In November, representatives in Bangkok of the International Committee of the Red Cross and of the United Nations Children's Fund indicated their wish to terminate their food distribution program both within Kampuchea and along the border with Thailand, the former by the end of 1980 and the latter by March 1981. A major improvement in conditions within Kampuchea was the official explanation given for this change of policy. A UNICEF representative maintained that the number of Kampucheans bringing ox carts to border points to pick up food and supplies had fallen from about 12,000 to 700 over a recent three week period.[4] Nonetheless, the problem of supplementary feeding had not been overcome. Although the government in Phnom Penh had undoubtedly made an effort to convey rice seed to the countryside, it has been estimated that only about 65% of the normal peacetime crop had been sown, which is unlikely to provide a sufficient harvest for basic needs in 1981.

If the spectre of famine has been lifted from Kampuchea, it remains a debilitated, broken, dependent state. Its administration comprises a heterogeneous group of survivors of Pol Pot's holocaust whose common denominators are rudimentary skills and, increasingly, acceptability to the Vietnamese. Its shortcoming in economic management were aired by Heng Samrin in August when he mentioned embezzlement, theft, graft, and bribery by government officials.[5] The shadow of the Khmer Rouge has not been removed from Kampuchea and continues to impose a terrible irony and contradiction on the protracted conflict over the state's identity. The Khmer Rouge represent the only viable direct military challenge to Vietnamese dominance but are an unacceptable political alternative for ASEAN members and their Western sympathizers who achieved an ephemeral diplomatic success in the United Nations in October. Nonetheless, resistance to Vietnam's design in Indochina requires the bloody instrument of the Khmer Rouge.

This conclusion represented the evident outcome of discussions conducted during the visit to China by Thailand's Prime Minister, General Prem Tinsulanond, at the end of October.

Notes

1. *The Times* (London), October 20, 1980.
2. Joel Henri in *The Times,* August 21, 1980.
3. Nayan Chanda in *Far Eastern Economic Review,* April 4, 1980.
4. *The Times,* November 13, 1980.
5. *International Herald Tribune,* August 18, 1980.

38

The Anguish of Cambodia

Some six years ago, I concluded a book on the foreign policy of Cambodia by suggesting that "Through determined, if unconventional, leadership, it [Cambodia] has been able to avoid the cauldron of conflict. Through a policy that combines long-term priorities and pragmatic day-to-day decisions, it has preserved an independent existence — no mean achievement in the environment of Indochina. This existence is still tenuous, and the danger is far from removed that the modern Khmer State will suffer the same unfortunate fate as its illustrious forebear."[1]

I cannot derive any comfort from the fact that the apprehensions so expressed have been confirmed by the events of the past three years; a period which has been marked by a tragic violation of a once self-styled "Peaceful oasis in the inferno of South-East Asia". Today, Cambodia is a stricken and broken state, its villages and towns have been ravaged by war, its capital has been subject to recurrent siege and

Reprinted from Michael Leifer, "The Anguish of Cambodia", *Asian Affairs* 60, no. 3 (1973): 270–79, by permission of Taylor and Francis Limited <http://www.tandf.co.uk/journals>.

its people have experienced a horrifying torment. The fact of Cambodia's state of anguish is very much self-evident and I do not propose to dwell upon this condition. What I hope to do is to consider the sources of this sorry state of affairs.

There is no doubt to my mind that the critical factor which brought Cambodia to its current tortured conditions was the deposition of Prince Norodom Sihanouk on 18 March 1970. Although his political downfall was essentially a product of domestic grievance, the circumstances surrounding this event, in particular the blatant challenge by his successors to the interests of the Vietnamese Communists, meant that the transfer of power from a quasi-monarch to a civil-military oligarchy — not in itself an exceptional happening — had immediate repercussions beyond the confines of the Khmer State which rebounded back on it in a devastating manner. The consequence was to draw Cambodia into the vortex of a conflict which had long afflicted the other states of Indochina.

The prior pacific condition of Cambodia, perched precariously on the sidelines of that conflict, had been preserved by Prince Sihanouk through a policy of political accommodation to the Vietnamese Communists premised on a belief that they would, in time, seize power in Saigon. They had come to use Cambodia as a military sanctuary and staging post, as a source of rice and as a corridor for the trans-shipment of military supplies; a facility provided through the good offices of both the Cambodian Government and Army. Following the military failure of the Tet offensive of January–February 1968, Cambodia became of increasing importance to the Communists as a sanctuary zone. However, from the early part of 1969, Prince Sihanouk began to articulate his second thoughts about the benefits accruing from his policy of accommodation as the alleged scale of Vietnamese Communist transgressions of Cambodian soil reached a level totally incompatible with their protestations of respect for the country's territorial integrity. Although Sihanouk complained publicly of these intrusions and modified the direction of his policy by closing the port of Sihanoukville to Communist military traffic and by re-establishing diplomatic relations with the United States, he refrained from pushing the issue to an open break because he was certainly aware that Cambodia did not possess the military resources with which to challenge the Communists. Indeed, his visits to Moscow and Peking in March 1970 were apparently intended to enable him to solicit diplomatic assistance over the matter of intrusions. Those who acted to depose Sihanouk, however, were less prudent. They used the issue of the Vietnamese Communist presence to dispute his authority and at the same time went far beyond the politic limits of Sihanouk's diplomacy.

The question of the degree of prudence displayed by Sihanouk's successors is a matter of some interest, as there has been both allegation and speculation about expectations of external assistance held by them in so blatantly challenging the Vietnamese Communists in the process of overthrowing the Cambodian head of state. It is difficult to find appraisals of this likelihood from either disinterested or untainted sources. However, Professor Milton Osborne has been able to establish the probability of prior collusion between Premier Lon Nol and Son Ngoc Thanh, Sihanouk's long-standing adversary and rival in exile in South Vietnam. Thanh is believed to have promised to furnish military assistance in the form of ethnic Cambodians serving with South Vietnamese Special Forces units to meet the possible danger of action by either Sihanouk loyalists in the Cambodian Army or Vietnamese Communists in the event of a coup attempt. This collusive association was confirmed by Son Ngoc Thanh in Phnom Penh during 1971 in interviews granted to Timothy Allman which were published in *The Guardian*. In one of these interviews Thanh went so far as to assert that the United States had pledged advance support for the coup group. What he meant by the United States, that is the level of authority concerned, has not been made clear. However, one should take note of Professor Osborne's comment on his own inquiries that if his source of information (the brother of Son Ngoc Thanh) was reliable then "This appears to be a solid reason for believing that the South Vietnamese military authorities and through them the United States military authorities must have had some advance notice of the intended confrontation (and subsequent coup) in Cambodia."[2] On the question of actual support, as far as I have been able to ascertain, some ethnic Cambodians serving with South Vietnamese Regional Forces were moved across the border before Sihanouk's deposition but units of Special Forces were not identified in Cambodia until April 1970.

I should point out, at this juncture, that I am not entirely convinced that the episode in Cambodia which began with inspired demonstrations against the Vietnamese Communists was necessarily predestined to lead to the overthrow of Prince Sihanouk. Indeed, the actual process of the coup had a less than planned look about it and appears to have been accelerated by the conduct of Sihanouk's supporters in Phnom Penh seeking to pre-empt such a prospect. However, irrespective of the precise design of those who toppled Sihanouk, whether they had intended initially to reduce him to a constitutional figurehead or whatever, the prior action of men who must have known full well the bedraggled condition of the Cambodian Army and who still persisted with risking a direct confrontation with the Vietnamese Communists leads me to suggest two possibilities, The blatant challenge was the product of either a Canute-like defiance or an expectation that appropriate external assistance would be forthcoming if necessary. Whatever the assumption,[3] those who deposed Sihanouk pushed the modification of his policy beyond the limits of accommodation and in the process roughly set aside an uneasy *modus vivendi* with the Vietnamese Communists.

The reaction of the Communists was an unequivocal assertion of their interests. It was alleged in Hanoi that: "The Lon-Nol-Sirik Matak Group, henchmen of the U.S., has staged a coup d'état which was a hostile act directed against the Cambodian people and the patriotic struggle of the Vietnamese people."[4] For the Vietnamese Communists, it became imperative to find a basis of legitimacy for their continuing essential use of Cambodia and which would facilitate a challenge to a government construed as a threat to their interests. The arrival of Prince Sihanouk in Peking on the morrow of his deposition proved to be a fortuitous event. The Chinese Government, eager to outbid the Soviet Union in competition for the political affections of the Vietnamese Communists, assumed the role of broker. They pandered to the affronted Sihanouk and, the day after his arrival in Peking from Moscow, brought him together with Pham Van Dong, the North Vietnamese Premier. The outcome of this sponsored meeting was the announcement on 23 March of a Cambodian National United Front under the titular leadership of Sihanouk. It was this body which was to provide the façade of national liberation for the military and political activities of the Vietnamese Communists in Cambodia.

The circumstances of military conflict in South Vietnam together with the expectation of armed intervention across the border, given the Cambodian Government's radical change of policy, made secure use of Cambodian territory a vital necessity to serve the long-standing priority of the Communists to seize power in Saigon. In response to signs of co-ordinated military action between South Vietnamese and Cambodian soldiers, the main force units of the Communist army moved deep into the north-east of the country away from the main threat, while smaller formations took action to neutralize the lesser one and in the process cut like scythes through the under-strength and ill-equipped Cambodian Army. They not only extended speedily their existing control in the north-east and undermined further the flimsy administrative structure linked to Phnom Penh, but also pressed close to the capital which by the end of April 1970 seemed to be in danger of falling into Communist hands. It was at this juncture that military intervention by South Vietnam and the United States appeared to stave off the prospect of imminent collapse and to stabilize the military situation, although, in effect, it did not serve as a major hindrance to Communist purpose in Cambodia.[5] In consequence, the sense of alarm in the Cambodian capital gave way to one of growing confidence and even a measure of euphoria, even though it was evident to disinterested observers that the initiative rested with the Communists who had succeeded in establishing an iron curtain across part of the country, behind which they could reorganize and refurbish their military machine and also set to work to promote a Cambodian insurgent force based on the Khmer Rouge movement which Sihanouk had sought to crush in the years preceding his overthrow.

If the popular reaction to the fall of Sihanouk within the Cambodian capital had been somewhat muted, the onset of physical confrontation with the Vietnamese Communists engendered a patriotic fervour and a sense of ethnic solidarity, especially among the young who rallied with enthusiasm to the support of the Lon Nol Government. Although the sudden transfer of power had been a confusing experience, in particular for the Cambodian peasantry, the Government had no difficulty in recruiting to expand its army from an ineffectual 30,000-odd. Indeed, the new recruits went off to war like children on a coach outing, although instead of coaches they were conveyed in Pepsi-Cola lorries.

The enthusiasm and indeed the solidarity which was so striking a feature of the middle of 1970 did not last for very long. And it was not many months before these feelings gave way to a sense of disillusionment which was succeeded in time by one of despair. The answer to the question, what went wrong, is not a pleasant one.

Fundamental to any explanation is the fact that irrespective of demonstrations of courage by Cambodian soldiers in facing traditional antagonists in new guise, they were rarely equal to the task. Military and economic assistance received from the United States and its allies was never sufficient in itself to compensate for the lack of elementary skill and experience in conducting military operations. And despite the provision of training facilities, the balance of military advantage was never at any time redressed. In addition, the initial sense of expectation of what could be achieved merely by putting recruits into uniform was quite mistaken in the circumstances. Perhaps the most serious miscalculation was the belief that it was possible to take an early and conventional military initiative with this people's army to force the Vietnamese Communists out of areas which they saw as vital to their purpose.

In September 1970 an offensive was launched northwards along route six in an attempt to relieve the siege of the provincial capital, Kompong Thom. By the end of the year it had become obvious that this action had failed because of an inability to match and master tactics well tested and applied by the Vietnamese Communists over many years. One result of that experience was a decision to forgo large-scale operations and to concentrate instead on smaller actions designed to clear territory in the vicinity of Phnom Penh. However, in the event, the lesson of operation Chenla I was not learnt by those who commanded Cambodia's Army. In September 1971 operation Chenla II was launched with, once again, the aim of securing route six through to Kompong Thom, at least for the period of the rice harvest. This operation had its outcome in a disorderly retreat in which the allegedly best trained units in the Cambodian Army were destroyed as a fighting force. The rout was so complete that the American Air Force was obliged to bomb abandoned equipment to prevent it falling into Communist hands. This disastrous episode shattered the morale of the Cambodian Army and undermined confidence in its leadership. And it does not appear to have recovered from what was then its worst defeat in 20 months of war. Indeed, only last week men from its allegedly crack Seventh Division deserted the western defences of the capital to demonstrate with firearms in its streets about arrears of pay.

In 1971 there was a marked decline in security. Phnom Penh became subject to intermittent rocket attack and terrorist violence, communications were regularly disrupted and the administrative subtraction of the countryside from the government in the capital continued without effective challenge. The economy of the city, swelled by an influx of refugees, was sustained only by infusions of external economic assistance. Vietnamese Communist purpose by this time was not the investment of the capital but the promotion of dissension within it. Signs of political decay became visible following the illness of Lon Nol in February 1971.

The political problems which have so beset the successor ruling group in Cambodia were a consequence in great part of the extension of war in Indochina. If Cambodia had not been caught up in the vortex of military conflict in the wake of Sihanouk's overthrow, then his successors might have been able to act with greater purpose and authority and to utilize the sense of political liberation felt by the urban élite of Phnom Penh to provide a semblance of good government. In the event, they were overwhelmed by the repercussions of their action in deposing Sihanouk. And in a context where legitimacy was an elusive quality, Cambodian political life reverted to the factional wrangling characteristic of the parliamentary system promoted in Phnom Penh by the French after the Second World War.

The failure of the successors of Sihanouk was a product also of the legacy which Sihanouk bequeathed to his country. The exiled Cambodian leader had possessed an ultra-Gaullist view of the state which he was unable to dissociate from his flamboyant person. He never made a serious attempt to institutionalize authority or to provide for the prospect of his political passing. For Sihanouk, the essential political relationship was between himself and the people, perceived as a constituency in the abstract. Thus, he castigated members of the French-educated urban élite, whom he suspected rightly of wanting to usurp his position, by charging that they were "neither Prince nor people" and therefore automatically excluded from effective participation in the political order which he had ordained.

By March 1970 the authority of Sihanouk had become eroded through his own egotistical and temperamental shortcomings. But it was an authority none the less which possessed a country-wide relevance. In removing him and at the same time opting for a confrontation with the Vietnamese Communists, his successors had removed a viable source of national authority in circumstances where the prospect of establishing an effective alternative with any speed was exceedingly unlikely. Initially, it did appear as if the political vacuum left by Sihanouk's overthrow might be filled by the person of Lon Nol whose demeanour and humble origins appeared suitable for the occasion. He appeared to enjoy the confidence of the people of Phnom Penh and especially that of the young educated but underemployed class who had so resented the suffocating omnipotence of Sihanouk with whom they associated the denial of their career prospects. Indeed, it was in an attempt to consolidate the loyalty of these young men that the cabinet which deposed Sihanouk was reshuffled in July 1970. It had not escaped notice that those who had united to remove Sihanouk had all served him in varying capacities and indeed were, in many respects, his place men. They could have been but little else in the political system which he had fashioned to his own design from 1955. The new rulers of Cambodia were not new brooms, if initially they sought to give the impression that their purpose was to sweep clean, especially the corrupt practices which had become a hallmark of Sihanouk's family circle.

The sense of euphoria which appeared to grip the urban élite of Phnom Penh in the middle of 1970 was allegedly matched by the measure of solidarity among Sihanouk's successors. Indeed, towards the end of the year a reputable British weekly reported that the unity and cohesion of government was refreshing and that the factionalism and intrigue of Saigon were lacking in Phnom Penh. The actual substance of this solidarity was shown to be fragile when Lon Nol returned to Phnom Penh in April 1971 from hospital in Hawaii, a frail and partially paralysed figure. With his illness, the reins of power had been taken up by his deputy, Sirik Matak, a cousin of Prince Sihanouk from the cadet branch of the Royal family. Sirik Matak's administrative style together with his Royal associations aroused resentment among the urban élite and in particular from a faction of the military led by Lon Nol's brother, Lon Non. The ensuing cabinet crisis of April 1971 not only brought above the surface the fragility of political association in Phnom Penh but also indicated that continuing adversity had begun to erode the apparent resilience of the people of Phnom Penh. The return of Lon Nol was marked by a wave of criticism about the alleged inefficiency and authoritarian tendencies of government. It was charged that too many of Sihanouk's nominees had remained in office and that corruption was as rife as ever. The enthusiasm which had been noted in the previous year had by now waned perceptibly, especially among the educated young men, and their criticisms and sense of alienation were reflected in the press and in the National Assembly.

The cabinet crisis had been precipitated by the resignation of Lon Nol which served as a means to dissolve the Government. Two weeks later, after much political wrangling, a cabinet was formed which included eight new faces as a sweetener to dissenting opinion. Sirik Matak, however, who had become a figure of some controversy, continued in office as acting Premier with Lon Nol retaining the titular position. This solution served only to intensify factional conflict in which Lon Non acted ostensibly in the interests of his stricken brother and contended for power from a military base, especially against Sirik Matak. The course of the war and the attendant disruption of the economy served only to encourage political dissent and the relationship between Government and National Assembly came to resemble the bickerings of two decades earlier which Sihanouk had found so exasperating. As the capital came to be cut off physically more and more from the provinces while subject to the intermittent terror of the Vietnamese Communists and their Khmer associates, the factional conflict in Phnom Penh was played out almost as if the state of war did not exist.

Concurrent with the onset of factional feuding, the Government assumed a more authoritarian position. Thus in October 1971 the National Assembly was stripped of its legislative powers and converted involuntarily into a constituent assembly whose endeavours were subsequently disregarded. A striking feature of this episode was a protest by Buddhist monks at the curtailment of the powers of the National Assembly. At the outset of the post-Sihanouk period, the Government had taken great care to associate the *Sangha* with its new political order as it was well aware of their status in Khmer society and of the extent to which Sihanouk had deferred to them. Indeed the bonzes were contemplated as a major resource for generating a sense of national resistance against the Vietnamese Communists. The fact of a Buddhist demonstration against the government of the day, however inspired, did not augur well. And by the end of the year government repression against its opponents in the capital was stepped up. It seems that the prospect of a coup following the military disaster of operation Chenla II, which was attributed to the ineptitude of Lon Nol, was staved off by an American threat to withdraw all assistance.

The resolution of one phase of factional wrangling took place in March 1972 when Lon Nol assumed the position of head of state and Sirik Matak was forced from office following student demonstrations directed against him. Presidential and general elections of a dubious kind succeeded each other in June and September and confirmed Lon Nol in office and made his brother's Social Republic Party the unopposed master of the National Assembly. By now the alliance of political forces which had overthrown Sihanouk was in disarray and government was concentrated in the ailing person of Lon Nol and in the hands of

Lon Non, even though the somewhat mysterious figure of Son Ngoc Thanh served for several months as Premier. This outcome had relevance only to a closed political circle and a more significant indicator of the decline of governmental fortunes was the food riot which took place in Phnom Penh in September 1972 and which was led by members of the Cambodian Army.

Following the signing of the Vietnam peace settlement in January 1973, there were expectations, expressed, for example, by Dr Kissinger, that a cease-fire would be instituted in Cambodia. Indeed, the Lon Nol Government took the initiative in unilaterally committing itself to a cease-fire and to negotiations with its Cambodian adversaries. The response was a military offensive which produced a situation even more threatening than in the closing days of April 1970, with the capital under siege and economic blockade. According to Prince Sihanouk, the point of the operation was not the military investment of the capital but the application of sufficient pressure to make it fall "like a ripe fruit". In the event, close support and carpet bombing by the United States Air Force and the provision of military cover for convoys of essential supplies up the Mekong staved off the immediate danger. However, one consequence of this offensive was to demonstrate that the Cambodian Government was in no position to contemplate negotiations unless the object was an unconditional surrender.

A further consequence within Phnom Penh was the resignation of the Government and the removal of Lon Non, most probably in response to American pressure. Such pressure was almost certainly responsible also for the decision by Lon Nol to suspend the one-party National Assembly and to form at the end of April a "High Political Council" composed of himself, Cheng Heng, the head of state after Sihanouk, Sirik Matak, his former deputy, and In Tam, his closest opponent in the presidential elections. This so-called broadening of the political base represented, in effect, a reassembly in uneasy coalition of the principal parties to the deposition of Prince Sihanouk and hardly a group capable of negotiating with an insurgent body which had just reaffirmed its support for the exiled Cambodian leader. In addition, the delay of almost a month in the formation of a coalition cabinet to be headed by In Tam was a clear indication of the political fissures within the Cambodian political élite. It would seem that mortal danger was less than sufficient to produce a measure of unity and cohesion among this discordant group whose aptitude for wrangling among themselves merits comparison with the fiddling of Nero. In three years a government of an apparently resolute kind has become a feeble mendicant maintained in office in its capital by an external patron who finds it necessary to devastate the countryside to save Phnom Penh.

Whether the successors of Sihanouk would have conducted themselves much differently if circumstances had been different is too academic a question and one which leads solely to speculation. What is evident is that Cambodia has become the victim of a wider conflict. For the United States it served initially as a buffer with which to facilitate the application of the Nixon Doctrine in Vietnam, but it has now become caught up in the complexities of the "peace with honour" formula. President Nixon has claimed that "The Cambodian situation is a serious threat to the hard-won peace in Vietnam" and has promised continued American air support and appropriate military assistance, as he put it, "if Hanoi still pursues aggression in Cambodia".[6] For the Vietnamese Communists Cambodia serves still as a military staging post and as a pressure point to assist their major political purpose. It would seem that, to this end, the Vietnamese Communists have been able to promote a Khmer political structure in the provinces and to recruit a Khmer military force of growing proportions. Certainly in the fighting this year in the vicinity of Phnom Penh, it appears that significant numbers of Cambodians have been engaged in concert with Vietnamese Communist stiffening.[7]

Following his return from a tour of the "liberated areas" within Cambodia which Prince Sihanouk claimed to have made in March this year through the good offices of the Vietnamese Communists, he announced that he had been recognized by the Khmer Rouge and the Vietnamese Communists as the leader of national resistance and as head of state. Such recognition might seem to be superfluous given the claims for unity made at the time of the formation of the National United Front. The need three years later to reaffirm recognition of the status of Sihanouk tends to confirm that there have been striking differences among the antagonists of the Lon Nol Government — as indeed Sihanouk himself has remarked on from time to time. It suggests also that the Khmer Rouge have found it expedient to set aside their true feelings for Prince Sihanouk because they have need of his personal authority to mobilize popular support. Whatever the intrinsic weakness of the United Front led by Sihanouk, it provides little comfort for the Government in Phnom Penh for his shadow remains over Cambodia. Whatever the deficiencies of his rule, it is one which Cambodians cannot but associate with peace by contrast to the present condition of their country which has been so laid waste by war in the three years since his overthrow.

The future of Cambodia is obviously bound up closely with the outcome of unresolved conflict in Vietnam. There would seem little prospect at the present time of the Government of Phnom Penh, irrespective of the scale of external assistance, being able to transform the situation to its advantage. It is a debilitated entity unable to break out of the vice-like grip applied by its antagonists. The prospect of any compromise solution to the present conflict is also unlikely given the weakness of the Government and the polarization of opposing forces. One prognosis which is relevant at the present time is suggested in the fatalistic comment made 10 years ago that "whether he is called Gia Long, Ho Chi Minh or Ngo Dinh Diem, no Annamite (or Vietnamese) will sleep peacefully until he has succeeded in pushing Cambodia towards annihilation, having made it first go through the stages of slavery".[8] These words came ironically from the same man who in April this year announced publicly that the Premier of North Vietnam was "one of the greatest heroes of our Indochina, one of the most noble supporters of Cambodia, one of the most admired among the most loved friends of the Khmer people and myself".[9] That man was Prince Norodom Sihanouk.

Notes

1. *Cambodia: The Search for Security* (New York and London, 1967), pp. 191–2.
2. Milton Osborne, "Effacing the God-King — Internal Developments in Cambodia since March 1970", in J. J. Zasloff and Allan E. Goodman, eds., *Indochina in Conflict* (Lexington, 1972), p. 77, footnote 14.
3. Since this lecture was given [on 23 May 1973], it has been revealed in testimony before the Senate Armed Services Committee that American B-52s had bombed Communist sanctuary areas in Cambodia from early 1969. This information throws considerable light on the expectations of those who not only deposed Sihanouk but also risked a direct confrontation with the Vietnamese Communists.
4. *Vietnam Courier*, Hanoi, 30 March 1970.
5. See the author's "Peace and War in Cambodia", *Southeast Asia*, Winter-Spring 1971.

6. *United States Foreign Policy for the 1970s.* A report by President Richard Nixon to the Congress (Washington, 3 May 1973), p. 75.
7. An interesting account of the "United Front" in Cambodia is provided in J. L. S. Girling, "The Resistance in Cambodia", *Asian Survey,* July 1972. For Sihanouk's account of the strength of the "Front", see his speech delivered in Hanoi on 10 April 1973 in *Bulletin d'Information* (Mission du Gouvernement Royal d'Union Nationale du Cambodge, Paris), No. 119/73, pp. 9–17.
8. *Cambodian News,* Phnom Penh, January 1963, p. 4.
9. *Bulletin d'Information, op. cit.,* p. 16.

39

Challenges Remain in Cambodia

Despite the inaugural meeting of a constituent assembly and agreement on an interim government, the Cambodian peace process is still in a fragile state. A new constitution and a viable government have to be created before the work of the United Nations is completed.

The root of the problem is that the accords concluded in Paris in October 1991 are based on assumptions that are not readily tenable in Indochina — or in other regions in which UN intervention may be required.

One irony of the Cambodian conflict is that the UN-supervised peace process was challenged by the government put in power by Vietnam in 1979 and not by the murderous Khmer Rouge that it displaced. Before elections in May, there was widespread concern that polling might be disrupted, or even prevented, by Khmer Rouge violence.

But peaceful and popular participation exceeded the expectations of the UN Transitional Authority in Cambodia. The results also

Reprinted from Michael Leifer, "Challenges Remain in Cambodia", *International Herald Tribune*, 24 June 1993, by permission of the New York Times Syndicate.

confounded the expectations of the governing Cambodian People's Party. It had assumed it would win an easy victory in polls that the Khmer Rouge had repudiated.

The gruesome record of the Khmer Rouge distracted attention from the willingness of the People's Party to use violence against its non-Communist opponents. The campaign of assassination and intimidation did not succeed, however. A near majority was secured by Funcinpec, the pro-royalist party founded by Prince Norodom Sihanouk and led by his son, Prince Norodom Ranariddh.

The People's Party tried without success to persuade the UN to set aside the results of the elections on the grounds that they had been fraudulently conducted. It refused to recognize them and began a campaign of threats to retain power.

The accord on the interim government is not the end of the power struggle. Although Prince Sihanouk has returned to center stage, his effectiveness as a power broker is limited. He may display the personal authority to patch things up in the short run; but, at age 70 and in indifferent health, he cannot ensure enduring accord.

The prince also suffers from the political disability of having sought to bring the Khmer Rouge into a political coalition. He had made it known that Cambodians should cease to regard the Khmer Rouge as their enemy. Should his brokered settlement founder, the Khmer Rouge will be ready like political vultures to pick the bones of civil conflict. The latest phase in the peace process has pointed to one of its basic weaknesses: an aversion to power-sharing among the factions.

The Paris conference was first held in July 1989 but was suspended partly because the factions could not come to terms over power-sharing arrangements before general elections.

The second phase of the conference, in October 1991, succeeeded only because the UN circumvented the power-sharing issue, taking responsibility for creating a "neutral" political environment in which free and fair elections could be held. The elections were to be the device through which national reconciliation would be achieved.

The elections were not conclusive, even without Khmer Rouge participation. Funcinpec won 58 of the 120 seats in the constituent assembly, while the People's Party won 51, with minor parties sharing the rest. The People's Party has shown itself reluctant to share power, while Funcinpec regards its entry into an interim government with deep mistrust. It remains to be seen whether the People's Party's control over the armed forces and the police will end.

To its credit, the United Nations refused to be intimidated into reconsidering its endorsement of the elections. It kept its nerve and called the bluff of the Phnom Penh government, which is running out of funds to pay the armed forces. But the United Nations does not have the mandate or power to do anything about a coalition deal that may be entered into with subversion in mind.

The Paris peace process was based on the assumption that its participants would adhere to electoral rules, win or lose. Cambodian politics have yet to work on that basis. Those who wield power are not normally disposed to relinquish it merely because of the result of a practice deemed legitimate in UN resolutions.

40

Tune Back In, Friends of Cambodia, the Crisis Show Isn't Over

The pomp and circumstance of royalty coexist in Cambodia with vehement denunciations of foreigners who have the temerity to point at dictatorial methods of government, at odds with a democracy ostensibly restored through United Nations intervention.

Norodom Sihanouk has been reinstated as king. The entire government and diplomatic corps attend at the airport as he and his consort set off on a state visit abroad. At the age of 73, despite failing health, he works the lineup like an old professional.

The assembled diplomats are concerned about more than being kissed on both cheeks by his majesty. The U.S. and French embassies have been threatened with violent demonstrations that recall acts of so-called spontaneous anger in 1964, when the U.S. and British missions were attacked.

It is Hun Sen, the second prime minister in the coalition government, who denounces foreigners. And he recently called out

Reprinted from Michael Leifer, "Tune Back In, Friends of Cambodia, the Crisis Show Isn't Over", *International Herald Tribune*, 21 December 1995, by permission of the New York Times Syndicate.

the tanks to place Prince Norodom Sirivudh, former foreign minister and the king's half-brother, under "protective custody" before he was formally arrested on a charge of plotting to assassinate him.

The first prime minister, Prince Norodom Ranarridh, eldest son of King Sihanouk, advised National Assembly members of his majority royalist party, of which Prince Sirivudh is secretary-general, to vote to remove the latter's parliamentary immunity so that he could be formally detained. He warned that if it were not removed, Prince Sirivudh's life could be at risk because of Hun Sen's intemperate personality.

That immunity was removed in a closed session. Foreign criticism of the violation of constitutional process provoked Hun Sen into making impassioned speeches threatening retaliation.

These days, King Sihanouk can only reign, not rule. He urged his half-brother to take the option of exile rather than risk trial and the ire of Hun Sen, a former member of the Khmer Rouge. Prince Sirivudh is to leave this Thursday for voluntary exile in France.

There are many interpretations of current Cambodian politics, including the likelihood of Hun Sen's fear of assassination. Cambodia has regressed politically since the heady days of UN intervention and the holding of democratic elections.

The UN transitional authority solved the Cambodian conflict as an international problem, and the Khmer Rouge have gone into political and military decline. However, Hun Sen's Cambodian People's Party which was put into power in January 1979 as the pro-Communist Kampuchean People's Revolutionary Party by the Vietnamese invasion force that ousted the Khmer Rouge regime has resumed its former dominant role, despite coming second in the elections to the royalists.

Before the elections, Hun Sen's party controlled the armed forces, the police, key ministries and much of the local administration. By threatening to use force to secure a dominant place in the coalition government with the royalists, it distorted the outcome of the elections conducted under UN auspices.

Prince Ranarridh evidently feels he has no choice but to work in an unholy alliance with Hun Sen. He does not have access to real power. His divided royalist party has failed to secure its share of military and administrative resources. For his part, Hun Sen is content to act in nominal junior partnership to sustain international recognition. The result is a strong-arm regime that intimidates opponents and lets unscrupulous foreign interests exploit natural resources.

The dictatorial style of government has shown itself unwilling to tolerate any legitimate challenge. This was exemplified by the removal from office last year of Sam Rainsy, the royalist finance minister, which prompted Prince Sirivudh's resignation as foreign minister in protest. Sam Rainsy was subsequently expelled from the royalist party and then from the National Assembly.

His move to create an opposition Khmer Nation Party has been the precipitating factor in the current political crisis. The opportunistic arrest and exile of his friend Prince Sirivudh served to create a climate of fear to fend off all challenge. It demonstrated to would-be dissidents the cost and futility of opposing the regime.

Sam Rainsy's party has been refused registration, and should he return from France, where he has been highly critical of Hun Sen, another political crisis is likely to follow. Hegel has been credited with saying that when history repeats itself, it does so first in tragedy and then in farce. Cambodia has had more than its fair share of tragedy. Its contemporary political scene displays undoubted elements of farce, but tragedy still hovers.

Those countries in Asia and the West which strongly supported the Paris peace agreement of October 1991 that paved the way for UN intervention seem reluctant now to assume their responsibilities under its terms. They have an obligation to tell the Phnom Penh government to observe the terms of Cambodia's democratic constitution.

Malaysia

INTRODUCTION

Nine articles on Malaysia were written by Leifer, but only five have been selected in this section: three are on Malaysian domestic politics and two on foreign policy. Constitutional stability and the concept of Malaysia are two important themes in his study of Malaysian politics. Recognizing the importance of leadership, Dr Mahathir took centre stage in Leifer's study of the country's foreign policy. Among others, Leifer examined the function of Malaysia's foreign policy, the issue of anti-Semitism, and Malaysia's relations with its former colonial masters.

Leifer began writing on Malaysia after the Federation of Malaysia was formed in 1963. He examined the alliance pattern of politics as the basis of constitutional stability in Malaysia. However, when the alliance broke down under electoral challenge, there was instability as reflected in the 1969 riots. He maintained that the inter-communal association had received a blow after the riots, and the future of parliamentary system was in doubt (Ch. 41).

In an article written after the 1969 riots, Leifer maintained that the source of tension lay in divergent and conflicting conceptions of

Malaysia as a political unit. He said, "Communal violence was not the product of any conventional clash of political interests but the outcome of irreconcilable views of the nature and identity of the Malaysian state." He further argued that if the Chinese continued to be alienated, it would benefit the Malayan Communist Party (MCP) (Ch. 42).

Tun Razak replaced Tunku Abdul Rahman as prime minister after the 1969 riots and succeeded in managing the communal conflict. Leifer was of the view that it was Tun Razak who was able to restore law and order by establishing the inter-communal national front coalition but communal tensions never disappeared. The MCP was exploiting the situation, especially after the passing away of Tun Razak. His successor, Hussein Onn, was able to hold the country together. Nevertheless, Leifer noted that Hussein Onn was a reluctant politician who followed in the steps of Tun Razak in pursuing multi-racialism in domestic politics and promoting ASEAN in his foreign policy (Ch. 43).

Hussein Onn was succeeded by Dr Mahathir bin Mohamad in 1981. Leifer was more interested in Mahathir's foreign policy rather than his handling of domestic politics, although it was clear that the two issues are closely linked. The most striking example was Malaysia's anti-Semitism during the Mahathir era (Ch. 44). Leifer noted that there was no Jewish constituency in Malaysia but the Mahathir administration was making a series of attacks on the Zionists and Jews. Mahathir was using this to garner Muslim support as Malay's support for the United Malays National Organization (UMNO) was declining. However, Leifer argued that Mahathir was also aware of the dangers of using this rhetoric — in terms of ASEAN unity and Malaysia's economic development — and hence abandoned it when he deemed it necessary.

Another major characteristic of Mahathir's foreign policy was "anti-British". There were two "Buy British Last" policies during his administration: one was in 1981 and the other in 1994 (Ch. 45). Leifer compared these two events and highlighted their similarities and differences. Both were launched during the Mahathir era but he noted that the first was a response to the British government's unfriendly remarks on Malaysia, especially towards Mahathir. The second was a response to the British press attacks on Mahathir and the British government's refusal to defend him publicly. Mahathir intended to use the policy to pressurize British companies and government to influence the British press, with limited successes. This was also done during the period when his position in UMNO was being challenged.

However, when there was a compromising mood on half of the British government, Mahathir seized the opportunity to drop the policy because he realized that it might harm the Malaysian economy in the long term. The policies reflect linkages in domestic politics and foreign policy. To have a comprehensive understanding of this issue, the article entitled "Anglo-American Difference over Malaysia" in Part I of this volume (Ch. 20) should also be consulted.

41

Politics and Constitutional Stability in Malaysia*

It is often salutary to regard constitutions as rule books which provide for the conduct of political activity as well as bodies of fundamental law. Their provisions may serve, for example, to indicate the strength of interests and the balance of political forces at the time of promulgation. Various founding documents are revealing in this sense: notable amongst them the constitution of the United States of America. Political practice, of course, need not and often does not correspond with constitutional precepts. It is not too difficult to cite instances of a gulf between such practice and precepts. One might, for example, mention the actual practice of politics in the Philippines which is in striking contrast to that country's democratic constitution. Here constitutional forms offer little insight into the ways of politics. There are also instances of states, especially in Africa and Asia, in which it has been found necessary to effect quite far reaching constitutional alterations to correspond with and also to underpin a political process

Reprinted from Michael Leifer, "Politics and Constitutional Stability in Malaysia", *Parliamentary Affairs* 22, no. 3 (1969): 202–209, by permission of Oxford University Press.

which bears little resemblance to that in existence on the morrow of independence. Here the pace of political change may be so fast that even an amended constitution will serve as a distorting mirror of political practice.

There is a circumstance, however, where prevailing political practice ensues from the time of constitutional promulgation in a manner so as to correspond closely to the norms of the founding document. The Federation of Malaysia in terms of constitutional form and political process may be seen as a genus of this ideal-type species, although it is important not to exaggerate the degree of political institutionalization that has been achieved since mainland Malaya became independent in August, 1957.[1] In the case of Malaya and Malaysia it is possible to point to a political system whose founding documents have not required fundamental alteration except in one contingency. The explanation for this condition of relative constitutional stability is that the character of the political system of Malaya continuing into Malaysia, as exemplified in what has become known by convention as the Alliance pattern of politics, has been of an enduring nature since before the promulgation of the constitution of 1957.

In the case of Malaysia, it is to be borne in mind that it was not quite a new federation that was set up in September 1963. It has been pointed out that "in no sense is it a brand new state that has come into being, but the old state (Malaya) has continued in an enlarged form and with a new name".[2] While this partisan statement is not strictly correct it does contain a strong element of truth for the old state has come to dominate the new. The process of politics in the territories which were linked with Malaya in 1963, with the obvious exception of Singapore which left the Federation in August, 1965, has been much influenced, if not determined, by the political system which took coherent shape in Malaya even before the transfer of power from colonial rule. The distinctive form of the Alliance pattern of politics of Malaya has been extended, though not necessarily entrenched, in the Borneo states of Malaysia. This Alliance pattern of politics, which can be interpreted as a euphemism for virtual one-party dominance by an intercommunal coalition is central to the political process in Malaysia; constitutional stability in the Federation may thus be seen as a function of the continuing existence of this distinctive pattern.

The key to an understanding of the stability of the Malayan and Malaysian constitutions is to be found in the fact that the prevailing governing system was firmly established in advance of constitutional discussions which preceded the grant of independence by the colonial power. In the plural society of Malaya an inter-communal political arrangement between Malay and Chinese political parties which was tried successfully at the level of municipal elections in 1952 was institutionalized at the national level with the general elections of 1955.[3] This arrangement, based on accommodation between communal leadership enabled attention to specific communal priorities to be squared with stable government based on majority rule. As a result, the Alliance coalition represented the only practical and sane choice for those who had the authority to grant full independence. The Reid Constitutional Commission, when it visited Malaya, was presented with but a single set of proposals from the Alliance party which represented an inter-communal compromise worked out behind closed doors. In view of this demonstration of inter-communal solidarity the Reid Commission treated the proposals of the Alliance with special consideration. And in the final process of bargaining before the Malayan Constitution was drafted for promulgation, it was the Alliance with one voice and not three which dealt directly with the British Government.[4]

The Constitution of Malaya, when it emerged, embodied the bargain struck within the Alliance coalition as to communal priorities. This coalition has since continued to enjoy a basis of consensus for political cohabitation and to attract majority support through a democratic electoral process. In so far as the governing coalition and its priorities have remained stable so has the constitution which it was instrumental in shaping. In other words, continued political success and a demonstrated ability to moderate communal extremes have made possible constitutional stability.

Constitutional stability, however, should not be taken to mean the absence of constitutional change. Nevertheless, the manner and nature of this change has been such as to ensure the perpetuation of the Alliance pattern which gave rise to the founding document of 1957 and later the Malaysian constitution of 1963. And in turn success in this endeavour has meant that in their most important aspect the original character of those documents prevails still.

In political terms the Malayan and Malaysian constitutions sought to provide in practical and symbolic form for an entrenched Malay dominance though in such a way as to avoid the alienation of the non-Malays whose numbers are such that they cannot be treated as an insignificant minority. Just a perusal of the 1963 document in terms of the rights and position of the Malays in relation to the non-Malays will confirm this objective.[5] Apart from an intra-Alliance crisis in 1959 over education and the allocation of electoral nominations, the commitment to a particular kind of communal compromise has continued to hold the Alliance leadership together. Alliance dominance has been sustained over opposition parties through electoral success although there has been a clear willingness to resort to emergency powers permitted under the constitution which are in part a product of the formative period of Malaya's political development. Their use might also be regarded as an expression of the government's belief that it has in some way a divine right to rule. Nevertheless, constitutional amendment in mainland Malaya, for example, to ensure that rural constituencies could embody only half the number of electors as in urban ones, was not solely intended to ensure the dominance of the Alliance as such against opposition parties but was to safeguard the balance of communal advantage as expressed in the unwritten Alliance bargain embodied in the Malayan Constitution of 1957.[6]

There has not yet been any serious electoral or other challenge to the Alliance pattern of politics originating within mainland Malaya. Opposition is in the main communally based and also fragmented and has failed to compete effectively. Opposition parties have not been successful in attempts to make a community-straddling appeal which is the special advantage of the Alliance. There has been only one considered challenge to the governing system and that arose after the establishment of Malaysia when Lee Kuan-yew, the Prime Minister of Singapore, sought to carry his ostensibly multi-racial message across the causeway that links the island to the mainland. However, his People's Action Party was able only to secure one seat out of nine contested in the mainland Malayan elections of 1964. The repercussions of this electoral intervention were, however, to lead in the following year to dramatic constitutional change. On the one other occasion when significant constitutional change was effected, the Alliance leadership in Kuala Lumpur sought to ensure that the Sarawak variant of the Alliance pattern was not disturbed unduly.

The formation of Malaysia may be seen as an attempt to perpetuate the Alliance pattern of dominance whilst at the same time providing by encapsulation for the security problem posed, so it appeared then, by Singapore.[7] The three states of Singapore, Sabah and Sarawak were to enjoy a constitutional relationship to the Federal Government of a different kind to that which had been the experience of the eleven states of Malaya. The distribution of powers, provision of formal constitutional safeguards and disproportionate parliamentary representation for the Borneo States were of a kind that the Malayan States had never enjoyed. Indeed, the limited constitutional powers of the Malayan States were demonstrated by the unsuccessful legal action by the State of Kelantan in 1963 to seek a declaration from the Federal Court that the Malaysia Act was null and void and not binding on the plaintiff.

It is not intended to consider here the actual distribution of powers between the Federal Government of Malaysia, Singapore and the Borneo States which made Malaysia an interesting variant of the more conventional Federal idea. These powers are set out in the Malaysia Agreement.[8] More important is the considered place of the states joining with Malaya in terms of the Alliance order of things.

Singapore was included in Malaysia of necessity though not with great pleasure. It was regarded essentially as a Chinese city-state whose communal political character was not capable of alteration. For this reason and also because of the suspicions felt towards the person of Lee Kuan-yew, the Prime Minister of Singapore, the island was publicly represented as the New York of Malaysia; a pointed indication of its political place. On the other hand, the Borneo States, which were seen as makeweights in an exercise to sustain an overall racial balance fell more naturally within the Alliance pattern even if the matter of ethnic identity should have led to greater caution. Even before the establishment of Malaysia the Alliance model was promoted in the Borneo States and came to dominate the political process there.[9] It was in the face of a challenge to the Alliance pattern in Sarawak that constitutional change was to take place.

In the case of Singapore, the Alliance parties were not prepared to tolerate a challenge to the governing system of which they were the beneficiaries. The electoral intervention of the Singapore based People's Action Party into mainland Malaya in 1964 was openly presented by Lee Kuan-yew as an attempt to displace the Chinese wing of the Alliance and their resentment of this intention was only too natural. The Malays in turn saw the prospect of P.A.P. success among the urban non-Malays as but the first step in a process whereby Chinese economic dominance in Malaysia would be translated to the sphere of politics.[10] As such, the principal communal wings of the Alliance had a vested interest in meeting the challenge of the P.A.P. before it reached uncontrollable proportions; at the same time concern with the prospect of violent inter-communal discord cannot be discounted as a factor in the motivation of the Alliance leadership. The initial electoral assault in 1964 was easily contained but Lee Kuan-yew did not cease to campaign for a fundamental change in the character of the Malaysian polity. As one author has commented, the P.A.P. slogan of a Malaysian Malaysia "was seen within Malaya as a direct and unprincipled assault on the fundamental constitutional basis of the country's independent existence."[11] At the time of this alleged assault Singapore's original *raison d'etre* for inclusion in Malaysia had ceased to exist. The extreme left-wing had been defeated in electoral contest and was in disarray. The P.A.P. was undoubtedly in a position of political dominance in Singapore. As a consequence the Prime Minister of Malaysia, Tunku Abdul Rahman, felt free to insist on a political divorce, Malay-style. Faced with no predictable alternative to formal secession, Lee Kuan-yew acquiesced and the enabling act passed through the Federal Parliament post-haste in one day's sitting and without dissent.[12] The difference in Alliance attitude between Singapore and the Borneo States was to be seen in the Tunku's hostile reaction to the suggestion that Sabah might follow the example of Singapore.

In the case of Sarawak, the recalcitrance of its Iban Chief Minister, Stephen Ningkan, on matters of communal import, was seen as an obstacle to the successful consolidation of the Alliance pattern, even though the ethnic composition of the population would not seem to permit Malay dominance. An initial attempt to remove Ningkan, who had apparently lost the support of the majority of the Sarawak Alliance coalition, by the (Malay) Governor of Sarawak in June 1966 was repulsed through local High Court action as being unconstitutional. The Federal Government then advised the Federal Head of State to declare a state of emergency in Sarawak on the grounds that the constitutional and political position there had deteriorated to such an extent that it posed a serious threat to Malaysia generally as well as to Sarawak itself. The existence of a state of emergency enabled the Malaysian Parliament in September to pass an act amending the Federal Constitution to allow the Sarawak constitution to be amended to give the Governor of Sarawak powers to call the State legislature and to dismiss the chief minister, should he lose the legislature's confidence. Ningkan was then dismissed from office for a second time. He was later to challenge this procedure in the Malaysian Federal Court but the case was decided against him in December 1967 because the judges were not prepared to treat as justiceable what they considered was, in constitutional theory, the discretionary power of the Head of State to declare a state of emergency, even though in practice he was clearly acting on ministerial advice.

It should be pointed out that the process of constitutional amendment in the case of Sarawak secured immediately the Alliance goal because the Governor of the State was tied in with the Alliance governing system and was willing to comply with demands from Kuala Lumpur. Ningkan successfully sought leave to appeal to the Privy Council who rejected his plea. In the meantime the Malaysian Parliament approved a bill to end the practice of appeal to the Privy Council on constitutional matters.

For the time being, the Alliance pattern of political dominance prevails certainly in mainland Malaya and also in Sabah where in 1967 a Muslim-Chinese coalition defeated an electoral challenge from a non-Muslim native party which has since dissolved its membership and advised that they join the other native but predominantly Muslim party within the Sabah Alliance.[13] In Sarawak, forthcoming elections will decide whether this Borneo variant of the Alliance pattern will prevail. So far, all but two by-elections at the District Council level held since June 1966 have been won by Ningkan's Iban based but communally mixed party. But it remains to be seen just how the electorate will respond in the first direct general elections on a state-wide level in the face of Federal Government threats of financial penalty in the event of a reverse for the Alliance.

In conclusion it can be suggested that constitutional stability has endured in important respects in Malaysia because the political system there has been sustained in a form that was institutionalized before the promulgation of the Malayan Constitution in 1957. This situation has endured with less consistency following the establishment of the Federation of Malaysia in 1963 for the obvious reason that Malaya and Malaysia are not the same in terms of political culture. In the case of Singapore, direct challenge was handled by secession and in the less pressing case of Sarawak by constitutional amendment albeit in spurious circumstances.

The Constitution of Malaysia is undoubtedly regarded by the ruling Alliance as an instrument which suits their political purpose. But it also reflects the basis of consensual bargain which enables an inter-communal coalition to co-operate to mutual and, one might suggest, national advantage. The continuation of a strong measure of constitutional stability depends above all on the stability of the Alliance pattern which in spite of undesirable features has demonstrated that viable government can function only on the basis of inter-communal accommodation. No other grouping within Malaysia has the prospect of doing the same.

Political change that has been initiated has, so far, taken place within the bounds permitted by the constitution. However, it should be pointed out that the constitution does permit great latitude to any ruling group that can command the necessary majority in the Federal legislature. There is no guarantee, of course, that the present situation of both political and constitutional stability will always exist. There could occur a fundamental split on communal lines within the ruling Alliance or an electoral challenge could leave the Alliance without a working parliamentary majority. In such circumstances the constitution could well be subject to radical alteration of the kind associated with a railway time-table. Such alteration might well have to be extra-constitutional because of formal restrictions on amendment. On the other hand, emergency regulations might suffice for those who command the support of the Head of State and the predominantly Malay Armed Forces.

In so far as the Constitution of Malaysia reflects certain realities of political life, it is an example of a special case. There is, of course, clear utility in examining constitutions as a means of inquiring into political behaviour. However, it should be fully obvious that not all constitutions offer such insights and to understand their real workings as opposed to their documentary sanctity it is more sensible to begin at the level of political systems and then to seek to assess the extent to which constitutional forms accord with political reality.

In Malaysia there is an example of a government of men who are willing to tolerate, within certain limits, a government of laws because such government of laws ensures what they earnestly believe to be the least objectionable way of running the public affairs of the country. To the extent that this government of laws continues to serve their political purpose, they are happy to work with a constitution that in principal respects is virtually identical to that promulgated in 1957.

Postscript

After this article went into proof, general elections were held in Malaysia on May 10th, 1969. In peninsular Malaya the Alliance, the governing inter-communal coalition, suffered a significant reduction in support compared to its performance at the previous elections in April 1964. On that occasion, it obtained 89 out of 104 seats contested for the Federal Parliament with 58.3% of the vote. In May 1969, it retained 66 seats with approximately 49%. The comparison with 1964 is somewhat unreal, however, because of the interposition of the issue of Indonesian confrontation in that campaign. A more reliable comparison would be with 1959 when the Alliance obtained 74 seats with 51.8% of the vote. Nonetheless, the 1969 results had disturbing implications for the governing coalition party. Its senior partner, the United Malays National Organisation (U.M.N.O.) suffered reverses in the home state of Prime Minister Tunku Abdul Rahman whose own majority was cut by some 8,000 votes. The beneficiary here was the Pan Malayan Islamic Party which is a passionate advocate of Malay supremacy. More striking was the collapse of support for the Malayan Chinese Association (M.C.A.) which lost 14 of its 27 seats to urban based opposition parties whose appeal was to non-Malays resentful of undue Malay dominance. A direct consequence of this change of political fortunes was the withdrawal, forced or otherwise, of the M.C.A. from the Alliance Cabinet thus terminating the Alliance pattern of politics instituted first in 1955.

The election campaign was notable for an excessive concentration on communal issues. On the evening of May 12th, supporters of the successful non-Malay opposition parties staged an electoral victory procession through the capital, Kuala Lumpur; an event which offended Malay sensibilities. The following day, the M.C.A. withdrew from the cabinet. That evening, U.M.N.O. leaders organised their own (counter) victory march but instead of a procession there ensued a communal riot which escalated into a full scale inter-racial confrontation mainly within the capital. For five days, Kuala Lumpur experienced murder, mayhem, arson and looting and when the military eventually restored order, the official toll of identified dead was put at 173 with many hundreds injured.

The day following the outbreak of violence, the Prime Minister announced the assumption by government of sweeping emergency powers which amounted to rule by decree. Parliament was suspended together with elections still proceeding in 31 constituencies in Sabah and Sarawak. In place of a cabinet there was substituted a military style National Operations Council as supreme executive with extraordinary powers necessitated, according to the Tunku, because

"A real attempt has been made by disloyal elements to overthrow the government by force of arms."

This is neither the place nor the time to provide a substantive analysis of the above events. There are, however, some relevant observations which can be made. First, the Alliance pattern of politics, the basis of constitutional stability, has broken down under electoral challenge. Secondly, inter-communal association has received a blow from which it may take decades to recover. Thirdly, the future of parliamentary government in Malaysia is in serious doubt. Finally, it would seem that for the time being constitutional change is not to be effected by alteration of the kind associated with a railway timetable; in the present situation the constitution has become of political irrelevance.

Notes

*This article is a revised version of a paper presented to a seminar on Post-Independence Constitutional Changes held at the Institute of Commonwealth Studies, University of London, in February 1968.

1. For the purpose of this article it has been found necessary to include Malaya and Malaysia within the compass of the same analysis.
2. Ghazalie Shafie, a member of the Cobbold Commission which inquired into feeling in the Borneo States about union with Malaya and also permanent head of the Malaysian Department of External Affairs, quoted by R. S. Milne in *Government and Politics in Malaysia*, Boston, 1967, p. 66.
3. See K. J. Ratnam *Communalism and The Political Process in Malaya*, Kuala Lumpur, 1965.
4. The two principal constituents of the Alliance were the United Malays National Organization and the Malayan Chinese Association. The Malayan Indian Congress became associated just before the general elections of 1955.
5. See Malaysia *The Federation Constitution*, Kuala Lumpur, 1964, and also the interpretation by Harry E. Groves *The Constitution of Malaysia*, Singapore, 1964.
6. A single explanation, however, might be advanced for the withdrawal of the power of the Election Commission to delimit constituencies by the Constitution (Amendment) Act of 1962. See T. E. Smith "The Administration of the Election" in K. J. Ratnam and R. S. Milne *The Malayan Parliamentary Election of 1964*. Singapore, 1967, pp. 60–1 and 65.

7. For an account of this aspect of the formation of Malaysia, see Michael Leifer "Politics in Singapore" *Journal of Commonwealth Political Studies*, May 1964.

8. *Malaysia — Agreement concluded between the United Kingdom of Great Britain and Northern Ireland, The Federation of Malaya, North Borneo, Sarawak and Singapore*, London, 1963. Cmnd. 2094.

9. The manifesto of The Sarawak Alliance, founded in November, 1962, could well have been written in Kuala Lumpur. It read in part "the best way of achieving inter-racial harmony and understanding, we believe, is for all racial problems to be settled by the various representative racial political bodies and then reconciled within an alliance of such racial political bodies..." *Sarawak Tribune, Kuching*, 4th June, 1963.

10. For an account of the P.A.P. challenge and the Alliance reaction see Michael Leifer "Singapore in Malaysia: The Politics of Federation" *Journal of Southeast Asian History*, September 1965.

11. Gerald S. Maryanov "Political Parties in Mainland Malaya" *Ibid.*, March 1967, p. 108.

12. Since the secession of Singapore an attempt was made by an opposition member of the Federal lower house to ensure that one month should elapse between the first and second readings of any bill to alter the constitution. This bill, however, was rejected on second reading.

13. See Gordon P. Means "Eastern Malaysia: The Politics of Federalism" *Asian Survey*, April 1968.

42

Adverse Conceptions of Malaysia
Consequences of Communal Violence

The communal violence which erupted in the capital of Malaysia on
May 13, 1969, demonstrated the fragile quality of political association
in the peninsular wing of the Federation. The violence, which took a
toll of nearly two hundred lives, followed a serious, though not
catastrophic, electoral reverse for the governing inter-communal
coalition, the Alliance. This coalition had provided the Government
of Malaya and then Malaysia continuously from before the grant of
independence. Its federal parliamentary majority was still not in any
doubt. Subject to challenge, however, was the position of its Chinese
constituent, the Malayan Chinese Association (M.C.A.) which had lost
fourteen of twenty-seven seats won at the previous elections of 1964.
Of lesser significance in terms of seats lost, but alarming, in terms of
the percentage increase in total vote gained by its principal communal
opponent, was the position of the United Malays National Organization
(U.M.N.O.), the dominant party within the Alliance.

Reprinted from Michael Leifer, "Adverse Conceptions of Malaysia: Consequences
of Communal Violence", *The Round Table*, no. 239 (1970): 285–93, by permission
of Taylor and Francis Limited <http://www.tandf.co.uk/journals>.

The result of the elections to the federal parliament within Western (peninsular) Malaysia was a major factor in the outbreak of violence which may be interpreted as a reaction to the electoral successes of predominantly non-Malay opposition parties. Crucial to an understanding of the precipitating cause, however, was the uncertain outcome of concurrent elections for the state government of Selangor within which the capital of Malaysia, Kuala Lumpur, is situated. This government had been assumed to be an exclusive Malay preserve reflected in the constitutional provision that the Chief Minister had to be a Malay. The elections indicated a deadlocked legislature and the prospect of an erosion of Malay control in the state which provided the country's capital — the symbolic seat of Malay rule — proved to be a catalytic factor in a situation charged with communal antagonism. This antagonism was of long standing but had been heightened by the nature of the electoral campaign, by results which indicated a significant non-Malay rejection of the Alliance pattern of political association and finally by celebratory processions in Kuala Lumpur, by supporters of the non-Malay opposition parties, which assumed a distinctive anti-Malay character.

In the early evening of May 13 a large crowd of Malays, some armed, gathered at the residence of the Chief Minister of Selangor, Dato Harun bin Haji Idris, with the purpose of participating in a counter-procession sponsored by the state branch of U.M.N.O. Incidents on the periphery of this assembly set up a process of communal violence in the capital which was not contained for five days. In its wake lay the shattered edifice of a tenuous inter-communal accord and of a parliamentary democracy replaced by an executive variant of pre-independence rule.

Communal Antagonism

To explain the precipitating circumstances of the violence of May 13 is to explain but a facet of the pathology of politics in Malaysia. To go on to say that the eruption reflected an underlying communal antagonism is to explain everything and yet next to nothing at the same time. Every commentator who has written on the politics of the peninsula has remarked on the mutual antipathy of Malays and Chinese who live in many cases in close proximity but in separate cultural compartments. There have been pessimistic analyses in plenty; particularly the more recent exercises which followed the relatively small-scale upheaval which had its source in Penang in November 1967. Such past analyses, however, have usually been qualified with sanguine appreciation of the apparently successful efforts of moderate political leadership to bridge the racial divide. The inevitability of major inter-communal confrontation has rarely been stated in unqualified terms. And yet within the political culture of the peninsula there has developed over the years a particular tension which, if institutionalized, could have no effect other than to promote an inexorable clash of political-communal forces. Hindsight is, of course, a fortunate perspective. Nonetheless, the tension in question came to underpin communal discord with the formation of Malaysia. It was sustained in the peninsula after the separation of Singapore in August 1965. It is this tension which needs to be laid bare in order to appreciate the full significance of the outbreak of violence on May 13 and the consequent governmental approach to the problem of political order.

The source of this tension lay in divergent and conflicting conceptions of Malaysia as a political unit. Communal violence was not the product of any conventional clash of political interests but the outcome of irreconcilable views of the nature and identity of the Malaysian state. Those who have followed the unhappy course of events in Northern Ireland should not have great difficulty in appreciating the order of the problem which in the simplest of terms revolves around the question of political participation. It centres on a clash between a political order founded on a clear hierarchy of political-communal interests and an aspirant order that is ostensibly egalitarian but which is regarded by the beneficiaries of the prevailing system as even more hierarchical.

The prevailing political order dates from 1955 before peninsular Malaya became independent. From that time up to May 1969 government was in the charge of an inter-communal coalition which sustained a rigid political pecking order between its Malay, Chinese and Indian constituents. U.M.N.O. — founded in 1946 in reaction to a British attempt to impose parity in communal rights — has been not only the senior partner in Alliance Government but also the prime determinant of the bounds of inter-communal compromise. In effect, it showed itself willing for practical reasons, associated with the prospect of independence and the number and economic contribution of the non-Malays, to tolerate a measure of inter-communal accommodation on the understanding that the underlying ethic of British colonial rule

— that Malaya was a Malay country — was carried over in symbolic and substantive form into the post-colonial situation. This ethic was expressed at the time of independence in constitutional provision for the special rights of the Malays which were entrenched, it was argued, in order to modify the disparate economic roles of Malays and non-Malays. In addition, Malay was established as the national and eventually as the official language. Islam was made the state religion, while the rotating monarch — chosen from among the Malay sultans — was empowered with responsibility and discretion under the constitution for the "special position" of his co-religionists. In return, the non-Malays were provided with access to citizenship and an unwritten promise that they were to be secure in their economic stake and not cast for a pariah role. Non-Malay interests were represented within the Alliance scheme through the M.C.A. and the Malayan Indian Congress (M.I.C.): domesticated and subordinate components of a political triad. The Alliance in concert postulated the formula for political-communal cohabitation. The role of the non-Malays was conceived in fairly static terms. It was implied by Prime Minister Tunku Abdul Rahman, in 1966, when he remarked of the Chinese that "business is their main concern". He meant, of course, that business ought to be their main concern and that politics was certainly not their concern, at least outside the framework of the Alliance system. This crudely expresses the essence of the governing system which was established in advance of independence. It has been described as a bargain. The nexus for Malay tolerance of the non-Malay economic stake was an entrenched Malay political dominance; a dominance reflected in the allocation of cabinet portfolios.

Discontent with Malay Malaysia

Such a bargain appeared to provide a viable basis for inter-communal accord at the time of independence. But with the passage of time its fundamental features were to fit less easily within the changing aspirational frameworks of competing communities. Non-Malays who sought and obtained educational qualifications became increasingly frustrated at what they regarded as the discriminatory features of the Malay special rights provisions, while the large working-class were not to regard themselves as beneficiaries of the Alliance system of communal representation. The Malays, for their part, came to associate a gap of credibility with a government which repeatedly told them that they were the *bumiputera* (sons of the soil). In their eyes, the Chinese and Indians continued to usurp the Malay inheritance. The independence bargain implied some prospect of divorcing economics from politics. In this respect it was founded on a sanguine view of reality.

The crystallization of conflicting perceptions of communal roles was to take place with the formation of Malaysia in 1963. This merger brought Singapore and the North Borneo territories within the political orbit of Kuala Lumpur. Sabah and Sarawak were conceived as amenable to the Alliance pattern of rule, while predominantly Chinese Singapore was provided with considerable local autonomy in exchange for self-denial of political ambitions outside the island. The Prime Minister of Singapore, Lee Kuan-yew, failed to observe this self-denying ordinance and arrogated to himself the role of leader of the non-Malays of Malaysia. Within months of the formation of the new Federation he launched a political campaign ostensibly in the cause of political democracy in order to transform what he was to describe as a Malay Malaysia into a Malaysian Malaysia.

In 1964, the ruling People's Action Party (P.A.P.) of Singapore led by Lee intervened in general elections on the Malayan mainland. The intended purpose was a token electoral appeal to the mainly urban-dwelling non-Malays to reject the subordinate parties within the Alliance, in particular the M.C.A. The abysmal failure of the P.A.P. on that occasion may be explained by failings in organization and by the existence of the state of confrontation being prosecuted by a notoriously anti-Chinese Indonesia. Although the P.A.P. gained but one seat out of nine contested, Lee persisted in an ideological campaign which in May 1965 was to have as vehicle an essentially non-Malay opposition coalition, the Malaysian Solidarity Convention. Lee reiterated his demand for a Malaysian Malaysia and his party proclaimed that it was not disposed to tolerate a situation where one race dominated the Federation. It went further to suggest that as a multi-racial socialist party it could best represent the interests of the have-nots of Malaysia who needed to realize "how much they have in common with each other despite differences of race, culture, language and religion". In the context of Malaysia's communal balance this species of advocacy fell most readily on the ears of the urban working class non-Malays increasingly resentful of what they perceived as a second-class status in a country to which they were expected to give their primary allegiance. To the Malays, however, the concepts of a multi-racial society and a Malaysian Malaysia as represented by Lee had a negative appeal. Such slogans and formulae were widely interpreted as but insidious ruses to erode cherished status and to translate Chinese economic dominance into political control. There was not to be any reconciliation of adverse positions. In August 1965 Singapore was summarily despatched from Malaysia and Mr. Lee was confined to his island republic.

The Tunku in providing a personal explanation for the violence of May 13 makes pointed reference to Chinese unwillingness to accept the Alliance pattern of Malay-dominated politics and the interrelated necessity for the expulsion of Singapore from Malaysia. His remarks merit extensive quotation:

> Then there is another class of young people among the Chinese, ambitious and articulate, the so-called intellectuals, fresh from the universities and now able to vote, young men and women who refuse to acknowledge the hitherto-accepted division of interests or balance of power as between political and economic forces for which the Constitution had so studiously and fairly provided. ...
>
> They aim to go into politics in a big way hoping ultimately to win undisputed leadership for the Chinese in both economic and political fields of Malaysia. They do not accept Malay dominance any more so they find the concept of Malaysian Malaysia, as advocated by Mr. Lee Kuan-yew, in line with their ambitions.
>
> They even manage to ignore the fact that it was for this same reason that Singapore was forced out of Malaysia.[1]

In his exegesis, the Tunku makes abundantly clear that Malay political dominance is the cardinal principle of the Malaysian governing system. Challenge to this principle will not be tolerated and will bring forth a reaction exemplified in the expulsion of Singapore.

Non-Malays of the Peninsula

The separation of Singapore from Malaysia was an exercise in crisis management; an adjustment to defuse a heightened conflict situation. Geography facilitated the exercise. But for peninsular Malaysia, where the arithmetical racial balance between Malays and non-Malays is roughly of the order 50:50, geography does not so readily permit a solution which follows the wisdom of Solomon. In the peninsula, the adverse conceptions of Malaysia were sustained because the ideas associated with the person of Lee Kuan-yew did not depart the Federation with the secession of Singapore. By then, they had become an essential component of the political organization which Lee had fathered on the mainland. Under the new title of Democratic Action Party (D.A.P.) and offered by citizens of Malaysia it continued to promote Lee's revisionist ideology.

In 1969, the D.A.P. contested the federal and state elections in circumstances different to those obtaining in 1964. There was no external crisis capable of influencing the urban Chinese to vote for the Chinese constituent of the Alliance which had a decreasingly representative aspect. The outcome was a substantial improvement of the federal parliamentrary position of the D.A.P. from one to thirteen seats. Additional inroads into the Alliance position in the urban areas was made by the new *Gerakan* party which was less diametrically opposed to the Alliance system and which had a measure of multi-racial following. The net effect, however, was to represent to Malay eyes a vigorous non-Malay challenge to the prevailing political order. The subsequent victory processions in Kuala Lumpur by the non-Malay opposition parties provided evidence, for those who sought it, that the election results foreshadowed the erosion of Malay political power and the prospect of aborigine status. In effect, there had been a polarization of communal support; the Pan Malayan Islamic Party (P.M.I.P.) had secured nearly a quarter of the total poll, although only twelve seats out of eighty-nine on the mainland. For the Malays of U.M.N.O., it was necessary to reckon with a seepage from a proprietary constituency. Overall the results represented a shattering of conventional mythology built around the linkage of the Alliance to the independence constitution. It was in this context of disruption of cognitive patterns, aggravated by the special post-electoral situation and the anti-Malay cast of non-Malay celebrations, which themselves indicated the end of an era, that communal tension pushed conflict beyond the bounds of political action.

The Restoration of Order

The reaction of government to the violence of May 13 was not immediate. The initial eruption produced a temporary paralysis of authority. The following day and the continuation of communal violence brought a royal declaration of a state of emergency with a suspension of the constitution and the parliamentary system as well as elections still proceeding in the Borneo states. Into this vacuum was inserted a Temple-like creation: the National Operations Council

(N.O.C.) under the direction of the Deputy-Prime Minister Tun Razak. The net effect was to freeze the political process and to gradually insulate those forces making for intercommunal confrontation. Government became rule by decree and those making the decrees were the leading figures in the U.M.N.O. political establishment backed by the arms of the Royal Malay Regiment. Ancillary to this body, there was established an Emergency Cabinet within which participated in junior positions Chinese and Indians from the electorally discredited non-Malay constituents of the Alliance. It has been this administrative structure of government which has sought to restore stability and confidence to a somewhat dazed country.

The principal priority of this governmental structure has been the maintenance of order and the damping down of communal tension. To this end, it has enforced curfews and initiated preventive detention and has succeeded in maintaining the peace with the exception of a brief interlude of violence at the end of June 1969. It should be pointed out, however, that its security problem was not of peninsula-wide proportions. Communal violence was confined in the main to Kuala Lumpur and succeeding outbreaks in other urban areas were both limited and quickly contained. It is significant, perhaps, that the island of Penang — the source of racial violence in November 1967 — was not affected and also that the non-Malays in the rural areas, where they are a minority, were not subjected to intimidation.

Order has been restored in Malaysia but not a political order. Tentative moves only have been made towards this end with the establishment in January 1970 of a nominated National Consultative Council. This body has a multi-communal representation and covers a functional spectrum of political and professional life with the significant exception of the D.A.P. which is engaged in a boycott because one of its nominees — organizing secretary Lim Kit-siang — is held in preventive detention. The function of the National Consultative Council is to inaugurate an inter-communal dialogue which, it is hoped, will lead to the formulation of agreed ground rules for the revival of political activity. The suggested outline for such a consensus has been indicated by the N.O.C. in its report on the May 13 violence. But before considering this suggestion and its significance, it is necessary to consider some of the other consequences of the events of May 1969.

Consequences of Violence

The outbreak of violence was a symptom of Malay anxieties and a reaction to the manner of non-Malay political participation. In its aftermath, the non-Malays appeared the most saddened and shocked. Quantitatively, they bore the brunt of the violence in terms of loss of life and property. In the N.O.C. report, the number of deaths recorded up to June 30, 1969, was 196. Of these 171 were non-Malay and of the non-Malays 143 were Chinese. The non-Malays have been angered by the semi-official and official explanations of the riots and particularly the charge that they were instigated by the communists which in Malaysia can only mean Chinese. In point of fact it is known that both the communists and the Government were equally taken by surprise by the outbreak of violence. They have been angered also by the initial behaviour of the forces of law and order who according to reliable accounts indulged in irresponsible conduct. Perceiving only the outbreak and the cause of the violence and not its background the non-Malays feel that they have been charged with responsibility for a pogrom in which they were the principal victims. Trust in government has declined as a consequence.

Non-Malay behaviour in the aftermath of the violence has indicated a certain resilience as well as demoralization. An apparently spontaneous boycott of Malay business enterprise did not last long. The non-Malays in the peninsula, especially the Chinese, have nowhere else to go and the indications are that they are trying to make the best of an unhappy situation; not a unique exercise in the history of the overseas Chinese. Apart from the D.A.P., the representatives of the opposition parties have recognized the utility of co-operating with the N.O.C. in the interests of communal peace.

The aftermath of May 13 has led to speculation that younger Chinese may take to the jungle and join with Chin Peng's guerrillas along the Thai border. There have been reports of young men disappearing concurrent with accounts of renewed communist activity in the north of the country. So far, however, such activity has been sporadic. An insurgency does not spring up entirely overnight and for the time being the security forces appear to have the upper hand. The prospects for Chin Peng will depend on the extent of Chinese alienation in the future.

The action of the N.O.C. has not transformed the position of the Malays, although it has provided assurance of political dominance. U.M.N.O. is certainly concerned about the erosion of its Malay base and measures have been taken to consolidate it. For example, besides recruiting three additional battalions to the Royal Malay Regiment, non-Malay citizenship rights have come under scrutiny and Malay-medium instruction is being introduced into all primary schools. A basic problem, however, is economic prospects. Although the economy has remained buoyant, because of external demand for primary products, the employment situation is not encouraging. In October 1969, there were nearly 160,000 officially registered as out of work. Malays moving from rural to urban areas make up a significant number of these. Early in 1970 Tun Razak inaugurated a National Youth Development Corps to cope with this problem. But the prospects of any early transformation of the Malay economic condition is not expected. Such a condition increasingly leads Malays to question whether the issue of special rights is relevant to their situation.

Shortly after the riots there arose a challenge to the position of the Tunku by a group of Malay militants who included in their demands the establishment of a system of apartheid. This challenge was dealt with expeditiously in particular through the expulsion from U.M.N.O. of a disgruntled defeated candidate. The Tunku appears to have recovered his personal position but his day of retirement cannot be far away. And there are some doubts as to whether his designated successor, Tun Razak, can overcome the role of longstanding Crown Prince. His future and perhaps the future of Malaysia depends on an ability to square the communal triangle. Malay economic demands require satisfaction and the status of *bumiputera* has to be substantive as well as symbolic. At the same time it is necessary to face the question of non-Malay political participation with which the Alliance system has been unable to cope.

With these factors in mind, one can consider the prescriptive aspect of the N.O.C. report. An irony of this report is that while it defends the suspension of the constitution because of exigency, it invests that self-same constitution with a hallowed sanctity as a basis for future political activity. In other words, the constitution did not fail the people. The people failed the constitution and, in order to restore a viable polity, it becomes necessary to return to its spirit. One passage from the report of the N.O.C. is extremely instructive — in terms of this argument. It reads:

The entrenched provisions in the Constitution are the result of agreement between all the communities in this country. They are the product of consultation and compromise. They represent binding arrangements between the various races in this country, and are the underpinnings on which the constitutional structure such as fundamental liberties, the machinery of government and a score of other detailed provisions are built. If these entrenched provisions are in any way eroded or weakened, the entire constitutional structure is endangered, and with it, the existence of the nation itself. It was the failure to understand, and the irresponsible and cavalier treatment of these extended provisions, that constituted one of the primary causes of the disturbance on May 13, 1969.[2]

This statement is quite explicit. Uncompromising in tone, it postulates the basic limits within which politics can take place within Malaysia.

In the preface to the report, Tun Razak speaks of the need "to construct a political framework which is realistic". The passage quoted demonstrates a stark realism congruent with the tolerable limits of compromise for those who command the forces of order in Malaysia. The National Consultative Council has been established by those who are adamantly unwilling to depart from the premise that their interpretation of the independence constitution is beyond challenge. In this respect, there is very little that the National Consultative Council can reasonably discuss. Its informal terms of reference call for ratification and not constitutional debate. The outcome of May 13 has not been to effect any genuine reconciliation of the adverse conceptions of Malaysia. It has made those still in power even more determined to underpin their own view of the state. They perceive communal compromise only within the framework of their interpretation of the constitution. They may well be right in this assessment. Chin Peng sits hopefully in the jungle in the expectation that they may be wrong.

Notes

1. Tunku Abdul Rahman, *May 13. Before and After* (Kuala Lumpur, 1969, pp. 19–20).
2. The National Operations Council, *The May 13 Tragedy. A Report* (Kuala Lumpur, 1969, p. 85).

43

Malaysia after Tun Razak
Tensions in a Multi-racial State

The achievements of Tun Abdul Razak as a devoted and faithful servant of his country are legion. He carried an excessively heavy burden of ministerial responsibility from 1955 when he resigned from the Malayan Civil Service to enter political life as the dedicated deputy of Tunku Abdul Rahman. In this role, he established the bases of educational policy and development administration and also guided the growth of Malaysia's defence establishment. But probably his greatest contribution was in shoring up the fragile structure of the multi-racial state after it had been beset by violent upheaval and then underpinning it with an enlarged inter-communal coalition which he forged as Prime Minister in his own right.

The great irony of the untimely and tragic death of Tun Razak is that it occurred so soon after the effective political consolidation of his position within Malaysia and also within its dominant party, the United Malays National Organisation (UMNO). In August 1974, the

Reprinted from Michael Leifer, "Malaysia after Tun Razak: Tensions in a Multi-racial State", *The Round Table,* no. 262 (1976): 153–60, by permission of Taylor and Francis Limited <http://www.tandf.co.uk/journals>.

National Front governing coalition which he had fabricated in piecemeal fashion won a resounding victory under his leadership in the federal elections. In June 1975, at the triennial General Assembly of UMNO, he had the satisfaction of seeing himself and his chosen deputy Prime Minister, Datuk Hussein Onn, returned unopposed to the positions of President and deputy President. In addition, he was able to secure the election of his favoured nominees for the three posts of vice-president of the organisation.

Tun Razak's death at the relatively early age of fifty-three years has left a political vacuum in Malaysian politics. The manner in which that vacuum is effectively filled will be of supreme importance because of the critical juncture which the country now faces. Interlocking challenges arise from the related revival of communal tension and Communist insurgency, and the mishandling of either problem could have incalculable consequences.

Communalism and Politics

The dominant feature of Malaysian politics derives from the plural nature of its society and the attendant tensions between the Malays and the non-Malays who are, in the main, Chinese in the peninsular part of the country. Although the society is plural, Malaysia has been governed increasingly as a Malay state. Indeed, in this respect, a political tradition has been sustained which served as the ostensible premise and justification of British colonial rule. Malay political predominance has taken both symbolic and substantive form. But in the wake of the communal violence of May 1969, which had followed general elections in which UMNO had lost significant support to its principal Malay rival, the special position of the Malays was more deeply entrenched in constitutional terms by the proscription of public questioning of so-called "sensitive issues".[1] Concurrently, the emphasis of the government's economic policy was shifted in order to reverse political seepage from an assumed proprietary constituency. This New Economy Policy incorporated within the second Five Year Plan gave prominence to the restructuring of Malaysian society and was designed, above all, to redress the economic imbalance between the Malays and the Chinese. The underlying political purpose was to curb the growing sense of grievance on the part of the Malay community which had been expressed, in-part, at the polls in 1969.

The New Economic Policy sought to provide the Malays with a 30 per cent stake in the management and ownership of the economy within a generation and was intended to establish a substantive economic underpinning to Malay political dominance which would put it beyond challenge from the non-Malay communities. This policy came to be identified by the exclusive term *bumiputra* (sons of the soil), by which the Malays had come to refer to themselves. It was predicated in theory on a rate of economic growth which would permit a redistribution of wealth without depriving the non-Malays of the fruits of their labours. In practice, the application of the *bumiputra* policy has had the initial impact of benefiting only a limited number of Malays but without necessarily producing an innovative and managerial class from among them. It has also attracted a sense of grievance on the part of non-beneficiaries within the Malay community whose economic expectations have been aroused but not fulfilled, especially in a period of economic decline. This sense of grievance has been articulated publicly by Malay students, themselves beneficiaries of preferential treatment in the form of easy access to university places and scholarships. They represent a new generation of involved and politically-conscious Malays whose rural origins make their own experience of life relevant to their political involvement.

Apart from its mixed impact among the Malays, the application of the exclusivist *bumiputra* policy has increased the sense of alienation of the non-Malay community who as non-*bumiputra* by definition have come increasingly to feel themselves to be second class citizens in a country to which they are expected to give their primary allegiance. In addition to a lingering resentment of the blame attached to them for communal violence and their lack of sympathy towards the entrenched status of the Malays expressed in preferential treatment in education and employment, the Chinese and Indians have felt a sense of bitterness at the fact that the large numbers of poor people within their communities have not received official recognition in past government policies.

The emphasis and presentation of the New Economic Policy which had given rise not only to non-Malay bitterness but also to some Malay resentment had been recognised as misplaced by Tun Razak in the last months of his life. Indeed, he had already begun to give a lead in reducing the significance attached to the special status of *bumiputra* and to replace the term's prominent position in the symbolic side of public life by stressing the concern of the government with the alleviation of poverty irrespective of race.

Communist Insurgency

The importance attached to the public modification of economic policy was a product in part of the revival of Communist insurgency in peninsular Malaysia. Ironically, that revival which began as far back as 1967 made an increasingly visible impact from the time of the visit to China by Tun Razak in May 1974. Central to the initiative in seeking diplomatic relations with China was a belief that such an accomplishment, together with the ritual reception of Tun Razak by Chairman Mao Tse-tung, would indicate to the large Chinese community of Malaysia that their interests would be served best by unreservedly extending their loyalty to their country of residence. The attempt to bring about the more effective political domestication of Malaysia's Chinese community was a direct consequence of the fact that the Malayan Communist Party (MCP) had always been predominantly Chinese in composition, and that its fortunes had, in turn, depended on the support which it could attract from its natural ethnic constituency.

Whether provoked or not by Tun Razak's visit to China, just prior to his departure for Peking, an insurgent force sabotaged a considerable quantity of road-building equipment at a work site on the route of the projected East-West highway. This highway represents not only a major development undertaking but also an intended means of tactical mobility for counter-insurgency forces along the border region with Thailand which serves as the base area for the MCP. Since that time, the MCP, which split into competing factions in 1970, has shown its hand increasingly in a number of dramatic ways, including the assassination of police officers.

Because of the association between the MCP and the Chinese community, the impact of the security measures taken by the Malaysian Government, given the increasing incidence of Communist insurgent activity, has been felt most acutely by the Chinese. In these circumstances, it became all the more imperative to modify the emphasis of economic policy in order to mitigate not only its effect among the non-Malays but also the impact of counter-insurgency measures. Tun Razak appeared to recognise the serious need to arrest the decline in the confidence of government by convincing all the people of Malaysia that it was concerned to protect their interests.

Political Succession

Tun Razak has been succeeded as Prime Minister of Malaysia by Datuk Hussein Onn who only assumed the post of deputy Prime Minister in August 1973 following the death of Tun Ismail. Datuk Hussein comes from a prominent political family. His father was a founder of UMNO and led the successful Malay nationalist campaign against the Malayan Union policy of the British. Although Datuk Hussein is regarded as a capable and virtuous man, he is not thought to be over-enthusiastic about assuming, for an indefinite period, the onerous burden which is the lot of the Prime Minister of Malaysia. Indeed, he is not in the best of health and is known to suffer from a heart condition.

In these circumstances of some uncertainty over enduring political succession, personal and factional conflict could well aggravate the communal situation which Tun Razak had latterly sought to contain. The Prime Minister of Malaysia has to be the leader of UMNO, and the principal qualification of the holder of such a post is that he must be seen to possess an unswerving dedication to the maintenance of Malay political dominance. Indeed, the father of Datuk Hussein discovered this harsh fact of political life when he sought, without success, over a quarter of a century ago, to convert UMNO into a multi-racial party. Any struggle for a more assured political succession is certain to involve competitive bidding for support within the Malay community which, by its very nature, would be certain to aggravate the apprehensions of the non-Malay communities, especially the Chinese who feel themselves to be increasingly under a cloud as insurgency continues without convincing evidence of the success of government in arresting it.

Such a course of events would only contribute to Malaysia's problems. Their solution depends, above all, on the management of communal tensions. While it is essential that the Malays have as Prime Minister a co-religionist who has a clear sense of their priorities, it is important also that he should be acceptable to the non-Malays who make up almost half the population. Tunku Abdul Rahman was such a man, at least until towards the end of his tenure of office, and if Tun Razak was less so, his position as leader was made acceptable because of his long apprenticeship as the deputy of the Tunku. The problem in a country like Malaysia where the communal divide has widened progressively is that men most suited to hold the middle ground of politics are not necessarily acceptable to those whose horizons are clouded by communal considerations.

There can be no doubt that Malaysia requires a stable political leadership underpinned by a strong personality. It faces a testing period given the generally unfavourable climate of economic circumstances and the dramatic impact of an insurgency which has had the intended effect of reducing popular confidence in the competence of government at a time when unease and uncertainty persist within non-Communist South-East Asia following the recent radical political changes within Indochina. An additional reason for the importance of a leadership manifesting both stability and strength is that Tun Razak had managed to contain, if not to control, two *enfants terribles* of Malaysian politics with the ambition to fill the vacuum left by his death, or to play a major role in its filling.

Political Recalcitrants

Tun Mustapha was, until the end of October last year, the Chief Minister of the Malaysian state of Sabah which he ruled like a mediaeval prince. Apart from his ostentatious and idiosyncratic style, his independent conduct of state affairs including involvement in the Muslim rebellion in the south of the Philippines placed a major strain on relations between the government in Kota Kinabalu and that in Kuala Lumpur. In order to curb his political pretensions and excesses, Tun Mustapha was persuaded to accept the post of Minister of Defence with third-ranking place in the Federal Cabinet formed after the elections of 1974. After this arrangement was made public, together with attendant speculation that its purpose was the political domestication of Tun Mustapha, he caused Tun Razak considerable political embarrassment by refusing to take it up on the grounds that the needs of Sabah took priority.

Relations between Tun Razak and Tun Mustapha deteriorated when, under the impact of a significant fall in timber prices, an initiative by the Sabah Government to act independently in securing external sources of loan finance was blocked by the federal authorities. Tun Mustapha responded by holding out the threat of Sabah seceeding from Malaysia. And this political defiance was countered by an inspired open challenge to the rule of Tun Mustapha within Sabah when, in

July 1975, an opposition political party, Berjaya, made its appearance from the ranks of the dominant United Sabah National Organisation (USNO). Its appearance and its open opposition to Tun Mustapha were facilitated by the action of the Federal Government in replacing Sabah's Commissioner of Police; a man with a reputation for a willingness to arrest the political opponent of Tun Mustapha.

In the event, the political crisis in Sabah and also in federal-state relations was resolved by Tun Mustapha agreeing to resign as Chief Minister in favour of his political associate of long standing, deputy Chief Minister Tan Sri Mohammed Said Keruak. But all this transpired only after Tun Mustapha had secured a vote of confidence in the Sabah legislature and consolidated his political position by Cabinet reshuffle so that twenty-four out of thirty-eight state assembly members held official posts as a consequence of his benefaction. Tun Mustapha resigned from office on October 31, 1975, but only as Chief Minister, and not as President of USNO which, like its counterpart in peninsular Malaysia, is the crucial base of political power. One indication of his continuing power outside of office is that the state assembly in a special bill voted him all the facilities of a Chief Minister.

The resignation of Tun Mustapha can be compared to the abdication of King Sihanouk of Cambodia in 1955 and of the Sultan of Brunei in 1967. Indeed, his political influence was felt after his resignation when USNO defeated the political challenge of the inspired defectors' party in two by-elections which Berjaya provoked. In January 1976, in the wake of these by-elections, and only days after the death of Tun Razak, the new chief Minister gave notice of the dissolution of the Sabah state legislature and the holding of general elections, ostensibly so that his government could secure a new mandate in order to implement its development programme. There is every prospect that USNO together with its subordinate Chinese partner within the ruling Sabah Alliance will win an overwhelming majority of seats. Should such a striking demonstration of the political resilience of Tun Mustapha take place, it could stimulate his ambition to make Datuk Hussein's life as Prime Minister that more difficult.

Another political recalcitrant has been Datuk Harun Idris, the former Chief Minister of the State of Selangor, who initially took leave of absence from his post while facing charges of corruption and malpractice. Datuk Harun is widely regarded in Malaysia as having played a notorious role in fomenting Malay agitation just prior to the outbreak of communal violence in May 1969. He had been regarded as a man of some political standing with a powerful constituency among the UMNO youth organisation. He only just missed securing the third place in the elections for the three posts of Vice-President at the UMNO General Assembly in June 1975. The Federal Government has been embarrassed, however, by the nature of his financial interests insofar as they have placed a harmful construction on the practice of the *bumiputra* economic policy.

Tun Razak sought to remove Datuk Harun from the Malaysian political scene by attempting to persuade him to accept a post at the country's mission to the United Nations in New York. It was upon his refusal that the charges of corruption were brought. He did not show any sign of a decline in self-confidence, however, despite this setback but seemed eager to defend himself in order to pursue political ambitions which could have been secured only through wider support within the Malay community. When it became known that Datuk Harun had been arraigned on charges of corruption, the Chinese of Kuala Lumpur were reported to have trembled at the prospect of young Malays from local *kampongs* going on the rampage to protest at this action against their patron and father-figure. On March 18, however, an emergency meeting of the UMNO Supreme Council resulted in the expulsion of Datuk Harun from the party — an indicator that Datuk Hussein is determined to exercise strong leadership, especially when political recalcitrance can aggravate communal tensions. Subsequently Datuk Harun resigned from the post of Chief Minister of Selangor.

The Need for Stability

The key to the future political well-being of Malaysia is the consolidation of effective leadership at a time when communal tensions serve the cause of the Malayan Communist Party. Tun Razak made a major contribution to that well-being by his promotion of the inter-communal National Front Coalition whereby political participation could be separated from undue popular passion. It would seem important for political stability in Malaysia in the near future for such a coalition to survive if only on the basis of co-existence. In this respect a major task which falls on the shoulders of Datuk Hussein is to provide the kind of leadership that will both sustain genuine intercommunal government; one consistent with Malay priorities, but ensuring also the co-operation of the non-

Malay communities through a demonstrable attachment to policies of moderation.

One indication of Datuk Hussein's priorities has been his appointment as deputy Prime Minister of the Minister of Education, Dr. Mahathir Mohammed, Dr. Mahathir has been a controversial figure in Malaysian politics. During the election campaign in 1969, he advised his Chinese constituents not to vote for him as he would not represent their interests in Parliament. In the event, he failed to secure re-election and then led a movement of younger Malays seeking to oust Tunku Abdul Rahman. In a personal letter to the Tunku, he wrote: "In truth, the Malays whether they are UMNO or PMIP supporters really hate you", and accused the former Prime Minister of making undue concessions to the Chinese. For this act of political *lèse-majesté*, he was expelled from the Executive Council of UMNO and then from the organisation itself. While in the political wilderness, he published a book entitled *The Malay Dilemma* in which he wrote that "the Malays are the rightful owners of Malaya and that if citizenship is conferred on races other than the Malays, it is because the Malays consent to this. That consent is conditional".

Dr. Mahathir was returned to the UMNO fold with the consolidation of Tun Razak's position. He re-entered Parliament and assumed cabinet office after the August 1974 elections. As Minister of Education, he has taken a strong line against undue political activity on the part of Malay students, some of whom now see him as a member of the UMNO establishment. His popularity within UMNO, however, was reflected in his attainment of the third post of Vice-President of the organisation at its General Assembly in June 1975. Although it would appear that Datuk Hussein has chosen as his deputy someone regarded by the non-Malays as a Malay ultra, it is almost certain that the responsibilities of high office will demand a moderation of his communal views. In this respect it is significant that the expulsion from UMNO of Datuk Harun came within two weeks of Dr. Mahathir's appointment and was intended in part to reassure the non-Malay communities of the new leadership's awareness of their political anxieties.

At the moment of political succession Datuk Hussein appeared overwhelmed by the harsh act of fate which had elevated him to high office. Yet he has not permitted himself to be overwhelmed by the immediate responsibilities of that office. Indeed, within a very short time, he demonstrated a sense of calm and stability which has begun to convey itself to an anxious political public. He was helped in making the enforced change of position by the expeditious way in which he was endorsed both by the UMNO Supreme Council and by the Council of the ruling National Front coalition. He has been assisted also by the fact that he has a reputation as a man of integrity without personal ambition. His re-entry into political life was a product of Tun Razak's persuasion and his own sense of duty. It may well be that his experience as an active soldier and as a lawyer will give him the qualities of decisiveness and judgment which Malaysia undoubtedly needs. The hour has often called forth the man, and providing his health — a major factor — and personal authority stand the test of any continuing manoeuvring for political advantage among UMNO luminaries, Datuk Hussein could do for Malaysia what Pope John did for the Church of Rome.

While it is much too early to make any lasting judgments, two features of Datuk Hussein's initial rule stand out. First, he is not the kind of man likely to aggravate consciously communal tensions. Indeed his former association with his father in seeking to encourage multi-racialism should stand him in good stead with the non-Malay communities. Secondly, he will not bring about any major change in Malaysia's foreign policy. His reaffirmation of a policy of regional co-operation within the context of the Association of South-East Asian Nations was exemplified by his early meetings with ASEAN leaders before the organisation's Summit Conference in Bali at the end of February at which he also demonstrated his commitment to continuity in foreign relations.

Note

1. See the author's "Adverse Conceptions of Malaysia", *The Round Table*, July 1970.

44

Anti-Semitism without Jews
The Malaysian Example*

Anti-Semitism without Jews is an unusual, if not unique, phenomenon. In the case of Malaysia, anti-Semitic sentiment has been identified specifically with Prime Minister Dr. Mahathir Mohammad. From the middle of 1986, Dr. Mahathir made a series of allegations charging that Zionists and Jews, without distinction, were trying to destabilise the country through a campaign in Jewish-controlled media. Whether from personal conviction or political opportunism, Dr. Mahathir's remarks indicated indulgence in a demonology whose modern origins may be traced back to the ill-framed forgery, *The Protocols of the Learned Elders of Zion,* reprinted in Malaysia in 1983. That demonology reached its peak during a speech delivered by Dr. Mahathir in October 1986 before the conference of Non-Aligned states in Zimbabwe. On that occasion, he asserted: "The expulsion of Jews from the Holy Land some 2,000 years ago and the Nazi oppression of Jews have taught them nothing. If at all, it has transformed the Jews into the very

Reprinted from Michael Leifer, "Anti-Semitism without Jews: The Malaysian Example", *Australian Institute of Jewish Affairs Survey* 4, no. 3 (1987): 3, by permission of the Australian/Israel & Jewish Affairs Council.

monsters that they condemn so roundly in their propaganda materials. They have been apt pupils of Dr. Goebbels".

By that juncture, Dr. Mahathir's *obiter dicta* about Zionists and Jews, employed interchangeably, had provoked international response including condemnation from the Anti-Defamation League of B'nai B'rith. Moreover, Malaysia was in the process of modifying its foreign investment laws in an attempt to revive a faltering economy. Significantly, by the time President Chaim Herzog of Israel visited neighbouring Singapore in November, generating political furore in Malaysia, Dr. Mahathir had ceased making either anti-Zionist or anti-Jewish statements. Indeed, by the following March, Dr. Mahathir had begun to change his public tune. He told the *New York Times* that his remarks about Zionism reflected only his opposition to an "extreme nationalism" manifested by some Jews. "I'm not anti-Jew", he said. "Henry Kissinger was just here (in Malaysia). We talk; we are friends. I have a lot of American businessmen who are my friends. They are Jews."

Dr. Mahathir's personal commitment to the cause of Palestinian nationalism is of long standing and reflects a sense of communal insecurity. Indeed, he has drawn a parallel between Britain's willingness, after the Second World War, to imperil the political birthright of the indigenous Malay-Muslim community and its corresponding behaviour in the case of Palestine. In his book *The Malay Dilemma,* first published in 1970, he points out: "In Palestine, for example, the whole country was taken from the Arabs and handed over to the Jews". That sentence, however, is only one of two referring to Jews in the entire volume. The other, if also isolated, betrays a crude stereotyping claiming: "The Jews for example are not merely hook-nosed, but understand money instinctively".

To try to get some grasp of the anti-Semitic disposition of Dr. Mahathir, it is necessary to take full account of political change within Malaysia over the past two decades. Whatever the personal prejudices of Dr. Mahathir, Malaysian politics have become increasingly dominated by the role of Islam in determining the identity of the Malay community. That community, which comprises a bare majority over more vigorous Chinese and Indian communities of migrant origin, has long felt vulnerable and embattled.

As the Islamic factor became a more central part of Malay identity, so there occurred an increasing identification with the Palestinian cause understood as a co-religionist issue. Initially, there had been a measure of ambivalence towards Israel. Recognition had been accorded but without the establishment of diplomatic relations. There was no Jewish community in Malaya/Malaysia. A cemetery in Penang houses the remains of one established under colonial auspices. For the brief period that Singapore was part of Malaysia, its declining community was subject to rule from Kuala Lumpur. The only Israeli presence of any kind, was a representative of the country's citrus board in Kuala Lumpur during the 1960s.

The June 1967 War and Israel's control of all of Jerusalem, including Muslim holy places, caused a stir throughout the Islamic world. Even before the visible impact of an Islamic resurgence within Malaysia, its first Prime Minister Tunku Abdul Rahman, noted for his multiracial outlook, played a leading role in publicising what he described at the United Nations as "The Muslim Cause". Malaysia's commitment to the Palestinians became more explicit and vocal when, under Tunku Abdul Rahman's successor Tun Abdul Razak, the country joined the Non-Aligned Movement in an attempt to establish a more progressive international identity. That support was expressed domestically in political display serving a useful function in the context of a growing Islamic assertiveness. For example, Palestinian Day and Al-Aqsa Day have become regular dates in the official calendar of state. Al-Fatah was given permission to open an office in Kuala Lumpur in April 1969 becoming a Palestine Liberation Organisation office in 1974. More significantly, in 1981, coincident with Dr. Mahathir becoming Prime Minister, that office and its representative were accorded full diplomatic status.

In the light of the role of Islam in Malaysia as the cornerstone of Malay identity and as a central factor in intra-Malay political competition, Dr. Mahathir's support for Palestinian nationalism and his strictures against Zionism serve a domestic function. His publicly expressed conviction that Zionism is a pernicious phenomenon capable of threatening the well-being of Malaysia may seem like national paranoia, but it reflects an established prejudice among the dominant Malay-Muslim community. Moreover, that prejudice does not make any distinction between Zionists and Jews.

Of some interest, however, was the disappearance of anti-Zionist and anti-Jewish rhetoric from Dr. Mahathir's statements in the public acrimony which arose with the visit to Singapore in November, 1986 of President Chaim Herzog. The official visit to the neighbouring island state by the President of Israel was interpreted in Malaysia as a provocative act. It was represented as a public flaunting of a politically unhygienic relationship prompting a formal diplomatic protest and the temporary withdrawal from Singapore of Malaysia's High Commissioner. Agitation in Malaysia was begun by the youth-wing of the United Malays National Organisation (UMNO) in Dr. Mahathir's home state of Kedah. Its momentum was sustained by an *ad hoc* action committee, comprising mainly left-wing and Islamic opposition elements, who relished the heaven-sent opportunity to mobilise public support over an issue which was beyond governmental reproach. The issue arose also at a time of some communal tension between Chinese and Malays over questioning of the prerogative position of the latter. Singapore has never been completely insulated from such tension because of its prevailing ethnic-Chinese social identity, as well as the persisting legacy of its stormy political interlude as a constituent state of the Malaysian Federation between 1963–65. The initial position adopted by the Malaysian government, that it did not have the right to protest over the visit because the matter was an internal affair of another country, was reversed in response to domestic pressure. The bad feeling on both sides of the causeway joining the two states has continued because of attention focussed in Singapore on the loyalty of its Malay community, which comprises fifteen per cent of the population. During the visit by President Herzog, many of their voluntary organisations identified with co-religionists across the causeway.

In a political sense, Dr. Mahathir was hoisted by his own petard. Irrespective of personal conviction, his use of anti-Zionist and anti-Jewish rhetoric had served to increase an Islamic appetite which indicated a potential to swallow him politically as well as endangering the cohesion of ASEAN, the regional grouping represented as the main pillar of Malaysia's foreign policy. His awareness of the dangers of undue personal association with anti-Zionist demonology was confirmed by his last minute absence from the opening ceremony of Palestine Week in March, 1987 held in Johor Baru at the Malaysian end of the causeway with Singapore. In the context of a struggle for political leadership within UMNO, he was also charged by former deputy Prime Minister Musa Hitam with hampering Malaysia's economic development by his criticism of Zionism.

Irrespective of personal conviction, perhaps fed by access to Jewish conspiracy literature from the United States, Dr. Mahathir would appear to have revised his view of the utility of playing the anti-

Zionist and anti-Jewish cards. Although he has sought to identify himself with the Islamic cause in the interests of political control, he is certainly aware of the vulnerability of UMNO to Islamic challenge because it has chosen to engage in intercommunal political partnership as a basis for stable government. To that extent, anti-Zionist and anti-Jewish demonology can rebound to his domestic political disadvantage, in addition to provoking international condemnation. Nevertheless, the political climate in which such rhetoric was employed has not changed, and anti-Semitism without Jews in Malaysia has not been expunged as an available political tool.

Note

* Adapted from a paper presented at the Second Asian-Jewish Colloquium by Professor Michael Leifer.

45

Anglo-Malaysian Alienation Revisited

In October 1981, Malaysia's Prime Minister, Dr Mahathir Mohamad, issued an instruction that all future governmental purchases from Britain would have to be referred to his office for final approval together with an alternative bid from a non-British source. This instruction inaugurated what became known as Malaysia's "Buy British Last" policy whereby British products would be purchased only as a last resort. That policy was a calculated riposte to conduct by the former colonial power deemed harmful to Malaysian interests. It expressed the personal animus of a newly appointed Prime Minister who was determined to register his political authority and national standing. The policy was reversed during the decade through the intervention of Britain's Prime Minister, Mrs Margaret Thatcher. She established a close relationship with Dr Mahathir which overcame his sense of injured national pride and which helped also to restore a flourishing Anglo-Malaysian trade relationship.

Reprinted from Michael Leifer, "Anglo-Malaysian Alienation Revisited", *The Round Table*, no. 331 (1994): 347–59, by permission of Taylor and Francis Limited <http://www.tandf.co.uk/journals>.

In February 1994, Anglo-Malaysian relations were disturbed dramatically for a second time, again through the direct initiative of Prime Minister, Dr Mahathir. Angered by allegations in the British press of his personal financial impropriety, Malaysia's cabinet decided that British companies would be excluded from tendering for any new government (construction) contracts. In March, in a letter to *The Financial Times,* Dr Mahathir expressed his personal bitterness over the way in which he and Malaysia had been maligned by the British press.[1]

The punitive action taken in 1994 was different from that adopted in 1981. British companies were excluded from all government contracts, irrespective of the competitiveness of their tenders. Moreover, the target of retaliation was quite unconnected in any way with the alleged defamatory press comment which had provoked Dr Mahathir's wrath. That comment had been beyond the control of British companies and the government in Westminster which had been held directly responsible for delinquencies in 1981. There is a further apparent difference in context between the two episodes. In October 1981, Dr Mahathir had occupied high office for only three months having recently succeeded Hussein Onn who had retired on grounds of ill-health. He had sound political reason then to put a personal stamp on the conduct of his new office. And what better way to do so than at the expense of the former colonial power against which he harboured unconcealed resentments. In February 1994, however, Dr Mahathir seemed a well established and self-confident leader who had no need to pick on a soft external target.

In February 1994, Dr Mahathir had occupied the office of Prime Minister continuously for nearly 13 years. As President of the United Malays National Organization (UMNO), he had led the politically dominant party to three successive electoral victories, despite a strong challenge to his leadership in 1987. Within Malaysia, he had asserted himself effectively against the press, the judiciary and the constitutional monarchy and had not been hesitant in employing the Internal Security Act against political opponents. He had also come to enjoy international acclaim as a combative champion of Third World causes. That role had been underpinned by Malaysia's impressive economic performance in export-led growth. His acerbic jibes in retort to alleged personal and national slights and the hypocrisy of the West had become commonplace. He had been enraged in particular by Western attempts to dictate a respect for human rights and the environment, while lacking resolve in the face of "ethnic cleansing" in Bosnia. The prospect of Malaysian trade sanctions against Australia had seemed likely for a time at the end of 1993 because Prime Minister Paul Keating had referred to Dr Mahathir as recalcitrant for not attending an informal summit of Asian-Pacific leaders in Seattle. The way in which he lashed out against innocent parties in response to British press comment was not totally out of character but it did suggest an extraordinary personal fury and lust for retribution. Besides causing consternation in London, his conduct appeared to disconcert cabinet colleagues as well as to embarrass regional partners within the Association of South-East Asian Nations (ASEAN).

This article is an attempt to assess the second round of Anglo-Malaysian alienation set against the experience of the first.[2] In addressing the motives for Malaysia's punitive policy, it will naturally consider Dr Mahathir's outrage at affronts to personal and national dignity. It will also take into account any expectations which might have been held of the government of John Major as well as the domestic political context within the Federation. Dr Mahathir may enjoy a bad press in Britain which has focused on his reputation for irascibility. However, although impulsive, strong minded and a political risk-taker, he is not normally given to inconsequential acts. Running through his political career has been an evident strain of pragmatism.

Buy British Last

The precipitating factor in the "Buy British Last" policy in October 1981 had been the decision to amend the take-over code of the London Stock Exchange to prevent "dawn raids". The Council of Securities Industry took action in the immediate wake of Permodalan Nasional Berhad, Malaysia's investment agency, securing control of Guthrie Corporation through such a procedure in September. The decision was construed in Kuala Lumpur as a deliberate attempt to prevent Malaysia from acquiring control of further of its British-owned national assets by legitimate means and as such a challenge to its economic policy. Shortly after announcing the "Buy British Last" policy, Dr Mahathir pointed out: "If they (the British) can change the rules of the game after we have just mastered them, so can we change the rules of the game".[3]

There were other factors which contributed to Dr Mahathir's punitive policy, including irritation at Britain's refusal to grant additional landing rights at Heathrow to Malaysia's national airline. Shortly before becoming Prime Minister, Dr Mahathir had been visibly angered by remarks made by Britain's newly appointed High Commissioner, William Bentley. He had served in Kuala Lumpur during the mid-1960s when the newly established federation was visibly dependent on the former colonial power in coping with Indonesia's intimidating policy of confrontation. Mr Bentley had made passing reference in a press interview to the contribution of British servicemen to Malaysia, harking back to the period of Communist insurrection. Such remarks were unwelcome to a politician of Dr Mahathir's background and generation who resented Britain's colonial role in fostering Chinese and Indian migration which had posed a fundamental threat to the political birthright of the indigenous Malays.

Dr Mahathir had been outspoken on behalf of the Malay cause after racial riots in May 1969 which had reflected his community's vulnerability and their loss of confidence in national leadership. He had been expelled from UMNO for his caustic criticism of Tunku Abdul Rahman, the country's first Prime Minister. He then wrote a political testament, *The Malay Dilemma,* which was judged so controversial in content and prescription that it was banned until August 1981 after Dr Mahathir had become Prime Minister.[4] Dr Mahathir differed from all three of his predecessors as prime minister by not sharing their common affection for Britain and its ways. They had all been educated in law at British universities and inns of court whereas Dr Mahathir had read medicine at the University of Malaya in Singapore where the colonial culture prevailed. They had also had been scions of higher or lesser nobility whereas he was the son of an Indian-Muslim migrant schoolteacher who had been obliged to overcome social and financial disadvantage in taking his life chance. His experiences of Britain both in the political wilderness and with his assumption of a ministerial career in the mid-1970s had been less than happy. His reception by ministerial counterparts in London did not always accord with his views of personal and national respect and he resented the mandarin style of Whitehall.

Dr Mahathir's first portfolio on returning to active politics in Malaysia was that of Education which gave him an appropriate background from which to appreciate the significance of Britain's change of policy in raising fees for overseas students in institutions of further and higher education. With some 12,000 students in post-secondary education in 1981, Malaysia provided the largest overseas number in Britain. Dr Mahathir as deputy-Prime Minister was incensed at the imposition of economic fees without consultation and at the special dispensation accorded to students from European Community states by contrast with those from the Commonwealth with which Britain claimed a special relationship. He assumed office with a very sour view of the Commonwealth and at one time contemplated withdrawing Malaysia from membership.

Dr Mahathir succeeded to the leadership of a far more assertive UMNO than that which had led the country to independence in 1957. In the wake of racial violence in May 1969, a New Economic Policy had been introduced with the deliberate intention of shifting the balance of material advantage in favour of the Malay community. Integral to that policy was a signal reduction of foreign ownership in the corporate sector. UMNO maintained its longstanding practice of inter-communal coalition as the prime vehicle for government but its *bumiputera* (literally, sons of the soil) policy was enforced in a way that Chinese and Indian partners were left in no doubt of their permanent subordinate position. In addition, foreign companies were pressed to reconsider their employment practices to take account of Malay economic expectations. Dr Mahathir had been a precursor of the New Economic Policy but he gave it a change of emphasis by an exhortation to "Look East" to Japan and South Korea for role models for development in place of the West where the drive to work had allegedly been lost.

By the time that Dr Mahathir had become Prime Minister of Malaysia in July 1981, the political culture and international outlook of the country had changed in a way that was not necessarily well appreciated in London. The "Buy British Last" policy therefore came as a shock and Mrs Thatcher took it on herself to bring about its reversal after her Foreign Secretary, Lord Carrington, had failed to make any impact on Dr Mahathir during a visit to Kuala Lumpur in February 1982. Ironically, the seeds of the second phase of Anglo-Malaysian alienation may be traced to the British Prime Minister's determination to reverse Dr Mahathir's policy and to seize every opportunity for promoting bilateral trade relations, including defence exports. Margaret Thatcher's determination and success has to be seen also in the context of the way in which politics and finance within UMNO had become increasingly entangled during Dr Mahathir's tenure.[5]

The "Buy British Last" policy became subject to change after a visit to London by Dr Mahathir in March 1983 during which he indicated a willingness to reconsider it. Later in the month, on his return to Kuala Lumpur, he informed the federal Parliament that Britain had adopted a more positive attitude towards Malaysia, particularly in trade and education. Early in April, Dr Mahathir rescinded his punitive instruction to government departments. The tone of the bilateral relationship improved noticeably from April 1985 when Mrs Thatcher paid her first visit to Malaysia during which an agreement was reached on improved landing rights for Malaysian Airlines. Talks were held also on aid, trade and arms sales which led on to the signature of a memorandum of understanding on defence procurements in September 1988 which became a matter of public controversy in Britain from early 1994. It has been suggested that one factor underlying Malaysia's signature of the memorandum of understanding was the British government's willingness to minimize the embarrassment to Kuala Lumpur arising from disastrous speculation in the Hong Kong property market by a subsidiary of Bank Bumiputera.[6]

The Pergau Dam

Tension in Anglo-Malaysian relations revived when Britain's aid funding for a 600-megawatt hydroelectric power station in Malaysia's east coast state of Kelantan became the subject of parliamentary and then press scrutiny. Although the Pergau Dam project had first received critical mention in the British press in May 1990, the matter only became one of major controversy when Sir Tim Lankester, the second Permanent Secretary of the Overseas Development Administration (ODA) within the Foreign and Commonwealth Office, gave evidence before the Public Accounts Committe of the House of Commons on 17 January 1994. Allegations had been made in the House of Commons in October 1990 that bribes had been paid to Malaysian agents of British companies which had prompted an investigation of the aid and trade programme of the Overseas Development Administration by the National Audit Office. Its report, which was released in October 1993, concluded that good value for money had not been obtained in the case of the Pergau Dam project which inspired the hearings of the Public Accounts Committee at which Sir Tim Lankester gave evidence. He revealed having warned ministers in early February 1991 that the aid package was unequivocally a bad one in economic terms and "an abuse of the aid programme". He disclosed also that the Foreign Secretary, Douglas Hurd, had overruled his advice on the ground that the highest level of understanding had been reached on the project with Malaysia and that to back down would be highly damaging to British trade. The final decision on the aid project had been made by the Prime Minister in late February 1991. John Major explained to the House of Commons early in January 1994 that he and Douglas Hurd had decided to honour a commitment given by Baroness Thatcher, while Prime Minister, in the wider context of maintaining exports to Malaysia.

In the light of the unprecedented revelations by Sir Tim Lankester, the British press broadened its attention from the merits of the dam project to alleged links between aid and defence procurements identifying companies said to be involved in both civil and military contracts in Malaysia.[7] Attention was directed, above all, to the memorandum of understanding on arms sales signed between Mrs Thatcher and Dr Mahathir in September 1988 and the possibility that aid for the Pergau Dam had been "a sweetener" to facilitate a deal for heavy weapons and defence construction projects worth more than a billion pounds. Such a direct link would have been in breach of the Overseas Aid Acts of 1966 and 1980. Attention was addressed also to a visit to Malaysia in March 1988 by George Younger, then Secretary of State for Defence, who had signed a protocol agreeing to a direct link between aid and arms sales. In early February 1994, Alastair Goodlad, Minister of State at the Foreign and Commonwealth Office, confirmed to the House of Commons that George Younger had, in fact, signed a protocol on 23 March 1988 which "contained figures relating amounts or percentages of civil aid to amounts of arms purchases" but that, on 26 June 1988, he had written to Malaysia's Finance Minister to point out that aid could not be linked to defence sales in an arithmetic or any other way.

In evidence before the House of Commons Select Committee on Foreign Affairs in March 1994, Douglas Hurd admitted that aid and defence deals had been "entangled" incorrectly for three months during 1988 but they had then proceeded separately. At issue, however, and unresolved was whether or not the link between aid and defence procurements had been sustained on an informal "nod and a wink" basis. For its part, the Public Accounts Committee concluded that the financial terms for the Pergau Dam were "most surprising and unacceptable".[8]

A link of any kind did not feature in the memorandum of understanding signed in September 1988. That document was leaked to *The Guardian* in February 1994 which published all relevant extracts to the great embarrassment of the British and Malaysian Governments. The significance of the memorandum was that it went beyond standard agreements on funding of defence exports thus indicating the lengths to which the British government of the day had been prepared to go in order to promote arms sales and secure defence construction projects in Malaysia.[9] A further departure from standard practice was the inclusion in the memorandum of an order of rating of suitable British defence contractors. In the month following the signing of the memorandum, Britain offered financial assistance by way of a concessionary loan for the Pergau Dam which was confirmed when Dr Mahathir visited Britain again in April 1989. The ultimate sum committed over 14 years in July 1991, when the first payment was made, was £234 million which proved to be the largest amount ever awarded for a single aid project.

The British press concentrated initially on the alleged link between the arms sales and the so-called aid "sweetener". Although the Malaysian government could not have been pleased at the nature and persistence of the investigative journalism, an official response from Kuala Lumpur was not forthcoming until towards the end of February 1994. Before then, the Pergau Dam affair had seemed to be essentially a domestic problem for the British government which had not entered the bilateral relationship. That certainly was the view of Malaysia's High Commission in London. For its part, the South-east Asian Department of the Foreign and Commonwealth Office appeared to be preoccupied with advising on answers to parliamentary questions than with the issue of likely damage to relations with Malaysia. Matters changed radically and dramatically in late February 1994 within days of an article appearing in the *Sunday Times* which claimed that the British construction company George Wimpey International had offered a bribe to Malaysia's Prime Minister in order to secure a contract for an aluminium smelter.[10]

Alienation Revived

On February 25, Malaysia's deputy-Prime Minister and Finance Minister, Anwar Ibrahim, called a press conference at which he announced that, in retaliation for allegations of corruption in the British media, his government would no longer award new contracts to British firms. Concurrently, Dr Mahathir received Britain's High Commissioner, Duncan Slater, to convey the same message. The decision to impose sanctions had been reached at a cabinet meeting two days before. Prior news of the impending announcement came as a surprise to the British government. It immediately took diplomatic measures to try to reverse the policy which went well beyond the "Buy British Last" practice of 1981 and which put in jeopardy contracts under negotiation worth more than £1 billion, including one for a new airport for Kuala Lumpur. Ironically, the boycott was announced within hours of the Royal Malaysian Air Force taking delivery of the first batch of 28 British Aerospace Hawk jet-fighter trainers which had been procured under the memorandum of understanding of September 1988.

In his statement to the press, Anwar Ibrahim indicated that particular offence had been caused by the allegation about special payments being offered by George Wimpey International. He commented that it was not just a normal newspaper story. "It is an issue that directly involves the integrity and credibility of our Prime Minister and the government and (is) not confined to one particular contract."[11] He drew particular attention to the story in the *Sunday Times* "as the most recent example of the international media's incorrigible and condescending attitude towards developing countries and their leaders". He went on to say that "we believe the foreign media must learn the fact that many developing countries, including a country led by a brown Muslim, has (*sic*) the ability to manage its own affairs successfully". A week later, Dr Mahathir explained that the punitive policy had its source in a sense of national frustration. He explained, "we have no quarrel with the British government and have no quarrel with any company ... We are only angry with the British press and we have no way of taking action against the British press", implying that British firms might find ways of doing so.[12] A preliminary remark to the effect that his government was disappointed over the British government's silence over the lies spread by the irresponsible British mass media was not well highlighted in the British press.[13] His comments as generally reported seemed to confirm the conventional wisdom in *The Guardian* that the hubris of one man was at the root of Anglo-Malaysian alienation. It was suggested that "The corruption taunt touched a raw nerve in a leader driven by a desire for local and international political acceptance and recognition of his ambitions for Malaysia".[14]

The crisis in Anglo-Malaysian relations was then aggravated by further press intervention by the *Sunday Times*. It merits mention that Dr Mahathir had earlier taken public exception to the purchase by its proprietor Rupert Murdoch of a controlling interest in the Hong Kong-based STAR satellite television network expressing the fear that it would lead to intrusion into the domestic affairs of regional states. The editor of the *Sunday Times*, Andrew Neil, in a letter to its companion newspaper, *The Times* maintained that he could not apologize for the offending article of 20 February because it had not implicated Dr Mahathir in allegations of business corruption.[15] Dr Mahathir responded by asserting that "It is quite clear from the inference that I had received money in order to give a contract to Wimpey".[16] More significant was a comment column in the next issue of the *Sunday Times* entitled "Stop grovelling and retaliate". It called on the British government to get tough with Malaysia's Prime Minister because grovelling would "serve only to reinforce Dr Mahathir's boast that bullying gets him noticed and produces results".[17] That issue was followed a week later by revelations of how Malaysians connected to Dr Mahathir had allegedly enriched themselves at the British taxpayers expense through windfall profits from the privatization of the electricity company which owned the Pergau Dam.[18] Four days later, Dr Mahathir responded personally with a long and angry letter to *The Financial Times* in which he repudiated as baseless the charges against Malaysia and himself and concluded by stating "For Malaysia, the die is cast. No contracts in exchange for British press freedom to tell lies".[19] This sequence of events dashed the prospects of a change in policy whose possibility had been indicated by a meeting in Kuala Lumpur on 8 March between former cabinet minister and chairman of GEC Lord Prior and Dr Mahathir as well as by a strong hint earlier from a Malaysian source that a personal intervention from John Major which vouched for the Malaysian Prime Minister's probity would be helpful.[20]

Anglo-Malaysian relations had been brought to their lowest point by an angry and punitive response to British investigative journalism which had offended personal and national dignity. Dr Mahathir seemed determined to inflict a collective punishment on British industry for the delinquencies of a press which reflected the prejudices of a society which had not expunged its colonial mentality. The conventional wisdom in London was that despite knowing full well the inability of the British government to control the press, Dr Mahathir was determined to teach Britain the lesson that a national price would have to be paid for tolerating its irresponsible overindulgence. His letter in *The Financial Times* merits closer consideration in that it also indicated a sense of grievance with the British government which had not been well highlighted in the British press. It is worth noting that the British Prime Minister's response to the boycott on returning from a visit to the United States in early March 1994 had been to say that the Malaysian action was short-sighted and unjustified. He may also have confirmed a Malaysian resentment of British condescension by adding that the reason Malaysia was within striking distance of becoming an industrialized country was due not least to the investment and trade of British companies.

In his emotive letter to *The Financial Times,* Dr Mahathir pointed out that "Press freedom is about telling the truth, not fabricating lies for whatever purpose. The contempt for the hurt inflicted on others seems to be condoned by the British Government and people".[21] Evident in the letter was the implication that there had been a deafening silence from the British government which could have acted to have put the record right, especially about the terms of aid for the Pergau Dam which had taken the form of a concessionary loan and not a grant. In making that point Dr Mahathir was only repeating his expression of disappointment of two weeks earlier over the British government's silence in response to "the lies spread by the irresponsible British mass media". Indeed, there is evidence to suggest that Dr Mahathir had held prior expectations of John Major in that regard which had been disappointed and over which he felt betrayed. For example, by early March there had been signs of a softening of attitudes from within the Malaysian cabinet. Deputy-Prime Minister, Anwar Ibrahim had suggested that the punitive policy could be reversed and that an earlier clarification of details of the Pergau Dam project might have avoided the boycott. He had also gone to pains to point out that the policy did not involve the private sector and education.[22] The Minister for International Trade and Industry, Rafidah Aziz, had also sought to differentiate the ban from the normal trading relationship and had commented "The British investors fully understand and in fact they're the ones feeling very upset the (British) government is not doing anything to control the damage further. In my opinion, they should do something positive to ensure the British media who started this problem understands the actual situation. A responsible government is a government able to influence and tell the truth to the press".[23]

Dr Mahathir's Motives?

In the light of these remarks, one possible explanation for Dr Mahathir's initial anger and sustained punitive action is that the British government had not lived up to certain private assurances. Indeed, it has been suggested that if only John Major had been willing to testify publicly to the probity of his Malaysian counterpart then the policy could be reversed in the same way that the "Buy British Last" policy had been. The source of this sense of betrayal may reside in discussions which took place between Malaysia's Foreign Minister Abdullah Ahmad Badawi and Douglas Hurd at the meeting of Commonwealth Prime Ministers in Cyprus in the latter part of October 1993. That meeting occurred concurrently with the appearance in the British press of details of the report of the National Audit Office report on the Pergau Dam. According to Malaysia's High Commissioner to London, Datuk Kamaruddin Abu, Britain's Foreign Secretary had provided assurances that his government would handle any (embarrassing) media intrusions into the arms for aid controversy. He revealed that "Hurd informed our Foreign Minister that they would make the necessary clarification over the issue", and also that the Malaysian government had been initially silent over the issue because of such assurances.[24] He was supported in this view two days later by the public comment of his Foreign Minister.[25] It is worth noting that in an interview on the British television programme *Whicker's World* in April 1994, Dr Mahathir in discussing the likely duration of the boycott said, "Well, it may sound final but we do expect the British papers and the British government (*sic*) to avoid telling lies about us and souring our relations".[26]

At issue is why the British government might have failed to live up to Malaysian government expectations causing it to initiate and then sustain its wrathful policy. The answer must lie in the realm of speculation but it is possible that John Major, who also has a reputation for harbouring strong feelings, resented the conduct of Malaysia's Prime Minister during a visit to Kuala Lumpur in September 1993. He had travelled to Malaysia to witness the signing of a memorandum of understanding for British involvement in the construction of a new airport to serve the Malaysian capital which then became a victim of the economic boycott. During that visit, John Major had been obliged to sit through a gratuitous tirade from his Malaysian counterpart on the hypocrisy of the West, including

Britain, over the Bosnian issue. The reticence of the British government to intervene on Dr Mahathir's behalf was almost certainly a product of its weak domestic political position over the Pergau Dam issue which had attracted strong criticism from within the Conservative party. In addition, there was probably a reluctance to be seen to be acting under duress as well as to be identified closely with a seemingly squalid Malaysian cause, especially given the concurrence of the enquiry being conducted by Lord Justice Scott over the sale of defence equipment to Iraq. It was difficult enough to have to explain away the alleged link between aid and arms transfers to Malaysia without becoming a hostage to the charges being levelled against Dr Mahathir. The only public defence of Dr Mahathir was mounted by Richard Needham, a junior minister at the Department of Trade and Industry. It is interesting to note that when John Patten, Britain's Secretary of State for Education, paid a prearranged visit to Malaysia in early April, he did not seek to defend the probity of the country's Prime Minister.

If Dr Mahathir had been angered by the delinquency of Britain's press and betrayed by its government's unwillingness to defend him publicly, he may also have been moved to lash out at British companies by his own domestic political circumstances. His position as head of UMNO was not as secure as his 13 years of continuous leadership might have suggested. Indeed, he was shown to have lost control of the party at its General Assembly in November 1993. Despite Dr Mahathir's initial opposition, Finance Minister, Anwar Ibrahim, had persisted in challenging deputy-Prime Minister Ghafar Baba for the office of deputy-President which automatically carries with it that of deputy-Prime Minister. His party support proved to be so overwhelming that Ghafar Baba resigned both posts so that Anwar Ibrahim was elected unopposed and was subsequently appointed deputy-Prime Minister. That loss of control was confirmed in elections for the three posts of party vice-president. Dr Mahathir had appealed for candidates to stand as individuals but political associates of Anwar Ibrahim stood collectively as a "vision team" to be easily elected to the Prime Minister's evident consternation. Dr Mahathir had brought Anwar Ibrahim into politics on UMNO's behalf for the federal elections in 1982 in which he employed his Islamic credentials in the party's interest. He has since enjoyed a meteoric political rise and, at the age of 46 compared to 68 for the Prime Minister, appeared to have inspired a change of political generations.[27]

Dr Mahathir appeared to have experienced a further political reverse in early February 1994, when the ruling federal National Front coalition lost state elections in Sabah in which he had invested considerable political capital. That result was reversed in the following month, after the punitive policy against British firms had been announced, when defections from the initially successful Sabah United Party caused it to lose its parliamentary majority. At the time, however, the electoral outcome was a serious blow to the Prime Minister who had to contemplate national elections within a year. At issue, therefore, was his political reputation as he faced up to the prospect of his last general election as prime minister. In the circumstances, it would be understandable for him to want to refute his critics, both foreign and domestic, and to reassert his authority through a resounding victory at the polls at the head of a united party.

Dr Mahathir's fury at the investigative journalism by the British press is well understood, although that anger may have been designed to obstruct further probing into the relationship between politics and finance in Malaysia. He was almost certainly resentful also of the deafening silence from the British government which has not gone to any lengths to defend Dr Mahathir from what he has represented as baseless slurs on his personal integrity. In addition, muckraking by the British press may well have provided Malaysia's Prime Minister with a convenient opportunity to attack a soft external target for domestic political reasons. He was able to pick on companies from the former colonial power with confidence in the strength of his country's economy and in the knowledge that Britain's business competitors would be only too ready to take up construction contracts that had fallen by the wayside.

Political Repair

By early April 1994, however, Malaysian political passions had appeared to have cooled, albeit without the punitive policy being reversed. Secretary of State for Education, John Patten was received very warmly in Kuala Lumpur by his counterpart Dr Daud Sulaiman who greeted him at the airport on his arrival in the early hours of the morning. Britain's offer to provide financial assistance for the establishment of an English Language Institute was greeted with enthusiasm, while Mr Patten made it clear that the initiative rested with Malaysia to lift the ban on public sector contracts for British companies.[28] A week later, Malaysia's Minister for Domestic Trade and Consumer Affairs, Abu Hassan Omar, held discussions with the President of the Board of Trade, Michael Heseltine, in the first visit to London by a senior member of his government since the embargo on British contractors had been announced in late February. Clearly a thaw in Anglo-Malaysian relations was being signalled but Malaysia's High Commissioner to London made it clear that the soonest the ban might be lifted would be "months rather than weeks".[29] Apparently, the Malaysian rescue of British soldiers lost during a survival exercise on Mount Kinabalu in Sabah, together with the robust role of Lt General Sir Michael Rose, the British commander of United Nations forces in Bosnia, had helped to begin the repair of mutual relations but without fully restoring them.

Foreign Secretary, Douglas Hurd, then acted publicly to encourage reconciliation. He turned his attention to Malaysia in a speech at the Lord Mayor of London's Easter Banquet on 13 April. He stressed Malaysia's importance to Britain and pointed to the exemplary support given by the Malaysian Armed Forces in the search for missing British servicemen in Sabah as proof of the strength of the underlying relationship. He commented that much nonsense had been said and written about Malaysia and revealed that "We are working hard in our contacts with the Malaysian government, and through the business community, to get things back on the even keel which is in the best interests of both countries". A week later, Lord Cranborne, a junior Defence Minister, led an 81-strong British business delegation to the Defence Services Asia '94 exhibition in Kuala Lumpur against a background of encouraging remarks from the Chief of Malaysia's Defence Forces, General Borhan Ahmad. He also met with Defence Minister, Najib Abdul Razak, who told foreign reporters that he was expecting a visit from Michael Heseltine, President of the Board of Trade. These attempts to repair the bilateral relationship proceeded in the absence of any fresh press comment of the kind which had so offended Dr Mahathir. Malaysian concern about its effect, however, led to invitations to British journalists to visit the country in order to counter negative publicity, especially from coverage by the *Sunday Times*. Such invitations indicated a longer term view of the Anglo-Malaysian relationship.

The revival of Anglo-Malaysian alienation was at one level a direct product of Dr Mahathir's bitter resentment of what was viewed as a malicious and patronizing British press. The episode was represented by him as a national failure to come to terms with the independence and dignity of the country which he had led for nearly 13 years. Indeed, he reminded Malaysians in mid-March 1994 that the West was still bent on colonization and that "If there is an opportunity, they will colonize us again". He went on to say that the West, which controlled the international media, always smeared the image of the Malaysian government because it wanted to undermine the political stability which was the country's strength.

His remarks should not be dismissed as mere paranoia but as serving a very practical political purpose. For example, he also pointed out that "If they (the Western media) are able to reduce the people's confidence in the government leadership, then the integrity and effectiveness of the government will be adversely affected". Referring to the British media, in particular, he remarked "If the accusation is not denied, Malaysians and even others will believe the allegations are true. Then the people's confidence in the government will wane. More than that, Malaysia's strong voice in the international arena will be muffled".[30] Wounded personal and national feelings apart, Dr Mahathir indicated in his pointed remarks a practical political basis for his apparent intemperate and indiscriminate riposte to British press comment as well as to his disappointment with the British government for not defending his personal integrity. For him, at least, the revival of Anglo-Malaysian alienation was functional and not inconsequential, especially if the domestic political context is taken into account.

As for the British government, the episode has exposed problems of propriety in managing an aid policy in a world in which competition for lucrative arms contracts has its own rules. More generally, it is obliged to live with the predicament that a Western democracy with a free press is always vulnerable to the manipulation of an external issue for domestic political purposes by a less democratic government.

Notes and References

1. *The Financial Times,* 17 March 1994.
2. For an account of the first round, see Michael Leifer, "Anglo-Malaysian alienation", *The Round Table,* January 1983.
3. See, *The Times,* 19 October 1981.
4. Mahathir bin Mohamad, *The Malay Dilemma* (Singapore, Donald Moore for Asia Pacific Press, 1970).

5. See, Edmund Terence Gomez, *Politics in Business: UMNO's Corporate Investments* (Kuala Lumpur, Forum, 1990); and also Philip Bowring, "Money and politics mix, in Malaysia as elsewhere", *International Herald Tribune*, 1 March 1994.

6. See, Bowring, *ibid.*

7. See, *Sunday Times*, 23 January 1994.

8. See, *Seventeenth Report of the Committee of Public Accounts*, Pergau Hydro-Electric Project (London, HMSO, March 1994).

9. The Memorandum stated, *inter alia*, "The total payment for any equipment procured under this (memorandum) will be provided by the Malaysian government but in the event that there is any shortfall in the funding, the United Kingdom government will assist in the arrangement of financial facilities provided by a United Kingdom bank or a group of banks and the United Kingdom will ensure that the interest to be charged will be at concessionary rates". *The Guardian*, 16 February 1994.

10. See, *Sunday Times* 20 February 1994.

11. *New Straits Times*, 26 February 1994. Anwar Ibrahim did concede that British companies may have been "conned" into parting with money to individuals claiming to represent the government or certain leaders.

12. *Bernama News Agency*, Kuala Lumpur, 2 March 1994.

13. Exceptions were *The Daily Telegraph*, 3 March 1994; and *The Guardian*, 7 March 1994.

14. See, *The Guardian*, 2 March 1994.

15. *The Times*, 4 March 1994.

16. *New Straits Times*, 5 March 1994.

17. *Sunday Times*, 6 March 1994.

18. *Sunday Times*, 13 March 1994.

19. *The Financial Times*, 17 March 1994.

20. See, *The Guardian*, 7 March 1994.

21. *The Financial Times, op cit*, Ref 19.

22. *New Straits Times*, 3 March 1994.

23. *Reuter*, 3 March 1994.

24. *New Straits Times*, 2 March 1994.

25. See, *Bernama News Agency*, 4 March 1994.

26. See, *New Straits Times*, 4 March 1994.

27. See, Ho Khai Leong "Malaysia: the emergence of a new generation of UMNO leadership", *Southeast Asian Affairs 1994* (Singapore, Institute of Southeast Asian Studies, 1994).

28. *New Straits Times*, 6 April 1994.

29. See, *The Guardian*, 14 April 1994.

30. See, *Bernama News Agency*, 16 March 1994.

Author's note 2 July 1994

In May 1994 Dr Mahathir announced that he had noticed an improvement in British media reporting on Malaysia especially after Andrew Neil, editor of the *Sunday Times,* had been transferred (to Fox TV in the United States). He went on to say that we will see whether his transfer will bring about a domestic difference in British media reports, and if we find that they report the truth and no longer print lies, there is no reason why we cannot resume business with British companies.

Editor's note 8 July 1994

Malaysia's Prime Minister Dr Mahathir said in Paris on 7 July 1994 that his country's ban on government contracts with British companies would continue selectively for the foreseeable future. The Malaysian Cabinet is known to have agreed that the ban on government contracts with British companies could be lifted. The timing of the change has been left to Dr Mahathir.

Singapore

INTRODUCTION

In maritime Southeast Asia, Leifer came to familiarize himself first with Singapore and Malaya/Malaysia. Since the early 1960s, he wrote many articles on Singapore, both on domestic politics as well as foreign policy. He realized that to properly understand Singapore, it was difficult, if not impossible, to confine oneself to Singapore's domestic politics without giving equal attention to its foreign policy, especially its special relationship with Malaya/Malaysia.

Leifer published more than twenty titles on Singapore (including one book) but because of space constraint, only seven articles are reproduced in this section. Three articles are on domestic politics, covering political history, Lee Kuan Yew's role, and problems of succession; another four articles cover Singapore's foreign policy, including Singapore's obsession with "vulnerability", the concept of exceptionalism, and the issue of Israel president's visit. Leifer was well known for his writings on Singapore's foreign policy and some of these concepts were developed in many articles that he wrote. It is hoped that this selection of articles will do him justice.

His essay on politics in Singapore, written in the early 1960s, discusses the first term (1959–63) of the People's Action Party (PAP) prior to its merger with Malaysia. He highlighted the role of the PAP in early Singapore politics, stressing the evolution of the post-colonial party. However, more important for our understanding of regional politics was the politics of Singapore in Malaysia (1963–65), which was characterized by the "politics of federation" (Ch. 46). Leifer analysed Singapore's intention to join Malaysia, its basic problem with Malay-dominated Peninsular Malaysia and Chinese-dominated Singapore, and the eventual departure of Singapore from the federation. At the time the article was written (early 1965), Singapore was still part of Malaysia. Nevertheless, Leifer accurately identified the serious problems in the new federation, pointing to the unacceptable arrangements and the irreconcilable attitude of the two major actors, the PAP and Alliance. In fact, the separation of Singapore from Malaysia was not a surprise.

Although focusing on the PAP in his analysis, Leifer highlighted the role of Lee Kuan Yew. He gave a lot of credit to the founder of modern Singapore. In the article written in 1990 when Goh Chok Tong became the prime minister succeeding Lee Kuan Yew, Leifer discussed that the survival of Singapore was largely due to the tough and pragmatic policy of Lee Kuan Yew. However, when Goh was about to take over, Leifer stated that "Lee has described Goh as 'no softie', implying that he will also be adept at political maintenance which has been the hallmark of PAP government ever since it came to power" (Ch. 47). However, in another article written at the same time, Leifer also realized that Lee would not retire. He would remain a "backseat driver" (Ch. 48). He quoted Lee's famous statement: "Even from my sick bed, even if you are going to lower me into the grave and I feel that something is wrong, I'll get up. Those who believe that when I have left the government as prime minister, that I've gone into permanent retirement, really should have their heads examined."

Singapore's foreign policy also has the imprint of Lee Kuan Yew and the "think-alike" elite. Nevertheless, apart from the continuity of the elite, there are also other factors which guaranteed Singapore's survival. Leifer's writings on Singapore's foreign policy can be summarized into two concepts: "vulnerability, but not insecurity" and "exceptionalism".

In Chapter 49, Leifer highlighted Singapore's fear of losing its competitiveness and its survival strategies and support of ASEAN, making it of "central importance as a structure of special relationships".

Leifer maintained that the tough-minded disposition of Singapore's general policy was due to the fact that there has been a constant awareness of the "innate vulnerability of the island-state" and its fear to fail. Nevertheless, the leadership was fully aware that "A wise nation will make sure that its survival and well-being are in the interests of other states."

Singapore has a special relationship with Malaysia, which is reflected in both Singapore politics and foreign relations. When Singapore invited Israeli President Chaim Herzog to Singapore in 1986, it resulted in friction with Kuala Lumpur (Ch. 50). See also Chapter 44 for the Malaysian perspective. Leifer correctly pointed out that the event highlighted the structural tension between Singapore and Kuala Lumpur. Malaysia considered the visit as being proof of the arrogance of the Chinese and insensitivity to Malay feelings, while Singapore considered the Malaysian pressure as "an unwarranted attempt to impose a veto on [Singapore's] foreign policy". However, being the closest neighbour, and at one time a part of Malaysia, Singapore had no choice but to exercise damage-control.

Chapter 51 addresses the issue of exceptionality in terms of Singapore's foreign policy. Singapore is seen as an exceptional state, which has innate vulnerabilities. This is probably the first time that Leifer used the term *exceptionalism* and he later developed it into a full argument in his book on Singapore's foreign policy. In fact, he applied the concept of vulnerability to other Southeast Asian countries, such as Vietnam, but the most frequent and extensive use was still in the context of Singapore (Ch. 52).

46

Singapore in Malaysia
The Politics of Federation

One feature of the Malaysia Agreement of July 1963 was the provisions designed to restrict the political role of Singapore in the new Federation. To this end, in return for a fair measure of local autonomy, Singapore was to accept a reduced representation in the Federal legislature together with a minor disability through a dual Malaysian citizenship.[1] While the government of Malaya, which was to assume the federal powers, was anxious to include Singapore in Malaysia so as to contain a subversive threat, it was concerned also to place limitations on a threat of a different order which seemed to be posed by the governing party in Singapore. The government in Singapore, which represented a predominantly Chinese electorate, was composed of men whose vision of a socialist society was not confined by the territorial bounds of the island-state. Indeed they had been long on record as to their ultimate objective.[2] The government in Malaya — founded on a loose communal coalition which reflected Malay political dominance —

Reprinted in abridged form from Michael Leifer, "Singapore in Malaysia: The Politics of Federation", *Journal of Southeast Asian History* 6, no. 2 (1965): 54–70, by permission of the History Department, National University of Singapore.

was conservative in complexion and made little secret of its protection of traditional interests and of its advocacy of private enterprise. It could not but look with disfavour on the Administration in Singapore, while attitudes towards its Prime Minister, Lee Kuan Yew, verged on the pathological.

The Singapore government, although accepting the limiting constitutional provisions of the Malaysia Agreement, was determined, despite the known objections of the Malayan government, to move from what it regarded as a parochial setting on to the national scene. And after the establishment of Malaysia, the prospect of attracting support from the mainland prompted it to take certain steps which were regarded in Kuala Lumpur not only as a challenge to the existing multi-racial Alliance regime but as a Chinese challenge to the governing system whereby a Malay ruling group enjoyed an entrenched political dominance. The principal consequence of this challenge has been to embitter federal-state relations and to bring into prominence the acute divisions between the racial communities within Malaysia: divisions which could have a greater potential for undermining the new Federation than the external threat posed presently by Indonesian Confrontation. Certainly the form of resolution of the conflict between the present Central government in Malaysia and that in Singapore will have a strong bearing on the future political and economic development of Malaysia and, of course, on its prospects for viability. To understand the present pattern of conflict it is necessary to return to the pre-Malaysia context.

During the final stages of the negotiations which preceded the establishment of Malaysia, the governing People's Action Party in Singapore was engaged in restoring a domestic position which had been undermined seriously by major defection from its left-wing.[3] The P.A.P. leadership had to face the prospect of the next elections with the knowledge that they had alienated many capable of soliciting mass support and also that in the previous elections of 1959 approximately 46% of the voting electorate had cast for other parties. The rift in the P.A.P. had crystallised as a consequence of the promulgation of the idea of a Malaysia by the then Malayan Prime Minister, Tunku Abdul Rahman, in May 1961. It was ironic that, at the same time, the Malaysia proposal offered the way of salvation for those in control of the formal party apparatus. They committed themselves whole-heartedly to the formation of Malaysia because they believed firmly in the intrinsic merits of the scheme but also because it represented a way to restore the political fortunes of the P.A.P. Singapore's Prime Minister set out to convince the electorate that union in Malaysia was vital to Singapore's survival as a viable economic and political entity and, at the same time, he ought to ensure that credit for the success of the venture would accrue to his party.

The urgent need for the P.A.P. government to regain lost political ground is a key factor in its subsequent stormy relationship with the Central Government of Malaysia. Political recovery in Singapore was related to internal imperatives and the government party there sought to overcome the hurdle of local political climate by exploiting almost last-minute negotiations on Singapore's financial terms of entry into Malaysia. But in the process further political hurdles were set up which the P.A.P. has, so far, been unable to overcome. The attempt to demonstrate to the Singapore electorate how effectively the P.A.P. government defended their interests aroused feelings of bitter antagonism in Kuala Lumpur which did not augur well for a harmonious relationship in Malaysia.

A simultaneous and related dispute broke out with the Malayan Chinese Association which had been a junior member of the Alliance coalition government since its initial establishment. Singapore's population (then approximately 1.7 million) was more than 75% Chinese and the P.A.P., although multi-racial in objective and appeal, presented the appearance of a Chinese party — most certainly to the Malay ruling group on the mainland.[4] Given the apparently entrenched Malay position in the Federal government based on rural representation, the prospects for the P.A.P. to even participate in the exercise of federal power would depend on its ability to convince the non-Malays in Malaya (of whom the vast majority were Chinese) that it was best suited to represent their interests. This could only come about at the expense of the M.C.A. and for this reason the M.C.A. regarded the P.A.P. as its natural enemy.

In 1963, the M.C.A., also hoping to exploit the prospect of Malaysia by using its governmental position among Chinese business interests, attempted to reorganise in Singapore. Lee Kuan Yew represented this initiative as an attempt by "merchant adventurers" to loot the material spoils of Singapore. Indeed a visit to Singapore by two M.C.A. senators in May lent substance to this charge. To the largely working class Chinese in Singapore, Lee played the role of thwarting the evil machinations of a political group that had become identified with the interests of the wealthy. It was in the context of this squabble that discussions on Singapore's financial terms of entry into Malaysia led to acrimonious exchanges between the Singapore Prime Minister and the Malayan Minister of Finance, Tan Siew Sin, who was also the Chairman of the Malayan Chinese Association. The ostensible problem at issue was the percentage of Singapore's revenue which was to be received by the Central government together with the amount of money Singapore would grant or lend the Borneo territories. The Singapore Prime Minister, whose main objective in the negotiations *per se* was to secure agreement on a common market for manufactured products within Malaysia, sought to demonstrate that Singapore enjoyed considerable autonomy from the government in Kuala Lumpur not only in the process of negotiations but also as a foretaste of the relationship to be expected within the impending federation. As a piece of political theatre, it was masterful and accomplished performance with acts played in Singapore, Kuala Lumpur and the finale in London. Although of imponderable impact, it certainly worked to the domestic political advantage of the P.A.P. During the course of the negotiations crisis appeared to follow crisis and even the Signature of the Malaysia Agreement in London seemed to be in jeopardy for a brief period. When the curtain fell on the final act in London, Lee Kuan Yew returned to Singapore to be feted as a heroic fighter for the rights of the island state. In Kuala Lumpur his performance received a more critical appraisal.

Before Malaysia was proclaimed officially and also before general elections were held in Singapore a further incident was to antagonise the government in Kuala Lumpur. As a consequence of the meeting in Manila in July–August 1963 between the heads of government of Malaya, the Philippines and Indonesia, it was decided in Kuala Lumpur to postpone the establishment of Malaysia beyond the nominated date of August 31. This delay was to enable a team appointed by the U.N. Secretary-General to make a determination of opinion in Sarawak and North Borneo in an effort to satisfy Indonesian and Philippine objections to the formation of Malaysia.

On August 31 the Singapore government proclaimed the then self-governing island-state *de facto* independent and announced that the *Yang di-pertuan Negara* (Head of State) would hold the federal powers in trust for the Central government until the official proclamation of Malaysia, by then postponed until September 16. This somewhat dramatic step was related to the internal political situation in Singapore as well as to some unfinished bargaining over Singapore's terms of entry into Malaysia. The announcement caused great offence in Kuala Lumpur where an emergency cabinet meeting was called to consider the situation. Despite this reaction, the Singapore Prime Minister insisted publicly on the rightfulness of his government's actions and went on to give even greater offence by making reference to the naive approach of some people to whom power was handed over "on a silver platter with red ribbons by British royalty in uniform."[5] Among the voices raised in anger was that of Syed Ja'afar Albar, then chief publicity officer of U.M.N.O. (United Malays National Organisation) — the senior partner in the Alliance government. In the future he was to achieve prominence as fierce critic and bitter antagonist of Lee Kuan Yew and was also to play a leading role in arousing the Malay community in Singapore against the P.A.P. government just prior to the communal riots which occurred first in July 1964. Meanwhile on September 7 the Malayan Prime Minister openly rebuked his Singapore counterpart for making statements regardless of their consequences.

Two days later the Singapore Prime Minister made a speech which did nothing to remove suspicion of him in Kuala Lumpur. It was regarded at the time as an attempt to split the Alliance coalition. The following year it was also remembered as how Lee Kuan Yew had failed to keep his word. During the speech in question Lee announced that the P.A.P. would not participate in the forthcoming mainland elections — not held until April 1964. He said "We want U.M.N.O. to win for there is no alternative government as tolerant and stable" but went on however, to predict defeat for the M.C.A. and ultimate co-operation between U.M.N.O. and the P.A.P. The speech, besides its immediate political impact, revealed the basically weak position of the P.A.P. as an erstwhile non-communal party with a national appeal. If the P.A.P. leadership had any confidence in their declared role as the apostles of non-communal nationalism in the plural society of Malaysia then they would have had to offer themselves as an orthodox opposition party. This would inevitably have necessitated a direct challenge to the Alliance government as a whole with the Tunku at its head. Such a step would certainly have further alienated the Malay electorate as well as exposing the P.A.P. to a charge of being disloyal at a time of crisis brought on by Indonesian Confrontation. Recognising the realities of the communal situation, and while not entirely giving up its multi-racial aspirations, the P.A.P. tactic was therefore, to try and replace the M.C.A. as the Chinese wing of the Alliance. The appeal was presented to urban voters who were predominantly Chinese. But this approach tended to confirm Malay suspicions that the P.A.P. from the predominantly Chinese island of Singapore was essentially a Chinese party.[6] Also the P.A.P. as a prospective Chinese partner had little, if any, attraction for U.M.N.O. which had worked fairly harmoniously with the M.C.A. since their first electoral arrangement in 1952. There was no pressing reason to dispense with an amicable associate in order to collaborate with one regarded with the utmost distrust. For the P.A.P. leadership it was to become apparent that argument on its own would be insufficient to persuade the Tunku and his Malay colleagues that the M.C.A. was a declining political force. It was necessary to supplement the cogency of argument with unavoidable facts. And it was probably for this reason that Lee Kuan Yew was to find it necessary in March 1964 to go back on his earlier statement that the P.A.P. would not participate in the forthcoming mainland elections. The P.A.P. had no alternative way to state a claim to federal recognition for at the end of September 1963 the Tunku had publicly defended the M.C.A. as "sound, honest, straight forward and absolutely trustworthy" and added that he resented any statement likely to cause a rift in the Alliance.

Relations between the Singapore and Central governments were not improved by the results of elections held in Singapore a few days after the establishment of Malaysia. In these elections the P.A.P. capitalised on Lee Kuan Yew's success in the Malaysia negotiations and was able also, because of its break with the extreme left, to draw on support that in 1959 went to opponents on the right. The result was a decisive victory for the P.A.P. Among the thirty-seven seats gained were three in predominantly Malay constituencies which had been regarded as the private preserve of the Singapore branch of U.M.N.O. As a result the only Malay representation in the Singapore legislature was through the P.A.P. — a somewhat humiliating situation for the U.M.N.O. leadership in Kuala Lumpur. The election result served only to confirm suspicions that the Singapore Prime Minister was out to capture eventually the Federal government of Malaysia.

The elections in Singapore followed immediately the breach in diplomatic and economic relations between Malaysia and Indonesia and the problems posed by Confrontation tended to keep differences between the governments of Singapore and the Federation somewhat in the background until the early part of 1964. Singapore, in particular, was concerned with the repercussions of the rupture of trade and financial ties with Indonesia at a time when its entrepot economy was only just beginning the process of transfer to a more stable industrial base.[7] But with the announcement on March 1, 1964, by Singapore's deputy Prime Minister, Dr. Toh Chin Chye, that the P.A.P. must consider itself a national party and to this end would play "a token part" in the forthcoming mainland elections, the political atmosphere was transformed dramatically. It is believed that this decision was taken only in the few weeks preceding the announcement, and at the time Lee Kuan Yew was out of the country on tour in Africa explaining the Malaysian position — a role which angered some U.M.N.O. leaders. In a speech made in the Singapore Parliament on December 9, 1963, in which he made reference to the prospect of an urban protest vote in Malaya being cast against the M.C.A., the Singapore Prime Minister had not indicated that his party would contest the elections to be held in Malaya only on April 24. Indeed he implied that the P.A.P.'s future course of action would be determined by that result.[8] It is possible, however, that the real prospect of a swing against the M.C.A. and towards the extreme left-wing and anti-Malaysian Socialist Front moved the P.A.P. to try and forestall any such happening. But as likely was the realisation that with state elections in Malaya being held concurrently with the Federal elections on the mainland, the P.A.P. would not have another opportunity to stake a claim to be more than just a Singapore party for probably five years. And only by increasing their representation in the Federal legislature at the expense of the M.C.A. could they expect to back effectively any demands for a working arrangement with U.M.N.O. and a change in the structure of the Central government. The P.A.P. made no secret of its ambitions in this respect. On March 15, 1964, following his return from Africa, Lee declared "Our enlightened self-interest demands that we should do nothing to hinder or embarrass the present Malay leadership ... But while the present Malay leadership of Tunku and Tun Razak is vital to the survival and success of Malaysia, the Chinese leadership in the Alliance as represented by the M.C.A. is not irreplaceable."

Within the Alliance the P.A.P. decision to contest the elections produced a most hostile response. The M.C.A. was convinced rightly that the P.A.P. was out to supplant it, while U.M.N.O. regarded the intervention as an attempt to subvert from within. An Alliance statement pointed out "The P.A.P. move in calling on the urban voters — who are mostly Chinese — was a clear indication that its participation in the election was to kill the M.C.A. and later force U.M.N.O. to accept the P.A.P. as a partner or compel U.M.N.O. to work with it. If the P.A.P. succeeds in destroying the M.C.A. it will no doubt later turn on U.M.N.O. itself."[9] The P.A.P.'s decision infuriated the Alliance leadership, particularly because of Lee's earlier public commitment to keep his party off the mainland. At the same time, it was regarded as an attempt to go back on the symbolic bargain whereby Malaya accepted Singapore in Malaysia, i.e., a federal representation of only 15 seats.[10] And the intellectual skill with which the Singapore leader so ably defended his party's action served only to increase the suspicions of his opponents, both Chinese and Malay. Further alarm was generated amongst them by the very large crowds that turned out to hear Lee when he came to campaign in Malaya.[11] On one such occasion he announced that the 1964 elections were a preliminary to those of 1969 and that if the voters demonstrated positively that they were "in favour of an honest government with a dynamic social and economic policy then the winds of change will begin to sweep through Malaysia." The imputation was too blatant for the Alliance government not to take offence.

The P.A.P. entered finally 9 candidates in the elections to the Federal lower house and there is every indication that the party's leaders expected fully to win a majority of the seats being contested. The result, however, confounded their expectations and confirmed the continued dominance of the Alliance government, together with its M.C.A. wing. Out of 104 seats the Alliance won 89, an increase of 15 from the elections of 1959. The P.A.P. gained one seat only and this by a narrow majority. Of the other 8 seats contested by the P.A.P. 6 were won by the M.C.A., 1 by the Socialist Front and another by the United Democratic Party.

One explanation for the poor showing of the P.A.P. has been that the fact of Indonesian Confrontation moved Chinese voters to cast for the Tunku's coalition. Indeed, the P.A.P. has claimed that the overriding reason why only one of their candidates was successful was "the sense of national solidarity in defence of Malaysia under threat from Indonesia.[12] Too much can be made of the Confrontation argument, for the M.C.A. victories by no means represented substantial pro-government swings. Indeed the anti-Malaysian Socialist Front polled an average of 15.95% and over 20% in six states: a higher percentage than in the 1959 elections. The fiasco of the P.A.P. intervention requires other explanations as well. It is of interest, for example, to note that in five of the seats contested by the P.A.P. (including its sole success) its intervention probably cost the Socialist Front a victory.[13] Also, there is little doubt that the P.A.P. leadership was too overconfident in its approach. It made few, if any, preparations for the contests. Some candidates were nominated before the establishment of party branches, while little care was taken in the selection process. It was certainly in too much of a hurry to write off the M.C.A. which, for all its alleged defects, was still a political going concern with an efficient organisation, and able to rely on solid U.M.N.O. backing to retain sufficient support to just see it through. It was argued effectively on the M.C.A.'s behalf that if its representation were reduced, then Chinese representation within the government would also be reduced because U.M.N.O. would treat only with the M.C.A. There is reason to believe that this argument would have been powerful, though perhaps not equally so, in the absence of Confrontation.

For the Alliance government, the immediate challenge from the P.A.P. had been contained, although it had gone on record as intending to persevere with its mainland activities.[14] The challenge, however, had been a disturbing influence in itself and was to produce repercussions which Malaysia could ill afford. The P.A.P. has admitted "It was unfortunate that the participation in the Peninsula elections was to exacerbate the fears of the Malay leadership which had barely recovered from the loss of the three Malay constituencies in the Singapore elections only six months ago."[15] The challenge was now to be reversed and to take a decidedly extreme-racial form. It was to be presented to the government in Singapore by U.M.N.O. non-governmental leaders who became involved in a campaign of agitation designed ostensibly to secure special privileges for the Malays who make up 14% of the island's population. This agitation which culminated under the direction of Syed Ja'afar Albar, now Secretary-General of U.M.N.O., led directly to the communal riots which erupted in Singapore in July and September 1964.

Malaysia had not brought the Malays of Singapore the special privileges enjoyed by their co-religionists on the mainland. Although the Singapore constitution recognised the special position of the Malays, the Malaysia Agreement stipulated that special privileges enjoyed by Malays in the former Federation of Malaya should not extend to Singapore. For example, there was to be no reservation of positions for Malays in the civil service, nor were they to enjoy any preference in the granting of permits and licences for the operation of any trade of business in Singapore.[16] There is every likelihood, however, that with the establishment of Malaysia, with a Malay-dominated Central government, the Malays in Singapore had some expectation of improving their general position relative to the other two principal races on the island,[17] — a position which had been further undermined by the economic effects of Confrontation.

Whatever expectations existed were stimulated by the Malay language newspapers, in particular, *Utusan Melayu*, whose motto is "To fight for religion, race and homeland." Besides constant harping on the depressed economic state of Malays in Singapore, for which there was some justification, it reiterated that Malays were being persecuted by the P.A.P. government led by "stepfather" Lee Kuan Yew against whom continual abuse was directed. Reference was also made to "the P.A.P.'s social revolution for the destruction of our race." The newspaper agitation for Malay rights came to a head in July over a decision by the Singapore government to evict and rehouse Malays from the Crawford area as part of its scheme of urban renewal. And here the financial interests of local landlords coincided with those seeking to assert Malay rights.

In an attempt to meet rising Malay demands, the Singapore Prime Minister invited non-political Malay organisations to meet with him on July 19 to discuss their grievances. This somewhat unfortunate move produced an immediate hostile reaction from the U.M.N.O. leaders in Singapore whose party was excluded from the meeting. In an attempt to forestall Lee, they called a Malay convention for July 12. This gathering, attended by a crowd estimated at twelve thousand, was addressed by the Secretary-General of U.M.N.O. Syed Ja'afar Albar, who claimed that the fate of the Malays in Singapore was worse than under the Japanese occupation. The Singapore Prime Minister was depicted as "an *Ikan Sepat* which lives in muddy waters only."[18] At this convention there was set up a Malay National Action Committee to be responsible for matters affecting the welfare of Malays in Singapore. Membership of this body included adherents of the Pan-Malayan Islamic Party and of the Peninsula Malay Union: groups noted for their racialism, bigotry and Indonesian sympathies.

On the day the convention was held, a communal disturbance occurred in Bukit Mertajam in Malaya in which two people were killed. This episode which aggravated the already unsettled communal situation in Singapore proved to be but a prelude to even more violent racial conflict. Meanwhile, on July 19, the Singapore Prime Minister held the pre-arranged meeting with representative of Malay organisations in spite of a call to boycott by the Action Committee which sought to insist that Lee negotiate only with them. At the meeting Lee promised that every effort would be made by his government to train and equip Malays to compete with non-Malays in finding jobs. But he made it clear that there could be no quota system in job allocation, the issuing of licences or the reservation of land for Malays.[19] To have agreed to such a request would have presented the Chinese opponents of the P.A.P. with an opportunity to exploit the communal issue for their own ends. But the meeting did nothing to satisfy the members of the Action Committee, whose chairman Singapore Senator Ahmad Haji Taff claimed that it was an insult to the Malays.

What followed demonstrates the dangerous undercurrents always just below the surface in Singapore and Malaya and also the consequences of seeking to channel them for political ends. On July 20, leaflets were circulated in Singapore which bore the heading "Singapore Malay National Action Committee." They claimed that Chinese in Singapore had drawn up a plan to kill Malays and concluded "Before Malay blood flows in Singapore, it is best to flood the state with Chinese blood." The following day, during the course of a Muslim procession to celebrate the birth of the Prophet, communal incidents between Malays and Chinese sparked off a full scale riot. It was several days before order was restored fully and not until twenty two people were killed and several hundreds injured. Early in September, a further serious outbreak took place, albeit on a lesser scale. On this occasion, circumstantial evidence would seem to suggest Indonesian complicity.

These bloody events marked the culmination of the reaction to the intervention and defeat of the P.A.P. in the mainland elections. They were the product of an ill-conceived attempt to leave no doubt as to who spoke for Singapore's Malay community and to inflict a further political defeat on the P.A.P. They also highlighted the fundamental weakness of the new Federation which the Indonesian government, already despatching instruders to the Malayan mainland, sought to aggravate through radio broadcasts.

The riots brought a temporary halt to feuding between the Alliance and the P.A.P. and saw their active co-operation to restore racial harmony. At the end of August, discussions were held between members of the two governments (in the absence of the Tunku in London) at which it was agreed to moderate their political rivalry. Public differences were sparked off again, however, during the following month. And the intensity of feeling generated would seem to suggest that the awful significance of the riots had not been fully appreciated.

During the second communal outbreak, the Singapore Prime Minister was in Europe attending an international socialist conference. Part of his time was spent in London. His presence there appeared to disturb the Central government who were suspicious of Lee's attempted dealings with British political leaders. These suspicions were confirmed for them by certain press reports from Britain,[20] which they felt certain had been inspired by Lee as a means of influencing the British government — which could exert leverage on the Central government as it was footing the major portion of the expense of countering Confrontation — to gain his own ends, in particular, P.A.P. representation in the Cabinet.[21] Indeed, they had reason to believe that Lee was appealing to British liberal sensibilities and idealism about the multi-racial structure of Malaysia with this object in view. While his arguments were germane, it was felt that the logic of his appealing analysis of racial problems in Malaysia could work only to the political advantage of Lee Kuan Yew and the Chinese. A week earlier, the Tunku had pointed out in a speech to the U.M.N.O. General Assembly that the Malay position in politics and administration was unrivalled. He said that Chinese and others did not aspire to giddy heights in politics because in this field the opportunity to make money was limited and they, therefore, went in for business. He continued with the ominous warning "Any attempt to try and force one side to give up their place in favour of the other is bound to meet with trouble." The reports in the British press appear to have been seen in this context.

On September 20, Lee Kuan Yew opened the new Chinese Chamber of Commerce building in Singapore. He marked the occasion by asserting with confidence that there was a future for the Chinese in the country if they were Malaysians and as long as there was a Malaysia. He also praised the Tunku and advised those present to put their trust in him. On the same day, in another part of the island, a reception was being held by the Singapore branch of the Alliance at which the Malaysian Prime Minister was the principal speaker. During his address, he aired issues which had been exploited by those agitating for Malay rights in Singapore prior to the riots, in particular the claim that Malays were being driven from their homes. He blamed Singapore politicians for creating the conditions for the riots and left no doubt as to the object of his criticism when he went on to attack the P.A.P.

for contending the mainland elections. He asserted that this action had been quite contrary to the agreement which established Malaysia. He also complained "There's an undercurrent to contest my leadership of the Malaysian people by trying to make out that I am leader of the Malays only."[22] The Tunku then called for the disbandment of goodwill committees, set up to restore racial harmony following the riots, claiming that they were composed of members of one party only and could not function properly. He announced he was setting up peace committees in their place. Finally, he uttered an implied warning to the Chinese community in informing them that "they don't have it so good anywhere else."

It is known that the Tunku's speech had been modified to a more moderate version shortly before delivery. Even so, coming soon after the riots there was a real prospect that it would carry relations between the Central government and the governing party in Singapore beyond the point of repair with all the consequences for communal antagonism that could ensue. Fortunately, the flashpoint potential of the situation was recognised and no response came from Lee Kuan Yew. Instead, a few days later, Lee and some of his senior colleagues met with the Tunku over dinner in Kuala Lumpur and agreed on what became known loosely as a truce. It was reported that both sides would not raise any sensitive issues regarding the respective positions of the communities in Malaysia and also that party differences would be relegated to the background for two years. The Singapore Prime Minister said that in the best interests of the country, there need not be a point by point reply to the Tunku's speech. Finally, it was announced that the peace committees, which the P.A.P. had suspected would be staffed with Malay agitators, would come under police control.[23]

It seems likely, however, that neither party quite appreciated what the other understood by the terms of the agreement. This became apparent about a month later when the Tunku was to interpret the agreement as only in respect of communal issues following a minor public argument which developed when the then Malaysian Minister of Agriculture and Chairman of the Singapore Alliance, Mohammed Khir Johari, stated that the Alliance was confident it would win sufficient votes to oust the P.A.P. and form the next government in Singapore. To the charge by the Chairman of the P.A.P. that this statement was a breach of the truce, Khir replied that he was not aware of any truce between the Alliance and the P.A.P. and that they must be prepared to face the occupational hazard of party rivalry.[24]

This, in turn, provoked the P.A.P. Chairman, Dr. Toh Chin Chye, into announcing that his party was to be "re-orientated and reorganised so that we can get at Malaya."[25]

The basic conflict situation remains unresolved in 1965, while the continuing bitter political climate is evidenced by the recurrent vocal reactions on the part of leading members of the Central government to what they regard as the provocations of the P.A.P., and vice versa. For example, the Tunku in his message for *Hari Raya* and the Chinese New Year, in a hardly disguised reference to Lee, spoke of politicians whose minds were obviously distorted and polluted. He was taking strong exception to a statement made by the Singapore Prime Minister at the beginning of 1965 in which he warned of the prospect of Malaysia breaking up through internal disintegration rather than as a consequence of external aggression. The Tunku described such talk as "Foolish and harmful and dangerous."[26] It would seem that even when Lee's arguments are, on the surface, cogent and plausible they are regarded with no less suspicion by the Central government who see, with some justification, a hidden purpose in their use. Such appeals are regarded solely as weapons to undermine the position of the Alliance government and its Malay majority who are very conscious that Malays make up only 39.2% of the population of Malaysia.[27] The P.A.P., for its part, is concerned that Singapore is being treated less as a constituent state of Malaysia than as a dangerous rival to be kept down. Substance for this belief can be found for example, in the dispute, early in 1965, over the allocation between Singapore and Malaya of the British textile quota at a time when there is unemployment in Singapore and, according to the Singapore Minister of Finance, no textile manufacturing capacity as yet in Malaya. The Singapore government has also expressed alarm over the demands of the Malaysian Finance Minister for a greater share of Singapore revenue and over his remarks that he might restrict the grant of pioneer status to industries newly established on Singapore's Jurong estate.

The present position of the Tunku and his Malay followers is that they refuse to consider working with Lee who they insist should regard himself as no more than the Mayor of Singapore.[28] However, any government in Malaysia has to command multiracial support if it offers any prospect of stability in the country. As long as the Alliance continues to demonstrate this support through electoral success then the P.A.P.'s bid for participation in the exercise of power will obviously fail. If, however, the P.A.P. is able to demonstrate electorally or in other ways that it represents an increasing proportion of non-Malay interests, its challenge can be disregarded only at the cost of racial discord. It could attract such support as a beneficiary of any governmental lack of consideration for non-Malays, for example, in an overzealous enforcement of Malay as the sole official language in 1967. The Tunku, however, has tended to adopt a moderate public stand on this issue and he must have taken note of the riots early in 1965 in Tamil speaking areas of India following the government's decision to impose the use of Hindi. But it is also possible for the P.A.P. to profit if it were felt in the Borneo territories that the Central government was interfering to promote the success of its Muslim nominees, as appeared the case in the crisis within the Sabah Alliance at the end of 1964. The P.A.P. is also well aware of the gradual but sure trend towards urbanisation which is likely to increasingly highlight class differences. It, therefore, places its multi-racial appeal on an ideological plane claiming that it can best represent the have-nots of Malaysia who need to realise "how much they have in common with each other despite differences of race, culture, language and religion." And if, in spite of present Malay suspicions of the P.A.P., the feeling developed that problems of rural poverty were not being tackled adequately, then the P.A.P. which has its own active Malay Affairs Bureau could well exploit the situation. Much, of course, will come to depend on the extent to which the Alliance government is prepared to initiate social and economic change in advance of rising discontent.

More than the success or failure of the P.A.P. or the Alliance is involved in the present conflict; it concerns the future prospects for a viable multi-racial Malaysia. A basic obstacle to a satisfactory resolution is that the concept of a multi-racial society, as expounded by the Prime Minister of Singapore, is regarded by most Malays as an insidious plan by which they gradually lose what they regard as rightful privileges to the more industrious Chinese. One can understand and sympathise with this feeling. But it may be too much to expect those Chinese who are not economic beneficiaries of the Alliance relationship to continue to conceal their dissatisfaction at their second class status in a country to which they are expected to give their primary allegiance. It might be argued, however, that if the P.A.P. gave up its national ambitions, racial harmony would be restored. But this would ignore the real prospect that any political discontent which it now attracts could then be re-directed towards those less concerned to see Malaysia survive.

Notes

1. The Malaysia Agreement differentiates between a Malaysian who is a Singapore citizen and a Malaysian citizen who is not a citizen of Singapore. And although it states that "citizenship of Singapore shall not be severable from citizenship of the Federation" (Singapore p. 20); the Agreement lays down that "A Singapore citizen is not qualified to be an elected member of either House of Parliament, except as a member for Singapore and a citizen who is not a Singapore citizen is not qualified to be a member of either House for or from Singapore" (p. 26).

2. The Manifesto of the P.A.P. promulgated in 1954 declared *inter alia* "Though, because of the division of Malaya into two territories, we are technically a political party operating in Singapore we shall in all our approaches to the problems of this country disregard the constitutional division. We are as actively interested in the problems of our fellow Malayans in the federation as we are in those of Singapore. When Malayans in the Federation who agree with our aims join us we shall work throughout Malaya".

3. For more detailed background to this episode see "Politics in Singapore" by the present author, *Journal of Commonwealth Political Studies* (May 1964).

4. "Although seeking to appeal to a multi-racial audience, the P.A.P., as must be the case with any mass party in Singapore, depends primarily on its ability to muster the Chinese vote." Milton E. Osborne, *Singapore and Malaysia*, Data Paper No. 53, Dept. of Asian Studies Cornell University, July 1964, p. 3. This work contains a wealth of information and mature observation on the period preceding and after Singapore's entry into Malaysia.

5. *Straits Times*, 4 September 1963.

6. Another difficulty facing the P.A.P. was highlighted in a paper presented to an M.C.A. Seminar of Secretaries and publicity officers held in March 1964: "Unless the P.A.P. toes the line of (*sic*) which the M.C.A. is doing at the moment, the P.A.P. can never dream to come into the fold of the Alliance and if the P.A.P. adopts the principle which we in the M.C.A. is (*sic*) practicing at the moment, is there any anxiety for the Chinese to elect and support the P.A.P. to replace the M.C.A."

7. Singapore's total imports for the first half of 1964 compared with the same period in 1963 fell by 23% and exports by 31%. This does not include transactions in the former barter trade with Indonesia. See *Far Eastern Economic Review* 26.11.64.

8. The speech in the Singapore Parliament did indicate the reasoning which the P.A.P. was to use publicly to justify its intervention in the mainland elections. "It is fairly obvious that if it were possible for the M.C.A. to hold

the towns in Malaya then the present structure to the Central government and the policies it pursues can be unchanged. But if the towns decisively reject all M.C.A. candidates then there must be a re-appraisal by U.M.N.O. They will then have to decide whether they can come to terms with a leadership that can command the loyalty of the sophisticated urban populations, Chinese, Indians, Eurasians, and others or govern without the partnership of the towns." *Legislative Assembly Debates*, Singapore, Vol. 22, No. 4, cols. 141/2.

9. *Straits Times*, 21 March 1964.

10. The Tunku said just this on 20th September 1964. *Ibid.* 21 September 1964. It is of interest that on 18 March the chairman of the Elections Commission, announced in Kuala Lumpur that only Federation citizens could take part in the election campaign. This would have excluded Malaysian citizens who were citizens of Singapore. The following day, however, the Attorney-General of Malaysia ruled that as Singapore citizens were Malaysian citizens they would not be committing any offence by campaigning in Malaya. This was probably a recognition that any prohibition of this nature would have to be reciprocal.

11. The Central Executive Committee of the P.A.P. was to admit "The fears and anxieties of the Malay rural base which would be aroused by large urban crowds mainly of Chinese and Indians rallying to our party banner was (*sic*) underestimated." *Our First Ten Years*, P.A.P. 10th Anniversary Souvenir, Singapore, 21 November 1964, p. 111.

12. *Ibid.*

13. Results in seats contested by the P.A.P.
    (a) Kluang Utara — (Johore)
        All. (M.C.A.) 19,138 S.F. 6,674 P.A.P. 1,276
    (b) Bandar Malacca — (Malacca)
        All. (M.C.A.) 13,789 S.F. 10,658 P.A.P. 3,461
    (c) Seremban Timor — (Negri Sembilan).
        All. (M.C.A.) 9,604 P.A.P. 5,410 S.F. 5,124 U.D.P. 1,670
    (d) Batu — (Selangor)
        S.F. 10,122 All. (MCA) 9,734 P.A.P. 2,459
    (e) Bukit Bintang
        All. (M.C.A.) 9,107 P.A.P. 6,667 S.F. 5,000 P.M.I.P. 650
    (f) Bangsar
        P.A.P. 13,494 S.F. 12,686 All. (MCA) 9,761 P.P.P. 2,219
    (g) Damansara
        All. (M.C.A.) 9,148 S.F. 8,602 P.A.P. 3,191
    (h) Setapak
        All. (M.C.A.) 12,292 S.F. 7,888 P.A.P. 4,214
    (i) Tanjong — (Penang)
        U.D.P. 12,928 S.F. 8,516 P.A.P. 778

14. *Straits Times*, 29 April 1964.
15. *Our First Ten Years*, op. cit.
16. *Malaysia* — Agreement concluded between the United Kingdom of Great Britain and Northern Ireland, the Federation of Malaya, North Borneo, Sarawak and Singapore. Cmd, 22 of 1963, Singapore, Government Printing Office, p. 46.
17. This has been admitted by Singapore's deputy Prime Minister, Dr. Toh Chin Chye. "The merger of Malaysia has possibly led a section of Malays in Singapore to anticipate that special rights for Malays as practised in Malaya will apply equally to them." *Out First Ten Years*, p. 126.
18. *Utusan Melayu*, 13, July 1964.
19. *Straits Times*, 21 July 1964.
20. What exercised the Central government above all else was an editorial in the *Sunday Telegraph*, 13 September 1964.
21. A further instance of this technique but in relation to the United States' government occurred in February 1965 with the expected reaction in Kuala Lumpur. See *Washington Post* February 5th and March 6th 1965.
22. *Straits Times*, 21 September 1964.
23. *Sunday Times* (Singapore) 27 September 1964.
24. *Straits Times*, 29 October 1964.
25. *Ibid.*, 2 November 1964.
26. *Siaran Akhbar*, 20 January 1965.
27. Musa bin Hitam, Political Secretary to the Minister of Transport in the Central government has claimed that all utterances of P.A.P. leaders on the racial problem are in themselves evidence of the party's communal base. "The very subtle insinuations of the P.A.P. leaders by propagation non-communalism and equality of status in Malaysia at the moment naturally provoke communal sentiments. And as long as the P.A.P. leaders imply in their speeches that no race should enjoy privileges and protection from the other so long will there be a hardening of attitudes in the different communities in Malaysia." *Straits Times.*, 9 February 1965.
28. See Lee Kuan Yew's letter *Straits Times*, 9 December 1964.

47

Triumph of the Will

After more than 30 years as prime minister, Lee Kuan Yew will step aside from office rather than step down. He will remain in the cabinet as senior minister, a rank directly after that of prime minister. While Lee's formal status may be reduced, his political standing will remain unchanged and indeed unchallenged.

Lee is a political phenomenon who combines modernising vision with a traditional Chinese style of rule, distinguished by an absence of tolerance and evident vindictiveness in the face of opposition. His great achievement, which is both respected and resented in Southeast Asia, is the flourishing city-state of Singapore. He is a man the philosopher Nietzsche would have admired because of his display of the power of human will. Lee is a political superman of his time, albeit in charge of a metropolis. To assess his record, it is important to understand his political qualities and outlook.

Reprinted from Michael Leifer, "Triumph of the Will", *Far Eastern Economic Review*, 15 November 1990, pp. 27–30, by permission of the Review Publishing Co. Ltd.

High intelligence and burning ambition go without saying, but these qualities on their own are not sufficient to produce a political leader of Lee's calibre. Relentless determination and ruthlessness would also seem to be necessary traits. Beyond these, he has the rare ability to command respect and loyalty based on an awesome personality. He is also able to inspire confidence and fear, reflecting a view of politics based on a belief in human fallibility. This belief reinforces the conviction held from the outset that Singapore suffers from an innate vulnerability which leaves little margin for error and no room for dissent.

That vulnerability has been shielded by great fortitude and skilful pragmatism on the part of Lee and his close colleagues. Crisis over an unanticipated independence from Malaysia provided the imperative for their expression, because the alternative to survival could not be contemplated. When the crisis of the 1960s passed and Singapore — under effective one-party rule — began to demonstrate astounding progress as a manufacturing and financial centre, the qualities of resolution realised in the founding experience were believed to be exclusive to the pioneer generation.

That foreboding has driven Lee ever since, and in turn has caused him to drive the people of Singapore in what he determines to be their own interest. His attitude derives partly from an understanding rare in tropical Asia; namely, the need for constant maintenance. Singapore's clean and attractive environment is a testament to the virtues of its practice, despite charges of sterility from peevish critics.

Constant maintenance and vigorous innovation is also central to Lee's approach to the body politic. Recurrent campaigns discouraging spitting and littering and encouraging courtesy and cleanliness assault the sensibilities of Singapore's citizens. In the way that the environment of Singapore is constantly subject to maintenance, so its citizens are constantly instructed and harried in order to prevent the political jungle from returning.

The politics of maintenance betrays a lack of confidence in the people of Singapore, who are thought not to have attained sufficient political maturity to appreciate just how vulnerable their material inheritance is. The remedy has been to reverse the conventional relationship which obtains in democracies between government and people. Instead of the government being held responsible to the people, the people are deemed to be responsible to a government which claims an infallible grasp of social priorities.

Lee's political pessimism is partly the product of a morbid personality and partly based on a judgment borne of experience about the perils of untrammelled liberal democracy, especially within a plural society where racial animosities are easily aroused. He has not concealed his views about the shortcomings of the racial communities which make up that society in Singapore.

The Indians — meaning all who hail from the Subcontinent — have been decried as contentious and relishing opposition for its own implicitly negative sake. Undoubtedly, the deeply irritating presence for a time in parliament of J. B. Jeyaretnam — depicted by Lee as a fly-by-night politician — served to reinforce that prejudice, even though some of his more important cabinet colleagues have a Subcontinental antecedence.

Because of the traumatic experience of eviction from Malaysia against a background of intense racial antagonism, Singapore's Malay Community has always been regarded with some suspicion. Confirmation that their loyalty as citizens of Singapore was shallow was demonstrated to Lee's consternation as a result of the visit by the president of Israel in November 1986, which provoked strong reaction across the causeway. His concern was reinforced by demographic trends revising the balance of population to the disadvantage of the Chinese community, regarded by Lee as Singapore's political bed-rock.

Ever since suffrage was extended in the mid-1950s beyond the direct beneficiaries of colonialism, elected government in Singapore has depended on Chinese voting support. The Chinese community has never been a perfect unity, acutely divided in the past into dialect groups and importantly into Chinese and English-educated. The English-educated group around Lee that founded the ruling People's Action Party (PAP) came to power through the votes of the Chinese-educated.

It has been a matter of policy to promote a greater unity within the Chinese community by encouraging a uniform cultural identity. Chinese culture espouses authoritarian values that place the interests of society before those of the individual; an imperative held by Lee. The active promotion of Confucian virtues also reflected a judgment that the Chinese do not naturally constitute a civic society. They had to be constantly exhorted to behave in the collective interest, otherwise disorder might ensue and undermine the fragile base of foreign investment on which Singapore's prosperity has depended.

In this mixed political culture, democracy is conceived as a process which permits periodic electoral judgment on the record of government. In effect, the exercise is designed to secure a renewal of a mandate that enables policy to be enunciated in a didactic manner and without challenge in a parliament where competent opposition has not been seen for over a generation.

Interest groups are regarded as potentially subversive and little better than united front vehicles of communist provenance. In effect, they are proscribed on the ground that the only proper point of entry into politics is by forming a party and putting up candidates for parliament; an intimidating prospect for all but the resolute and the foolhardy.

The maintenance model of politics deemed necessary by Lee in the national interest, and as the price required for the good life, has not really been modified over the years of his rule. One reason is that the past decade has been particularly troubling as new voters have come to their majority without the formative experience which had given their seniors the habit of political obedience. Jeyaretnam's by-election victory in October 1981 was a political turning point of a kind by demonstrating it was possible for an opposition candidate to win a parliamentary seat.

The outcome of the December 1984 general elections, with their 12.6% swing against the government as well as the return of the detested Jeyaretnam to parliament, came as a greater blow to Lee. The measure of political alienation at the time, despite sustained economic progress, was indicated in the correspondence columns of *The Straits Times,* the usually self-censoring English-language vehicle of government.

For a short time it became a sounding board of public opinion, undoubtedly at government behest. Controversial policies over pensions and eugenics were important in prompting the electoral swing. Strong resentment was also expressed at the way such policies "were seen to be rammed down our throats." The government's ruling style also drew criticism. One correspondent wrote that "for many the PAP government is seen as unnecessarily overbearing and overly paternalistic. It seems to know everything best and it is as uncompromising as it is arrogant."

The December 1984 elections were not salutary for Lee in the sense they inspired a change of political heart. One of his initial responses, prompted by canvassing on racial grounds, was to raise the prospect of re-examining the one-person, one-vote system. Clearly the people had failed the government and threatened to imperil the smooth transfer of political generations just as Lee was beginning his sixth cycle in life.

For Lee the issue was the preservation of his achievement against the electorate's fickleness, which required heavy political maintenance. To this end a virtual onslaught was launched against dissenting views, including those carried by the foreign press whose alleged intervention in domestic politics were portrayed in paranoid terms. It should have been known that the reason why some foreign publications were read so avidly by a highly educated constituency was that *The Straits Times*, while an excellent source for regional news, was regarded as a supine rag in its local reporting.

On one occasion, its editor tried to persuade students at the university otherwise by giving a talk entitled The Press in Singapore: Faith, Hope and the Future. Despite the conformist culture of education in Singapore, students have a pungent sense of humour reminiscent of the Soviet Union. One wag quipped at the title: "They have no faith, we have no hope; that's the future." Shortly after, the well-meaning editor was removed from his job.

The Law Society was also purged and diminished in role because it had the temerity to raise objections over legislation empowering the government to effectively ban foreign publications should they be judged to have engaged in domestic politics. Concurrently, Jeyaretnam's political head was hunted with relentless ferocity. The climax of this exercise in intimidation was the arrest of members of an alleged clandestine Marxist network, many of whom were active in Catholic social organisations, in May 1987 under the Internal Security Act.

This sordid story — together with its sequels — has been well recounted in [the *Far East Economic Review*], which has felt Lee's litigious wrath as a consequence. The reason for an episode which brought unnecessary misery to a number of decent families was said to be national security — a justification that failed to register credibility in Singapore, where it is well understood that silencing dissent is executed in the interests of stable political succession. That purpose was reiterated with the public denigration of Devan Nair, Singapore's former president and an acolyte of Lee's, for his audacious re-entry into politics after having brought disgrace on his office and country by public misconduct. By and large, these exercises in heavy political maintenance had the desired effect, as foreign business interests —

as Lee correctly calculated — were not perturbed by detention without trial.

In the September 1988 general elections, the swing against the government was arrested to the extent it increased by only 1.1% of the valid votes cast. The prime minister was relieved and became more relaxed as he contemplated the first stage of his retirement. Lee had the good sense to know he had to pass on the reins of power in one form or another, but has yet to demonstrate the confidence to let go completely. Instead he has sought to institutionalise his practice of political maintenance within a new office of executive president with wide reserve powers, including a role in internal security.

Lee's achievement in the quarter of a century since Singapore became independent has been remarkable by any standards. A man who once asserted that "island-nations are jokes" has, through an act of will, transformed an entrepot cast out by Malaysia into an international by-word for efficiency and excellence. He has done this by not suffering fools gladly and insisting on the highest standards, by eschewing sentimentality and rooting out corruption and by responding savagely to those believed to have betrayed the confidence placed in them.

In his pursuit of excellence, Lee has sought to mobilise and mould talent from a so-called limited gene pool. The academic performance of Singapore students overseas is evidence of success in this endeavour. A notable shortcoming, however, is that talent does not necessarily stay in Singapore as open governmental concern with emigration indicates. Moreover, there does not seem to be a ready willingness to understand just why skilled citizens should want to leave their green, prosperous and peaceful island for alien lands. The conventional wisdom is that they leave Singapore to advance careers attracted by material advantage, though that explanation is not sufficient in itself.

People also migrate from Singapore because they wish to be free of the constant constraints and harassment which are part of everyday life in a country small and compact enough for the hand of government to hover over the shoulder of every citizen. They are not prepared to pay the price in political and social control which Lee believes is absolutely necessary to preserve a stable and prosperous Singapore into the 21st century.

Perpetuating Lee's level of achievement will depend on the soundness of that judgment. His designated successor Goh Chok Tong brings a different style and reputation to high office. Goh has promised to loosen the reins of government while carrying a jockey's whip, an unfortunate analogy between goading horses to perform better and chastising the people of Singapore in their own interest. Lee has described Goh as "no softie," implying that he will also be adept at political maintenance which has been the hallmark of PAP government ever since it came to power.

48

Backseat Driver

Political succession has long been an obsession with Lee Kuan Yew. He has never concealed his anxiety that the inevitable passing of Singapore's founding political generation will weaken the republic's characteristic spirit of resolve. He has expressed personal reservations about his successor Goh Chok Tong, accepted as the choice of the second generation of leadership. Still in his 40s, Goh is a graduate in economics from the former University of Singapore who made his managerial mark in shipping.

At issue is what kind of political succession will take place with a man of Lee's ability and temperament still in the cabinet. Some have argued that the prospect for Goh as prime minister is very uncertain. He does not convey those qualities of determination and ruthlessness which have been the hallmark of Lee's tenure. He faces the task of registering his authority, knowing full well that Lee's impatient presence will be at his side.

Reprinted from Michael Leifer, "Backseat Driver", *Far Eastern Economic Review*, 15 November 1990, pp. 30–31, by permission of Review Publishing Co. Ltd.

Although Lee will no longer be prime minister, his personal influence will be all-powerful should he choose to use it. He is not likely to stay silent should he believe that the hand on the political tiller of Singapore is less than firm, especially if economic circumstances were to change adversely.

In a speech in August 1988, Lee warned his countrymen: "Even from my sick bed, even if you are going to lower me into the grave and I feel that something is wrong, I'll get up. Those who believe that when I have left the government as prime minister, that I've gone into permanent retirement, really should have their heads examined."

Goh is faced with a quandary. He is not one of nature's hard men, by contrast with the prime minister's eldest son, Lee Hsien Loong, who retired as a youthful brigadier-general in 1984 to rise like a rocket in politics. However, part of Goh's attraction to the people of Singapore is that he represents a contrast in style to that of Lee Senior.

The common man and woman can identify with an able individual who is seen as kind and compassionate, and even less than perfect, and therefore human. It has been suggested that the reason why the ruling People's Action Party (PAP) arrested its electoral decline in 1988 was the popular understanding that Goh was Lee's designated successor. But what may suit a changing electorate may not suit Lee Kuan Yew, and there is the rub.

It would be premature, however, to write off Goh as a political has-been even before he takes up the highest office. Political power has an intoxicating attraction and Goh may well come to enjoy its exercise more than he appears to do as first deputy prime minister. Moreover, he does possess majority support among his cabinet colleagues, especially the more experienced of them. One perceptive head of a local diplomatic mission has observed that Goh will probably have a longer shelf-life than many imagine.

Pressing him hardest is Lee Hsien Loong (or BG Lee) whose intellectual capability is beyond question. His political style and judgement is another matter, while he has a capacity for abrasive self-assertion which does not go down well with less senior but older political colleagues. He is undoubtedly a prime minister-in-waiting but his time has yet to be determined. His political turn was indicated in February 1989 when he was elected to the newly created post of second assistant secretary-general of the PAP.

There has been considerable speculation in Singapore about the new political pecking order from 28 November. That speculation is now mainly academic with the announcement by Goh that there will be two deputy prime ministers of equal rank, one of whom will be BG Lee and the other Ong Teng Cheong, the incumbent second deputy prime minister.

Although co-equal in protocol, BG Lee has been given the political edge by being nominated as acting prime minister in the event of Goh's absence from the country.

A new rising star is former brigadier-general George Yeo, currently minister of state for both finance and foreign affairs, who is to be the acting head of the new Ministry of Information and the Arts.

Speculation will probably continue about the political future of Ong, who may well become the first ambassador to China, leaving a space for someone of Subcontinental origin — possibly current Minister of Law S. Jayakumar — in order to overcome alienation among the Indian community.

Goh may not be entirely happy with the younger Lee breathing down his neck, and with his father also at his elbow. But it would seem logical to give him his political head. As Goh's principal deputy, he will be joined publicly in fullest responsibility for the failures as well as the successes of government. His future career will be linked inextricably to his partnership with Goh.

Irrespective of cabinet hierarchy, the immediate issue will be Lee Kuan Yew's interpretation of his new role as senior minister. Will he be content to act as an avuncular elder statesman holding his counsel until and only if it is requested, or will he be incapable of changing the habits of a political lifetime?

One indication of his intent will be whether or not he takes on the office of elected president which is the subject of legislation now before parliament. In the election campaign of 1988, Lee assured the people of Singapore that he would not be the first person to hold that office.

The terms of the pending legislation would permit the incumbent ceremonial President Wee Kim Wee to exercise executive powers until the end of his current term. Clearly, there would be opportunity for Lee Kuan Yew to step into the new office when the current presidential term ends or should Wee decide to retire early, and still honour the letter of his election pledge. His assumption of such office would provide concrete evidence of an inability to let go politically. Indeed, a confirmed cynic might suggest that Lee Kuan Yew's personal dominance is so deeply entrenched in Singapore that only an act of God and not of mere man can truly decide effective political succession.

49

Overnight, an Oasis
May Become a Desert

In Singapore, the memory of Sir Stamford Raffles still commands respect. His vision and enterprise are commended to a rising generation by latter-day founding fathers. It is to another Englishman, however, of pre-colonial vintage, that Singapore's practitioners have turned for general guidance on the conduct of foreign policy.

Ideas of the 16th-century philosopher, Thomas Hobbes, have been cited by Singapore leaders to convey the eternal nature of relations among states. His view of the uncertain life of man in the absence of common government has been quoted by Foreign Minister Suppiah Dhanabalan in a speech he made to the National University of Singapore in November 1981.

"International relations ... resemble a Hobbesian state of nature, where each is pitted against all," he said. "In the absence of order, the life of states would be as the life of men in the state of nature — 'nasty, brutish and short'."

Reprinted from Michael Leifer, "Overnight, an Oasis May Become a Desert", *Far Eastern Economic Review,* 8 January 1987, pp. 52–55, by permission of the Review Publishing Co. Ltd.

Acting Minister of Trade and Industry Lee Hsien Loong speaking in his capacity as minister of state for defence, perhaps reflecting his father, Prime Minister Lee Kuan Yew's brooding pessimism, has asserted in the same vein that "the world of states shares many characteristics of the world of beasts."

Those in charge of the destiny of Singapore never take its future existence for granted. They are moved by the apprehension articulated by Lee Hsien Loong that "overnight, an oasis may become a desert," and by the conviction that "goodwill is no substitute for self-interest." An attendant tough-minded pragmatism has been the characteristic feature of foreign policy, exemplified by the remark in July by First Deputy Prime Minister and Minister for Defence Goh Chok Tong that a S$2 billion (US$913 million) defence budget during a period of recession was a clear signal that Singapore had the will to protect itself.

The single-minded pursuit of self-interest, however, has become less crudely displayed. More than 20 years since the island's enforced independence, tough-mindedness has become combined with greater self-assurance. Fewer blatant expressions of waspishness are needed nowadays. Although concerned still to demonstrate a credible defence capability — indicated in provision for emergency food distribution and air-raid shelters, as well as state-of-the-art military technology — the earlier emphasis on Singapore's indigestible qualities has been toned down.

In place of a calculated abrasiveness, deemed necessary to register Singapore as an established fact of international political life, a more conciliatory outlook has emerged. This has been shown, above all, in relations with regional partners, notwithstanding the unanticipated discord generated by the visit in November of Israel's president. To some outside observers, ASEAN may not seem to be an institution of much substance. For the government of Singapore, however, ASEAN has become of central importance as a structure of special relationships.

The particular merit of that structure is that it serves to reinforce the regional acceptability and hence political durability of the republic. Unity of a kind within ASEAN mitigates the hostile Hobbesian environment of states. In Singapore's case, membership of an evolving diplomatic community has been of signal political advantage.

As an articulate advocate for ASEAN in the protracted Cambodia conflict, the government of Singapore has been able to advance both corporate and individual interests. Fundamental to the association's diplomatic challenge to Vietnam's continuing occupation has been a sustained commitment to uphold the sanctity of national sovereignty. In a speech on Cambodia delivered before the UN General Assembly in October 1986, Minister of State for Foreign Affairs Yeo Cheow Tong dwelt on those principles of international law bearing on the security requirements of small states.

He urged that "to make the world safer for other small states we must prove that no state, not even Vietnam, can be allowed to violate these fundamental principles. If Vietnam succeeds, other aggressors might be encouraged and make the world a more dangerous place for small states." The implications of his message for Singapore are self-evident. In addition, ASEAN's commitment to the principle of national sovereignty over the Cambodia issue reinforces indirectly the respect of ASEAN's partners for Singapore's independence.

For Singapore, membership of ASEAN was a step in the political dark. After nearly 20 years, participation has become a matter of both political prudence and advantage. Despite a self-styled representation as a global city, Singapore cannot change its geographic location and scale, its prevailing ethnic identity and, in many respects still, its regional economic role. It is lodged there, wedged between Malaysian and Indonesian sea and air space. Active membership of ASEAN serves to confirm Singapore's legitimate and enduring place within that uncertain environment.

An abiding source of environmental uncertainty is political change among regional partners, whose attitudes can shift from friendly to hostile overnight. The unpredictability of regional change was testified to by Lee Kuan Yew in July when he admitted in the case of the Philippines: "I never envisaged the events that transpired." In order to cope with more predictable generational political change below the level of top leadership, attention has been paid to strengthening bilateral relationships at lower levels with nearest neighbours.

For example, assiduous attempts have been made to cultivate a range of subordinate ministerial and bureaucratic ties with Malaysian counterparts on the model of the ostensible working relationship between prime ministers Lee Kuan Yew and Datuk Seri Mahathir Mohamad. The objective of this collaboration, which even includes sporting fixtures, is to try to ensure good relations will continue into the 21st century.

At the highest level, the relationship withstood well the strain of a Singapore court imposing a custodial sentence in August on

Tan Koon Swan, the president of Malaysian Chinese Association and a member of Malaysia's federal parliament. But it was seriously tested by the official visit in November of Israel's President Chaim Herzog.

In the case of Indonesia, a corresponding network has yet to be established, though a significant sign of military cooperation was the presence of Maj.-Gen. Winston Choo, chief of general staff of Singapore's armed forces, as guest of honour at the ceremony in Jakarta in October commemorating Indonesia's Armed Forces Day.

An attempt to promote contact between second-generation leaders was the declared purpose of a seminar in Bali in July, held under the joint auspices of Singapore's Institute of International Affairs and Indonesia's Centre for Strategic and International Studies.

Of more immediate political purpose was the visit in July to Manila by Lee Kuan Yew. It was both significant and characteristic that he was the first — and so far only — ASEAN head of government to visit the Philippines in the wake of the dramatic transfer of power in February which brought Corazon Aquino to the presidency.

Lee remarked on that occasion: "I have come here to be able to know you and to know the men and women who serve in your government." That remark points to the overriding preoccupation with the region and an attempt to influence it out of proportion to the size and population of the island state.

If Singapore has sought to come to terms with its more immediate regional locale, its political leaders have never been inclined to rely for security solely on harmonious regional relationships. At the time of independence, Singapore was confronted with the spectre of an unpalatable local-power dominance which has since been lifted but not eliminated. Its first head of state pointed to a prevailing concern within months of independence. The late Yusof bin Ishak explained: "So many of our neighbours and we ourselves would not have a separate existence if purely Asian forces were to settle the shape of decolonised Asia."

The Singapore Government has long sought to make the survival of the island less dependent on the region. In foreign economic relations, such a course became imperative from the outset, because of a declining entrepot role and the loss of an anticipated hinterland. The concept of Singapore as a global city, pioneered by the first foreign minister, Sinathamby Rajaratnam, has become even more important because of the recession.

Senior ministers, including Lee, have conducted personal diplomacy in Washington, London, Paris, Bonn and Tokyo, battling against protectionism and extolling the virtues of free trade. They have sought to encourage overseas investment appropriate to Singapore's declared role as a stable and efficient centre of high technology and financial and information services.

Although economic circumstances have changed, the general emphasis of extra-regional diplomacy has been sustained. Lee has argued that Singapore's foreign policy had to encourage the major powers in the world to help the island state, or at least to see that its situation did not worsen. Accordingly, it was said to be necessary for Singapore to offer the world a continuing interest in the type of society it projected. In addition, Lee insisted that it was imperative always to have "overwhelming power on our side."

Continuity has prevailed in an abiding concern to ensure that the regional balance of power conforms to Singapore's advantage. In ideal terms, the objective of foreign policy has been to overcome the spectre of an adverse change in the regional balance by cultivating countervailing external relationships.

Events moved against Singapore in 1975 with the success of revolutionary communism in Indochina and the special relationship which developed between Vietnam and the Soviet Union. It is the waxing role of the Soviet Union in Asia that causes most anxiety in Singapore's Foreign Ministry.

The US has long been regarded by Singapore as the critical external makeweight in the regional balance. The shrill insistence on the communist threat to the rest of Southeast Asia in the late 1970s and early 1980s was designed in part to try to jolt the government in Washington out of a perceived sense of complacency.

If the message is no longer communicated in the same tone, the underlying position is the same. In an address before the Council on Foreign Relations in New York in June, Lee Hsien Loong urged the US to preserve the strategic balance in Southeast Asia by maintaining a military presence in the region and by supporting ASEAN's stand over Cambodia.

The Cambodia question is now pursued less intensively. Nonetheless, a dogged diplomatic attack has been sustained by Vietnam's failure to achieve a conclusive victory. In this undertaking, shared interests with China have been upheld, based on a revised assessment of capability and threat. But the ultimate regional intent of a modernised People's Republic has not been discounted. In political terms, the relationship with China has been kept at a working distance.

Although special emphasis has been placed recently on external economic relations, the foreign policy of Singapore reflects a continuity of purpose which in turn reflects the continuity of leadership. If its current foreign minister, drawn from the bureaucracy via banking, gives more scope to his bureaucrats than his predecessor, the terms of reference of foreign policy have not changed fundamentally since independence, despite significant changes in the region.

In order to survive and prosper, Singapore is obliged to learn to live with its neighbours whatever ideals may be entertained about managing the competing external powers. That priority in foreign policy was indicated by Lee Hsien Loong, who has pointed out that "a wise nation will make sure that its survival and well-being are in the interests of other states."

To that end, Singapore has sought to make itself a regional asset within ASEAN. On the other hand, as Lee remarked, "goodwill is no substitute for self-interest." That view has been reinforced by Goh's comment: such relations will only last if founded on mutual respect and understanding. He maintains: "I believe in being friendly but no one shall mistake this as being weak."

50

Israel's President in Singapore
Political Catalysis and Transnational Politics

A foreign visit by a non-executive head of state at a counterpart's formal invitation is not normally an exceptional event. Such a visit would indicate either diplomatic good standing between governments or a mutual interest in promoting such a condition. Its political significance would be primarily symbolic because it is not the practice on such occasions for heads of states who are not heads of government to raise matters of substance in a bilateral relationship. The symbolism of a state visit is not without importance, however. A visiting head of state embodies the perceived virtues and vices of country and countrymen. Accordingly, he would not normally be invited abroad if his representative presence were deemed highly objectionable either by a significant constituency within the host state or by the government of a friendly neighbouring one. When President Chaim Herzog of Israel was invited to pay a state visit to Singapore in November 1986

Reprinted in abridged form from Michael Leifer, "Israel's President in Singapore: Political Catalysis and Transnational Politics", *Pacific Review* 1, no. 4 (1988): 341–52, by permission of Taylor and Francis Limited <http://www.tandf.co.uk/journals>.

by President Wee Kim Wee, the worst expectation in the island-republic was that it would be received "with cold displeasure in Malaysia".[1] In the event, his visit served to arouse very strong political feelings on both sides of the Strait of Johor.

Strictly speaking, catalysis is the effect produced by an agent that without undergoing change itself facilitates a chemical reaction and change in other bodies. Political catalysis was the effect produced by President Herzog because his state visit was the agent responsible for a marked adverse change in relations between Singapore and Malaysia and to a very much lesser extent between Singapore and Indonesia and Brunei. The visit was one of acute controversy becoming engaged emotively in the domestic politics of both Malaysia and Singapore, which are linked transnationally. Indeed, the domestic repercussions of the visit were disturbing for both governments which have been longstanding regional partners within the Association of South-East Asian Nations (ASEAN) established in 1967, as well as within the Five Power Defence Arrangements which replaced the Anglo-Malaysian Defence Agreement in 1971. In its wake, they have sought to limit political damage and to restore a working relationship which neither party can really afford to jeopardise beyond repair. At issue is why Chaim Herzog's presence in Singapore should have generated political furore, bringing relations with Malaysia to their lowest ebb since constitutional separation in August 1965. This article addresses that question, taking into special account the close interrelationship between domestic context and foreign policy which distinguished the stormy episode.

President Herzog's visit to Singapore was deemed provocative and not only by partisan interests who perceived Israel as a pariah-state. The best informed and most dispassionate regional publication commented after the event: "Observers find it difficult to believe that the bilateral relationship (with Israel) is of such importance that it (Singapore) would offend its important neighbours".[2] It should be stated, at the outset, that the invitation by the president of Singapore to his Israeli counterpart was not a calculated act designed to give offence. Such a feature of Singapore's practice of foreign policy had been evident shortly after independence when neighbouring governments appeared to require reminding that the island-republic enjoyed sovereign status. Over two decades after an enforced independence from Malaysia, Singapore has moderated a testy diplomacy. Its government, under the continuous leadership of Prime Minister Lee Kuan Yew, has long appreciated the utility of Singapore's membership of ASEAN. Institutionalised regional cooperation has been valued because it contributes to the security and welfare of an innately vulnerable Singapore. Part of the reasoning behind a willingness to extend an invitation to President Herzog was that intra-ASEAN relationships were deemed sufficiently sturdy and resilient for the visit not to disturb any of them unduly. Left out of that calculation, however, was the contradiction between the value placed on a regional structure of special relations and an interest in sustaining a longstanding association with Israel.

The Politics of Damage Limitation

The major initiative in political damage limitation was undertaken by Singapore with other regional protestors and the Arab-Islamic states also in mind. During the course of a speech at a banquet for Chaim Herzog, Singapore's president made a special point of publicly urging Israel to withdraw to its pre-1967 borders, to return Jerusalem to its original status and to recognise the rights of the Palestinians to self-determination. In April 1987, it was found politic to provide a venue for a United Nations regional conference on Palestine organised by the Organisation's Department of Public Information. This conference in Singapore was attended by Zehdi Terzi, the PLO's permanent representative to the UN, who publicly reiterated the point of an earlier communication in January from Yasser Arafat that the government of the island-republic had the right to invite whomsoever they pleased. Nearly a month after the visit by Israel's president, Prime Minister Lee went out of his way publicly to soften the blow to his Malaysian counterpart's sense of self-esteem. He half-apologised for any slight and implicitly regretted the episode. He shifted the burden of responsibility onto officials of Singapore's ministry of foreign affairs who were misled or beguiled into believing it was a routine decision. He pointed out that if he had been kept better informed, he would have postponed the visit because of his "personal relationship with Dr Mahathir". He went on to make a plea in mitigation: "So I would not wish to slight him. But once it was announced, we could not without horrendous consequences to ourselves and to our foreign policy, cancel it because of demonstrations in Malaysia. It is not the way you behave if you want to be taken seriously".[3] Well before Lee Kuan Yew had indicated regret, Malaysia's government had taken steps to contain continuing agitation over President Herzog's visit.

Dr Mahathir went out of his way to instruct the Johor branch of the *ad hoc* action committee to cease their protests because their activities were threatening the safety of Singaporeans visiting Malaysia by causeway and by inference the livelihood of shopkeepers and hoteliers in Johor. He expressed doubts about the committee's motives, questioning whether their purpose was to pressure Singapore or the Malaysian government. By early December 1986 the Foreign Minister, Datuk Rais Yatim, had advised that the two countries should live and let live because of their interdependent relationship. Within days of Lee Kuan Yew's address at the National University, Dr Mahathir was reported as saying: "I feel we just forget the matter *(sic)*".[4]

Among the three states of ASEAN which protested at the president of Israel's visit to Singapore, only Malaysia continued to be at odds with the island state after his departure. Relations with Brunei and Indonesia were not at all seriously disturbed. Indeed in February 1987, President Suharto made a cordial visit to Singapore, travelling across the causeway from Malaysia which had been his first call. The repercussions of President Herzog's visit continued to rumble on for a while because of the way in which the politics of Singapore and Malaysia were joined. For example, a public remark later in February by the prime minister's elder son, Lee Hsien Loong, in his capacity as second Minister of Defence questioning the loyalty of Malays in Singapore's armed forces revived contention just as intra-party contention within UMNO was reaching a peak.[5] Later in the year, an incursion into Malaysia's coastal waters by a small group of national servicemen from Singapore had a corresponding, albeit lesser, effect indicating an intrinsic fragility in the relationship.

Despite that fragility both governments sought to repair matters. The strained political climate was not allowed to stand in the way of practical cooperation. For example, joint naval exercises were conducted in the South China Sea in April 1987. Malaysia's Minister of Defence Tengku Ahmad Rithaudeen visited Singapore towards the end of the year and ratified an agreement on exchanging students in respective defence colleges. Close cooperation between internal security services is believed to have been displayed concurrently with arrests in Malaysia under the Internal Security Act in October 1987. Prime Minister Lee met with Dr Mahathir during the Commonwealth Heads of Government Meeting in Vancouver earlier in October where they discussed issues of controversy in the bilateral relationship and also water and natural gas supply from Malaysia to Singapore. These discussions were continued in December 1987 in Manila when both heads of government attended the third ASEAN summit. Progress was reported on the linked issues of water and gas supply from Malaysia to Singapore. The momentum of *rapprochement* was sustained when Dr Mahathir paid a one-day visit to Singapore in January 1988, after which he announced a new agreement on the supply of additional fresh water from Malaysia and one in principle by Singapore to buy Malaysian natural gas.[6] These agreements, confirmed when Prime Minister Lee visited Kuala Lumpur in June, were symptomatic of the order of priorities of both leaders, each of whom faced domestic problems which made it important to avoid ensnaring their bilateral relationship. Prime Minister Lee, at a time when he was thinking seriously of shifting further the burden of political responsibility to a younger generation of leaders, had been confronted with primordial facts of life. He was obliged to confess "Superficially we have become Singaporean", later encouraging a revision of the constituency system for parliamentary elections whereby special provision would be made for minority race candidates.

In the case of Malaysia, Dr Mahathir had been struggling to reassert his political authority in the face of a challenge which had split UMNO in an historically unprecedented way. In the event, he used the opportunity of a rise in racial tension in October 1987 to employ the Internal Security Act against political enemies. Subsequently, a high court decision (arising from a challenge to the conduct of the UMNO elections of April 1987), which declared the Malay party to be an illegal organisation, led Dr Mahathir to set up a new national organisation with the power to vet all prospective members. In his context, he saw no political profit in pursuing a feud with Singapore arising from an anti-Zionist obsession which he had by then dropped, partly because of its adverse effect on attracting American business interests to Malaysia.

President Chaim Herzog's visit to Singapore in November 1986 gave rise to an exceptional episode in that country's relations with Malaysia. As a catalytic event, it served to generate a strain which had not been so intensely evident since constitutional separation in August 1965. The Israeli interest was in widening a breach in an Arab-inspired wall of diplomatic containment. Singapore conceded a willingness to participate in such an exercise because of the longstanding benefits derived from the Israeli connexion. What was intended as a ceremonial undertaking backfired politically. Dr Mahathir's anti-Zionist demonology reinforced a hostile political climate in Malaysia to make Chaim Herzog's visit appear a gratuitous provocation. Indeed the apparent flaunting of a politically unhygienic relationship was taken as a personal affront by Dr Mahathir whose leadership of UMNO was subject to growing challenge. Apart from the element of opportunism in Malaysian reactions, the visit also highlighted the transnational communal linkage between the domestic politics of both states. In Malaysia, Singapore viewed as an offshore symbol of Chinese challenge to Malay political birthright was made more insidious by the Israeli connexion. In Singapore, Malaysian demands at ministerial level to reconsider the visit were construed as an unwarranted attempt to impose a veto on foreign policy and also subversive of the loyalty of Malay citizens. Accordingly, the episode became a test of national sovereignty. An editorial in *The Straits Times* in March 1987, in response to criticism of Lee Hsien Loong's remarks about the position of Malays in Singapore's armed forces, pointed out: "This goes to show that some 22 years after Singapore left Malaysia, not everyone in Malaysia has accepted the Republic as a sovereign state."[7]

In the event, after a decent interval and an apology of a kind from Lee Kuan Yew, practical attempts were made to restore equilibrium to a relationship liable to disruption because of structural tensions. Symbolic reconciliation was expressed in the first ever official visit by a Malaysian king in July 1988. In Singapore, the Herzog episode has had a salutary effect up to a point. Speaking to Singapore journalists while in Manila in December 1987, Prime Minister Lee recalled his conversation with Dr Mahathir in Vancouver in which Malaysia's prime minister had expressed the view that in discussing its domestic affairs, Singapore should try and avoid subjects that were also sensitive in Malaysia. Mr Lee cautioned that should Singapore be ignorant of Malaysia's problems and discuss its own problems in isolation of Malaysia's search for, and implementation of, its own solutions, "then it may cause problems between us".[8] A declared sensitivity to Malaysian interests in Singapore should not be interpreted, however, as a formula for appeasement on the part of a government which is concerned not to give the impression that friendship may be construed as weakness. For that reason, the Israeli connexion has been maintained, if reduced in profile. Private visits to Singapore by senior Israeli military officers shortly after Chaim Herzog's controversial visit underpinned the comment once made by Lee Hsien Loong that "goodwill is no substitute for self-interest". An Israeli presence will not be allowed to play a politically catalytic role in the future but given Singapore's conspicuous ethnic identity and geopolitical vulnerability, that presence will not be willingly sacrificed on the altar of friendship with Malaysia. Moreover, transnational linkages between domestic politics, and a mutual insecurity have not so altered as to deny the prospect of their ever against disrupting the bilateral relationship across the Straits of Johor. President Chaim Herzog's visit to Singapore demonstrated paradoxically the potential for such disruption as well as a mutual interest in both managing and overcoming it.

Notes

1. Letter to *The Straits Times*, 17 December 1986, by Singapore's Senior Minister and former Foreign Minister, Sinnathamby Rajaratnam.
2. *Far Eastern Economic Review*, 27 November 1986.
3. Lee Kuan Yew, *The Straits Times*, 15 December 1986.
4 *The Straits Times*, 20 December 1986.
5. During a constituency tour Lee Hsien Loong remarked, in response to a question why were there no Malay pilots in the air force: "If there is a conflict, if the SAF is called to defend the homeland, we don't want to put any of our soldiers in a difficult position where his emotions for the nation may come into conflict with his emotions for his religion." *The Straits Times*, 23 February 1987.
6. See *Far Eastern Economic Review*, 11 February and 18 February 1988.
7. *The Straits Times*, 31 March 1987.
8. *Singapore Bulletin*, January 1988.

51

Singapore in Regional and Global Context
Sustaining Exceptionalism

The Shadow of Vulnerability

Singapore enjoys the reputation of an exceptional state both within and beyond its regional locale. As in essence a city, it is without a contemporary comparator in the range and quality of its material accomplishments. Those accomplishments do not require rehearsing here. They have also been widely acknowledged; for example, by the Swiss based World Economic Forum in its annual Global Competitiveness Report for 1997 in which Singapore was ranked first among 53 economies, ahead of Hong Kong and the United States. Its circumstances and condition as a city-state, however, are *sui generis* in the modern world and do not provide support for the fashionable argument that rising cities pose a challenge to declining states. Indeed, in foreign policy, Singapore's problem is dealing with states.

Reprinted from Michael Leifer, "Singapore in Regional and Global Context: Sustaining Exceptionalism", in *Singapore: Re-engineering Success*, edited by Arun Mahizhnan and Lee Tsao Yuan (Singapore: Oxford University Press, 1998), pp. 19–30, by permission of the Institute of Policy Studies, Singapore, and Marshall Cavendish International (S) Pte Ltd.

Singapore's material accomplishments associated with a strong and effective political leadership have given the island-state a unique international standing. They have also attracted a measure of envy and resentment, especially within regional locale, in part, for the self-congratulatory way in which those accomplishments have sometimes been celebrated. Moreover, the social and political model which Singapore's government has deliberately chosen in the common good has not been uniformly well received in the West where it is seen to be at odds with the concept of a civil society inherent in Liberal Democracy. Prime Minister Goh Chok Tong has claimed that the overwhelming electoral victory of the ruling People's Action Party (PAP) in January 1997 demonstrated that Singapore's voters had rejected Western-style Liberal Democracy.

The very fact that the so-called Singapore model of development has been held up for emulation in a country such as China has compounded its problems with the West. For its part, Singapore defends its corner and its chosen course with ferocity and doggedness and some hubris which may be a problem for a small vulnerable state which cannot be a total master of its own destiny. At issue for Singapore in the 21st century is the extent to which its government and society are able to continue to cope imaginatively and constructively with those underlying adverse circumstances visited on the island-state by and at an unanticipated independence in August 1965 and which have not changed since. Limited size, confined location and prevailing ethnic-Chinese identity do not in themselves add up to destiny but they are facts of geopolitical life which have to be addressed on a continuing basis from generation to generation without their necessarily being bound together by a shared experience and, therefore, by the same depth of common awareness that the independence of the island-state can never be taken for granted. Such was the message articulated by a former Defence Minister, Lim Kim San, on celebrating his eightieth birthday in November 1996.

The Republic of Singapore was established against all expectations and against the conventional wisdom of its ruling PAP. Indeed, its first Prime Minister, Lee Kuan Yew, when in opposition, had pronounced that "island nations are political jokes". However, independence in the wake of a turbulent experience within Malaysia was not a laughing matter. From the outset, the problem was how to address and to overcome an innate vulnerability compounded by a pattern of tensions based in regional locale but with roots also in the colonial inheritance.

In essence, that situation has not changed, which has served to provide a strong strain of continuity in the premises and practice of foreign policy.

At the outset, and with an acute vulnerability much in mind, regional locale was treated as a menacing environment exemplified by the felt need to articulate an indigestible "poison shrimp" idiom and to display a deliberate combativeness towards likely predators close at hand. Moreover, the initial stage of regional cooperation within an embryonic Association of South-east Asian Nations (ASEAN) was regarded with both scepticism and suspicion against the background of recent Confrontation and the registration of a common Malay identity by Indonesia and Malaysia in bringing that dispute to a conclusion. With that experience in mind, it has been a consistent principle of foreign policy that Singapore should never find itself solely at the mercy of regional forces. The notion of balance of power, in the sense that access to countervailing external influences and support was continuously required, was built into the calculations of policy from the very outset. It was with this consideration in mind that Singapore reached out beyond regional locale to attract multinational enterprises in an imaginative industrial venture which provided the economic foundations for realizing its vision of becoming a "Global City". That concept was articulated by the island's first Foreign Minister, Sinnathamby Rajaratnam, in February 1972. He explained then that "we draw sustenance not only from the region but also from the international economic system to which we as a Global City belong and which will be the final arbiter of whether we prosper or decline".

Singapore has sought to ensure its economic base and prosperity by transcending its regional context and constraints wherever practical but without being able to retain close access to countervailing military support of the kind provided once by a British presence. During the Cold War, a recurrent rhetoric about the utility of an American regional military presence was not a substitute for direct provision for national security which has been addressed through an expensive self-defence policy financed through the fruits of economic success. And although that military presence has come to enjoy a greater immediacy from the 1990s through the provision of limited facilities within Singapore, it does not in itself constitute a satisfactory and assured source of external countervailing power in the interest of perpetuating independence. Singapore is hardly a central factor in the strategic calculations of the United States which is well understood within the island and also a source of continuing concern.

In the wake of independence and after an initial hesitation, and also without giving up its stark strategic outlook and defensive self-reliance, Singapore's government came to see the complementary merits of a constructive regional policy, despite its shortcomings in economic cooperation. That modified perspective roughly coincided with the establishment of a professional foreign service as opposed to a mixture of seconded civil servants and gifted amateurs. An ability was developed to identify with the concerns of regional partners, especially from the mid 1970s which saw the success of revolutionary communism in Indochina. A special effort was made to cultivate close personal relations with political leaders in Indonesia and Brunei which has been a more difficult undertaking in the case of Malaysia from which Singapore continues to draw an essential supplementary supply of water. Moreover, it soon came to be realized that in a multilateral context such as ASEAN, a small country with a clearly defined agenda pressed by skilled and articulate ministers and officials could punch diplomatically above its weight.

Singapore demonstrated that facility with extraordinary success during the course of the Cambodian conflict during the 1980s when its diplomats turned to national advantage the undue burden of corporate responsibility carried in mobilizing voting support at the United Nations (UN). With the end of the Cold War and the attendant resolution of the Cambodian conflict, fresh opportunity was identified and initiative taken to promote greater cooperative security through the vehicle of the Asia Pacific-wide ASEAN Regional Forum (ARF), while Singapore's more conspicuous role in encouraging the Asia-Europe Meeting (ASEM) has served corresponding interests. Both of these enterprises, as well as Asia Pacific Economic Cooperation (APEC), have provided institutionalized forms of multilateral engagement in regional locale which has been a prime long-standing objective of Singapore's foreign policy.

In taking such regional initiatives both during and after the Cold War, Singapore's ministers and officials have been able to reconcile regional and global policies to national advantage. Indeed, although Singapore would not seem to have given up its realist international outlook with an innate vulnerability perpetually in mind, it has managed to combine such an outlook with liberal internationalist and cooperative security policies with a singular measure of success. The object of the multiple exercise has been to cope with a predicament visited on the island-state on independence by a cluster of policies which converge to serve the same end — that of multilateral engagement within regional locale so as to underpin independence. The dominant idiom remains that of the balance of power which was the prescription for security in a post-Cold War Asia Pacific offered by Senior Minister Lee Kuan Yew, in his keynote address to the annual conference of the International Institute for Strategic Studies held in Singapore in September 1997.

Driving the Region?

Singapore has exemplified the logic of globalization and has learned how to benefit from that uncertain process and double-edged sword in attracting multinational enterprises in manufacturing and services of an increasingly sophisticated kind. Its leaders have preached the sermon that the world does not owe Singapore a living. Public policy has been designed to sustain the international competitiveness and comparative advantage of the island-state with a greater emphasis on investment in upgrading human resources and also on holding open the door to foreign talent. A good sense of adaptation has been demonstrated in the measure of flexibility over immigration whereby the full population of the island has risen to 3.6 million and includes some 560,000 foreigners who have been described by Prime Minister Goh Chok Tong as "intellectual capital". An abiding apprehension about limitations of the talent pool among a native population of some 3 million has not, so far, been borne out by a flagging performance. Indeed, creativity of the Nobel Prize kind may not be required for Singapore to continue on its successful way. Sensitive political leadership and diplomatic skills will be required in continuing measure, however, to cope with an uncertain future, especially as inevitable political change within close regional locale will bring new problems. These problems have been pointed up with the onset of the Asian economic crisis from mid 1997 to which Singapore has responded by trying to mitigate the adverse condition of close neighbours with which it is joined in economic and strategic interdependence. Interdependence, however, is not in itself a foolproof recipe for a viable foreign policy.

How should Singapore seek to cope with a region and a world beyond any kind of direct control by a state of its limited dimensions? For a start, its diplomats should report fearlessly about the way in which the Republic is regarded in its regional locale and beyond. Although Singapore is valued for its intellectual contribution to regional initiatives and cooperation, there has been a recurrent tendency on the part of some of its political leaders to address the region in a didactic manner which has been resented. Such resentment was one dimension of the furore within the Philippines in March 1995 over the hanging in Singapore of a Filipina maid found guilty of murdering a young child in her charge as well as a fellow countrywoman. Indeed, such resentments tend to be stored up so that when an episode of some tension arises, whether through perceived sins of commission or of omission, the measure of fury directed at Singapore has seemed to be out of all proportion to the presumed offense. That certainly seemed to be the case when a row erupted with the government in Kuala Lumpur in early 1997 over a statement made to a Singapore court over a libel action by Senior Minister Lee Kuan Yew, which appeared to be disparaging of public order in Johor Bahru, Malaysia, where a political opponent named in the libel action had fled, claiming to be in fear for his life. In the case of Malaysia, a structural tension was exposed and that requires continuous management.

The fact of the matter is that Singapore's success is not necessarily enjoyed by all around and when that success is combined with an articulated sense of superior achievement by contrast with close neighbours, then trouble has to be expected. Such trouble has to be identified in advance and addressed in a constructive way, especially should it interpose in critical relationships beset by a structural tension. Moreover, in its perpetual condition of vulnerability, Singapore cannot afford more than a measure of such trouble. A small dose may be useful for mobilizing domestic support and for demonstrating the facts of political life to a sceptical public without direct experience of past adversity. Beyond that, business confidence, both locally and beyond, may begin to be affected even if the same may be said for the locus of the trouble. Damage limitation is not a good enough preoccupation for a professional foreign service which may be ill-served, at times, by a lack of sensitivity on the part of its political masters. An essential requirement for the future is the development of a far more conscious measure of political sensitivity in the day-to-day practice of foreign policy, especially in relations with Malaysia which have always been problematic. This is not to suggest adopting a culture of dependence and subservience and any display of weakness, but rather, to think of how to advance interests without causing offense and attendant alienation. A connected matter is to avoid giving the impression of employing double standards by engaging in gratuitous criticisms of foreign countries beyond immediate locale whether or not as part of a calculated practice of managing domestic social forces.

That said, those responsible for Singapore's foreign policy will be obliged also to consider the implications of a changing regional context of which the degree of enlargement of ASEAN is one dimension. The rhetoric of enlargement has worn thin with the political embarrassment of having to postpone Cambodia's entry scheduled for July 1997 because of the bloody coup in that country. Enlargement to nine members, however, has brought with it a greater political diversity and greater problems of building the consensus by which the Association proceeds. ASEAN cannot be compared to the European Union (EU) with its treaty-based supranational dimension. ASEAN has always been about upholding national sovereignty which becomes a more complex undertaking with enlargement. Moreover, the Association can no longer enjoy the cosy intimacy of scale and quasi-familial cultures which distinguished the grouping before Vietnam's entry in July 1995 removed the logjam to new admissions. Such changing circumstances place Singapore in a position whereby its politicians and officials will require great skill in positioning themselves in respect of changing patterns of alignment which are likely to appear within an enlarged and far more disparate Association. Moreover, ASEAN, and Singapore with it, has become involved in a very different kind of regional issue to that which united the Association, up to a point, over Cambodia during the 1980s.

Singapore was in the forefront of a diplomatic campaign to challenge the legitimacy of the government installed by Vietnamese force of arms in Phnom Penh in January 1979 in defence of the principle of the sanctity of national sovereignty. The direct connection between that territorial violation and the integrity of Singapore was matched by the Republic's response to Iraq's invasion of Kuwait in August 1990. In July 1997, however, Singapore supported postponing Cambodia's entry into ASEAN on the grounds of the violation of constitutional sanctity, which is a very different issue indeed. The matter of principle was articulated by the Foreign Minister, Professor S. Jayakumar, when he stated that "where force is used for an unconstitutional purpose, it is behaviour that ASEAN cannot ignore and condone". The new diversity of ASEAN is such that such a principle is at variance with the political cultures of many member states and the principle invoked is also inconsistent with a fundamental working convention of the Association which upholds the sanctity of national sovereignty by repudiating any intervention into the domestic affairs of member states. ASEAN's stake in the viability of the Paris Peace Accords of October 1991 and the integrity of the constitution arising from their implementation is well understood. However, the stand taken in response to the Cambodian coup, although genuine in terms of Singapore's interest, marks a move into unchartered political waters which could well rebound on ASEAN with considerable adverse consequences, especially as it is inconsistent with that adopted over Myanmar.

ASEAN has become important to Singapore as a security structure based on political dialogue and cooperation but the attempt to build consensus around a radical principle for the Association could well prejudice its utility. Once a judgement had been made in the early 1970s about the utility for Singapore's security of its fellow members' commitment to the Association, and in particular by Indonesia, it came to be realized how participation and the attendant development of a practice of confidence-building could contribute to the regional acceptability of the Republic. The quality of political cooperation displayed from the mid 1970s, despite Singapore's evident disappointment at an inability to match that political cooperation economically, served to overcome concerns that the Republic would find itself subject to the diktat of its larger close neighbours. The multilateral quality of ASEAN and the whole emphasis of the Association on reinforcing national sovereignty has enabled Singapore to take political comfort from the extent to which membership could contribute to the independence of the island-state. The multilateral structure has also enabled Singapore to play a regional role on the basis of an authentic regional identity. That experience, above all in the case of Cambodia, indicated that Singapore would be able to take an active role whenever an appropriate mandate had been accorded by the Association which was notably the case with the initiative to found the ARF. Since the onset of the new complicating issue of Cambodia, however, coincident with institutional enlargement, the problems of consensus-building are likely to make it more difficult for Singapore to find the diplomatic space for corresponding initiatives.

The underlying significance of the initiative over the ARF, which occurred when Singapore occupied the chair of ASEAN's Standing

Committee, was that it marked an attempt to seek national advantage from regional uncertainties over changes in the balance or distribution of power in East Asia attendant on the end of the Cold War. The initiative for the ARF, which caught the regional mood, was not the exclusive inspiration of Singapore but Singapore's Foreign Ministry assumed a vigorous leading role. It has also been most active in support of ASEAN assuming and sustaining a diplomatic centrality within the ARF. In its degree of success in this endeavour, Singapore has managed to engage in a remarkable balancing exercise. By helping to promote the ARF, its Foreign Ministry has enabled Singapore to embed itself more deeply within a wider regional structure of political cooperation and, therefore, a more desirable pattern of power. At the same time, by taking a strong position on ASEAN's diplomatic centrality within the ARF, Singapore has shown itself to be a reliable regional partner within its more limited South-east Asian context.

The same measure of skill may be said to have been demonstrated over the successful initiative to set up the ASEM convened first in Bangkok in March 1996 and which may be seen as a complementary multilateral structure of cooperation that contributes also to underpinning Singapore's international status. Moreover, the composition of the Asia side of the ASEM process has enabled ASEAN to assume a corresponding diplomatic centrality to that realized in the case of the ARF which Singapore has supported. In the light of the degree of success of those post-Cold War initiatives, it is possible to suggest that Singapore has not only been able, up to a point, to drive its region but also to do so in a way which encourages a greater degree of interest and engagement by a range of states which serves the goal of an ideal multiple balance. Sustaining the ASEM process has become more problematic, however, with the dramatic reversal of East Asian economic fortunes.

Coping with the Wider World

Internationally, beyond South-east Asia, Singapore looks to the major powers to take a benign interest in its economic activities and in its survival in viable form. It has been notably successful in developing a working relationship with China with which formal diplomatic relations were only established in late 1990 in deference to Indonesia which only re-established ties earlier in the year. The nature of the association, however, including the degree of investment in mainland

Chinese enterprise, has revived suspicions within the region as to the Republic's true affinity, especially in the light of encouragement for gatherings of Overseas Chinese. However, opportunities have been found to register and reiterate the axiom that Singapore is a separate and totally different political identity to China and that its policies have to reflect that identity which is based in important part on the rightful place of non-Chinese minorities and on its South-east Asian regional locale. It was Singapore's Senior Minister Lee Kuan Yew, who, exceptionally within ASEAN, expressed his outspoken concern about the utility of China engaging in intimidating military display in March 1996 in order to influence the outcome of Presidential elections in Taiwan. Nonetheless, managing the relationship with China is a critical matter for Singapore because of the mixed feelings entertained towards the island-state within the region on account of its prevailing ethnic identity and also because of the geopolitical shadow increasingly cast over South-east Asia by China as a rising power with an irredentist agenda in the South China Sea. Moreover, the economic crisis which has afflicted the states of Southeast Asia since July 1997 with attendant financial loss, have served to revive animosity towards local Chinese business interests whose natural regional locus is seen to be in Singapore.

The relationship between Singapore and the United States is, for the time being, more important but in some ways even more problematic. Singapore contemplates the United States in terms of an ideal regional security buffer role. A working security relationship to that end was signalled in the bilateral Memorandum of Understanding concluded in 1990 which marked the first regional initiative to provide America's military with a measure of compensating access to limited facilities in return for the loss of major ones in the Philippines. Its multinational companies have long been active in the Republic and access to America's market is critical to Singapore's economic buoyancy. Problems have occurred, in particular, since the end of the Cold War when the United States enunciated a policy of enlarging market democracies as an alternative to the defunct one of containing communism. Partly in reaction to a concern that America's new agenda for world order brought with it a licence to intervene in the domestic affairs of states which did not share Washington's public value system, the Republic through a variety of spokespersons took it upon itself to enunciate an alternative set of communitarian values deemed more appropriate for Asian societies. The attendant repudiation of Western liberal political values together with a robust critique of the social pathology of Western societies was received with some offense, irrespective of its degree of justification. Controversial episodes involving American nationals in Singapore have served to widen the cultural gap and to reinforce alienation. Moreover, representations of the political process in Singapore in the American press, and especially the way in which government ministers have resorted to the courts against political opponents, have served to blemish Singapore's reputation. Such blemish has added to the difficulties encountered by Singapore's representatives in seeking a hearing in Washington's parochial political arena, although President Clinton's choice of Prime Minister Goh Chok Tong as a golfing partner in Vancouver for the APEC summit in November 1997 would suggest the reversal of an adverse diplomatic trend.

Japan is, of course, of continuing major importance, given the strong long-standing economic links and the extent to which its bilateral security relationship with the United States is regarded as the foundation stone of Asia Pacific regional security. Singapore has declared an interest in Japan sustaining a security policy which does not extend beyond its home islands which is, in part, a legacy of the Pacific War. Concern has been expressed about the extent to which a regeneration of the American-Japan security relationship, expressed in revised guidelines for defence cooperation, will raise tensions with China because of their inferred application to Taiwan. Singapore is not in a position to influence those revised guidelines but can act with its regional partners within ASEAN to register its concern over their interpretation. The fact of the matter, however, is that Singapore can do little on its own to shape the relationships among the major Asia Pacific powers. It is obliged to work within a multilateral context which is a mixed blessing from which, however, some practical benefits have been drawn suggesting the direction of future policy. At issue is how to avoid circumstances where Singapore is obliged to choose between the United States and China on a matter such as Taiwan which has become an increasing source of tension affecting the wider Asia Pacific region.

Its role within ASEAN notwithstanding, Singapore's prevailing ties are still with a Western constellation of states which help to underpin its economic achievement. However, Singapore's government does not seem inclined or likely to modify its political culture to suit the interests of Western non-government organizations (NGOs) and the Western press. Accordingly, a problem exists which relates to the very essence of Singapore's foreign policy; namely, how to ensure that sufficient major powers take sufficient interest in its continued independence. The problem with living with vulnerability is that there is a natural and strong inclination not to display any undue signs of accommodation lest they be mistaken for appeasement and weakness and so compromise the position of the Republic. In that respect, Singapore is encased in a political mould which does not show any signs of change with the approach of the 21st century.

Singapore's immutability may cause discomfort to some Western governments but it does not, so far, discourage forein companies which have been attracted by the Republic's comparative advantage in efficiency in manufacturing and service facilities and non-corrupt business climate. Sustaining exceptionalism will depend, above all, on an ability for adaptation in economic activities in response to global changes. Success in that endeavour will be critical in upholding a remarkable international standing. As Deputy Prime Minister Lee Hsien Loong pointed out in May 1997, should the Republic be overtaken and made irrelevant, its influence and international standing would go down. To that extent, foreign policy begins at home.

Conclusion

In so many respects, little has changed in over three decades since an unanticipated independence. A minuscule Singapore is still wedged within a confined sea and air space, access to which is controlled by neighbours which are not fully trusted. The need to assert sovereign status is still strongly felt and matched by a reluctance to appear to make concessions under any kind of duress for fear of creating an unwholesome precedent. Accordingly, balance of power considerations still underlie the calculations of those responsible for the conduct of foreign relations even if they are expressed, at times, in ideas about cooperative regional and international enterprise. Of course, problems of foreign policy have become more complex with changes in the international system, but their dominant expression of globalization has been in tune with the constant national aspiration to keep the Republic out of the play of solely regional forces. That aspiration, based on an underlying premise of vulnerability, has run as a continuous seam through the course of Singapore's international experience. The goal of "re-engineering success" will have to be addressed in the light of that fundamental continuity.

52

Coping with Vulnerability

The condition of Singapore at the beginning of the twenty-first century stands in marked contrast to that which obtained on the morrow of independence in 1965. A new state without a hinterland has succeeded in making a hinterland of the global economy with conspicuous success. Moreover, the way in which the regionally contagious economic adversity was addressed at the end of the last century demonstrated an underlying resilience based on a system of governance respected for its efficiency and probity. Singapore has superseded its past as a colonial entrepôt to give new and modern meaning to the concept of entrepôt in an age of globalisation. An underlying continuity of geopolitical circumstance and outlook has gone hand in hand with that change, however.

It is notable, for example, that the economic adversity, which required popular belt-tightening at the end of the 1990s, was not permitted to become a constraint on defence expenditure based on a

Reprinted from "Conclusion: Coping with Vulnerability", in *Singapore Foreign Policy: Coping with Vulnerability*, by Michael Leifer (London and New York: Routledge, 2000), pp. 157–62, by permission of the publisher.

constant percentage of gross national product. While a necessary austerity obliged regional neighbours to neglect their defence establishments, Singapore sustained a programme of arms procurements, including the purchase of four submarines from Sweden, and defence training. Minister of Defence, Dr Tony Tan, remarked in March 1998 that Singapore had to continue its long-term investment in defence, even during regional economic turmoil, if it wanted to avoid paying the price of being caught unprepared. That indication of priorities pointed to a basic continuity in governmental perceptions of Singapore's strategic circumstances. In crudest geopolitical terms, those circumstances of size and location have not changed for a minuscule island without any defence in depth. Moreover, towards the end of the 1990s, relations with its most immediate neighbours were returned to a problematic state because of domestic circumstances in both Indonesia and Malaysia, which were well beyond Singapore's influence. The management of relations with those neighbours has been a perpetual core consideration of Singapore's foreign policy.

For a quarter of a century, relations with Indonesia were conducted on a relatively stable basis because of an understanding reached between former Prime Minister Lee Kuan Yew and former President Suharto. President Suharto's effective depoliticisation of his country meant that an underlying suspicion and resentment of Singapore in Jakarta was rarely translated into open bilateral tensions. With his political downfall in May 1998, the condition of bilateral relations became vulnerable to Indonesia's new-found competitive politics, while interim-President Habibie made no secret of his personal grudge against Senior Minister Lee Kuan Yew for publicly casting doubt on his credentials for vice-presidential office. Fortunately for Singapore, at least in the short run, Dr Habibie failed in his bid to retain the presidency. His successor, Abdurrahman Wahid, has acknowledged Singapore's potential role in his country's economic recovery and has held out the hand of friendship. As long as he remains the President of Indonesia, Singapore can expect a similar quality of relationship to that which obtained under former President Suharto.

In the case of Malaysia, a structural tension in bilateral relations has been the normal condition but has been aggravated either when it has suited Prime Minister Dr Mahathir for domestic political purposes, or when statements emanating from Singapore or issues between the two governments have entered the domestic domain. That underlying circumstance is not expected to change with a change in Malaysia's leadership. The country's domestic domain is set in its mind against Singapore, as demonstrated when Singapore's national team was booed at the Commonwealth Games in Kuala Lumpur in September 1997. That said, neither Indonesia nor Malaysia have been in a position to threaten Singapore in military terms either because of limits to capability or because of the likely damage to self-interest that would occur. That judgement assumes, of course, that rational calculations prevail in Jakarta and Kuala Lumpur. Such rationality is not taken for granted in Singapore, which helps to explain Dr Tan's remarks cited above. Singapore's leaders display a notable ambivalence as they seek to build viable relationships with close neighbours whose unpredictable politics require that the island-state never lowers its guard.

Indonesia's more recent tribulations, in particular, have extended beyond the bilateral relationship with Singapore to touch on the viability and utility of ASEAN, once regarded as a valuable forum for mediating and mitigating regional tensions. Under the stable authoritarian rule of President Suharto, Indonesia provided a locus of leadership for ASEAN, albeit exercised in a low-key and acceptable way. With acute economic adversity and political turbulence, Indonesia's capacity for regional leadership was diminished and so, correspondingly, was the international standing of ASEAN. ASEAN has been much affected also by the aggregation of the adverse economic circumstances of its key states and by the problems of managing consensus attendant on its enlargement of membership to coincide with geographic South-East Asia. In consequence, a framework of multilateral dialogue set up to serve the cause of managing regional tensions and which evolved into a diplomatic community has been weakened considerably, to Singapore's disadvantage.

Singapore's government has not been addicted to multilateralism in foreign policy for its own sake. It has promoted its prime interests through bilateral arrangements in defence and economic cooperation. Nonetheless, ASEAN has been very much at the centre of its foreign policy practice, permitting a collective diplomacy which has served the interests of the Republic well. ASEAN demonstrated its utility over the Cambodian conflict, albeit in exceptional circumstances, and served as a vehicle for successful initiatives leading to the ARF and to ASEM, for example. Through ASEAN, Singapore sought to embed itself regionally as a political partner of governments that exhibited mixed feelings towards it. That facility for political solidarity has been weakened through the institutional failings of an enlarged Association and its lack of a common focus post-Cambodia, without any substantive compensation for Singapore, so far, from the advent of the ASEAN Regional Forum. The ARF has not progressed beyond a minimal confidence-building role, although it still serves Singapore's interests through providing an institutional locus for dialogue among the major Asia-Pacific powers, especially the USA and China.

Set against the failings of ASEAN and the limitations of the ARF, Singapore's policy-makers can take some comfort from the absence of acute conflicts within South-East Asia since the end of the Cold War. There is, of course, the exception of the potential inherent in that over the islands in the South China Sea, where it is not a claimant state. Moreover, as long as sources of energy in commercial quantities are not discovered beneath the sea-bed, the contention over the Spratly Islands, in particular, should not get out of hand. In addition, although within a wider East Asia, the issues of Taiwan and the Korean Peninsula continue to display a potential for armed confrontation, the strategic environment has remained relatively stable, in part, because of the degree of Sino-American accommodation. In Singapore, it is believed that China would not have had the temerity to seize Mischief Reef in the Spratly Islands had the USA not withdrawn previously from its military bases in the Philippines. Correspondingly, the display of resolve by the Clinton administration in March 1996 in deploying two carrier groups to the vicinity of Taiwan in response to China's attempt to influence the outcome of presidential elections through armed intimidation was quietly welcomed as a demonstration of the viability of a regional balance of power predicated on an American military presence. Singapore has contributed to that balance, or, more accurately, distribution of power by providing facilities for America's airforce and navy. And, in the case of China, a policy of engagement has been advocated as the most practical way of giving the People's Republic a stake in regional stability. It is well understood in Singapore that the island-state is primarily a spectator to the evolving pattern of power in the Asia-Pacific, which is why the American military connection is highly valued.

The more local distribution of power has been served up to a point by the Five Power Defence Arrangements in collaboration with Malaysia, Britain, Australia and New Zealand. These arrangements have suffered from ups and downs in the relationship across the causeway, but have been sustained by the growing interest of Australia in playing a role, in the interest of regional stability. They are valued in Singapore because of the Australian connection in particular, and because of the additional indirect link to the USA with which Australia is in an alliance relationship. They also provide a channel of communication between Singaporean and Malaysian defence counterparts. The Five Power Defence Arrangements do not provide a security guarantee for Singapore. They are regarded as a vehicle for confidence-building of a limited kind, and also as a barometer of the state of relations with Malaysia, with which Singapore has experienced the most turbulent exchanges. For example, Five Power joint exercises were called off in September 1998, when Malaysia withdrew at short notice citing economic difficulties, but were then resumed in April 1999. They are valued most of all, however, because they continue to draw in countries in addition to Malaysia with which Singapore has enjoyed long-standing good relationships.

With the devastating impact of regional economic adversity at the end of the twentieth century, Singapore's scope for initiative within collective diplomatic frameworks involving its regional partners has been considerably reduced, although Prime Minister Goh Chok Tong has promoted the idea of an Asia-Latin American forum to match ASEM. In the case of ASEAN, expectations have been downgraded to await a possible restoration of regional economic vibrancy. In that context, Singapore's main initiative at the turn of the new millennium has been in the realm of foreign economic policy where government-directed initiatives towards liberalisation in banking and financial services have been intended to improve the international competitive economic edge of the Republic. At issue is the judgement that it is necessary to prepare for an anticipated regional return to economic crisis by tapping the potential of global markets. In addition, Singapore's Ministry of Foreign Affairs has set its sights, for the first time, on a non-permanent seat on the United Nations Security Council in the year 2001.

Beyond such minimal initiative, Singapore displays continuity in the influence on foreign policy of Senior Minister, Lee Kuan Yew. His political perspective, including the conviction that Singapore cannot take its independence for granted and that continual adaptation is required for survival, is part of the conventional wisdom of the successor generation of political leaders. As noted above, Lee Kuan Yew has combined a razor-sharp intellect and a remarkable experience with a disposition for speaking his mind on political matters which has not always helped in managing relations with Singapore's closest neighbours, Malaysia and Indonesia. Indeed, some of his *obiter dicta* have served to point up the persisting vulnerability of the Republic through the hostile reactions of those governments.

Vulnerability is not necessarily the same as insecurity, however. Singapore conducts its foreign policy on the basis of an underlying vulnerability but the island-state does not enter the twenty-first century in a condition of insecurity because of its considerable economic strengths. Those strengths enable a corresponding defence capability, which fulfils a deterrent function. Nonetheless, the goals of foreign policy remain governed by the same concerns that were evident at independence; namely, that size and location should not add up to destiny and that every effort should be made to keep the fortunes of the Republic out of the play of solely regional forces that cannot be fully trusted. In that respect, although Singapore's foreign policy has not come full circle completely in its environmental circumstances, the bases of its practice have remained remarkably constant. That practice has been predicated on the premises of the balance of power, albeit without conceiving of its application in a crudely mechanical way. In addition to securing access to the countervailing military strength of the USA and developing its own deterrent capability, Singapore has participated in multilateral security dialogue and multilateral economic cooperation. It has done so as a way of engaging the interest of extra-regional states in its environment and in its continued independence. Balance of power has also been expressed in adaptive Social Darwinist terms in the need to attract foreign talent as a way of remaining globally competitive and exceptional. Lee Kuan Yew pointed out in August 1999 in respect of such potential skilled migrants: "If we don't welcome them, make them stay, we will be out of the race because conditions have changed. ... So if we just stay in our little pond, we will perish."

In one obvious sense, Singapore has no alternative but to stay in its little pond. That has been its geopolitical fate ever since August 1965 and is the source of its abiding vulnerability. It is also the source of an extraordinary political morbidity about addressing the viability of the island-state. In seeking to cope with an innate vulnerability, there are no illusions about the task involved, despite an innovative culture that has been responsible for an extraordinary achievement. Indeed, Singapore copes with vulnerability by trying to be extraordinary in the way in which its achievements are projected and perceived well beyond its little pond. In the process, nothing is taken for granted and nothing is guaranteed. Lee Kuan Yew gave voice to the sombre philosophy underlying foreign policy in a statement of October 1981, which still applies. He pointed out then that: "In an imperfect world, we have to search for the best accommodation possible. And no accommodation is permanent. If it lasts long enough for progress to be made until the next set of arrangements can be put in place, let us be grateful for it." This epigraphic statement encapsulates the essence of Singapore's practice of foreign policy.

Indonesia

INTRODUCTION

Leifer's understanding of Indonesia's politics was profound. He was sensitive to Indonesian history and political culture and attempted to understand Indonesian politics from these perspectives. In addition, as a student of political science he was interested in the examination and application of political science concepts, particularly the use of nationalism, the problems of political stability, succession, civil society, and democracy.

Leifer wrote one book and about twenty articles on Indonesia, making it difficult to select his "representative works". Since Part II of this volume focuses on domestic politics and foreign policies, four items on domestic politics have been selected, covering his interpretation of Indonesian nationalism, problem of succession, civil society, and a commentary on the fall of Soeharto. With regard to foreign policy, three articles were selected: a chapter from his book on the characteristics of Indonesia's foreign policy, Islamic factor in Indonesia's foreign policy, and the dilemma of "engagement" with China. These three items show Leifer's insight into Indonesia's policy as well as his contributions to foreign policy conceptualization using Indonesia as the example.

He pointed out that Indonesian nationalism manifested itself in various forms. Different governments in Indonesia, from Sukarno to Soeharto and beyond, have used different aspects of nationalism to serve their own objectives (Ch. 53). Leifer also recognized that Indonesian politics was unstable, partially due to under-institutionalization. Succession was a major problem, and the authoritarian nature of Indonesian politics was at its roots. He noted in 1990 that Soeharto had been in power for a quarter of a century and there was rising opposition to his rule. Leifer foresaw the difficulty for him to remain in power due to social change (Ch. 54).

Leifer also noted the necessity of creating a civil society in Indonesia, but at the same time he recognized Indonesia's different history and political culture from those of the West where the concept was developed. He therefore maintained that civil society in Indonesia could only be realized slowly and the characteristics might be different from that of the West (Ch. 55).

Leifer witnessed the fall of Soeharto and pointed out the problems that the new Indonesia faced. In an article written a few days after Soeharto's fall, Leifer noted that Indonesia would not be able to find political and economic solution "by turning to any simplistic model of Western liberal democracy" (Ch. 56). He argued that honesty, public trust, and public accountability were more relevant.

If Leifer provided history and political culture as a background to understanding domestic politics of Indonesia, he also used the same perspective when dealing with Indonesia's foreign policy. He clearly pointed out the close relationship between domestic politics and foreign policy (Ch. 57). He further discussed the characteristics of Indonesia's foreign policy from Sukarno to Soeharto, pointing out its similarities and differences.

The nature of Indonesia's foreign policy vis-á-vis Islam was the focus of his excellent article reproduced as Chapter 58. In that article, he stated that being a country with the largest number of Muslim population, Indonesia had a non-Islamic foreign policy. This could be explained in terms of the nature of Indonesian Islam and the historical development of the Indonesian modern state. Nevertheless, Leifer saw the dilemma of the Indonesia's foreign policy makers in keeping a balance between a "secular" and an "Islamic" foreign policy. He was among the first who addressed this important issue in a substantive article. The article was published in 1983, and in 1994 he published an article entitled "The Peace Dividend" (Part I, Ch. 26), depicting Israel's changing relationship with Southeast Asia, including Indonesia, where he discussed the short and "unofficial visit" of Prime Minister Rabin to Indonesia. However, the visit only brought temporary benefit for both sides as it did not develop into normalization of ties.

China loomed large in Indonesia's foreign relations, which was linked to the domestic political, socio-economic, ethnic, and security issues. Leifer was fully aware of the importance of the People's Republic of China (PRC) in the foreign policy of Indonesia, especially during the Soeharto era. Noting that Indonesia's foreign policy makers were critical of China, they also realized a need to engage the PRC in order to achieve regional stability (Ch. 59). In this article, Leifer discussed the concept of "engagement of China" as implemented by Indonesia and its limitation. He noted that both China and Indonesia tended to be self-centred and that the Indonesian style of engagement was not the conventional engagement but multilateral dialogue and supplemented by the balance of power. Nevertheless, it has serious limitations.

53

Whither Indonesian Nationalism?

Indonesia acquired statehood as an exemplar of civic nationalism and also as an exponent of revolutionary struggle as the most appropriate mode through which to define and express national identity against an obdurate colonial power. The late President Sukarno expropriated the rhetoric and symbols of a revolutionary nationalism in his own political interests. The effect was to extend the phase of nationalist struggle over two decades past the proclamation of independence. With the succession of President Suharto, Indonesian nationalism was deliberately made mute in its public expression and lost its exhibitionist quality in the interest of a radically revised political economy. Indeed, since then, nationalism, as a centrifugal activity within the archipelago, has been more of challenge to Indonesia than Indonesian nationalism has been to either regional or international order, despite the frustrated sense of regional entitlement held in Jakarta. The extent to which

Reprinted in abridged form from Michael Leifer, "The Changing Temper of Indonesian Nationalism", in *Asian Nationalism,* edited by Michael Leifer (London: Routledge, 2000), pp. 153–69, by permission of the publisher and the Asia Research Centre, London School of Economics.

Indonesia under Suharto was willing to accommodate to economic dependence, instead of repudiating it Sukarno-like in his well-known statement "to hell with your aid", was demonstrated in the way in which national pride was not allowed to get in the way of economic priorities. That pragmatic outlook was not revised by the interim administration of President Habibie. Indeed, that administration found itself in a corresponding position of dependence to that experienced by former President Suharto in 1966, albeit in a very different strategic environment. It is one in which the West had lost its fear of a communist take-over and therefore could be uninhibited over applying economic pressure on Jakarta over self-determination in East Timor.

In recapitulation, Indonesian nationalism in challenging Dutch rule consciously repudiated an ethnic rationale defining itself exclusively with reference to the colonial territorial legacy. Post-independence, the nationalist ideal was sustained in a romantic irredentist phase whose rationale was to complete the revolution in its territorial extent as well as to keep alive its original spirit. An underlying motivation for employing revolutionary symbols and imagery was to serve a domestic function in a competitive political context in Sukarno's particular interest.

From the mid-1960s, however, Indonesian nationalism assumed a muted quality for reasons of political economy and regional co-operative security. None the less, the government of President Suharto was protective of national interests. That protectivism was displayed in the cases of Irian Jaya, Indonesia's archipelagic status and East Timor as well as in assuming the chair of the Non-Aligned Movement. It was displayed also in the view that Indonesia was entitled to a permanent seat on the United Nations Security Council.

The last truly robust expression of Indonesian nationalism occurred, however, during the early to mid-1960s driven by the competitive condition of domestic politics. Indonesia has now reached the end of a political era during which a quasi-monarchical ruler placed the highest premium on political demobilisation and stability and in which the only political competition was among courtiers. In the event, the provisional transfer of power in May 1998, that was accompanied and precipitated by violence, was relatively orderly compared to the bloody circumstances of 1965–1966 that had preceded President Sukarno's political downfall. President Habibie, as incumbent vice-president, succeeded to high office virtually by default, partly because it suited the armed forces leadership to make a constitutional virtue out of a political necessity in the interest of public order. Moreover, there was a notable absence of any exhibition of nationalist symbolism either among the beneficiaries of the transfer of power or among advocates of political reform.

That said, the exit of President Suharto raised popular expectations of political reform that is certain to mean greater political competition among Indonesia's cultural diversity, which includes an important Islamic dimension. Indeed, forty-eight political parties took part in the parliamentary elections in June 1999, although only five made a significant showing. Politics in Indonesia has become a much more open activity and political leadership will face demands for greater accountability from a legislature with genuine legitimacy. That development was demonstrated in the rejection of President Habibie's account of his stewardship by the MPR and his consequent decision to withdraw from the presidential contest, then won by Abdurrahman Wahid in October 1999. It is in such circumstances that a more strident nationalism could enter the political arena should opportunistic forces seek to exploit its mobilising potential. Indonesia's regional context is very different now, however, to that during the Sukarno era. There are no colonial presences to interpose in regional relationships, while those relationships have become encompassed within institutionalised structures of dialogue and co-operation, albeit weakened by economic adversity. And Indonesia after having been afflicted by an acute economic adversity has not recovered sufficiently to strike nationalist postures of the kind that enabled it to replace the IGGI with the CGI in 1992.

Indonesian nationalism persists as a political tradition and has revived to a degree with the political downfall of President Suharto. But it has become far more difficult to define and express with reference to an external other that provided its original source. Australia, with a population the tenth of Indonesia's, may seem a politically pretentious and irritating neighbour over East Timor but it has yet to inspire a unified nationalist passion, probably because it is difficult to regard as a serious threat. Moreover, the circumstances of the political downfall of President Suharto obliged his interim successor to concentrate on domestic economic priorities: a responsibility assumed also by President Abdurrahman Wahid. In such an exercise, which requires external, including IMF and World Bank support, any attempt at a romantic nationalist revival would be self-defeating for those in power in a more accountable political context. The circumstances of the political downfall of President Suharto and the dramatic events in East Timor would suggest that the nationalist card has not been played with any effect, and certainly not in the interest of managing a competitive domestic politics.

Fifty years after international acknowledgement of its independence, Indonesia's nationalism is most likely to be expressed through attempts to reassert a regional diplomatic role. Such a leading role was diminished by the impact of economic adversity and political turmoil. To reclaim such a role, Indonesia would need to demonstrate substantive evidence of economic recovery, which requires an inter-dependence with the global economy and its institutions. That conditional requirement places an obligation on Indonesia's new political leadership to conceive of the Republic's role in a similar way to that understood by former President Suharto. In August 1969, as indicated above, he had declared that: "We shall only be able to play an effective role if we ourselves are possessed of a great national vitality". Some three decades later, President Abdurrahman Wahid is confronted with the same challenge which also requires sublimating a romantic nationalist tradition.

54

Uncertainty in Indonesia

As Indonesia moves toward the end of a remarkable era in its history, this vast archipelago of 180 million people has become absorbed by the politics of succession. How the succession question will be resolved is also a subject of great interest and speculation beyond Indonesia's borders.

At issue is the seeming determination of President Suharto to soldier on in office, thereby increasing the likelihood that ultimate political change will be less than orderly. Such an outcome would not only represent a serious setback for Indonesia, it would also be ironic, given the president's consistent concern with national harmony since assuming power nearly a quarter of a century ago.

The succession battle will be fought and decided by a small circle comprised of Suharto, the military, and other members of the ruling elite. In this respect, the wave of democratization now sweeping the world has left Indonesia surprisingly untouched, prompting neither a more assertive opposition nor a more open and accommodating government.

Reprinted in abridged form from Michael Leifer, "Uncertainty in Indonesia", *World Policy Journal* VIII, no. 1 (1990–91): 137–57.

President Suharto is currently serving his fifth unopposed term of office. His term expires in March 1993, at which time he will be nearly 72 years old. Suharto is widely believed to be intent on serving another five years despite his age (retirement is normally at age 55 in Indonesia) and despite signs of dissent within the armed forces, which have been his power base from the outset. Insistence on a further term of office could possibly provoke a coup attempt with adverse consequences for national unity and international business confidence in Indonesia. Indeed, factional conflict within the armed forces could unleash cultural tensions in the political heartland of Java, thus giving greater impetus to separatist movements in outlying Irian Jaya, East Timor, and Aceh.

Even if Suharto should secure another full term in 1993, national unity might still be tested. On the one hand, should he die or become incapacitated in office, a destabilizing factional struggle for power might ensue if the vice-president who succeeded him were a controversial choice. (Article 8 of the constitution provides for the essentially ceremonial vice-president to succeed the president.) On the other hand, should Suharto survive a sixth term without making adequate provision for transferring the presidency to a nationally acceptable figure, the problem of succession would persist in acute form. As he aged in office, confidence in his political competence would undoubtedly wane.

The manner of political succession is critical for the republic, which has experienced succession only once since independence in 1945. That transfer of power occurred against a background of violent disorder — an abortive coup in 1965 that exposed divisions within the armed forces and was followed by extensive bloodletting. At the time, the integrity of this culturally diverse archipelago-state was in doubt as the prospect of civil war loomed.

The condition of Indonesia in 1990 is very different from that in 1965. The most important difference is the absence of intense political competition between the army and the Communist Party. The Communist Party no longer exists, and a more professional officer corps is extremely conscious of the dangers of a breakdown of formal constitutionalism. Political succession will nonetheless be a major test of the republic's political maturity. Its manner will demonstrate whether or not the system of government created by Suharto over the past quarter of a century is more than just an instrument of personal rule.

Although public interest in political succession has been strong ever since Suharto was last reelected in March 1988, he has gone out of his way to restrict discussion of the issue. In August 1990, a dissident group of retired officers and politicians suggested that the president step down in March 1993 and that his successor be permitted a maximum of two terms in office. Barely concealing his anger, Suharto argued that all such discussion was premature and usurped the role of the constitutionally supreme People's Consultative Assembly, which meets every five years to choose a president and vice-president. Suharto's veiled indications of his intention to retain the presidency stand in contrast to his recurrent stress on phasing out the founding generation of leaders identified with the independence struggle against the Dutch. He appears to regard himself as an exception to this rule, which has been applied strictly in the armed forces and selectively in the civil sector.

Suharto is believed to be motivated by a sense that his mission is still incomplete. He is also said to be concerned with ensuring a favorable place for himself in history and with protecting the well-being and extensive financial assets of his family, whose burgeoning business activities have become a national scandal. (For example, in October 1990 it was revealed that Bank Duta, the country's second largest bank, had lost $420 million because of improper foreign-exchange dealings. A business group run by one of Suharto's sons has been one of Duta's main customers.) Suharto's excessive indulgence of his family has been a major cause of the military establishment's political alienation.

Despite growing resistance in the armed forces and elsewhere to another term of office, Suharto retains considerable political advantages and skills that should not be underestimated, including the power to influence key military appointments. His renewal in office may require greater effort than on previous occasions, but it is well within his grasp, especially if he avoids choosing a vice-presidential running mate against whom the military might unite.

But such a political triumph might be short-lived if the issue of succession is deferred rather than confronted. Much depends on whether time is on Suharto's side. The longer he delays grasping the nettle of succession, the greater the prospect of a power struggle that might well subvert his purpose and priorities — and that might tarnish his reputation, as indeed was the experience of his predecessor.

Indonesia's first decade and a half after the attainment of independence was marked by political turbulence and economic decay. Many put the blame for the country's economic and political instability on the tempestuous personality of the country's first president, Sukarno. By contrast, the past quarter of a century has been distinguished by stability and economic development. These achievements have been attributed to the political sobriety and managerial skills of Indonesia's second and incumbent president, Suharto.

In October 1965, as a major-general in charge of the army's strategic reserve in Jakarta, Suharto crushed a coup attempt conventionally attributed to Indonesia's Communist Party. In March 1966, as lieutenant-general and commander of the army, he masterminded the transfer of executive power to himself from a discredited Sukarno and then Sukarno's formal removal from office. At the time, Suharto was 44 years old and virtually unknown outside of Indonesia. Within a year of initially displacing Sukarno, he became acting president and in March 1968 was officially made head of state.

Suharto has subsequently dominated Indonesian politics in a unique way, setting the country on a new and quite successful course in economic and foreign affiars without facing any effective challenge to his position. It needs to be stressed, however, that his political dominance has been maintained by authoritarian practices and at the expense of human rights. Furthermore, the benefits of economic development have been very unevenly distributed. Thirty million of some 180 million Indonesians live below the World Bank poverty line, and 60 percent of Indonesian currency in circulaton is reported to be in the capital, Jakarta.[1]

Over the past 25 years, Indonesian society has changed significantly as the nation has developed economically. Urbanization and the emergence of a middle class concentrated in Jakarta have been two important consequences. Although the middle class has enjoyed the benefits of economic growth, it has resented the strict limits placed on political participation. Yet because of the repressive nature of the government, including strict controls on the press, and the absence of well-developed interest groups and political parties, there has been little open expression of that resentment. Highly dependent on government patronage, indigenous business groups have also been quiet. The only dissenting voices heard — and then only occasionally

— are those of the small number of retired officers and politicians who came to some prominence a decade ago after they charged that Suharto had falsely interpreted the *Pancasila*.

Stresses have also arisen as a result of conspicuous urban consumption that generates a natural jealousy among the poor and unorganized who live in urban *kampongs* or villages. The acute issue of a more equitable distribution of wealth was raised at the annual meeting in July 1990 of the Indonesian Economists Association. Economic discontent has been kept partly at bay because the government has ensured that the staple food — rice — is readily available.

While Islam is no longer the burning issue it once was, it has enjoyed growing popular appeal at a time of disturbing economic and social changes. A politicized Islam is seen by some as an alternative to the failure of Sukarno's socialism and the inequities of Suharto's capitalism. Since the Islamic revolution in Iran, the government has been especially determined to deny any opportunity for popular mobilization around an Islamic issue that might serve as a catalyst for political challenge on the part of other disaffected groups, including the urban underclass. The last significant outburst of Islamic dissatisfaction was the 1984 riot in the port areas of Jakarta, which the government violently suppressed.

In addition to the government's hostility to a politicized Islam, there are other factors that explain why Islam is not a strong force in Indonesian politics today. To start, Muslims in Indonesia do not share a homogenous culture; nor does Islam express itself in monolithic social and political organizations. Islamic identity has been further diluted by the obligation that all Indonesian organizations accept the *Pancasila* as their sole ideology. Muslim solidarity was diminished when the traditionalist *Nahdatul Ulama* (Muslim Scholars) faction withdrew from the Islamic United Development Party and public politics in general, thus harming the party's electoral fortunes. Suharto has also been successful in his cultivation of the Islamic constituency, as evidenced most recently when 21 Muslim leaders publicly endorsed him for another term.

Despite the aforementioned stresses, violent political challenge persists only at the periphery of the state and bears no comparison to the convulsion that have beset modern India. Nation-building has proceeded because of the continuing centrality of Indonesia's victory over the Dutch, a common language, and a deferential political culture.

The political glue is provided by the archipelago-wide presence of the armed forces, still the most important national institution. The government has controlled opposition by repression and cooptation, including the dispensing of patronage through *yayasans*, nonprofit foundations that are ostensibly vehicles of philanthropy. Besides the armed forces, the government has been able to rely on the loyalty and obedience of a vast civil service that administers the state in an elitist tradition. For all these reasons, serious political change is most likely to come from near the top of society.

Although Indonesia's bureaucratic structures and practices have become more complex and skilled as the country functions increasingly like a modern state, the political system has progressed more in terms of form than substance. In justifying its severe limits on public participation, the government has argued that untrammeled politics is a contentious process that would lead in Indonesia's case to disorder and disunity rather than the stability required to sustain international business confidence. Suharto has not been completely oblivious to the wave of democratization that has swept much of the world. In August 1990 he made some public statements in favor of greater democracy, but his remarks drew cynicism, not enthusiasm.[2]

On the surface, Indonesia abides by constitutional proprieties, including regular elections to a national parliament responsible for enacting legislation. Members of parliament together with military and political appointees comprise the People's Consultative Assembly, whose primary function is to elect an executive president and a ceremonial vice-president every five years. In principle, the democratic expression of popular views is an intrinsic part of the political system. In practice, regular elections do not provide a free and fair choice among political alternatives.

The president is chosen by an electoral college, more than half of whose 1,000 members are nominated by the government. Moreover, in all of Suharto's 25 years in office, there has never been a choice of presidential candidates. He has always been the sole nominee, elected every five years by unanimous acclamation.

Indonesia's opposition parties have been manipulated and harassed, while their distinctive identities have been blurred virtually beyond recognition by mergers and ideological dilution. General elections to the parliament have been managed to the exclusive advantage of Golkar, ostensibly an association of functional groups within society founded during the Sukarno era. Golkar serves as the political arm of the government and has been employed as an electoral vehicle acting in its interest.³ Working in alliance with appointed members from the armed forces, Golkar has dominated the parliament and the People's Consultative Assembly.

That working relationship has begun to change recently as political differences between Suharto and the armed forces have emerged. Moreover, members of parliament have begun to take their responsibilities more seriously, for example by questioning the terms of proposed legislation. That said, popular and parliamentary demands for political participation have been relatively restrained and well below any crisis point so far. The net effect has been that the constitutional process has retained its long-standing ritual quality. It has served to validate governmental authority without obliging the government in any practical sense to conform to conventional forms of democratic accountability. For example, after each re-election, Suharto has insisted on exercising his right to rule without constitutional constraints until his term expires. Only when the end of his five-year term is drawing near does he feel obligated to provide a formal accounting of his stewardship to the next People's Consultative Assembly, which could, in principle, then withhold its mandate — but has yet to do so.

Suharto's style of leadership lends itself to differing interpretations of the exercise of power in Indonesia. One view is that a thin veneer of constitutionalism facilitates Suharto's near-naked exercise of power on behalf of a military establishment in whose interest Sukarno was ousted. The political entitlement and centrality of that establishment have their origins in Indonesia's experience of national revolution against the Dutch. Having no confidence in the competence of civilian authority and viewing its own state-building role as critical, the military staked out a political function beyond the conventional responsibility for national security during the decade following independence.

This claim to a dual function was realized partly in July 1959 with the introduction of Sukarno's authoritarian system of "Guided Democracy," which replaced parliamentary politics. With the abortive coup in 1965, that system collapsed and was succeeded by Suharto's "New Order." Under Suharto, dual function came to enjoy much fuller expression as members of the military increasingly staffed economic enterprises and ministerial, bureaucratic, and diplomatic offices. Over the past quarter of a century, Suharto, a retired general who counts the armed forces as his key base of support, has protected the military's privileged position in Indonesia.

Although Suharto has undoubtedly exercised power in the interests of the armed forces, which have been conspicuous beneficiaries of his rule, that generalization requires some qualification. First of all, the armed forces have never exhibited perfect unity. They have always been subject to internal rivalries and factionalism based on personality, regional affiliation, and military function. Sukarno exploited such intramural differences for his own political advantage. Since the turbulent days of his downfall, however, those differences have been contained as the armed forces have become more professional and as successive batches of officers have been indoctrinated in the importance of the dual function ideal — of upholding both corporate and national interests.

There is no way of being absolutely sure just how the armed forces as a whole would behave in a domestic crisis, especially one linked to the succession. Of importance would be the extent to which Suharto himself would be a contentious factor and the extent to which the armed forces believed he was either serving or undermining the dual function ideal. The issue has been put in these terms because over time Suharto has appeared to have consolidated his personal authority, thus making him less dependent on direct military support. Indeed, in many respects, he has been able to determine the nature and terms of the dual function, as reflected in his controversial choice of State Secretary Sudharmono for vice-president in March 1988, a choice that went against the prevailing military sentiment.[4]

An alternative view of Indonesian politics at this juncture is that constitutionalism and the practice of dual function ceased to serve as a façade for military rule during the Suharto era. Instead, they have become a means for exercising personal power. Stripped of its constitutional trappings and semblance of institutionalization, Indonesian politics functions like a modern-day version of the traditional Javanese polity, with power concentrated in the hands of a king-like figure.

In such a polity, prearranged succession is not part of the political process because of the presumed divinity of political leadership. The president rules in the style and manner of a Javanese monarch, who would be reluctant to appoint a political successor for fear that such an act would create an alternative locus of power capable of undermining the established political order. Although Suharto is aware of his own mortality, he has told close confidants that his initial assumption of power and consolidation of position were the result of divine intervention. While nominally deferential to Islamic interests, the president is steeped in Javanese cultural values, including mysticism.

At issue as the Suharto era draws to a close without a terminal date in sight is the extent to which these two alternative models of Indonesian politics constitute competing forces in the struggle for succession. A third genuinely constitutional and pluralistic model would seem out of the question because political demobilization at the expense of organized interests has been successful and because, factionalism aside, the armed forces remain united over the principle of dual function. They still regard politics as too important a matter to be left exclusively to civilians.

Two other factors also probably contribute to Suharto's reluctance to leave office: concern for his family and for his place in history. Suharto's rule has been marked by the construction of an elaborate and far-reaching structure of patronage and by the concentration of power. The president has conspicuously indulged his family, as well as a network of ethnic Chinese business partners. This practice has caused popular resentment as the country's economic achievements have flowed disproportionately to his family and the "conglomerates," a code word for ethnic Chinese business enterprises. In an attempt to neutralize such resentment, Suharto recently called on ethnic Chinese to transfer 25 percent of their corporate holdings to cooperatives run by indigenous Indonesians.

What has come to distinguish the final phase of Suharto's rule is the extent to which his indulgence of family business interests has alienated senior members of the officer corps. The rapacity with which those interests have been pursued is a political Achilles' heel for the president, one that he does not appear to appreciate. Suharto, however, seems to regard any questioning of the business role of members of his family as a direct challenge to his political authority. In this way, his personal priorities have become relevant to the political process.

Although none of Suharto's sons has followed him into the armed forces and could therefore be considered a contender in the succession stakes, his sons, daughters, and other kin together add a quasi-dynastic dimension to Indonesian politics. Indeed, a brother-in-law, Maj. Gen. Wismoyo Arismunandar, has been made third in command of the army with his appointment as head of Kostrad, the strategic reserve command, and a former aide, Brig. Gen. Kentot Harseno, has been appointed commander of the Jakarta garrison.

This convergence of family interests and military appointments is relevant to the succession question. One would not expect the president's family, on whom he dotes, to encourage him to give up office as long as he is capable of exercising it to their economic and political advantage. Moreover, because his family's economic stake has become so extensive, there is a shared concern about protecting it after the eventual transfer of presidential power. Related to that concern is the important matter of providing for the physical security of the president's family, which could be at risk in the future as old scores are settled.

These considerations are likely to cause Suharto to be cautious about retiring from high office until he can be sure that appropriate protection can be provided through a political successor acceptable to him. Suharto is also reluctant to leave office without ensuring that his reputation and the correct version of his historical record are preserved for posterity. He has let it be known that he regards himself as the virtual savior of Indonesia from political and economic calamity. Accordingly, its citizens should be appropriately grateful and certainly not begrudge his family its economic activities, which, according to Suharto, have contributed to the nation's well-being.

Suharto's own view of his place in history was apparent in an autobiography published in April 1989.[5] One student of his rule has said that this book reveals Suharto's conceited, mean-spirited, graceless, and insecure side.[6] A striking feature of the autobiography is his defense of the economic indulgences of his six children and his unwillingness to acknowledge any contribution to his New Order by other leading Indonesians, in particular members of the military. This self-centered attempt to rewrite the historical record has embittered some senior and retired officers, who now feel that Suharto has increasingly used and abused the armed forces for the benefit of himself and his family. That discontent was manifest in an August 1990 petition signed by 58 prominent Indonesians, including retired generals, who called on Suharto to give up office in March 1993.[7]

Suharto's unprecedented tenure in office and the skill with which he has managed all political challenges have clearly engendered in him a great deal of hubris. Encouraging Suharto in his obduracy, despite evident disaffection within the military establishment, is a vivid memory of the last and only other Indonesian experience of political succession. Sukarno was politically dispossessed, and his historical reputation as a nationalist leader was subsequently besmirched. His family and his political associates were stripped of their wealth; some were put on trial and sentenced to prison and death. The example of Sukarno's fate bolsters Suharto's reluctance to give up office until he can be assured that he will not meet a similar fate.

Over the years Suharto has taken steps to reinstate Sukarno's reputation. He sanctioned the construction of a tomb over his grave site, accorded him and former vice president Hatta the title of "proclamators" of independence, and named Jakarta's international airport after them. It would seem that Suharto is haunted by the specter of Sukarno's historical fate and has sought to make amends for his own role in that episode by propitiating his immortal spirit.

Ironically, in his attempt to avoid Sukarno's fate, Suharto may be ensuring a similar one for himself. His greatest problem is that time is running out, and his support from the military, which has been the key to his political power, is eroding. Suharto has responded by trying to rise above the military by wielding power without consulting the armed forces. His insistence on having Lieutenant-General Sudharmono chosen as vice-president in March 1988, despite opposition from within the armed forces, is a glaring example.

Sudharmono, a retired soldier, was not regarded as a representative of military interests. A lawyer by training, he had been influential as state secretary and also as general chairman of Golkar; his tenure in both posts was perceived by members of the armed forces to be against their interests. (As state secretary, he controlled the allocation of funds, and as general chairman, he appeared to be building a civilian power base.) While his candidacy was clearly opposed by the armed forces faction within the People's Consultative Assembly, the issue was not pressed to the point of confrontation. Nonetheless, it added to the tension caused by the earlier removal from office of Gen. Benny Moerdani, the commander of the armed forces.

Moerdani was removed not long after his term had been extended for a year and in advance of the regular cabinet reshuffle that followed the re-election of the president in 1988. Moerdani is a distinguished soldier with both field and intelligence experience whose loyalty to the president had been thought rock-solid. Indeed, he owed his more recent military career to presidential favor. Their relationship had a father-son quality to it, but had become strained because of Moerdani's attempt to warn Suharto about the adverse political consequences of his indulging his venal family.

As a Catholic with a German grandparent, Moerdani has been ruled out as a presidential contender. Nevertheless, he does command considerable respect as a soldier and had been influential in military appointments. Suharto kept him in the government, giving him the post of minister of defense. (The position did not grant him operational control of the military, however.) Although a member of the cabinet, Moerdani has become increasingly outspoken in his calls for political change. For example, in a May 1990 speech in Yogyakarta, he is said to have made it clear that he favored a change of leadership at the end of Suharto's current term in 1993.[8]

Working to Suharto's advantage is the military establishment's evident concern over the prospect of a breakdown of order caused by internecine strife. Irrespective of personal and factional differences, the Indonesian officer corps has sustained a strong sense of corporate identity. Corporate interest, of course, is not necessarily the same as national interest — with the doctrine of dual function a case in point. However, the senior echelons of the armed forces appear to be governed by an awareness of the necessity of restraint so as to avoid the violent disorder of the 1965–66 presidential succession.

Ideally the officer corps would prefer that Suharto step down in March 1993 in favor of an acceptable successor with a military background. A compromise alternative would be for Suharto to stand unopposed for another term of office, but with a vice-presidential running mate from within the military establishment who had the general support of the armed forces. The conventional wisdom about this scenario is that the vice-president and eventual successor would be Gen. Tri Sutrisno, the incumbent commander of the armed forces. Tri has been an aide to the president and is well known for his close personal ties and loyalty to Suharto. He is also known to be close to Moerdani and gives the impression of deferring to his seniority and greater experience. In addition, Tri is believed to be acceptable to the orthodox Muslim community, whose numbers have been increasing in Indonesia.

The difficulty with this scenario is that, while it may be acceptable to the military establishment, it may not necessarily be acceptable to Suharto. Tri is an engineering officer and not in the mainstream of military experience. He is also thought to be lacking the right kind of military spirit, especially when it comes to making hard political decisions. While the military establishment may be willing to tolerate Tri, Suharto may not. Loyalty is not the issue. Suharto's reservations about Tri stem from a concern that he would not be a strong enough figure to protect Suharto's reputation and his family's wealth and security after the president leaves office.

Suharto, like Indonesia, continues to confound critics. In March 1966, there was no expectation that a barely known soldier would be able to consolidate power, let alone exercise it without serious challenge for a quarter of a century. Suharto's system of rule combines personal and institutional factors, but the personal would seem to be the more important. Indeed, Indonesia's constitutional apparatus has a camouflage-like quality that lends legitimacy to the exercise of personal power.

Suharto has amassed his enormous personal power with the support of the armed forces, which have been employed as an instrument for intimidating civilian political groups, including parties from the Sukarno era, and have been decisive in molding Indonesia's political system. While the military has backed Suharto's management of Indonesia's political and economic order, the question is whether he can count on that support indefinitely. The armed forces are probably Indonesia's only truly national institution. Political succession, therefore, will depend on the cohesion of its senior echelons and the extent to which they share a sense of common purpose in keeping Indonesia on the political and economic course set by Suharto since the mid-1960s.

Although the armed forces have become more professional, there is no sign that the military establishment intends to give up its guardian role in the political sphere, which is an integral part of its corporate tradition. Accordingly, the armed forces are virtually certain to be the decisive factor in political succession. The key to an orderly succession would seem to lie in the choice of a vice-president come the spring of 1993. Should Suharto fail to act in a politic manner in his choice of a running mate, then the prospect could arise of some kind of military ultimatum to the president, with the key consideration being whether or not corporate solidarity prevails. The stakes will be very high because political change will result in an important change in the patronage structure. The armed forces will probably close ranks in the face of a national crisis, but nothing is assured, in part because Suharto refuses publicly to confront the pressing issue of political succession, raising tensions as a consequence.

Suharto may well confound his critics once again through an imaginative initiative, of which he has shown himself to be capable in the past. The political stability and economic health of Indonesia depend on his willingness and ability to act in advance of events. If they overtake him and Indonesia, it may expose the extent to which he has created an ephemeral rather than an enduring political system, despite his considerable economic achievements over the past quarter of a century.

Notes

1. See Professor Juwono Sudarsono in the *International Herald Tribune*, September 8, 1990.
2. See *The Indonesian Observer*, August 24, 1990.
3. For an excellent assessment of the nature and role of Golkar, see Leo Suryadinata, *Military Ascendancy and Political Culture* (Athens, Ohio: Center for International Studies, Ohio University, 1989).
4. For an informed analysis of changing military interests, see Harold Crouch, "Military-Civilian Relations in Indonesia in the Late Suharto Era," *The Pacific Review*, Vol. 1, No. 1 (1988).
5. Suharto, *My Thoughts, Words and Deeds* (Jakarta: P. T. Citra Lamtero, Gung Persada, 1989).
6. See David Jenkins, *Sydney Morning Herald*, July 4, 1989.
7. See an account by Reuters in *The Straits Times* (Singapore), August 15, 1990. The episode was not reported by Indonesia's press.
8. See Michael Vatikiotis, "A Stir in the Ranks," *Far Eastern Economic Review*, July 5, 1990.

55

The Challenge of Creating a Civil Society in Indonesia

It should be understood from the outset, that the concept of a civil society is one that exists at the level of political ideals and not as a perfect working model of political practice which is suitable for application to all societies at all times. Indeed, in practice, many states which may be represented as exemplars of a civil society tend only to approximate to the ideal rather than fulfill all of its conditions. The concept of a civil society is a powerful symbol, however. It stands for human freedom and dignity and the right not to be subject to political oppression which is a universal human aspiration, not one confined to a particular continent or culture.

Historically, civil society is a concept that originated in a European context concurrent with the emergence of the notion of modernity involving the application of reason in the interest of human improvement and progress. It registered a belief in the ability of man to become the master of his own destiny. It was the product of

Reprinted from Michael Leifer, "The Challenge of Creating a Civil Society in Indonesia", *The Indonesian Quarterly* XXIII, no. 4 (1995): 354–60, by permission of the Centre for Strategic and International Studies.

scientific discovery and the industrial revolution and in intellectual terms is regarded as one of the products of the Eighteenth Century "Enlightenment" which marked a fundamental jump in philosophical ideas. The initial revelation spawned by the enlightenment and stimulated by the intoxicating experience of the French Revolution was followed, however, by a salutary experience of terror, dictatorship and empire which was responsible in part for the genesis of the Marxist alternative which has only recently been totally discredited long after its own experience of terror, dictatorship and empire. Indeed, it is in the context of the failure of Marxism to provide for human progress and dignity that the notion of a civil society has revived and has reappeared in the political lexicon attracting great interest in Eastern Europe in particular and in other parts of the world as well as generating debate over whether it is appropriate and even arrogant for Western political traditions to be translated to and applied in countries which have different political cultures. Indeed, when one thinks back to the facile way in which it was taken for granted that Westminster or Washington models of government could be transplanted without great difficulty in the wake of decolonisation, it is only too apparent why there should be caution in applying this political ideal of Western provenance.

Whatever the reservations of context, civil society is about pluralism and the freedom to associate and choose in political terms and choice is the essence of personal and political freedom. The most succinct definition of civil society which I have come across may be found in a recent book by Professor Ernest Gellner entitled "The Conditions of Liberty". He defines a civil society as one that contains that set of diverse non-governmental institutions which is strong enough to counterbalance the state and, while not preventing the state from fulfilling its role of keeper of the peace and arbitrator between major interests can nevertheless prevent it from dominating and atomizing the rest of society. Another way of putting it would be to suggest that a civil society is one where the rights of individuals and groups to organise within the law but free of state corporate intervention are fully protected.

The question may be legitimately asked: what has all this got to do with Indonesia, especially as its people are celebrating the fiftieth anniversary of the proclamation of their independence which they achieved through their own revolutionary struggle. Why should a concept which is of European provenance, and which appeared first in the title of a book written by an eighteenth century Scottish philosopher called Adam Ferguson, have any bearing on how Indonesians order their political system, especially when they have enjoyed over a quarter of a century of stability which has been responsible for remarkable economic achievement and an enhanced international standing.

The answer to the question lies partly in that very economic achievement which has been responsible for generating an attendant social change, including the emergence of a small but growing educated and sophisticated urban middle class who want to have greater account taken of their interests by a government which is not used to the kind of constant application of checks and balances to be found in Western political practice. In other words, as one commentator has noted: "economic consumers now seek to become political consumers". Evidence of demands from this relatively new and growing constituency may be found in the phenomenon of Non-Government Organisation (NGO) which has been replicated in other parts of industrialising East Asia. It is important to take full cognizance of that NGO phenomenon which focuses on issues which may not necessarily seem to be of political significance but which almost invariably touch on matters of conflict of interests which is the stuff of politics. Its advent may have been inspired by Western example but its appearance, expansion and activism over a wide range of social and politically-related issues has been a product of local circumstances and initiative, especially the fundamental social changes which have been induced by rapid and successful economic development. It has been engendered also by the negative aspects of rapid economic development affecting the countryside as well as the towns. To that extent, political consumerism has spread beyond the middle-class.

It is of interest to note that a recent study of the nature and activities of NGOs in Asia Pacific and published in the region is entitled "Emerging Civil Society". It should be noted also that in the case of Indonesia, the number of NGOs has been estimated as up to six thousand. The NGO phenomenon, which encompasses a diversity of interests, should be understood as a symptom of a process of change as much as an agent for change. Morever, the clock cannot be put back on the kind of social change generated by such successful economic development of the kind which has been an important part of the Indonesian experience. The goal of sustained economic development continues to be upheld by Indonesia's government in the national interest. And to the extent that its momentum is maintained, the effect will almost certainly reinforce the process of social change which I have identified with attendant political consequences. In that respect, Indonesia is going to have to face up to the political outcome of its own economic success which is an example of the old adage that for every solution there is a problem. In such changing circumstances, old established political formulae may not be enough to sustain the stability which is essential to underpin continuing improvement in social welfare which is an important basis of the legitimacy of government.

The second answer to the question also lies in Indonesia's experience and in this respect there is an interesting comparison with Europe, even though there are important cultural differences which need to be noted and respected. In addressing the concept of civil society, we are really talking about the degree of political choice and democratisation suitable for different and diverse countries. In the case of the West, political tradition has placed great emphasis on the rights of the individual in the context of successful historical challenges to royal absolutism and dynastic succession once justified in terms of a divine right to rule. The argument for democracy as it emerged, for example, during what is known as the English Revolution in the Seventeenth Century when the Republican Roundheads triumphed over the Royalist Cavaliers, was based on the assumption that all men and women were created equal in the sight of God. To that extent, they were entitled to a say in decisions which affected their everyday lives and those of their families. The legitimacy or moral authority of governments which are part of that tradition has its origins in that assumption.

There have been strong challenges of late to that interpretation of democracy on the grounds that in East Asia the long-standing tradition is quite different. It is said to be one of respect for authority with the individual under a powerful obligation to the family, group or society by contrast with the West where the individual tends to be the centrepiece of a democracy which has been designed to disempower government. What is at issue here is the appropriate balance between the rights of the individual and those of the state. In the case of Indonesia, the challenge of creating a civil society relates to shaping the appropriate balance between the rights of the individual and those of the state in the context of social change without prejudicing the understandable requirement to uphold political order.

That said, respect for the rights of individuals may not be so alien to Indonesian political tradition as might be inferred from the argument about the different emphasis placed on such rights in so-called East Asia compared to the European tradition. Indeed, a basis for such rights may be identified in a parallel doctrine to that of civil society, namely the state philosophy of Pancasila which pivots on the obligation of every Indonesian to believe in a single deity. In the case of the single supreme God in which Indonesians are enjoined to believe, particularly if they are Muslims or Christians, both of these religions are based on the notion of a community of equal believers. All such equal believers are said to find the same quality of grace in God's sight and deserve corresponding respect from government. Pancasila also imposes important obligations on the state beyond the provision of respect for religious pluralism, including social justice and democracy which share corresponding assumptions. It is possible to argue, therefore, that Indonesia in its state philosophy shares the same underlying assumption of the English democratic revolution which was based on the belief that men and women are created equal in the sight of God. Indeed, Pancasila may be described as the Indonesian expression of the concept of a civil society.

To that extent, it is possible to suggest that the concept of a civil society is not totally alien to Indonesian values and that it is not a doctrine which is being imposed from outside arising from the nature of the end of the Cold War. It is, of course, well understood that the attempt by the Clinton Administration to apply a new doctrine of enlarging market democracies in place of the defunct one of the containment of international communism was received with some skepticism in South-East Asia as a devious attempt to impose conditions for aid and trade. However, the content and ideals of Pancasila are not the constructs of an alien Western mind. They constitute standards which relate to human dignity which are entrenched in the Indonesian constitution and Indonesian governments will be judged in Indonesia by the extent to which they are upheld.

Without seeking to offer gratuitous advice, I would, nonetheless, like to identify three related problems which would seem to arise in seeking to create a civil society in the Indonesian version and which Indonesians might address:

1. One fundamental challenge or obstacle would seem to arise from the very roots of the current political order which has been

responsible for such remarkable economic success. The New Order was established out of political and economic chaos and decay in the context of a subversive challenge with an external dimension which required placing a high premium on security defined in terms of internal threat to the identity of the state. Not only was it deemed necessary to define and address security in terms of the restoration of order but with the important change of national and international priorities it was deemed necessary also to conceive of security as a critical precondition to economic development itself seen as the key to future stability. To that end, political activity was strictly controlled and with some justification. That strictness has been modified over time but only up to a point.

It is, of course, well understood that democracy underpinned by a civil society is not only an ideal goal but it is also a politically intoxicating potion. Democracy in its plural form engenders strong debate and contention and is therefore capable of causing divisions within society which can be destructive, especially if there are preexisting religious and communal differences which can be easily inflamed. Without seeking to apportion blame for shortcomings in the role of the United Nations and any individual states in the conflicts in the former Yugoslavia, the human tragedy there arising from acute religious and cultural tensions which have their roots deep in history is only too apparent and a salutary lesson for all countries with human diversity contained within their bounds. Indonesia's goal has been that of unity in diversity since independence and national experience particulary during the course of the 1950s served to point up the problems of fulfilling that ideal aspiration. It is understandable, therefore, for any government in Jakarta to continually bear in mind its heavy responsibility for upholding the cohesion and integrity of the state. Moreover, there is also the thought that the educated middle class, however noble in intentions, are a privileged section of society and that government has to look well beyond that limited constituency in fulfilling its national responsibilities.

In that respect and bearing in mind the origins and priorities of the New Order, then one obstacle to civil society is the extent to which a political approach required at one historical juncture is maintained intact despite deep-seated economic and social change. A long-standing concern with a set political order based on a culture of security arising from Indonesian circumstances, which has encouraged depoliticalisation in the interest of a related stability and economic development, is one evident obstacle to the measure of progessive political relaxation which would serve the objects of a civil society. To that extent, the ideal virtues of a civil society may be seen to represent not only a step into the political unknown but also one which taken may be difficult to retrace should the state run into difficulty.

2. Closely related to the question of the preservation of political order so as to avoid the release of primordial and other destructive social forces and to underpin economic priorities, there is the sensitive matter of corporate entitlement. We all know full well the circumstances in which the doctrine of *dwi fungsi* was conceived, developed and applied. Its origins go back to the time of national revolution when the judgement was made that the political leadership of the Republic had compromised its ideals in too readily owing to Dutch *force majeure*. From that moment, the view was born that politics was too serious a matter to be left to politicians and the Indonesian political system has reflected such a view. *Dwi fungsi* has evolved over time but it exists in essence as a prerogative and privileged status. At issue, however, is to what extent can such a status be maintained and justified with the kind of social change that comes with strong economic development. That is not for me to say but for Indonesians to debate among themselves. Some observers have argued that the extent to which any armed forces devotes itself unduly to political activity, then there is a strong probability of its professional competence and military role being undermined as a consequence. Moreover, to the extent that a political role is sustained beyond historically appropriate circumstances, then the national standing of the institution may itself be damaged particularly if the popular view emerges that what is being protected is corporate privilege rather than national interests. However, it may be justified, the concept of *dwi fungsi* is based on a prerogative role which is not easy to reconcile with the notion of a civil society. As I have said, that is a subject for Indonesians to debate among themselves. Their very ability to debate it constructively will be one indicator of the prospects for a civil society.

3. Another sensitive subject is that of political succession which has to be faced by all governments of mortal men. It is no secret that

Indonesia has had only one experience of such fundamental political change and that was highly traumatic. There is a conventional wisdom which would argue strongly that in order for such change to take place in the fullness of time in an orderly way so that the achievements of the decades of stable government are not prejudiced then the Pandora's box of political excitement ought not to be opened up. In that way, a volatile open political process would be avoided.

How the process of change is managed ultimately is again a problem for Indonesians to solve but the concurrence of that problem with continuing significant social change may well mean that a choice will have to be made between conceding and containing demands for a more civil society in the interest of stable political order.

In addressing some of the reasons why civil society may have to be subordinated to other priorities, there is a danger, however, of failing to recognise the degree of social change which has been the experience of Indonesia during the past three decades as well as the change at the global level which has discredited the Marxist model of political economy and which has undermined its attractiveness for dissident groups. Communism has not only failed as a political system but also as a model of political economy which is why it is possible to be somewhat confident about its loss of appeal and diminished threat to national security.

Conclusion

I would add by way of conclusion, that one overall challenge to the realisation of an Indonesian version of civil society to suit and serve Indonesian circumstances is whether or not government continues to address issues of the Twenty First Century in terms of a particular traumatic defining experience of the mid-Twentieth Century. A failure to revise ideas and concepts which were appropriate and necessary to the conditions of stability and economic success at an earlier historical juncture could give rise to unanticipated political difficulties particularly when a new-generation of political leaders is obliged to assume the heavy responsibility for steering the Indonesian ship of state in a changing social context. To that extent, the notion of openness which has become the code-word for democratisation, also lends itself to debate. It has been interpreted as requiring responsibility, which is understandable. However, there is a sense in which that responsibility is deemed to be owed only by the practitioners of openness to government, whereas there is a danger of neglecting a corresponding obligation on the part of government to its citizens to provide a credible form of accountability. There is a danger of governments assuming a fixed mind-set, so that the very phenomenon of opposition which is one dimension of the concept of civil society may be perceived in terms of disloyalty to the state and even incompatible with the virtues of Pancasila.

The very idea of loyal opposition may seem unduly Western and alien to Indonesian culture and circumstances and I am not recommending it. But, the great danger that the very process of conceiving of political choice and opposition in negative terms may give rise to a self-fulfilling prophecy with adverse consequences for political order by encouraging the very disloyalty which the government seeks to prevent. Even more so is the danger of assuming that new generations of Indonesians are not capable of understanding the responsibilities as well as the rights which obtain under the general rubric of civil society. Indeed, it would seem appropriate to point out during this period of commemoration of the fiftieth anniversary of independence, that one of the arguments advanced for denying independence, and not only to Indonesians, was their the people of the colonised country were not ready to assume their responsibilities but required continuing tutelage. It would be a terrible irony, if fifty years after the proclamation of Indonesia's independence, Indonesians were to be denied greater political emancipation on the basis of a similar argument to that once employed by the former colonial power.

Note

Paper presented at the Seminar on "Indonesia and the World at the Beginning of 21st century," organised by CSIS and the *Jakarta Post*, 17 October 1995.

56

Lessons from a Downfall

There is a terrible irony in the circumstances of the political downfall of President Suharto within weeks of his seventy-seventh birthday.

The man who led Indonesia for over 32 years and who was honoured as "Father of Development" has fallen victim to national economic adversity and almost certainly to his own sense of hubris.

After trying to step down from office on his own terms, President Suharto was obliged to revise his timetable for a managed succession; almost certainly pushed by the IMF, although the message was conveyed politely in almost Javanese ambiguity by US Secretary of State Madeleine Albright.

The final decision was precipitated by a withdrawal of support from the armed forces. However, in order to avoid a complete political vacuum and the appearance of a coup, Indonesia's constitution has been called into play to countenance the succession of Dr Habibie, even though its strict letter does not provide for the resignation of a president.

Reprinted from Michael Leifer, "Lessons from a Downfall", *Straits Times*, 23 May 1998, p. 53, by permission of the copyright-holder.

At issue, initially, is how will a man who has never been taken seriously as a political leader address the acute problems which confront the republic?

Indonesia faces a troubled future with a former vice-president who only acceded to that subordinate and ceremonial office last March because the president had insisted pugnaciously on his nomination and election.

Apart from a limited urban Islamic constituency, Dr Habibie is a contentious and controversial figure who is deeply mistrusted as a long-standing personal and political crony of Suharto by the student protest movement.

Moreover, his eccentric economic views and his dissipation of national resources on grandiose projects have discredited him among the technocratic community on whom Indonesia will need to rely in the immediate future.

Dr Habibie is not respected either by the armed forces leadership which only tolerated his election as vice-president because of a prior continuing commitment to Suharto. They have been willing to suffer him now in highest office because of a concern that political change should not be disorderly which was the case at the end of the turbulent rule of the late President Sukarno in the mid-1960s.

The question arises as to whether Dr Habibie may be able to redeem himself and Indonesia in the process. He has acted speedily to appoint a new Cabinet but apart from removing the most conspicuous personal associates of the former president, there is considerable continuity with its predecessor, with the same coordinating ministers for all responsibilities, including economy and finance as well as armed forces chief, General Wiranto, continuing in dual defence ministry role.

It would be argued that the new president has missed a great opportunity to make a truly fresh start, above all, by appointing a prime ministerial figure with proven economic competence and an integrity untouched by close association with the Suharto regime which would attract national and international confidence.

The composition of the Cabinet lends itself to mixed and not necessarily charitable interpretations both within and outside Indonesia. For example, should its composition give the impression that President Habibie is acting as a proxy for the interests of former President Suharto, seen as attempting to manipulate events behind the scene, then the politics of the street could erupt again to national disadvantage.

Equally controversially, should Dr Habibie seek to assert himself politically and to impose his own idiosyncratic economic views, then any limited revival of international confidence will quickly drain away.

That international confidence is essential because Indonesia is in such a stricken economic and social condition. Inflation and unemployment continue to rise and there is a growing food shortage compounded by the disruption of the distribution system. Moreover, the economic damage done by the victimisation of the local Chinese community has been considerable.

In such circumstances, statesmanship is required and, despite initial misgivings over the Cabinet, President Habibie will have to prove himself capable of steering the process of promised democratic reforms without unleashing centrifugal political forces.

An additional problem which he will have to face is the likely demand for some political accounting, especially as prisoners emerge from detention and questions are raised about the scale and location of the alleged inordinate wealth of the Suharto family.

One of the reasons why Suharto sought to manage his own political exit was to avoid the ignominy and humiliation experienced by his ill-fated predecessor who ended his days under house arrest. In Suharto's case, there are almost certainly far more scores to be settled and while a deal may have been struck with the armed forces over his personal security and those of his family circle, the momentum of political protest has been fuelled by a deep-seated popular anger at the scale of greed and corruption which has pervaded and distinguished the Suharto regime. Indeed, the term corruption does not do justice to the scale of plunder which is better described as grand larceny.

Because President Habibie has been so closely identified for so long with the indulgences and excesses of the Suharto era, he is in a difficult position from which to try to restore political confidence and economic activity. At best, he will be an interim figure subject, in particular, to the guidance of the armed forces leadership. So far, their corporate unity has held and their political balancing act in supporting Suharto until he had become a proven national liability without attracting popular anger has enabled them to reiterate their traditional dual function with a prerogative influence at the centre of politics.

A paternalistic armed forces watching over the diminutive figure of an unlikely president cannot be sufficient on its own as a formula for a new beginning for Indonesia. The military may be necessary to hold the state together but the past three decades have produced considerable social change whose fruits in informed political participation and in civil society have been frustrated by the demobilising policies of Suharto's rule.

Indonesia is also not going to find political and economic salvation by turning to any simplistic model of Western liberal democracy. But if it is going to have another chance, its new government must learn the lessons of the downfall of the last; namely, that standards of honesty in public life, respect for the rule of law and public accountability provide the best way to earn popular trust and legitimacy in bad times as well as good.

57

Indonesia's Foreign Policy
Change and Continuity

Nearly four decades have elapsed since the late President Sukarno proclaimed Indonesia's independence. In that period, the Republic has experienced the upheaval of national revolution and a succession of political systems beginning with a febrile Parliamentary Democracy. Parliamentary Democracy gave way to the romantic and volatile authoritarianism of Guided Democracy and this, in turn, was replaced, by a more sober authoritarianism which has styled itself *Pancasila* Democracy.

The course of Indonesia's foreign policy has reflected this uneven political progress. First, changes in political system have given rise to corresponding changes in the idiom of foreign policy. For example, under Guided Democracy, the precept of an independent and active foreign policy was discarded. In its place was enthroned an alternative notion of progressive New Emerging Forces, with Indonesia depicted as their vanguard. That notion was based on a view of the international

Reprinted from "Conclusion: Change and Continuity", in *Indonesia's Foreign Policy*, by Michael Leifer (London: George Allen & Unwin, 1983), pp. 172–81, by permission of the Royal Institute of International Affairs.

system totally at variance with the one which had underpinned the original independent and active formula. That formula was reinstated, however, with the collapse of Guided Democracy and has been maintained as official doctrine. Second, changes in political system have been accompanied by changes in the pattern of external associations and alignments. For example, on the morrow of independence, an ideal commitment to an independent and active foreign policy was combined with a qualified disposition towards the Western constellation of states. That tendency was revised during the changing course of Parliamentary Democracy in favour of a more assertive and explicit non-alignment. With the advent of Guided Democracy, and as a consequence of confrontation over West Irian and Malaysia, an association was cultivated with communist states at the expense of the West — first with the Soviet Union and then with the People's Republic of China. Alignment with the latter was reinforced by repudiation of membership in the United Nations. Such a pattern was speedily reversed when Guided Democracy was succeeded by the New Order, or *Pancasila* Democracy, inaugurated by General Suharto. Special relationships were then established with the United States and Japan and an unprecedented initiative was underaken in regional association in company with conservative neighbouring states.

Finally, changes in political system have been matched by changes in the style of conduct of foreign policy exemplified by the prosecution of Indonesia's claim to West Irian and its challenge to the international status of Malaysia. In the former case, although unwavering in objective, governments during the period of Parliamentary Democracy were content, in the main, to pursue the claim by conventional diplomatic means. By contrast, during Guided Democracy, which was dominated by the personality and pronouncements of Sukarno, a flamboyant coercive diplomacy was adopted. Such practice was employed successfully in the case of West Irian, but not in that of Malaysia. At an early stage in the establishment of the New Order, accommodation with and to Malaysia was reached by informal and formal negotiation. Subsequently, Indonesia resumed membership of the United Nations and its foreign policy has been conducted with greater deference to the conventions of the international system.

If change has been evident, however, it does not constitute the sum of Indonesia's foreign policy. Such change has been more than matched by a strong strain of continuity. That continuity, expressed in international outlook and policy goals, has been the direct product of a shared experience on the part of post-colonial successor elites. A Java-centric view of the regional standing and vulnerability of archipelagic Indonesia which was formed during the struggle for independence has been sustained since its attainment. The political generation whose mental attitudes were affected most deeply by the impact of national revolution have not departed completely from public life. Indeed, both President Suharto and vice-President Adam Malik were actively involved in the independence struggle, if each in different ways.

Nationalist challenge to the restoration of Dutch rule precipitated a protracted and bitter struggle in which the vulnerability of the embryo Republic was exposed and exploited. The experience of upholding independence in both domestic and international dimensions generated an abiding concern for the integrity of a state beset by social diversity and physical fragmentation. That concern was reinforced by a conviction about the country's attractiveness to external interests because of its bountiful natural resources and important strategic location. A common and consistent theme of Indonesia's foreign policy has been the need to overcome an intrinsic vulnerability. Paradoxically, however, a continuous sense of vulnerability has been combined with an equally continuous sense of regional entitlement based on pride in revolutionary achievement, size of population, land and maritime dimensions, natural resources and strategic location. That sense of regional entitlement has been less than consistently displayed in open form; it has persisted none the less.

In the years since the attainment of independence, the spectre of external intervention has haunted the Indonesian state. Foreign policy priorities have been determined accordingly. For example, Sukarno pursued the claim to West Irian for a variety of motives but not least from a suspicion that the Dutch had retained a peripheral foothold from which to assert influence in the event of political collapse within the Republic. He was supported in this endeavour by the leadership of the armed forces which had been engaged, during the 1950s, in crushing Islamic and regional rebellion, the latter having attracted external support. Sukarno appointed as commander of the final phase of the West Irian operation the very man who succeeded him as president. If President Sukarno had questioned the requirement for a test of opinion in West Irian provided for in the settlement of August 1962, his successor, President Suharto, was prepared to tolerate such an exercise only as a formality. The so-called act of free choice conducted in 1969 did not permit an authentic expression of self-determination. It was conducted in a sober manner without the public display characteristic of the Sukarno era, but the priority of ensuring the integrity of the archipelago and of denying any precedent for separatism was firmly maintained. The subsequent conduct of the Suharto administration over the controversial issue of East Timor served to confirm a strong attachment to a strategic perspective which existed before the internal transfer of power in March 1966. Indeed, a sense of strategic imperative overrode deference to the conventions of the international system.

As indicated above, the group of soldiers led by general Suharto who deposed and succeeded Sukarno did not constitute a new political force. They were the product of the same military and political experience attendant on the creation of the Indonesian state out of a Dutch administrative frame. The armed forces had never been fully subordinate to civilian authority during the period of national evolution. After independence, the officer corps, although beset by factional and regional divisions, had exhibited a sense of guardianship towards affairs of state. They derived a perception of political entitlement from their military endeavours during the national revolution and subsequently in holding the post-colonial state together. They played an influential part in inaugurating Guided Democracy and have claimed the right to a political role because of their contribution to the creation and preservation of the Republic. Charged with the defence of the state, they have been more conscious than their civilian predecessors of the innate vulnerability of the Republic, especially to any conjunction between internal dissension and external interference.

The leadership of the armed forces repudiated the domestic and international alignments of Sukarno and claimed that they were restoring the Republic to its true course in foreign policy. That was correct in so far as idiom, outlook and style were concerned but it was contingent on an attempt to recover the confidence of those Western states whose assistance was essential for economic recovery. A necessary concession to secure such assistance was the cessation of confrontation with Malaysia. Accommodation to the reality of Malaysia had been made possible, above all, by domestic political change and facilitated by the prior separation of Singapore from the federation. The armed forces had not differed from Sukarno in opposing the advent of Malaysia, at least not at the outset. As the course of confrontation appeared to serve the interests of the Indonesian Communist Party, and had led on to an unpalatable alignment with the People's Republic of China, the leadership of the armed forces reappraised their interests. Malaysia had been suspect because of the manner of its formation, the conspicuous role of Britain as patron of the undertaking, and also the pivotal position which Singapore appeared to occupy. Its advent was deemed to pose a threat to the security of Indonesia; it offended also against the Republic's sense of regional entitlement. Accordingly, the ending of confrontation in August 1966 marked a break in continuity in the light of a policy enunciated three and a half years previously. For some within the armed forces, acceptance of Malaysia was, initially, a bitter pill to swallow. None the less, the strategic perspective which had contributed to confrontation was not discarded with the settlement of the dispute between Indonesia and Malaysia.

When Indonesia led by acting President Suharto appeared to confirm a change in international course in August 1967 by helping to found ASEAN, it displayed an outlook which had been shared, in part, by the administration of President Sukarno. The special interests which the Indonesian delegation managed to get incorporated within ASEAN's inaugural declaration had been articulated and endorsed at those conferences which convened in Manila in 1963 to deal with the contention aroused by the prospect of Malaysia. The qualified proscription of foreign military bases set out in that declaration reflected one of the basic objections to the formation of the federation. The Manila documents to which Subandrio and Sukarno had put their names also expressed a clear sense of regional entitlement. The incorporation of clauses dealing with regional order within the ASEAN declaration expressed a corresponding outlook. The difference between Manila in 1963 and Bangkok in 1967 was one of the context and degree. The constituents of an Indonesian-inspired strategic perspective had been sustained and an unprecedented willingness to engage in regional association indicated an attempt to use alternative means to attain abiding priorities. A recognition by the Suharto administration of the underlying weaknesses of Indonesia has meant a grudging disposition to adjust to prevailing realities. None the less, that administration has persisted with attempts to prescribe for regional order based on a limited and diminishing role for external powers. Such a view was central to the declaration by the ASEAN Foreign Ministers in November 1971 in favour of a Zone of Peace, Freedom and Neutrality, which was incorporated within the Declaration of

ASEAN Concord promulgated in February 1976. It was incorporated also in the joint statement issued by President Suharto and the Malaysian Prime Minister, Datuk Hussein Onn, in March 1980, if received without enthusiasm by other regional partners.

Further confirmation of an underlying continuity in foreign policy expressing both a sense of weakness and one of entitlement has been indicated in maritime initiatives. An archipelagic principle was enunciated in December 1957 after the introduction of martial law had suspended Parliamentary Democracy. It was reaffirmed as part of municipal law by decree in February 1960 during the first year of Guided Democracy. It was further incorporated as one of the guidelines of state policy in March 1973 by the People's Consultative Assembly during *Pancasila* Democracy. Moreover, the Indonesian government has pressed its claim to archipelagic status with evident success during the course of the Third UN Conference on the Law of the Sea.

The argument for continuity must not be pressed to the exclusion of all other factors. There are obvious differences between civilian and military-based governments and between a charismatic leader like Sukarno and a cautious military figure like Suharto. Moreover, environmental circumstances change which may require changes in policy. For example, Islam has become a more important factor in foreign policy considerations. During the administration of President Suharto, Islam has burgeoned as an international phenomenon with domestic significance. Accordingly, the government has been obliged to be especially careful to strike a balance in external associations in order to appease domestic Islamic opinion without appearing to enhance its national standing in political terms. Yet, that requirement stems from unresolved problems about the identity of the Indonesian state which were the subject of public debate before the proclamation of independence. The communal divisions which express the absence of a single great cultural tradition have determined the constituencies of political life. They have direct relevance to the conduct of foreign policy. Indeed, they constitute an immutable feature of a fragmented social fabric only matched by a fragmented physical structure. Indonesia in its present form cannot escape it social diversity, in respect of which the national motto "Unity in Diversity" represents a statement of aspiration rather than achievement. It also cannot escape a geographical configuration which, combined with social diversity, encourages centrifugal political tendencies. Moreover, it cannot escape a location in which fundamental problems of state and nation-building have been heightened by intrusions on the part of external powers.

The dominant theme of Indonesia's foreign policy arises from the interplay of all these factors and the constant, if uneven, attempt by governments in Jakarta to overcome an attendant condition of subordination. The administration of President Suharto has sought to overcome that condition, in part by promoting economic development which, if reversing a conspicuous internal debility, has also aggravated social tensions. In terms of rhetoric, that administration has proclaimed the concept of national resilience which amounts to a call for spiritual, as well as political, self-reliance which has been echoed, to an extent, by ASEAN partners. Like the motto of "Unity in Diversity", this concept expresses an aspiration rather than an accomplished fact. None the less, the exhortations to both national and regional resilience indicate more than a mere declaratory desire for national and regional self-determination. The government's undoubted objective is to serve as the foundation of a regional grouping of its own promotion which would be independent of the substantive influence of outside powers. It is in this context that the independence of Brunei and its future membership of ASEAN have been welcomed.

In this endeavour, Indonesia faces untold difficulties arising from its own relative weakness and that of its regional partners. Moreover, those regional partners do not necessarily share its strategic perspective to the full. For example, Thailand entertains a very different perception of external threat, and this has been responsible for a pattern of external alignments, incorporating China, which is viewed with deep suspicion in Jakarta. And although Singapore under Prime Minister Lee Kuan-yew has developed a practical working relationship with the Suharto administration, its government has never sought to hide a concern that a regionally determined balance of power might give rise to an unpalatable local dominance. Accordingly, Singapore has indicated a preference for an ordered involvement of external powers which would neutralize both of them and any threat posed by a potentially dominant regional state. Furthermore, for all its achievements, ASEAN remains no more than a diplomatic community which has been more successful in accommodating than in reconciling divergent intramural interests. In practical terms, it is a sub-regional association obliged to share an aspirant managerial role with a constellation of Indochinese states in which the dominance of Vietnam is in no way matched by Indonesia's position within ASEAN. In the light of intra-regional polarization since the end of the Second Indochina War, which has been aggravated with the onset of renewed conflict, the Indonesian government has been obliged to moderate its plans for regional order, which continue to be affected also by the competing interests of major and global powers.

Indonesia has never been able to overcome the difficulties involved in confronting problems posed by the intrusion of such powers. For example, should the global powers ever be in accord, then their willingness to act in concert would certainly prove an insuperable obstacle to the realization of Indonesia's regional vision. Indeed, an example of such accord has been displayed over passage of naval vessels through straits used for international navigation and, specifically, over the Straits of Malacca and Singapore. However, should the global powers be at odds, which is their normal condition, then there is a reasonable prospect that they will have competitive interests to pursue in South-East Asia. In such circumstances, a country like Indonesia would be obliged to make a choice if only because it is almost certain to perceive each global power in a different light. This has been the case during the course of its foreign policy since independence. In so far as its pattern of external alignments has fluctuated, this has reflected changing relations with the major powers and has also indicated attempts to employ conventional balance of power techniques.

Under the Suharto administration, the longstanding suspicion of all external powers has been sustained but tempered with an evident pragmatism, especially in relations with the United States and Japan. Indeed, regional circumstances since the end of the Second Indochina War in 1975 have reinforced a strategic dependence on the United States, despite a declining confidence in its ability to resume a military role in South-East Asia. The result has been an evident paradox in attitudes. On the one hand, Indonesia would prefer, ideally, to do without an American military presence just over the horizon as a counter to that of the Soviet Union which has been extended from the Indian Ocean to the South China Sea. On the other hand, because of adverse changes in the balance of external influences bearing on the region, especially the expression of Sino-Soviet rivalry, there has been strong private criticism of the United States as insufficiently resolute in its superpower role and also for placing global priorities before regional ones, especially in dealings with China over the transfer of military technology. In other words, the Indonesian Government would prefer the least objectionable superpower to be on tap and not on top. Preferences, however, have had to give way to pragmatism. For example, during the Carter Administration, irritation at the prominence given to the issue of human rights did not obstruct an extensive release of political prisoners deemed necessary to assuage the political sensibilities of the White House and Congress.

Indonesia's ambivalence towards the United States has been more than matched by its relationship with Japan, which has played an increasingly prominent role in the economic life of the Republic. Given the development strategy which it has employed, the Indonesian government cannot do without Japanese capital investment and technical expertise. Japan is also a major market for raw materials, especially oil and liquified natural gas. Yet Japan and its ubiquitous businessmen are generally perceived as engaged in the exploiting role that the Nipponese forces set out to undertake in 1942. Indeed, a visit by a Japanese Prime Minister in 1974 provided a justification for public disorder in Jakarta. The economic relationship with Japan is endured because it serves the requirements of political elites committed to development policies which rest on Indonesian participation in the international capitalist economy. However, despite the measure of dependence which this might appear to entail, there has been no inclination to endorse America's encouragement of Japan to assume a military role in Asia. Japan is tolerated as a necessary economic partner but is not regarded with any enthusiasm as a prospective regional one. Australia is a less daunting neighbour but is also viewed with mixed feelings of amity and irritation.

Since 1966, Indonesia has maintained unchanging priorities in assessing the merits and demerits of external powers. If the United States and Japan have been regarded with a mixture of forebearance and reserve, the Soviet Union has been contemplated with suspicion because it is a communist superpower which has displayed a growing capability to project military means within Indonesia's maritime bounds. Asylum for exiled members of the PKI and inept attempts at espionage have served to reinforce such suspicion. Moreover, to the extent that a country like India appears to enjoy a special relationship with the Soviet Union, that suspicion has been carried over in relations with New Delhi and pointed up by differences over Kampuchea. Rivalry over competing claims for influence in the Indian Ocean has been mitigated, to the extent that the government in New Delhi has demonstrated a genuine willingness to assume the role of maritime watchdog. In addition, Indonesia shares with India a profound apprehension of China.

It is well appreciated in Jakarta that China does not possess the requisite military capability to pose a threat to Indonesia. The People's Republic is not contemplated in terms of conventional threat but in respect of a presumed access to Indonesia's resident Chinese community. Concern over the political reliability of a Chinese minority of approximately three and a half million has its roots both in colonial experience and in the period of national revolution. It has been sustained because of the influential role which that minority has continued to play in the management of the economy. For its part, the Chinese government has served to vindicate Indonesian suspicions by providing asylum for exiled members of the PKI and by a persistent refusal to renounce party-to-party relations while dealing on a governmental basis with non-communist administrations in South-East Asia. The administration in Indonesia which charged China with complicity in the abortive coup of October 1965 has been ambivalent about resuming diplomatic relations suspended since October 1967. For example, in March 1978, shortly before his re-election by the People's Consultative Assembly for a further five-year term, President Suharto indicated his government's intention to prepare the way for restoring diplomatic relations with China. This announcement drew critical response from the Muslim United Development Party and the initiative was stopped. The following year China's military act of punishment against Vietnam and the continuing exodus of ethnic Chinese refugees from that country served to delay further any serious consideration of the matter. There is no doubt that Indonesia's relationship with China is as much a matter of domestic politics as of foreign policy. However, given the long-term sense of threat associated with China and the perceived absence of tangible advantage likely to accrue from the presence of a Chinese embassy in Jakarta, the issue of restoring diplomatic relations has been recurrently deferred.

Within South-East Asia, Indonesia has sought, without conspicuous success, to prevent its regional environment from becoming an arena of conflict for outside powers. Such an ideal has remained well beyond its grasp. Its limitations were pointed up during the course of the first two Indochina wars in which first France and then the United States sought to determine post-colonial political succession. The outcome of the second of those conflicts has had a profound influence on the balance of external influences bearing on South-East Asia. At its conclusion, Indonesia and its regional partners were not in a position to seize the opportunity to translate an ideal design for a Zone of Peace, Freedom and Neutrality into an orderly structure of regional relations. Initially, the legacy of that conflict in the form of Vietnamese suspicions of ASEAN was interposed between Indonesia and its regional partners on the one hand, and the revolutionary successor governments in Indochina on the other. And then a revival of pre-colonial antagonisms combined with ideological incompatibility in a manner which served to aggravate already deteriorating Sino-Vietnamese relations perceived in Peking and Moscow as an adjunct of Sino-Soviet relations. One dramatic outcome was Vietnam's invasion of Kampuchea, involving the violation of a principle which Indonesia had sought to make the basis of a system of regional order. Moreover, an attendant competitive engagement of external power interests appeared to return the region virtually full circle to the very condition which the Indonesian government had laboured diplomatically to prevent.

Despite this major setback, Indonesia has retained its regional vision based on an exclusive pattern of relations among resident states. But it is still some distance from assuming the position of a regional power centre able to shape that pattern. Within the Republic, it is regarded as the logical candidate for such a role and current development strategy is related to that end. The gap between aspiration and achievement remains, none the less, and has been sustained because, in certain important respects, quantitative assets such as population and territorial scale remain liabilities — thus ensuring that continuity prevails over change. Indeed, the Achilles heel lies in the economy, which has yet to overcome the burden of a population whose constant growth cancels out achievement. President Suharto's comment in 1969 cited earlier that "We shall only be able to play an effective role if we ourselves are possessed of a great national vitality" is likely to remain valid for the rest of the twentieth century.

58

The Islamic Factor in Indonesia's Foreign Policy
A Case of Functional Ambiguity

Although approximately 90 per cent of Indonesia's population of some 150 million are Muslims in one sense or another, the Republic is not an Islamic state. Indeed, one feature of its foreign policy has been a conscious attempt to disabuse all abroad of such an assumption. Spokesmen for Indonesia have insisted that the Republic is "neither a theocratic nor a secular state". Moreover, Indonesian governments, especially from the advent of the New Order inaugurated by General Suharto, have taken great care not to allow foreign policy to be dictated by Islamic considerations. This position has been determined by domestic circumstances. Islam, however, is not without influence on Indonesia's foreign policy but that influence has been expressed much more in the form of constraint than in positive motivation. To understand the precise relationship between Islam and Indonesia's foreign policy, it is necessary to appreciate the complexity and

Reprinted in abridged form from Michael Leifer, "The Islamic Factor in Indonesia's Foreign Policy: A Case of Functional Ambiguity", in *Islam in Foreign Policy*, edited by Adeed Dawisha (London: Cambridge University Press, 1983), pp. 144–59, by permission of the Royal Institute of International Affairs.

contentiousness of religious–cultural identity within the distended archipelago. It is essential also to take account of attendant governmental concern that incautious engagement in any international Islamic issue might feed back with adverse consequences into the domestic political process. Finally, it is important not to exaggerate the Islamic factor in assessing, for example, Indonesia's relationship with Arab–Islamic states. Conciliation towards them is as likely to indicate interest in General Assembly votes over East Timor or Kampuchea as in any matter with an identifiable Islamic dimension.

Invariably foreign policy begins at home. To assess the Islamic factor in Indonesia's foreign policy, one is obliged to begin by noting the absence of a single great cultural tradition within the post-colonial state. The national motto, "Unity in Diversity", constitutes a statement of aspiration rather than one of established fact. The most fundamental source of diversity is the communal division between nominal and observant adherents of the Islamic faith which is most acute on the pivotal island of Java which contains almost two-thirds of the country's population. That division has its origins in the arrival and acceptance of Islam in the archipelago. In many parts of East and Central Java, Islam was only superimposed on a syncretic cultural tradition which drew its inspiration from entrenched Hindu–Buddhist beliefs. The uneven impact and degree of penetration of Islam has left a divided cultural legacy which continues to trouble the cohesion of a state which has enjoyed more than thirty years of independence.

The attendant communal divisions within Indonesian society, as well as divisions within orthodox Islam, have been dealt with ably and at length in the corresponding chapter to this in the companion volume, *Islam in the Political Process*. In that chapter, the point has been well made, that "For all the overwhelming number of Islam's formal adherents in Indonesia, which makes it on paper the world's largest Muslim nation, Islam in any strict sense is a minority religion."[1] Nevertheless, Islam's faithful adherents within Indonesia have never accepted that view. Their claim to religious primacy has constituted the principal source of contention over the identity of the state which became a matter of public debate even before the proclamation of independence in August 1945. The protagonists of Islam had sought to entrench an obligation for all Muslims to observe *sharia'a* law in the constitution of the embryo state. However on 1 June 1945, future President Sukarno enunciated five principles before the Investigating Committee for the Preparation of Independence, which in effect frustrated Islamic expectations. These principles have served since as the philosophical bases of the Indonesian state.

Sukarno represented an example, *par excellence,* of the alternative Javanese cultural tradition to that of orthodox Islam. Although he acknowledged adherence to Islam,[2] his dominant values were drawn from pre-Islamic spiritual precepts which had taken deep root in East and Central Java. His five principles, or Panca Sila, were intended to provide a harmonizing frame for Indonesian diversity. One of them, above all, was intended to ensure religious pluralism and tolerance expressed in a belief in a single deity which would in turn permit every Indonesian to "believe in *his own* particular God".[3]

Foreign policy in Indonesia is in the formal charge of a government department. However, ultimate sanction for its conduct comes from a military establishment whose formative experience has produced a strong disposition against an Islam regarded as a danger to national unity. Heavy military representation in senior diplomatic posts and within the higher echelons of the Foreign Ministry provided visible assurance that the external priorities of the armed forces will not be disregarded. However, the civilian section of the Foreign Ministry has been permitted freedom of initiative in areas where matters of security do not impinge too directly. Relations with Arab–Islamic states fall under this heading but have not proved to be a matter of controversy because the consensus which pervades the armed forces over the issue of Islam extends to the Foreign Ministry.

For the greater part of its independent existence, Indonesia has been governed by administrations which have reflected the alternative pre-Islamic cultural tradition associated with East and Central Java. For short periods during Parliamentary Democracy (1950–7), identifiably Islamic prime ministers from Masyumi led unstable coalition governments within which power was shared with secular parties. There have been three such prime ministers. Mohammad Natsir (September 1950 to April 1951); Sukiman Wirjosandjojo (April 1951 to April 1952); and Burhannuddin Harahap (August 1955 to March 1956). An examination of programmes presented to Parliament by these prime ministers does not indicate any Islamic content. A particular disposition toward the Western constellation of states and a vigorous anti-communism on the part of Sukiman may have derived in part from religious conviction but hardly expressed Islamic interests. Moreover, all governments during the parliamentary period were obliged to cope with the *Dar ul-Islam* insurrection which, by its very nature, placed identifiably Islamic prime ministers in a difficult position. The only period in which Islam has served as a positive element in foreign policy occurred during Indonesia's struggle for independence but only as part of a general diplomatic strategy designed to secure recognition and international endorsement for the embattled Republic. Thus, after attendance at the Asian Relations Conference held in New Delhi in March 1947, a conspicuously Islamic Deputy-Foreign Minister, Haji Agus Salim, who enjoyed fluent command of Arabic, travelled to Cairo where he set up a mission with the object of soliciting recognition from Arab League states. He was successful in his endeavours to the extent that he was able to conclude treaties of friendship on behalf of the Republic with Egypt and Syria and secure recognition from Iraq and Lebanon.

With the attainment of independence in December 1949, no evident Islamic strain was manifested in foreign policy. Indeed, foreign policy as such constituted a secondary priority at the outset, the most important foreign policy issue was the recovery of the western half of the island of New Guinea (Irian Barat) which early governments sought to achieve by quiet diplomacy. Nonetheless, there was a propensity for international issues to penetrate the domestic political process; most dramatically exemplified when the Sukiman government was brought down because its foreign minister, Achmad Subarjo, concluded a military-aid agreement with the United States on terms deemed offensive to national dignity and an independent and active foreign policy. Accordingly, there was no disposition to offend orthodox Muslims who identified with co-religionists in the Arab–Islamic world, especially given the revival of links with Middle Eastern seats of leaning and of the *hajj* after the Japanese occupation and the struggle for independence. Recognition was not accorded to the state of Israel, but support for the cause of the Palestinians was extended on the ground of the right to national self-determination. Support for the independence of other Arab–Islamic peoples, for example, in the case of Morocco, was extended on the same basis and not on the ground of co-religionist affinity. At the historic Asian-African Conference in Bandung in 1955 both Nehru and U Nu opposed the inclusion of the Palestinian issue on the agenda but Prime Minister Ali Sastroamijoyo (whose secular nationalist party was a bitter rival of Masyumi) argued successfully in favour.[4] An invitation was not extended to any Palestinian delegation, although the Grand Mufti of Jerusalem was among the invited guests. The final communiqué of the conference called for support for the rights of the Arab people of Palestine and for the implementation of United Nations resolutions designed to achieve a peaceful settlement. Subsequently, Indonesia accorded strong support for President 'Abd al-Nasir during the Suez crisis on the ground of anti-colonial solidarity.

If no offence was given to Muslim opinion by the practice of foreign policy during the parliamentary period, even less opportunity was provided for criticism during Guided Democracy, given its domination by issues of colonialism and neo-colonialism. The issue of West New Guinea (Irian Barat) assumed crisis proportions and culminated in a successful exercise in coercive diplomacy. Confrontation pursued against Malaysia, where Islam was the official religion, was a failure and contributed to Sukarno's downfall. During the period of Guided Democracy, foreign policy served the evident domestic function of sustaining an unstable political equilibrium but Islam had no special place. In August 1962 a stormy episode occurred, arising in part from the exclusion of Israeli athletes from the Asian Games which were being held in Jakarta. Their exclusion in response to Arab pressure cannot be separated from the concurrent exclusion of athletes from Taiwan. Indeed, the double exclusion fitted easily at the time into Sukarno's representation of the struggle of the New Emerging Forces. If exclusion of Israeli athletes did not constitute deference to a specifically Islamic cause, the action may be construed as a sweetener to Indonesia's Muslim community who, together with the Communist Party and leftist affiliates, had been expected to oppose Israeli participation.[5]

The Indonesian Foreign Ministry's conduct over the Asian Games provided a further indication of a pragmatic approach to any international issue which might provoke or serve to mobilize the Muslim community. With the collapse of Guided Democracy and its succession by the New Order, there was a greater requirement both to contain and take account of domestic Muslim potential and opinion. Political Islam was perceived to pose a major threat to national unity in the light of its adherents' capacity for violence demonstrated in the process of liquidating the Indonesian Communist Party and the revival of claims to incorporate a mandatory obligation for Muslims to practise their faith in the preamble to the constitution. Compared to Sukarno at the peak of his powers, General Suharto was less assured of his ability to contain the Muslims. Muslim mobilization had been affected also by the increasing impact of Islam in the international environment which served to influence the attitude of the Indonesian government. Islamic solidarity had been stimulated by Israel's dramatic victory in June 1967 in which all of Jerusalem, including the Temple Mount, was captured. The moment for greater self-assertion was seized by Saudi Arabia, especially with the burning of the al-Aqsa Mosque in Jerusalem in August 1969. The first meeting of Muslim heads of government convened in Rabat in September and addressed the wider question of Jerusalem. In March 1970, a meeting of Islamic foreign ministers took place in Jidda, which set up a permanent secretariat. In March 1972, delegates met again in Jidda to compile and promulgate a charter of the Islamic Conference, whose first objective was "to promote Islamic solidarity among member states". In respect of membership, the Charter stated that "every Muslim state is eligible to join the Islamic Conference on submitting an application expressing its desire and preparedness to adopt this Charter". In other words, membership of the Organization of the Islamic Conference (OIC) was deemed to constitute an affirmation of state identity.

Indonesia sent a delegation to the conference in Jidda in March 1972 but it declined to seek formal membership of the OIC and pointedly refused to sign the Islamic Charter in contrast to its ASEAN partner, Malaysia. Indeed, participation itself was controversial within Indonesia, and Foreign Minister Adam Malik was obliged to issue a press statement at the end of 1972, to the effect that the government was not yet prepared to sign the Islamic Charter and that the Republic was not an Islamic country. His statement attracted mildly critical comment from the influential, newly-formed Centre for Strategic and International Studies, a government-sponsored "think-tank" known to be unsympathetic to the cause of political Islam. It was pointed out that:

> Mr. Malik's statement is thus an important affirmation that Indonesia is not an Islamic country or any other form of a theocratic state directly governed by Islamic or other religious laws. It is, rather, if one rejects the term "secular", a theo-democratic state, indirectly governed by God's laws through sound human reason and common sense.
>
> On that basis, it can surely be argued that Indonesia should not have sent a delegation to the Jeddah conference in the first place. At least the delegation should have only had the status of an observer rather than a full participant. It is possible, however, that the delegation was sent with the understanding that it represented a Moslem country merely in the sense that it is predominantly Moslem populated, so

that the interests of the Moslems in general, which the conference was surely meant to serve, would also be the interests of the Indonesian Moslems.[6]

This comment serves to indicate the dilemma of the Suharto administration which prefers to keep the Arab–Islamic world at a distance lest it establish an unhealthy junction with volatile political forces within Indonesia. On the other hand, it is only too conscious of a requirement to express at least nominal solidarity when appropriate in order to contain those forces and deny them an issue which might mobilize their strength. For example, the Indonesian government cannot divorce itself from a matter such as the status of Jerusalem. Indeed, General Suharto has publicly criticized the government of Israel for its unilateral revision of that status which he acknowledged publicly had "offended the feelings of the Islamic community throughout the world". Moreover, it was obliged in April 1982, in the middle of a turbulent election campaign, to heed the late King Khalid's call for a one-day strike in protest at a shooting on the Temple Mount in Jerusalem by a Jewish gunman. Nonetheless, where it has had a choice, the Indonesian government has sought to restrict involvement in Islamic issues and to maintain a balance in external associations designed to fulfil a domestic function in both positive and negative senses. In May 1981, Foreign Minister Mochtar Kusumaatmadja was questioned during the course of an interview as to why Indonesia as a Muslim country had not signed the Charter of the OIC. Apart from reiterating that Indonesia was "not a Muslim country in the sense that it is an Islamic state", he indicated satisfaction with the position of ambiguity which permitted Indonesia to participate in the activities of the OIC without being obliged to undertake a commitment to unacceptable principles. In response to persistent questioning as to his government's specific objections to the Islamic Charter, he replied:

You are a South Asian but in South-East Asia we are not nitpickers, I am sorry to say that, because I see this always with my South Asian friends. They love to quarrel about one word and spend hours and waste a lot of time. South-East Asians are more practical. They say that what is this, you want to co-operate in this, what is the objective, all right. We are not so particular about details. I prefer the South-East Asian way. It is more productive. It is more pleasant. It does not involve any recriminations, debates, long waste of time and a big fat zero in the end. So the South-East Asian way has much to commend.[7]

Professor Mochtar was, in effect, engaged in the diplomatic equivalent of "stonewalling" in cricket. He was unwilling to discuss openly and frankly an issue that exposed could serve only to impair Indonesia's relations with the Arab–Islamic world with attendant adverse domestic consequences. The point at issue is that the administration of President Suharto has committed itself to a syncretic cultural design for the Indonesian state which does not admit a special public place for Islam. Yet, it is conscious of the capacity of Islam for political challenge and disruption and cannot afford to appear to neglect Muslim opinion above all over domestic issues, but also over international ones. For example, Professor Mochtar drew his interviewer's attention to Muslim opposition to any restoration of diplomatic relations between Indonesia and China, pointing out that, "In fact, there are two important sections in Indonesian political life — the Muslims and the armed forces. We cannot ignore that."[8] The requirement to pay attention to what has become "the sole effective voice of opposition"[9] has meant that Islam enters into the foreign policy-making process primarily as a factor of constraint. Because of an abiding concern lest the international and domestic dimensions of Islam fuse and establish a political junction, the Suharto administration treads warily. It engages in Islamic occasions and issues in as far as it is necessary to appease Muslim opinion, but not in a way and to an extent which might arouse it. The objective is domestication and the means adopted take a variety of forms. At the symbolic level, for example, President Suharto and his party, when on overseas visits, always wear the *pici* (Muslim black velvet cap) and are photographed so adorned for domestic consumption.[10] Indonesians are permitted to participate in Qur'an reading contests abroad, in Mecca as well as in Kuala Lumpur, while the *hajj* to Mecca is facilitated under government control. The cities of Jakarta and Jidda entered into a twinning agreement in March 1982. In the same month, the Ministry of Religion extended support for the establishment of an international Islamic university but to be located in Malaysia. In addition, the government has tolerated expressions of solidarity by Muslim organizations with co-religionists in Afghanistan since the Soviet invasion. Where matters of substantive political interest are involved, the government has displayed a pragmatic caution.

There are many recent examples of such caution. When the Camp David agreement was reached in September 1978, Indonesia sought to sustain a neutral position in response to appeals from Egypt and Jordan (representing its opponents). The Indonesian government had been sympathetic to President Sadat's earlier dramatic initiative in November 1977, which President Suharto described as bringing "a new hope for peace", but was unwilling to indicate its explicit support because of the scale of opposition in the Arab world. For example, in March 1978 President Suharto made the equivocal statement that, "as a fellow sovereign country, we know that our brothers in the Middle East will adopt the best possible decision for themselves. As a friend, we fully support any decision whatever they make." The revolution in Iran constituted a disturbing phenomenon for an Indonesian government apprehensive at the impact of an Islamic resurgence which drew strength from the dissatisfaction with the values of development. Accordingly, a formal statement was not issued when the Shah was ousted; nor was one issued on the release of the American hostages, over which Foreign Minister Mochtar had refused to be drawn as to the possibility of Indonesia serving as mediator.[11] It has been pointed out that

> In Indonesia and Malaysia particularly, this official silence reflects the dilemma of being caught between the pragmatic considerations of the government's support for the principles of international law and the emotional identification on the part of many Indonesian and Malaysian citizens with the idea of the creation of a just and egalitarian state in Iran.[12]

In the case of the Soviet invasion of Afghanistan in December 1979, Indonesia endorsed the condemnation pronounced by the OIC meeting in Islamabad in January 1980 but there was a conscious effort to avoid defending Afghanistan as a wronged Islamic state. Indonesia went out of its way to stress that the Soviet Union had invaded a fellow non-aligned state and sought to avoid any commitment to defend Islamic principles which might be exploited by domestic Muslim groups.[13] For many Indonesians, there is a tendency to associate Arab with Islamic. For this reason in part, Indonesia has refused to allow the Palestine Liberation Organization to open an office in Jakarta — by contrast with Malaysia which has accorded it full diplomatic status. Officially, Indonesia supports the Palestinian cause. For example, in his address to the House of People's Representatives in August 1981 on the occasion of the 36th anniversary of the proclamation of independence, President Suharto stated, "our attitude toward the problems of the Middle East has always been clear from the beginning, that is, we stand on the side of the Arab peoples and that of the people of Palestine who are fighting for their just rights against the arrogant aggression of Israel". Evidently that clear attitude does not include tolerating a mission for the organization widely acknowledged to represent the interests of the Palestinians. In effect, the position of the Indonesian government toward the PLO has been influenced not only by the possible impact which the opening of its mission might have on the Muslim community. It has been affected also by concern lest intra-Arab rivalries be extended to the streets of its capital city and by apprehension at the communist connections of the PLO. In addition, it would probably not be pleased at the prospect of an office in Jakarta which might be used to monitor unofficial dealings between its military establishment and Israel, whose armed forces are admired for their military doctrine and proficiency. Indeed, in September 1979, Indonesia entered into an agreement with Israel for the purchase of 14 A-4 Skyhawk ground-attack fighter aircraft, together with two TA-4 Skyhawk trainers.[14] Indonesia has been willing to defer publicly to Arab and domestic Muslim sensibilities over the Palestine question only by attending appropriate meetings and endorsing declaratory resolutions. For example, in February 1982, its delegation voted in favour of a resolution before the General Assembly of the United Nations which called on members to "totally isolate Israel in all fields" as a riposte to its annexation of the Golan Heights. And in the following June, its Foreign Ministry denounced "Israel's aggression against Lebanon". Nonetheless, in practical dealings, often of necessity, covert rather than overt, the Suharto administration has sought to pursue alternatives to an association with the Arab–Islamic states which requires an anti-Israeli nexus.[15]

International Islamic issues closer to home than the Middle East have also engaged the concern of the Indonesian government. Muslim-based insurgencies exist in Thailand and the Philippines, regional partners within ASEAN. In both cases, Indonesia does not want to breach the principle of non-intervention, to appear to support separatism, or to impair the cohesion of a regional association which has been represented as the cornerstone of its foreign policy. Yet it has faced domestic pressure to remedy the grievances of co-religionists, especially in the case of the Southern Philippines, which is proximate to Indonesia and where the conflict is most serious. Indonesian Muslims have suggested that their government has not done sufficient to resolve that conflict. In effect, the Indonesian government has sought to engage in mediation while at the same time defending the Philippines in the OIC. Because of the priority attached to ASEAN by Indonesia, it cannot be seen to exercise pressure on President Marcos. At the same time, it sustains an apprehension lest Muslim revolt in the Philippines becomes an issue in domestic politics with the charge levelled that persecuted co-religionists are being neglected. In as far as the viability of ASEAN takes pride of place, the Indonesian government remains vulnerable to such a charge. That vulnerability constitutes a special case of a general condition which arises from domestic circumstances.

The Islamic factor in Indonesia's foreign policy has become more significant over the decades since independence because of the greater convergence of international and domestic Muslim dimensions. Islam within Indonesia has become a bitter, beleaguered force with a sense of denial of rightful political entitlement. Although permitted formal expression within a controlled political system, it has been denied a place in the symbols of state. Indeed, it has been obliged to defer to a state symbolism which arouses resentment rather than an intended sense of harmony. Islamic resurgence is nevertheless a fact of life stimulated by the domestic impact of a development policy based on Western orthodoxies and also by international associations and solidarity. The Indonesian government has been conscious of the need to take account of Muslim feeling in the conduct of foreign policy. As one senior diplomat remarked, "Do not underestimate Muslim public opinion in Indonesia. If neglected, it will be cultivated by extremists". Accordingly, the government has sought to strike a balance in foreign policy where Islamic issues are concerned in an attempt to appease that opinion without appearing to enhance the standing of political Islam or to validate its domestic political claims. In that delicate exercise, there is a limit beyond which the Suharto administration will not go. Such a limit has been indicated by its persistent refusal to sign the Islamic Charter and by the conspicuous absence of President Suharto from Islamic summit conferences.

In Indonesia, Islam has entered the foreign policy process more by way of challenge than by way of support. Domestic circumstances have been responsible for this state of affairs. Correspondingly, successive governments have made a conscious attempt to excise a co-religionist dimension from foreign policy wherever possible because of its perceived threat to national unity. Because of these same domestic circumstances, it has been found necessary also to engage cautiously in Arab–Islamic issues internationally as a practical means to neutralize political challenge willing to exploit a co-religionist dimension. In addition, such cautious engagement has been used to secure international support over matters deemed vital to Indonesia's interests. However, Islam does not provide a natural meeting ground between Indonesia and other states. Indonesia prefers to keep the Arab–Islamic world at a distance, because Islam remains a divisive symbol and force within the Republic, the more to be feared because of its international resurgence.

Notes

1. Ruth McVey, "Faith as the Outsider: Islam in Indonesian Politics", in James P. Piscatori, *Islam in the Political Process* (Cambridge: Cambridge University Press, 1983), p. 200; see also Harold Crouch, "Indonesia", in Mohammed Ayoob (ed.), *The Politics of Islamic Reassertion* (London: Croom Helm, 1981) and H. J. Benda, "Continuity and Change in Indonesian Islam", *Asian and African Studies: Annual of the Israel Oriental Society,* 1 (1965), and Michael Leifer, *Indonesia's Foreign Policy* (London: Allen and Unwin, 1983).

2. 'We are Moslems, myself included — a thousand pardons my Islamism [*sic*] is far from perfect — but if you open up my breast, and look at my heart, you will find it none other than Islamic,' *Lahirnja Pantjasila* (*The Birth of Pantjasila*): *An Outline of the Five Principles of the Indonesian State.* President Soekarno's Speech. (Ministry of Information, Republic of Indonesia, Jakarta, 1952), pp. 24–5.

3. Ibid., p. 28.

4. Ali Sastroamijoyo, *Milestones on My Journey,* edited by C. L. M. Penders (St. Lucia: University of Queensland Press, 1979), p. 289.

5. See Ide Anak Agung Gde Agung, *Twenty Years of Indonesian Foreign Policy 1945–1965* (The Hague: Mouton, 1973), p. 513.

6. "Indonesia and the Islamic Charter", *Monthly Review,* Centre for Strategic and International Studies, Jakarta (November–December 1972), 7.

7. *Impact International,* London (22 May–11 June 1981), 9.

8. Ibid., p. 7. Note also his remarks in *Far Eastern Economic Review* (15 December 1978).

9. McVey, "Islam in Indonesian Politics", p. 205.

10. The *pici* is not an exclusively Muslim symbol. It has long been associated also with the secular Indonesian Nationalist Party (PNI).

11. See Leo Suryadinata and Sharon Siddique (eds.), *Trends in Indonesia II* (Singapore: Singapore University Press, 1981), p. 49.

12. Sharon Siddique, "Contemporary Islamic Developments in ASEAN", in *Southeast Asian Affairs 1980* (Singapore: Institute of Southeast Asian Studies, 1980), 90.
13. See Hans H. Indorf and Astri Suhrke, "Indochina: The Nemesis of ASEAN?" in *Southeast Asian Affairs 1981* (Singapore: Institute of Southeast Asian Studies, 1981), 63.
14. *The Military Balance 1980–1981*, International Institute for Strategic Studies, London (1980), p. 106.
15. For a discussion of the ambiguity in attitudes toward Israel, see Franklin B. Weinstein, *Indonesian Foreign Policy and the Dilemma of Dependence* (Ithaca: Cornell University Press, 1976), pp. 125–30.

59

Indonesia's Dilemmas of Engagement with China

The concept of engagement is both ambiguous and alien as a criterion for assessing Indonesia's changing relationship with China. It is replete with alternative meanings in the English language and, more to the point, does not have an equivalent in Indonesia's vernacular lexicon of foreign policy. In Jakarta, the concept of engagement with reference to China has entered into the discourse of international relations because it has been employed by the government in the United States to describe its policy towards the People's Republic. Indonesia's policy towards China fits within America's parameters only up to a point, however. It differs from them in one very important respect. The underlying objective is to try to influence the external conduct of China and not the way in which the People's Republic orders its domestic politics.

Reprinted in abridged form from Michael Leifer, "Indonesia's Encounters with China and the Dilemmas of Engagement", in *Engaging China: The Management of an Emerging Power,* edited by Alastair Iain Johnston and Robert S. Ross (London and New York: Routledge, 1999), pp. 87–108, by permission of the publisher.

Indonesia's policy towards China has also been driven in part by very different considerations to those of its two closest regional neighbours and partners, Malaysia and Singapore. Indonesia's position is distinguished, above all, by an incipient geopolitical rivalry with China which does not obtain in the cases of Malaysia and Singapore. That rivalry has its roots in Indonesia's foreign policy elite's sense of standing and entitlement within Southeast Asia based on an extensive geographic scale, a strategic location, a large population as well as on a national revolutionary tradition. It has been based also on an economic promise which has been set back dramatically from the second half of 1997. That prerogative stance has been combined, in some contradiction, with a sense of national vulnerability arising from the fissiparous physical and social condition of the archipelagic state which has been the source of a shared concern with its close regional neighbours about the hegemonic potential and intent of a rising China. That concern has its source also in Indonesia's experience of past encounters with China which has generated an adverse perspective of the People's Republic and which has informed the practice of engagement.

Indonesia's version of engaging China has been distinguished in the main by participation in multilateral dialogues with a view to encouraging the government in Beijing of the advantages of regional cooperation and good citizenship. It has also been supplemented by a limited measure of balance of power practice. Indonesia's political reopening to China after a break in direct diplomatic ties of some twenty-three years has never been envisaged as sufficient in itself to cope with the rising power and influence of the People's Republic. The break and restoration of diplomatic ties occurred during the long tenure of President Suharto which came to an end in May 1998. His resignation from office against a background of economic adversity and political turmoil, and his succession by his Vice-President, Dr B. J. Habibie, has not made any appreciable difference in national outlook and policy towards China.

Dilemmas of Engagement

For Indonesia, the restoration of diplomatic relations with China in August 1990 may be construed as a form of engagement without explicit employment of that concept. Direct diplomatic contact was seen as a way of becoming better informed about the People's Republic, although the linguistic skills of Indonesia's embassy staff in Beijing have been limited. Indeed, within Indonesia, the teaching of Chinese language and the use of its characters remain tightly restricted. As indicated above, from the mid-1980s, the lack of direct diplomatic contact with Beijing was considered to be an impediment to Indonesia promoting a resolution of the Cambodia conflict and also to its assumption of the chair of the Non-Aligned Movement. It is doubtful, however, if much more was anticipated of the restored relationship by way of securing China's practical endorsement of Indonesia's vision of regional order. This vision had been articulated by ASEAN's foreign ministers in November 1971 in a collective commitment to make Southeast Asia a "Zone of Peace, Freedom and Neutrality" (ZOPFAN) which would be "free from any manner of interference by outside powers." This statement had been precipitated by the People's Republic's assumption of China's seat in the United Nations in October with Indonesia abstaining in the decisive vote. It was a declaratory way of announcing to external powers that the ASEAN states reserved the exclusive right to define the terms of their own regional order and was directed, among others, at China. Indeed, for Indonesia, ASEAN has always been regarded as a political shield of a kind against an assertive China.

Despite mixed feelings among ASEAN's governments about the utility and appropriateness of ZOPFAN, it has become part of the official security doctrine of Indonesia and its regional partners. Although China has been supportive of that doctrine in principle, it has not been willing to endorse all of ASEAN's expressions of its application. For example, China, together with the United States, raised practical objections to the terms of a Southeast Asian Nuclear Weapons-Free Zone (SEANWFZ) Treaty concluded by the ASEAN states in December 1995 which was represented as integral to the realization of ZOPFAN. Although China has encouraged ASEAN's role as a vehicle for promoting multipolarity in Asia-Pacific within which it is obliged to cope with troubling relationships with the United States and Japan, the Association has not made any headway in persuading Beijing to moderate its irredentist agenda. Moreover, within ASEAN there are differences of strategic perspective towards China with Thailand, for example, more concerned about Vietnam's intentions within Indo–China and willing to rely on China's regional countervailing power as a check to its possible ambitions. For this reason, in part, ASEAN has not been a robust vehicle of engagement to the extent of being able to effect a substantive change in China's conduct. For example, ASEAN did not take a collective stand on Vietnam's behalf in an oil-drilling dispute with China in March/April 1997 in contested waters between Danang and Hainan Island.[1]

Nonetheless, ASEAN has demonstrated some utility in its collective engagement with China to Indonesia's satisfaction. For example, ASEAN and China have begun a series of annual security dialogues at the level of senior officials. It was at the first of these dialogues held in Hangzhou in April 1995 that the ASEAN side made known its strong objections to China's seizure of Mischief Reef. The outcome was a political accommodation in form by China in the context of its acute tensions with the United States and Japan with an evident temporizing for a time over any further pressing of its maritime claims by show of force.[2] Such a response may be judged to have been a success of a kind, albeit determined by China's assessment of the disadvantages of driving ASEAN into a united front against its interests. For Indonesia, however, ASEAN has served in the main as a quasi-familial undertaking in cooperative security from which China is excluded as a non-regional state. Indonesia has also supported the progressive enlargement of ASEAN to include all other Southeast Asian states, including those which have been at odds with China and those over which China is seen to enjoy undue influence. To this end, Vietnam became a member in July 1995 and Myanmar and Laos joined in July 1997, with Cambodia's entry being postponed because of an intervening violent *coup* which was a source of acute political embarrassment. Despite its limitations as a diplomatic community, an enlarged ASEAN, speaking with one voice, has been regarded in Jakarta as likely to be a more effective instrument for managing relations with a China regarded with apprehension and some foreboding. Indonesia has also suggested expanding ASEAN cooperation "to include a security dimension," without pressing its regional partners on the matter.[3]

In its limited engagement of China, Indonesia is faced with a dilemma not experienced by other regional partners within ASEAN. Indonesia shares a mirror image with China in its view of its rightful place within its regional environment. In geopolitical terms, there is a sense in which they may both be described as "middle kingdoms," and therefore natural geopolitical rivals within an East Asia incorporating a fused Northeast and Southeast Asia, especially since the end of the Cold War. For its part, at least until its economic tribulations from late 1997, Indonesia has sought to occupy the role of prime manager of regional order within Southeast Asia; a call for a greater assertiveness to that end was endorsed by members of its foreign policy establishment at a seminar in 1988 to commemorate the fortieth anniversary of Mohammad Hatta's seminal statement.[4] Indonesia's initiative to restore diplomatic relations with China was one expression of that greater self-assertiveness in foreign policy, but it was taken in the light of changes in the regional balance or distribution of power seen to be working to the advantage of the People's Republic. To that extent, there was evident interest in cooperating with like-minded governments which argued for trying to incorporate China constructively within a post-Cold War regional order based on shared norms of interstate conduct. The problem for Indonesia has been how to reconcile such incorporation with its own long-standing sense of regional entitlement. Such a perspective rules out an intervening role for external powers, especially for a territorially dissatisfied and menacing China which is not regarded as a resident Southeast Asian state.

It was with this dilemma in mind that in May 1993 in Singapore, Indonesia joined in an unprecedented joint meeting of ASEAN's senior officials and their counterparts from dialogue partners among the industrialized states which participated in the Association's annual Post Ministerial Conference (ASEAN-PMC). At its fourth summit in January 1992, ASEAN's heads of government had decided to address regional security cooperation through "external dialogue." In May 1993, in Singapore, the senior officials recommended extending the ASEAN-PMC with security in mind to include, among other countries, China and Russia. Indonesia was among a number of governments represented which exhibited some nervousness about extending the multilateral dialogue beyond the familiar context of the Western-aligned grouping. In the event, Indonesia's representatives were persuaded of the merits of trying to encapsulate China within a structure of relations which would include the United States and Japan as well as ASEAN. At a special dinner meeting in Singapore the following July, Indonesia's Foreign Minister, Ali Alatas, together with seventeen counterparts, including China's Foreign Minister, Qian Qichen, agreed to inaugurate the ASEAN Regional Forum (ARF) as a multilateral security dialogue.[5]

By the time the ARF had convened for its first working session in Bangkok in July 1994, an institutional change had occurred within Asia Pacific Economic Cooperation (APEC), a multilateral forum set up in 1989 to promote greater regional free trade and investment to which Indonesia and China were both parties. As a result of an initiative by President Clinton in mid-1993, annual meetings of its heads of government were convened after the regular meeting of its finance ministers. With this change in format, APEC acquired an enhanced significance and an informal security relevance given the opportunity for heads of government to address matters of mutual concern in private conversation. President Suharto did not have any qualms about participating. Indeed, he volunteered Bogor as the venue for the second APEC summit in 1994. APEC registered the dynamism of the time among the economies of Asia-Pacific and the incentive and likely constraining influence of interdependence for a country like China with pressing domestic economic priorities. APEC was therefore seen as an underpinning complementary structure to the ARF which was viewed as the security analogue of APEC. Indonesia went along with this cooperative approach to regional security which well fitted its declared philosophy of foreign policy, but with the ARF constituted geographically on a far more extensive basis than ASEAN.

Indonesia accepted the logic of employing the vehicle of multilateral security dialogue underpinned by institutionalized economic cooperation as a way of playing on China's sense of self-interest. In order to accelerate the momentum of economic development, the official view in Beijing has been that a stable regional environment is required. Indonesia has been encouraged by the extent to which the ARF is itself predicated on the security model and experience of ASEAN and to a degree by China's willing and sustained participation in inter-sessional dialogues on confidence-building, however limited their practical accomplishments. At issue for Indonesia, however, has been a concern that in engaging with China through the ARF, ASEAN may come to lose its distinct and distinctive identity and become subordinate to the wider Asia-Pacific multilateral enterprise which could then serve as the equivalent of a "Trojan horse" for the intervening attentions of external powers. In other words, the price of engaging China may be at the expense of Indonesia's exclusivist vision of regional order. That view has also been reinforced by the way in which, so far, China's participation within the ARF has not appeared to have affected the steely rectitude with which it has asserted its irredentist agenda in the South China Sea.

For Indonesia, what passes for engagement is both a process and a goal. The process has been expressed in the restoration of diplomatic relations and participation with China in multilateral enterprises within the Asia-Pacific. That process may be seen as an attempt to promote an entanglement on China's part because of the expectation that self-interest, both economic and security, will influence its conduct to Indonesia's advantage. Such an entanglement would seem directly related to the goal of engagement which has not been articulated explicitly but which may be inferred as an attempt to secure China's respect for norms of state conduct that have come to distinguish the collective culture of ASEAN and which serve the cause of a stable regional order. That said, Indonesia's government is not naive about the limitations of engagement through multilateral security dialogue within the ARF. Its salutary experience of frustration in the workshops on the South China Sea as well as concern over the incipient conflict of maritime interests with China have served to confirm an underlying apprehension which has not been assuaged by the experience of engagement. In addition, Indonesia has not come to terms with the prospect of China being able to play a leading role in Southeast Asian affairs through the vehicle of engagement.

Supplementing Engagement

Indonesia cannot be described as an enthusiastic advocate of engagement with China. The decision by President Suharto to restore diplomatic relations did not express a full consensus on the part of the foreign policy elite with evident misgivings registered by the military establishment which constitutes its dominant part. Moreover, there was a grudging quality about the response of Indonesia's Department of Foreign Affairs to the advent of the ARF within which the Republic would have to cope with the diplomatic weight of the three major Asia-Pacific powers, including China. With those reservations in mind, it is important to take note of the measure of change in Indonesia's regional security policy, albeit without any declared change in principle.

Outright containment of China has never been considered a realistic proposition by Indonesia. Indeed, its defence establishment would be quite inadequate for such an ambitious undertaking. The Republic's security doctrine has been overwhelmingly inward-looking, with its navy geared primarily to coastal defence. It has been noted that, with the possible exception of the Philippines, "Indonesia still affords less attention to external security than probably any other state in Southeast Asia."[6] Moreover, it was pointed out in 1997 by the Department of

Defence and Security that "in the medium-term instability will tend to be caused by internal rather than external factors."[7] That said, limited measures of collective external defence have been entered into by way of compensation for military weakness. For example, an initial irritation with Singapore for concluding a memorandum of understanding on military access with the United States in November 1990 gave way to a common outlook. The government in Jakarta speedily came to terms with the underlying intent of providing limited facilities to offset its significant loss in the Philippines as a way of helping to sustain America's military deployment in the region. Indonesia followed up with an offer of limited repair and port visit facilities at the headquarters of its Eastern Fleet in the port of Surabaya.[8] Whatever the view, in principle, of the undesirability of major external powers playing a role in Southeast Asian affairs, the United States was judged to be a necessary informal defence partner as the only countervailing force capable of balancing a rising China.

A more striking example of Indonesia's conversion to the merits of the balance of power has been registered in the security agreement concluded with Australia in December 1995, to the surprise of the Republic's Department of Foreign Affairs as well as that of its ASEAN partners. The accord, which exhibits the spirit of an alliance, states *inter alia* that the two parties will consult "in the case of adverse challenges to either party or to their common security interests and, if appropriate, consider measures which might be taken either individually or jointly and in accordance with the processes of each party."[9] The terms of the treaty would seem to violate the traditional tenets of Indonesia's foreign policy as well as to be out of keeping with the spirit of multilateral security dialogue which both Indonesia and Australia had viewed as a prime vehicle for engagement. Moreover, the treaty had been concluded within only months of President Suharto vacating the chair of the Non-Aligned Movement; his tenure having been represented as one of the concluding triumphs of his long rule. In that respect, the treaty may be viewed as the most significant break in continuity in Indonesia's foreign policy since the late President Sukarno embarked on his ill-fated axis with China in the mid-1960s. It is important to note that, for Indonesia, the decision to conclude the treaty was made by President Suharto in great secrecy in much the same way as he had made the decision to restore diplomatic relations with China.

Indonesia's primary motivation for concluding the agreement with Australia was to institutionalize the changing dynamics of the bilateral relationship. However, China's new-found strategic latitude and rising power is believed to have played some part in Jakarta's change of course.[10] The security agreement with Australia does not have the potential for transforming Indonesia's defence capability with China's maritime assertiveness in mind but it serves to enhance it to a degree, as well as communicating an important political point to Beijing. In addition, the agreement has provided an additional linkage in defence ties with the United States with which direct defence cooperation and sales had become less reliable because of the interposing issue of East Timor. Such additional linkage was indicated in July 1996 when Australia stepped up its defence cooperation with the United States.

The bilateral security agreement between Indonesia and Australia did not in itself repudiate the ARF process. Indeed, in July 1996, Indonesia's capital served as the venue for its third working session. At issue, however, is the utility of the ARF and its related processes in an undeclared role of seeking to restrain regional assertiveness on China's part. By concluding an unprecedented security agreement with Australia, Indonesia's former president indicated his reservations about engagement through the vehicle of the ARF and conveyed a willingness to commit his government to complementary undertakings with national security in mind. Moreover, within days of concluding this accord in December 1995, President Suharto backed a proposal by Singapore's Prime Minister, Goh Chok Tong, at the meeting of ASEAN's heads of government in Bangkok that India should become a dialogue partner of the Association and also, by implication, a member of the ARF on the grounds that it would provide an element of balance to China.

A more conspicuous signal was communicated by Indonesia to China through unilateral action. Indonesia could not have failed to have noted, with some concern, China's use of military display in March 1996 in the Taiwan Strait with the object of exercising an intimidating influence on the island's presidential elections. Limited steps had already been taken for greater surveillance and protection of the Natunas and their waters by increasing air patrols from the main island of Greater Natuna and by augmenting its small garrison. In August 1997, Indonesia ordered twelve Russian Sukhoi SU-30K fighters which, according to its Air Force Planning Director Air Vice-Marshall Richard Haryono, would be deployed to assist in the maritime defence of the Natuna Islands.[11] In the previous September, Indonesia's armed forces had engaged in a conspicuous military display through combined military exercises in and around the Natuna Islands involving nearly 20,000 armed servicemen supported by fifty-four aircraft and twenty-seven naval vessels.

Irrespective of the efficacy of these operations, the largest of their kind ever staged in the Republic, it was an attempt to demonstrate Jakarta's resolve and willingness to use military force should its national resources be subject to challenge. At the time, one well-informed Indonesian commentator explained that the Republic's officials had "begun to reappraise this policy of engagement which they adopted from their neighbours" because of the growing evidence that China was "not going to be deterred" from pursuing its regional territorial ambitions. He went on to suggest that the Republic's "wariness does not mean it will deviate from a policy of constructively engaging China. But it reveals the country's growing assertiveness in shaping security arrangements in the Asia-Pacific region."[12] Moreover, it seemed more than coincidental that during the period in which the combined exercises were being conducted, Indonesia's Foreign Minister Ali Alatas was willing to receive his Taiwanese counterpart John Chang, albeit disclaiming any official status for the meeting.

This meeting provoked Chinese protest in the light of Beijing's sensitivity over President Lee Teng-hui's controversial presence in the United States the previous June and also his so-called "vacation" visit to Indonesia in February 1994. In August 1996, President Suharto had taken the unusual step of commenting publicly on the prospect of China becoming a threat to Asia, at least in economic terms, explaining that he was "concerned that it may dominate the global market with its economic power which is capable of producing low-priced goods."[13] Indeed, it had been President Suharto's astonishment at the pace and extent of China's economic development during his visit in November 1990 and his attendant concern about its regional implications, as well as recognition of the economic opportunities involved, that had influenced his government to support initiatives within ASEAN for a wider framework for regional security dialogue beyond the limited bounds of the Association.

It should be pointed out that the underlying reserve towards China on Indonesia's side has not obstructed the development of a working relationship of a kind. Reciprocal visits of senior political and military figures have taken place. Coincidentally or not, Major-General Prabowo Subianto, then Commander of Indonesia's Special Forces and President Suharto's son-in-law, was present in Beijing concurrently with the onset of the combined military exercises in and around the Natuna Islands but without attracting hostile attention. Moreover, Foreign Minister Ali Alatas and State Secretary Moerdiono were invited to attend the ceremonies marking the reversion of sovereignty of Hong Kong to China at the end of June 1997. Trade has been a rising factor in the relationship with its two-way value put at around US$3.23 billion in 1995, with a small surplus in Indonesia's favour, compared with only US$232 million in 1984.[14] Despite presidential encouragement for increased trade relations, Indonesia's misgivings about China rise regularly above the surface, as they did when Foreign Minister Ali Alatas appeared before a Commission of Indonesia's Parliament in September 1996. He registered national concerns about its maritime assertiveness, while expressing hope that the People's Republic's participation within the ARF would have a moderating influence.[15] For its part, China has gone out of its way to strengthen the bilateral relationship. For example, US$200 million in export credit facilities has been extended, in addition to US$400 million in stand-by loans as part of an IMF rescue package. In addition to avoiding any impression of interfering in Indonesia's internal affairs over the predicament of its ethnic-Chinese community, forbearance has been shown at visits by senior figures from Taiwan where the matter at hand has been trade and investment. Such forbearance was displayed in January 1998 when Taiwan's Prime Minister Vincent Siew visited Jakarta.

The Limits of Engagement

Indonesia's post-Cold War relationship with China has been conducted on the basis of evident misgivings and within a context of national limitations. Irrespective of the Republic's long-standing sense of regional entitlement, it is not capable of embarking unilaterally on a policy towards China which would be able to keep the People's Republic at a distance and so assuage deep-seated anxieties about its mid- to long-term intentions. Indeed, President Suharto's decision to restore diplomatic relations reflected, in part, a pragmatic recognition of the political utility of direct communications with the government in Beijing as the Cold War was coming to an end. Beyond a diplomatic opening as a form of engagement, Indonesia was persuaded, albeit with some reluctance, of the complementary merits of encapsulating China within the framework of a multilateral regional security dialogue in an attempt to influence its external behaviour.

Indonesia had objected strongly nearly a quarter of a century before to Malaysia's proposal for the neutralization of Southeast Asia based on the guarantees of the major powers, including China. It had been argued in Jakarta that such a proposal would take the management of regional order out of the hands of its resident states and allocate virtual policing powers to those from outside. It was an alternative to neutralization in the classical sense that in 1971 ASEAN's foreign ministers were persuaded to endorse the alternative ZOPFAN concept which was in keeping with Indonesia's regional vision.[16]

The ARF, to which Indonesia has been a party from the outset, has been based on ASEAN's model of regional security. However, its far more extensive geographic remit threatens the integrity of the ZOPFAN concept because it holds out the prospect of ASEAN's prerogative role becoming subordinate within the multilateral enterprise and with it the loss to Indonesia of a valued diplomatic centrality reflected symbolically in the location of ASEAN's Secretariat in Jakarta. Accordingly, the endorsement of the ARF has represented a pragmatic accommodation to the change in regional strategic circumstances attendant on the end of the Cold War, and especially the disturbing emergence of a new distribution of power to the apparent advantage of China. A compelling argument in favour of the ARF was not only that it would locate China within a multilateral structure of dialogue with the prospect of influencing its external conduct. It was maintained correspondingly that the collateral participation of the United States would encourage its continuing post-Cold War interest in the region as a factor in the regional balance. To that extent, Indonesia was disposed to acquiesce in the extension of cooperative security arrangements beyond the ambit of Southeast Asia because they would incorporate a balance of power factor with China in mind. Such acquiescence did not register strong enthusiasm for engagement in the sense articulated in Washington.

Indonesia has sustained its long-standing declaratory commitment to an "independent and active foreign policy" which is fully compatible with its involvement in both the ASEAN and ARF versions of cooperative security. There has been a measure of revision in Jakarta's practice, however, in the form of limited collective defence measures complementary to the process of engagement, while unilaterally asserting a determination to protect national assets against Chinese predatory intent. The purchasing order for advanced Russian fighter aircraft in August 1997 should be viewed in that light. Naval access facilities granted to the United States and the security treaty with Australia are indications also of how Indonesia has sought to mix a measure of balance of power policy with that of engagement in managing its relations with China without being a party to any overt acts of containment.

China is not perceived as an imminent security threat in Jakarta, but it is viewed as casting a growing shadow which has begun to encroach on the periphery of Indonesia's archipelagic and strategic bounds. For the time being, engagement as a way of trying to encourage China in cooperative practice serves economic and, up to a point, security interests. Moreover, it is not deemed to be costly in political terms. For its part, China has responded positively up to a point. Stereotypes of China die hard in Jakarta, however, and the displays of regional good citizenship by government in Beijing have not served to dispel them. For Indonesia's foreign policy elite, engaging China is a stratagem undertaken without any deep-seated conviction in its merits and also without much enthusiasm for its outcome.

Acknowledgements

In writing this chapter I have benefited, in particular, from the helpful comments of Alan Dupont and Yuen Foong Khong.

Notes

1. See Michael Richardson, "China–Vietnam Dispute Revives Regional Fears", *International Herald Tribune*, 14 April 1997.
2. Note the revival of maritime assertiveness in the first half of 1997 with the establishment by China of hut-like structures on Scarborough Shoal to the north of the Spratly Islands and the passage of Chinese warships close to Philippines-occupied islands in the Spratly group. See *The Economist*, 24 May 1997.
3. See *The Policy of the State Defence and Security of the Republic of Indonesia 1997* (Department of Defence and Security, Jakarta, 1997), p. 4.
4. See Michael Leifer, *Indonesia's Foreign Policy* (London: George Allen & Unwin, 1983), p. xv and *passim*, and *The Jakarta Post*, 6 September 1988.
5. For an account of the origins and role of the ARF, see Michael Leifer, *The ASEAN Forum. Extending ASEAN's model of regional security*, Adelphi Paper No. 302, International Institute for Strategic Studies, London, 1996.

6. See Alan Dupont, "Indonesian Defence Strategy and Security: Time for a Rethink?", *Contemporary Southeast Asia*, Vol. 18, No. 3, December 1996. For an official public statement of Indonesia's defence doctrine, see *Policy of the State Defence and Security of the Republic of Indonesia, 1997*, and Robert Lowry, *The Armed Forces of Indonesia* (St Leonards, Australia: Allen & Unwin, 1996). For an account of Indonesia's order of battle involving fewer than 300,000 military personnel (excluding police and reserves) out of a population of around 200 million with a responsibility for defending a distended archipelago with sovereign jurisdiction over an area of land and sea of almost ten million square kilometres, see *The Military Balance* (London: The International Institute for Strategic Studies, 1997/98), pp. 179–81.

7. *Policy of the State Defence and Security of the Republic of Indonesia, 1997*, p. 12.

8. For an Indonesian interpretation of this security burden-sharing exercise, see Jusuf Wanandi, "ASEAN's China Engagement: Towards Deeper Engagement", *Survival*, autumn 1966, p. 120.

9. The text of the treaty has been reprinted in Desmond Ball and Pauline Kerr, *Presumptive Engagement. Australia's Asia-Pacific Security Policy in the 1990s* (St Leonards, Australia: Allen & Unwin, 1996), Appendix 5. See also Rizal Sukma, "Indonesia's *Bebas-Aktif* Foreign Policy and the 'Security Agreement' with Australia", *Australian Journal of International Affairs*, Vol. 51, No. 2, 1997.

10. See the discussion in Bob Lowry, *Australia–Indonesia Security Cooperation: For Better or Worse*, Strategic and Defence Studies Centre, Working Paper No. 299 (Australian National University, Canberra, August 1996), and also in Alan Dupont, "The Australia–Indonesia Security Agreement", *Australian Quarterly*, Vol. 68, No. 2, 1996.

11. *The Australian*, 6 August 1997.

12. Rizal Sukma, "Indonesia Toughens China Stance", *Far Eastern Economic Review*, 5 September 1996.

13. In a rare interview in Jakarta to the Japanese publication *Nihon Kezai Shimbun* reprinted by *Agence France Presse*, Jakarta, 14 August 1996.

14. See *Jakarta Post*, 10 September 1996.

15. See *Suara Pembaruan*, 12 September 1996.

16. See the discussion in Leifer, *Indonesia's Foreign Policy*, pp. 147–54.

Vietnam, Brunei, the Philippines, and Thailand

INTRODUCTION

Leifer's writings also cover some other countries in Southeast Asia, namely Vietnam, Brunei, the Philippines, and Thailand, but the number is small. A selection of these writings have been put together in one section.

Leifer argued that Vietnam had a dilemma prior to the end of the Cold War. On one hand it would like to continue to occupy Cambodia, but on the other hand the Cambodian issue isolated Vietnam from the international community and drained Vietnamese resources. When the Soviet Union was no longer able to aid Vietnam, *Doi Moi* or the open door policy was introduced but because of its policy towards Cambodia, economic recovery was not attained. After the disintegration of the Soviet Union, Vietnam had no other choice but to reorient its foreign policy and adjust its policy towards the major powers and ASEAN (Ch. 60). The basic problem of Vietnam was its sense of vulnerability and in the post-Soviet era, Vietnam finally overcame this vulnerability, at least temporarily, and managed new relations with the major powers. Vietnam's predicament was its strained relations with China, its historical adversary (Ch. 61). In the post-Soviet era,

Vietnam had no alternative but to come to terms with its northern neighbour in order to improve domestic economy, and China was responsive to the Vietnamese overture because it would assume the role of the regional power. Nevertheless, the basic problem of vulnerability of Vietnam was not really resolved.

With regard to Brunei, Leifer correctly pointed out that its predicament on the eve of its independence was the nature of the Brunei Sultanate polity (Ch. 62). The interest of Brunei was interpreted "in terms of the narrow aristocratic group and their political beneficiaries". The undemocratic nature of the regime made the Sultanate unpopular in the international community. Even in the wake of independence, this predicament persisted. Leifer stated that, "the real political process in the sultanate is virtually a closed activity". This characteristic was also reflected in its foreign policy (Ch. 63). The Sultanate wanted to be left alone and without external intervention.

Leifer wrote a monograph on the Philippine claim to Sabah but never wrote a book or a major article on Philippine domestic politics proper. In his shorter article on the Philippines and Sabah (Ch. 64), Leifer examined the origins of the claim on Sabah and its relations with the domestic politics of the Philippines. Despite Marcos's gesture to resolve the dispute, the claim was not abandoned. On the contrary, it was intensified domestically. The so-called Corregidor Incident, the training of Muslims in Correigdor Island, which was believed to have been endorsed by Marcos and meant to subvert Sabah, was uncovered because of a mutiny. The revelation of this project caused deterioration in the Manila–Kuala Lumpur relationship, leading to the eventual rupture of diplomatic relations.

Leifer did not write much on Thailand. This volume includes his two short commentaries on this country, one written in 1965 and the other in 1993. It was well known that Thailand was ruled by the military in the late 1950s and 1960s. Field Marshal Sarit died and was succeeded by his deputy, Thanom Kittikachorn, who was also a general. Thanom tried to dissociate himself from the previous corrupt regime without much success (Ch. 65). In 1993, Thailand became more democratic. Leifer analysed the kingdom in early 1990s (Ch. 66), when it was returned to the civilian government led by Chuan Leekpai. Nevertheless, Leifer wondered if the Thai democracy would last as the Thai military had had a long history of political intervention, and it might not be satisfied to be kept away from politics.

60

Vietnam's Foreign Policy in the Post-Soviet Era
Coping with Vulnerability

Vietnam's foreign policy has been transformed almost beyond recognition within a relatively short span of time.[1] It has been driven by pragmatism at the expense of ideology in the interest of regime and national security. Both of these core goals were in some jeopardy by the mid-1980s and more so by the turn of the decade, with the Cold War ending and an attendant loss of external patronage. Revolutionary Vietnam had always enjoyed such patronage. The post-Soviet era has been distinguished by its conspicuous absence. For Vietnam, the central issue of foreign policy has been how to overcome an acute problem of vulnerability that had not been contemplated in April 1975 with the triumphal attainment of national unification.

Few states can match Vietnam's recent experience of falling from international grace. Lionized as a symbol of national liberation struggle,

Excerpted from Michael Leifer, "Vietnam's Foreign Policy in the Post-Soviet Era: Coping with Vulnerability", in *East Asia in Transition: Toward a New Regional Order,* edited by Robert S. Ross (Armonk, NY: M. E. Sharpe; Singapore: Institute of Southeast Asian Studies, 1995), pp. 267–92, by permission of the publisher.

it became a virtual diplomatic pariah within only a few years of reunification. Relative isolation during the early 1980s aggravated economic distress induced by dogma and made necessary a radical reversal of domestic course in mid-decade. Concurrent changes in the pattern of global politics reinforced a vulnerable condition and impelled the change of domestic course, with signal consequences for foreign policy. With the astounding loss of Soviet patronage, Vietnam's political leadership had little alternative but to come to terms fully with a national debility that threatened its political order. A foreign policy of regional and international accommodation became the only rational choice, despite a formal attachment to ideological virtues expressed, for example, in the name of the state, the Socialist Republic of Vietnam.

An important part of Vietnam's difficulties arose from miscalculating the so-called correlation of forces in deciding to invade Cambodia in December 1978.[2] That decision reflected a strategic perspective in which the security of Vietnam was tied closely to its ability to determine the political identity of neighboring Laos and Cambodia within an Indochinese domain. In the event, Vietnam failed to realize its strategic purpose. After more than a decade of costly military engagement, it was obliged to withdraw its forces from Cambodia and to abandon the government that it had installed in January 1979. It did so, ironically, for the very reason that had obliged the United States to withdraw from Vietnam: a loss of political will arising from domestic circumstances.

Vietnam, both as a revolutionary movement and as a state, had been instrumental in shaping the pattern of international politics in Southeast Asia for more than four decades. The Cold War provided the overall context for its role, particularly after the outbreak of hostilities in Korea in 1950. Vietnam's significance was that its potential for enforcing changes in political identity within Indochina became coupled to the prospect of far-reaching changes in the regional and global balances of power. The assumption, held above all in Washington, that a resolution of internal conflict in Indochina to communist advantage would have disturbing strategic consequences provided the rationale for a fruitless and costly military intervention.

The Communist Party of Vietnam had made a corresponding domino-like judgment. The military experience of confronting the French after the Pacific War had persuaded its leadership to incorporate all the countries of Indochina within a common strategic perspective. That perspective, expressed in a prerogative special relationship with

Laos and Cambodia, became invested with an imperative quality in the late 1970s as the changing pattern of Cold War politics disinterred a historical antagonism with China.[3] Moreover, Pol Pot's Cambodia came to be regarded as China's bridgehead of aggression in Indochina, which had to be eliminated in the interest of national security.

In its confrontation with France, Vietnam's Communist Party had been able to attract material support from China, proffered out of self-interest. In its confrontation with the United States, the party had enjoyed both Chinese and Soviet material benefaction in mixed measure as well as attracting wider international backing. Against China, the Soviet Union fulfilled the critical supporting role. As Vietnam's sole external patron of any substance, it provided access to material aid and countervailing power for more than a decade. Assistance from the Soviet Union and its Eastern European bloc allies, with some help from India, proved crucial after 1979. The ultimate loss of such access with the end of the Cold War, and then the disintegration of the Soviet Union and the failure to realize a compensating normalization with the United States, substantially diminished Vietnam's capacity to shape the regional pattern of power. Moreover, with the end of the Cold War, that pattern in Indochina lost its international significance, which Vietnam had used to advantage by exploiting major power rivalries. In consequence, the ruling party in Hanoi has come full circle to the circumstances of the Geneva Conference on Indochina of 1954, when the political interests of Vietnam were compromised as a result of major power accommodation. Vietnam has been obliged to fend for itself by forging new relationships with countries that were its prime adversaries during the Cambodian intervention.

The international settlement of the Cambodian conflict in Paris in October 1991 eased Vietnam's vulnerable condition, but did not overcome it. Its government still has to cope with an intimidating China, which seemed determined to chasten Vietnam for its political impertinence since reunification and to ensure that it knew and kept its subordinate regional place. As of this writing, a long-sought countervailing normalization of relations with the United States has been frustrated because of the sustained salience in U.S. domestic politics of the issue of American servicemen missing in action (MIAs) from the Vietnam War. Hanoi's considerable cooperation in searches for remains of American servicemen enabled President Clinton to withdraw objections to lending to Vietnam by multilateral institutions in July 1993. In February 1994, he lifted a trade and investment embargo that had been imposed on the entire country with the fall of Saigon in 1975. This important step toward normalization was coupled, however, with the condition that the establishment of diplomatic relations would require further progress on the MIA issue.

Confronting Vulnerability

As indicated above, the turning point in foreign policy for Vietnam was its Cambodia war.[4] Assuming that it was possible to reconcile priorities of external security and economic doctrine because of assurances of Soviet backing, Vietnam's Politburo committed the country to a punishing and ultimately fruitless ordeal. They failed to anticipate the international coalition that mobilized against their attempt to reshape the regional balance of power. Instead of being applauded as a benefactor for having rid Cambodia of a political pestilence, Vietnam found itself denounced at the United Nations for having violated the cardinal rule of the society of states. More seriously, its ruling party failed to calculate the prospect, pace, and likely consequences of political change within the Soviet Union until it was too late.[5]

By the mid-1980s, Vietnam's Communist Party was facing a crisis of confidence and legitimacy as the long-heralded economic promise of the revolution failed to materialize. A notable expression of political dissent was the establishment in the southern part of the country in May 1986 of the Club of Resistance Fighters by disgruntled military veterans. The party's radical solution to economic distress was to jettison its centralist planning model in favor of a market-based alternative under the guidance of a new and reformist general secretary, Nguyen Van Linh. The decision of its Sixth National Congress in December 1986 to adopt a policy of *Doi Moi*, or renovation, was an attempt to cope with economic failure and its political consequences in an increasingly uncertain international environment influenced by the impact of Mikhail Gorbachev's "new political thinking." In Hanoi, there was almost certainly the initial expectation that economic reform would not only counter material decline and political alienation but also permit the sustained pursuit of external security goals in Indochina. Preserving the regime established in Cambodia by force of arms in January 1979 appeared to remain a prime objective.[6] But by the Party's Seventh National Congress, which convened in June 1991, it had become impossible to reconcile those two priorities, a judgment registered in a toned-down assertion of a special relationship with the lesser states of Indochina.[7] The overriding priority of *Doi Moi* was impeded nonetheless by the problem of Cambodia, which came between Vietnam and a desirable full access to the international economy, which its coalition adversaries could deny. Cambodia had once been represented as the key to Vietnam's national security, with its post-invasion condition described as irreversible. Vietnam's involvement there became instead a fundamental obstacle to economic recovery, which was the only way to overcome an underlying problem of regime security. A declared unconditional withdrawal of troops from Cambodia in September 1989 eased relations with adversaries but failed to bring about a transformation of Vietnam's international position. Hanoi's insistence on preserving the administration implanted in Phnom Penh and denying roles in a political settlement to the Khmer Rouge and the United Nations led to an inconclusive outcome at an international conference in Paris in July–August 1989. In the meantime, the United States remained obdurate in tying normalization to Vietnam's active cooperation in promoting a Cambodian settlement, while the Soviet Union became a rapidly declining asset. In the circumstances, Vietnam was obliged to make a critical choice between internal and external priorities in favor of the former.

That choice was expressed in Vietnam's grudging acquiescence to a settlement of the Cambodian conflict, mediated by the United Nations Security Council, that it had previously resisted.[8] The terms of that settlement included participation by the Khmer Rouge in the Supreme National Council, a symbol of Cambodia's sovereignty that had been devised to circumvent the problem of power sharing among the country's four warring factions by delegating authority to the United Nations. The world body would assume a quasi-administrative role during a transitional period before elections to choose a new government. Such provisions diminished the status of the administration in Phnom Penh that had been set up in Vietnam's interest. However much the terms of the Cambodian peace settlement were resented, economic necessity reinforced by international isolation determined Vietnam's political choice. The long-held strategic priority of a special relationship with the lesser states of Indochina had to be relinquished, at least in the case of Cambodia. That with Laos could be sustained only through looser fraternal ties because Vietnam could not fulfill the obligations of a patron.

With the end of the Cold War, Indochina has ceased to enjoy its former strategic coherence, which Vietnam inherited from France. Nonetheless, geopolitical considerations will oblige Vietnam to maintain continuing interest in political change in both Cambodia and Laos, but with little early prospect of influencing it in either state. The more immediate practical priority of foreign policy has been to cope with a vulnerability rooted in problems of economic development.[9] Vietnam's leaders have been confronted with a choice similar to that faced by a bankrupt Indonesia in March 1966, when General Suharto assumed executive authority from President Sukarno. Indonesia chose the road of development based on a close engagement with the international capitalist economy but had the good fortune to attract the immediate support of the United States and Japan and the major international financial agencies. Indonesia was able also to take an early initiative in promoting a structure of regional reconciliation, the Association of Southeast Asian Nations (ASEAN), which could serve as a vehicle through which to influence the shape of regional order. Vietnam has not enjoyed such corresponding good fortune; it did not embark on market reforms with the full engagement in the international economy that Indonesia enjoyed, and it has still to assume membership in ASEAN. Moreover, Indonesia was not obliged to confront a major problem of national security. Vietnam, by contrast, has had to deal virtually unaided with an overshadowing and testy China, which, despite formal rapprochement, seems to want to settle an old political account in a way that leaves no doubt of the unequal nature of the bilateral relationship.

The fact of the matter is that Vietnam has ceased to count regionally in the way it once did. Foreign policy is dictated by the imperative of economic reform and employing its benefits to maintain a political monopoly for the Communist Party, which is seen as synonymous with upholding socialism and national independence. To that end, the Politburo in Hanoi has been obliged to behave in a pragmatic manner to the best of its limited ability. Regional acceptance has been encouraged by dissipation of an earlier fear of Vietnam and the specter of a reassertive China. The problem for Vietnam is that growing regional acceptance does not offer an opportunity to participate in a structure that might readily withstand China's blandishments. ASEAN has never aspired to become an alliance with a capability for projecting collective military power against a common adversary. Vietnam, with Laos, in acceding to ASEAN's Treaty of Amity and Cooperation in

Southeast Asia in Manila in July 1992, took an important symbolic step toward regional rehabilitation and ultimate membership. But that act of accession did not presage an expansion of a security regime as an alternative source of external countervailing power. To that extent, Vietnam's sense of vulnerability has been mitigated but not overcome.

At issue for the government in Hanoi is how to manage changes in international relationships required by imperatives of political economy. Before discussing those problems of management, it is pertinent to comment in passing on the subject of foreign policy itself.

For any country, foreign policy is a matter of internal debate whose participants and terms depend on the nature of the political system. In the case of Vietnam, that debate has never really reached the public domain. Moreover, Vietnam's Communist Party has enjoyed a remarkable record of concealing intramural contention and avoiding in the main the kind of political turbulence and purges that other fraternal parties have experienced. Analysis of alleged tension between pro-Soviet and pro-Chinese factions within the Politburo has never been particularly illuminating or rewarding, although it should not be discounted altogether.

During Vietnam's adjustment to the emerging post-Soviet era, there was certainly a debate about preserving the socialist model of economic development, which was won by reformers, who showed their strength with the political rehabilitation of Nguyen Van Linh in the office of Communist Party general secretary in December 1986. A more fundamental debate came to the fore at the turn of the next decade, reconciling economic reform with a forward policy in Indochina. One signal of the way in which that internal debate was resolved was the announcement at the Seventh National Congress in June 1991 of the resignation from office and from all party positions of Foreign Minister Nguyen Co Thach. Nguyen Co Thach had enjoyed a reputation as a Sinophobe, and his removal was interpreted as a necessary concession to Beijing in the interest of rapprochement on terms that could no longer be denied because of Vietnam's intrinsic vulnerability.

China's intentions have remained a matter of concern, but for the time being, vigorous debate on that dimension of foreign policy seems to have become muted. Vietnam's leaders have been obliged to come to terms with living under China's intimidating shadow without access to their accustomed countervailing power. A mitigating factor has been the assurance that the ruling party in Beijing has an undoubted interest in perpetuating a socialist regime in Hanoi, given the acute difficulties faced by its remaining fraternal partners in Pyongyang and Havana. Consequently, debate in Vietnam has been directed toward the internal political consequences of foreign economic policy. It expresses itself over the management of attendant external influences on domestic life, with concern registered in a strengthening of the state's internal security apparatus.

Notes

1. For indications of that transformation, see the report by Foreign Minister Nguyen Manh Cam to the National Assembly on December 11, 1991, in British Broadcasting Service (BBC), *Summary of World Broadcasts (SWB)*, FE/1259, pp. B/3–4, and the address to that body by the general secretary of Vietnam's Communist Party, Do Muoi, on September 19, 1992, in BBC, *SWB*, FE/1493, p. B/7. See also, "Ho Chi Minh's Thought — The Foundation of Vietnam's Foreign Policy," *Vietnam Courier* (Hanoi), no. 31 (May 1992).
2. It merits noting that in January 1979, Ha Van Lau, Vietnam's permanent representative to the United Nations, informed his Singaporean colleague: "In two weeks, the world will have forgotten the Kampuchean problem." Quoted in Kishore Mahbubani "The Kampuchean Problem: A Southeast Asian Perception," *Foreign Affairs*, Winter 1983/84, p. 410.
3. For a Vietnamese view, see *The Truth about Vietnam-China Relations over the Last Thirty Years* (Hanoi: Ministry of Foreign Affairs, 1979). See also Robert S. Ross, *The Indochina Tangle: China's Vietnam Policy 1975–1979* (New York: Columbia University Press, 1988); Anne Gilks, *The Breakdown of the Sino-Vietnamese Alliance, 1970–1979* (Berkeley, CA: Institute of East Asian Studies, University of California, 1992).
4. An excellent summary of the changing course of Vietnam's foreign policy may be found in Michael C. Williams, *Vietnam at the Crossroads* (London: Pinter Publishers for The Royal Institute of International Affairs, 1992), chap. 5. See also Michael Leiter and John Phipps, *Vietnam and Doi Moi: Domestic and International Dimensions of Reform*, Discussion Paper No. 35 (London: The Royal Institute of International Affairs, 1991).
5. See Leszek Buszynski, *Gorbachev and Southeast Asia* (London: Routledge, 1992).
6. The Political Report of the Sixth National Congress in December 1986 affirmed that consolidating and developing Vietnam's special relationship

with Laos and Cambodia was "a sacred duty and a task of strategic importance to the vital interests of independence, freedom and socialism in our own country and on the Indochinese peninsula as a whole." BBC, *SWB*, FE/8447, pp. C1/11.

7. The Political Report of the Seventh National Congress in June 1991 stated, "We will ceaselessly consolidate and develop the special relationship of solidarity and friendship between our party and people and the fraternal parties of Laos and Cambodia." BBC, *SWB*, FE/1109, pp. C1/11.

8. The full terms of the Cambodian settlement may be found in *Agreement on a Comprehensive Settlement of the Cambodia Conflict*, October 23, 1991, Cm 1786 (London: HMSO, December 1991).

9. For a discussion of those problems, see Borje Llunggren, ed., *The Challenge of Reform in Indochina* (Cambridge, MA: Harvard Institute for International Development, 1993).

61

Vietnam's Changing Relations with China

Fundamental to Vietnam's predicament in foreign policy has been its strained relationship with a neighboring and overshadowing China, which since the end of 1978 has turned on the issue of Cambodia. That tormented country served as the arena of indirect conflict between former allies over the balance of power in Indochina. China was prominent among Vietnam's adversaries in insisting that its occupation be liquidated and also that its political legacy be expunged. Virtually from the outset, Vietnam's policy toward Cambodia had been to offer concessions on military withdrawal in return for being able to consolidate the position of the government that it had brought into the country almost literally in the saddlebags of its army. Its effective military withdrawal from Cambodia by the end of September 1989 failed to satisfy its Chinese adversaries. They seemed determined then

Excerpted from Michael Leifer, "Vietnam's Foreign Policy in the Post-Soviet Era: Coping with Vulnerability", in *East Asia in Transition: Toward a New Regional Order,* edited by Robert S. Ross (Armonk, NY: M. E. Sharpe; Singapore: Institute of Southeast Asian Studies, 1995), pp. 267–92, by permission of the publisher.

that the government in Phnom Penh should be dismantled and that the Khmer Rouge should become a legitimate party to a political settlement.

The eventual political settlement to the Cambodian conflict, which was endorsed by an international conference that reconvened in Paris in October 1991, involved major concessions by Vietnam, but not a total abdication of its position. Innate weakness obliged it to tolerate the Khmer Rouge as a member of the symbolically sovereign Supreme National Council and the intervening quasi-administrative role of the United Nations Transitional Authority in Cambodia, or UNTAC, which was empowered to conduct general elections to determine the political future of the country. The incumbent government in Phnom Penh, albeit diminished in status, remained in place after UNTAC began its work in March 1992 without attracting Chinese protest. Indeed, UNTAC's failure to exercise the measure of supervision and control of key ministries required by its mandate provoked Khmer Rouge anger but not China's public displeasure.

China's reaction to the invasion of Cambodia had been to view Vietnam as a willing proxy of a menacing Soviet Union. Its limited but punitive military intervention in Vietnam in February 1979 was intended to convey a geopolitical message, which Vietnam has been obliged to take to heart in the post-Soviet era. Sino-Soviet rapprochement and the withdrawal of Soviet support from Vietnam brought about a revision of China's earlier view of the country as an oriental Cuba. In addition, the political distance from Vietnam demonstrated by the government in Phnom Penh and its deference to Prince, now King, Norodom Sihanouk further reduced Chinese concerns about the balance of power in Indochina. In mid-October 1991, just before the International Conference on Cambodia in Paris, the ruling Kampuchean People's Revolutionary Party convened in extraordinary congress, without participation by fraternal delegates, at which its name was changed to that of the Cambodian People's Party in apparent repudiation of its once-declared lineal descent from the ruling party in Hanoi. In fact, a practical compromise appeared to be accepted in Beijing whereby Vietnam relinquished control over Cambodia, while its implanted administration continued in place, with the Khmer Rouge in a legitimate but marginal role, all subject to United Nations supervision in the transitional period before national elections. The subsequent repudiation of those elections in May 1993 by the Khmer Rouge failed to attract China's support. China's government endorsed the political outcome of the election, a coalition of all Cambodian parties except the Khmer Rouge.

Whatever the misgivings of the government in Hanoi, the Paris settlement of October 1991 removed the burning issue of Cambodia from Sino-Vietnamese relations. A process of rapprochement set in train in the late 1980s appeared to culminate on November 10, 1991, with a meeting of party and state leaders in Beijing, at which agreements on trade and border cooperation were signed.[1] The meeting was represented as a high-level one rather than as a party-to-party occasion, which was symptomatic of an underlying coolness in the new relationship. Despite the apparent convergence of the interests of the two regimes, shocked by the course of events in Eastern Europe and determined to reconcile market economies with authoritarian politics, an underlying tension has remained.[2]

Problems in the relationship have arisen in acute form over territorial and maritime jurisdiction in the South China Sea. Vietnam had concealed its differences with China over competing claims to jurisdiction until after its unification, by which time China had assumed total control over the contested Paracel Islands.[3] Indeed, in 1958, Pham Van Dong, as prime minister of the Democratic Republic of Vietnam, had communicated his government's endorsement of all of China's territorial claims in the South China Sea. Vietnam's reversal of position in 1976 in contesting jurisdiction provoked strong comment in Beijing. China began to challenge Vietnam's measure of control over islands in the Spratly Archipelago in early 1988 — significantly, without arousing any active Soviet response — while Vietnam's diplomatic protests fell on deaf ears.[4]

In February 1992, the Standing Committee of China's National People's Congress adopted a new law on territorial waters and their contiguous areas that reasserted long-standing claims to maritime jurisdiction in the South China Sea and beyond.[5] This maritime initiative had implications for a number of regional states in dispute with China. However, in reasserting its claims, China has acted with a measure of discrimination directed against Vietnam. Its government has taken evident care to avoid direct confrontation with Brunei, Malaysia, and the Philippines, all of which have claims to some of the Spratly Islands. The promulgation of the new maritime law was followed by the occupation of an additional reef in the Spratly Archipelago, but territories claimed by Brunei, Malaysia and the Philippines were not affected. In addition, China has appeared to be attempting to exploit American-Vietnamese alienation. In May 1992, the Chinese authorities entered into a contract with the Denver-based Crestone Energy Corporation to explore for oil and natural gas in 25,000 square kilometers of what the Vietnamese claim is the Tu Chinh bank on the country's continental shelf, but which the Chinese maintain is part of the maritime domain of the Spratly chain. A Crestone spokesman was reported as saying that China had promised the use of naval power to protect the offshore exploration.[6] China pointedly chose to conclude the agreement with Crestone during a visit to Beijing by the former general secretary of Vietnam's Communist Party, Nguyen Van Linh. It also took place in the presence of an American diplomat, albeit one of junior status.

Li Peng paid a visit to Vietnam at the end of November 1992, the first by a Chinese prime minister since that Zhou Enlai in 1971. He made a series of conciliatory statements, stressing that both countries were engaged in socialist construction and that China would neither seek to fill any so-called regional vacuum nor seek to impose hegemony.[7] Despite the positive tone that Li Peng conveyed, the two governments were unable to reconcile any of their territorial differences. In March 1993, Nguyen Dy Nien, Vietnam's deputy foreign minister, revealed a continuing absence of progress over territorial differences despite the onset of negotiations between expert officials the previous October.[8] An agreement on basic principles for "the settlement of border territory issues" was concluded in October 1993, followed in November by the first visit to China by a Vietnamese head of state since that by Ho Chi Minh in 1959. However, President Le Duc Anh and his counterpart Jiang Zemin failed to signal any progress concerning their governments' competing claims to sovereignty. A return visit to Vietnam by President Jiang Zemin in November 1994 produced an agreement to set up a joint expert group to deal with rival claims to the Spratly Islands — without any indication of compromise on either side.

A Vietnam obliged to concentrate on economic reform has not been in any position to engage in military confrontation over territorial differences with a China that enjoys overwhelming advantages. Vietnam's military machine has fallen into disrepair and lacks in particular a naval and air force capability able to match that of China, which has begun to purchase SU-27 long-range jet fighters from Russia for probable deployment in the South China Sea from their base on Hainan Island and enhanced its naval and amphibious capability.[9]

Further potential for military deployment into the South China Sea was indicated with the publication by *Yomiuri Shimbun* in August 1993 of a satellite photograph showing a Chinese airfield on Woody Island, the largest territory in the disputed Paracels group.[10]

Vietnam's armed forces leadership has been disinclined to make public China's acts of assertiveness in the South China Sea, preferring to engage in private communication through military attaches' offices. The foreign ministry in Hanoi has prevailed in the interbureaucratic squabble and has not allowed the country's case to go by default, despite its inability to advance it in any material sense. For example, in April 1993, the anniversary of national liberation was marked by Vice Premier Tran Duc Luong paying a well-publicized visit to the Spratly Islands and by a reassertion of sovereignty over both the Spratly and Paracel groups. In April 1994, Vietnam signed contracts with a consortium of American and Japanese companies led by Mobil for exploration in and adjoining westerly field within the area of China's claim to the *Tu Chinh* bank.

Contention over maritime jurisdiction has been only the most prominent of a number of issues that are symptomatic of the underlying tension in the Sino-Vietnamese relationship despite the formal reestablishment of party-to-party ties. Vietnam has been obliged to suffer Chinese interference in maritime traffic and oil drilling operations, consoling itself with the knowledge that Beijing is not out to destroy the regime in Hanoi, but only to demonstrate that regime's subordinate position. China has also intervened to limit Vietnam's burgeoning relationship with Taiwan by limiting the right of Taipei's flag carrier to fly to major cities. It has not, however, sought to constrain the scale of Taiwan investment.

China intimidates but also tolerates Vietnam. In the changed circumstances after the end of the Cold War, it would not be in China's interest to encourage the collapse of Vietnamese communist power into an Eastern European-like chaos. It suffices for the lesson of February 1979 to have been conspicuously learned — namely, that whereas France, Japan, the United States, and most recently the Soviet Union have been obliged to retreat back across the seas, China and Vietnam march together in perpetuity. On his assumption of the office of president of Vietnam in September 1992, General Le Duc Anh, a senior Politburo member, made a point of stressing publicly his government's interest in peaceful and friendly relations with China. He pointed out, "We need peaceful and friendly coexistence very much."[11] The problem for Vietnam is that it is not in a position to determine the terms of such peaceful and friendly coexistence. The fact that coexistence was used to describe the appropriate relationship is an indication of the continuing vulnerability of Vietnam in the post-Soviet era and the mixed quality of the postrapprochement ties with China. That coexistence has developed a working quality, however, is indicated by a series of agreements on economic and scientific cooperation, by a progressive opening of border crossings, and by China's being allowed to establish a consultate in Ho Chi Minh City.

Overcoming Vulnerability

Vietnam has emerged quite rapidly from a virtual pariah condition since the international resolution of the Cambodian conflict. That conflict brought to a head in particular a deterioration in relations between Vietnam and China, which had been precipitated by Hanoi's sense of betrayal at the nature and terms of Sino-American rapprochement in the early 1970s. The erstwhile Sino-Vietnamese alliance had been forged out of expediency in order to cope with a common threat from the United States. As such, it constituted a deviation from a historical pattern. Vietnam's prevailing experience has been one of resistance to and struggle with a one-time suzerain power whose Confucian culture it shared but against which it had long defined its national identity. Indeed, a formal and grudging relationship of deference to China had been broken only with the intervention of French colonialism in the latter part of the nineteenth century. Ho Chi Minh expressed authentic national priorities when, after the end of the Pacific War, he indicated his preference for the return of the French as a less objectionable alternative to the continued presence north of the sixteenth parallel of the rapacious army of General Chiang Kai-shek, which had been charged with taking the surrender of occupying Japanese forces. The antagonism with China, which came to a head over Cambodia and which was marked by a clash of arms, returned the relationship to one characteristic of past centuries. Moreover, during that conflict, China was able to exploit a conjunction of global and regional interests to Vietnam's disadvantage, which became acute when countervailing Soviet patronage was lost.

In the post-Soviet era, Vietnam no longer faces the problem of international isolation because of its disengagement from conflict in Cambodia. The relationship with China remains the most problematic, however, because of the intrinsic mistrust and inequality that distinguishes it and the two countries' immutable close proximity. At the end of the 1970s, China embarked with success on a program of economic modernization, which has been sustained through close engagement with the international economy, despite the bloodletting in Tiananmen Square in June 1989. Moreover, the end of the Cold War, with its evident effect on America's strategic perspective and deployments in East Asia, and the breakup of the Soviet Union have permitted the People's Republic a measure of latitude in regional affairs that is quite unprecedented since its establishment in 1949. Success in economic modernization has enabled China to embark on a military buildup that has enhanced its potential for force projection beyond its mainland into the South China Sea.[12] That buildup, however, justified in terms of replacing aging equipment, has been taking place at a time when China is not subject to any apparent external threat. Vietnam, in contrast, is not capable of matching China's growing military strength. Its budget cannot provide for corresponding modernization, let alone adequate provision for spare parts for its antiquated Soviet equipment. Opportunity has arisen for access to countervailing regional relationships, but access to countervailing power is another matter.

Under the circumstances, Vietnam has little alternative but to concentrate its efforts on rebuilding its economy as the most effective way to cope with vulnerability. Although perturbed by the fragile condition of the Cambodian peace process, the government in Hanoi has avoided any initiative that might appear to reinstate it as a party to the continuing conflict. There has been strong public condemnation of Khmer Rouge killings of Vietnamese residents in Cambodia, with corresponding pleas to the United Nations to take action to protect them. But in April 1993, at a dinner in Tokyo given by Japan's prime minister, Kiichi Miyazawa, Prime Minister Vo Van Kiet provided an unequivocal assurance that "Vietnam does not intend to again dispatch its army to Cambodia."[13] A resumption of power by the Khmer Rouge and a return to the situation of the late 1970s in which their forces engaged in murderous violations across the common border would create a problem of different order. However, the public remarks made in May 1993 by Vice Minister of Foreign Affairs Le Mai are also worth noting. He reiterated: "I resolutely emphasize that we will not walk into this trap. Vietnam will not repeat its Cambodian intervention in any circumstances."[14]

Vietnam's current options in foreign policy are limited, and a realistic single-minded attention has been given to economic priorities. That policy has not been without its domestic political risks. Market economics has revived the importance of Ho Chi Minh City, which has reverted to being Saigon in everything but name and could become a locus of power rivaling Hanoi. The easing of regulations that was required for economic liberalization has brought with it demands for political reform, with agitation growing among Buddhist monks, whose dissent has taken the form of periodic demonstrations. The ruling party has responded by tightening the apparatus of repression and has been unresponsive to appeals from human rights organizations. There is no doubt that there is a smoldering crisis of ideological confidence and authority within the Communist Party of Vietnam which is subject to a declining membership but is adamantly opposed to relaxing the reins of political control. Domestic stability, with obvious implications for foreign relations, has not been subject, so far, to even moderate disturbance. There have been no signs of the kind of challenge to political order experienced by the government in Beijing in June 1989. For the time being, the Communist Party as the only political organization holds on to its monopoly of power without great additional effort. Nonetheless, the underlying situation, distinguished by the momentum of economic activity, contains within it the seeds of fundamental political change, which deeply troubles a Politburo that has no alternative but to continue along the road of reform chosen in 1986.

Given the abrupt withdrawal of Soviet bloc benefaction, the progress of economic reform has been remarkable, despite a continuation of loss-making state enterprises, an antiquated bureaucracy, an inadequate legal system, and burgeoning corruption. Growth rates of around 8 percent GDP were registered in 1992 and 1993 and were close to 9 percent in 1994. Galloping inflation has been brought under control, and the value of the dong, which has long been freely convertible, has been strengthened and stabilized. Underpinning the economy have been exports of oil and rice, with Vietnam having gone in a short space of time from a rice deficit country to the third largest exporter in the world, behind the United States and Thailand. Until February 1994, trade and investment had been hampered by the American embargo. Nonetheless, Vietnam had been able to generate a modest trade surplus of around US$70 million in 1992, its first for decades, which was succeeded by a deficit of

US$300 million in 1993. A liberal foreign investment law, in operation since the late 1980s, has attracted major capital flows from Hong Kong, Taiwan, and South Korea in particular, and more recently from Japan, with overall commitments of US$10.9 billion made by the end of 1994. Significantly, the Primal Corporation of Brunei, with royal family backing, has indicated interest in large-scale investment in oil and natural gas exploration. Vietnam's target is to double living standards from an average per capita income of around US$200 by the turn of the century. Prime Minister Vo Van Kiet informed the National Assembly in December 1992 that the country required an additional infusion of US$40 billion to achieve this goal. The key to successful economic development is the repair and rehabilitation of the country's infrastructure, which has begun to be undertaken. But this priority can be fully addressed only with the active cooperation of the international financial institutions, which resumed lending in the latter part of 1993.

That cooperation was held up because of American objections. In the circumstances, Vietnam had no alternative but to wait patiently for a change in American position determined by domestic political considerations. Correspondingly, Vietnam has enjoyed limited scope for foreign policy initiatives beyond an expansion of ties, which have been actively sought. Long-standing fraternal ties with North Korea were not allowed to obstruct the establishment of diplomatic relations with South Korea, while the presence of a Palestinian diplomatic mission in Hanoi did not prevent matching relations with Israel. It is not without significance that both states enjoy a special link with the United States. In 1993, Prime Minister Vo Van Kiet visited Australia and New Zealand and then France, Germany, Britain, and Belgium, and a residual association with India was cultivated as both countries engaged in corresponding economic reform.

An assiduous courting of ASEAN governments has been maintained in the hope of demonstrating a growing convergence based on corresponding models of developmental authoritarianism and finding a welcome place in a regional network of international standing. On his return from the annual meeting of ASEAN's foreign ministers held in Singapore in July 1993, Nguyen Manh Cam indicated a regional receptiveness to Vietnam's early membership in the association.

Within ASEAN, the most problematic of relationships is likely to be that with Thailand, with which Vietnam has had a long-standing rivalry for influence over the trans-Mekong region that reached a flash point over Cambodia. In the late 1980s, Thailand began to engage in a forward economic policy within mainland Southeast Asia that reflected a newfound confidence based on developmental performance. That policy, expressed in the concept of a "Golden Peninsula," suggested hegemonic aspirations that caused concern in Hanoi. Thai investment has been welcomed along with that of other ASEAN countries, but Vietnam is not likely to tolerate being treated as a source of raw materials for Thai exploitation in the way that Burma and Cambodia have been abused. Correspondingly, there is no enthusiasm for Thailand's playing the role of exclusive economic interlocutor. Thai economic penetration of Cambodia and Laos must also be a matter of concern, but there are not direct countervailing economic measures available, especially in Cambodia, where the Vietnamese presence generates hostility. Thailand poses a problem for Vietnam, but it will be addressed by permitting a share of economic access within an extensive network of relationships.

Vietnam is not expected to be a disruptive factor in regional order in the remaining years of the twentieth century. It was once depicted with alarm as the Prussia of Southeast Asia, but it is no longer in a position to challenge the national sovereignty of its neighbors, and it has been evidently reluctant to engage in a clash of arms with China in response to encroachments in the Spratly Islands or its continental shelf. Vietnam's strategic vulnerability suggests that a better analogy now would be to think of it as the Finland of the region (recalling the way that Nordic state was overshadowed by the Soviet Union). With a population of around 70 million that is still rising, Vietnam is a weak state that is more likely to be influenced by the regional pattern of power than the other way around. Its ruling party, which associates its own survival with provision for national welfare, in much the same way as the ruling party in China does, is driven by the imperative of development, for which there is only one economic model in the post-Soviet era. Foreign policy has become primarily a matter of serving this necessary goal, which requires a welcoming open door to all those who can help in the development process. Accordingly, any discussion of Vietnam's wider regional interests and ambitions can only be somewhat academic. For the time being, its foreign policy begins and ends at home, with development the overriding imperative in the cause of underpinning national independence.

It has been indicated above that debate over foreign policy would seem to have been muted by the constricting circumstances in which

Vietnam has been placed in the post-Soviet era. Those circumstances are made up in particular of having China as a foreboding neighbor against whom a welcoming ASEAN, an opportunistic Japan, and a reluctant United States do not provide an alternative to a pragmatic accommodation. A policy debate would certainly revive should China again become actively assertive in the Spratly Islands or should the Khmer Rouge resume power in Cambodia. It would become most acute should a realignment occur between a Khmer Rouge–dominated Cambodia and a China still led by the political generation that sought to teach Vietnam a lesson. The restoration of that worst-case prospect — namely, Vietnam appearing to be squeezed in a strategic vice, which was the situation in 1978 — does not seem at all likely in the different circumstances of the post-Soviet era. There is, of course, no certainty about its external environment, but the sights of Vietnam's foreign policy have been lowered in a realistic adjustment to a transformation in national circumstances. The overriding imperative is national economic recovery and development in the interest of a conservative political stability. That domestic priority shapes the future direction of Vietnam's foreign policy and, if sustained, can only be of positive benefit to regional order.

Notes

1. For the terms of the Sino-Vietnamese communique, see BBC, *SWB*, FE/ 122, pp. A3/1–2. See also Martin Gainsborough, "Vietnam: A Turbulent Normalization with China," *The World Today*, November 1992.
2. A succinct account of Vietnam's difficulties with China may be found in Carlyle A. Thayer, "Vietnam: Coping with China," in *Southeast Asian Affairs 1994* (Singapore: Institute of Southeast Asian Studies, 1994).
3. For the background to Sino-Vietnamese differences over maritime jurisdiction, see Lo Chi-kin, *China's Policy toward Territorial Disputes — The Case of the South China Sea Islands* (London: Routledge, 1989).
4. Vietnam's position on both the Paracel and Spratly Islands may be found in *The Hoang Sa and Truong Sa Archipelagoes and International Law* (Hanoi: Ministry of Foreign Affairs, 1988). For an account of China's role, see John W. Garver, "China's Push Through the South China Sea: The Interaction of Bureaucratic and National Interests," *The China Quarterly*, no. 132 (December 1992).
5. For the text, see BBC, *SWB*, FE/1316, pp. C1/1–2.
6. *The New York Times*, June 18, 1992. See also the justification of Crestone's position in a letter by its chairman and president, Randall C. Thompson,

to the *Far Eastern Economic Review,* November 5, 1992. Crestone announced that it had begun exploration in April 1994. See *International Herald Tribune,* April 21, 1994.

7. For the text of the joint communique, see BBC, *SWB,* FE/1557, pp. A2/1–2.

8. In an interview with Michael Richardson, in *International Herald Tribune,* March 15, 1993.

9. See the report in *International Herald Tribune,* August 24, 1992, and also David Shambaugh "In Shanghai's Busy Shipyards, a Warning about Chinese Might," Ibid., January 15, 1993.

10. See *International Herald Tribune,* August 5, 1993.

11. BBC, *SWB,* FE/1501, pp. A2/7.

12. For a report of American intelligence calculations of China's military expenditure, see *International Herald Tribune,* July 31–August 1, 1993.

13. *Kyodo News Service,* April 25, 1993, in BBC, *SWB,* FE/1648, pp. A1/2.

14. BBC, *SWB,* FE/1690, pp. A2/3.

62

The Predicament of the
Brunei Sultanate

The government of Brunei, whose policies are determined by the former Sultan, regards the issues of decolonisation and international status, which have been raised at the United Nations and which trouble Britain, as misconceived. It would argue that the predicament of Brunei arises not from its lack of international status in terms of legal sovereignty, but rather from its lack of sufficient capability to enable the Sultanate to ward off the unwarranted attentions of neighbouring Malaysia. Thus, for the time being, the battalion of Gurkhas serves as an effective deterrent against any external military intervention in alleged support of an internal popular challenge to rule by the royal family of Brunei. Correspondingly, Britain's stiffening of the two battalions of the Royal Brunei Malay Regiment and the local police force and special branch serves to sustain internal political order. Furthermore, an expatriate community plays a crucial role in maintaining essential services which Brunei's own population is not

Excerpted from Michael Leifer, "Decolonization and International Status: The Experience of Brunei", *International Affairs* 54, no. 2 (1978): 240–52, by permission of Oxford University Press.

fully able to do, in part because a significant proportion of its limited pool of manpower is more attracted by the terms of service in the army and the police.

This problem of Brunei as represented by Malaysia at the United Nations is put in terms of the issues of decolonisation and international status. It is maintained that the British connection sustains an anachronistic political system and accordingly denies self-determination and independence. But from the point of view of the government of Brunei, the issue at stake is the kind of independence which the Sultanate wishes to enjoy, given the perceived existence of an external predator. Like a number of micro-states which do enjoy an internationally acknowledged status, Brunei exhibits a strong sense of vulnerability and seeks sustained access to external countervailing capability and expertise. In its case, the exclusive diplomatic relationship with Britain is contemplated not as an expression of a dependent association but as a way of ensuring the neutralisation of hostile external influences. Indeed, there is a parallel of sorts between the experience of Brunei and that of Kuwait, although ironically Kuwait's delegation at the United Nations voted in 1977 in favour of Malaysia's resolution calling for self-determination and independence for the Sultanate.

This interpretation of the predicament of Brunei is, of course, couched in terms of the interests of a narrow aristocratic ruling group and their political beneficiaries. Despite the munificent social policies which follow from a liberal use of oil and liquid natural gas resources to the order of £450 million annually, some underlying political dissatisfaction is present. It arises from resentment of the manner of rule and from a belief that a fundamental alteration in the relationship with Britain would provide a range of openings and career prospects for those whose claim to preferment is based on meritocratic criteria. Indeed, such a prospect would be a likely outcome of the institution of the kinds of political change urged publicly by the United Nations and privately by the British government. But such a transformation in the political structure of the Sultanate would not necessarily work to the advantage of Malaysia.[1] On the contrary, political change within Brunei could even serve once again as a catalyst within Northern Borneo; this time in reviving separatist sentiment possibly for a North Borneo state as advocated in December 1962 by the leadership of the very same Partai Ra'ayat which ironically has become the political beneficiary of the Malaysian government. It is even possible that the government of Brunei hopes to capitalise on such incipient sentiment within Malaysian Borneo in an endeavour to find an acceptable alternative political format, given the inevitability of Britain's relinquishment of its current responsibilities.

The concept of decolonisation, which has been used as a standard with which to challenge the international status of Brunei, is not really applicable to the experience of the Sultanate. This is because of the reluctant role of Britain and the obdurate determination of the government of Brunei to retain the bilateral association as long as possible in order to overcome an intrinsic vulnerability which persists despite the considerable wealth at its disposal. The basic issue in the case of Brunei is not an absence of independence but an absence of democracy. However, it hardly behoves the General Assembly of the United Nations, of all bodies, to be self-righteous on that account. The credentials of Brunei have been challenged because of the British connection and because Malaysia has been able to attract support from its non-aligned and Islamic associates. In consequence the international status of Brunei is not acknowledged. Yet neither is it sought by Brunei because a formal derogation of sovereignty has been willingly accepted in the interest of overcoming an intrinsic vulnerability. There is a real prospect, however, of international status being thrust upon Brunei against its will as a consequence of British act of volition. In this event, deprived of the justification of a tainted colonial association, the General Assembly can only condemn the Sultanate on the ground of its autocratic political system. The adoption of a resolution along these lines would constitute a most interesting undertaking for the world body.

Note

1. It is of interest to note the comment in *Utusan Melayu*, 1 December 1977, "... it is necessary to stress that any efforts to establish a parliamentary democratic government in Brunei should be carefully planned so as to prevent the country from becoming a new communist base and a political pawn of the Powers."

63

Brunei
Domestic Politics and Foreign Policy

The international outlook of the government of Brunei has been conditioned by the geopolitical circumstances of the minuscule but wealthy sultanate and, correspondingly, by a salutary experience of the interrelationship between domestic political challenge and external support. That experience had a profound impact during the course of the nineteenth century, but its modern expression dates from December 1962 when an abortive rebellion in opposition to Brunei's joining the projected Federation of Malaysia served as the initial justification of Indonesia's policy of confrontation. A further experience of external support for internal dissidence occurred during the mid-1970s when the government of Malaysia assumed a subversive role in a second attempt to subsume the sultanate within its federal structure. Although both Indonesia and Malaysia under different leaderships have reversed their policies toward Brunei, which they have welcomed as a regional

Reprinted from Michael Leifer, "Brunei: Domestic Politics and Foreign Policy", in *ASEAN in Regional and Global Context,* edited by Karl D. Jackson, Sukhumbhand Paribatra, and J. Soedjati Djiwandono (California: Institute of East Asian Studies, 1986), pp. 183–93, by permission of the publisher.

partner within ASEAN, the legacy of those relatively recent experiences continues to inform the external priorities of the sole remaining ruling monarchy in Southeast Asia. On resuming sovereignty in January 1984, the sultanate of Brunei has sought to protect a traditional identity and a fragile independence, in part by sustaining access to external sources of countervailing power and by actively soliciting recognition and endorsement of its international legitimacy. There is thus a very clear and direct relationship between domestic politics and foreign policy in Brunei. The object of the latter is not only to secure the independence and integrity of the microstate but also to ensure that a traditional political system is maintained intact.

Brunei has long been concerned with the threat posed by external predators, who have sought to exploit internal dissidence. Indeed, the experience of the sultanate during the greater part of the nineteenth century was of considerable territorial contraction effected principally in favor of a British political adventurer who became Raja of Sarawak. Brunei retained a separate identity as a territorial vestige of a historical empire only through the imposition of official British protection in 1888. That model of colonial rule secured the residual integrity of the sultanate with the notable exception of the still-disputed district of Limbang, now in Sarawak, whose annexation by Raja Charles Brooke in 1890 split Brunei into two enclaves, connected only by a maritime bridge. That residual integrity survived Japan's occupation during the Pacific War, while British protection, both formal and informal, continued uninterrupted, if diminished, until January 1984 when the transfer of the responsibility for external affairs restored the sultanate to full international status.

Brunei's experience of recovering independence has been unique within Southeast Asia. It has also been indicative of an international outlook that has not changed in substance since Brunei's government assumed responsibility for the conduct of its foreign policy. It was a reluctant aspirant for national liberation, resisting for many years attempts by successive British governments to cast it adrift politically. A fascinating illustration of that reluctance is the Treaty of Friendship and Cooperation concluded between the British Crown and the Sultan of Brunei in January 1979, which states in parenthesis on its title page that "the Treaty is not in force" and which contains in its text the statement that "this treaty shall enter into force five years from 31st December 1978."[1] Grace periods are associated normally with the repayment of debts. In Brunei's case, a reversion to full sovereignty was delayed for five years, and that period of delay and preparation was a negotiated minimum. The government of Brunei actually sought a much longer extension of a quasi-colonial status quo because of an abiding sense of vulnerability.

In effect, when the Treaty of Friendship and Cooperation came into effect, it produced only a change of legal form rather than one of political substance. Under the terms of an earlier agreement in September 1959, Brunei promulgated a new constitution. Internal political autonomy was restored, leaving Britain with responsibility for external affairs and defense (including internal security) and retaining only a formal prerogative — never exercised — to advise the sultan on all matters connected with governing the state. That agreement was amended in November 1971 to remove that formal prerogative and remaining vestige of Britain's control of internal affairs. The British government retained some responsibility for defense, excluding internal security, but only on a consultative basis corresponding to those diminished obligations assumed concurrently under the Five-Power Defense Arrangements, which superseded the Anglo-Malaysian Defense Agreement.

Only in external affairs was any formal derogation of sovereignty sustained. The amended agreement stipulated that "Her Majesty shall continue to enjoy jurisdiction to make for the state laws relating to external affairs."[2] But this external affairs power was never exercised in a policy-making sense, but only in a representative capacity. Decisions affecting the international status and affiliations of the sultanate were made, if by veto, in Bandar Seri Begawan and not in Whitehall. Any derogation of sovereignty was freely tolerated by the government of Brunei. Ironically, independence was demanded by the putative colonial power, which wished to free itself of an entangling political embarrassment. It was resisted with vigor and diplomatic skill by the putative subject state. Irony was compounded by the difficulty faced by British Labour governments in trying to withdraw the battalion of Gurkha Rifles, which had been deployed continuously on a rotating basis in the sultanate ever since the abortive rebellion in 1962. An insistent demand to retain an alleged mercenary presence came from Brunei, and that insistence has born fruit in the form of the postindependence relationship with Britain.

Brunei's insistence on enjoying a measure of informal British protection is the direct consequence of its experience of external support for internal political challenge in the recent past by Indonesia and

Malaysia. The political downfall of Sukarno and the attendant termination of the confrontation policy removed an immediate threat to the traditional system of royal family rule, but a lingering suspicion of Indonesia's intent has remained despite the transformation of the republic's political identity and international orientation, brought about by the advent and consolidation of President Suharto's New Order.

Moreover, if provoked by Brunei's revival of the Limbang claim, an active role was adopted by Malaysia in supporting proscribed rebels and in challenging the international status of the sultanate in the United Nations within only the last decade. That challenge was supported by Indonesia, as well as by the Philippines and Thailand, but not by Singapore.[3]

An uninterrupted process of reconciliation with its two former adversaries was set in motion after May 1978 when President Suharto and Prime Minister Datuk Hussein Onn met in Labuan and issued a joint disclaimer of ill-intent, indicating a willingness to welcome Brunei as a member of ASEAN when it became independent. Brunei has been an active party to such reconciliation, responding positively to regional initiatives, but has relied on more than expressions of goodwill to safeguard its security.

For Brunei, foreign policy has a prime domestic dimension. Its priority is to sustain the identity as well as the territorial integrity of the bifurcated microstate. That identity is conceived in terms of perpetuating a royal absolutist political system despite the degree of social change attendant not only on the immense wealth of the sultanate but also on the expansion of educational opportunity beyond the traditional governing class. There has been no indication of a desire for constitutional reform that might enable a return to a measure of popular political participation. Indeed, the elections of August 1962, in which the now proscribed Partai Ra'ayat secured all elective seats in the Legislative Council, are regarded by the royal family as an example of the dangers of democracy. All attempts since then by Britain's Foreign and Commonwealth Office to encourage progressive democratization have been resisted, although elections for ten of the twenty-one seats in the Legislative Council were held in March 1965. Democracy has been identified with political instability and external intervention, a view reinforced by the experience of East Timor since April 1974.

It has been made quite clear in Bandar Seri Begawan that there are no plans for new elections and party politics or indeed to return to the terms of the 1959 constitution to replace the emergency powers introduced in 1962, which permit the sultan to continue to rule by decree. Just prior to independence, acting Chief Minister Pehin Abdul Aziz Umar (now minister for Education and Health) remarked: "We do not want to be ruled by laborers and taxi drivers. We want to be governed by those who know how."[4] At independence, the sultan, Sir Muda Hassanal Bolkiah, assumed the offices of prime minister and the head of Internal Affairs and Finance. His father, the former sultan, who abdicated in favor of his son in 1967, assumed the Defense portfolio; his brother, Prince Mohamad, became minister for foreign affairs; and another brother, Prince Jefri, became minister for culture, youth, and sports, as well as deputy finance minister. Government and politics in Brunei are very much a family affair, and the purpose of the sultanate's foreign policy is to keep it that way.

The political status quo is maintained in part by employing the bounty enjoyed from the exploitation of oil and liquified natural gas to maintain an ideal welfare state in the form of free education and health care, subsidized loans for housing, cars, funerals, and pilgrimages to Mecca, sweetened further by an absence of an income tax. An awareness of the prospect of frustration among meritocratic commoners has been matched by a rapid indigenization of the upper echelons of government, while a measure of social control has been exercised by employing Islamic symbolism, which fundamentalist dissidents find difficult to use against the sultan, whose office combines religious and secular roles.

External defense and internal security are provided by the Royal Brunei Armed Forces (formerly Malay Regiment), founded in 1961 and trained and staffed in part by British officers and other loan service personnel. It is at present under the command of a British brigadier-general, himself subject to the authority of Brunei's minister of defense. Concurrent with the conclusion of the Treaty of Friendship and Cooperation with Britain, there was a corresponding exchange of notes concerning in part the continued provision of assistance to the armed forces of Brunei by Britain. Although Brunei does not purchase its arms exclusively from Britain, it plays a continuing dominant role in training troops and in servicing equipment. In the sense that the external relationship with Britain is directly connected to the general efficacy of Brunei's armed forces, it constitutes a source of countervailing power.

At the time of independence, Brunei's armed forces of some 4,000 men included two infantry battalions under local command, with a third in the process of formation. Supporting services consisted of an engineering and signals squadron, an armed reconnaisance squadron, and an air defense battery employing Rapier surface-to-air missiles. Equipment included sixteen Scorpion light tanks, two Sultan armored cars, twenty-four Sankey armored personnel carriers, and sixteen 81mm mortars. Air support took the form primarily of helicopter squadrons including gunships, while a small navy deployed fast patrol craft, three of which were armed with Exocet missiles.[5]

Given the propensity for intervention on the part of armed forces in new states, the well-equipped Royal Brunei Armed Forces constitutes a double-edged sword. Indeed, its capability is probably more suitable for launching a coup than in providing for external defense. There is no doubt that its officer corps is monitored closely for signs of political disaffection. At the same time its material needs are well cared for, while career prospects have improved with a reduction in the complement of British officers. But there is the prospect that dissatisfaction with the narrow absolutist structure of politics could engender dissent within the meritocratic strata of the bureaucracy, which in turn could find matching expression in the armed forces — as happened in Thailand in 1932.

Apart from a police force with a paramilitary element some 1,750 strong, internal security is maintained both directly and indirectly through access to external sources of countervailing power. A near unique relationship obtains with the government of Nepal whereby former Gurkhas who have served in the British army have been recruited to form a specially constituted Gurkha Reserve Unit or paramilitary force of some 900 men, who are employed to guard key installations, including prisons, the liquified natural gas plant at Lumut, and the magnificent new royal palace, whose buildings cover fifty acres and contain 1,788 rooms. This palace, which may well have cost $500 million and which overlooks the capital, represents a symbol of royal expectations that continuing generations of sultans beyond the incumbent twenty-ninth in line will continue to rule as well as reign. The Gurkha Reserve Unit is at the sultan's disposal, although there is no reason to believe that its presence is welcomed generally within the state.

This mercenary presence is supplemented in a primarily internal deterrent role by the continued deployment at Seria of a battalion of

Gurkha Rifles from the British army on a rotating basis from their brigade headquarters in Hong Kong as well as a company of Royal Marines. Before independence, the Gurkha deployment was maintained by a private exchange of letters with Whitehall. Certainly since 1971, the Gurkha presence, ostensibly serving a training function, has never been committed officially either to the internal or external defense of the sultanate. However, because the role of the battalion has never been publicly defined, its presence has an informal deterrent function. Internally, the fighting prowess and record of the Gurkhas is well understood and serves as a major constraint on possible political adventurism on the part of any faction within the Royal Brunei Armed Forces. Its presence has served also as a factor in the calculations of external adversaries, but external deterrence no longer possesses practical relevance.

Successive British governments — especially when the Labour party has been in office — have been concerned at the alarming prospect of finding a Gurkha battalion interposed between the Brunei royal family and a popularly based local military uprising. The current Conservative administration led by Margaret Thatcher has been more willing to live with that prospect because the Brunei government pays for the full cost of maintaining the rotating Gurkha battalion, which represents an important contribution to sustaining intact the Gurkha Brigade based in Hong Kong. In the year preceding the ultimate transfer of sovereignty, protracted and contentious negotiations took place over the terms on which the British battalion would remain in the sultanate. It would appear that the government of Brunei wanted to be able to exercise some form of veto over the deployment of the Gurkhas out of the sultanate, say, in the event of a breakdown in public order in Hong Kong — if not to enjoy a commanding role. A private agreement was reached in September 1983 which ensured that the role of the Gurkha battalion in Brunei would remain unchanged and undefined.[6] In the process, Britain was obliged to sacrifice an incumbent high commissioner and also forfeited a monopoly role for its Crown agents as manager of Brunei's multibillion pound investment portfolio in favor of Morgan Guaranty and Citibank.

Although the Gurkhas are almost certain to remain in their ambiguous role, at least until after the next general election in Britain, their longer term future is uncertain because of the strong likelihood that the fate of the Gurkha brigade will be linked to Britain's tenure in Hong Kong. In the meantime, the Gurkha presence and Britain's continuing training and servicing role for the Royal Brunei Armed Forces serve as a major constraint on any local attempt to challenge royal absolutism. If the external relationship with Britain has a deliberately ambiguous connection with internal security, seen as the key to the revival of any external threat, a newer special relationship with Singapore has a marginal security relevance.

The political relationship between Brunei and Singapore developed in the wake of the latter's separation from Malaysia in August 1965. The two states, if strikingly different in terms of prevailing cultural identity, identified with each other because of their similar size, sense of vulnerability, and sources of external threat. Apart from establishing an informal diplomatic presence in the sultanate during the 1970s, the government of Singapore has been permitted to deploy a rotating company of troops in the easternly Temburong enclave and to enjoy access to the Gurkha jungle training school near Seria. Military cooperation has been sustained since the transfer of residual sovereignty, expressed, for example, in joint exercises with the Singapore navy. The economic relationship has flourished, with Singapore becoming Brunei's third most important trading partner.

Long before and since full independence, Brunei has employed external relationships with a view to stiffening internal military capability and securing access to sources of countervailing power. Although military capability possesses an evident external defense dimension, internal security enjoys a higher priority, partly because of the conviction that the most likely circumstances in which an external threat could arise would be in response to an internal challenge. Long-standing external relationships with Britain and Nepal — with a special if minor role for Singapore — have been conceived with internal security in mind. With independence, Brunei has embarked on a range of wider diplomatic relationships, which also have relevance to security, but the prime object of the exercise has been to establish the international legitimacy of the sultanate. Certainly, membership in ASEAN was directly related to this objective.

Within a week of the transfer of residual sovereignty, Brunei, in its full title, *Negara Brunei Darussalam*, became the sixth member of ASEAN and only the first new entrant since its formation in August 1967. Any earlier reluctance to contemplate membership in an association that included Indonesia and Malaysia was overcome by the persuasive efforts of other members of ASEAN who were not seen as potential threats. Moreover, membership was not an overnight affair. Foreign minister designate Prince Mohamad had been attending meetings of the foreign ministers of ASEAN since 1981 in the role of an observer. Indeed, preparation for membership had begun as soon as the Treaty of Friendship and Cooperation with Britain had been concluded and the process of independence for the sultanate set in motion.

In considering the utility of membership in ASEAN, it should be understood that Brunei did not join because of its economic record. Economic cooperation within ASEAN has been a modest undertaking, while Brunei can purchase human skills and technology from wherever its government pleases. Moreover, it is not likely to invest its surplus wealth in any of its new regional partners unless there are sound economic grounds for doing so. Neither did Brunei join ASEAN in order to enjoy the benefits of a collective defense enterprise. Although defense cooperation does take place among ASEAN's members, primarily on a bilateral basis, it is conducted outside the auspices of the organization. Indeed, it has become an article of faith among the members that ASEAN is not an alliance. Brunei has joined ASEAN primarily in order to uphold the international legitimacy of the fledgling state.

The record of ASEAN in managing intermural tensions has been encouraging. Underpinning the quality of relationships based on an assiduous attention to bureaucratic and ministerial consultation has been an overriding commitment to respect the sovereign independence of member states. Indeed, ASEAN's founding declaration in August 1967 affirmed the intention "to promote regional peace and stability through abiding respect for justice and the rule of law in the relationships among countries of the region," while the Kuala Lumpur Declaration of November 1971, which articulated a commitment to a regional zone of peace, recognized "the right of every state, large or small, to lead its national existence free from outside interference in its internal affairs." The cardinal principle of the international society of states has also been enshrined in a Treaty of Amity and Cooperation signed by ASEAN's heads of government in February 1976. That treaty serves as the justification for ASEAN's collective diplomatic challenge to Vietnam's invasion and occupation of Cambodia. By joining ASEAN, Brunei has put itself in a position whereby the same standards of international conduct that have been applied to Vietnam can also be applied to regional partners, especially to those geographically most proximate. In other words, Brunei has sought to secure advantage from a self-imposed structure of corporate constraint implicit in the public philosophy of the organization.

Because of the conflict over Cambodia, the collective commitment to the non-violation of national sovereignty has become the central feature of ASEAN's corporate identity. Consequently, any display of aggressive intent toward Brunei by one of its new regional partners would bring ASEAN into disrepute in terms of its declared public philosophy. Indeed, from Brunei's perspective, ASEAN takes on the features of a traditional collective security organization like the League of Nations, whose main ideal purpose was to prevent aggression on an intramural basis. Indeed, it was with such a conception in mind that Thailand's former foreign minister, Thanat Khoman, suggested that collective political defense was ASEAN's major achievement. Brunei hopes to become a beneficiary of that form of defense. Membership in ASEAN is intended to institutionalize the process of reconciliation with Indonesia and Malaysia but correspondingly to provide in the process for the continued integrity and independent identity of the sultanate.

International legitimacy has been sought also by embarking on a restricted range of diplomatic relationships, confined to states with whom Brunei has some sense of political affinity. Apart from the other ASEAN states, diplomatic missions have been opened in London and Washington. In Bandar Seri Begawan, apart from Britain and the ASEAN states, diplomatic missions have been opened by the United States, South Korea, and Australia and a representative office by Japan.[7] A special coreligionist relationship without an exchange of missions appears to have been established with Pakistan, whose advice has been taken on the internal application of Islamic values, which serve in part as an instrument of social control. Such considerations of wider identity may have been responsible for the July 1984 visit by Yasser Arafat, chairman of the Palestine Liberation Organization.

Beyond ASEAN, Brunei has joined the Organization of the Islamic Conference, the Commonwealth, and the United Nations. It has also been recognized by the Soviet Union, Vietnam, and the People's Republic of China. International recognition has been extended without question, in contrast to Brunei's experience a decade ago when its status was the subject of adverse resolutions in the U.N. General Assembly: in September 1984, it became member 159 without a dissenting vote, jointly sponsored by all ASEAN states and Britain.

International legitimacy, however, cannot depend on external recognition alone: it requires a basis in established political fact, which in the case of Brunei is less than certain. In a speech on attaining full independence, the sultan stated that Brunei would remain a Malay Islamic monarchical state. Of those three qualities, that of monarchy is most likely to be subject to challenge as the educational base widens and when a bilingual (Malay-English) education system is established by 1988. Because Brunei is an absolute monarchy — with no attempt to emulate the Thai model or even the more contentious Malaysian one — political change could well occur in a sudden, if not totally unexpected way. Moreover, the great wealth of the sultanate — some $4 billion annually from the exploitation of oil and natural gas — may not be able to buy off political discontent.

Brunei has not experienced domestic violence for over twenty-three years, but its absence is not an indication in itself of the strength and resilience of its political institutions, which in no way mask the self-indulgence and the ostentatious lifestyle of the royal family. Brunei has made it quite clear that it will resist any demands for political change. One justification for an unwillingness to widen the basis of political participation is a belief that domestic turmoil may follow, which might then prompt a larger neighbor to intervene, ostensibly to uphold regional order. There has been no public cognizance of the alternative prospect — that a rigid resistance to political change could bring about the very scenario that is feared the most, namely, domestic upheaval and external intervention, probably in the form of an ASEAN peacekeeping force.

That prospect is not an immediate expectation while a Gurkha battalion is deployed in an ambiguous role; however, if in its absence the Royal Brunei Armed Forces were to overcome traditional loyalties and royal manipulation and decide to intervene politically, the structure of external relationships could not serve to sustain the complete identity of the microstate. The threat to a monarchical identity does not lie in a revival of the Partai Ra'ayat, whose exiled leadership no longer receives external support. Indeed, nearly half the Malay population of Brunei — some 120,000 — is under twenty, so that living memory of the 1962 revolt has faded with the passing of time. More significant are the deep currents of change beneath the surface of welfare-induced stability, the source of the observation that "there is a restlessness among the younger Malays coupled with a growing nationalism which is most marked in returning students."[8]

External threats per se to the security and identity of Brunei do not possess any real immediacy. Brunei's common stand with its new partners over Cambodia represents an expression of necessary corporate solidarity and an attachment to practical principle, not a pressing sense of apprehension because the most proximate major city is Ho Chi Minh. In the current climate of intra-ASEAN conciliation, any maritime dispute with Malaysia over the delineation of the international boundary of Brunei Bay can be contained, while the sultanate has been cautious in avoiding entanglement in the multilateral contention over the Spratly Islands. Moreover, while the status and even livelihood of the vast majority of Brunei's Chinese community of some 60,000 has been put in jeopardy by the assumption of full sovereignty, it does not constitute a political threat capable of being manipulated by the PRC. Indeed, it is significant that discrimination against Brunei's Chinese community has not prompted any external response either from outside or within ASEAN. British attempts to make provision for their assured future before surrendering the external affairs power failed conspicuously.

In Bandar Seri Begawan the burgeoning of new foreign relationships does not serve directly as a security policy, but it does reflect the view of geographic neighbors that regional stability will be promoted best by encapsulating Brunei within an exclusive structure of international relations. For Brunei that collective view provides a measure of assurance that gratuitous acts of interference will not take place. But that view cannot guarantee that developments within the sultanate will not be seen to pose a threat to the interests of regional partners. At a seminar in Jakarta in October 1974, Tan Sri Ghazalie Shafie, then Malaysia's minister for home affairs, drew attention to "the security issues that revolve around the continuing existence of vestigial colonial territories in our region." He warned that "their existence, besides being historically anomalous, also makes them the foci of local discontent and foreign intrigue. The security issues that they pose may be peripheral to the ambit of our concern here, but they are nevertheless potential areas of instability."[9] Brunei is no longer a "vestigial colonial" territory, nor historically anomalous, but the measure of concern expressed over a decade ago has not completely disappeared.

Mention has been made above to a growing nationalism in Brunei marked among returning students. That nationalism draws its sustenance from a sense of lineal descent from a historical empire, which gave its name in English to an island of continental proportions now comprising mainly Indonesian and Malaysian territory. The declared goal of the rebellion in 1962 of a unitary state of North Borneo to incorporate present-day Sarawak and Sabah reflected a nationalist impulse, as did the irredentist claim to the district of Limbang by the former sultan, Sir Omar Ali Saifuddin, which has never been formally repudiated. Accordingly, future political change within Brunei could serve once again as a catalyst within North Borneo, depending on the nature of the relationship between the two distant wings of Malaysia. Such a worst-case scenario must occasionally merit consideration in Kuala Lumpur, which was in part the source of the expression of concern by Tan Sri Ghazalie Shafie over a decade ago.

Such an irredentist scenario is almost certainly not contemplated by the absolute monarchy in Bandar Seri Begawan because it could most likely occur only at its expense. Indeed, external priorities are governed by domestic considerations, which is why the most important external relationships are those which have the most immediate relevance to perpetuating the political status quo. It is of interest therefore to take cognizance of a new Brunei law which states that "outside armed forces stationed in the Sultanate by mutual agreement might be used to control public order."[10] Britain's military association with Brunei has been based, however, on the assumption that the very presence of the Gurkhas should make their use unnecessary. Should it ever seem likely that they would find themselves engaged in defense of an absolute monarchy against a popularly based uprising, then strong parliamentary pressure would be applied to bring about their withdrawal. In other words, the key external relationship that serves as a critical sanction against internal political challenge is based on a bluff, which could be called in the near future.

In this context, the political good health of Brunei is not easy to assess because the real political process in the sultanate is virtually a closed activity. Any personal or factional rivalries within the royal circle have had limited public expression. The Legislative Council with a nominated majority meets only once a year to hear a royal address and to approve legislation. Decision making is confined to an exclusive royal circle, with the former sultan or Seri Begawan playing an important paternal role. That practice has been confirmed by the attainment of independence, not established as a consequence of it. The central institution of the state is a monarchy of historical long-standing, which is a regional anomaly. Foreign policy has been governed primarily by a determination to preserve that royal house within its vestigial territorial domain, which is upheld more by a postimperial relationship than by new-found regional associations, however important. When that residual postimperial relationship comes to end, almost certainly by 1997, the political identity of Brunei will depend in great part on the loyalty of the Royal Brunei Armed Forces despite any continuing private arrangements with the government of Nepal.

It is the constancy of that loyalty more than anything else that is likely to influence any revision in a foreign policy directed currently toward a linked international legitimacy and domestic political continuity. In other words, political change within Brunei would be required before alternative foreign policies of either integration within Malaysia or a separate North Borneo are likely to be contemplated seriously. For now, the relationship between domestic politics and foreign policy can be expressed in one sentence taken from the acceptance speech of the sultan on the occasion of the admission of the state to the United Nations: "We wish to be left alone, and free from foreign intervention."

Notes

1. Cmnd. 7496, HMSO (London, 1979), p. 7.
2. Cmnd. 4932, HMSO (London, 1972), p. 4.
3. For a discussion of Brunei's international status at that juncture and subsequently, see Michael Leifer, "Decolonization and International Status: The Experience of Brunei", *International Affairs* 54, no. 2 (April 1978) 240–252, and Timothy Ong Teck Mong, "Modern Brunei: Some Important Issues", *Southeast Asian Affairs 1983* (Hampshire, England: Gower, 1983). See historical account of the international position of Brunei by D. S. Ranjit Singh, *Brunei, 1839–1983: The Problems of Political Survival* (Singapore: O.U.P., 1984).
4. *Daily Telegraph,* December 29, 1983.
5. For full details of Brunei's military establishment, see *The Military Balance, 1984–1985* (London: International Institute for Strategic Studies, 1984), p. 97.
6. Richard Lace, minister of state at the Foreign and Commonwealth Office, explained that a Gurkha battalion would remain in Brunei "under essentially the same arrangements that apply at present" (*Financial Times,* September 23, 1983).

7. Diplomatic relations with ambassadors accredited to Brunei from either Malaysia or Singapore have been established with Bangladesh. Belgium, Canada, Egypt, France, West Germany, India, Italy, Nepal, the Netherlands, New Zealand, Oman, Pakistan, Papua New Guinea, Turkey and Sweden.

8. A. J. Crosbie, "Brunei in Transition." *Southeast Asian Affairs 1981* (Singapore: Heinemann Asia, 1981), p. 88.

9. Tan Sri Muhammad Ghazali bin Shafie. "ASEAN's Response to Security Issues in Southeast Asia," in *Regionalism in Southeast Asia* (Jakarta: Center for Strategic and International Studies, 1976), p. 23.

10. *Asia 1984 Yearbook* (Hong Kong: Far Eastern Economic Review, 1983), p. 134.

64

The Philippines and Sabah Irredenta

By January of this year there was good reason to assume that the territorial claim by the Philippines to the Malaysian state of Sabah had been relegated to the limbo of lost causes. Two months later, however, this assumption was dispelled as a consequence of a dramatic episode, the implications and repercussions of which have probably impaired a trustworthy relationship between Malaysia and the Philippines for many years to come.

Sabah, known formerly as the British Crown Colony of North Borneo, was incorporated into the Federation of Malaysia in September 1963. It was the provisional decision the previous year to include North Borneo in the new federation which was responsible for the timing of the Philippine claim. In June 1962, in response to an admonitory Foreign Office note, President Macapagal stated his Government was in dispute with the British Government "regarding the ownership and sovereignty" of North Borneo. The claim was based

Reprinted from Michael Leifer, "The Philippines and Sabah Irredenta", *World Today* 24, no. 10 (1968): 421–28, by permission of the Royal Institute of International Affairs.

largely on the Filipino interpretation of a document of January 1878 by which the Sultan of Sulu had transferred most of present-day Sabah to the predecessors of the British North Borneo Company.[1] This company, founded in 1882, had exercised the administration until it was assumed by the British Crown in July 1946, the very month in which the Philippines became independent.

The urging of the claim soon became entangled in the diplomacy to resolve the more violent conflict between Indonesia and Malaysia over the legitimacy of the new Federation. And in this exercise a mixture of Filipino opportunism, desire for recognized Asian identity, and concern over matters of regional security served to lend some cover to the ambitions of President Sukarno. The claim dwindled in significance with the more active phase of Confrontation and in the light of the association of limited endurance which became known as the Peking–Djakarta axis. With the abortive *coup* in Indonesia in October 1965 and the consequent transformation of the political system in that country, the prospect for Filipino exploitation of the state of Indonesian-Malaysian relations to national ends became less likely. And by the time that Sukarno was displaced following the formal termination of Confrontation, the Philippine Government had already re-established full diplomatic relations with Kuala Lumpur. Macapagal's successor President Marcos, who came to office in January 1966, was believed to hold different priorities from those of his defeated electoral opponent and appeared eager to renew harmonious relationships with the partner of the Philippines in the Association of South-East Asia (ASA).

Although the claim was not officially withdrawn, there was assumed to be little advantage and much disadvantage in pressing the matter. Besides, the Government in Manila had ceased to enjoy any political leverage through which to tease concessions. Diplomatic relations between Kuala Lumpur and Manila, broken in September 1963, were restored in June 1966, and Malaysia entered into a formal agreement in September 1967 to assist the Philippine Government in combating smuggling across the Sulu Sea. A measure of the degree of reconciliation between the two countries was the official visit by President Marcos and his wife to Malaysia in January this year which passed without untoward incident and apparently in a cordial manner. And yet while this visit was taking place, certain developments were under way within the Philippines which, when made public, were to pose serious doubts as to the importance placed by President Marcos on a continuing and harmonious relationship with Malaysia.

The Corregidor Affair

On 21 March 1968 the press in the Philippines began to release information concerning an incident which served to upset all previous prognostications about the state of Malaysian-Philippines relations. It appears that a young Muslim from the Sulu region had presented himself in a distressed state at the residence of Governor Montano of Cavite Province with a seemingly incredible tale of the stranger than fiction variety. He claimed to be one of more than a hundred young Muslims recruited in the Sulu region in 1967 by an Air Force Major Martelino (a convert to Islam taking the name of Abdul Latif), head of the Civil Affairs Office of the Philippine Department of National Defence. The ostensible purpose of this recruiting campaign was to set up civic action centres in provincial capitals, but according to the testimony of the young Muslim, Jibin Arula, the real purpose was to train those enlisted in "Special Forces" techniques in preparation for infiltrating Sabah. Arula was to testify before an investigating committee of the Philippine Congress "If we were able to go to Sabah, we were to destroy the oil fields and electric plants and banks which we were told to rob" (*sic*). He claimed also that he was instructed to persuade Filipinos resident in Sabah to join the insurgents in order to seize the territory.

The training programme began, so it was reported, in the latter part of 1967 on Simunul of the Tawi-Tawi group of islands in the south of the Philippines and trainees included some members of the 25,000 strong Philippine community resident in Sabah. In January 1968 the trainees were moved to a Philippine army camp on the island of Corregidor located in Manila Bay — the scene of the memorable last stand of Filipino and American soldiers following the Japanese invasion of the Philippines during the second World War.

According to Arula, he was the sole survivor of a massacre in which eleven of his fellow trainees had been killed in cold blood by their officers. His testimony gave rise to the interpretation of events that the trainees had been shot in the act of mutiny following demands for pay which had not been forthcoming for two months. However, other witnesses added only confusion and contradiction to this evidence; the number of those allegedly killed rose to over sixty and then fell to six and finally it was suggested that there had not been any killings at all. Another interpretation was that those trainees liquidated included agents infiltrated by the Malaysians. Despite the confusion and conflicting evidence over what actually happened on Corregidor[2] the episode brought to public notice the existence of the training programme and the associated project known as "Operation Merdeka".

The purpose of the training programme was given additional confirmation when the Malaysian Government announced that early in March it had arrested twenty-six Filipinos in possession of small arms and explosives. They were said to have been apprehended on Banggi island, a Malaysian possession some thirty miles to the north of Sabah and about thirty miles to the south of the southernmost Philippine island of Balabac. It was made known later by the Malaysian Prime Minister that at least seventeen of those arrested had received military training in the Philippines.[3]

The Claim Revived

On 23 March the Malaysian Government reacted to the news of Corregidor incident by lodging a formal protest with the Philippine Government at the apparent breach of good faith and friendly relations together with a request for an explanation. It also instructed its representative at the United Nations to inform the Secretary-General of the arrest of infiltrators in Sabah. The Malaysian Government made it quite clear that it was taking a very serious view of what was regarded as a direct threat to national security. It was to announce the strengthening of the regular garrison in Sabah, that vigilantes and local defence corps were to be formed, and that all men between the ages of eighteen and twenty-eight in Sabah were to be registered in preparation for selective call-up.

Reaction to the incident within the Philippines tended to reflect party political affiliation. However, in reply to the Malaysian note, the Philippine Foreign Ministry stressed that the matter was "purely an internal affair" and gave no indication of regret. Indeed, President Marcos made it known that he had instructed the Philippine representative at the United Nations, Salvador Lopez, to seek the good offices of the U.N. Secretary-General to persuade the Malaysian Government to agree to a peaceful settlement of the Sabah claim, preferably through the International Court of Justice. A solution through the International Court of Justice has been a persistent objective of the Philippines almost from the time that the claim was first advocated. However, such a mode of settlement is dependent on the acquiescence of the Malaysian Government which has never shown itself disposed to become a party to litigation before the World Court.

The formal revival of the claim to Sabah at this juncture did not suggest a preconceived exercise but rather a reactive attempt to divert attention from the implications of the Corregidor affair to an issue on which the Philippines could pose, with more justice, as the aggrieved party. In the Malaysian press this initiative was represented and resented as "a counter-attack in the absence of an adequate reply to Malaysia's protest and request for information". Retorts in the Philippine press served also to disturb relations which were further aggravated early in April by distorted news stories about the interception of a Filipino motor boat off the Sabah coast.

The attitude of the Malaysian Government to the revival of the claim to Sabah was to treat the matter separately from the Corregidor episode. After limited exchanges it was agreed that two panels of Malaysian and Philippine representatives would meet in June in Bangkok to begin discussions on a mode of settlement of the claim.

Inquest and Exegesis

In the meantime in the Philippines a process of inquiry had begun into the Corregidor affair. The initial explanation of the Government to the revelations was that the preparations on Simunul and Corregidor had no bearing on Sabah but were designed to enable the Government to cope with any upsurge of communist activity in the Muslim south of the country. However, with the commencement of Congressional investigation a variant of this explanation was put forward by witnesses connected with the Government. The training programme was explained as a pre-emptive exercise to forestall any action that might be taken by the so-called "Free Sabah Militia" of the late congressman Ombra Amilbangsa, who claimed the title Sultan of Sulu and the territory of Sabah.

The various accounts of and explanations for the Corregidor affair tend, however, to cloud one strong likelihood. Given the nature of the political process in the Philippines, there is most probably only one person who could have authorized the financing and the establishment of "special forces" type camps and the recruitment of Muslim trainees; that is President Marcos.[4] However, to suggest that President Marcos promoted the training scheme to provoke a revolt in Sabah in order to back the claim to the territory is a romantic notion. Marcos, of course, has a courageous record as a guerrilla leader against the Japanese during the World War and it is possible to speculate, if a little wildly, about the revival of former roles in a vicarious manner. Yet it would seem a bizarre initiative in terms of practicability and in contrast to steps being taken, in which the Philippines has been closely involved, to promote more effective regional co-operation within South-East Asia. Certainly the Corregidor affair and its aftermath have retarded seriously the progress of such attempted co-operation.

There can be little doubt that the training camp and the recruits there have some connection with Sabah. And yet President Marcos, up till the recent revelations, had not displayed any public enthusiasm for the claim which was sponsored initially by his predecessor and political rival, ex-President Macapagal. It is perhaps ill-advised to seek the answer to the mystery in speculation, but for the time being there is little alternative. Three hypotheses present themselves. First, there is evidence that the President had become disturbed at the political state of the Muslim south of the country following years of promises and administrative neglect.[5] It is possible that "Operation Merdeka" was designed to channel Muslim energies away from concern with their economic condition which was the responsibility of Manila towards dreams of Sabah irredenta. For the Philippines, Sabah might stand in relation to the Sulu region as the Malay peninsula stood in relation to Sumatra for the Indonesian Government during Confrontation. In other words, there might well be concern in Manila that the Muslims of the Southern Philippines are becoming attracted by the far more prosperous Sabah dominated by a predominantly Muslim political party. Secondly, there is the related possibility which derives from Marcos's concern, like all Philippine Presidents, about his prospects of re-election. It is possible that he foresaw the prospect of creating some set of diversion involving Sabah prior to polling in November 1969 which might assist his main political purpose to become the first Philippine President since independence to be elected for a second term of office. Finally, there is the crude explanation that Marcos planned a campaign of insurgency designed to lead to the detachment of Sabah from Malaysia, because he wished to succeed where his predecessor had failed.[6] Such speculation can produce a variety of further hypotheses around similar themes, but it offers little intellectual profit or satisfaction. It is more important to note that good relations with Malaysia took second place in the order of priorities of whoever initiated what stumbled into public light as the Corregidor affair.

Negotiations in Bangkok

On 17 June officials from the respective Foreign Ministries of Malaysia and the Philippines met in Bangkok to discuss the matter of the claim to Sabah. From the outset the two delegations were completely at cross purposes. The Malaysian interpretation of the object of the meeting was that it should clarify first the nature of the claim and the substance of the evidence and arguments upon which it is said to rest. This position is supported by the argument that the Philippine Government has yet to file its grounds of claim with Malaysia; nor has it specifically set out the map reference points in relation to the area claimed. Before such clarification was offered the Malaysians refused to discuss a mode of settlement. The Filipinos, for their part, were single-minded in their determination to press for the reference of the claim to the International Court of Justice.

The sessions very quickly became bogged down over procedural matters and it became apparent that the members of the Philippine delegation had very limited powers of negotiation and were obliged to refer back constantly to Manila, necessitating frequent adjournment. Finally in the middle of July after a month of fruitless discussions, the Malaysian delegation announced that they rejected outright the Philippine claim and that as far as they were concerned the talks were "over and done with"; the following day, 16 July, they quit the conference room in what was described by the Filipinos as a walk out. A subsequent attempt by the Philippine President to suggest that the head of the Malaysian delegation did not have the authority to break off the talks was rejected out of hand by the Malaysian deputy-Prime Minister Tun Razak.[7]

During the discussions neither side had moved basically from its initial negotiating position. Although the Filipinos appeared to agree in principle that the matter of clarification of the claim should take precedence over discussion on a mode of settlement, no new information on the grounds of the claim was forthcoming. The Malaysians for their part stuck rigidly to their refusal to consider an approach to the I.C.J. in spite of the claim by the Philippines that Tunku Abdul Rahman, the Malaysian Prime Minister, had privately given his word on such an approach to ex-President Macapagal in

February 1964. The Philippine demand for the matter to go to the I.C.J. certainly has great force because it is based on the inference that if Malaysia is confident in her sovereign position in Sabah she has nothing to lose by going to The Hague. However, the Malaysians have good reason not to let the matter go to litigation. Irrespective of any doubts that they may have as to their title in Sabah, the Malaysians are determined to resist any challenges to the legality of the incorporation of Sabah into the Federation. Federal-state relations have been subject to some degree of strain which has not been completely healed in spite of the outcome of the Sabah elections of 1967.[8] There are issues which still divide Kota Kinabalu from Kuala Lumpur and therefore there is no desire in the Federal capital to give the impression that the people of Sabah, who have not shown any enthusiasm for association with the Philippines, are being made the subject of any political or legal bargain or even a sell-out. For Malaysia, the possession of Sabah is seen as much more than nine-tenths of international law.

Diplomatic Rupture?

The immediate outcome of the breakdown of the talks in Bangkok was the decision by the Philippine Government to recall its Ambassador and all but one of his staff in Kuala Lumpur. This decision did not appear to cause any great alarm in the Malaysian capital; however, the Malaysian Government responded by recalling its Ambassador in Manila for consultation, it being announced that this was not to be interpreted as a reciprocal act. For the time being the state of relationship between the two countries resembles the situation at the time of the inauguration of Malaysia, when the Philippine Government refused to establish full diplomatic relations with the new Federation unless there was a clear undertaking to agree to a definite procedure for the settlement of the Sabah claim.

It has been suggested that it is possible that an attempt at conciliation will be made by the Association of South-East Asian Nations (ASEAN) to which both Malaysia and the Philippines belong. However, it has also been pointed out that "one difficulty is that the Philippines Government has already lost so much face through its uncertain conduct of the affair that it will be a difficult task to make any appeal to reason.[9] The whole affair is bedevilled by considerations of face and of internal politics. President Marcos, having found himself obliged to resume the claim in the face of evident political embarrassment, is in no position to back down, especially with his sights set on re-election in 1969. The Malaysian Government for its part feels obliged to stick rigidly and doggedly to a static position which offers no room for compromise. For the student of South-East Asian politics with his mind continually on the more heart-rending conflict in Vietnam and the prospects of settlement there, the whole episode cannot but take on the magnitude of farce. It is to be hoped, however, that somewhere cooler counsels[10] will prevail to prevent farce from turning into tragicomedy.

Notes

1. The only collection of pleadings and documents relating to the claim published by the Philippine Government is *Philippine Claim to North Borneo*, Vol. 1, Manila, Bureau of Printing, 1963.
2. One commentator reported: "For all the noisy and elaborate rituals of the current congressional investigation — floodlights, searching TV camera eyes, witnesses, tall piles of affidavits and secret documents — the truth about the Corregidor massacre and the 'secret army' is no more visible to the public than it was at the start of the congressional probe three weeks ago." Napoleon G. Rama, "The Corregidor Affair", *Philippines Free Press*, Manila, 13 April 1968.
3. *The Straits Times*, 4 April 1968.
4. Major Martelino was to testify "The project was approved by the Chief-of-Staff of the Armed Forces and I would also assume, by the Commander-in-Chief himself." *Philippines Free Press*, 6 April 1968. Former Defence Under-Secretary, Manuel Syquio, allegedly in charge of the project in response to the question whether the President had a hand in it replied: "It is possible he may have known about it." *Ibid.*, 4 May 1968.
5. See E. R. Kiunisala, "Republic of Mindanao?", *Philippines Free Press*, 1 June 1968.
6. Within the Philippines there has also been speculation about the personal stake of the President in the claim following the revelation that on 1 February 1968 the heirs of the Sultan of Sulu signed a power of attorney in favour of President Marcos, additional to their so-called surrender of sovereign rights to the Philippine Government in 1962, giving him authority to act on their behalf regarding proprietary rights in Sabah.
7. Tun Razak told the press "There is no point in talking any further. The question has been disposed of". *Straits Times*, 19 July 1968.
8. See Gordon P. Means, "Eastern Malaysia: The Politics of Federalism", *Asian Survey*, April 1968.
9. *The Times*, 22 July 1968.

10. The prospects for reconciliation have not been improved by the recent passage by the Philippine Congress of a Bill to include Sabah within the territory of the Philippines. This Bill has since been signed into law by President Marcos.

65

Thailand
The Politics of "De-Stalinization"

In December 1963, the death occurred of Marshal Sarit Thanarat, Prime Minister and virtual military dictator of Thailand from 1958. Since his decease, Thailand has been passing through a period of political transition which bears some resemblance to the phase in recent Soviet history which followed the revelation by Khrushchev of the enormity of Stalin's crimes. Marshal Sarit's successor as Prime Minister, Thanom Kittikachorn, is also a Field Marshal but is no Khrushchev. He also does not enjoy the distinctive qualities of the late Prime Minister of Thailand. Marshal Sarit was a strong and forceful personality with an evident will to govern and, in spite of certain shortcomings which have been ventilated widely since his death, gave Thailand a sense of stability. For this he was respected, albeit, not loved. Prime Minister Thanom is, by temperament, a milder man, less determined and certainly less ruthless than his late predecessor and accordingly he receives corresponding deference on the Thai political

Reprinted from Michael Leifer, "Thailand: The Politics of 'De-Stalinization?'", *The Australian Outlook* 19, no. 1 (1965): 97–100, by permission of the Australian Institute of International Affairs.

scene. Because of his very close connection with the late Prime Minister (he was Deputy P.M.) Thanom cannot altogether avoid being associated with the much publicised misdeeds of the past regime. However, like Khrushchev in 1956, he would seek to present himself as a scourge against evils — in Thailand's case large-scale corruption — which have their origin in the past and which can be laid conveniently at the feet of the dead.

Considerable pitfalls face Thailand's Prime Minister in this attempt to create for himself the role of a man of integrity. He is, yet, to appear convincing as such and has, so far, not demonstrated the political skill which could enable him to substantiate his pretensions to probity. As with the process of de-Stalinization in the Soviet Union, the inevitable questions "Where were you" and "What part did you play" are likely to be levelled against Sarit's former associates who, with Thanom, make up the bulk of the present government. And there is the possibility that the process of de-Stalinization in a Thai context may not stop with the dead. Subtle references to some of the notable living of Sarit's associates have already appeared in the Thai language press which, in spite of the existence of a state of martial law, has been enjoying a remarkable degree of freedom. There has been one resignation from the cabinet, that of the Minister of Agriculture, General Surachit, although it took place over a scandal unrelated to the Sarit affair.[1] If Thanom is unable or unwilling to protect his cabinet colleagues from charges arising out of their former association with Sarit, then his own position could become very insecure indeed. In such circumstances he could well be confronted by a military group within his own cabinet who would have every reason to protect their personal interests. It should be pointed out that Thailand is an example, *par excellence*, of Mao Tse-tung's dictum that power grows out of the barrel of the gun. He who controls the army controls Thailand. Prime Minister Thanom's political success will, no doubt, depend in large part on his ability in this direction.

Public feeling about the corrupt practices of Marshal Sarit's regime existed in Thailand before his death. However, it was only in the more liberal political atmosphere that came with his decease that the issue was ventilated. While Sarit's body was beginning to putrefy, according to Buddhist custom, in an urn prior to cremation, stories began to appear in the newspapers about large sums from state funds which had been diverted for his own use by the late Prime Minister. At the same time, mention was made of the many women, referred to as minor-wives, whom the late Prime Minister had taken under his patronage. The revelations originated with a court action by Sarit's widow, the Lady Vichitra, to ensure that she would enjoy in full her position as the late Prime Minister's legal wife and was therefore entitled to claim his entire estate. This action was disputed by two of Sarit's sons by an earlier marriage.

The Thai language press soon filled with daily reports of huge sums allegedly filched from the coffers of the state. These stories did not cease with the cremation of Sarit, one hundred days after his death, but continued in so sensational a manner that the government set up a commission to enquire into the whole affair. Prime Minister Thanom declared subsequently that the government would use its powers under article 17 of the constitution to restore misappropriated funds. In the meantime a report of the commission in the form of a white book is awaited eagerly within Thailand, although concern has been expressed in the press that the white book will not include the names of recipients of monetary gifts from Marshal Sarit. Indeed, reports have already indicated that the government has decided to withhold the names of certain Generals who had received funds for secret service operations. Cynics have suggested that the government has no intention of making the white book available for public release, given the expectation that it could very well embarrass members of the present cabinet.

Towards the end of 1964, further stories of corruption appeared in Bangkok's newspapers and the name of the late Prime Minister was associated with this renewal of public scandal. At the beginning of October, one of the largest insurance firms in Thailand, the Nakorn Luang Life Company, went into voluntary liquidation because it was unable to meet its commitments. The Thai language press reported the Prime Minister as saying that Marshal Sarit had utilised fourteen million baht[2] of N.L.L.I.C. funds for his personal investments. A former managing director of the Company disclosed that he had been ordered by Marshal Sarit to transfer eighteen million baht from Nakorn funds to stabilise the Bank of Asia in which the late Prime Minister had a large interest. It was also reported that the N.L.L.I.C. had been forced to make exorbitant gifts to Sarit, while some of his associates used its funds for their own purposes.

A further unsavory affair involved Sarit's mother-in-law, Mrs Prathieb Cholasap. It was alleged in the press that she received eighteen million baht from the Degremont Company for her part in arranging a government contract for laying water-supply pipes in Bangkok and Thonburi. The government has begun to investigate the matter and Mrs Cholasap has since revealed that the Degremont Company had allocated one hundred and seventy million baht for gratuity purposes and that the sum she had received was very small indeed compared to that given to one unnamed individual who she said had collected ninety million baht. Meanwhile the press have made subtle references to the Finance Minister, Sunthorn Hongladorom, in connection with the affair and derogatory writings have appeared on the walls of the house of the Director of Public Works.

Yet another matter of public concern has been the high price of pork. This is sold in Bangkok and Thonburi under a monopoly by the Live-stock Trading Cooperative Company, a semi-public body whose Chairman of Board of Directors is the Under-Secretary for the Interior, Thawin Sunthornsarathoon. Growing rumours about the role of the Ministry of the Interior may have been responsible for the announcement on the 7th October 1964 that the Deputy Prime Minister and Minister for the Interior, General Praphas Charusathien (who was recently made Commander-in-Chief of the army) was selling his fifteen per cent share holding in the Live-stock Trading Cooperative Company to the Bangkok municipality. It is most significant that General Praphas should seek, by the sale of his shares, to dissociate himself from growing public criticism over the price of pork. He is the one man most closely associated with the "extra-mural" activities of the late Prime Minister and there has been much speculation of late as to whether the process of "de-Stalinization" is going to touch him. It is of interest that General Praphas withdrew from the Chairmanship of the Board of Directors of the Nakorn Luang Life Insurance Company at the beginning of 1964, possibly when it was realised that the firm was no longer solvent.

So far, revelations about corruption have troubled almost exclusively the ashes of the late Prime Minister. His successor, Thanom Kittikachorn, appears to be encouraging the process of public cleansing now in operation, at least to the extent that it reflects on the dead rather than on the living. At the same time, he would seek to stand aside from any public antagonism being generated by the ventilation of such matters.

Prime Minister Thanom's attempts to show himself as a man of integrity have been received within Thailand with a certain amount of justifiable scepticism. He has yet to overcome popular feeling that he is only trying to protect himself. His past association with the Sarit regime has been too close for him to be able to effectively differentiate himself from his activities, that is, unless like Khrushchev he is prepared to indict an "anti-party group" who can serve conveniently as scape-goats for the sins of the former regime. Thanom has yet to demonstrate that he can match the strength of the obvious candidates for this role, particularly General Praphas Charusathien. In the meantime he has already had to face the prospect of a coup from military officers who may have been excluded from the material benefits of Sarit's regime. Since the demise of Sarit there had been recurrent rumours of an impending coup. Before his death in Japan, in June this year, rumours circulated to the effect that former Prime Minister, Pibun Songkhram, would return to lead a revolt. An in August, General Praphas flew back suddenly to Bangkok during a visit to West Germany because he apparently believed that a coup was imminent. At the beginning of December 1964, a series of arrests of military officers took place. Their numbers included eventually an Air Chief Marshal. They were accused by the Prime Minister of plotting a coup d'etat to coincide with the annual parade of the Royal Guard for the King's birthday celebrations.

In the meantime, popular attention is being engaged by the prospects of a new constitution which is expected to be promulgated some time in 1965. Some have been vocal that this will usher in a period of civilian rule. Indeed, the Minister for National Development, Pote Sarasin, has spoken publicly of the need to form political parties which he implied would be able to function without military intervention. His reported statements on this issue have given some heart to intellectual circles and adherents of formerly defunct political parties. More sceptical observers believe, however, that Prime Minister Thanom is behind Pote's kite-flying about political parties, and that he has no real intention of permitting complete civilian control of the country. But they are also of the opinion that a political party with military backing may serve as a necessary safety valve. It would prevent the use of force which has been a recurrent factor in Thai political life and could even bring into being a limited form of constitutionalism.

Constitutional progress, however, faces serious obstacles. It is possible that the programme for the adoption of the promised constitution may be upset because either the process of "de-Stalinization" goes beyond the dead and produces a reaction from among the living who fear its progress, or yet another military group may make a bid for power with the aim of restoring the country's prestige which has been somewhat sullied by so much unwelcome publicity of late, although the latter prospect has diminished following the December arrest — 1964. But even if a constitution is introduced it need not necessarily be operative for very long if Thai politicians begin their traditional squabbles over who gets what. Indeed, a period of constitutionalism may well provide only a brief breathing space whereby new personalities will emerge within the military and who, with the name of Sarit forgotten, will assume control in the name of order and good government.

One person who could inject a sense of greater stability into the present period is the King of Thailand, Bhumibol Adulyadej. He has come to enjoy ever increasing popular regard and reverence since the beginning of Marshal Sarit's period of office. And soon he will be able to reap the full benefit of his maturity and long tenure on the throne. However, he has shown, so far, little inclination for intervention in politics and there would seem to be no immediate prospect that he would lend his personal prestige to the underpinning of constitutional rule.

A further factor that is always present and that could introduce, once more, Sarit-style military rule in Thailand is a shift in Thai foreign policy. If, for example, the United States position in South Vietnam became untenable, then a coup could come about as a preliminary to the withdrawal of Thailand from the Western Alliance. And in this context there may well be special significance in the message from Chou En-lai to the Thai Prime Minister in October 1964 assuring him that China had no aggressive intentions in becoming a nuclear power.[3]

In the meantime the situation continues as one of flux and the process of "de-Stalinization" in Thailand continues along its unpredictable path.

Notes

1. The Thai Foreign Minister, Thanat Khoman, sought to resign in October 1964 but then withdrew his resignation. However, this was believed to be related solely to his desire to shed a burdensome office which he had held for many years.
2. £1 is equivalent to approximately 57 baht.

3. The Chinese however would seem to be playing a dual game. In December 1964, a radio station (operated from Laos) calling itself the voice of the people of Thailand announced the formation of a Thai independence movement. This news, together with the manifesto of the movement, was given wide publicity in the Chinese press and radio.

66

Can Democracy Last in Thailand?

Since the end of absolute monarchy in Thailand, parliamentary democracy has been the exception rather than the rule. Civilian democratic government, set aside by a coup in February 1991, was restored through elections in September 1992 after the military failed to hold on to power by resorting to brute force. Unresolved, however, is whether democracy in Thailand is any more than a recurrent interlude between periods of military-based administration.

At the moment, the armed forces are licking their wounds following the bloody confrontation in Bangkok in May that led to the humiliation and downfall of former army commander, General Suchinda Kraprayoon. His successor, General Wimol Wongvanich, has been depicted as a more professional soldier with respect for the virtues of constitutional authority.

But General Wimol has been no less outspoken and robust than his predecessor in his public defense of military interests. For example, he has inspired a virtual legal crusade against a newspaper alleged to

---

Reprinted from Michael Leifer, "Can Democracy Last in Thailand?", *International Herald Tribune*, 8 March 1993, with permission of the publisher.

have sullied the reputation of the army. The recent visit to Thailand by eight Nobel Peace Prize winners to campaign for the release from detention by Burma's military regime of fellow laureate Daw Aung San Suu Kyi also provoked an outburst from General Wimol. Partly concerned about relations with Burma and China, he advised the civilian government to put Thailand's house in order before interfering in a neighbor's internal affairs over the issue of human rights.

For the civilian prime minister, Chuan Leekpai, the presence of the Nobel Peace laureates served to reaffirm the liberal credentials and the independence of his government. Moreover, their reception by King Bhumiphol Adulyadej (but without the Dalai Lama to avoid undue provocation to China) underscored the constitutional monarchy's commitment to democracy. The King's intervention had been crucial in obliging the military to give up power in May.

An elected civilian government in Thailand does not necessarily mean dynamic and efficient rule. So far, the performance of Mr Chuan's administration has been somewhat ineffectual in the face of tensions between the parties in his coalition and carping criticism from opposition politicians. It has certainly not matched up to the performance of the two technocratic caretaker governments in 1991–92 headed by Anand Panyarachun that did not have to overcome the constraints and frustrations of Thailand's raucous democratic process.

Still, the current shortcomings of the Chuan government do not provide a ready opportunity for a return to military rule. For example, the charge of wholesale corruption, which was used by the armed forces to justify the overthrow of Prime Minister Chatichai Choonhavan's administration in February 1991, cannot be revived with any credibility. In addition, the vibrant private sector of the economy seems to have recovered from the shock and damage caused by the street violence in May.

Nonetheless, Thailand's military establishment continues to believe that it is entitled to play a political role and also to share in the material spoils of public life. It is this persisting corporate view that poses an underlying threat to democracy.

But Thailand, with its remarkable burst of economic development in recent years and corresponding social and educational change, is not Burma. Military rule in Bangkok would require an army that was fully prepared to shoot down educated middle-class demonstrators in cold blood. Thai soldiers do not appear to have the stomach for such cruel self-indulgence.

Military commanders know that there would be extensive coverage by the electronic media of any attempted coup. Images of any bloodletting would be transmitted around a world in which human rights has become an established part of the international agenda, especially since the end of the Cold War. An even more important deterrent would be the economic consequences of a recurrence of forcible intervention by the military that would impair its own extensive business interests.

Of course, soldiers, like politicians, do not always act rationally, even in modern Thailand, where the pace of economic growth and social transformation seems to have made coups an increasingly counterproductive method of changing governments. Probably only when young men discover that the military academy does not provide the key to great personal wealth will democracy have a more assured future.

Such a change in expectations has yet to take place because the armed forces continue to act to self-advantage as a trading company rather than a professional fighting force. The more a civilian government seeks to curb their material appetite, the greater the prospect of a military backlash at democracy's expense.

Bibliography

The content of this bibliography is arranged in alphabetical order according to sections that complement the organization of this book. Interviews with Michael Leifer, his reviews on the works of others, others' reviews on his works, and tributes and obituaries on him are listed at the end of this bibliography.

Southeast Asia: General

Asian Nationalism, edited by Michael Leifer. London and New York: Routledge, 2000.

Dictionary of the Modern Politics of South-East Asia. London and New York: Routledge, 1995.

Dictionary of the Modern Politics of South-East Asia. 2nd ed. London and New York: Routledge, 1996.

Dictionary of the Modern Politics of South-East Asia. 3rd ed. London and New York: Routledge, 2001.

Dilemmas of Statehood in Southeast Asia. Singapore: Asia Pacific Press, 1972.

"Expanding Horizons in Southeast Asia?". *Southeast Asian Affairs 1994*, pp. 3–21. Singapore: Institute of Southeast Asian Studies, 1994.

The Foreign Relations of the New States. Camberwell, Vic.: Longman Australia, 1974.

"In Asia, a Post-colonial Status Quo". *International Herald Tribune*, 27 August 1992, p. 24.

"The Individual and the State: Asian's Debate Will Continue". *International Herald Tribune*, 21 May 1996, p. 28.

"Malaysia, Brunei and Singapore". In *The Annual Register*. London: Longmans, 1967–2000.

Nationalism Revolution and Evolution in South-East Asia, edited by Michael Leifer. Hull Monograph on Southeast Asia, No. 2. Zug: Inter Documentation Company, 1970.

"Political and Governance Challenges in Southeast Asia: Outlook 2001", by Abdul Aziz and Michael Leifer, pp. 12–19. ISEAS Trends in Southeast Asia no. 3. Singapore: Institute of Southeast Asian Studies, 2001.

"The Political and Security Outlook for Southeast Asia". ISEAS Trends in Southeast Asia no. 2. Singapore: Institute of Southeast Asian Studies, 2000.

"The Security of Southeast Asia". *Pacific Community* 7, no. 1 (1975): 14–27.

"So Far, So Good? Political Change and the Asia Crisis". *World Today* 54, no. 3 (1998): 69.

"Some South-East Asian Attitudes". *International Affairs* 42, no. 2 (1966): 219–29.

"South-East Asia". In *The Oxford History of the Twentieth Century*, edited by Michael Howard and Roger Louis, pp. 227–39. Oxford and New York: Oxford University Press, 1998.

"Tigers, Tigers, Spurning Rights". *Times Higher Education Supplement*, 21 April 1995.

Part I: International Relations

Southeast Asia: Conflict and Co-operation

Conflict and Regional Order in South-East Asia. London: International Institute for Strategic Studies, 1980.

"Keselamatan Asia Tenggara". *Dewan Masyarakat* 14, no. 4 (1976): 48–53.

"The Limits of Functionalist Endeavour: The Experiences of Southeast Asia". In *Functionalism: Theory and Practice in International Relations*, edited by A.J.R. Groom and Paul Taylor, pp. 278–83. New York: Crane Russak, 1975.

"Problems and Prospects of Regional Cooperation in Asia: The Political Dimension". *Indonesian Quarterly* 4, no. 2–4 (1976): 92–104.

"Regionalism, the Global Balance and Southeast Asia". In *Regionalism in Southeast Asia*, pp. 55–70. Jakarta: Centre for Strategic and International Studies, 1975.

"The Vietnam War and the Response of Southeast Asian Countries". In *International Affairs in Asia and the Pacific: Their Past, Present and Future*, pp. 345–66. Tokyo: Japan Association of International Relations, 1986.

ASEAN and Regional Order

"ASEAN and the Problem of Common Response". *International Journal* 38, no. 2 (1983): 316–29.

ASEAN and the Security of South-East Asia. London; New York: Routledge, 1989.

"ASEAN as a Model of a Security Community?". In *ASEAN in a Changed Regional and International Political Economy*, edited by Hadi Soesastro, pp. 129–42. Jakarta: Centre for Strategic and International Studies, 1995.

"ASEAN: Bigger Doesn't Mean More Clout". *Straits Times*, 3 July 1997, p. 19.

"ASEAN Enlargement: Solution or Problem". *Trends* 82 (28–29 June 1997): III.

"ASEAN: Ensuring Stability for Development". *Euro-Asia Business Review* 6, no. 1 (1987): 10–14.

"ASEAN: First Seventeen Years". *Asia Pacific Annual Review* (1985): 41–42.

"ASEAN: Now for the Next 25 Years". *International Herald Tribune*, 13 August 1992.

"The ASEAN Peace Process: A Category Mistake". *Pacific Review* 12, no. 1 (1999): 25.

"The ASEAN Regional Forum: A Model for Cooperative Security in the Middle East". Working Paper No. 1998/1. Canberra: Research School of Pacific and Asian Studies, Australian National University, 1998.

The ASEAN Regional Forum: Extending ASEAN's Model of Regional Security. London: Oxford University Press for the International Institute for Strategic Studies, 1996.

"The ASEAN States and the Progress of Regional Cooperation in South-East Asia". In *Politics, Society and Economy in the ASEAN States*, edited by Bernhard Dahm and Werner Draguhn, pp. 3–16. Wiesbaden: Otto Harrassowitz, 1975.

"The ASEAN States: No Common Outlook". *International Affairs* 49, no. 4 (1973): 600–607.

ASEAN's Search for Regional Order. Singapore: G. Brash for Faculty of Arts and Social Sciences, National University of Singapore, 1987.

"ASEAN under Stress over Cambodia". *Far Eastern Economic Review* 124, no. 24 (14 June 1984): 34.

"Asia: Two Models for a Broader Security Umbrella". *International Herald Tribune*, 18 May 1993, p. 24.

"A British View of ASEAN as a Diplomatic Community". *Korean Journal of International Studies* 14, no. 3 (1983): 211–17.

Expanded Model of Regional Security. Phnom Penh: Cambodian Institute for Cooperation and Peace, 1995.

"The Extension of ASEAN's Model of Regional Security". In *Nation, Region and Context: Studies in Peace and War in Honour of Professor T.B. Millar*, edited by Coral Bell, pp. 73–90. Canberra: Strategic and Defence Studies Centre, Australian National University, 1995.

"The Forum Makes a Perfunctory Start?". *International Herald Tribune*, 25 July 1994, p. 24.

"International Dynamics of One Southeast Asia: Political and Security". *Indonesian Quarterly* 24, no. 4 (1996): 357–64.

"Is ASEAN a Security Organization?". In *The ASEAN Reader*, pp. 379–81. Singapore: Institute of Southeast Asian Studies, 1992.

"The Issue Is ASEAN". *Far Eastern Economic Review* 158, no. 48 (30 November 1995): 34.

"Multilateral Structures: Where Are They Leading?". Paper presented at the 473rd Wilton Park Conference, Wiston House, Steyning, West Sussex, 9–12 July 1996.

"The Paradox of ASEAN". *Round Table* 271 (July 1978): 261–68.

"The Progress and Problems of Multilateral Security Cooperation in Asia". Paper delivered at the 28th London School of Economics and Political Science, International Social Economics Forum, Japan, 27 January 2001.

"Regional Order in South-East Asia: An Uncertain Prospect". *Round Table* 225 (July 1974): 309–17.

"Regional Security in a New Light". *The Star*, 10 February 1994, p. 18.

"Regional Solutions to Regional Problems?". In *Towards Recovery in Pacific Asia*, edited by Gerald Segal and David S. G. Goodman, pp. 119–31. New York: Routledge, 1999.

"The Role and Paradox of ASEAN". In *The Balance of Power in East Asia*, edited by Michael Leifer, pp. 119–31. Basingstoke, Hampshire: Macmillan, 1986.

"Trends in Regional Association in South East Asia". *Asian Studies* 2 (1964): 188–98.

"Truth about the Balance of Power". In *The Evolving Pacific Power Structure*, edited by Derek da Cunha, pp. 47–51. Singapore: Institute of Southeast Asian Studies, 1996.

"Whither ASEAN?". *Foreign Relations Journal* 2, no. 2 (1987): 45–55.

"Will ASEAN Pay the Price for Peace?". *Business Times*, 28 July 1993, p. 14.

"Will the ARF Work?". *Business Times*, 20 July 1994, p. 12.

The Cambodia Conflict

"The Balance of Advantage in Indochina". *World Today* 38, no. 6 (1982): 232–38.

"Cambodia". In *The New Interventionism, 1991–1994: United Nations Experience in Cambodia, Former Yugoslavia, and Somalia*, edited by James Mayall, pp. 59–93. New York: Cambridge University Press, 1996.

"Cambodia: A Fresh Start, with Help Still Needed". *International Herald Tribune*, 15 November 1993, p. 26.

"Cambodia and Laos: Critical Issues in Southeast Asia". Paper presented at US-ASEAN Conference on Economic, Political, and Security Issues in Southeast Asia in the 1980s.

"Cambodia in Regional and Global Politics". In *Vietnam's Withdrawal from Cambodia: Regional Issues and Realignments*, edited by Gary Klintworth, pp. 4–18. Canberra: Strategic and Defence Studies Centre, Research School of Pacific Studies, Australian National University, 1990.

"Cambodian Conflict: The Final Phase?". In *Rivalry and Revolution in South and East Asia*, edited with an introduction by Partha S. Ghosh, pp. 27–56. Brookfield, Vt.: Dartmouth, 1997.

"Conflict over Kampuchea: The Issues at Stake". Speech delivered at an inter-faculty Seminar on International Conflicts and their Resolution with Special Reference to the Kampuchean Problem, National University of Singapore, 1988.

"The Course of Conflict in Cambodia". *Viertal Jahres Berichte* 88 (June 1982): 127–32.

"Indochina and ASEAN: Seeking a New Balance". *Contemporary Southeast Asia* 15, no. 3 (1993): 269–79.

"The Indochina Problem". In *Asian-Pacific Security after the Cold War*, edited by T.B. Millar and James Walter, pp. 56–68. Canberra: Allen & Unwin, 1993.

"The International Dimensions of the Cambodian Conflict". *International Affairs* 51, no. 4 (1975): 531–43.

"The International Representation of Kampuchea". *Southeast Asian Affairs 1982*, pp. 47–59. Singapore: Institute of Southeast Asian Studies. 1982.

"Kampuchea and Laos: Critical Issues for ASEAN". In *Economic, Political and Security Issues in Southeast Asia in the 1980s*, edited by Robert A. Scalapino and Jusuf Wanandi, pp. 13–22. Berkeley, CA.: Institute of East Asian Studies, University of California, 1982.

"Obstacles to a Political Settlement in Indochina". *Pacific Affairs* 58, no. 4 (1985–86): 626–36.

"Obstacles to Peace in Southeast Asia". Paper presented to the Global Community Forum, Kuala Lumpur, 2–4 December 1984.

"Post-mortem on the Third Indochina War". *World Today* 35, no. 6 (1979): 249–58.

"Power Sharing and Peacemaking in Cambodia?". *SAIS Review* 12, no. 1 (1992): 139–53.

"The Road to Phnom Penh is Blocked by Moscow". *Far Eastern Economic Review* 134, no. 52 (25 December 1986): 30.

"The Stakes of Conflict in Cambodia". *Asian Affairs* 21, no. 2 (1990): 155–61.

"The Third Indochina Conflict". *Asian Affairs* 14, no. 2 (1983): 125–31.

"Tune Back In, Friends of Cambodia, the Crisis Show Isn't Over". *International Herald Tribune*, 21 December 1995, p. 28.

"The UN is Losing in Cambodia". *International Herald Tribune*, 30 April 1993, p. 27.

External Actors and Southeast Asia

"Anglo-American Differences over Malaysia". *World Today* 20, no. 3 (1964): 156–67.

"Astride the Straits of Johore, the British Presence and Commonwealth Rivalry in Southeast Asia". *Modern Asian Studies* 1 (1967): 283–96.

The Balance of Power in East Asia, edited by Michael Leifer. Basingstoke, Hampshire: Macmillan, 1986.

"The Balance of Power in the Pacific". *Ditchley Journal* 8 (Spring 1981): 34–44.

"China and Southeast Asia". *Pacific Community* 9, no. 1 (1977): 84–95.

"China and the US: Common Standards of Engagement?". *Trends* 77 (25–26 January 1997): IV.

China in Southeast Asia: Interdependence and Accommodation. Taipei: Chinese Council of Advanced Policy Studies, 1997.

"De Gaulle and Vietnam: A Conception of Political Pathology". *International Journal* 23, no. 2 (1968): 221–33.

"East Asia: Drawing New Lines". *International Herald Tribune,* 27 January 1993, p. 24.

"East Asia Fears Chinese Hegemony as U.S. Presence Ebbs". *International Herald Tribune,* 27 January 1993, p. 26.

"External Powers and Domestic Stability in Southeast Asia". Paper presented at the Conference on the United States, Japan, and Southeast Asia: The Issues of Interdependence, Maui, Hawaii, 14–18 December 1983.

"Great Power Intervention and Regional Order". In *Conflict and Stability in Southeast Asia,* edited by Mark W. Zacher and R. Stephen Milne, pp. 181–201. Garden City: Doubleday, 1974.

"Halting the Glacier: ASEAN's China Problem". *Straits Times,* 20 June 1995, p. 18.

"Need for Japan on Tap, Not on Top". *The Star,* 12 February 1994, p. 18.

"The Nixon Doctrine and the Future of Indochina". *Pacific Community* 2, no. 4 (1971): 742–53.

The Peace Dividend: Israel's Changing Relationship with South-East Asia. IJA Research Reports, no. 1, pp. 2–13. London: Institute of Jewish Affairs, 1994.

"The Soviet Union in Asia". *Soviet Jewish Affairs* 15, no. 1 (1985).

"The Soviet Union in South-East Asia". In *The Soviet Union and the Third World,* edited by E. J. Feuchtwanger and Peter Nailor, pp. 164–82. London: Macmillan, 1981.

"Taiwan: A Studied Exercise in Vacation Diplomacy". *International Herald Tribune,* 11 February 1994, p. 26.

"Taiwan and South-East Asia: The Limits to Pragmatic Diplomacy". *China Quarterly* 165 (March 2001): 173–85.
"Who's It That Really Needs to be Engaged?". *Bangkok Post*, 9 February 1997, p. 2.

Between Regions: ASEAN and the EC/EU

"Europa und Sudostasien: Aus Europaischer Perspektive" [In German]. In *Europa und Asien-Pazifik: Grundlagen, Entwicklungslinien und Perspektiven der Europaisch-asiatischen Beziehungen*, edited by Hans W. Maull, Gerald Segal and Jusuf Wanandi, pp. 245–51. Munchen: R. Oldenbourg Verlag, 1999.
"Europe and Southeast Asia". In *Europe and the Asia Pacific*, edited by Hans Maull, Gerald Segal and Jusuf Wanandi, pp. 198–205. London; New York: Routledge, 1998.
"The European Union, ASEAN and the Politics of Exclusion". *Trends* 89 (31 January–1 February 1998): 7.
"Regional Decision-making and Corporate Foreign Policies". In *ASEAN-EC Economic and Political Relations*, edited by R. H. Taylor and P. C. I. Ayre, pp. 63–71. London: School of Oriental and African Studies, University of London, 1986.
"Regionalism Compared: The Perils and Benefits of Expansion". In *The Asia Pacific in the New Millennium: Political and Security Challenges*, edited by Mely C. Anthony and Mohamed Jawhar Hassan, pp. 499–504. Kuala Lumpur: Institute of Strategic and International Studies, 2001.

Security and Order: The Maritime Dimension

"Chinese Economic Reform and Defense Policy: The South China Sea Connection". Paper presented at the IISS/CAPS Conference, Hong Kong, July 1994.
"Chinese Economic Reform and Security Policy: The South China Sea Connection". *Survival* 37, no. 2 (1995): 44–59.
"Chinese Economic Reform: The Impact on Policy in the South China Sea". In *Chinese Economic Reform: The Impact on Security*, edited by Gerald Segal and Richard H. Yang, pp. 141–56. London; New York: Routledge, 1996.
"Conflict of Interest in the Straits of Malacca". Co-authored with Dolliver Nelson. *International Affairs* 49, no. 2 (1973).
Malacca, Singapore and Indonesia. Alphen aan den Rijn: Sijthoff & Noordhoff, 1978.
"The Maritime Regime and Regional Security in East Asia". *Pacific Review* 4, no. 2 (1991): 126–36.
"The Security of Sea-lanes in South-east Asia". In *Security in East Asia*, edited by Robert O'Neill, pp. 166–74. New York: St. Martin's Press for the International Institute for Strategic Studies, 1984.

"Southeast Asian Sealanes: Security in 3 Issues". *Nation Review*, 21 and 22 October 1981. p. 5.

"Stalemate in the South China Sea". In *Perspectives on the Conflict in the South China Sea*, edited by K. Snildal, pp. 1–9. Oslo: Centre for Development and the Environment, University of Oslo, 1999.

"The Straits Are Not Protected". *International Herald Tribune*, 23 January 1993, p. 24.

Part II: Domestic Politics and Foreign Policy

Cambodia

"The Anguish of Cambodia". *Asian Affairs* 60, no. 3 (1973): 270–79.

"Cambodia and China: Neutralism, Neutrality and National Security". In *Policies toward China: Views from Six Continents*, edited by A. M. Halpern. pp. 329–47. New York: McGraw-Hill, 1965.

"Cambodia and Her Neighbors". *Pacific Affairs* 34, no. 2 (1961): 361–74.

Cambodia and Neutrality. Ann Arbor, Mich: University Microfilms, 1971.

"Cambodia and SEATO". *International Journal* 17 (1962): 122–32.

"Cambodia in Search of Neutrality". *Asian Survey* 3, no. 1 (1963): 55–60.

"Cambodia Looks to China". *World Today* 20, no. 1 (1964): 26–31.

"Cambodia: The Limits of Diplomacy". *Asian Survey* 7, no. 1 (1967): 69–73.

"Cambodia: The Politics of Accommodation". *Asian Survey* 4, no. 1 (1964): 674–79.

Cambodia: The Search for Security. London: Pall Mall Press, 1967.

"Cambodian Elections". *Asian Survey* 2, no. 7 (1962): 20–24.

"Cambodian Opposition". *Asian Survey* 2, no. 2 (1962): 11–15.

"Challenges Remain in Cambodia". *International Herald Tribune*, 24 June 1993, p. 26.

"Failure of Political Institutionalization in Cambodia". *Modern Asian Studies* 2 (1968): 125–40.

"Historical and Economic Survey". In *South-East Asia: An Introduction — Essays on the Geography, History and Economy of the Region*, pp. 49–55. London: Europa, 1973.

"Kampuchea 1979: From Dry Season to Dry Season". *Asian Survey* 20, no. 1 (1980): 33–41.

"Kampuchea in 1980: The Politics of Attrition". *Asian Survey* 21, no. 1 (1981): 93–101.

"The Khmer Rouge Have a Hard Foot in the Door". *International Herald Tribune*, 23 July 1993, p. 26.

"A New Orientation for Cambodia?". *World Today* 25, no. 6 (1969): 234–37.

"Peace and War in Cambodia". *Southeast Asia* 1, no. 1–2 (1971): 59–73.

"Political Upheaval in Cambodia". *World Today* 26, no. 5 (May 1970): 46–55.
"Problems of Authority and Political Succession in Cambodia". In *Nationalism, Revolution and Evolution in South-East Asia*, edited by Michael Leifer, pp. 148–74. Zug, Switzerland: Inter-Documentation Co., 1970.
"Rebellion or Subversion in Cambodia?". *Current History* 56 (February 1969): 88–93.
"Sihanouk: A Prince among Neutrals". *Australian Quarterly* 34, no. 4 (1962): 38–49.
"Sihanouk Won't Be a Panacea". *International Herald Tribune*, 17 February 1993, p. 28.
"Vietnam's Intervention in Kampuchea: The Rights of State v. the Rights of People". In *Political Theory, International Relations, and the Ethics of Intervention*, edited by Ian Forbes and Mark Hoffman, pp. 145–56. New York: St. Martin's Press in association with the Mountbatten Centre for International Studies, University of Southampton, 1993.

Malaysia

"Adverse Conception of Malaysia". *Round Table* 60 (July 1970): 285–93.
"Anglo-Malaysian Alienation". *Round Table* 285 (January 1983): 56–63.
"Anglo-Malaysia Alienation Revisited". *Round Table* 331 (July 1994): 347–59.
"Anti-Semitism without Jews: The Malaysian Example". In *The Jews and Asia: Old Societies and New Images*, pp. 62–65. Melbourne: Asia Pacific Jewish Association, 1989.
"Anti-Semitism without Jews: The Malaysian Example". *Australian Institute of Jewish Affairs Survey* 4, no. 3 (1987): 3.
"Mahathir Has Other Concerns". *International Herald Tribune*, 10 March 1994, p. 24.
"Malaysia after Tun Razak: Tensions in a Multi-racial State". *Round Table* 262 (April 1976): 153–60.
"Malaysia and Indonesia: The Myth of Blood Brotherhood". *News Letter (The Institute of Race Relations)* 1, no. 3 (1967): 123–26.
"Politics and Constitutional Stability in Malaysia". *Parliamentary Affairs* 22, no. 3 (1969): 202–209.

Singapore

"Backseat Driver". *Far Eastern Economic Review* 150, no. 46 (15 November 1990): 30–31.
"Communal Violence in Singapore". *Asian Survey* 4, no. 10 (1964): 1115–21.
"The Conduct of Foreign Policy". In *Management of Success: The Moulding of Modern Singapore*, edited by Kernial Singh Sandhu and Paul Wheatley, pp. 965–81. Singapore: Institute of Southeast Asian Studies, 1989.

David Marshall: Letters from Mao's China, edited with an introduction by Michael Leifer. Singapore: Singapore Heritage Society, 1996.

"Different Mind-sets Cause Strains in Relations". *Straits Times*, 25 September 1998, p. 20.

"Independence Balanced by Good Neighbour Policy: Wary Acceptance". *Far Eastern Economic Review* 150, no. 46 (15 November 1990): 34.

"Israel's President in Singapore: Political Catalysis and Transnational Politics". *Pacific Review* 1, no. 4 (1988): 341–52.

"Overnight, an Oasis May Become a Desert". *Far Eastern Economic Review* 135, no. 2 (8 January 1987): 52.

"Politics in Singapore: The First Term of the People's Action Party 1959–1963". *Journal of Commonwealth Political Studies* 2 (May 1964): 102–19.

"Singapore". Co-authored with N. Balakrishnan. *Far Eastern Economic Review* 150, no. 46 (15 November 1990): 27–35.

"Singapore in Malaysia, the Politics of Federation". *Journal of Southeast Asian History* 6 (September1965): 54–70.

"Singapore in Regional and Global Context: Sustaining Exceptionalism". In *Singapore: Re-engineering Success*, edited by Arun Mahizhnan and Lee Tsao Yuan, pp. 19–30. Singapore: Oxford University Press, 1998.

Singapore's Foreign Policy: Coping with Vulnerability. New York: Routledge, 2000.

"Triumph of the Will". *Far Eastern Economic Review* 150, no. 46 (15 November 1990): 27.

Indonesia

"Ali Moertopo: Regional Visionary and Regional Pragmatist". *Indonesian Quarterly* 13, no. 4 (1985): 524–30.

"The Challenge of Creating a Civil Society in Indonesia". *Indonesian Quarterly* 23, no. 4 (1995): 354–60.

"The Changing Temper of Indonesian Nationalism". In *Asian Nationalism*, edited by Michael Leifer, pp. 153–69. London: Routledge, 2000.

"Continuity and Change in Indonesian Foreign Policy". *Asian Affairs* 60, no. 2 (1973): 173–80.

"Habibie Choice a Power Play". *Business Times*, 4 March 1998, p. 18.

Indoneshia no gaiko: Henka to renzokusei. Co-authored with Tomoko Shuto. [In English and Japanese.] Tokyo: Keiso Shobo, 1985.

"Indonesia and Malaysia: The Changing Face of Confrontation". *World Today* 22, no. 9 (1966): 395–405.

"Indonesia and Malaysia: The Diplomacy of Confrontation". *World Today* 21, no. 6 (1965): 250–60.

"Indonesia in ASEAN: Fed up Being Led by the Nose". *Far Eastern Economic Review* 130, no. 39 (3 October 1985): 26.

"Indonesia Waives the Rules". *Far Eastern Economic Review* 143, no. 1 (5 January 1989): 17.

"Indonesia's Encounters with China and the Dilemmas of Engagement". In *Engaging China: The Management of an Emerging Power*, edited by Alastair Iain Johnston and Robert S. Ross, pp. 87–108. London: Routledge, 1999.

Indonesia's Foreign Policy. London and Boston: Allen & Unwin for the Royal Institute of International Affairs, 1983.

"Indonesia's Future Role". *World Today* 26, no. 12 (1970): 512–19.

"Indonesia's Regional Vision". *World Today* 30, no. 10 (1974): 418–25.

"The Islamic Factor in Indonesia's Foreign Policy". In *Islam in Foreign Policy*, edited by Adeed Dawisha, pp. 144–59. Cambridge and New York: Cambridge University Press in association with the Royal Institute of International Affairs, 1983.

"Lessons from a Downfall". *Straits Times*, 23 May 1998, p. 23.

"The Non-toppling of Sukarno". *Venture* 17, no. 11 (1965): 13–15.

Politik Luar Negeri Indonesia. [In Indonesian.] Jakarta: Penerbit PT Gramedia, 1989.

"A Post-Suharto Indonesia Still Troubles the Region". *Trends* 93 (30–31 May 1998): 9.

"The Process of Political Change in Indonesia". *Royal Central Asian Journal* 54 (1967): 266.

"Uncertainty in Indonesia". *World Policy Journal* 8, no. 1 (1990–91): 137–58.

Vietnam, Brunei, the Philippines, and Thailand

"Brunei: Domestic Politics and Foreign Policy". In *ASEAN in Regional and Global Context*, edited by Karl D. Jackson, Sukhumbhand Paribatra and J. Soedjati Djiwandono, pp. 183–93. Berkeley: Institute of East Asian Studies, University of California, 1986.

"Can Democracy Last in Thailand?". *International Herald Tribune*, 8 March 1993, p. 26.

"Decolonisation and International Status: The Experience of Brunei". *International Affairs* 54, no. 2 (1978): 240–52.

The Philippine Claim to Sabah. Zug, Switzerland: Inter Documentation Co., 1968.

"The Philippines and Sabah Irredenta". *World Today* 24, no. 10 (1968): 421–28.

"Thailand: The Politics of 'Destalinization'". *Australian Outlook* 19 (April 1965): 97–100.

Vietnam and Doi Moi: Domestic and International Dimensions of Reform. Co-authored with John Phipps. RIIA Discussion Paper No. 35. London: Royal Institute of International Affairs, 1991.

"Vietnam and the Premises of Intervention". *Pacific Affairs* 45, no. 2 (1972): 268–72.

"Vietnam's Foreign Policy in the Post-Soviet Era: Coping with Vulnerability".
In *East Asia in Transition: Toward a New Regional Order*, edited by Robert S.
Ross, pp. 267–92. Armonk, N.Y.: M. E. Sharpe; Singapore: Institute of
Southeast Asian Studies, 1995.

Miscellaneous

"Australia, Trusteeship and New Guinea". *Pacific Affairs* 36, no. 3 (1963): 250–
64.
Constraints and Adjustments in British Foreign Policy, edited by Michael Leifer.
London: Allen and Unwin, 1972.
"Human Rights in the European Community". *Australian Outlook* (August
1961): 169–87.
"Maintain APEC on its Economic Trajectory". *International Herald Tribune*,
8 November 1993, p. 28.
"North America and the Asia-Pacific Region in the 21st Century: The
Political, and Strategic Dimensions of Interaction". Paper presented at
the MAAS International Conference on North America and the Asia-
Pacific Towards the 21st Century: Facing the Challenges of Promoting
Cooperative Security and Prosperity, Petaling Jaya, Malaysia, 7–8
November 1995.
"A Personal Note". In *Elie Kedourie CBE, FBA, 1926–1992: History, Philosophy,
Politics*, edited by Sylvia Kedourie, pp. 29–30. London and Portland, OR:
Frank Cass, c1998.
"Reviving the Dinosaur?", *Far Eastern Economic Review* 155, no. 34 (27 August
1992): 21.
"Zionism and Palestine in British Opinion and Policy, 1945–1949". Ph.D.
dissertation, London School of Economics, 1959.

Interviews

"Academic Backs SM's Account of Racial Riots". [BBC interview.] *Straits Times*,
18 September 1998, p. 14
"Indonesia Needs Firm but Democratic Hand". *Straits Times*, 8 January 2000.
p. 25.
"A Lack of Trust over Mindanao". [BBC interview.] *Straits Times*, 1 June 2000,
p. 21.
"Legitimacy Is the Issue, Says Expert". [BBC interview. *Straits Times*, 16 April
1999, p. 38.
"Malaysia's Reaction Reinforces SM Lee's Point". [Radio interview with the
BBC.] *Straits Times*, 19 September 1998, p. 44.
"Possible Political Dimension to Aceh Violence". [BBC interview.] *Straits Times*,
6 May 1999, p. 10.

"Year 2000 'Blows Winds of Harmony to ASEAN-10'". *Jakarta Post*, 12 June 1997, p. 5.

Book Reviews on Works of Others

Abdullah Ahmad. "Tengku Abdul Rahman and Malaysia's Foreign Policy 1963–70". *Contemporary Southeast Asia* 8, no. 4 (1987): 335–36.

Abueva, Jose Veloso. "Foundations and Dynamics of Filipino Government and Politics". *Public Affairs* 43 (1970): 470–71.

Acharya, Amitav. "The Quest for Identity: International Relations of Southeast Asia". *Pacific Review*, 14, no. 3 (2001): 484–86.

Adams, Nina S. and Alfred W. McCoy, eds. "Laos: War and Revolution". *Journal of Asian Studies* 32 (1972–73): 121–24.

Allen, James de V. "Malayan Union". *Bijdragen tot de Taal-, land- en volkenkunde* 124 (1968): 302–303.

Andre, Pamela. "Australia and the Postwar World: The Commonwealth Asia and the Pacific, Documents 1948–49". *Journal of Imperial and Commonwealth History* 27, no. 3 (1999): 195–97.

Antolik, Michael. "ASEAN and the Diplomacy of Accommodation". *International Affairs* 67, no. 3 (1991): 628.

Aptheker, Herbert. "Mission to Hanoi". *Journal of Southeast Asian History* 8 (September 1967): 347–48.

Ba Maw. "Breakthrough in Burma, Memoirs of a Revolution, 1939–1946". *Journal of Southeast Asian Studies* 1, no. 2 (1970); 132–33.

Bilveer Singh. "Whither PAP's Dominance? An Analysis of Singapore's 1991 General Elections". *Far Eastern Economic Review* 155, no. 47 (26 November 1992): 46.

Burchett, Wilfred G. "Vietnam North". *Journal of Southeast Asian History* 9 (1968): 175–76.

Butwell, Richard A. "Southeast Asia: A Political Introduction". *Pacific Affairs* 48, no. 3 (1975): 461.

Camilleri, Joe. "Security and Survival: The New Era in International Relations". *Pacific Affairs* 47, no. 3 (1974): 405.

Chanda, Nayan. "Brother Enemy: The War after the War". *Far Eastern Economic Review* 134, no. 52 (25 December 1986): 38.

Chandler, David P. "The Tragedy of Cambodian History: Politics, War, and Revolution since 1945". *Journal of Asian Studies* 51, no. 4 (1992): 977–78.

Chawla, Sudershan, Melvin Gurtov, and Alain-Gerard Marsot, eds. "Southeast Asia under the New Balance of Power". *Pacific Affairs* 48, no. 2 (1975): 280–82.

Chin Kin Wah, ed. "Defence Spending in Southeast Asia". *Pacific Affairs* 62, no. 3 (1989): 425–26.

Colbert, Evelyn Speyer. "Southeast Asia in International Politics, 1941–1956". *Journal of Asian Studies* 38 (1978–79): 207–208.

Crone, Donald K. "The ASEAN States: Coping with Dependence". *Pacific Affairs* 57, no. 1 (1984): 168–69.

Djiwandono, J. Soedjati and Yong Mun Cheong, eds. "Soldiers and Stability in Southeast Asia". *Pacific Affairs* 62, no. 3 (1989): 425–26.

Dommen, Arthur J. "Conflict in Laos: The Politics of Neutralization". *Journal of Asian Studies* 32 (1971–72): 121–124. *Journal of Southeast Asian Studies* 3 (1972): 166–67.

Dzurek, Daniel J. "The Spratly Islands Dispute: Who's on First?". *China Quarterly* 153 (March 1998): 167–68.

Falk, Richard A. "Vietnam War and International Law. Vol. III". *Public Affairs* 46 (1973): 170–71.

Field, Michael. "Prevailing Wind: Witness in Indo-China". *Journal of Southeast Asian History* 7 (March 1966): 145–47.

Fifield, Russell Hunt. "Americans in Southeast Asia: The Roots of Commitment". *Pacific Affairs* 46, no. 4 (1973): 600–601.

Fistie, Pierre. "L'evolution de la Thailande Contemporaine". *Bulletin. University of London. School of Oriental and African Studies* 31 (1968): 429–30.

Fitzgerald, Stephen. "China and the Overseas Chinese, a Study of Peking's Changing Policy, 1949–1970". *Journal of Southeast Asian Studies* 4 (1973): 327–29.

Frost, F. "Vietnam Foreign Relations: Dynamics of Change". *Australian Journal of Political Science* 29, no. 3 (1994): 606–607.

Golay, Frank H, ed. "The United States and the Philippines". *Modern Asian Studies* 1 (1967): 303–304.

Grant, Jonathan S. and A. G. Laurence. "Cambodia: The Widening War in Indochina". *Journal of Asian Studies* 32 (1972–73): 121–24; *Pacific Affairs* 44, no. 4 (1971): 645–47.

Greenfield, Jeanette. "China's Practice in the Law of the Sea". *International Affairs* 69, no. 1 (1993): 177.

Haas, Michael. "Cambodia, Pol Pot, and the United States: The Faustian Pact". *Journal of Asian Studies* 52, no. 1 (1993): 216–18.

———. "Genocide by Proxy: Cambodian Pawn on a Superpower Chessboard". *Journal of Asian Studies* 52, no. 1 (1993): 216–18.

Hancox, D. J. and Victor Prescott. "A Geographical Description of the Spratly Islands and an Account of Hydrographic Surveys amongst those Islands". *China Quarterly* 153 (1998): 167–68.

Hood, Steven J. "Dragons Entangled: Indochina and the China-Vietnam War". *China Quarterly* 137 (1994): 244–45.

Hsiung, James Chieh, ed. "Asia Pacific in the New World Politics". *China Quarterly* 141 (1995): 242–43.

Hyde, Douglas Arnold. "Confrontation in the East: A Background Book". *Modern Asian Studies* 1 (1967): 102–104.

Iriye, Akira and Warren I. Cohen, eds. "The United States and Japan in the Postwar World". *International Affairs* 66, no. 2 (1990): 441–42.

Jansen, G. H. "Afro-Asia and Non-alignment". *Journal of Southeast Asian History* 8 (1967): 347–48.

Kaplan, Lawrence S., Denise Artaud, and Mark R. Rubin, eds. "Dien Bien Phu and the Crisis of Franco-American Relations, 1954–1955". *English Historical Review* 108, no. 428 (1993): 773–74.

Kaplan, Morton A., et al. "Vietnam Settlement, Why 1973 Not 1969?". *Public Affairs* 47 (1974): 393–94.

Kirk, Donald. "Wider War: The Struggle for Cambodia, Thailand and Laos". *Journal of Asian Studies* 32 (1972–73): 121–24.

Kulick, Elliott and Dick Wilson. "Thailand's Turn: Profile of a New Dragon". *TLS — The Times Literary Supplement* 4714 (6 August 1993): 25.

Lee Kuan Yew. "From Third World to First: The Singapore Story, 1965–2000: Memoirs of Lee Kuan Yew". *Straits Times*, 15 October 2000.

Longmire, R. A. "Soviet Relations with South East Asia: An Historical Survey". *Soviet Studies* 42, no. 3 (July 1990): 593–94.

Mcmahon, R. J., H. D. Schwar, and L. J. Smith, eds. "Foreign Relations of the United States, 1955–1957. Vol. 22 — Southeast-Asia". *English Historical Review* 108, no. 428 (1993): 773–74.

McVey, Ruth Thomas. "Rise of Indonesian Communism". *Modern Asian Studies* 1 (1967): 102–104.

Mauzy, Diane K. "Politics in the ASEAN States". *Pacific Affairs* 58, no. 3 (1985): 557–58.

Muscat, Robert J. "Thailand and the United States: Development, Security, and Foreign Aid". *Political Science Quarterly* 106, no. 3 (1991): 567–68.

Neher, Clark D. and Ross Marlay. "Democracy and Development in Southeast Asia: The Winds of Change". *Journal of Southeast Asian Studies* 28, no. 1 (1997): 174–75.

Noble, Lela Garner. "Philippine Policy towards Sabah: A Claim to Independence". *Pacific Affairs* 52, no. 1 (1979): 156.

Palmer, Norman Dunbar. "The New Regionalism in Asia and the Pacific". *Millennium Journal of International Studies* 20, no. 3 (1991): 571–72.

"Priorities and Political Order in Malaysia and Singapore". *Journal of Commonwealth Political Studies* 11, no. 2 (1973): 176–79.

Pym, Christopher. "Mistapim in Cambodia". *Pacific Affairs* 36, no. 2 (1963): 204–205.

Reid, Robert H. and Eileen Guerrero. "Corazon Aquino and the Brushfire Revolution". *TLS — The Times Literary Supplement* 4907 (18 April 1997): 26.

Riaz Hassan, ed. "Singapore: Society in Transition". *Journal of Southeast Asian Studies* 9 (1978): 148–50.

Robison, Richard, Kevin Hewison, and Richard Higgott. "Southeast Asia in the 1980s: The Politics of Economic Crisis". *International Affairs* 64, no. 4 (1988): 734.

Rohwer, Jim. "Asia Rising: How History's Biggest Middle Class Will Change the World". *International Affairs* 73, no. 3 (1997): 607.

Ross, Robert S. "The Indochina Tangle: China's Vietnam Policy, 1975–1979". *China Quarterly* 117 (1989): 168–69.

Scalapino, Robert A. "Asia and the Road Ahead: Issues for the Major Powers". *Pacific Affairs* 49, no. 3 (1976): 523–24.

Searle, Peter. "Politics in Sarawak 1970–1976". *Political Studies* 33, no. 3 (1985): 513.

Segal, Gerald. "Rethinking the Pacific". *Government and Opposition* 26, no. 1 (1991): 120–21.

Selvan T. S. "Singapore: The Ultimate Island (Lee Kuan Yew's Untold Story)". *Asian Affairs* 23, no. 1 (1992): 96.

Seow, Francis T. "To Catch a Tartar: A Dissident in Lee Kuan Yew's Prison". *Bulletin of the School of Oriental and African Studies, University of London* 59, no. 1 (1996): 200.

Shibusawa, Masahide, Zakaria Haji Ahmad, and Brian Bridges. "Pacific Asia in the 1990s". *International Affairs* 68, no. 2 (1992): 385–86.

Simon, Sheldon W. "The ASEAN States and Regional Security". *Pacific Affairs* 56, no. 1 (1983): 182.

Smith, Roger M. "Cambodia's Foreign Policy". *Public Affairs* 38, no. 3 (1965): 435–36.

Solidum, Estrella D. "Towards a Southeast Asian Community". *Pacific Affairs* 48, no. 2 (1975): 282.

"Southeast Asian Affairs, 1979". *Journal of Southeast Asian Studies*, 12, no. 2 (1981): 546–48.

Stevenson, Charles A. "End of Nowhere, American Policy toward Laos since 1954". *Public Affairs* 46 (1973): 171.

Tan Kah Kee. "The Memoirs of Tan Kah-Kee". *Bulletin of the School of Oriental and African Studies, University of London* 59, no. 3 (1996): 612–13.

Tarling, Nicholas. "Sulu and Sabah: A Study of British Policy towards the Philippines and North Borneo from the Late Eighteenth Century". *Pacific Affairs* 52, no. 1 (1979): 154–55.

Taylor, Jay. "China and Southeast Asia: Peking's Relations with Revolutionary Movements". *Pacific Affairs* 48, no. 2 (1975): 280–82.

Thompson, W. Scott. "Unequal Partners: Philippine and Thai Relations with the United States, 1965–75". *Pacific Affairs* 50, no. 1 (1977): 168–69.

Tooze, Ruth. "Cambodia: Land of Contrasts". *Public Affairs* 36 (1963): 204–205.

Tow, William T. "U.S. Foreign Policy and Asian-Pacific Security: A Transregional Approach". *Pacific Affairs* 56, no. 1 (1983): 117–18.

Trager, Frank N. "Burma: From Kingdom to Republic, a Historical and Political Analysis". *Asian Studies* 6 (1966): 658.

———. "Why Viet Nam?". *Journal of Southeast Asian History* 9 (1968): 175–76.

United States Department of Defense. "Pentagon Papers, the Secret History of the Vietnam War". *Pacific Affairs* 45, no. 2 (1972): 268–72.

Vasil, R. K. "Politics in Plural Society: A Study of Non-communal Political Parties in West Malaysia". *Journal of Commonwealth Political Studies* 11, no. 2 (1973): 176–79.

Vertzberger, Yaacov. "Coastal States, Regional Powers, Superpowers and the Malacca-Singapore Straits". *Pacific Affairs* 59, no. 2 (1986): 350–51.

Wilcox, Wayne. "Asia and the International System". *Pacific Affairs* 46, no. 2 (1973): 304.

Williams, Maslyn. "Land in Between: The Cambodian Dilemma". *Pacific Affairs* 44, no. 1 (1971): 149–50.

Willmott, William E. "Chinese in Cambodia". *Pacific Affairs* 40, no. 3 (1967): 404–405.

Wu, Yuan-li. "Strategic Land Ridge: Peking's Relations with Thailand, Malaysia, Singapore and Indonesia". *Pacific Affairs* 49, no. 1 (1976): 164–65.

Others on Michael Leifer's Works

ASEAN and the Security of South-East Asia. London; New York: Routledge, 1989.
Reviewed by Brian Bridges in *International Affairs* 65, no. 3 (1989): 581–82.
Reviewed by Chung In Moon in *Third World Quarterly* 11, no. 4 (1989): 340–42.
Reviewed in *Journal of Strategic Studies* 13, no. 4 (1990): 100–101.
Reviewed by Patrick M. Mayerchak in *Conflict* 11, no. 1 (1991): 89–91.
Reviewed by W. Nester in *Millennium Journal of International Studies* 20, no. 2 (1991): 311–13.
Reviewed by Donald E. Weatherbee in *Pacific Affairs* 62, no. 4 (1989): 569–71.

The ASEAN Regional Forum: Extending ASEAN's Model of Regional Security. London: Oxford University Press for the International Institute for Strategic Studies, 1996.
Reviewed by Michael Lawrence Smith in *Asian Affairs* (London) 28, no. 2 (1997): 273–74.

Asian Nationalism, edited by Michael Leifer. London and New York: Routledge, 2000.
Reviewed by Lee Hock Guan in *Contemporary Southeast Asia* 23, no. 1 (2001): 177–81.
Reviewed by Gary D. Rawnsley in *International Affairs* 77, no. 4 (2001): 1022–23.

David Marshall: Letters from Mao's China, edited with an introduction by Michael Leifer. Singapore: Singapore Heritage Society, 1996.
Reviewed by Frank Cibulka in *Southeast Asian Journal of Social Science* 25, no. 2 (1997): 213–15.

Dictionary of the Modern Politics of South-East Asia. London and New York: Routledge, 1995.

> Reviewed by Philip Bowring in *International Herald Tribune*, 25 February 1995.

> Reviewed by Victor Funnell in *Asian Affairs* (London) 26, no. 2 (1995): 228–29.

> Reviewed by Habibul Haque Khondker in *Southeast Asian Journal of Social Science* 26, no. 2 (1998): 126–27.

> Reviewed by Leo Suryadinata in *Asian Journal of Political Science* 3, no. 1 (1995): 108–109.

Dilemmas of Statehood in Southeast Asia. Singapore: Asia Pacific Press, 1972.

> Reviewed by Milton Osborne in *Pacific Affairs* 46, no. 2 (1973): 342–43.

Indonesia's Foreign Policy. London and Boston: Allen & Unwin for the Royal Institute of International Affairs, 1983.

> Reviewed by Donald S. Zagoria in *Foreign Affairs* (Summer 1983).

> Reviewed by Sheldon W. Simon in *Pacific Affairs* 57, no. 1 (1984): 171–72.

Malacca, Singapore and Indonesia. Alphen aan den Rijn: Sijthoff & Noordhoff, 1978.

> Reviewed by M. B. Hooker in *Third World Quarterly* 4, no. 1 (1982): 184–85.

> Reviewed by Francis Lai in *Journal of Southeast Asian Studies* 13, no. 1 (1982): 203–205.

> Reviewed by R. McVey in *International Affairs* 56, no. 2 (1980): 392–93.

> Reviewed by John Norton Moore in *American Journal of International Law* 74, no. 1 (1980): 231–33.

Singapore's Foreign Policy: Coping with Vulnerability. New York: Routledge, 2000.

> Reviewed by Jorn Dosch in *Asian Affairs* (London) 32, no. 2 (2001): 233–34.

> Reviewed by N. Ganesan in *Pacific Affairs*, 74, no. 4 (2001/2002): 620–21.

> Reviewed by Terada Takashi in *International Relations of the Asia-Pacific* 2 (2002): 160–62.

> Reviewed by Stein Tonnesson in *Journal of Peace Research* 40, no. 6 (2003): 750.

Tributes and Obituaries

Asad Latif. "Tributes to Scholar Who Educated a Generation". *Straits Times*, 28 March 2001.

———. "A True Friend of Singapore". *Straits Times*, 1 April 2001.

Chin Kin Wah. "In Memoriam: Professor Michael Leifer: 1933–2001". *Asian Journal of Political Science* 9, no. 1 (2001): 1–3.

Ch'ng Kim See. "A Personal Tribute to Michael Leifer". Unpublished. Institute of Southeast Asian Studies Library, Singapore, 2004.

da Cunha, Derek. "In Memoriam: Michael Leifer, 1933–2001". *Contemporary Southeast Asia* 23, no. 1 (2001).

Dewitt, David. "From the Chair: Tribute to Dr Michael Leifer". *PISA News* (Summer 2001): 1.

IDSS-LSE Conference on "The Unending Search for Regional Order: Essays in Memory of Michael Leifer", Marina Mandarin Hotel, Singapore, 13–14 May 2004.

"In Memoriam: Professor Michael Leifer". *Times*, 28 March 2001.

Leifer, Jeremy. Closing remarks at the IDSS-LSE Conference on "The Unending Search for Regional Order: Essays in Memory of Michael Leifer", Marina Mandarin Hotel, Singapore, 14 May 2004.

Leifer, Richard. Closing remarks at the IDSS-LSE Conference on "The Unending Search for Regional Order: Essays in Memory of Michael Leifer", Marina Mandarin Hotel, Singapore, 14 May 2004.

"Professor Michael Leifer — Obituary". *Times*, 28 March 2001.

Roberts, Adam. "Obituary: Professor Michael Leifer". *Independent*, 9 April 2001, p. 6.

Smith, Trevor. "Michael Leifer: Political Scientist with Unrivalled Knowledge of South-East Asia". *Guardian*, 3 April 2001.

Wanandi, Jusuf. "Michael Leifer, Friend and Critic of Southeast Asia". *Jakarta Post*, 30 April 2001, p. 4.

Yahuda, Michael. Closing remarks at the IDSS-LSE Conference on "The Unending Search for Regional Order: Essays in Memory of Michael Leifer", Marina Mandarin Hotel, Singapore, 14 May 2004.

———. "Obituary". *The London School of Economics and Political Science News and Views* 25, no. 1 (2001).

———. "Professor Michael Leifer: Analysing the Politics of Southeast Asia over Thirty Years". *Times*, 28 March 2001.

Index

713